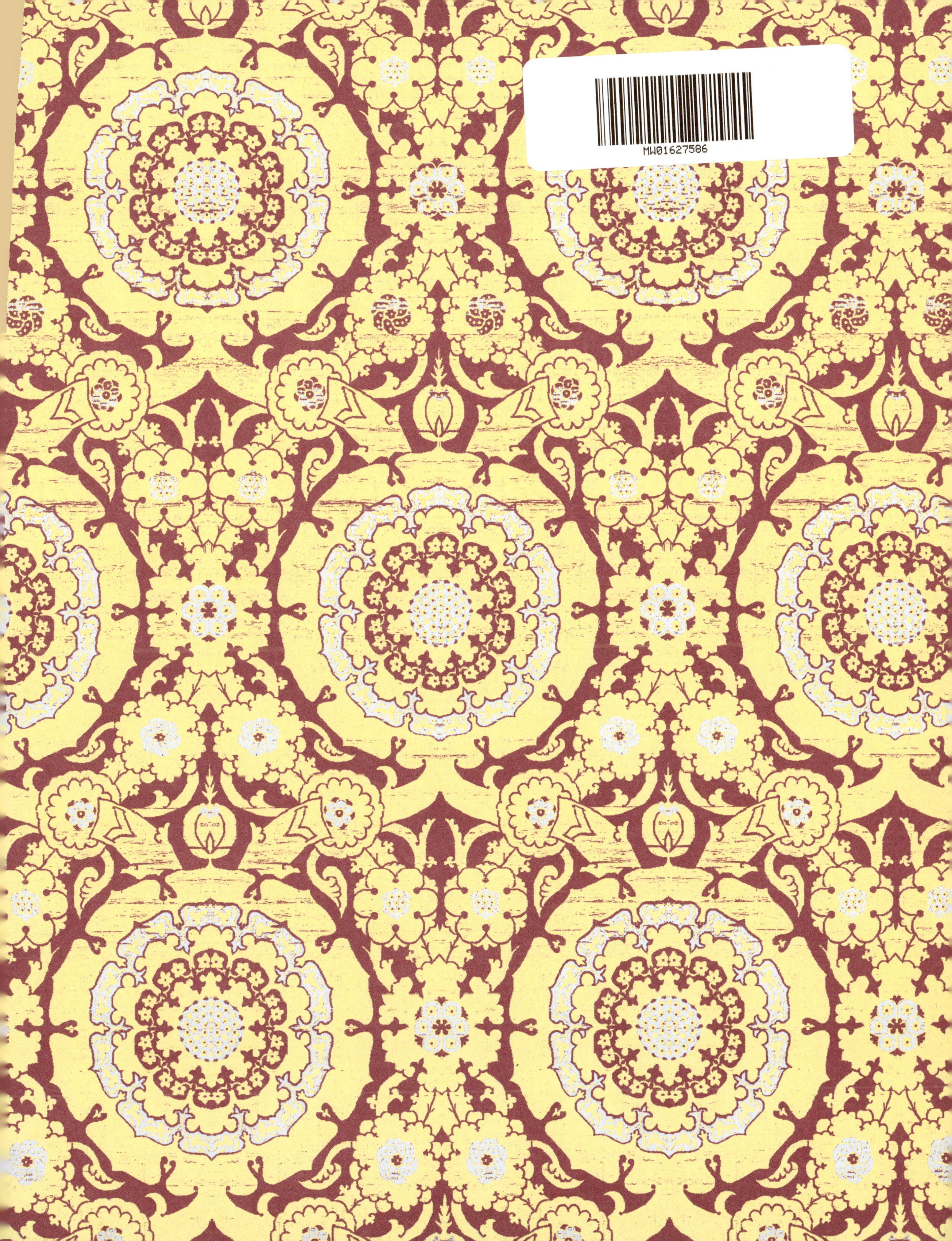
MW01627586

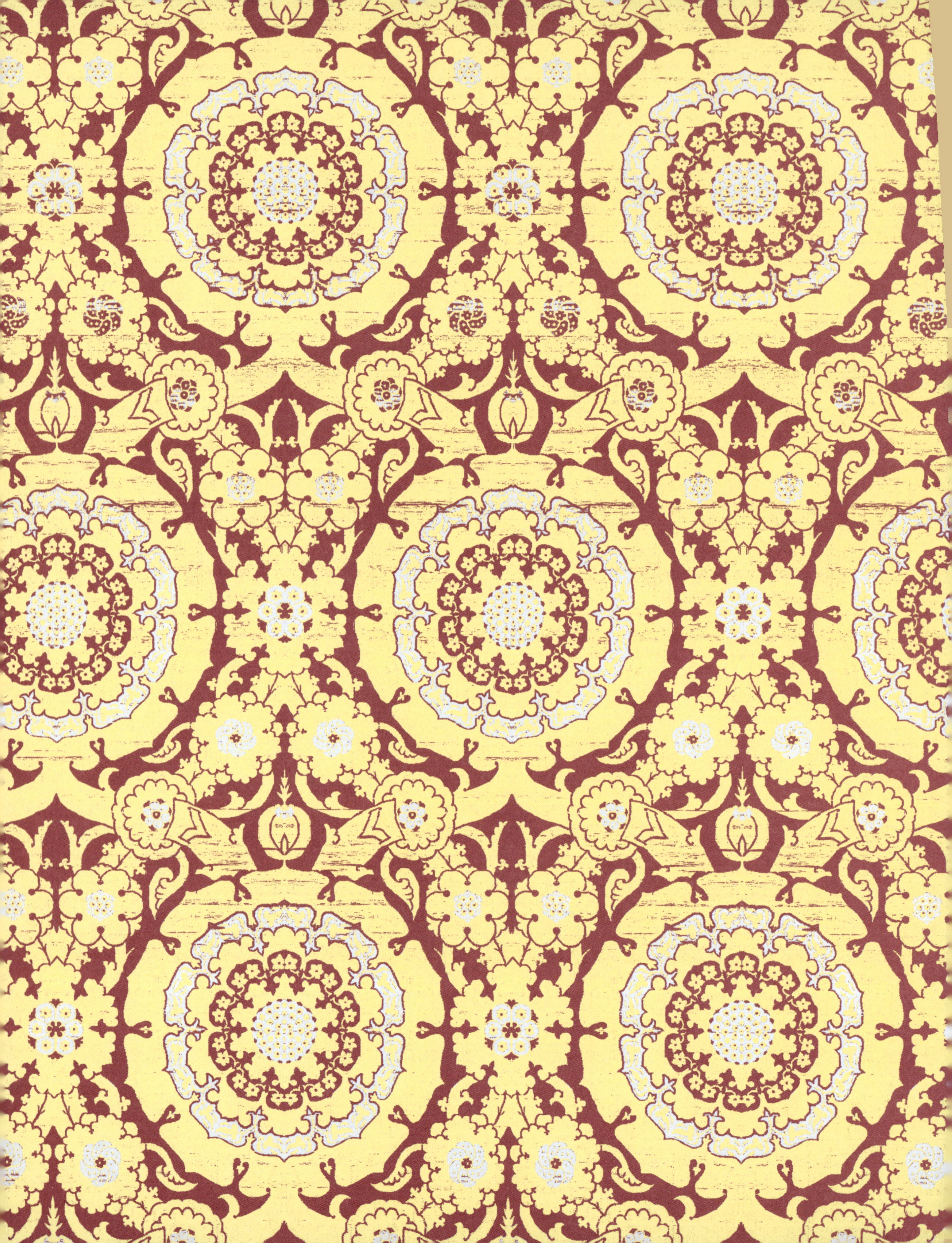

MASTERPIECES

from the Department of Islamic Art
in The Metropolitan Museum of Art

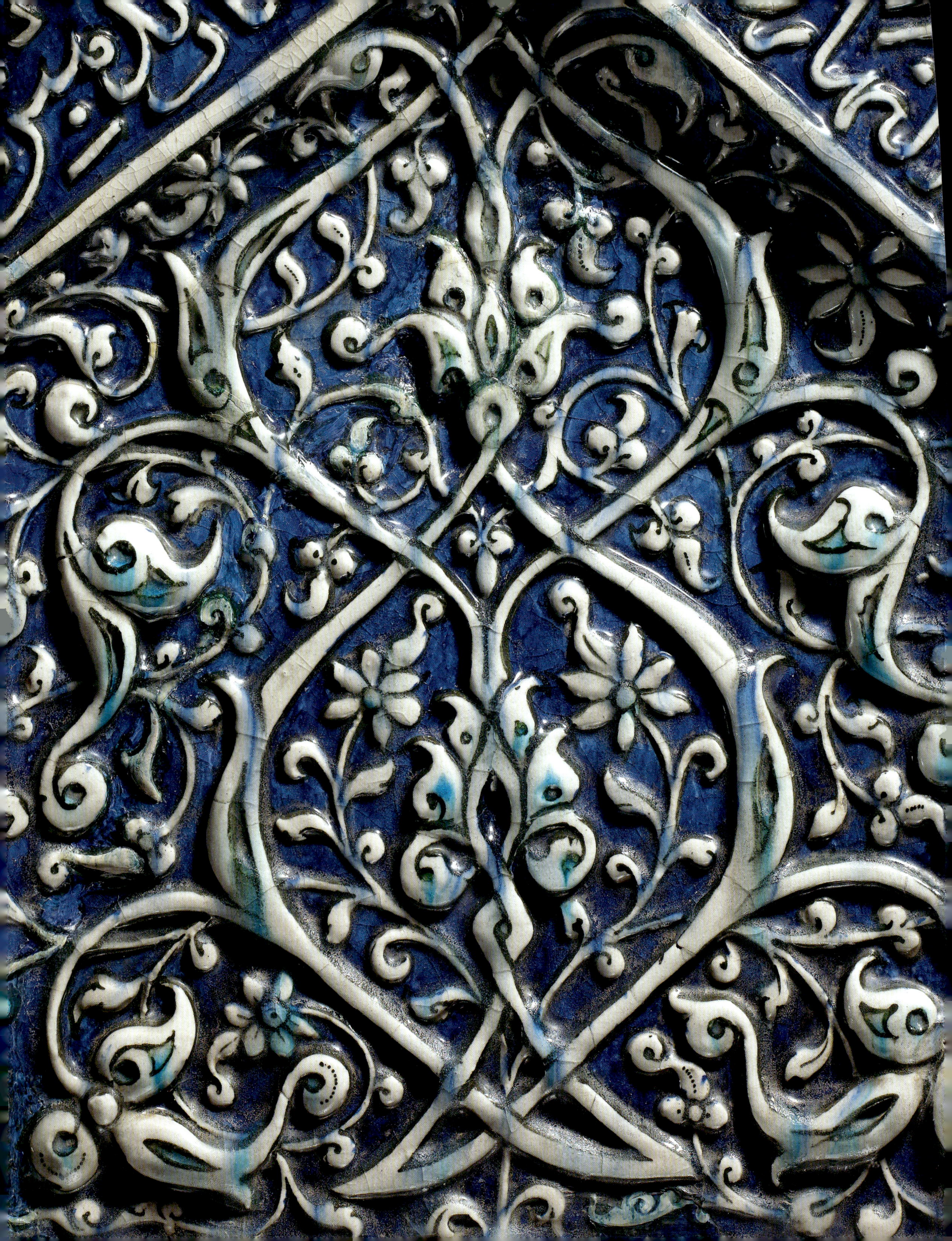

MASTERPIECES
from the Department of Islamic Art in The Metropolitan Museum of Art

EDITED BY

Maryam D. Ekhtiar, Priscilla P. Soucek,
Sheila R. Canby, and Navina Najat Haidar

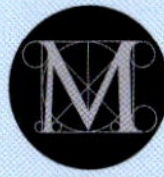

The Metropolitan Museum of Art, New York

Distributed by Yale University Press, New Haven and London

This catalogue is published in conjunction with the reopening of the Galleries for the Art of the Arab Lands, Turkey, Iran, Central Asia, and Later South Asia on November 1, 2011.

This publication is made possible through the generous support of Sharmin and Bijan Mossavar-Rahmani.

Published by The Metropolitan Museum of Art, New York
Mark Polizzotti, Publisher and Editor in Chief
Gwen Roginsky, Associate Publisher and General Manager of Publications
Peter Antony, Chief Production Manager
Michael Sittenfeld, Managing Editor
Robert Weisberg, Assistant Managing Editor

Edited by Cynthia Clark and Margaret Donovan
Designed by Bruce Campbell
Bibliography by Penny Jones
Production by Jennifer Van Dalsen
Map by Anandaroop Roy
Floor plans by Brian Cha (fig. 1) and Constance Norkin (fig. 27)

Typeset in LTC Deepdene, Poetica Std, and Lotus Linotype by Eriksen Translations Inc., Brooklyn, New York
Printed on 130 gsm Magno Satin
Separations by Professional Graphics, Inc., Rockford, Illinois
Printed and bound by Die Keure, Brugge, Belgium

Front jacket/cover illustration: Detail of *Rosette Bearing the Names and Titles of Shah Jahan*, from *Four Folios from the Emperors' Album* (cat. 250 A–D)
Back jacket/cover illustration: Detail of *Pair of Doors* (cat. 113)
Frontispiece: Detail of *Tile from a Mihrab* (cat. 80)
Endpapers: Detail of *Kaftan Back* (cat. 227)

Photographs of works in the Metropolitan Museum's collection are by The Photograph Studio, The Metropolitan Museum of Art; new photography for this publication is by Anna-Marie Kellen and Katherine Dahab.

Additional photography credits: p. 20: Dome of the Rock, Jerusalem, 691 (photo: Courtesy Scala/Art Resource, NY); p. 53: Prayer hall, Great Mosque of Cordoba, 8th–16th century (photo: Walter B. Denny); p. 86: Samanid Mausoleum, Bukhara, ca. 914–43 (photo: Walter B. Denny); p. 136: Mosque of al-Aqmar, Cairo, 1125 (photo: Walter B. Denny); p. 170: Dome, Shaikh Luftallah Mosque, Isfahan, 1590–1602 (photo: Walter B. Denny); p. 285: Selimiye Complex, Edirne, 1568–74 (photo: Walter B. Denny); p. 338: Mausoleum of Mumtaz Mahal, Taj Mahal Complex, Agra, 1632–48 (photo: Wayne B. Denny)

First printing, 2011

The Metropolitan Museum of Art
1000 Fifth Avenue
New York, New York 10028
metmuseum.org

Distributed by
Yale University Press, New Haven and London
yalebooks.com/art
yalebooks.co.uk

Cataloging-in-Publication Data is available from the Library of Congress.
ISBN 978-1-58839-434-7 (hc: The Metropolitan Museum of Art)
ISBN 978-1-58839-435-4 (pbk: The Metropolitan Museum of Art)
ISBN 978-0-300-17585-1 (hc: Yale University Press)

CONTENTS

DIRECTOR'S FOREWORD

Since the closure of the galleries of the Department of Islamic Art for renovation in 2003, Museum staff and outside researchers have been engaged in a thorough reassessment of the collection. This work has taken the form of art-historical and scientific research. Often the results have led to discoveries about the makers, patrons, or materials of objects in the collection. This handbook, published in conjunction with the opening of the refurbished, renamed Galleries for the Art of the Arab Lands, Turkey, Iran, Central Asia, and Later South Asia, presents the latest findings on the finest works of art from these regions in the Metropolitan Museum's collection. In addition, many objects acquired since 2003 are presented here for the first time.

The publication of this book is generously supported by Sharmin and Bijan Mossavar-Rahmani. It has involved numerous editors, curators, and conservators and contains contributions from more than twenty-five authors. During the long evolution of this handbook, Maryam Ekhtiar, Senior Research Associate, Professor Priscilla Soucek, and Navina Haidar, Curator and Coordinator of the Gallery Project, have guided authors and have edited its content. Sheila Canby, Patti Cadby Birch Curator in Charge of the Department of Islamic Art, contributed to the effort in its later stages.

While no experience can replace that of seeing the actual works of art, this handbook will enhance and deepen the reader's understanding of the interconnections and particularities of the art produced from Spain to India between the seventh and late nineteenth centuries. Books such as this volume represent one of the core activities of a universal museum. Departmental curators, researchers, and consultants as well as a number of the Metropolitan's conservators have analyzed the most significant objects in the Museum's permanent collection in light of recent scholarship and have presented their findings in a manner that is of scholarly interest to experts, but is also accessible to nonspecialists. In the several decades that have elapsed since the Metropolitan Museum published a book dealing with the whole range of objects in the Department of Islamic Art, the study of Islamic art has expanded, as has global awareness of the regions from which the collection comes. What has remained constant is the beauty and importance of the finest works of art from the Arab Lands, Turkey, Iran, Central Asia, and Later South Asia, many of which are presented here.

Thomas P. Campbell
Director, The Metropolitan Museum of Art

PREFACE

From the Atlantic to the Indian Ocean, from Rabat to Dhaka, as populations adopted Islam from the seventh century onward they adapted local artistic idioms to the new forms and requirements associated with the new faith. Alongside the official symbols of Islam—the mosque, Qur'an manuscripts, and coinage—new art forms evolved in part due to the changing political realities in western Asia and North Africa. The Arab conquest of Egypt and Iran brought religion, a new language and alphabet, and a realignment of trade between the recently Islamized regions that resulted in creative artistic cross-fertilization. Yet, as strong an example as the Umayyads at Damascus or the Abbasids at Baghdad, Raqqa, or Samarra set, slavish copies of their art in other regions of the Islamic world are the exception rather than the rule.

Thanks to over a century of scholarship on Islamic art, the specific character of the art from different regions with large Muslim populations has come increasingly into focus. As a result, the new galleries of the Metropolitan Museum's Department of Islamic Art have been given a geographical name: Arab Lands, Turkey, Iran, Central Asia, and Later South Asia. This name reflects the shift away from the perception of Islamic art as a unicum to the recognition of the variety of forms and meanings that characterize each period and locale. In addition, Islam today is practiced by large numbers of people in sub-Saharan Africa and Southeast Asia. As the new galleries do not contain the art of either region, the new name more precisely defines what the visitor can expect to find in them. The nomenclature and organization of galleries along geographical lines in no way negate the existence of what is commonly called "Islamic art." Works of Islamic art have been identified as such because of the unique combination of their properties—such as Arabic calligraphy, geometric ornament, and the use of the vine scroll—from Spain to South Asia, from the seventh to the end of the nineteenth century. While most of the regions represented in the Department of Islamic Art were once dominated by ancient empires, a new era accompanied the advent of Islam, and with it came the distinctive approaches to ornament that characterize Islamic art.

This book treats a number of objects that have entered the Museum's collection since 1975. While some have been exhibited at the Museum, others acquired since the Islamic Department's galleries closed in 2003 have not been published or seen by the public. The team of authors who have written entries and chapter introductions have presented the collection within the context of modern scholarship, drawing on a body of literature that has expanded in the past thirty years. Moreover, advances in scientific research have enabled conservators and researchers to pinpoint dates of production and aspects of technique that were previously elusive.

While the question of where and when an object was made continues to concern historians of Islamic art, increasingly these scholars are asking why a particular piece was produced, even when the patron is known. With the understanding of the complexity of the societies in which these objects were conceived has come the question of the extent to which non-Muslims created and used the same objects as Muslims. Along with the luxurious works that originated in court ateliers for royalty and nobility, large numbers of fine ceramics, glassware, metalwork, textiles, and carpets of very high quality were the property of anonymous people who represent the population at large of the lands from Spain to India. What is remarkable is how appealing and fresh so many of these objects appear hundreds of years after they were made.

In today's world, attention to the areas represented in the Met's new galleries mostly concerns dynamic political events, such as the Arab Spring or the conflicts occurring in North Africa, the Middle East, and South Asia. Meanwhile, interest has grown in the burgeoning contemporary art scene and the position of Dubai as a center for artists from across North Africa and the Middle East to show their art. The originality and depth of work produced by contemporary artists, who invariably refer to themselves by the region from which they come or in which they live, not by their religion, does have some parallels with the art of the past. Then as now, artists were not deterred by times of strife and weak leadership. Their work almost always continued in spite of political instability. While the subject matter and forms of art in contemporary North Africa, the Middle East, and Central and South Asia have changed, the human spirit has continued to find expression in works of art, both humble and grand, sacred and profane.

Sheila R. Canby
Patti Cadby Birch Curator in Charge, Department of Islamic Art

ACKNOWLEDGMENTS

The present volume is the first major publication in this century devoted to the collection of the Department of Islamic Art, appearing in celebration of the reopening of the permanent galleries in 2011. The reinstallation of the new Galleries for the Art of the Arab Lands, Turkey, Iran, Central Asia, and Later South Asia and this accompanying publication are the result of several years of planning and execution representing the dedicated efforts of numerous individuals within and outside the Metropolitan Museum. We would like to take this opportunity to express gratitude to all those whose invaluable roles contributed to the vision and the making of the new galleries and this book.

Our Director, Thomas P. Campbell, has provided unwavering institutional backing for this endeavor at every turn. We are also grateful for the support of Emily Rafferty, President; Jennifer Russell, Associate Director for Exhibitions; Carrie Rebora Barratt, Associate Director for Collections and Administration; and Nina Diefenbach, Vice President for Development and Membership, and her team. The gallery reinstallation project was initiated under Philippe de Montebello, Director Emeritus, who oversaw its early development along with Mahrukh Tarapor, former Associate Director for Exhibitions and Director for International Affairs; J. Nicholas Cameron, former Vice President for Construction; Jeffrey Daly, former Senior Design Advisor to the Director; and Doralynn Pines, former Associate Director for Administration. We also express thanks to Sharon Cott, Senior Vice President, Secretary, and General Counsel; and Jeffrey Blair, Senior Associate Counsel.

In the course of preparing the works of art for display and publication the Museum's conservators and scientists have undertaken important research on the collection leading to a deeper scholarly and technical understanding and many new discoveries. The conservators involved in objects conservation under Lawrence Becker, Sherman Fairchild Conservator in Charge, included Mechthild Baumeister, Jean-François de Lapérouse, Lisa Pilosi, Karen Stamm, Vicki Parry, Beth Edelstein, Sarah McGregor, Amy Jones, Daniel Hausdorf, Rudolph Colban, Sarah Barack, Janis Mandrus, Drew Anderson, Nancy Britton, Pascale Patris, and Marijn Manuels. Textile conservation under Florica Zaharia, Conservator in Charge, included Janina Poskrobko, Kisook Suh, Yael Rosenfield, Midori Sato, Giulia Chiostrini, Julia Carlson, Olha Yarema-Wynar, Emilia Cortes, Kristine Kamiya, Kathrin Colburn, and Sarah Pickman. Paper conservation under Marjorie Shelley, Sherman Fairchild Conservator in Charge, included Yana van Dyke, Valerie Faivre, Martin Bansbach, Rebecca Capua, and Angela Campbell. We also thank Christine Giuntini in the Department of the Arts of Africa, Oceania, and the Americas for her work on textiles. The scientists involved in scientific research under Marco Leona, David H. Koch Scientist in Charge, included Nobuko Shibayama, Adrianna Rizzo, Mark Wypyski, Tony Frantz, Masahiko Tsukada, and Julie Arslanoglu. For the examination, conservation, and installation of the Damascus Room and Spanish Ceiling we also thank Timothy Hayes, Anke Scharrahs, Melanie Brussat, Arianna Gambirasi, Miguel Garcia, Ross Keppler, Emy Kim, Ursula Kugler, Stephanie Massaux, Batyah Shtrum, Erin Toomey, Wilson Santiago, Julia Schultz, Consider Vosu, Lauren Fair, Jan Hempelmann, and the people from Traditional Line Ltd., especially Jim Boorstein and Joe White. For their valuable work in designing and fabricating mounts as well as installing the collection we thank Sandy Walcott, Fred Sager, Warren Bennett, Jenna Wainwright, and Matthew Cumbie. We are grateful as well to the many conservation interns who worked on the collection during this project, including Alisa Eagleston, Jennifer Dennis, Kari Kipper, Emily Hamilton, Greg Bailey, and Kristina Werner. For research assistance on the Damascus Room we thank Deborah Pope, Sharon Littlefield, and Maja Clark at the Doris Duke Foundation for Islamic Art, Honolulu, as well as Annie-Christine Daskalakis-Mathews and Stefan Weber. For similar assistance on the Spanish Ceiling we thank Enrique Nuere and Mary Levkoff.

Colleagues across the Museum provided much support during the many phases of the gallery reinstallation project. Though space does not permit a complete list of the many members of the staff, past and present, I should like in particular to mention the following: from Administration, Missy McHugh, Whitney Donhauser, Ashley Williams, and Betsy Wilford; from Development and Special Events, Amy O'Reilly Rizzi, Christine Begley, Kristin MacDonald, Ashley Potter Bruynes, Aiza Keesey, Eileen Destri, and former Development staff Kerstin Larsen and Savita Monie. Among our curatorial colleagues, we also thank Peter Barnet and Charles Little, Kurt Behrendt, and Ian Wardropper. In addition, we are grateful to our colleagues from Education, Peggy Fogelman and her group, including Joseph Loh, Merantine Hens, William Crow, Claire Moore, Vivian

Wick, special consultant Zeyba Rahman, and the people at Antenna Audio, including Sandy Goldberg; from Concerts and Lectures, Limor Tomer and her team; from Digital Media, Erin Coburn and her staff, especially Christopher Noey, Paco Link, Teresa Lai, Stella Paul, Matthew Morgan, Morgan Holzer, and Eileen Willis; from External Affairs and Communications, Harold Holzer, Elyse Topalian, Tom Schuler, Donna Williams, Egle Zygas, and their colleagues; from the Registrar, Aileen Chuk and her team; from the Antonio Ratti Textile Center, Giovanna Fiorino-Iannace and Melinda Watt; from General Counsel, Melissa Oliver-Janiak and Rebecca Gideon; and from Security, John Barelli and his staff. From our Merchandise Department we thank Brad Kauffman, David Wargo, Michael Nash, Atif Toor, Narmeen Husain, Ruben Luna, Will Lach, Ronald Street, Valerie Troyansky, Marilyn Jensen, Sandra Wiskari-Lukowski, and Karen Klink among many others.

For the splendid design of the galleries we thank Michael Batista, Linda Sylling, Clint Coller, Richard Lichte, Constance Norkin, Sophia Geronimus, Brian Cha, Aaron Maestri, and other present and former members of the Design Department. For architecture we thank Kevin Roche, Jim Owens, and Garry Leonard. For the construction of the galleries we thank Tom Javits, Eric Hahn, Paul Cunningham, Phil Tharel, and Mahan Khajenoori as well as Stuart Koshner, Michael Trumino, Karim al-Hindi, James Papcun, and the staff at RC Dolner LLC. For the gallery graphics we also thank Pamela Barr, Pamlyn Smith, and Philomena Mariani. For lighting design we thank Richard Renfro, Eileen Pierce, and Rick Jellow. For the beautiful display cases we thank Till Hahn and his team at Glasbau Hahn, including Jamie Ponton and Jörg Stübinger. For the Moroccan Court we thank Adil Naji and the Naji family and craftsmen of Arabesque Inc., Fez, as well as Nadia Erzini and Achva Benzinberg Stein. For other special gallery features we thank al-Nadim, Cairo; Fred Bauerschmidt; and Pier Glass, Brooklyn. For installation work in the galleries we thank Tom Scally, Taylor Miller, Crayton Sohan, Franz Schmidt, and all the Museum Riggers.

We gratefully acknowledge our academic and other colleagues for their invaluable advice, among them Oleg Grabar, Marilyn Jenkins-Madina, Steve Kossak, Finbarr Barry Flood, Jerrilyn Dodds, Terence McInerney, Lisa Golombek, Asok Kumar Das, and Ghiora Ahironi. We also thank the Hispanic Society of America, particularly Director Mitchell Codding, for its partnership in the galleries.

In the Department of Islamic Art many present and former members have contributed to the reinstallation of the new galleries and to this volume. Navina Najat Haidar has coordinated the curatorial side of the gallery project from its inception. In addition, department contributors include Maryam D. Ekhtiar, Ellen Kenney, Marika Sardar, Denise-Marie Teece, Professor Walter B. Denny, Professor Priscilla P. Soucek, Stefan Heidemann, Deniz Beyazit, Annick Des Roches, Timothy Caster, Kent Henricksen, Warren Bennett, Ria Breed, Melody Lawrence, Courtney Stewart, Michelle Ridgely, Julia Rooney, Rina Indictor, and Patricia Sclater-Booth, with special thanks to Marie Lukens Swietochowski. For research and other assistance we thank Elena Chardakliyska, Kendra Weisbin, Ayşe Pinar Gokpinar, Karin Zonis, Rashmi Viswanathan, Mariam Otkhmezuri, Eda Aksoy, Madeleine Cassella, Ariana Muessel, and Paola Chadwick. Special thanks are due to our former senior colleagues Daniel Walker, Michael Barry, and Stefano Carboni. Among our many supporters we thank our Visiting Committee, the Friends of Islamic Art, volunteers, docents, and walking-tour guides.

The head of the Editorial Department, Mark Polizzotti, and his predecessor, John O'Neill, have brought this volume to fruition together with other members of the department, in particular editors Cynthia Clark and Margaret Donovan, Gwen Roginsky, Peter Antony, Michael Sittenfeld, Robert Weisberg, Elizabeth Zechella, Jennifer Van Dalsen, Penny Jones, and Mary Jo Mace; Eriksen Translations Inc., Brooklyn, typeset the English text as well as the Arabic and Persian inscriptions, and Steve Chanin handled text corrections. In the Photograph Studio we are grateful to Barbara Bridgers and her staff, particularly Anna-Marie Kellen, Wilson Santiago, Thomas Ling, and Katherine Dahab for the photography of the objects. For the maps in the galleries as well as in this publication we thank Anandaroop Roy. For the reading and translation of inscriptions we thank Abdullah Ghouchani, Wheeler Thackston, Stefan Heidemann, Maryam Ekhtiar, and Deniz Beyazit. Maryam Ekhtiar and Priscilla Soucek have been the principal coordinators of this volume in the Islamic Department, and we are especially grateful for their efforts.

Particular gratitude is expressed to the many authors of this volume who have contributed their expertise to the discussion of the objects. In addition to staff, interns, and volunteers from the Department of Islamic Art, Museum colleagues who contributed to this book include Helen Evans, Eric Kjellgren, John Guy, Florica Zaharia, Janina Poskrobko, Daniel Hausdorf, Mechthild Baumeister, Beth Edelstein, Jean-François de Lapérouse, James Watt, and Stuart Pyhrr. We extend our gratitude to the following outside authors: Priscilla Soucek, Walter Denny, Daniel Walker, Olga Bush, Stefano Carboni, Francesca Leoni, Paola Chadwick, Qamar Adamjee, Abdullah Gouchani, Yumiko Kamada, Elisa Gagliardi Mangili, Marta Becherini, Jochen Sokoly, David Alexander, and Rebecca Lindsey.

A consortium of donors made this project possible at the Metropolitan Museum. They are a reminder that any institution is only as vital as the people who support it. We are grateful to the following contributors to the renovation and reinstallation of the new galleries: Sharmin and Bijan Mossavar-Rahmani; The Hagop Kevorkian Fund, particularly Ralph Minasian; Vehbi Koç Foundation; Patti Cadby Birch; The Patti and Everett B. Birch Foundation; Iranian–American Community; Seran and Ravi Trehan; Institute of Museum and Library Services; Tinku and Ajit Jain; Dr. and Mrs. Richard R. Lindsey; The Selz Foundation; Victor and Tara Menezes; Usha M. and Marti G. Subrahmanyam; Girish and Rasika Reddy; Younghee Kim-Wait and Jarett F. Wait; Amita and Purnendu Chatterjee; Anita and Ash Gupta; Alexander Shashaty Family Foundation; and Slomi and Rajiv Sobti.

We would also like to recognize the following donors for their support of educational programming in conjunction with the new galleries: Sharmin and Bijan Mossavar-Rahmani; The Patti and Everett B. Birch Foundation; Doris Duke Foundation for Islamic Art; The Andrew W. Mellon Foundation; Lavori Sterling Foundation, Inc.; Aga Khan Trust for Culture; American Institute of Iranian Studies; and the Moroccan-American Cultural Center. Finally, we thank Sharmin and Bijan Mossavar-Rahmani for their support of this publication and the educational mission of the Metropolitan.

Throughout the course of this historic enterprise, the assistance of our many friends and colleagues has been an inspiration to every member of the Department of Islamic Art.

Sheila R. Canby
Patti Cadby Birch Curator in Charge, Department of Islamic Art

CONSERVATION WORK FOR THE NEW GALLERIES

The renovation of the Department of Islamic Art galleries provided curators, conservators, and conservation scientists with an extraordinary opportunity to examine the collection in its entirety and to assess its conservation needs. Artworks from Islamic lands were among the earliest acquisitions by the Museum, and well over four-fifths of the present holdings were obtained before the 1970s, when the technical examination of works of art prior to their entering the collection became standard practice. As a result, the condition of many objects, textiles, and works of art on paper and parchment had never been fully ascertained, and their technical descriptions were often unverified or incorrect. Some treatment work had taken place before the opening of the previous galleries in 1975 and in the succeeding years, but these efforts were not as comprehensive in scope as the project that has accompanied the current reinstallation. In addition, past treatments often involved the use of materials that we now know to be unstable as well as outdated mounting methods that did not adequately protect the art. Finally, recent advances in scientific analysis and expertise in the Museum have allowed us to glean more information than ever before about the materials and production methods used by Islamic artists and craftsmen.

Many discoveries, both minor and major, have been made during this project. For example, among the smaller objects in this volume, it was found that dark layers of tarnish on the surface of a silver cup with *kufic* inscriptions (cat. 83) since its acquisition had concealed the fact that the interior was gilded by the amalgam process while the exterior was not. Now that it has been cleaned, the intended coloristic contrast between both sides can be fully appreciated. On a much larger scale, a thorough examination of the Damascus Room (cat. 238) revealed that in the previous installation the wall panels had been rearranged from their original configuration to suit the available gallery space. Now that the entrance door and windows have been returned to their correct location along the same wall, a sense of the sun-filled courtyard this audience chamber once overlooked has been restored. In addition, the proper sequence of the calligraphic text that runs from right to left in the upper part of the wall panels has been reestablished.

At the same time, some less felicitous discoveries were made in the course of this project. Examinations revealed the incorporation of extraneous fragments and/or excessive restoration in some cases, while the decorative program of others had been over-embellished by past restorers. Such restorations often cast a discolored veil that partially obscured original compositions. In other instances, the restorations themselves—some executed over a century ago—have acquired historic value. Working together, conservators and curators discussed how to deal with these modern interventions on a case-by-case basis, keeping in mind the integrity of the original fabric and artistic conception. Understandably, this process influenced final decisions about which art works were selected for exhibition.

Textile conservators identified twenty-seven of the most important textiles and carpets in the collection that required comprehensive treatment, including the removal of previous restorations, cleaning, stabilization, and in-depth fiber and structure analysis. Within this group, the Emperor's Carpet (cat. 181) was the focus of an intensive three-year project. Over one hundred textiles also required extensive consolidation and protection in enclosed mounts to ensure adequate structural support and a microclimate with a stable relative humidity. Many of these textiles were lined on the reverse and/or stitched onto a fabric that had been specifically dyed to a compatible color. Mounting systems for an additional two hundred fifty textiles and carpets were designed and implemented by conservators so that they could be safely displayed.

For paper conservators the closing of the galleries provided a rare opportunity to examine the bound manuscripts in the collection that had regularly been on view and to address any needed stabilization to their miniature paintings and bindings. Over three hundred folios, including those from the incomparable *Shahnama* of Shah Tahmasp (cat. 138 A–G), were also thoroughly examined, treated as needed, and rehoused in archival mounts. Given their light-sensitive nature, these folios cannot be exhibited for more than a few weeks at a time. As a result, over seven hundred works of art on paper and parchment will be displayed on a rotating basis each year in the new galleries.

In 2008 object conservators were awarded an Institute of Museum and Library Services matching grant to treat the more than four hundred glass, ceramic, and stucco finds from the Museum's archaeological excavations at Nishapur, many of which had been restored with unstable adhesives and could not be safely handled. Over five hundred additional objects of various media from the collection were examined and treated to assure their stability and improve their appearance with the removal of old adhesives, discolored restorations, and deteriorated metal coatings. Hundreds of ingeniously supportive but unobtrusive mounts were made by preparators and metalworking staff, often in consultation with conservators.

With the de-installation of the former galleries, the long-standing need for the structural stabilization, cleaning, and consolidation of actively flaking paint layers and metal-leaf decoration in the Damascus Room and Spanish Ceiling could finally be addressed. These architectural projects presented considerable challenges given their size and complexity, calling on the collaboration of conservators, construction staff, architects, and specialists for the installation of historic architecture. After the conservation work was completed, wall and ceiling panels were remounted using more appropriate supporting frameworks and fastening systems, with full access provided for monitoring and maintenance.

Less visible but crucially important to the long-term preservation of the collection is the considerable attention that has been devoted to case design, environmental systems, and climate monitoring for the new galleries. In the decades since the former galleries were installed, the deleterious effects of unstable wood products, fabrics, and adhesives on works of art have been noted and investigated. While in some cases this damage can be acute and readily apparent, in others the alterations can occur at an insidiously slow rate and may not be noticeable in the short term. Consequently, all of the materials proposed for use in the casework for these galleries were tested by conservation scientists, and only those approved have been incorporated. In addition, all case designs were reviewed and modified when necessary by conservators and conservation scientists.

Before and during conservation treatments, analytical information was obtained by nondestructive means or by sampling at break edges or other inconspicuous locations. The results of these analyses were used to determine appropriate treatment strategies and to provide material identifications for object records and gallery labels. Dissemination of the significant technical discoveries and related studies conducted during the course of this project has begun and will continue in lectures and scholarly publications. It is hoped that this knowledge will increase appreciation of the technical skill and artistic mastery evident in this extraordinary collection.

Jean-François de Lapérouse
Conservator, Sherman Fairchild Center for Objects Conservation

CONTRIBUTORS TO THE CATALOGUE

QA Qamar Adamjee, Associate Curator of South Asian Art, Asian Art Museum, San Francisco

DGA David Alexander, Independent Scholar, Puycelsi

MB Mechthild Baumeister, Conservator, Sherman Fairchild Center for Objects Conservation, The Metropolitan Museum of Art, New York

MaB Marta Becherini, Former Research Assistant, Department of Asian Art, The Metropolitan Museum of Art, New York

OB Olga Bush, Visiting Scholar, Kunsthistorisches Institut–Max-Planck-Institut, Florence

SRC Sheila R. Canby, Patti Cadby Birch Curator in Charge, Department of Islamic Art, The Metropolitan Museum of Art, New York

SC Stefano Carboni, Director, Art Gallery of Western Australia, Perth

PC Paola Chadwick, Research Assistant, Department of Islamic Art, The Metropolitan Museum of Art, New York

EC Elena Chardakliyska, 2010–2011 Kress Interpretive Fellow, Departments of Islamic Art and Education, The Metropolitan Museum of Art, New York

WBD Walter B. Denny, Professor of Art History, University of Massachusetts at Amherst

BE Beth Edelstein, Associate Conservator, Sherman Fairchild Center for Objects Conservation, The Metropolitan Museum of Art, New York

ME Maryam D. Ekhtiar, Senior Research Associate, Department of Islamic Art, The Metropolitan Museum of Art, New York

HCE Helen C. Evans, Mary and Michael Jaharis Curator of Byzantine Art, Department of Medieval Art and The Cloisters, The Metropolitan Museum of Art, New York

AG Abdullah Ghouchani, 2008–2009 and 2009–2010 Andrew W. Mellon Fellow, Epigrapher, Department of Islamic Art, The Metropolitan Museum of Art, New York

PG Ayşe Pinar Gokpinar, Intern, Department of Islamic Art, The Metropolitan Museum of Art, New York

JG John Guy, Florence and Herbert Irving Curator of Southeast Asian Art, Department of Asian Art, The Metropolitan Museum of Art, New York

NNH Navina Najat Haidar, Curator and Administrator, Department of Islamic Art, The Metropolitan Museum of Art, New York

DH Daniel Hausdorf, Assistant Conservator, Sherman Fairchild Center for Objects Conservation, The Metropolitan Museum of Art, New York

SH Stefan Heidemann, Associate Curator, Department of Islamic Art, The Metropolitan Museum of Art, New York

YK Yumiko Kamada, Assistant Professor, Waseda Institute for Advanced Study, Tokyo

EK Ellen Kenney, Assistant Professor, Department of Arab and Islamic Civilizations, American University in Cairo

EPK Eric P. Kjellgren, Evelyn A. J. Hall and John A. Friede Associate Curator, Department of the Arts of Africa, Oceania, and the Americas, The Metropolitan Museum of Art, New York

JFL Jean-François de Lapérouse, Conservator, Sherman Fairchild Center for Objects Conservation, The Metropolitan Museum of Art, New York

FL Francesca Leoni, Assistant Curator of Islamic Art, Museum of Fine Arts, Houston

EGM Elisa Gagliardi Mangili, 2006–2007 Sylvan C. Coleman and Pamela Coleman Memorial Fund Fellow, Department of Textile Conservation, The Metropolitan Museum of Art, New York

JP Janina Poskrobko, Associate Conservator, Department of Textile Conservation, The Metropolitan Museum of Art, New York

SWP Stuart W. Pyhrr, Arthur Ochs Sulzberger Curator in Charge, Department of Arms and Armor, The Metropolitan Museum of Art, New York

MS Marika Sardar, Research Associate, Department of Islamic Art, The Metropolitan Museum of Art, New York

JS Jochen Sokoly, Gallery Director and Assistant Professor, Department of Art History, Virginia Commonwealth University, School of the Arts in Qatar, Doha

PS Priscilla P. Soucek, John L. Loeb Professor, Institute of Fine Arts, New York University, New York

DMT Denise-Marie Teece, Research Associate, Department of Islamic Art, The Metropolitan Museum of Art, New York

RV Rashmi Viswanathan, Department of Islamic Art, The Metropolitan Museum of Art, New York

DW Daniel Walker, Pritzker Chair and Curator of Asian Art, Chair and Christa C. Mayer Thurman Curator of Textiles, Art Institute of Chicago

JCYW James C. Y. Watt, Curator Emeritus, Department of Asian Art, The Metropolitan Museum of Art, New York

KW Kendra Weisbin, Department of Islamic Art, The Metropolitan Museum of Art, New York

KrW Kristina Werner, Intern, Sherman Fairchild Center for Objects Conservation, The Metropolitan Museum of Art, New York

FZ Florica Zaharia, Conservator in Charge, Department of Textile Conservation, The Metropolitan Museum of Art, New York

KZ Karin Zonis, Department of Islamic Art, The Metropolitan Museum of Art, New York

NOTE TO THE READER

For the transliteration of Arabic, Persian, and some Turkish words, we are using a simplified version of the *IJMES* (*International Journal of Middle Eastern Studies*) system. *Ayn* and *hamza*, letters of the alphabet, are marked, but other diacritical signs are not used. We have attempted to retain the phonetic integrity of the individual languages. For example, the name *Sulaiman* is used in an Arabic or Persian context, but *Süleyman* in a Turkish one. In most instances, we use the modern Turkish spelling for Turkish words. In addition, the Persian silent *h* (ه) is transliterated as *a*, as in *Shahnama*, as is the Arabic *ta marbuta* (ة), as in *mashraba*. When an Arabic, Persian, or Turkish word is found in *Webster's Encyclopedic Unabridged Dictionary* with a standard English spelling, this form is used. We have chosen to keep the names of cities untransliterated.

Dates are given in the Gregorian calendar unless an object carries a precise Hegira date. In that case, dates are given in both eras. References to the Qur'an follow the numbering used in the Egyptian standard edition of 1924, which has been widely used in the Muslim world. English translations of the Qur'an are taken from Arthur J. Arberry's *The Koran Interpreted* (New York, 1966). It is worth noting that the verse numbering in Arberry's translation often differs from that in the Cairo volume, which was based on an edition of the Qur'an first published by Gustav Flügel in 1834 (*Corani textus arabicus*; Leipzig, 1834).

Throughout the catalogue, dimensions are given in the following sequence: height precedes width precedes depth. When necessary, the abbreviations H. (height), L. (length), W. (width), and Diam. (diameter) are used for clarity.

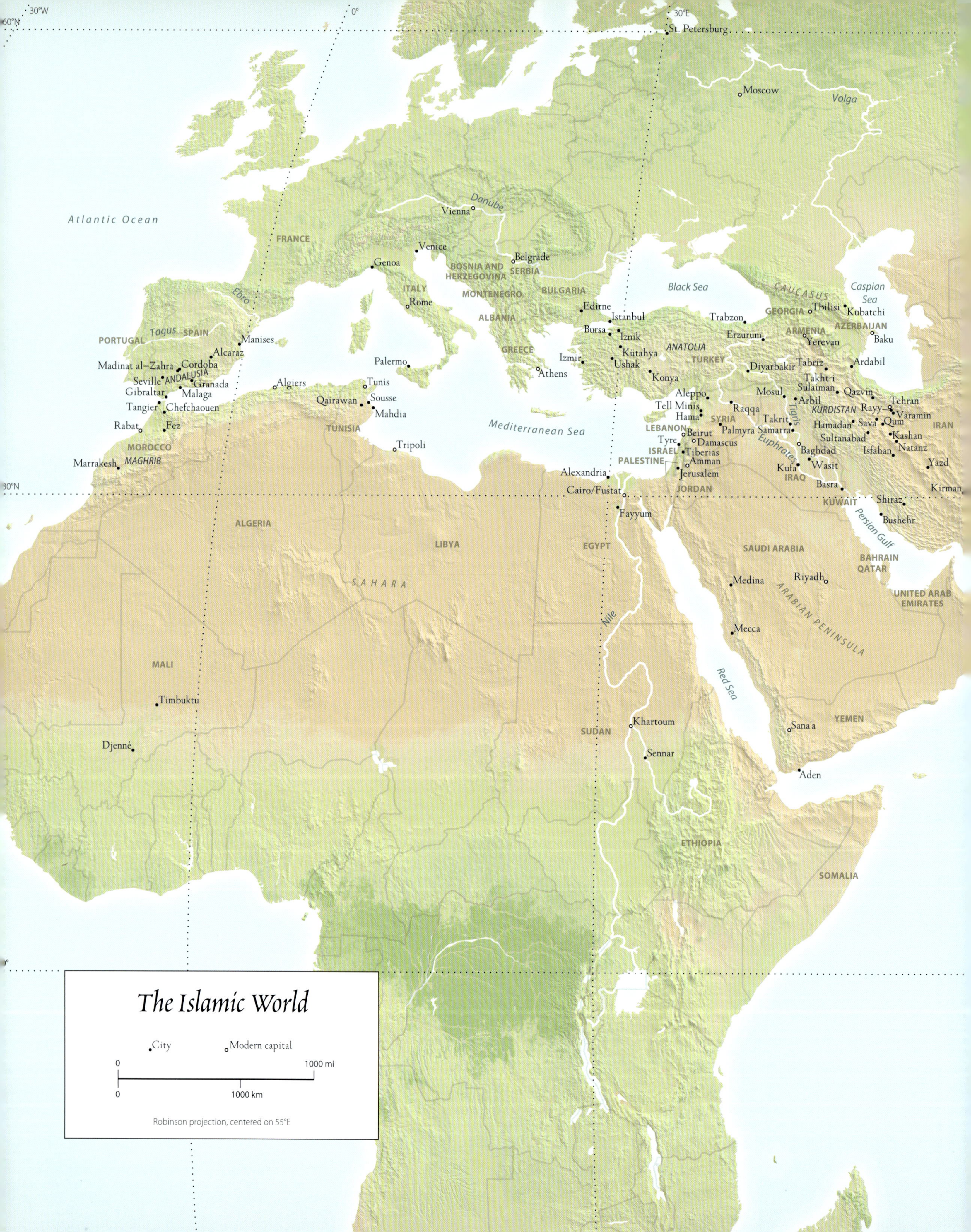
30°W
0°
30°E
60°N
St. Petersburg
Moscow
Volga
Atlantic Ocean
Danube
Vienna
FRANCE
Venice
Belgrade
Genoa
BOSNIA AND HERZEGOVINA
SERBIA
Ebro
ITALY
MONTENEGRO
BULGARIA
Black Sea
CAUCASUS
Caspian Sea
Rome
ALBANIA
Edirne
Istanbul
Trabzon
GEORGIA
Tbilisi
Kubatchi
PORTUGAL
Tagus
SPAIN
Manises
Bursa
Iznik
Erzurum
ARMENIA
AZERBAIJAN
Alcaraz
GREECE
Kutahya
ANATOLIA
Yerevan
Baku
Madinat al-Zahra
Cordoba
Palermo
Izmir
Ushak
TURKEY
Diyarbakir
Tabriz
Ardabil
Seville
ANDALUSIA
Granada
Athens
Konya
Takht-i Sulaiman
Gibraltar
Malaga
Algiers
Tunis
Mosul
Qazvin
Tangier
Chefchaouen
Qairawan
Sousse
Aleppo
Arbil
Tehran
Mahdia
Tell Minis
Raqqa
Tigris
KURDISTAN
Rayy
Varamin
Rabat
Fez
Hama
SYRIA
Takrit
Hamadan
Sava
Qum
IRAN
Mediterranean Sea
LEBANON
Beirut
Palmyra
Samarra
Kashan
TUNISIA
Tyre
Damascus
Euphrates
Sultanabad
MOROCCO
Tripoli
ISRAEL
Tiberias
Baghdad
Isfahan
Natanz
Marrakesh
MAGHRIB
PALESTINE
Amman
Yazd
Alexandria
Jerusalem
Kufa
Wasit
IRAQ
30°N
Cairo/Fustat
JORDAN
Basra
Kirman
KUWAIT
Shiraz
Fayyum
Persian Gulf
Bushehr
ALGERIA
LIBYA
EGYPT
SAUDI ARABIA
BAHRAIN
QATAR
Medina
Riyadh
SAHARA
UNITED ARAB EMIRATES
ARABIAN PENINSULA
Nile
Mecca
MALI
Red Sea
Timbuktu
Khartoum
YEMEN
Sana'a
Djenné
SUDAN
Sennar
Aden
ETHIOPIA
SOMALIA
0°
The Islamic World
City
Modern capital
0
1000 mi
0
1000 km
Robinson projection, centered on 55°E

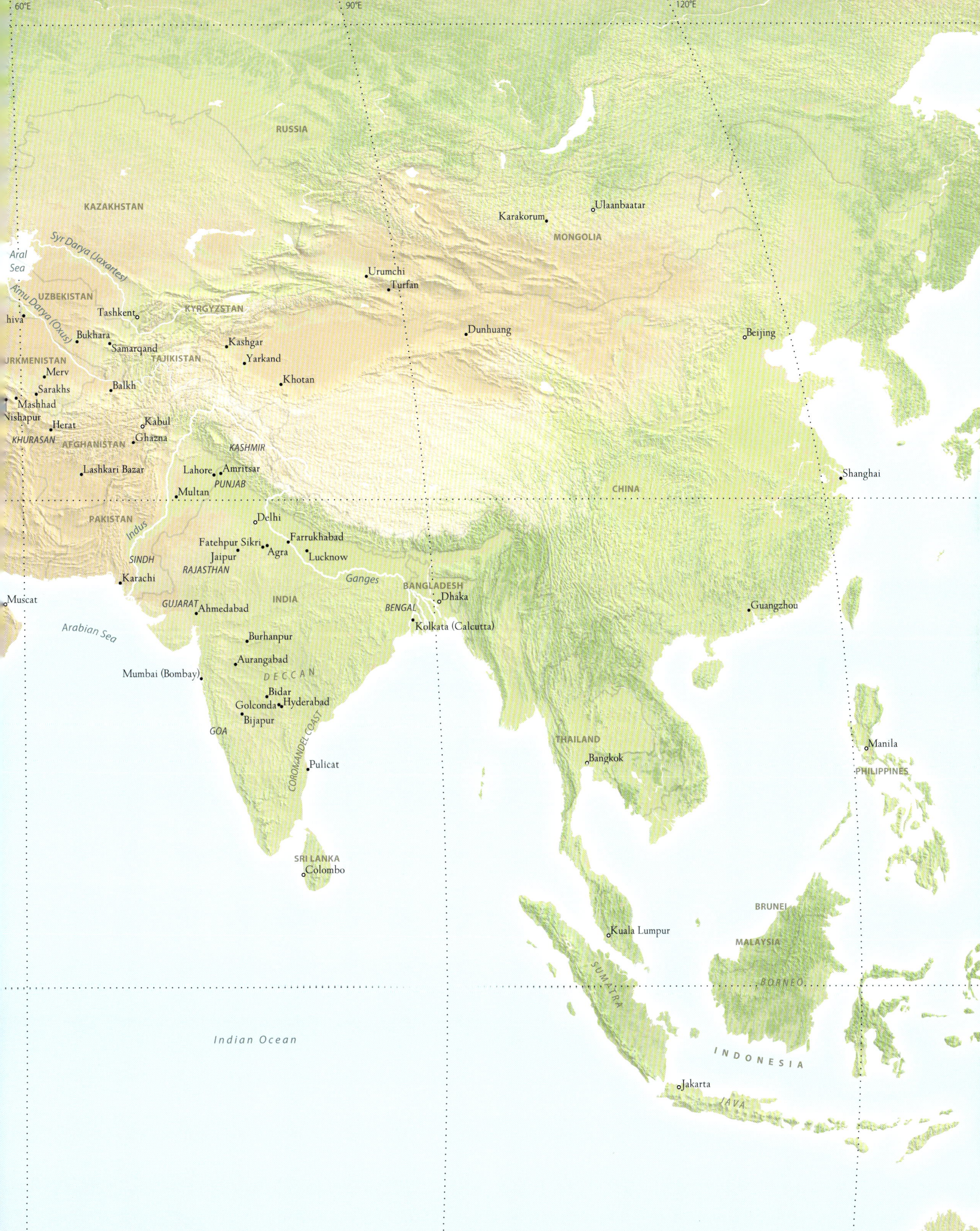

60°E
90°E
120°E
RUSSIA
KAZAKHSTAN
Karakorum
Ulaanbaatar
MONGOLIA
Aral Sea
Syr Darya (Jaxartes)
Amu Darya (Oxus)
UZBEKISTAN
Khiva
Tashkent
KYRGYZSTAN
Urumchi
Turfan
Bukhara
Samarqand
TAJIKISTAN
Kashgar
Yarkand
Dunhuang
Beijing
TURKMENISTAN
Merv
Sarakhs
Balkh
Khotan
Mashhad
Nishapur
Herat
Kabul
Ghazna
KHURASAN
AFGHANISTAN
KASHMIR
Lashkari Bazar
Lahore
Amritsar
PUNJAB
Multan
Shanghai
CHINA
PAKISTAN
Delhi
Indus
Fatehpur Sikri
Agra
Farrukhabad
Lucknow
Jaipur
SINDH
RAJASTHAN
Karachi
Ganges
BANGLADESH
Dhaka
Muscat
GUJARAT
Ahmedabad
INDIA
BENGAL
Guangzhou
Kolkata (Calcutta)
Arabian Sea
Burhanpur
Aurangabad
Mumbai (Bombay)
DECCAN
Bidar
Golconda
Hyderabad
Bijapur
GOA
COROMANDEL COAST
THAILAND
Bangkok
Manila
PHILIPPINES
Pulicat
SRI LANKA
Colombo
BRUNEI
Kuala Lumpur
MALAYSIA
SUMATRA
BORNEO
Indian Ocean
INDONESIA
Jakarta
JAVA

MASTERPIECES

from the Department of Islamic Art
in The Metropolitan Museum of Art

Introduction

Building a Collection of Islamic Art at the Metropolitan Museum, 1870–2011

PRISCILLA P. SOUCEK

More than twelve thousand objects from the Islamic Near East, Central Asia, the Indian subcontinent, and the Islamic West—Spain, North Africa, and southern Italy—are currently preserved in the Metropolitan's Department of Islamic Art, reflecting the taste, enthusiasm, and generosity of the Museum's donors as well as the expertise of its curators and the skill of its archaeologists. During the first phase of its development—in the decades that intervened between the Metropolitan's foundation in 1870 and the establishment in 1932 of a separate department devoted to the art of the Near East—this collection was formed largely by donations and bequests.[1] A second stage in the collection's development—the decades between 1932 and the designation in 1963 of an independent Department of Islamic Art—marks the Museum's participation in Near Eastern archaeology, initially in Iraq at Ctesiphon and then in Iran at Nishapur. These activities substantially augmented the department's holdings; nearly half of the objects in the department's custody derive from these excavations. The third stage in the collection's life began in 1975, when a suite of rooms on the second floor of the Metropolitan's southeastern wing was chosen to house its permanent installation; it is to that space that the objects have now returned (see the following essay on the new galleries by Navina Haidar).

The collectors whose donations and bequests laid the foundation for the Museum's Islamic collection reflect the expanding cultural horizons of American, and particularly New York society in the later nineteenth and twentieth centuries. Most of them visited Europe repeatedly or even settled there; a few ventured to the Near East and beyond to South and East Asia. The earliest and most comprehensive of these collections was that formed by Edward C. Moore (1827–1891), head designer at Tiffany and Company from 1868 until his death.

Moore's collection, which arrived as a bequest in 1891 and was first put on view the following year, covered a wide range of periods and media, including Greek and Etruscan vases, metalwork (cat. 104), glass, ceramics, and textiles of various periods and regions. The terms of Moore's bequest required that the entirety

A Century of Installations: A Photo Essay

REBECCA MERIWETHER LINDSEY

These photographs from the Museum's Archives record installations over the last one hundred years of objects now in the Department of Islamic art. They provide a long view of the changing contexts and interpretations of the collection.

In presentation, the pictures follow historical developments. Initially most works of art from the Islamic world were considered to be industrial or decorative rather than fine art, and were displayed as such. At the same time, major donations began to prompt the dedication of a permanent display of such material. Thus "Donors and Decorative Arts: The First Displays, 1907–20" assembles images of the first installations, which were heavily dependent on early benefactors. By contrast, the period covered by "The Near Eastern Department: Establishment and Expansion, 1921–49" saw refinement of displays, with a clear focus on Near Eastern art driven by curatorial expertise as well as donations, purchases, and excavations at Nishapur. The section "Postwar Displays, 1949–70" reflects the growing recognition of the field of Islamic art, culminating in the 1963 establishment of the Department of Islamic Art and its first permanent galleries in 1975.

The displays shown here have primarily been installed in two areas on the second floor of the Museum: from about 1907 to 1970, on the north side of the building, in Wings D, E, and H (now the Asian Department); and since 1975 in Wing K, above the Greek and Roman galleries. Since 1963 the objects have belonged to the Department of Islamic Art. Before that, they were part of the Department of Decorative Arts (1907–22) and its sub-department of Near Eastern Art (1923–31), and then of the Department of Near Eastern Art, which was created in 1932 with two divisions, Ancient Near Eastern Art and "Art of the Islamic Near East, comprising Moorish Spain and North Africa, Egypt under the Arabs, Turkey in Europe, the Caucasus, Asia Minor, Syria, Mesopotamia, Arabia, Persia, West Turkestan, Afghanistan, India, Indonesia, and Indo-China."

Museum archival records, including some referred to here, provide varying dates for the building and administrative divisions.

of his collection be displayed in a contiguous space (figs. 2, 6).[2] Moore's broad taste was characteristic of the Aesthetic Movement, which focused on the qualities of the individual object without respect to its time and place of origin. This eclecticism encouraged him and others to integrate elements from various periods, cultures, or regions in their own artistic creations.[3]

In 1902 the Museum received a collection, described as "bric-à-brac" in the *New York Times*, amassed by William B. Osgood Field (1823–1900), a New York businessman and philanthropist who lived for many years in Rome. Upon his death the collection was bequeathed to his wife, Katherine Parker, then to the Metropolitan after her death in 1901.[4] Into the Museum came Turkish (cats. 215, 218A), Chinese, and European ceramics along with a pair of Italian clocks and some Indian shields.

Also donated in 1902 were jade objects belonging to Heber Reginald Bishop (1840–1902). Bishop, who made his fortune in Cuban sugar and Minnesota iron ore, was an avid collector of carved jades and other hard stones. Shortly before his death he arranged for this collection to be given to the Metropolitan Museum, stipulating that it be displayed in a setting that replicated the ballroom in his house in which it had been on view. He also provided for the publication of a book about jade and similar stones, including the twenty-seven jades attributed to Central Asia (cats. 133, 258) or India that are now on display in the Islamic galleries.[5]

Although most closely associated with the library and museum that bears his name, John Pierpont Morgan (1837–1913) played several distinct roles at the Metropolitan. One of the Museum's initial supporters, he joined its Board of Trustees in 1889 and served as its fourth president (1905–12).[6] His tenure in that capacity was instrumental in the institution's transformation from an enterprise run largely by volunteers to a professional organization with full-time employees.

Morgan preferred to purchase groups of objects amassed by others, one such example being the George Hoentschel collection of decorative arts that arrived at the Museum as a loan in 1910.[7] The size and quality of this group prompted the Museum to construct a new gallery for its display, in anticipation of its eventual donation.[8] Although Morgan died before the collection's status had been clarified, objects purchased by him, now in the Islamic Department, were donated in 1917 by his son, J. P. Morgan, Jr. Among them were a magnificent ivory casket from southern Italy

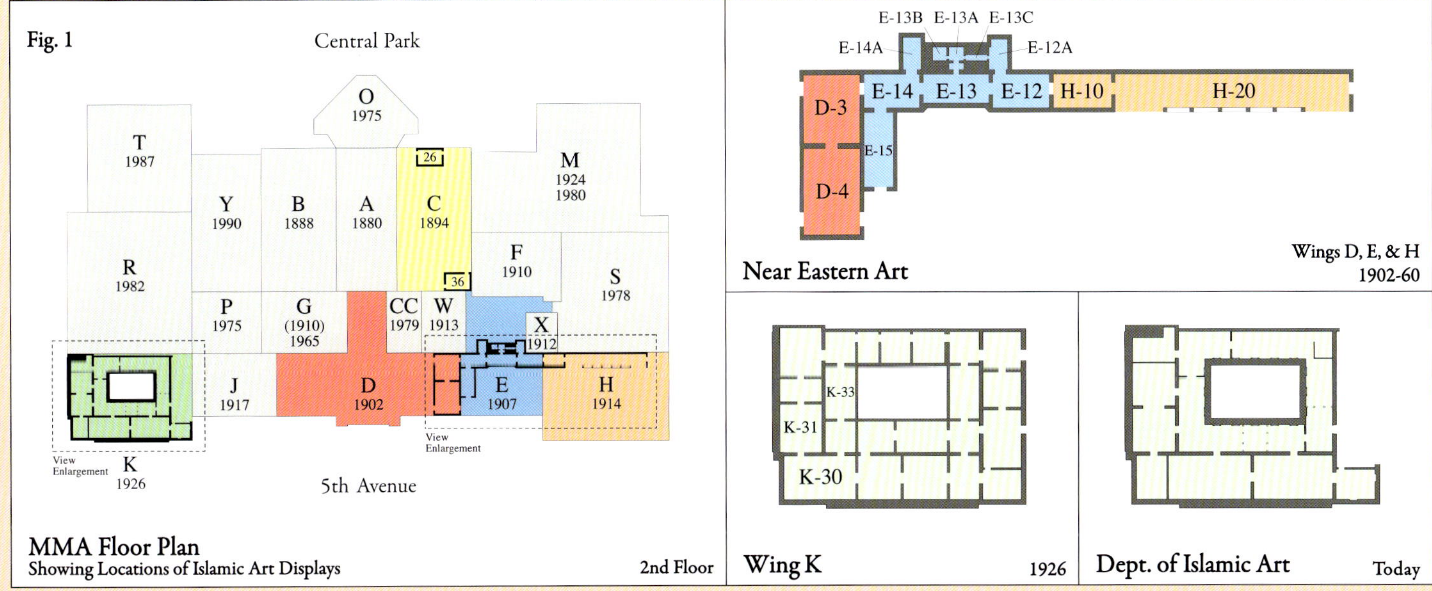

Fig. 1

MMA Floor Plan
Showing Locations of Islamic Art Displays

(cat. 39), a pair of Indian carpets (cat. 262), an ecclesiastical vestment made from an Ottoman textile, a group of enameled and gilded mosque lamps from Mamluk Egypt (cat. 109), and panels of colorful tiles from Ottoman Iznik.

Alexander Smith Cochran (1874–1929) donated a collection of illustrated manuscripts (fig. 17). Twenty-four manuscripts as well as thirty single-page pictures, given in 1913 (cats. 123A–C, 135), were accompanied by a published catalogue compiled by A. V. Williams Jackson and Abraham Yohannan.[9] Cochran, who had inherited carpet mills from his maternal grandfather, was most active as a yachtsman and competed in numerous races. In 1907 Cochran and Jackson, who were neighbors in Yonkers, traveled together to Iran. Containing illustrated versions of Persian literary classics as well as texts in Turkish and a copy of the Qur'an, Cochran's manuscript collection was probably formed with Jackson's advice.

The bequest of William Milne Grinnell (1858–1920) combined some twenty paintings, including a dozen from Firdausi's *Shahnama* (cat. 239A, B), with an impressive variety of ceramic vessels and tile panels (cat. 130).[10] Grinnell, who came from a well-established New York family of Huguenot origin, had graduated from Yale University in 1881; subsequently, he trained as an architect at Columbia University and practiced this profession for some years. A brief sketch of his life, however, published in a history of Yale graduates written in 1910, placed particular stress on his years of travel, suggesting that he had visited "every country in the world."[11] Describing the Grinnell bequest in 1920, Joseph Breck indicated that many of the donor's purchases had been made in Cairo, "where he spent several winters."[12] If so, the preponderance of Persian ceramics, ranging in date from the twelfth to the nineteenth century, in his collection is noteworthy; his Egyptian examples consist mostly of fragments from luster-painted bowls.[13] Grinnell also collected Syrian, Turkish, and Central Asian vessels.[14]

Near Eastern and Indian rugs, widely popular, came to the Museum from several donors. Merchant Benjamin Altman (1840–1913) gave some sumptuous Persian carpets made of silk (cats. 182, 183) and Indian rugs of *pashmina* (cat. 265).[15] Having long coveted Altman's painting collection, which included pictures attributed to Rembrandt, Museum officials accepted his requirement that they be displayed, along with the donor's own portrait, in a room surrounded by the remainder of his collection—carpets, Turkish ceramics (cat. 210), Chinese porcelain, Japanese metalwork and lacquer, European sculpture, rock crystal, and furniture as well as an extensive array of snuff bottles (figs. 3, 13).

During the 1920s the Museum's growing importance as a repository of Near Eastern art began to attract the attention of more specialized collectors. In the fall of 1921 James F. Ballard (1851–1931), a lifelong resident of St. Louis, selected the Metropolitan Museum as the venue for a temporary exhibition of sixty-five examples from his rug collection.[16] Ballard, who had made a fortune through the sale of patent medicines, particularly "Ballard's Snow Liniment," was in equal measure self-promotional and

Donors and Decorative Arts: The First Displays, 1907–20

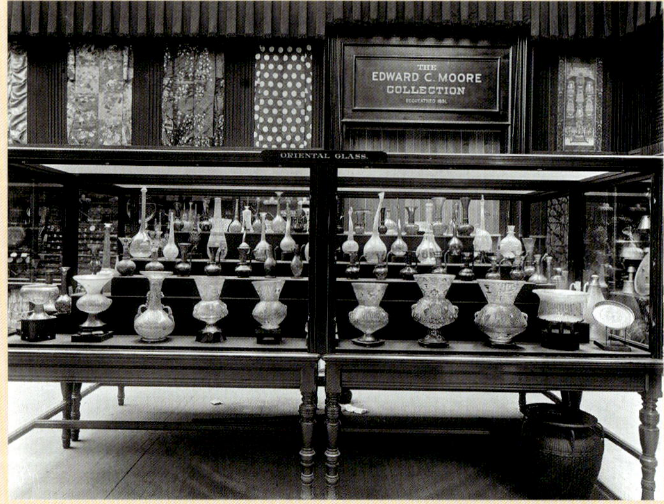

Fig. 2 May 9, 1907: Wing C, The Edward C. Moore Collection of Oriental Glass. This is the Museum's earliest photograph of objects now in the Islamic Department.

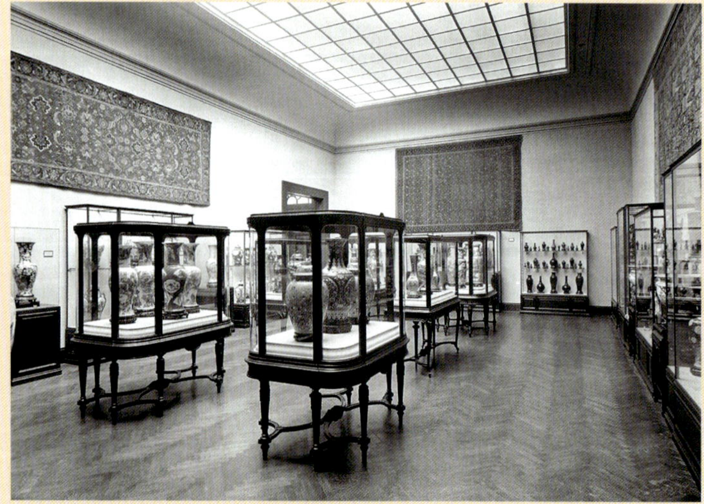

Fig. 3 November 11, 1914: Wing C, The Benjamin Altman Collection, which included sixteen oriental carpets, Safavid and Ottoman ceramics and metalwork, and Chinese porcelain. In 1926 the Altman Collection moved to galleries K-30-36.

passionate about the moral, historical, and artistic significance of the rugs he owned.[17] Between 1916 and 1921 he arranged for public exhibitions of his rugs in St. Louis, New York, Chicago, Indianapolis, Minneapolis, Pittsburgh, and Buffalo. After this flurry of publicity, he donated to the Metropolitan 112 rugs (figs. 10, 11; cats. 51, 236, 237) along with several other textiles (cat. 198A, B). He also wrote and published catalogues that combined colorful descriptions of the rugs on display with tales of his own harrowing adventures as a collector in the Near East.

Maurice Sven Dimand (1892–1986), the Museum's first specialized curator for Near Eastern art, had a strong personal interest in the study of rugs.[18] He joined the Museum in 1923 after completing a doctoral dissertation on Coptic wool tapestries at the University of Vienna under the tutelage of Josef Strzygowski.[19] Starting with a catalogue of the Metropolitan's Coptic textiles, Dimand's thirty-seven-year career provided the study of Near Eastern art a solid professional foundation. He gave lectures, mounted exhibitions, and published collection guides in addition to important reference works. The years of Dimand's service also witnessed major acquisitions by the Near Eastern Department. Among the more focused collections of this period was that of George Dupont Pratt (1869–1936). Donated in 1929 and 1931, most of these textiles were inscribed but varied in technique (cats. 26, 27, 29). Many had embroidered *tiraz* inscriptions signaling their production in official state-sponsored workshops; others had woven, stamped, or printed texts.[20]

Some donors enriched multiple departments of the Museum. Theodore M. Davis (1837–1915), primarily known for his archaeological projects in Egypt, bequeathed to the Near Eastern Department an impressive album of seventeenth-century Persian and Indian paintings (cat. 190) along with more than eighty objects from Spain, Turkey, Iran, and India—these include two capitals from Madinat al-Zahra in Spain and carpets from Iran and the Caucasus. Due to legal challenges to his will, this bequest only reached the Museum in 1930.[21]

While donations by the Havemeyers to the Museum's collection of European paintings are well known, the family also owned works from the Near East. The original impetus to collect examples of "decorative art" appears to have come from the family patriarch, Henry Osborn Havemeyer (1894–1907), who had become fascinated with objects from distant regions that he had seen at international fairs and expositions.[22] The family's initial gift, in 1929, was given in his memory and is known as the H. O. Havemeyer Collection. It included Persian, Syrian, and Turkish ceramics along with some Persian manuscript pages (cats. 43A, B, 53). The family's generosity to the Metropolitan was continued by Horace Havemeyer (1886–1956), son of Henry and Louisine; the final installment of his gift arrived as a bequest in 1956.[23] His collection was composed largely of ceramics and included objects that had once belonged to his parents (cat. 97); his own purchases were made with advice from the dealer and collector Dikran Kelekian (1869–1951).[24]

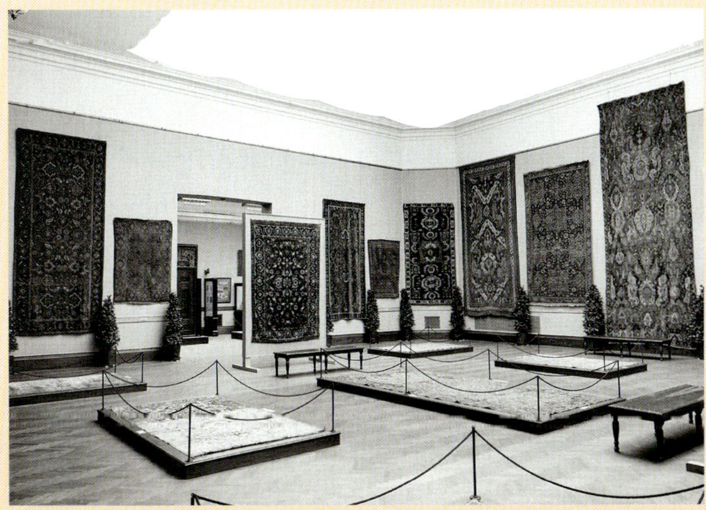

Fig. 4 November 5, 1910: "Early Oriental Rugs." Several pieces shown here at this first Islamic art special exhibition at the Museum later entered the permanent collection. The total exhibition costs of $4,000 included $100 for rental of the topiary bay trees from Bloomingdale's department store.

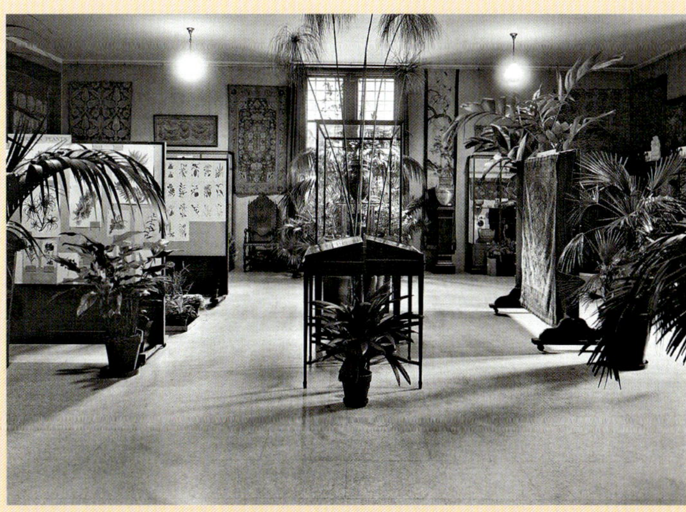

Fig. 5 March 21, 1919: "Plant Form in Ornament," a special exhibition in collaboration with the New York Botanical Garden, was conceived during World War I as a patriotic means "to give art designers a new trend and inspiration . . . better than Germany and Austria." It included nineteen objects from the Islamic world, including ceramics from the 1902 Osgood Field donation. (Letter, Britton to Kent, September 4, 1918)

Another important donor of the Dimand era was Cora Timken Burnett (ca. 1865–1957). Her father, Henry Timken (1831–1909), born in Germany, had emigrated to St. Louis in 1847. After a number of years in farming, he turned to the manufacture of carriages and made a fortune from the patent he held for the tapered ball bearings used in carriage axles. (Today, the Timken Company that he founded in 1889 continues to operate in several countries.)[25] In 1897 the Timken family moved to San Diego, where Cora was active as a painter and sculptor, although no work by her appears to survive.[26] Following her July 1920 marriage to an osteopathic physician named John Clawson Burnett, Cora traveled extensively and collected works of art. After her death in January 1957, her collection was divided between the San Diego Museum of Art, an institution supported by other members of her family, and the Metropolitan Museum. San Diego received Japanese woodblock prints and Indian sculptures;[27] the portion of her Metropolitan Museum bequest that is now in the Islamic Department included more than twenty-five single-page pictures and album leaves (cats. 55, 59, 92, 120–21, 202). Some of these had passed through the collection of F. R. Martin (1868–1933), who appears to have obtained them in Istanbul.[28]

By the 1950s the Metropolitan's collection of carpets was sizable, yet its range and quality were much enhanced through gifts and bequests from Joseph V. McMullan (1896–1973), whose generosity to the Museum extended from 1955 to 1974. McMullan's collection was particularly strong in rugs from Turkey (cat. 235), the Caucasus, and Central Asia, but he also gave the Museum key examples from Iran, India, and Spain. While some of these came from important court production centers, McMullan had a particular affection for works with unusual designs of nomadic or village origin (fig. 18).[29]

Notable objects for the Near Eastern Department were also acquired by purchase under Dimand's leadership. These included a Mamluk enameled glass bottle formerly in the collection of the Habsburgs (cat. 111),[30] two carpets from the collection of Edith Rockefeller, one of which has come to be known as the Emperor's Carpet (cat. 181),[31] and a majestic, lion-shaped incense burner dated to 1181–82 (cat. 85).[32] Dimand's tenure also marked the beginning of the department's close working relationship with the Kevorkian Foundation and its successor, the Kevorkian Fund.[33]

The 1930s and 1940s witnessed the Museum's establishment of a Near East Expedition to conduct archaeology in the region. Two of this group's founding members, Walter Hauser and Charles K. Wilkinson (1897–1986), had previously worked in Egypt; the third, Joseph M. Upton, came from the Decorative Art Department. Their initial venture, in 1931, was to participate in the German-led expedition to Ctesiphon in Iraq.[34] In 1932 and 1933–34 the group worked at Qasr-i Abu Nasr in Iran near Shiraz.[35]

After these rather modest ventures, the group accepted an invitation from the Persian government to shift its attention to the site of Nishapur near the modern city of Mashhad, where they had expected to find remains of the pre-Islamic period. What they

The First Displays, 1907–20

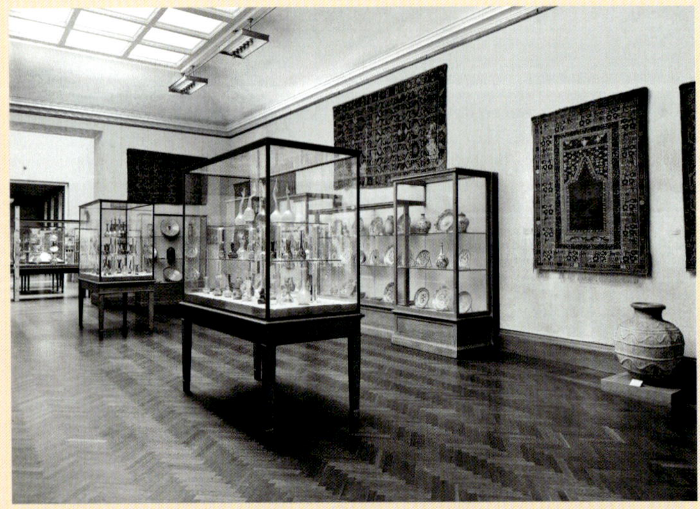

Fig. 6 June 27, 1918: Gallery E-12, showing glass from the Moore Collection and 19th-century carpets. After Wing E opened in 1910 the Museum gave Near Eastern art separate galleries in Wings D, E, and, after 1912, H. At the north end of Wing E, galleries E-12, E-13, and E-14 served as the three primary display rooms for Islamic objects for approximately fifty years.

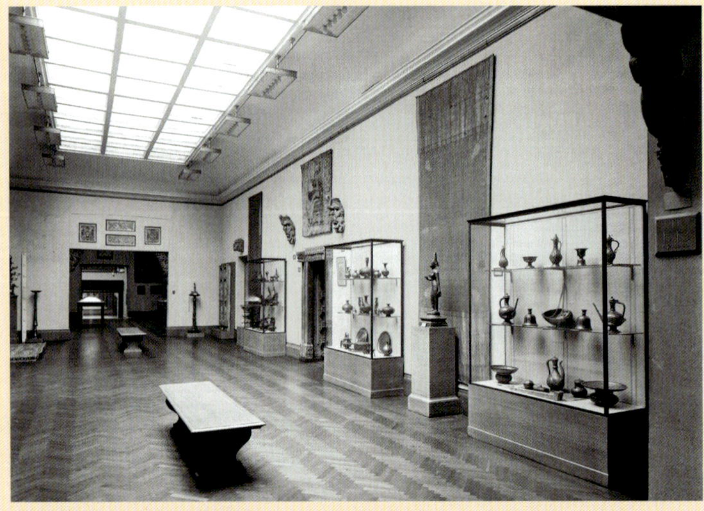

Fig. 7 June 26, 1918: Gallery E-13, looking south into E-14. Although called the "Central Persian" gallery, E-13 displayed mostly Indian art and was one of the three large Near Eastern art galleries from 1910 to 1958. During those years the terms *Persian* and *Assyrian* were also in use, often to distinguish Islamic-period from ancient Near Eastern art. A Museum trustee wrote, "It may be necessary eventually to separate the Persian and the Assyrian and have different experts in charge." (Letter, Coffin to Breck, October 14, 1931)

found instead were substantial quantities of high-quality ceramic vessels, many of which were embellished with Arabic inscriptions. They also discovered the remains of substantial buildings, including a mosque. These structures had walls decorated with painted plaster, carved stucco, and glazed ceramic tiles. The terms of their agreement with the Persian authorities allowed the Museum to keep half of the materials unearthed, which helped greatly to expand the Near Eastern Department's holdings (figs. 16, 21). In 1939 international turmoil caused them to suspend operations, but in 1941 the expedition returned to Iran for a short concluding season. It fell to the group's youngest member, Charles Wilkinson, to publish detailed descriptions of the ceramics (cat. 68), wall decorations (cat. 60), and architectural remains (cat. 61) that they had unearthed at Nishapur.[36]

Following Dimand's retirement in 1960, Wilkinson was chosen to head the Near Eastern Department, whose collection at that time ranged from prehistory to the nineteenth century. Wilkinson's tenure was brief, however, as he himself retired in 1962. His departure marked the end of an era and led to the creation of two new departments, the Department of Ancient Near Eastern Art and the Department of Islamic Art.

Ernst J. Grube became the first head of the new Islamic Department.[37] In conjunction with this change, a selection from the collection was reinstalled in the Museum's north wing in a chronological sequence, an innovation that acknowledged the distinctive historical phases of Islamic culture (fig. 24). During Grube's leadership the collection was augmented by important purchases of ceramic and glass vessels.[38] He also founded The Friends of the Islamic Department, a support group that continues to assist the department in building its holdings.[39]

In December 1966 the sudden death of James Rorimer (1905–66), director of the Metropolitan, also led to changes in the Islamic Department. Rorimer's successor, Thomas Hoving (1931–2009), entrusted the direction of the Islamic Department to Richard Ettinghausen (1906–1979), a professor at New York University who previously had been a long-time curator at the Freer Gallery in Washington, D.C.

The Ettinghausen era was marked by important acquisitions as well as a major reinstallation of the Islamic collection on the second floor of the Museum's south wing (fig. 25). This display featured interior wall and ceiling panels from an eighteenth-century Damascus reception room (cat. 238) and a marble-inlaid basin and fountain donated by the Kevorkian Fund.[40] The Museum's centennial year, 1970, saw the purchase of an exceptional carpet from Mamluk Egypt (cat. 116) notable for is elaborate geometric design and its unusually varied color scheme.[41]

Notable bequests of the 1970s included fifty-two carpets from Joseph McMullan, the final stage in his generous gifts to the Museum.[42] A very special presentation of the Ettinghausen years was the 1972 exhibition of ninety-eight pages from an extraordinary copy of Firdausi's *Shahnama* belonging to Arthur Houghton (cat. 138A–G). Seventy-six of these had been given to

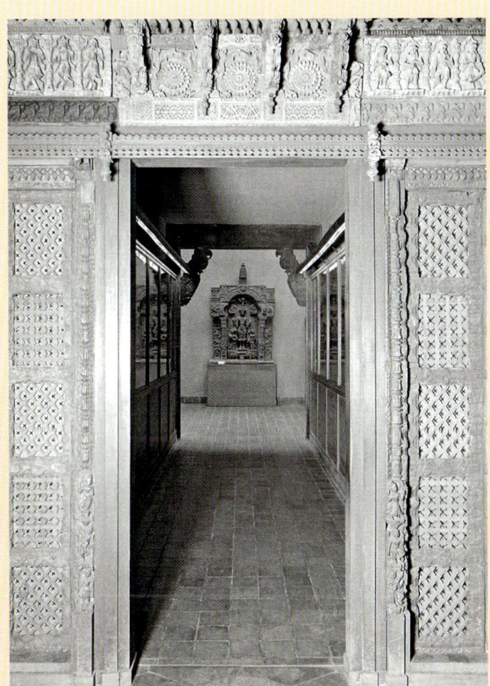

Fig. 8 April 19, 1921: Gallery E-13C. A small passageway built parallel to E-13 was pressed into service as a display gallery in 1919, when Museum acquisitions resumed after World War I. Here it is seen with Indian jewelry cases lining both walls, looking north into E-12A, which showed Indian sculpture.

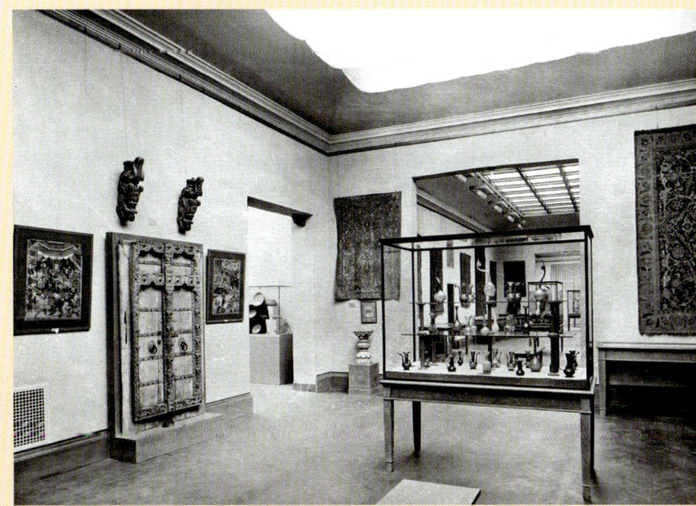

Fig. 9 October 2, 1912: Gallery E-14, the "Persian Room" looking north into E-13, pictured here in a Museum postcard. Note the draperies over the skylight to protect the art from direct sunlight.

the Museum in 1970; the exhibition was commemorated by the handsomely illustrated monograph *A King's Book of Kings* by Stuart Cary Welch.[43] A number of gifts in this period also came from Ettinghausen's private collection.[44]

In October 1979 leadership of the Islamic Department passed to Stuart Cary Welch.[45] Art from the Indian subcontinent became prominent in the purchases and donations of his time, among them remarkable paintings by Indian artists of various periods as well as a pierced marble window screen and a marble basin from a Mughal monument.[46] These new objects were featured in the international loan exhibition "India," held at the Museum in 1985–86.[47] Welch's enthusiasm for Indian art encouraged Alice Heeramaneck and others to donate several works to the Metropolitan, among them a charming study of a lion at rest and a child's coat from nineteenth-century Punjab made from wool tapestry decorated with a grapevine (cat. 284).

During the 1980s the collection and study of jewelry also increased. Acquisitions, particularly those made with funds provided by Patti Cadby Birch in addition to the objects purchased with help of the Louis E. Seley Foundation, reflect this emphasis.[48] By 1982 the Museum's collection of jewelry was sufficient to be used as the basis for a monograph written by Marilyn Jenkins and Manuel Keene.[49] Further purchases of jewelry included a necklace fashioned from sheet gold and set with gems (cat. 88).[50]

In recent decades the bequest of Louis E. Seley (d. 1986) has been of critical importance for the growth of the department's collection (fig. 25; cat. 185). Some curatorial purchases have added key objects to the already substantial collections of ceramics, jewelry, and metalwork, while others have strengthened holdings linked to Islam's religious practice, such as pages from Qur'an manuscripts, prayer books, and pilgrimage guides. Another innovation made possible by funds from the Seley bequest and other donors is the purchase of single-page paintings from the eighteenth and nineteenth centuries produced in India, Iran, and Turkey, challenging the common view that identifies Islamic art with the medieval period.[51]

With the arrival of Daniel Walker as departmental head in 1988, the study of carpets assumed a renewed prominence, evident in gifts, departmental purchases, and program of exhibitions. Among these were a "Chessboard" rug fragment presented by the Wolf Foundation and a carpet showing pairs of confronted quadrupeds attributed to fourteenth-century Anatolia (cat. 234). Walker continued to build the department's holdings of art from the Indian subcontinent, notably such architectural elements as a wooden calligraphic roundel (cat. 278B) and a pair of *jalis* or pierced sandstone window grills, as well as diverse pieces of metalwork, including a sculptural brass water flask, an iron elephant goad inlaid in gold and silver, and a wooden writing box overlaid with both metal plaques and patterned silk (cat. 276). A 1988 agreement with the family of Stuart Cary

The Near Eastern Department: Establishment and Expansion, 1921–49

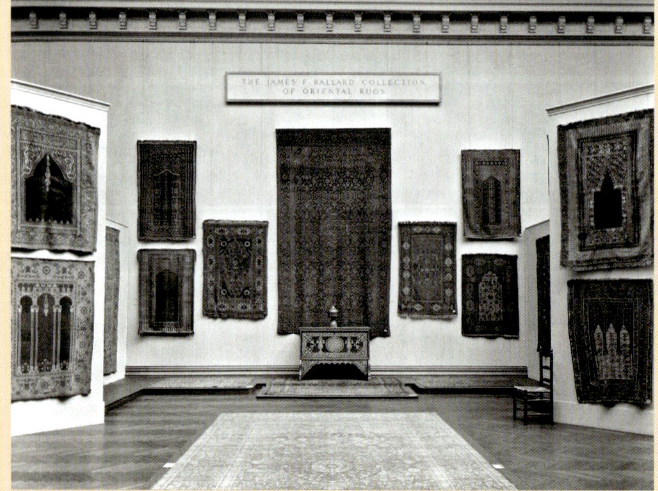

Fig. 10 October 3, 1923: The Ballard carpet donation. "There is a majesty and grandeur in these imperishable colors, mellowed but uneffaced by time and in the exquisite designs which render them a thing to love and cherish beyond any other form of art and when seen under proper light, each one seems bent on outdoing his neighbor in an effort to display every regal charm of beauty." (Letter, Ballard to Museum trustees, May 20, 1922)

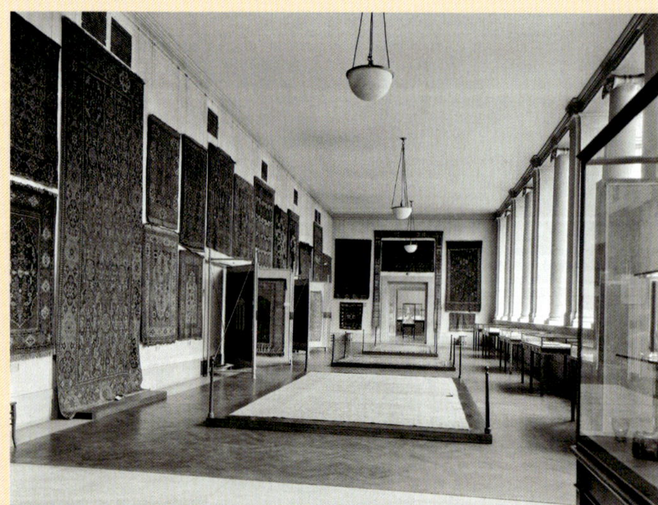

Fig. 11 March 31, 1925: Gallery H-20. Wing H was added to the north of Wing E in 1914, and one of its largest galleries, H-20, was devoted to "Oriental" carpets and textiles, including several Ballard Transylvanian rugs, at left. Note the swinging panels on walls for the display of small carpets.

Welch was significant for allowing a remarkable picture in their collection, by the sixteenth-century painter Sultan Muhammad, to be shared between the Metropolitan's Islamic Department and Harvard University Art Museum (cat. 137). Walker's connections with the Wolf Foundation were instrumental in their decision to donate a collection of Turkmen silver to the Museum (cat. 199). Their donation of more than two hundred fifty objects has given the department a new strength. A fully illustrated monograph about this collection was published in 2011 by Layla S. Diba.[52] Walker also initiated the development of plans for the reinstallation of the Islamic Department's collection prior to his departure in 2005 to become director of the Textile Museum in Washington, D.C.

Since 2005 the department's energies have been focused on the study and reinstallation of its collection. The magnitude of this task required the establishment of a new administrative framework within the department. Walker's successor as Consultative Chairman, Michael A. Barry (2005–8), contributed to the conception that shaped the collection's reinstallation. In 2005 Stefano Carboni became Departmental Administrator, a role he filled until his departure in the summer of 2008. Navina Haidar was overall coordinator of the multifaceted gallery reinstallation project from 2005 until its completion in the fall of 2011 and administered the department in 2008–9.

In 2009 Sheila R. Canby assumed leadership of the department. Since her arrival, Canby has renewed collecting activity with such major acquisitions as a Mughal painting and an elaborate Indian dagger.[53] Owing to her initiative, for the first time the department is acquiring works by contemporary Middle Eastern and South Asian artists.

For more than a century, building the Department of Islamic Art at the Metropolitan Museum has been a collective enterprise. The Aesthetic Movement encouraged collectors to trust their personal taste and served to widen their appreciation of diverse artistic traditions. Early collectors valued Islamic objects for their beauty, but paid little heed to the circumstances in which they had originated. As knowledge about the region and its artistic traditions grew more widespread, additions to the collection became more focused and served to augment the department's holdings in a particular medium or period. Objects acquired through the Museum's excavations opened new vistas onto the art and culture of the Near East. Looking to the future, the department seeks to broaden appreciation not only of the objects themselves but also of the cultural and religious contexts from which they derive.

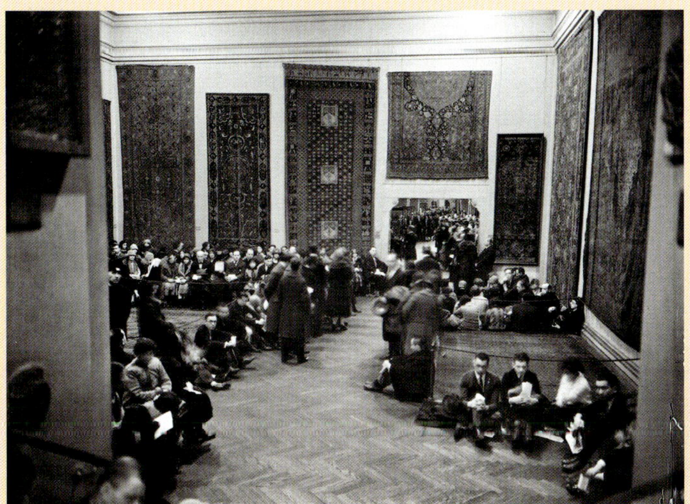

Fig. 12 January 9, 1926: Carpet Gallery D-3. For forty years David Mannes led free symphony concerts from the Great Hall balcony (seen through doorway at rear); here, overflowing Museum audiences sit on the carpet platforms to hear Beethoven, Bach, Lully, Gluck, Tchaikovsky, Saint-Saens, Brahms, Strauss, and Smetana.

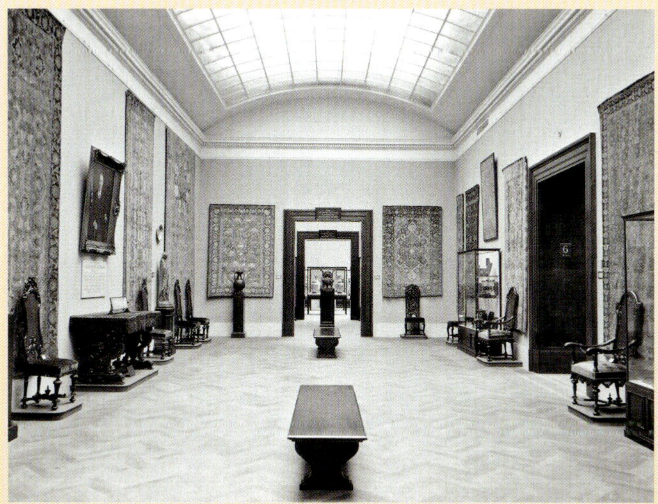

Fig. 13 April 13, 1926: Wing K, Gallery K-33, at the opening of this grand space originally built for the Altman Collection. The 1953 decision by the Altman trustees to allow the collection to be displayed with other related objects elsewhere in the Museum paved the way for the eventual use of the space by the Islamic Department.

The New Galleries for the Art of the Arab Lands, Turkey, Iran, Central Asia, and Later South Asia

NAVINA NAJAT HAIDAR

The new Galleries for the Art of the Arab Lands, Turkey, Iran, Central Asia, and Later South Asia mark a fresh interpretative approach to collections that had previously been on permanent display in the same wing from 1975 until 2003 (fig. 25).[54] The reinstallation, which occupies an expanded area of nineteen thousand square feet, underscores the artistic and cultural diversity of the art of the Islamic world in fifteen galleries grouped by geographical region overlooking the Roman court below. A new emphasis on region is reflected in the geographic title of the galleries, a departure from the previous designation of Islamic Art, which remains a term used widely within the installation and accompanying didactic program.[55] A map of the Islamic world in close proximity to the gallery entrance further conveys the underlying rationale for the works of art brought together.

Drawn from a permanent collection of over twelve thousand works, the approximately one thousand objects on display have been chosen for their aesthetic merit, rarity, condition, and art-historical importance. The largely chronological organization of material within each gallery highlights artistic centers and follows the historical sweep of Islamic civilization through the Arab world, Turkey, Iran, Central Asia, and later South Asia from the seventh century onward. This arrangement aims to impart a clear sense of place and time to the visitor, crucial elements for the understanding of the historical and cultural contexts of the collection and in keeping with the prevailing approach of the Museum as a whole.

While there is a principal didactic chronological route through the galleries, multiple entrances allow for the varied experiences of the visitor. Care has been taken, however, to ensure that the display is visually and contextually meaningful regardless of point of access. As in the previous galleries, the display cases feature groups of stylistically or historically related mixed media. These are occasionally interposed by groupings of objects that explore particular themes, such as the development of styles of calligraphy, the advancement of science across the medieval Islamic period, or techniques of ceramic production, among others.

Interconnections, Contexts, Regions

The open plan and new circular path of the expanded gallery space allow for wide-ranging cultural interconnections to be discerned throughout the display (fig. 27). These are particularly meaningful in light of the charged geopolitical climate during the time in which this reinstallation project has been undertaken and the global audiences it seeks to address.[56] The emergence of

Near Eastern Department Initiatives, 1930s–40s

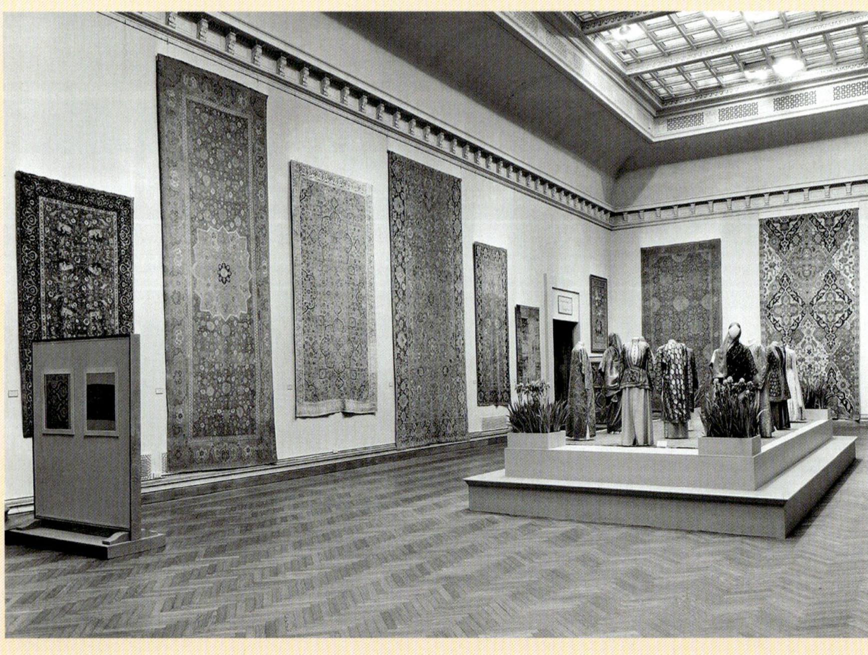

Figs. 14 and 15 May 15, 1935: The "Oriental Rugs and Textiles" exhibition. This may have been the only exhibition in the Museum's history to have used live models to display many of the Indian costumes that were shown (see below).

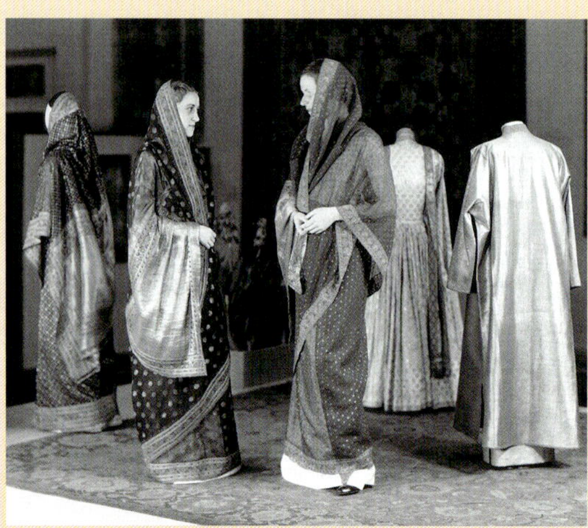

Islamic art from its pre-Islamic heritage and its profound artistic exchanges with wider contemporaneous traditions, notably those of Europe and the Far East, present Islamic culture as both a recipient and a disseminator of broad influences, with many and separate points of origin and development. A new space (457) for the Islamic West (Spain, North Africa, and southern Italy) just off the introductory gallery highlights eight centuries of Islamic art and culture in premodern Europe. A second entrance into the galleries is provided through a space for later South Asia (464; mainly Jain, Rajput, Pahari, and related traditions), which lies outside the footprint of the main galleries but is connected to them through the adjoining Mughal and Sultanate galleries. This spatial innovation allows for the unified presentation of the later arts of the Indian subcontinent as related to, but also independent from, Islamic traditions.[57] Another historically meaningful point of entry into the galleries connects medieval Egypt and Syria to the Museum's nineteenth-century "Orientalism" galleries exhibiting European artists' treatment of Middle Eastern subjects (454).

The challenge of achieving a balance between two important cultural forces—region and religion—presents a constant tension in the installation. Islamic tradition itself recognizes the duality between unity of belief and diversity of peoples as expressed in its sacred text: "We created you nations and tribes that ye may know one another" (Qur'an 49:13). Interpretation of the works as part of the Islamic tradition rather than a phase in the long artistic development of a particular region or culture is independently stressed through the fresh floor plan, new juxtapositions of works, integration of key objects from other departments, and updated didactic labels and texts. In light of the complex political and historical networks and numerous exchanges through trade, travel, people, and ideas, regional boundaries are not dogmatically asserted but made flexible according to the nature of the material. Links across borders are also demonstrated by the incorporation of post-Sasanian, Coptic, and Byzantine objects with early Islamic-period works; Jewish, Christian, and Islamic manuscripts displayed together with other works from Islamic Spain; and Chinese ceramics shown alongside Persian or Ottoman adaptations, among other examples. This treatment of the subject expands conceptual parameters to reflect modern scholarship and highlights the multifaceted nature of Islamic art, which includes Muslim and non-Muslim artists and patrons.[58]

Contextualization of art styles within the courtly patronage of Islamic dynasties has become central to the approach of the broader scholarly field and is consequently reflected within the galleries, as before. Nomenclature such as Ottoman Turkey, Safavid Iran, or Mughal India helps locate the works within such cultural parameters. Equally, tribal and nomadic art, commercial production, interregional trade, and foreign patronage are given their places within each sphere. (For example, in three adjoining spaces the Ottoman wing showcases the court arts of imperial Istanbul; the Damascus Room, an eighteenth-century

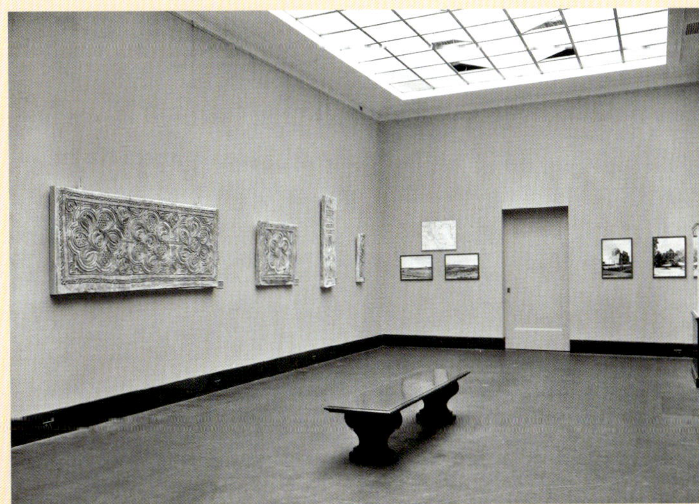

Fig. 16 October 25, 1937: Gallery E-15. The Near Eastern Department expanded its space by converting an airshaft. Gallery E-15 opened with the first temporary display of archaeological material from Nishapur, where Museum excavations were then active. Visible are stucco dado panels from Sabz Pushan and photographs of the excavation sites.

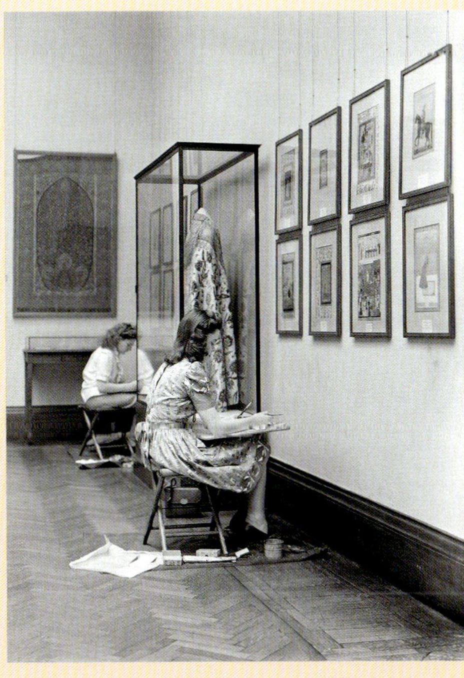

Fig. 17 May 18, 1943: Gallery E-13. After the attack on Pearl Harbor in 1941, the Museum sent most of its large and fragile art objects to a rural Pennsylvania location thought to be safer from air raids, and some galleries were closed because staff were serving the war effort. The Near Eastern galleries remained open with limited displays, while educational programs continued unabated, here with Mughal miniatures from the Alexander Smith Cochran Collection.

domestic interior from the Ottoman provincial center at Damascus; and classical and village carpets.) The installation thus attempts to weave together and synthesize these wide contexts, allowing for the broadest and most nuanced understanding of the material. This approach represents a shift in emphasis from the underlying unity and greater linearity that characterized the previous Islamic galleries to rooting the art in the distinctive geographic, cultural, and linguistic realms of the Islamic world.[59] At the same time, care has been taken to preserve a sense of the timeless permanence of the objects themselves and the many seasons of human history and varied interpretations through which they have endured.

Past Legacies and Present Design

The previous installation history of this material at the Museum goes back almost a century, leading up to the creation of the Department of Islamic Art in 1963.[60] The immediate predecessor of the present galleries, established in the same space in 1975, represented at the time the first major and most extensive display dedicated to Islamic art in any museum in North America.[61] This celebrated installation of ten galleries created by Richard Ettinghausen and other members of the Islamic Department provided a stimulating visitor experience as well as a teaching tool for generations of art historians and students.[62] The display underscored the unity of artistic expression through an interwoven presentation of the material spanning a period of a thousand years. Special areas within the galleries included a dedicated section for archaeological finds from Nishapur, a room for religious arts, and the installation of the Damascus period room, in addition to outer galleries for the later arts of Iran, Turkey, and the Indian subcontinent. Many of the most-admired features of these former galleries have been retained in the present installation, including seated areas for the viewing of paintings, carpet platforms for oversize rugs, the use of mixed media in display cases, and maintenance of large open spaces. The present installation also retains much of the basic outline of the original McKim, Mead, and White floor plan of Wing K (fig. 1).[63]

In styling the new galleries, one of the principal aims has been to create an appropriate setting for the objects in keeping with the overall emphasis on regional diversity.[64] Texture and color have been used to convey a sense of individual place. The stones for the floors in the galleries have largely been sourced from the regions represented, with white marble employed in transitional spaces as a common material.[65] A pair of sixteenth-century Mughal *jali* screens set in the east wall of the introductory gallery (450) provide inspiration for the room's inlaid cartouche-and-medallion floor pattern. These classic Mughal architectural motifs are also found all over the Islamic world in a variety of media, from carpets to bookbindings.

The arch-shaped portals between some galleries and the stepped banding of the ceiling design find prototypes in Islamic

Near Eastern Department Expansion, 1930s–40s

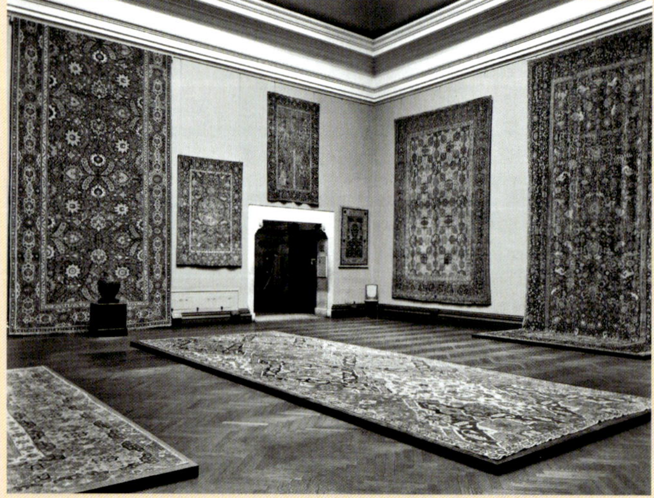

Fig. 18 December 2, 1944: Gallery D-3. When the Museum brought back objects sent away after Pearl Harbor, the Near Eastern Department celebrated with an exhibition, "20 Great Rugs of the Orient." Shown at right is the Emperor's Carpet (before 2011 displayed only twice), along with rugs from the Morgan and McMullan gifts.

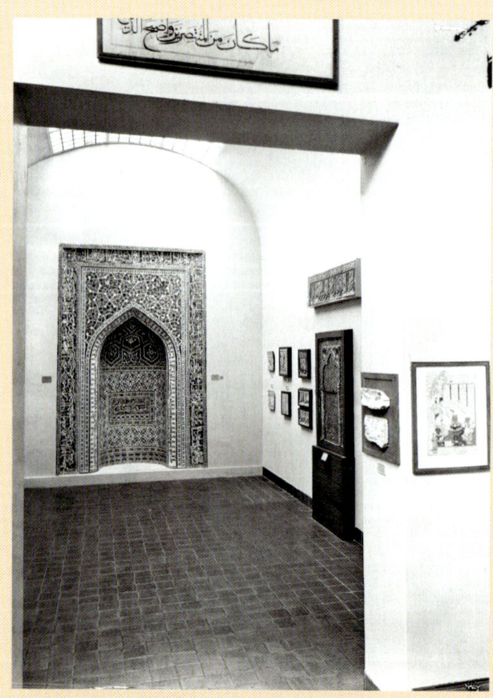

Fig. 19 September 12, 1939: Gallery E-14A. The first display of the 1354 *mihrab* from the Madrasa Imami, Isfahan. It has been on virtually continuous display since its acquisition and remains an iconic piece.

architecture, including the Damascus Room. Modern glass mosque lamps suspended in the gallery for medieval Syria and Egypt (454) mark the space as another point of entry into the gallery suite.[66] Window openings in the clerestory around the Roman court allow for long views of the sculpture below seen through pierced wooden *mashribiyya* screens, encouraging historical connections for the early Islamic material and introducing the visual and symbolic element of filtered light.[67] The aural and visual effects of water in the live fountains of the Damascus Room and Moroccan Court are intended to animate the gallery setting and evoke a unifying symbol of the Islamic world.

A Maghribi-Andalusi medieval-style court created by artisans from Fez is a special feature of the new galleries (fig. 26).[68] This Ibero-Moroccan Court is an area of repose, filled with light and color, and acts as an extension to the adjoining gallery for the arts of Spain, North Africa, and the western Islamic world. Bordered by original Nasrid-period columns from the Museum's holdings, the decoration of the court combines traditional *zilij* tiles, carved plaster, cedar woodwork, and a low marble fountain basin. Representing a living craft tradition of the Islamic world, the court is conceived around design elements and a color palette closely based on Marinid and Nasrid models of the fourteenth and fifteenth centuries.[69] The design of the wall tiles is adapted from a tile panel from the Alhambra palace that was displayed at the Metropolitan Museum in 1992.[70]

Processes, Strategies, Discoveries

The present organizational approach to the galleries evolved from the investigation of many alternative ideas, several of which were explored in early designs.[71] The participation of the wider academic community in developing the present scholarly approach, as well as the input of other groups toward understanding audience and visitor experience was sought throughout the reinstallation process.[72] Strategies included academic meetings;[73] an ongoing program of special installations, exhibitions, lectures, and symposia;[74] exchanges with a variety of audience groups;[75] and visitor surveys.[76] Among the more significant results were: the consensus among many Islamic art historians of the shortcomings of the term *Islamic art*, especially within a museum context;[77] the wide interest in the presentation of intercultural connections; the powerful resonance of the idea of western Islamic art; the public interest in conservation work; the degree of public unfamiliarity with the history and ruling dynasties of the Islamic world; and the prevailing misconceptions about the role of figural imagery in the arts of the Islamic world. Visitor surveys also revealed a heightened level of interest in the region and material due to current events.

The process of preparing for reinstallation led to significant new scholarship on the collection by staff and researchers and has been shared more widely through the Museum's educational and information systems.[78] A major survey of the holdings resulted not just in the rediscovery of many works previously only rarely,

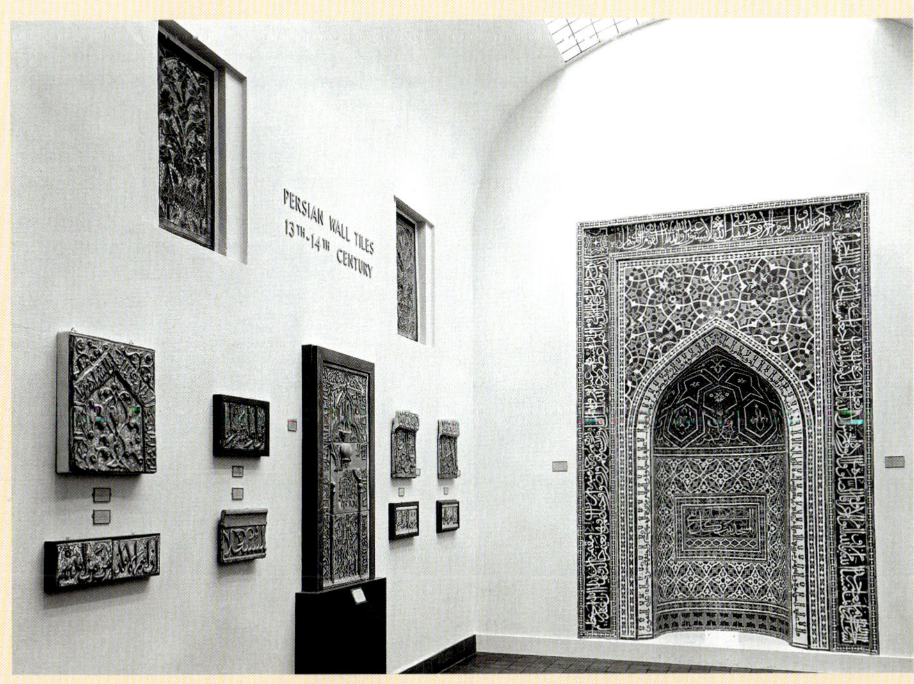

Fig. 20 May 20, 1949: Gallery E 14A. After a complete closure in 1947–49, the slightly enlarged Near Eastern Department galleries reopened in the same space with new signage and expanded displays. Sadly, between 1958 and 1962 all of the Near Eastern galleries closed again due to Museum rebuilding; only one reopened before the construction of the 1975 galleries. Eighteenth-century Ottoman stained-glass windows at top left remain unchanged from the post-World War I installation.

or in some cases never, displayed, but also in new digital photography and updated records for global Internet access. In addition, the opportunity to undertake substantial conservation work on the collection led to significant improvements in the condition of many objects as well as a better understanding and some new discoveries.[79] Among them, an analysis of the original structure and decoration of the 1707 Damascus Room resulted in a new configuration, closer to the original layout of the room. The restoration of the early sixteenth-century Emperor's Carpet (cat. 181) from Iran allowed for improved knowledge of its structure and palette and its introduction into the gallery display on a long-term basis. Other notable conservation projects included the restoration of an important eighteenth-century Ottoman silk banner and numerous manuscripts and paintings. Archaeological material from the Nishapur excavations and later *mina'i* ceramics from Iran, among other objects, were closely examined, and new approaches to their restoration and presentation were jointly developed by the conservation, scientific, and curatorial departments.

Information on the collection is conveyed by a variety of means in the galleries, from the traditional object label in the vitrine to the latest technological methods such as electronic handheld devices or audio guides.[80] The general aim has been to stack information to serve a variety of interest levels, with a concise and lively delivery in the object labels, making use of diagrams and other nonwritten methods to impart detail, and more in-depth offerings on the accompanying touch-screen monitors, handheld devices, Teacher Resource Guide, catalogue, and the Museum website. Wall labels, maps, and illustrations of architecture in the galleries serve to contextualize the collection within historical and cultural parameters and to help the visitor grasp the complex geography related to the collection.

The New Galleries (Galleries 450–464)

The introductory gallery (450) has been envisioned as a space to feature masterpieces and new acquisitions from the collection and serves as a vantage point from which a viewer can discern the scope of the interior by offering visual and physical access into two wings around the central court, as well as views into the adjacent South Asian galleries through sixteenth-century Mughal *jali* screens. Objects on display include a pair of carved ivory inlaid *minbar* doors from Mamluk Egypt donated in the late nineteenth century by Edward C. Moore, one of the founders of the collection. Recently restored monumental Timurid Qur'an pages, a carved Ilkhanid *rahla* (book stand), and a group of calligraphic and painted folios, several of which have been recently acquired, represent the collection's strength in the arts of the book. A powerful inscribed black-on-white slip Nishapur vessel of the tenth century, a molded and glazed Kashan ceramic *mihrab* fragment with springing vines, a calligraphic stone panel from Sultanate Bengal, and other works demonstrate the quintessential elements of the arts of the region and express the underpinning Islamic influence.[81]

The Postwar Displays, 1949–70

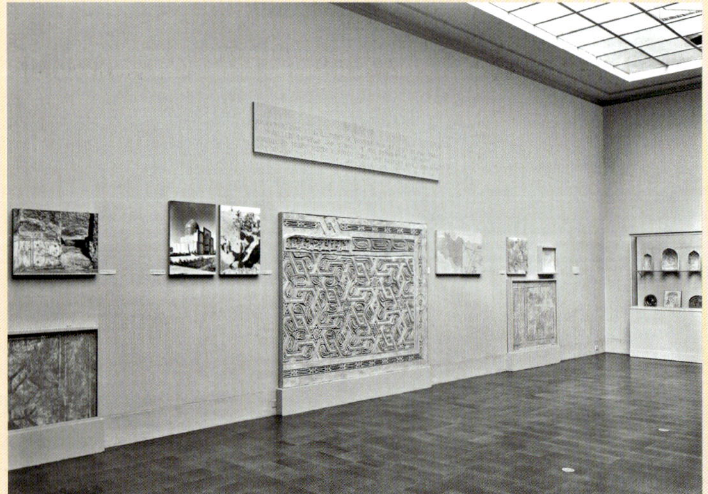

Fig. 21 May 20, 1949: Gallery E-15. A highlight of the Near Eastern Department's new 1949 gallery installations was the first permanent display of objects excavated at Nishapur. Stucco panels, ceramics, and photographs of the tomb of Umar Khayyam near the site are visible.

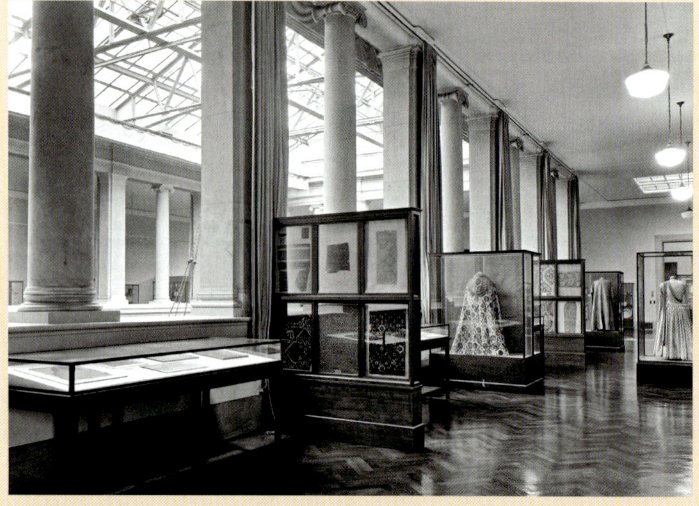

Fig. 22 1949: Gallery H-20, the postwar installation. Ottoman and Safavid silks are shown in the cases. H-20 had curtains that could be drawn to protect textiles and paintings from sunlight and offered views into the Near Eastern armor installation below.

Arab Lands (Galleries 451, 454, 456, 457)

Leading through an early Islamic-style triple-arch colonnade, the main route off the introductory gallery initiates the visitor through the materials of the Umayyad (661–750) and Abbasid (750–1258) periods in the eastern Mediterranean and Iran, regions that came under Arab sway in this early phase (451). Transitions from Late Antique and Sasanian traditions toward a new idiom under the influence of Islam are shown through Coptic textiles, post-Sasanian Persian metalwork, and examples of Late Classical-influenced woodwork. A consolidated display of early and medieval Qur'an pages explores the birth and evolution over four centuries of Arabic calligraphy, underscoring the most prestigious of Islamic artistic traditions. The art of the Abbasids centered at Baghdad and their far-reaching cultural impact is seen in the Museum's "beveled-style" carved wood from Samarra, as well as in luster ceramics from various centers at Raqqa, Cairo, and, later, Kashan. The Museum's collection of epigraphic textile fragments (*tiraz*) gives an indication of the luxury textiles produced by royal workshops at several centers in Egypt, Yemen, and Iran in this early period.

The southward route off the introductory gallery leads into a space for the arts of Spain, North Africa, and southern Italy (457), extending into the adjoining Moroccan Court (456) through Spanish Nasrid columns. This combined area represents a new conception in the overall scheme, a space in which the artistic culture of eight hundred years of the Islamic West is presented. A collaboration with the Hispanic Society of America has strengthened the display through a long-term loan of important objects. Highlights include a group of early carved ivories from the period of Umayyad rule in Spain (756–1031) and a later group from southern Italy, including the Morgan Casket, one of the earliest objects to have entered the collection. A special grouping of manuscripts explores the shared exchanges in book decoration between different faith traditions during the Nasrid (1232–1492) and other periods.

The arts of medieval Egypt and Syria are presented in a further gallery (454) that connects with the Orientalist painting gallery of the nineteenth-century European wing through an independent entrance. Among the highlights on display are works made for Mamluk (1250–1517) and Rasulid (1228–1454) rulers, including gilded and enameled glass, inlaid metalwork, manuscripts, and paintings. Fatimid (909–1171) and Ayyubid (1171–1260) precursors include textile fragments and carved wooden architectural elements. The expanded Kevorkian Fund Special Exhibitions Gallery (458) lies off this portal, providing space for temporary exhibitions.

Turkey (Galleries 459, 460, 461)

The galleries devoted to the arts of the Ottoman world have effectively tripled in size from their previous representation. The main

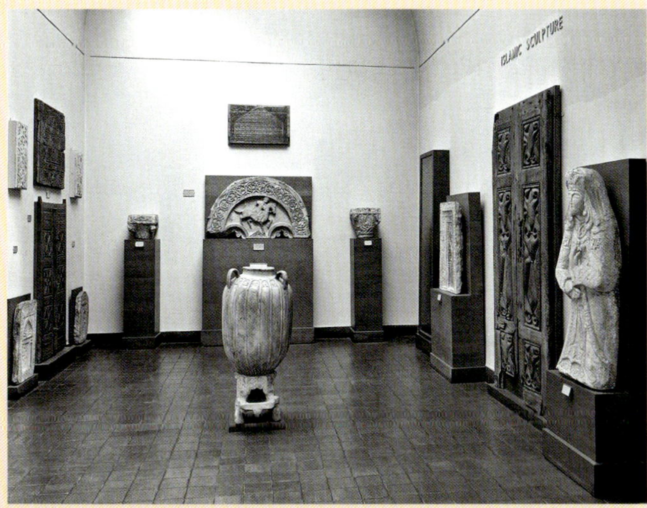

Fig. 23 May 20, 1949: Gallery E-13A, the newly arranged "Islamic Sculpture" gallery. The title draws attention to the collection of carved and relief works on display.

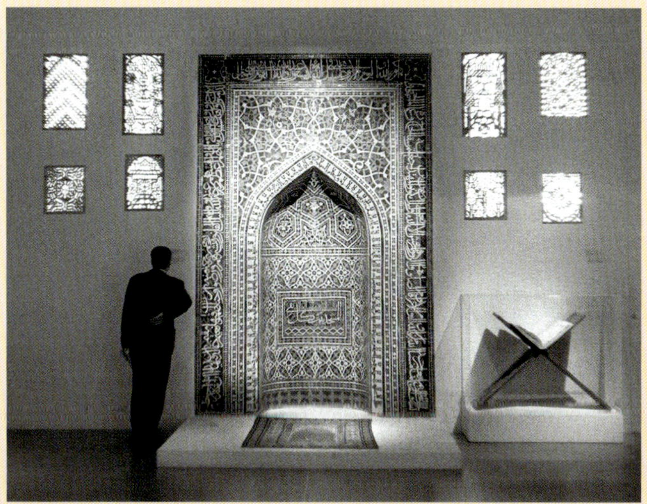

Fig. 24 1965: After years with no objects on display at all, the Islamic Department, established in 1963,was given a single temporary gallery created by combining the principal Near Eastern galleries, E-12–14. From then until shortly before the 1975 galleries opened, this modernist-feeling space showed representative objects from various places and eras.

goal of this expansion is to adequately reflect the span of the Ottoman Empire (1299–1923) as well as to display more effectively the depth of the collection in this area. Three adjoining spaces now show different levels and traditions of Ottoman art: Istanbul and the courtly arts in the central gallery (460); carpets and textiles of Anatolia and other regions (459);[82] and the period room dated 1707 from Ottoman Damacus (461).[83] Augmenting the display is material on loan from the Arms and Armor Department.

The central gallery draws together works from the classical Ottoman period, including the imperial *tughra* (monogram) of Süleyman the Magnificent (r. 1520–66), a collection of Iznik ceramics spanning almost two hundred fifty years, and a group of important manuscripts, some recently attributed to Ottoman Baghdad. A thorough investigation of the reconfigured Damascus Room has provided fresh readings and identifications of the inscriptions, a better understanding of the complex techniques of the painted wooden decoration, and a reattribution of the fountain to the earlier Mamluk period (1250–1517). The flanking carpet gallery is crowned by a painted-and-gilded ceiling with interstellar geometric patterns from sixteenth-century Spain, below which a modular carpet platform permits the most fragile Turkish carpets of various shapes and sizes to be shown; space on the walls allows for the display of tribal and nomadic rugs of the wider Ottoman world.[84] Visually, the resulting efflorescence of medallions, stars, and geometric-based ornament expresses a fundamental formal element of Islamic art.

Iran and Central Asia (Galleries 452, 453, 455, 462)

The arts of Iran represent almost 60 percent of the collections and are shown in at least four of the galleries in the total suite.[85] Iranian art therefore runs as a thread through the installation and is reintroduced at several points. Early Iranian works following the Arab conquest of the region are displayed along with other works of the early Islamic period together in the first gallery (451). Archaeological material excavated by the Museum between 1935 and 1940/47 from the important medieval city of Nishapur and a reconstruction of an interior space with carved stucco dado panels from the site of Sabz Pushan are shown together in the following gallery (452).[86] A further survey of works from Iran, Central Asia, and Afghanistan shows the patronage of the Samanid (819–1005), Ghaznavid (977–1186), Ghurid (1000–1215), and Seljuq (1040–1194) dynasties (453).

Following the Mongol invasions of the early thirteenth century, the arts of Iran reflect renewed connections with the Far East, developing a style that came to have a major impact on the arts of the Ottoman, Safavid, and Mughal worlds. A gallery (455) displaying Iranian and Central Asian works from the Mongol Ilkhanid (1256–1353), Turkmen (1380–1508), and Timurid (1370–1507) worlds lies on the route to the galleries for the later empires. The arts of the book from this classic age form a major part of the display. This gallery also holds the Museum's well-known blue cut-tile *mihrab* from a *madrasa* at Isfahan dated

A New Identity for the Department of Islamic Art, 1975–2011

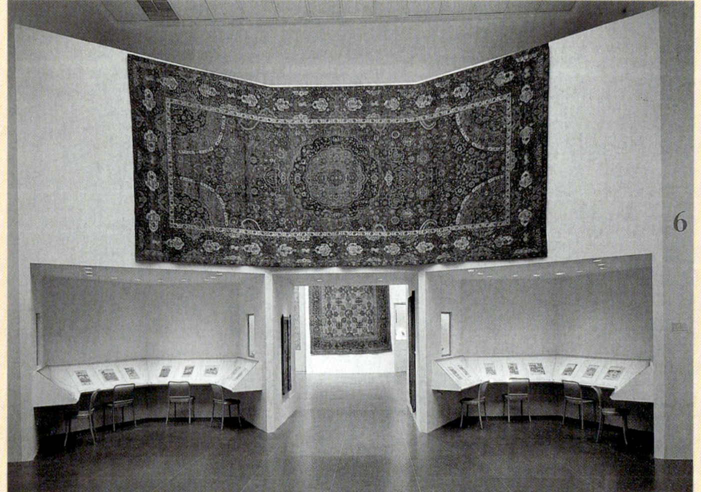

Fig. 25 September 24, 1975: Gallery K-31. The Islamic Department's first permanent galleries, a major suite of ten rooms, opened in September 1975. This space, known as Gallery 6, contained Timurid and Safavid art, including the Seley Carpet, with seating at desks for the viewing of miniatures, a popular feature retained in the new galleries.

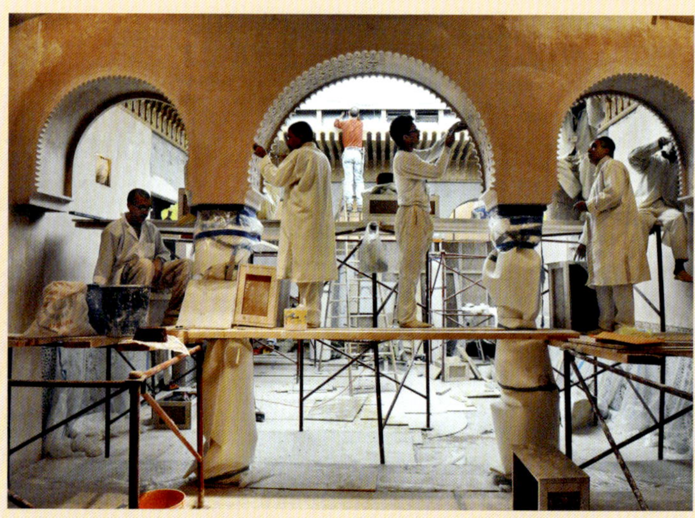

Fig. 26 March 1, 2011: Wing K, Gallery 457 (see fig. 27). Craftsmen from Fez create the Moroccan Court in the 2011 installation of the Art of the Arab Lands, Turkey, Iran, Central Asia, and Later South Asia.

1354. Safavid magnificence is the main focus of the largest of the Iranian galleries (462), which also displays works from successive periods up until the late nineteenth century.[87] Among the masterpieces here are the Emperor's Carpet, folios from the Tahmasp *Shahnama*, and a dedicated "connoisseur's corner" for the display of Persian drawings. Connections with China, India, and Europe are explored through ceramics, painting, and the artistic patronage at Isfahan.

Later South Asia (Galleries 463, 464)

Two galleries for the arts of later South Asia unify the collections of the Islamic and Asian departments in adjoining spaces, which together display objects from the many artistic centers of the Indian subcontinent from about the early fifteenth century. Works of art are arranged chronologically and grouped by court or region, with a concentration of Sultanate, Mughal, Deccan, and later Mughal works in one gallery (463) and Rajput, Punjab Hills, British "Company," and some late South Indian traditions in the second (464). A number of new acquisitions join the existing strengths of the collection, including a late sixteenth- or early seventeenth-century gilded Golconda dagger with zoomorphic hilt, a painting of the goddess Bhairavi of about 1635, attributed to the Mughal master Payag, and a study of an Indian fruit bat (cat. 285), dated about 1780. An oversize glass wall case for the display of Indian textiles shows the Museum's multiple-niche Mughal tent panel at eye level for the first time, providing a quasi-architectural climax to the space.

A significant feature of the galleries for later South Asia is their physical position within the overall suite, which includes an independent entrance off the main vestibule area. By maintaining a position beyond the footprint of the rest of the galleries, the space allows for the free and intermixed display of objects from a variety of streams of later Indian tradition, with the powerful impact of Mughal art (1526–1858) apparent throughout.

As with any installation, the new Galleries for the Art of the Arab Lands, Turkey, Iran, Central Asia, and Later South Asia are conceived not as a definitive statement but as an adaptable space in which a growing collection and new interpretations can find future room. Allowance for change and evolution within the space acknowledges the dynamic changes in the art of the regions represented, the rise of new expressions, and the rediscovery of forgotten traditions. From the perspective of the Museum's overall organization, the upper floor of the building can now be seen to offer a long view of the art of Asia, east and west, with earlier traditions displayed in the north and central section and with the present suite of galleries at the south end bringing the Museum's collections closer to our present moment.

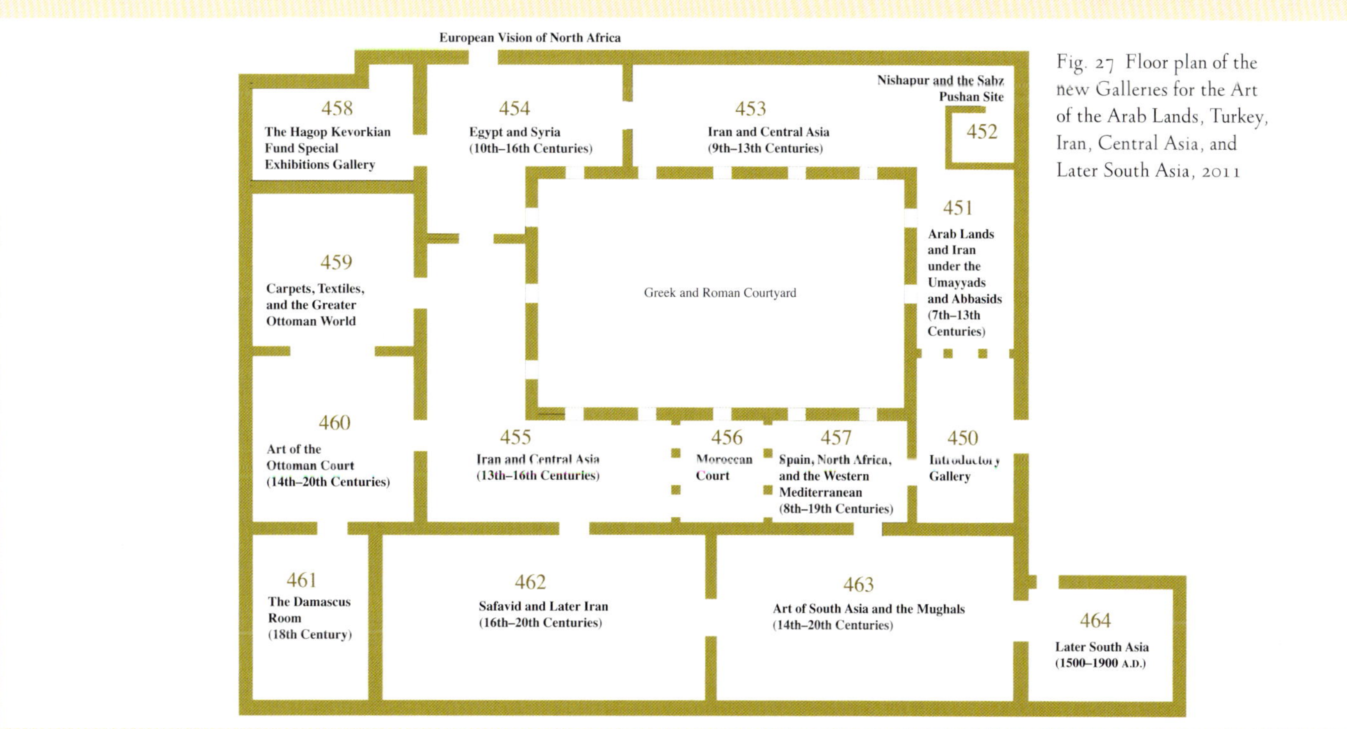

Fig. 27 Floor plan of the new Galleries for the Art of the Arab Lands, Turkey, Iran, Central Asia, and Later South Asia, 2011

1. Breck 1932.
2. Hewitt 1907; *MMA Annual Report* 23 (1892), p. 552.
3. Stein 1986–87.
4. *New York Times* 1901.
5. Despite display in the Islamic galleries, these objects are under the custody of the Department of Asian Art. For Bishop's biography, see *New York Times* 1902a, b; on his collection, see Kunz 1903 and *Bishop Collection* 1909, pp. 82–86.
6. Howe 1913, p. 289.
7. Ibid., p. 310.
8. This wing, designated by the letter "F" in schematic plans of the Museum, was also called the Morgan Wing. At present it displays the Museum's collection of arms and armor.
9. Valentiner 1913; Jackson and Yohannan 1914.
10. Breck 1920.
11. Daggett 1910, pp. 311–13.
12. Breck 1920.
13. Objects said to come from Egypt include nine shards: acc. nos. 20.120.192–201, and a green-glazed bowl: 20.120.207.
14. His Syrian examples seem to have come from Raqqa; see Jenkins-Madina 2006, p. 122; additional Syrian examples include acc. nos. 20.120.202, 20.120. 220–224, and 20.120.226.
15. Dimand 1955; Dimand and Mailey 1973, pp. 41, 43, 96, 101–4, 111–14, 130–32.
16. *New York Times* 1921; New York 1921.
17. Ballard 1916; Minneapolis 1922; Chicago 1922–23; Pittsburgh 1923; Buffalo 1926.
18. New York 1930; New York 1935; New York 1961; New York 1966.
19. Dimand 1924.
20. Dimand 1932b; Dimand 1933a.
21. *MMA Bulletin* 1930.
22. Havemeyer 1993, pp. xiv–xv, 16, 70–76, 297; Frelinghuysen 1993, pp. 101–2.
23. Dimand 1957.
24. Jenkins-Madina 2006, pp. 19, 124–39, 146–57; Frelinghuysen 1993, pp. 107–13.
25. On the history of this firm, see Pruitt 1998.
26. Her own works are said to have been destroyed by a fire at her New Jersey residence in March 1939; on the bequest, see *MMA Annual Report* 87 (1956–57), p. 68.
27. A number of the prints donated by Cora Timken were included in a recent exhibition of Japanese prints from the San Diego Museum of Art, "Dreams and Diversions: 250 Years of Japanese Woodblock Prints," Founders Hall, University of San Diego, February 26–June 5, 2011.
28. Roxburgh 1998, pp. 50–57, figs. 9–10.
29. Ettinghausen 1970a; McMullen 1965.
30. Dimand 1944b.
31. *MMA Annual Report* 74 (1943–44), pp. 37–38; Dimand and Mailey 1973, p. 101, no. 12, fig. 76, acc. no. 43.121.1; pp. 109–10, no. 37, fig. 104, acc. no. 43.121.2.
32. Dimand 1952.
33. He compiled a catalogue for an exhibition of rugs belonging to the Kevorkian Foundation (New York 1966).
34. Fino 2010; finds from Ctesiphon in the custody of the Islamic Department include 174 ceramic fragments and 20 glass objects or fragments.
35. Whitcomb 1985; Frye, ed. 1973.
36. Wilkinson 1973; Wilkinson 1986.
37. Ernst J. Grube in *MMA Annual Report* 94 (1963–64), pp. 74–76.
38. Ibid., 95 (1964–65), pp. 63–65; 96 (1965–66), pp. 83–84; 97 (1966–67), pp. 74–78.
39. Ibid., 98 (1967–68), p. 103.
40. Richard Ettinghausen in *MMA Annual Report* 99 (1968–69), pp. 79–81; donation of the "Nur-al-Din" room (now called the Damascus Room) is mentioned in ibid., 100 (1969–70), pp. 84–85.
41. Ibid., 100 (1969–70), pp. 83, 86.
42. Gifts of carpets by McMullan occurred in 1970 (ibid., pp. 84, 85), in 1972 (*MMA Annual Report* 102 [1971–72], pp. 44, 45), and in 1973 (ibid., 104 [1973–74], p. 47).
43. *MMA Annual Report* 102 (1971–72), p. 45; New York 1972.
44. *MMA Annual Report* 106 (1975–76), pp. 12, 47–49; 107 (1976–77), p. 55.
45. Stuart Cary Welch in *MMA Annual Report* 110 (1979–80), pp. 38–40.
46. The seventeenth-century basin is acc. no. 1984.213 and the marble screen is 1984.193. Important donors of Indian objects include Wendy Findlay and Alice C. Heeramaneck; for a listing of acquisitions, see Welch in *MMA Annual Report* 112 (1981–82), pp. 33–34; 113 (1982–83), pp. 36–37; 114 (1983–84), pp. 36–37; 115 (1984–85), pp. 39–40; 116 (1985–86), pp. 30–31; Daniel Walker in *MMA Annual Report* 118 (1987–88), pp. 29–30.
47. New York 1985–86.
48. Jewelry purchased by funds from Patti Cadby Birch include acc. nos. 1981.222.1–6 and 1976.405–406; Objects purchased with Seley funds include acc. nos. 1978.141–2, 1979.7.1–4.
49. New York 1983.
50. This object was discussed in New York and Los Angeles 2002–3, pp. 86, 275, no. 148, fig. 89.
51. Purchases of religious texts include acc. no. 1990.265, a prayer scroll dated to 1810.
52. Diba et al. 2011.
53. The ca. 1635 painting of the goddess Bhairavi is attributed to Payag; the dagger (acc. no. 2011.236) has a gilded zoomorphic hilt.
54. See the photo essay by Rebecca Lindsey in this chapter, as well as a website feature with expanded information at www.metmuseum.org.
55. The term *Islamic Art* remains in use as recognition of the wider academic field and as the identity of the department.
56. The Museum's reinstallation project was undertaken in the aftermath of the events of September 11, 2001, and continuing changes in worldwide political events. Coincidentally, several other major museums were also completing, or have recently completed, similar projects. For a partial overview, see Bloom and Blair 2009.
57. This gallery is the result of collaboration with the Department of Asian Art, which presently oversees part of the later South Asian collections along with early sculpture.
58. The last thirty years of scholarship in the field have seen the development of major specializations in textile studies, codicology, and metalwork, as well as new work on cultural interconnections.
59. Ettinghausen et al. 1975a, p. 4, offers perspectives into the philosophical approach of the previous installation. Adamova 1999, pp. 7–8, discusses the issue of exhibiting unity versus diversity in Islamic art. In the same volume, other approaches and displays are also explored.

60. In addition to the preceding photo essay and essay, Jenkins-Madina 2000 provides insights into the early history of the collection. In the same volume other authors discuss related topics. Wider discussions are found in Vernoit, ed. 2000.
61. Ettinghausen et al. 1975a accompanied the gallery opening. *MMA Annual Report* 106 (1975–76), pp. 9, 47, contains an official report of the opening of the galleries.
62. Responses to the previous installation include Grabar 1976 and Goldin 1976. These responses are discussed along with a summary of developments and new thoughts in Komaroff 2000.
63. See Heckscher 1995 for a history of the building including Wing K. The original plans included three windows overlooking the Roman court, which have been reopened along with other later openings above the court.
64. The design for the new galleries was created collaboratively between the Museum's curatorial and design departments and Kevin Roche John Dinkaloo Associates. A few outside architects were invited to give informal input, records of which are maintained in the Islamic Department files. The construction was completed by RCDolner.
65. Michael Spink's suggestions of employing color and texture are gratefully acknowledged here. Stone for the floors was sourced from Turkey, Egypt, Spain, and India, among other places.
66. These mosque lamps were created by Kevin Kutch and Mary Ellen Buxton of Pier Glass, New York.
67. These screens were manufactured in Cairo, Egypt, by Adham Nadim and colleagues of Al-Nadim Company.
68. The Moroccan Court was created by the artisanal firm Arabesque Moresque, run by the Naji family of Fez, Morocco. The scholarly guide for the project was Nadia Erzini, curator of the Luqash Madrasa Museum in Tetouan. The court design was by Achva Benzinberg Stein of City College, New York, in collaboration with Museum gallery designer Michael Batista and Garry Leonard of Kevin Roche John Dinkaloo Associates. An extensive didactic program, including a documentary film and forthcoming publication, records and discusses the concept and making of the Moroccan Court.
69. The stucco and ceiling designs are largely adapted from the 'Attarine Madrasa and the Bou 'Inania Madrasa in Fez.
70. For the *zilij* pattern and tile panel, see Granada and New York 1992, p. 375, no. 119.
71. Records of suggestions and alternative plans are preserved in the Department of Islamic Art private records. In addition, grateful acknowledgment is made here of the many informal contributions and suggestions of Museum colleagues, academics, designers, artists, and friends that are reflected in the concept, design, and execution of the galleries.
72. Recent pertinent discussions on the topic of Islamic art in museum installations are found in Blair and Bloom 2003, Folsach 2006–7, and Crill and Stanley 2006. Guha-Thakurta 2004 offers a critical survey on museum practices in nineteenth- and twentieth-century India.
73. On October 27, 2004, and November 18, 2004, the Museum held roundtable meetings including scholars as well as select curators and others. Internal minutes recording these discussions are preserved in the Department of Islamic Art files. In addition, the department has maintained a list of more than forty scholars who were shown the evolving plans and whose input was considered.
74. During the reinstallation period (2003–2011) a variety of objects from the Department of Islamic Art were shown in other parts of the Museum. Exhibitions and special installations included "Pearls of the Parrot" (October 14, 2005–March 12, 2006), "Venice and the Islamic World" (March 27–July 8, 2007), and "Masterpieces of Islamic Calligraphy" (June 2, 2009–September 1, 2009). Lectures and symposia included the annual Schimmel and Wilkinson lectures and the symposium "Art of India's Deccan Sultans" (October 24–25, 2008).
75. Formal and informal exchanges included those with local, national, and international cultural groups, official bodies, and academic advisers, sometimes in collaboration with the Museum's Multicultural Audience Initiative (MADI) and other departments.
76. Visitor surveys were conducted during the spring of 2009, with analysis of results preserved in the Department of Islamic Art files. The responses came from a variety of visitors aged from their late twenties to late seventies and included local and foreign residents, Muslims and non-Muslims, and a range of cultural, professional, and linguistic backgrounds. Topics included reasons for interest; understanding forthcoming expectations; familiarity with art-historical, historical, geographic, and other terminology; responses to label styles and content; responses to conservation issues; and existing misconceptions about Islamic art, tradition, or history.
77. A number of sometimes varying definitions of Islamic art exist in scholarly literature, a sampling of which can be found in Ettinghausen, Grabar, and Jenkins-Madina 2001, p. 3; Brend 1991, p. 10; Ettinghausen 1984; Issa 1994; Grabar 1987a, pp. 1–18; Burckhardt 1976, p. 31; and Folsach 2001, pp. 19–21. One of the strongest challenges to the concept of Islamic art is expressed in Melikian 2001, p. 94.
78. See the Museum's website, www.metmuseum.org.
79. See the remarks by Jean-François de Lapérouse in this volume for an outline of the conservation work undertaken for this project.
80. Canby 1999a outlines some of the philosophical and practical issues around the question of labels, didactics, and information in museums.
81. Komaroff 1992a provides an overview of the previous set of galleries. In 1976 the installation was accompanied by a special *Bulletin* as well as a slim booklet, *Notes on Islamic Art in Its Historical Setting* (Ettinghausen et al. 1975a, b).
82. These two galleries are named the Koç Family Galleries.
83. The Damascus Room is part of the Kevorkian Fund gift to the Museum.
84. Shtrum et al. 2010, pp. 29–50.
85. The large number of Iranian works in the collection is due to the substantial findings of the Nishapur excavations. They also reflect the roots of the Islamic Department, which grew out of the Near Eastern section and its strong component of Iranian materials.
86. This gallery is named after the Iranian American community.
87. This gallery is named the Sharmin and Bijan Mossavar-Rahmani Gallery.

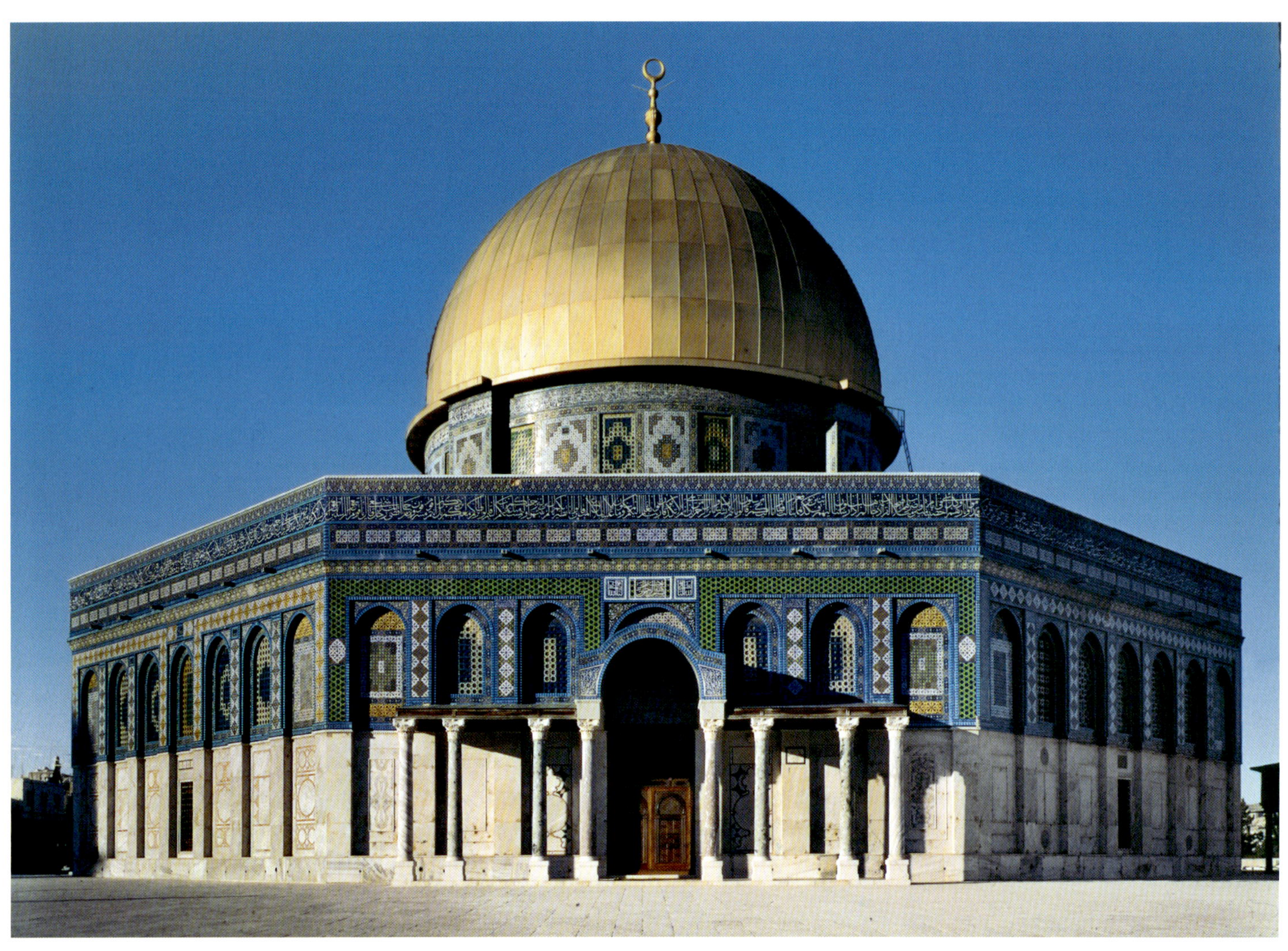

Art of the Early Caliphates (7th to 10th Centuries)

MARYAM D. EKHTIAR

The story of early Islamic art and architecture begins well before the advent of Islam. In recent years, scholars have attempted to reframe the art and culture of this transitional period by integrating it into the study of the Late Antique world.[1] This more inclusive and nuanced approach has allowed for an increasingly pluralistic, interdisciplinary consideration of the late Roman, Sasanian, and early Islamic societies by breaking down barriers of geography and periodization.[2] From this point of view, the advent of Islam in the early seventh century is no longer seen as a drastic break from Late Antique culture, which is believed to have extended well into the early ninth century.

Long before the birth of Islam the two greatest cultural, political, and military forces in the Near East, the Byzantine and Sasanian empires, had developed a shared visual and cultural language of legitimacy. The cross-cultural exchanges between these two realms encompassed both friendly interchange and hostile, combative statements of competition;[3] the rock reliefs at Bishapur showing the Sasanian Shapur I triumphing over the Roman emperor Valerian in 260 A.D. are prime examples of this second type of interaction.[4] Various processes of interconnection and influence included forced migrations as a result of war, skilled craftsmen and artists seeking new opportunities, and direct diplomatic contact, as well as gift exchange and trade between the lands of the Mediterranean, West and Central Asia, and the Indian Ocean. The similarities in style and decorative vocabulary among the arts of the fifth and sixth centuries—exemplified by the architecture and domestic mosaics from Roman Antioch, Sasanian seals, and decorative and utilitarian objects that on the basis of style could have originated in either empire—all show evidence of selective appropriation and the convergence of artistic taste.

The fall of the Sasanian Empire and the loss of control by the Byzantines of their eastern territories provided a fertile ground for the emergence of a new faith in Mecca on the Arabian Peninsula and eventually a new political order in the Near East. Islam was based on the divine message revealed to the Prophet Muhammad through the Archangel Gabriel, beginning around the year 610. These revelations were later collected and compiled to form Islam's holy book, the Qur'an. Within twenty years of his receiving the revelations, Muhammad's message had gained a following in both Mecca and Medina; its main objective was to free the inhabitants of the Hijaz region of the peninsula from pagan worship in favor of the belief in one God (in Arabic, Allah).[5] Including elements of both Judaic and Christian beliefs, Islam is the last of the monotheistic religions. The arrival of Islam in the Near East placed Muslims on an equal footing with Jews and Christians as "people of the book" and as the ultimate inheritors of the Abrahamic tradition.

The year 622 A.D., the date of the *hijra*, or flight of the Prophet Muhammad and his followers from Mecca to Medina, marks the beginning of the Islamic calendar, which is based on a lunar year. From the Arabian Peninsula the Muslim conquest soon spread to surrounding areas in the Byzantine and Persian Sasanian empires. By 714 the Arabs had pushed the frontiers of Islam as far west as Spain and as far east as India and China, incorporating vast territories into their new realm.

The death of the Prophet Muhammad in 632 was followed by the rule (632–61) of the four "Rightly Guided Caliphs," who were chosen from the Prophet's immediate circle. During this period the new Muslim rulers reportedly annexed or built new structures in close proximity to Christian churches and Zoroastrian temples, intending these buildings for use as mosques, or Muslim places of worship. In this way, the caliphs physically aligned themselves with the local religious communities in the conquered cities.[6] In 651, nineteen years after the death of the Prophet, 'Uthman (r. 644–56), the third caliph, ordered a group of scholars to produce a standard written copy of the text of the Qur'an, often referred to as the 'Uthmanic recension. This text, which was divided into 114 chapters (Suras), has remained fundamentally unchanged and continues to serve as the standard form for the Qur'an today.

Although the date of the *hijra* marks the beginning of the Islamic era, it does not necessarily correspond to the beginning of a new artistic tradition. The development of an Islamic artistic identity was a slow and incremental process. In fact, the art of the earliest Islamic period is not drastically different from that of the artistic traditions that preceded it.[7] Artists and craftsmen who had formerly worked under Byzantine and Sasanian patronage continued to follow preexisting conventions under Muslim patrons. Textiles produced in Egypt during this period, for example, mirrored the long-established Coptic tradition,[8] and early Islamic glass and metalwork from Iran are often indistinguishable from their Late Antique and Sasanian antecedents. Given the centuries of interaction between the two powers prior to the Arab conquests, it is rarely possible in specific cases to identify one or the other as the sole source of artistic inspiration.

In the attempt to date and attribute these early Islamic works of art, scholars have relied on various forms of technical analysis, stylistic comparisons with datable architectural monuments, and a few dated or datable objects found in archaeological excavations. For instance, the incised decorative scheme on the so-called Marwan ewer excavated at Abu Sir al-Malak in Egypt, where the last Umayyad caliph, Marwan II (r. 744–50), was reportedly killed by the Abbasids in 750, closely resembles designs on a woven textile fragment with an Arabic inscription in *kufic* script that contains Marwan's name.[9] This visual evidence has aided the attribution of the Metropolitan Museum's very similar ewer with a cock-shaped spout (cat. 7) to roughly the same time. In much the same way, paleographic comparisons using decorative inscriptions from the Dome of the Rock in Jerusalem (about 690) have aided the dating of early Qur'an manuscripts and folios.[10]

New paleographic evidence documenting the emergence of Arabic script from its Nabatean origins in Syria at sites such as Zabad (512), Jabal Usays (529), and Harran (568) has led to the more accurate dating of early epigraphic material, providing us with the ability to date the first extant Arabic papyrus documents (643) and the first fragmentary Qur'an manuscripts on parchment, or *mushaf* (from 633 to 644–56), and the emergence of *hijazi* (678), one of the earliest Arabic scripts, as well as *kufic*. This research has also revealed close affinities between early Qur'an manuscripts and Syriac, Hebrew, and Greek Bibles and scribal traditions.[11]

Mosaics of the eighth century found near the Jordanian town of Umm al-Rasas and other sites, produced for Christian patrons during the first centuries of Islam, not only reflect a continuum with Late Antique mosaics but also serve as historical documents that are as equally informative as literary texts, inscriptions, coins, sculptures, and buildings.[12] They contain inscriptions in Greek and depict classical cityscapes in addition to scenes from classical mythology. These mosaics reflect the persistence of Greco-Roman taste in the territories newly conquered by Islam.

The Umayyads (661–750)

In 661 the first Islamic dynasty—the Umayyads—came to power and established a capital at Damascus in Syria. The founder, Mu'awiya (r. 661–80), made the succession to the caliphate hereditary, putting an end to the elective system that had chosen the "Rightly Guided Caliphs." Umayyad rule was a period of Arab supremacy, and Arabic was the language of polity, administration, and scholarship in most parts of the new empire.

The codification of the Qur'an in written form had an indelible impact on manuscript production and on the development of Arabic calligraphy as an art form. The Umayyad 'Abd al-Malik (r. 685–705) instituted reforms of coinage in A.H. 77/676–77 A.D., eventually eliminating the depiction of human figures and substituting for them purely epigraphic text (cats. 8, 9). He also patronized the construction of mosques that were devoid of figural representations.[13] Another development in coinage that occurred during this period was the unification of two monetary zones, that of the Byzantine Empire, which had minted coins in gold and copper for centuries, and that of the Sasanian Empire, whose currency was the most widespread silver coin in the Near East.[14]

As caliph, 'Abd al-Malik commissioned the construction of a shrine, the Dome of the Rock, in Jerusalem, completed in 691 and considered to be the earliest surviving Islamic monument and the first major artistic endeavor of the Umayyad dynasty. Mount Moriah, the site of the Dome of the Rock on the eastern side of Jerusalem, had important associations for all three monotheistic religions, endowing the new structure with layers of sanctity and meaning.[15] Much of its interior is covered with glass mosaics—a well-established Byzantine practice appropriated by 'Abd al-Malik. These mosaic designs incorporate an amalgam of pre-Islamic Persian and Byzantine insignias of royal power, such as crowns and jewels, along with vegetal motifs; the inclusion of Qur'anic texts and litanies vividly reflects the vision and religious convictions of the Umayyad caliphs. As the earliest extensive monumental Arabic inscriptions, they establish a watershed in the use of *kufic* script on such a scale.

Historical and physical evidence affirms that several sections of the Umayyad Mosque of Damascus, built during the first decade of the eighth century by the caliph al-Walid ibn 'Abd al-Malik (r. 705–15), were covered with lavish glass mosaics representing landscapes and buildings.[16] As with the Dome of the Rock, the decoration of this mosque was distinguished by a complete absence of human and animal imagery. Through the exclusion of such depictions from religious buildings, the Umayyad caliphs initiated a practice that has characterized Muslim religious architecture to the present day. This conscious avoidance of figural imagery in religious contexts was not limited to architecture and was seen in coinage, Qur'ans, textiles, and other artistic media. Since the Qur'an itself does not mention figural art, the Umayyads relied upon the hadith, teachings of the Prophet, for justification of this practice. In addition, the Umayyads pursued a distinct visual identity that would not only assert their power and legitimacy but would also set them apart from their Byzantine rivals and Sasanian predecessors: religious buildings without figural decoration signaled their control over recently conquered territories.

Among a wealth of secular art and architecture commissioned by the Umayyads, agricultural estates with hunting villas, such as Qusayr 'Amra (eastern Jordan) and Qasr al-Hayr West (Syria, southwest of Palmyra), and the grand palaces of Mshatta (Jordan) and Khirbat al-Mafjar (Jordan, near Jericho) reflect the royal and aristocratic tastes of their Muslim patrons. These were places of retreat, where the rulers went to hunt and to escape from city life and palace protocols. Like mosques and religious structures of this period, the plans, forms, and techniques originated in the architectural vocabulary of Late Antiquity. The reuse of fragments from earlier structures in these buildings was common—columns, column bases, and capitals were often antique elements adapted to suit Umayyad taste and improved to fit into the newly constructed structures.[17] These villas contained a remarkable variety of figural and nonfigural mosaics, wall paintings, and even three-dimensional figural sculpture illustrating royal themes that originated in pre-Islamic times, indicating that the avoidance of figural imagery was restricted to religious buildings. The divide between the religious and the secular was among the earliest developments in the history of Islamic art.

For centuries both the eastern Mediterranean region and Iran had flourishing luxury textile industries. One of the most significant contributions of the Umayyad workshops was the production of epigraphic textiles, many of which were embroidered in gold and colored threads and bore the names and titles of caliphs and the Umayyad elite. These workshops also produced luxurious robes of honor to be given to high officials and foreign dignitaries. The earliest textual evidence for such royal textile workshops, called *tiraz*, in the Islamic era dates to the Umayyad caliph Hisham (r. 724–43), while the earliest dated textile example is a fragmentary silk from a *tiraz* workshop in Ifriqiya (present-day Tunisia) with an inscription from the reign of Marwan II.[18] Under the Umayyads such weaving establishments were not centralized and seem to have been administered locally.[19] Designs and patterns from Syria, Iraq, and Persia appear in these textiles, demonstrating the universality of artistic language during this early period in Islamic history. Glass production during this time further illustrates the persistence of Sasanian and Greco-Roman techniques, shapes, and motifs. Glass mosaic (*millefiori*) as well as cut and molded glass continued

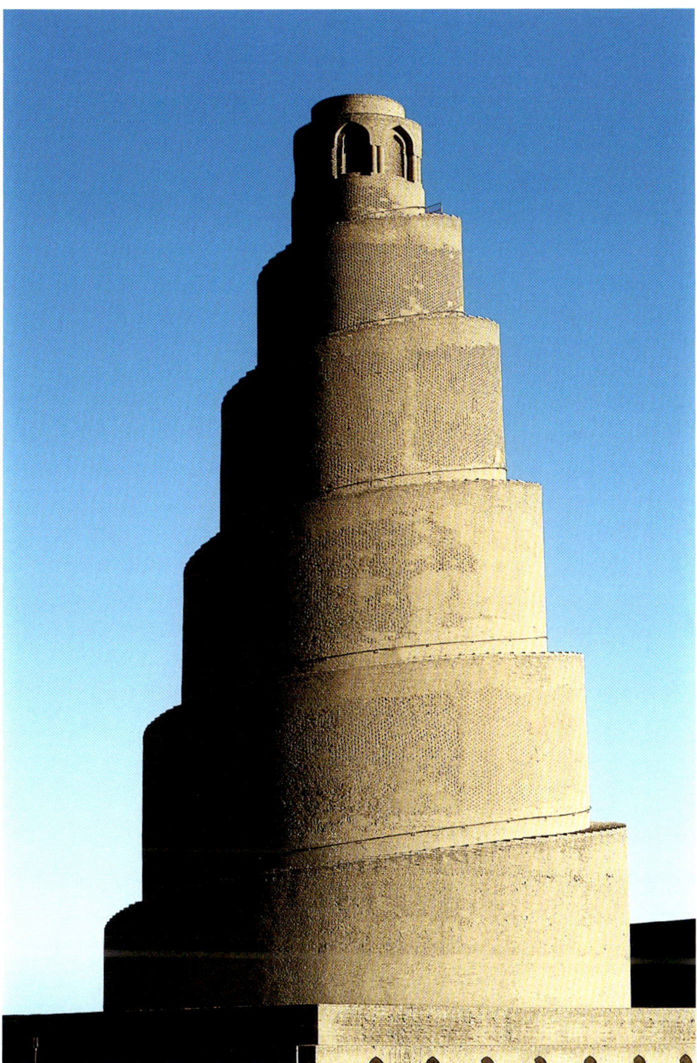

Fig. 28 Minaret, Mosque of Abu Dulaf, Samarra, 859–61. Photo: De Agostini/Getty Images

to be employed. The same is true of techniques used in early Islamic metalwork and carved wood.

Umayyad art has been characterized as a product of the novel distribution and reinterpretation of artistic forms from all over the dynasty's dominion along with the introduction of a limited number of innovations; as illustrated by the architectural structures and objects discussed above, it was eclectic, experimental, and propagandist.[20] Toward the end of the Umayyad period, however, a gradual movement away from pre-Islamic artistic models began with the emergence of an "Abbasid style."

The Abbasids (750–1258)

In 750 the Abbasids succeeded the Umayyads; a revolt, largely by non-Arab Muslims (*mawali*) and Shi'is, led to the Umayyads' demise and the transfer of the caliphal capital from Syria to Baghdad in Iraq. This period witnessed a turning away from the arts of the Late Antique as a direct artistic source and the gradual emergence of a new artistic identity.[21] Under the Abbasids, Arab supremacy was diluted. Non-Arab Muslims, such as the Persians, became the pillars of the new *umma* (community of believers). Persian *dihqans* (the local landed gentry) emerged as the backbone of the new Islamic state and sought to re-create the opulence and rich court culture of their Sasanian predecessors.[22] The Abbasid capital, Baghdad—the palace city, Madinat al-Salam, or City of Peace—with its circular wall, owed very little to the great cities of the Roman Empire: it was a later incarnation of the round cities of Assyria, Iran, and Central Asia.[23] Significantly, Baghdad was only about twenty-two miles (roughly thirty-five kilometers) north of the former Sasanian capital at Ctesiphon, making a relationship with the earlier culture both predictable and appropriate.

The first three centuries of Abbasid rule are considered to have been a golden age, during which distinctively Abbasid artistic developments arose that were to have a marked impact for centuries to come.[24] Although the Abbasid capital was first established at Baghdad, it was relocated to Samarra in 836 because of conflicts between the Turkish palace guards of the Abbasid caliphs and the other residents of Baghdad. The vicissitudes of history, as well as twentieth-century excavations at that site, have led art historians to focus on objects from Samarra to explain the evolution of early Abbasid art. Among the new artistic developments of Abbasid Baghdad and Samarra the most prominent was "the beveled style" (a technique with a distinctive slanted cut), used primarily to embellish large expanses of walls in palaces and mosques. Although decoration in the beveled style was originally formulated for stucco, it was soon applied to other media, such as carved wood (cat. 23), molded glass, and cut rock crystal. The "Samarra style" of surface decoration (which included the beveled style) eventually spread to regions as far away as Iran, Egypt, and Central Asia, where it was adapted to local tastes.

Under the Abbasids, *tiraz* weaving workshops multiplied and extended beyond the court to the marketplace. Most were concentrated along the Egyptian delta, which had been a thriving center of textile production in pre-Islamic times. Egyptian textiles survive in greater numbers than those from Spain, Yemen, Iraq, or Iran. Many inscribed *tiraz* textiles from this period include the caliph's name, which has aided in their accurate dating. Although most of the inscriptions are embroidered, some are tapestry woven, painted, or even block printed.[25]

The Abbasid period also saw a dramatic expansion of international trade, in particular the opening of a direct sea route from Iraq to the Indus Valley, Sind, and China that transformed Iraq into an international marketplace in which prized Chinese and Southeast Asian goods such as silk, paper, tea, ceramics, and teakwood were sold.[26] The wide distribution of Chinese ceramics in the Abbasid realm introduced into the Near East new techniques and styles of pottery. Chinese-inspired ceramics with a tin-opacified glaze and a light-colored body produced by artisans under Abbasid patronage survive in quantity. Another innovation in ceramic production during this period was the introduction of luster-painted pottery. Although luster-painting on glass had first appeared in the sixth or seventh century, potters in ninth- and tenth-century Iraq, in an effort to emulate gold and silver metalwork, applied metallic glazes to the surfaces of ceramic vessels.[27] Techniques such as these were applied to objects in a myriad of shapes and styles and were soon disseminated far beyond Iraq to Egypt, Iran, North Africa, and Spain.

By the ninth century the central authority of the Abbasid caliphate had weakened. Independent Muslim centers of power emerged, with provincial rulers paying nominal allegiance to the Abbasid caliph in Baghdad. As they became more powerful and self-sufficient, these regional rulers followed the caliph's model by minting coins and commissioning *tiraz* textiles inscribed with their own names. The fragmentation of the empire resulted in the further dissemination of the Abbasid style, initiating another phase in the development of early and medieval Islamic art.

1. Of special interest are the following recent studies: Hoffman 2007, Bowersock 2007, Bowersock 2006, Canepa 2009, Brown 1989, George 2010, and Cutler 2009. Other studies include: Grabar 1987a, Allen 1988, Ettinghausen, Grabar, and Jenkins-Madina 2001, Fowden 1993, and Fowden 2004.
2. According to Eva Hoffman, this also includes the breaking down of misleading categories such as East and West; Byzantine and Islamic; Jewish, Christian, Muslim, and Zoroastrian; and Late Antique and Medieval. Hoffman 2007, p. 1.
3. Canepa 2009, p. 7.
4. Ibid., p. 188.
5. Brown 1989, p. 190.
6. Genequand 2008.
7. According to Prudence Harper, "with little surely dated material surviving, the transition from the pre-Islamic to the Islamic period is still, in terms of existing monuments from Mesopotamia, Iran and Asia Minor, an almost invisible one." New York 1978, p. 153.
8. The Copts were the Christians of Egypt whose ancestors embraced Christianity in the first centuries after Christ. Over the centuries, the word *Copt* has come to refer to an Egyptian Christian.
9. Whelan 1990a, pp. 42–43; O'Kane, ed. 2006, pp. 20–21.
10. Ettinghausen, Grabar, and Jenkins-Madina 2001, pp. 15–79; George 2010, pp. 55–93.
11. George 2010, pp. 27–28 and 33–38. See also Déroche 2004a, Déroche 1992, Déroche 1999, Roxburgh 2007, pp. 8–9, Déroche 2004b, and Blair 1998.
12. Bowersock 2006, p. 5.
13. The transition to the aniconic, epigraphical coin types and their meaning were recently the focus of three studies, each with a different approach. Heidemann 2010, Bacharach 2010, and Treadwell 2009.
14. I would like to thank Barry Flood for suggesting that I include this interesting point. See also Hillenbrand, R. 1999, p. 20, Heidemann 1998, and Treadwell 2009.
15. Ettinghausen and Grabar 1987, p. 28; Raby and Johns, eds. 1992.
16. For an extensive study on this mosque, see Flood 2001.
17. Allen 1988, pp. 47–48.
18. Fragments of this textile are housed at the Victoria and Albert Museum, London, and the Brooklyn Museum, New York; until 1960, in the Whitworth Art Gallery, Manchester, the Musées Royaux des Arts Décoratifs, Brussels, and the Pushkin Museum, Moscow. See also Whelan 1990b, no. 20, and Kühnel and Bellinger 1952.
19. New York 1992–93.
20. Grabar 1987a, p. 197. See also Hillenbrand, R. 1999, p. 34.
21. Hoffman 2008; Northedge 2005.
22. Brown 1989, p. 201.
23. Ibid., p. 202.
24. In an effort to destabilize the East–West opposition that was stressed at the beginning of the twentieth century, Eva Hoffman has suggested that the art of the Abbasid period was not necessarily a watershed, as Ernst Herzfeld had proposed, but rather a period of "active integration"—a series of dynamic networks of interaction and connections that brought together Eastern and Western artistic conventions. She postulates that the clear labeling of West (Byzantine/Greco-Roman) for Umayyad art and East (Sasanian Persian and Central Asian) for Abbasid art is an oversimplification of a much more complex set of factors. See Herzfeld 1923 and Hoffman 2008.
25. New York 1992–93.
26. See Flood 2009.
27. Luster-painting involved the use of a paste of silver and copper oxides mixed with fine clay that was applied to a previously fired ceramic surface, often over an opacified glaze. After the decoration was completed, the object would be refired in an atmosphere with low oxygen, causing the metal oxides to reduce to metallic form and migrate into the glaze. Once the object was removed from the kiln, the surface was polished to remove the clay residues and reveal the metallic luster. For early history of the technique, see Carboni 2001, p. 200, and Corning, New York, and Athens 2001–2, pp. 209–11.

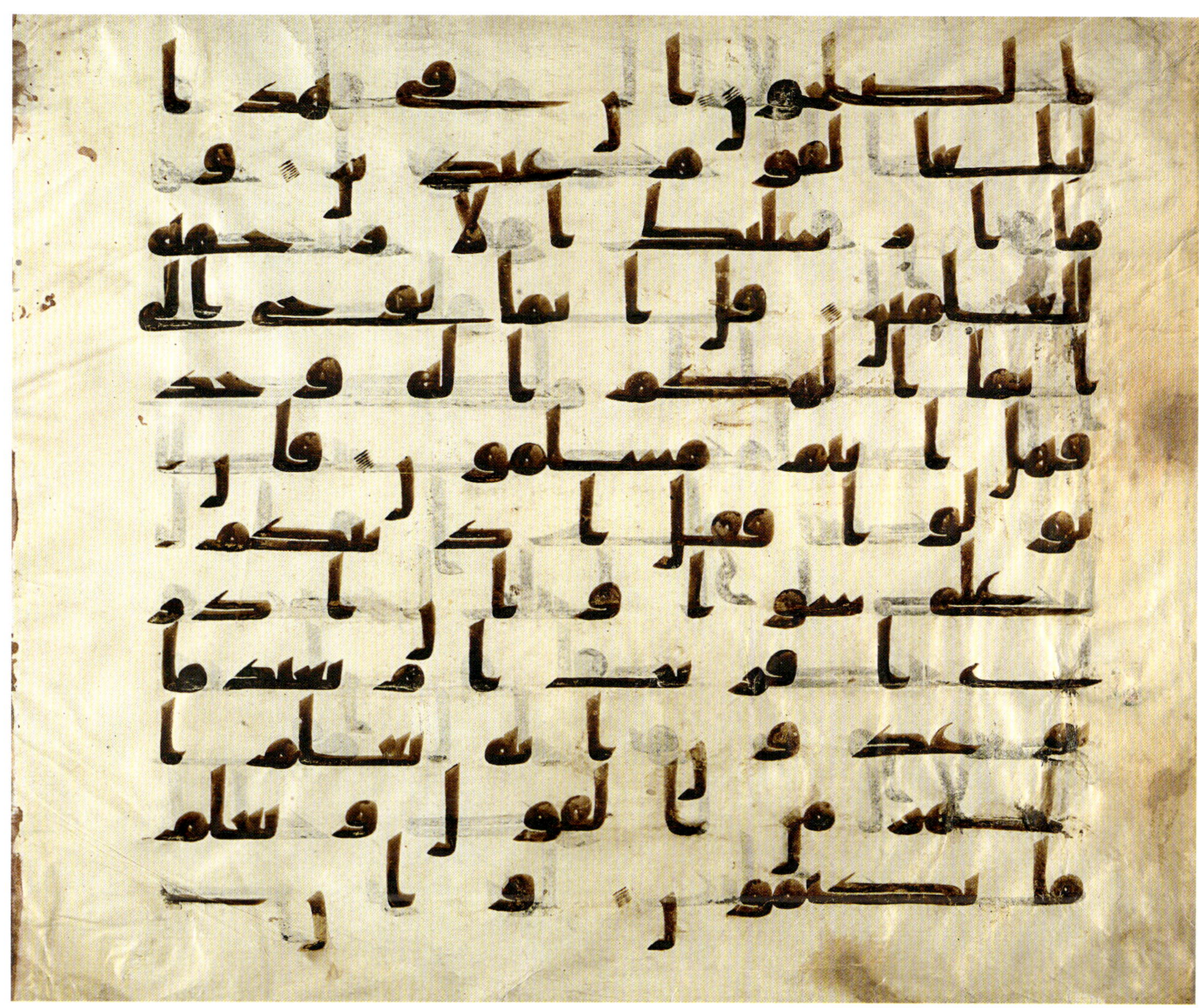

1. Monumental Qur'an Folio

Syria or North Africa, late 8th–early 9th century
Ink on parchment
21 5/8 × 27 1/2 in. (55 × 70 cm)
Purchase, Lila Acheson Wallace Gift, 2004 2004.87

This oversize folio comes from one of the oldest Qur'an manuscripts in existence. Often referred to as the ʿUthman or Tashkent Qur'an, this monumental manuscript is possibly the largest extant Qur'an on parchment. The text, which is from Sura 21 (*al-Anbiya*, "The Prophets"), verses 103–111, contains twelve lines in *kufic* script. Only two illuminated folios from this manuscript survive (one in Paris, the other in Gotha);[1] the remainder of the folios, like this one, are devoid of both illumination and diacritical marks.

The script used here is an early version of *kufic*. In fact, the verticality and the slight slant of the shafts of the letters and their position on the baseline demonstrate possible traces of the *hijazi* script (a script used before the development of *kufic*). Although its origin remains uncertain, we do know that *hijazi* was still in use in Cairo, Damascus, or Sanaʿa during the late eighth or early ninth century.[2] Based on orthographic studies and carbon dating, a number of scholars have dated this manuscript of the Qur'an to the end of the eighth and the beginning of the ninth century.[3] One scholar has drawn parallels between the rows of arches in the surviving illuminated folio in Paris and those in a folio of the Sanaʿa Qur'an,[4] contending that these images resemble the shimmering mosaics of the Dome of the Rock and the Great Mosque of Damascus and were, in all likelihood, illuminated and executed by outstanding artisans trained in Byzantine (or Syriac) scriptoria.[5]

The largest portion of the manuscript to which this folio belongs is presently kept in a *madrasa* library attached to the Tellya-Shaikh Mosque in an area of old Tashkent. The story of how it arrived there is not entirely clear, but most likely it was carried along the Silk Road from the Near East or North Africa via Merv, Bukhara, and Samarqand.[6] It was taken to St. Petersburg in 1868 after the Russian conquest of Central Asia and housed in the Imperial Library there (now the Russian National Library),[7] at which time a number of pages were separated from the rest, including this one. After the Bolshevik Revolution, Vladimir Lenin, in an act of goodwill to the Muslims of Russia, reportedly gave the Qur'an to the people of Ufa, in modern Bashkortostan. Following repeated appeals by the people of Turkestan, the Qur'an was returned to Central Asia in 1924, where it has since remained.[8] From 1905 to 1971 this exceptional Qur'an was subjected to extensive paleographic research, providing valuable insight into early *kufic* Qur'an manuscripts and their historical trajectories.[9]

ME

1. Forschungs- und Landesbibliothek, Gotha (Or. A462) and Bibliothèque Nationale de France, Paris (BN Arabe 324c). See Déroche and Gladiss 1999, p. 20, no. 5; and Paris 2001–2, p. 37, no. 14.
2. Déroche 1992, pp. 27–33. See also George 2010, pp. 87–88.
3. A companion folio was carbon-dated at Oxford, showing a 68 percent probability of a date between 640 and 765 and a 95 percent probability of a date between 595 and 855, confirming the stylistic dating. See Fendall 2003, p. 12.
4. This Qur'an, dating to 649–90 A.D., is in the Dar al-Makhtutat al-Yamaniyya (House of Manuscripts) in Sana'a, Yemen. See Amsterdam 1999–2000, pp. 101–4.
5. George 2010, pp. 87–88. For an image of the illuminated page in the Bibliothèque Nationale de France, Paris (BN Arabe 324c), see ibid., fig. 57.
6. See Déroche 1999.
7. In St. Petersburg it was studied in depth by A. F. Shebunin. See Fendall 2003, pp. 12–13.
8. MacWilliam 2006.
9. A facsimile of the manuscript was published in 1905 by Uspenskii and Pisarev, and a thorough paleographic study of the remaining section of the manuscript was carried out in 1971 by Salahuddin al-Muhajjid. See Pisarev 1905.

PROVENANCE: Private collection, Norway; [Sam Fogg, London, until 2004; sold to MMA]

2. *Qur'an Juz'*

Syria or Iraq, late 9th–early 10th century
Ink, opaque watercolor, and gold on parchment
4 × 6¾ in. (10.2 × 17.1 cm)
Gift of Philip Hofer, 1937 37.142

The Qur'an is customarily divided into thirty *juz'*, or sections of equal length, and those divisions are often reflected in the copying of the text. This intact example of the second *juz'* (2:142–252) retains the two pairs of decorated folios that separated and protected the text pages from the binding (fols. 1b–2a, 100b–101a). Each set of these folios has a distinct design of interlacing gold bands that enclose stippled red and green dots mimicking designs derived from weaving or embroidery. A golden treelike plant projects into the outer margin of the short side of each page. In both design and size, these pages bear a close resemblance to an illuminated folio from a Qur'an in the National Library, Tunis, that had been preserved in a storeroom at the Great Mosque of Qairawan.[1] A group of discarded bindings decorated with interlace patterns that were discovered in the same mosque suggest that the design of the now-lost binding of this *juz'* may have resembled that of its opening and closing illuminations.[2]

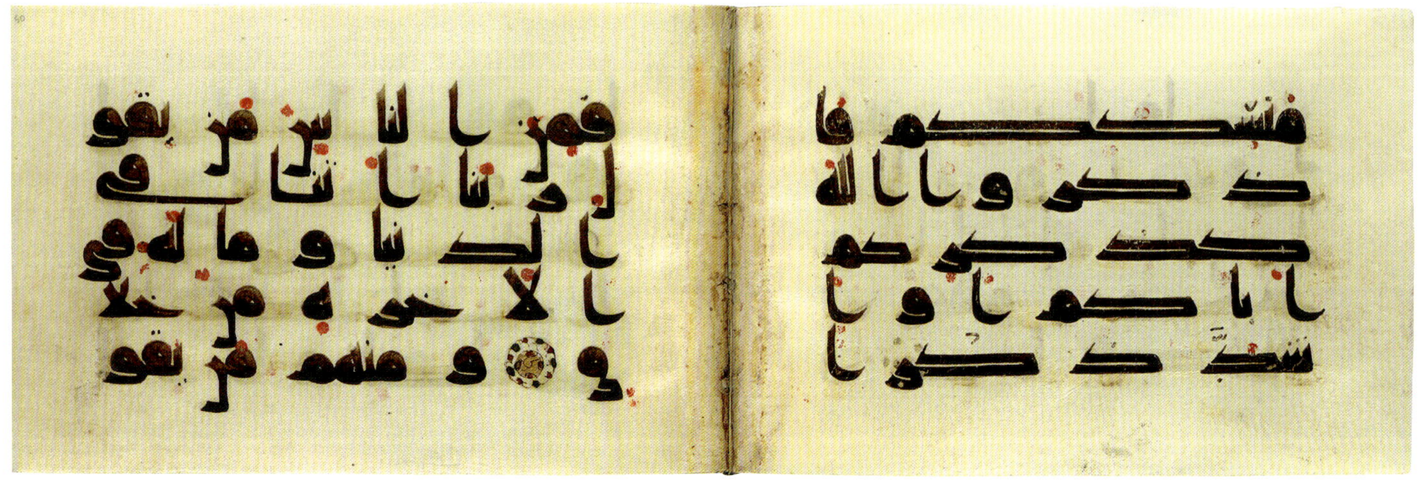

The excellent state of preservation of this manuscript allows for a detailed analysis of its script. Each page bears five lines of text, with both the inner and outer margins justified in most cases. The hand is notable for its aesthetic consistency and for the careful way in which a harmonious design is achieved by balancing the vertical and horizontal elements on each page. The letter forms and their proportions resemble those in a select group of manuscripts dating from the late ninth and early tenth centuries that were donated to mosques. These include two Qur'ans given to the Great Mosque of Damascus: the first in 876 by Amajur, an Abbasid governor of that city (r. 870–78), and the second in 911 by a certain 'Abd al-Mu'min.[3] The illuminated pages of the later Qur'an are strikingly similar in design and execution to those of the present manuscript.[4]

Its majestic script and kinship with Qur'ans known to have been donated to mosques place the Metropolitan Museum's *juz'* among the most accomplished examples of early Abbasid calligraphy. Qur'ans of this type have been attributed to both Syria and Iraq.[5]

PS

1. Paris 1982–83, pp. 258–59, no. 343.
2. Marçais and Poinssot 1948–52, vol. 1, pls. 13b and 21; Petersen 1954, fig. 16.
3. Déroche 1992, pp. 36–37; Blair 2006, pp. 105–6, 111.
4. Arberry 1967, Ms. 1421, p. 8, no. 16, and pls. 19, 20.
5. Whelan 1990b, pp. 119, 124–25.

PROVENANCE: Philip Hofer, Cambridge, Mass. (until 1937)

3. Folio from a Qur'an Manuscript

Central Islamic Lands, 9th century
Ink, opaque watercolor, and gold on parchment
1 1/2 × 2 7/8 in. (3.8 × 7.3 cm)
Rogers Fund, 1962 62.152.2

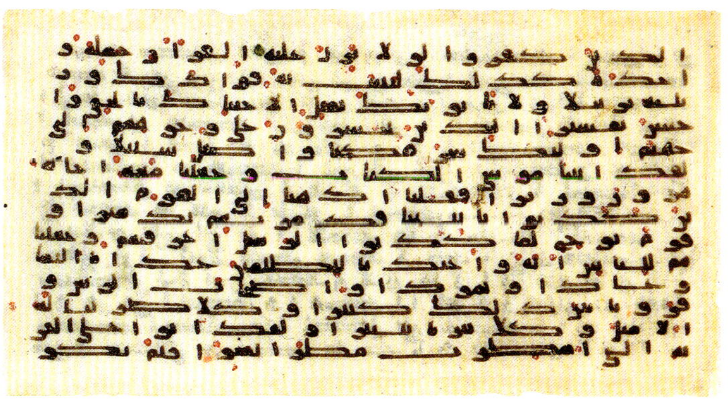

In many periods and regions, small-scale copies of the Qur'an served as amulets, worn or carried in special cases, and the manuscript from which this folio derives may have been made for such a purpose. The page contains verses 22–40 of Sura 25 (*al-Furqan*, "The Criterion"); the side illustrated here bears verses 32–40.

The history of copying the Qur'an has yet to be reconstructed, but this particular page from a manuscript on parchment has distinctive features linking it to versions that are much larger in size. Among these are the even number of lines on each page (fourteen in this case) and a script that exaggerates the horizontal elongation of letters while compressing their vertical elements. Imparting a marked density, which accentuates the horizontality of the page, these characteristics link the Metropolitan Museum folio with a group of Qur'an fragments studied by Estelle Whelan and designated by her as Group 2.[1]

Perhaps because of the small size of the folio, the only diacritical signs employed are red dots to indicate the short vowels. The manuscript is also notable for the translucency of its ink, which is brown rather than the opaque black seen on most early copies; later manuscripts from North Africa and Spain are written in the same ink. Other folios from this manuscript are now in the collection of the New York Public Library.[2] Those folios contain the last sections of Sura 4 and the beginning of Sura 5 and mark the transition between the two with a gold inscription written over the text. The presence of such an addition demonstrates that Sura headings were not part of the original design of this manuscript.

PS

1. Blair 2006, pp. 111–16; Whelan 1998.
2. Schmitz et al. 1992, p. 251, fig. 296; Q 4:172–76, 5:1–7.

PROVENANCE: William Ivins Jr., New York (until d. 1961); his daughter, Barbara Ivins, Milford, Conn. (1961–62; sold to MMA)

4. Throne Leg in the Shape of a Griffin

Probably western Iran, late 7th–early 8th century
Bronze; cast around a ceramic core and chased
22 3/8 × 3 3/8 in. (57 × 8.7 cm)
Purchase, Joseph Pulitzer Bequest, 1971 1971.143

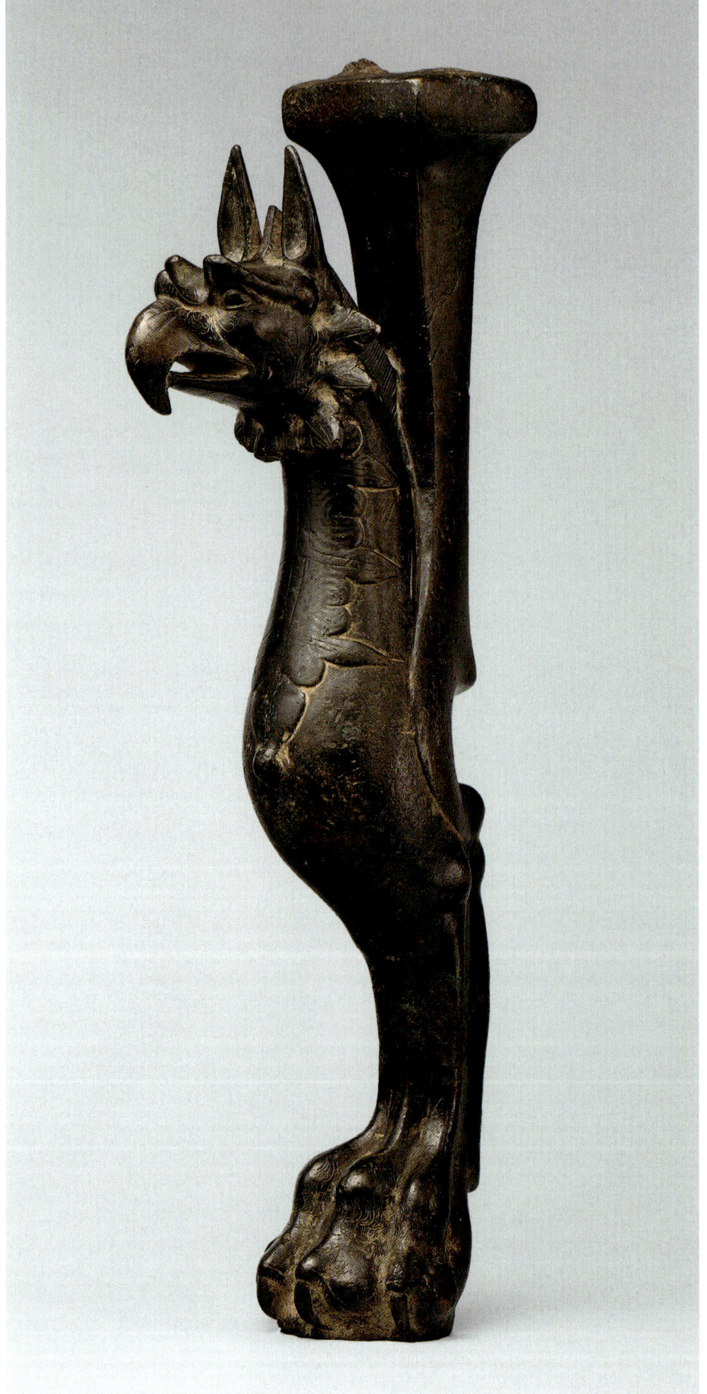

Shaped as the forepart of a griffin, a formidable hybrid creature, this throne leg was cast in leaded bronze; the strut, which originally supported the throne with two iron rods, rises from behind the griffin's neck. The head, chest, and paws are decorated with chased plant motifs, including leaf patterns and floral details, while the fur on the griffin's face and paws is delineated by curvilinear designs. Continuing a long history of fantastic animal forms in Sasanian and post-Sasanian thrones and other decorative works, this object represents the symbolic identification of winged and particularly powerful animals (real and imaginary) with royalty. In pre-Islamic times the griffin, a combination of two solar symbols (the lion and the eagle), was seen as a vehicle of ascension, implying the ruler's deification. In the early years of the Islamic period, these royal and religious symbols were appropriated to project an aura of power and legitimacy.[1]

Allegedly one of a pair,[2] this leg stands apart stylistically from other extant related examples.[3] Its attribution and dating have been complicated by the fact that no examples of Sasanian thrones survive. The closest counterparts are two griffin supports, one in the State Hermitage Museum, St. Petersburg, and the other in the Nizami Museum of Literature in Baku, Azerbaijan.[4] Although the attribution of the Metropolitan's leg remains inconclusive, the vegetal decoration on the griffin's chest offers some useful clues. There is no precedent for this particular combination of forms and motifs in the western reaches of the Sasanian Empire. However, wall paintings and sealstones from Panjikent (present-day Tajikistan) dated to the fifth and sixth centuries show enthroned figures supported by a leg with a griffinlike head bearing foliate decoration. This iconography and distinct decorative detail may have been introduced to Iran during the last century of the Sasanian period, when contacts with Soghdian Central Asia increased. Like the Museum's silver plate (cat. 6), this throne leg fits comfortably into the category of post-Sasanian art. ME

1. Welch, S. C., et al. 1987, p. 15.
2. Orbeli 1938–39, p. 719, pls. 240 B, C. According to New York 1978, pp. 97–100, both illustrations may show the same, rather than two different, pieces.
3. New York 1978, p. 99. Prudence Harper, Curator Emerita, Department of Ancient Near East, Metropolitan Museum of Art, studied this piece in great detail in 1978 and published the results in ibid., pp. 97–100.
4. Bretanitskii and Veimarn 1976, p. 40 (Nizami Museum throne leg). See New York 1978, p. 99.

Provenance: D. David-Weill, Paris (by 1938–71; sale, Hôtel Drouot, Paris, June 16, 1971, lot 49, to MMA)

5. Ewer

Iran, 7th century
Bronze; cast, chased, and inlaid with copper
H. 19⅛ in. (48.5 cm); Diam. 8¼ in. (21.1 cm)
Fletcher Fund, 1947 47.100.90

With its elegant profile and imposing size, this ewer stands out among the metal vessels produced during the early period of Islam. The ovoid body has a cylindrical neck and rests on a ring-shaped molding atop a domical base. Two heads of ducks in profile encircle the lip of the vessel. Its handle is shaped as a sinuous panther whose front paws rest on the rim, while the animal's body and legs extend down the side of the ewer. The smooth surface of the neck and handle contrasts with the undulating surface of the body, which is covered with rows of stylized lobed and bud forms originally inlaid with copper. Lotus petals surround the base of the body, and the same motif is repeated on the foot, arranged in two overlapping bands.

The elongated ovoid shape of this ewer is seen frequently in the metalwork production of Sasanian Iran from the third to the seventh century. This form was especially popular in the silverwork production of the later Sasanian period, in which it appears combined with smaller bases and narrower necks often terminating in spouted rims.[1] The ewer's decoration, which has been interpreted as a stylized mountainous landscape, has also been connected with Sasanian production.[2] Mountains and plants, sometimes visible at the bases of the vessels but more often arranged in overlapping bands covering most of the objects' surfaces, appear in more naturalistic fashion on a number of late Sasanian ewers and plates, often accompanied by animals and hunters.[3]

In the early centuries of the caliphate, the continuation of pre-Islamic forms was common in the production of metalware, particularly in the eastern part of the Islamic world where a solid tradition of metalwork had been in place for centuries. Along with specific types of vessels, a wide range of vegetal and zoomorphic motifs continued to be employed in the decades following the Muslim conquest. This continuity has complicated the dating of objects produced in the phase of transition from the Sasanian Empire to the Islamic caliphate. The present ewer, for example, was long considered to be one of the last masterpieces of Sasanian metalwork production. At the same time, its monumental proportions, larger foot, and more bulbous profile, along with the stylized nature of its decoration—whose rhythm and repetitive quality foreshadow two distinctive traits of Islamic ornamentation—create an aesthetic that departs from previous tradition. Thus it likely belongs to the transitional phase of metalwork production in Iran during the first decades of Islam, when forms and motifs inherited from preexisting traditions were adopted and refashioned to respond to a new sensibility. FL

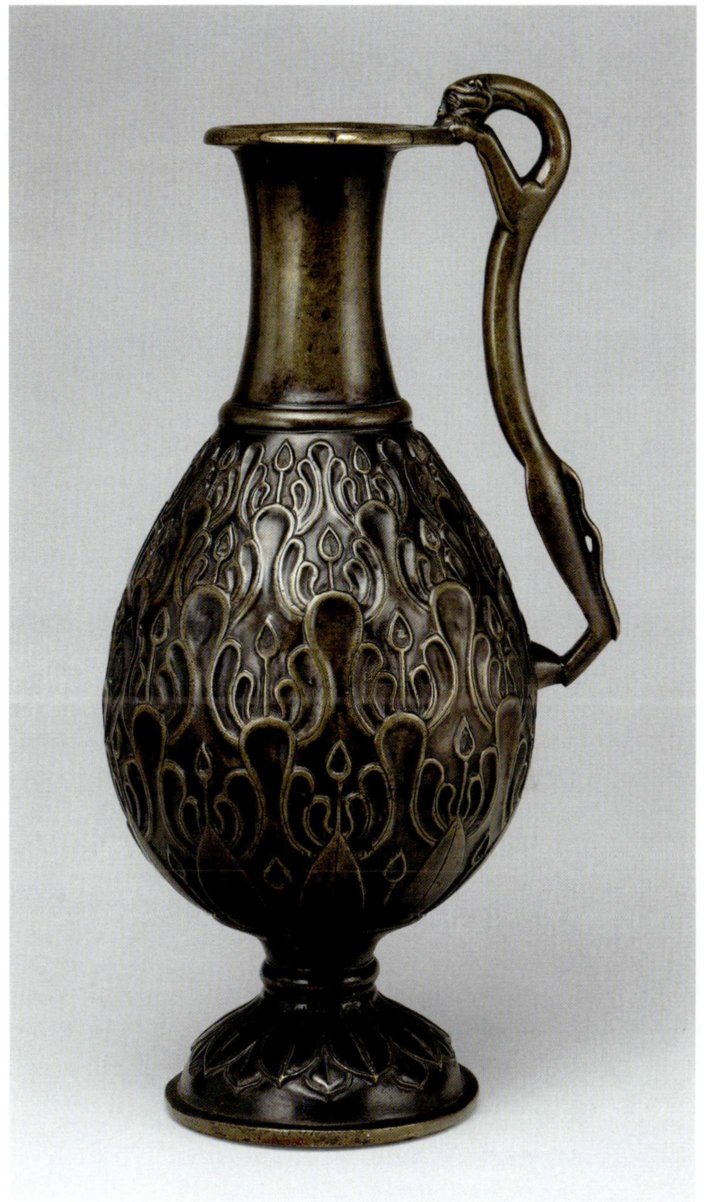

1. Ann Arbor 1967, pp. 105–6, nos. 18–19; New York 1978, pp. 60–61, no. 18.
2. New York 1978, p. 66.
3. Ibid., p. 33, no. 3; p. 39, no. 6; pp. 58–59, no. 17; pp. 65–67, no. 22; Ann Arbor 1967, p. 111, no. 24.

PROVENANCE: Prince Orloff, Russia (probably by 1912); [G. J. Demotte, New York]; [Brummer Gallery, Inc., New York, by 1940–47; sold to MMA]

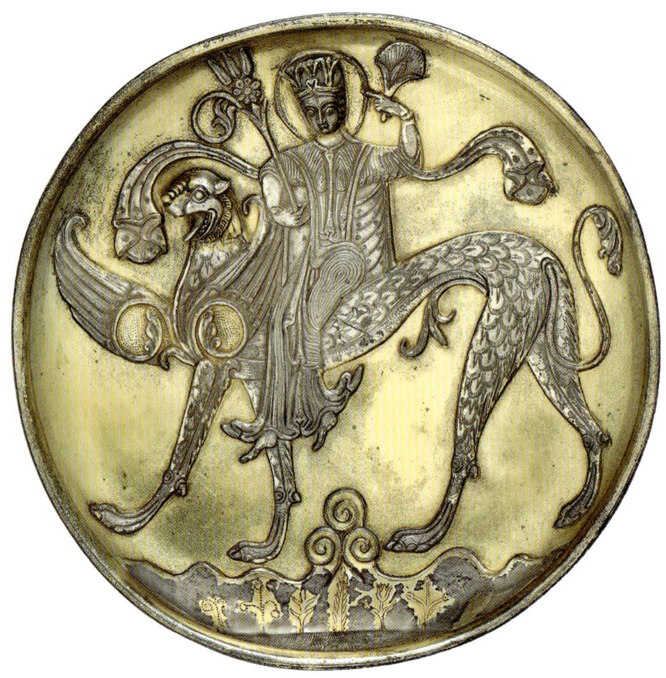

6. Silver Plate

Iran, probably 8th century
Silver; gilded, chased, and engraved, with applied elements
Diam. 8 1/8 in. (20.6 cm)
Harris Brisbane Dick Fund, 1963 63.186

Emblematic of post-Sasanian metalwork, this handsome silver plate depicts a female figure, possibly a goddess, who wears a three-pointed crown with a halo and rides a fantastic winged creature with a lean feathered body, feline head, and canine legs; the heads of both figures are crafted in high relief. The female's pose as she rides the mythological beast, the slender and elongated bodies, and the foliation on the animal are all features seen in wood sculptures of the late seventh or early eighth century from Panjikent (present-day Tajikistan) in Central Asia.[1] In addition, the formalized and awkward position of the woman's arms and the hand gesture (mudra) are fairly common in the art of Central Asia, particularly on wall paintings; on the lower part of the plate, a stylized representation of earth, water, and sky is also reminiscent of imagery in cave paintings of Central Asia. (This is not to suggest that the Museum's plate was produced in Soghdian territories but rather that these aspects are evidence of artistic exchanges with that region.)[2] The six-petaled flower with a long stem the goddess is holding is a motif again seen on two silver ewers, one in the National Museum of Iran, Tehran, and the other in the British Museum, London, each assigned to the Sasanian period,[3] while the unusual drapery of the goddess's garment, notably the coiling technique used to delineate the ample folds, also appears on a silver ewer of the Sasanian period depicting Dionysus/Anahita in the collection of the Metropolitan Museum.[4]

Both the design and the manufacture of this dish are complex and ambiguous, giving rise to detailed discussions about its attribution and place of production.[5] The plate's resemblance to a number of silver objects in the collection of the State Hermitage Museum, St. Petersburg, that were found at various sites in the Urals has been helpful in attributing it to post-Sasanian eastern Iran.[6] In fact, the closest parallel to the woman's pose occurs on a silver-gilt plate in the Hermitage from Tomyz, Viatka (in the present-day Republic of Tatarstan in southern Russia) with an inscription in Pahlavi, a script that continued in use in parts of Iran well into the eighth century.[7] This plate, with its abundance of influences, serves as a testament to the extent of cultural exchange between Iran and neighboring areas during the eighth century; perhaps its meaning can be best interpreted within that context.

ME

1. Harper 1972.
2. Ibid.
3. Marshak 1971, pl. 29.
4. Metropolitan Museum (acc. no. 67.10).
5. Harper 1972.
6. Ibid.
7. Harper 1972, p. 154.

PROVENANCE: [J. J. Klejman, New York, until 1963; sold to MMA]

7. Ewer

Syria, 8th–early 9th century
Bronze; cast and pierced
H. 15½ in. (39.4 cm)
Samuel D. Lee Fund, 1941 41.65

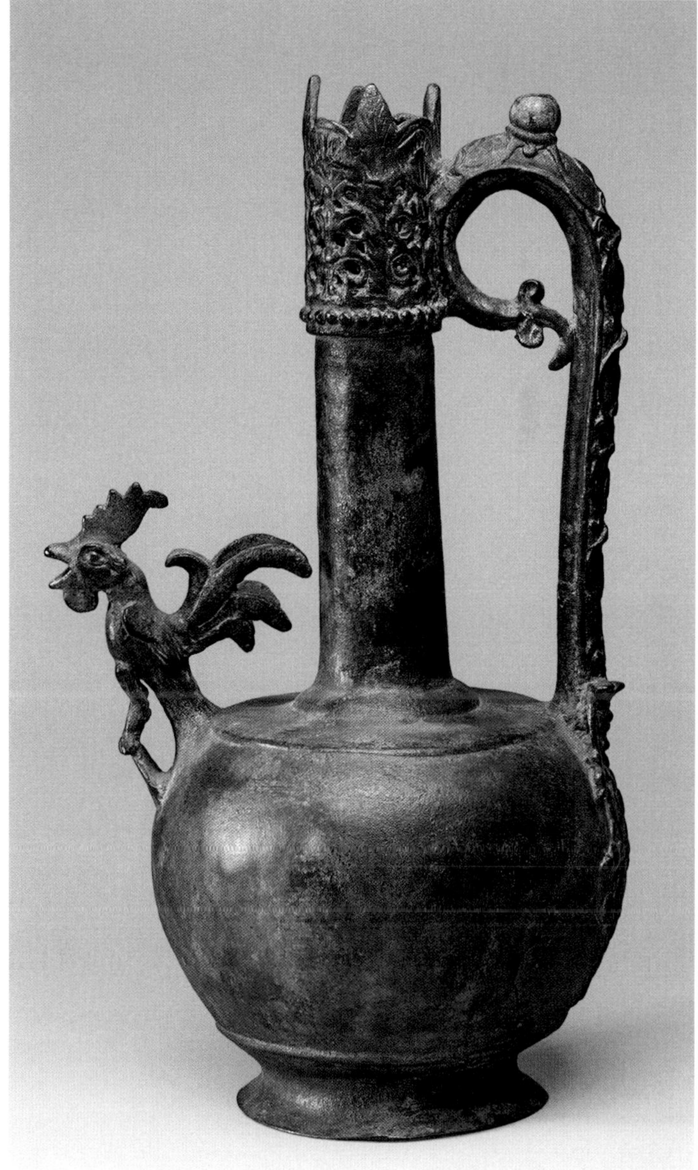

This ewer is one of five vessels with a globular body on a splayed foot, a long cylindrical neck, and a straight handle that have been related to the so-called Marwan ewer, now in the Museum of Islamic Art in Cairo.[1] Smaller in size than its famous counterpart, the Metropolitan's example exhibits a similar decorative program without the same level of refinement and detail. The upper section of the neck is emphasized by an openwork band of palm trees in relief. A scrolling vine bearing fruit runs along the handle and continues on the body, blossoming into a combination of half palmettes with pomegranates flanked by stylized dolphins. Finally, like the Cairo example, a rooster in the round sits on the spout, his beak open to release the liquid contained within.

Scholars have pointed out parallels between the present ewer's peculiar shape and Byzantine glass bottles, such as those excavated at Hanita, Beth She'arim, and Beth Ras, Israel, suggesting a Near Eastern origin for this form.[2] Its decoration also elaborates on vegetal and zoomorphic forms drawn from the Late Antique world: the rooster was a popular motif in classical antiquity, when it was associated with royalty, and its iconography was popular in the regions of the Mediterranean that became part of the Islamic caliphate.[3] Evident as well is the impact of Eastern decorative motifs; the half palmette with pomegranates that descends from the handle probably originated in Sasanian Iran, where it appeared in stucco and stone decoration.[4] The Marwan ewer in Cairo shows similarly inspired elements, particularly its pearl-roundel ornamentation, which can be found in Sasanian stuccos and textiles. A Sasanian silk textile with the same pearl-roundel motif dates to the reign of Marwan II (744–50), thus helping to determine the date of the ewer in the Cairo museum, and, by extension, the present example.[5]

The incorporation of pre-Islamic forms and motifs is characteristic of metalwork production during the first centuries of Islam, reinforcing an early date for this ewer and others like it. The association of the Cairo ewer with the last Umayyad caliph, Marwan II, is based on the fact that it was found in the surroundings of Abu Sir al-Malak in the region of Fayyum, where the ruler was assassinated and buried.[6] Unfortunately, no historical or archaeological proof yet exists that confirms a direct connection between this vessel—or those related to it—and the Umayyad ruler. FL

1. Museum of Islamic Art, Cairo (no. 9281); see O'Kane, ed. 2006, p. 21, no. 11. A list of the ewers, with bibliography, is provided in Fehérvári 1976, p. 33.
2. Baer 1983, p. 86 n. 198.
3. In the Islamic period, the cock came to be associated with religious rituals, becoming God's way to announce and regulate the practice of daily prayers.
4. Examples are attested in Kish and Ctesiphon. See New York 1978, p. 107, no. 40.
5. For a fragment of this textile, see Brend 1991, p. 43, fig. 23 (Victoria and Albert Museum, London). Another fragment is in the collection of the Brooklyn Museum, New York.
6. Sarre 1934.

Provenance: Bobrinsky Collection, Russia; Henry Harris, London (by 1931–38; to Brummer); [Brummer Gallery, Inc., New York, 1938–41; sold to MMA]

8. Coin (Dinar)

Syria, dated A.H. 79/698–99 A.D.
Gold
Diam. 7/8 in. (2.1 cm)
Bequest of Joseph H. Durkee, 1898 99.35.2386

Obverse
Inscription in Arabic in field:
لا اله الا الله وحده لا شريك له
There is no god but God alone. He has no associate.

Inscription in Arabic in margin:
محمد رسول الله ارسله بالهدى ودين الحق ليظهره على الدين كله
Muhammad is the Messenger of God, who sent him "with the guidance, and the religion of truth to show that He may uplift it [Islam] above every religion." (variation of Qur'an 9:33)[1]

Reverse
Inscription in Arabic in field:
الله احد الله الصمد لم يلد ولم يولد
God is one. "God, the Everlasting Refuge, / who has not begotten, and has not been begotten." (excerpt from Qur'an 112)

Inscription in Arabic in margin:
بسم الله ضرب هذا الدينار في سنة تسع وسبعين
In the Name of God, this dinar was struck in the year A.H. 79.

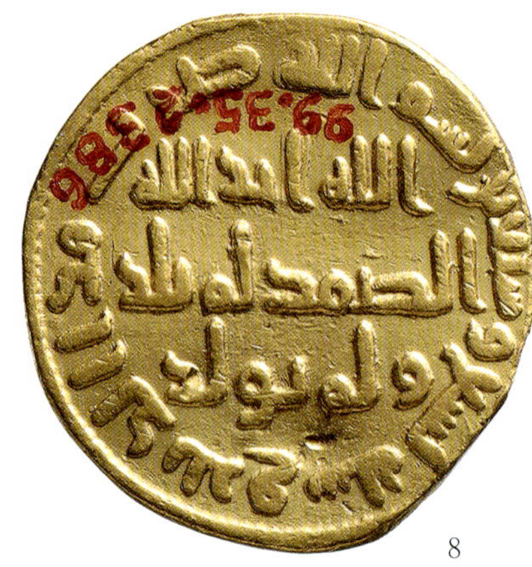

8

9. Coin (Dirham)

Iraq, Wasit, dated A.H. 93/711–12 A.D.
Silver
Diam. 1 1/8 (2.7 cm)
Gift of Darius Ogden Mills, 1904 04.35.3343

Obverse
Inscription in Arabic in field:
لا اله الا الله وحده لا شريك له
There is no god but God alone. He has no associate.

Inscription in Arabic in margin:
بسم الله ضرب هذا الدرهم بواسط في سنة ثلث وتسعين
In the name of God, this dirham was struck in Wasit in the year A.H. 93.

Reverse
Inscription in Arabic in field:
الله احد الله الصمد لم يلد ولم يولد ولم يكن له كفواً احد
God is one. "God, the Everlasting Refuge, who has not begotten, and has not been begotten, and equal to Him is not any one." (Qur'an 112)

Inscription in Arabic in margin:
محمد رسول الله ارسله بالهدى ودين الحق ليظهره على الدين كله ولو كره المشركون
Muhammad is the Messenger of God, who sent him "with the guidance and the religion of truth, that He may uplift it [Islam] above every religion, though the unbelievers be averse." (variation of Qur'an 9:33)

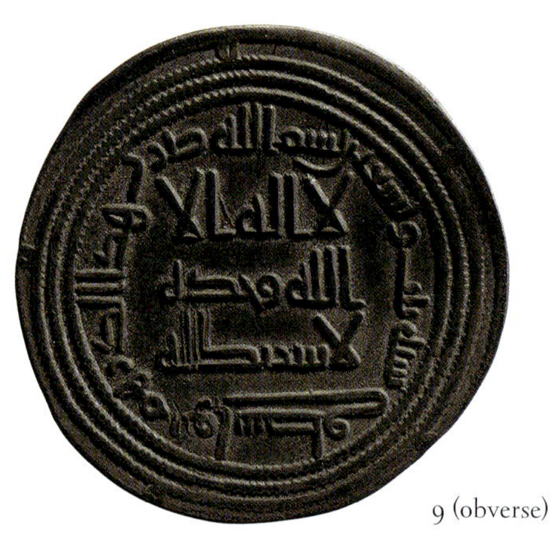

9 (obverse)

9 (reverse)

For the first few years after the establishment of the Umayyad dynasty, its coins were based on those of its predecessors—the Byzantine emperors in the western part of its empire and the Sasanian kings in the east. In 697, however, the caliph 'Abd al-Malik (r. 685–705) issued new gold dinars bearing only writing, which included phrases from the Qur'an and the statement that there is only one God and Muhammad is his messenger. The following year silver dirhams in the same style were minted in the eastern provinces.[2] Although earlier Umayyad coins had had Arabic writing and versions of the affirmation of faith on them, neither the Qur'an nor any other holy text had ever appeared on the coins of this region. Images such as fire altars, crosses, and portraits, rather than written statements, had always been the standard indicators of the issuing authority's religious and dynastic affiliations.

Many scholars have speculated about why the switch to all-epigraphic coins was made. Most recently it has been suggested that 'Abd al-Malik settled on an iconographic system that did not borrow too heavily from symbols associated with the earlier Byzantine and Sasanian rulers yet was understandable in both of these cultural realms where the coins would circulate, resulting in one unique Umayyad creation to be used across his domains.[3] Another hypothesis, based on the historical context of the specific moment in which these coins appeared, proposes that their message was aimed directly at 'Abd al-Malik's greatest rival at that time, the Byzantine Empire: the coins bear a version of the affirmation of faith stating that God has no partner, a refutation of the Christian doctrine of the trinity, most relevant in the political arena of the western Umayyad empire.[4] Ultimately, however, their success and their continued use have been ascribed to market factors over other considerations.[5]

The dinar illustrated here has the same format as the earliest known all-epigraphic coin, which it postdates by two years;[6] the dirham, from fourteen years later, reflects changes that resulted from the differences between the denominations of the two coins and their dates of issue. While both coins bear essentially the same text, the dinar, as a smaller coin, includes neither the name of the mint (but believed to be Damascus) nor the full text of the Qur'anic verses of Suras 9:33 or 112 on it. On the dirham, Sura 9:33 appears on the margin of the reverse rather than the margin of the obverse.[7] In addition, on the obverse of the dirham the writing is located within three serrate circles, with five annulets in the border, while on the reverse the field text is surrounded by a solid circle, and the marginal text by a serrate circle with five annulets. Although these elements are borrowed from the silver Sasanian coins that they were meant to replace, they are markers of the mint administration and differ from issue to issue.[8] MS

1. Only the quoted phrase is from the Qur'an; it also appears in Sura 25:14 and Sura 61:9.
2. Important analyses of Umayyad coins include Walker, J. 1941, Walker, J. 1956, and Bates 1986. The last several years of scholarship on this subject, including a new chronology of the silver issues (previously thought to have appeared starting in A.H. 79), is summarized and augmented in three recent studies of Umayyad coins: Treadwell 2009, Heidemann 2010, and Bacharach 2010. I would like to thank Dr. Bacharach for sharing the text of his article with me before its publication.
3. Treadwell 2009, p. 379.
4. Bacharach notes that although scholars often mention that the "affirmation of faith" appears on certain coins, we cannot assume what the exact text is because there are differences between the seventh- and twenty-first-century versions, as well as between various seventh-century formulations. Based on the evidence of coins from the east, he suggests that there the formulation was "In the name of God, there is no god except God, Alone, Muhammad is the Prophet of God"; based on coins, architectural inscriptions, and milestones in the west, the formulation there was "There is no god except God, Alone, He has no partner." See Bacharach 2010.
5. For Bacharach's application of Gresham's Law to this situation, see Bacharach 2010. He stresses that the ultimate success of these coins, and the adoption of their basic format by almost all subsequent Muslim dynasties, cannot be applied backward to our understanding of the circumstances of their appearance and acceptance of these coins in the market at that time.
6. American Numismatic Society, New York (no. ANS 1002.1.406), published in Bates 1982, p. 14.
7. This format became standard after A.H. 79/698–99 A.D. See Orientalisches Münzkabinett Jena (no. 305-H10), dated to that year; published in Heidemann 2010, p. 185.
8. This pattern of borders and annulets is standard until the year A.H. 99/717–18 A.D. Possible reasons for the later changes are discussed in DeShazo and Bates 1974.

Provenance

Cat. 8: Joseph H. Durkee, New York (until d. 1898)
Cat. 9: Darius Ogden Mills, New York (until 1904)

10. Bowl with Cobalt-Blue Inscriptions

Iraq, probably Basra, 9th century
Earthenware; painted in blue on opaque white glaze
Diam. 8 in. (20.3 cm)
Harris Brisbane Dick Fund, 1963 63.159.4

Inscription in Arabic in *kufic* script:
غبطة / غبطة
Felicity / Felicity

Chinese stonepaste and porcelain ceramics of the Tang period (618–907) were exported in quantity to western Asia in the mid-eighth and ninth centuries. Excavated examples found at various sites throughout Iraq serve as evidence of the popularity of these wares at the Abbasid court. In an attempt to imitate the hard body of Chinese high-fired porcelain, ninth-century Iraqi potters rediscovered the earlier technique of coating earthenware vessels with tin oxide mixed with a clear lead glaze, which created a fine opaque white surface onto which a wide array of designs could be painted. Since there were no tin mines in the region, this metal was imported by sea from Southeast Asia.[1] Iraqi potters often decorated their wares with blue (cobalt), green (copper), and manganese purple. They also sought to replicate the shapes of the Chinese ceramics, the majority of which, like this example, are bowls with low feet, flaring sides, and everted rims.

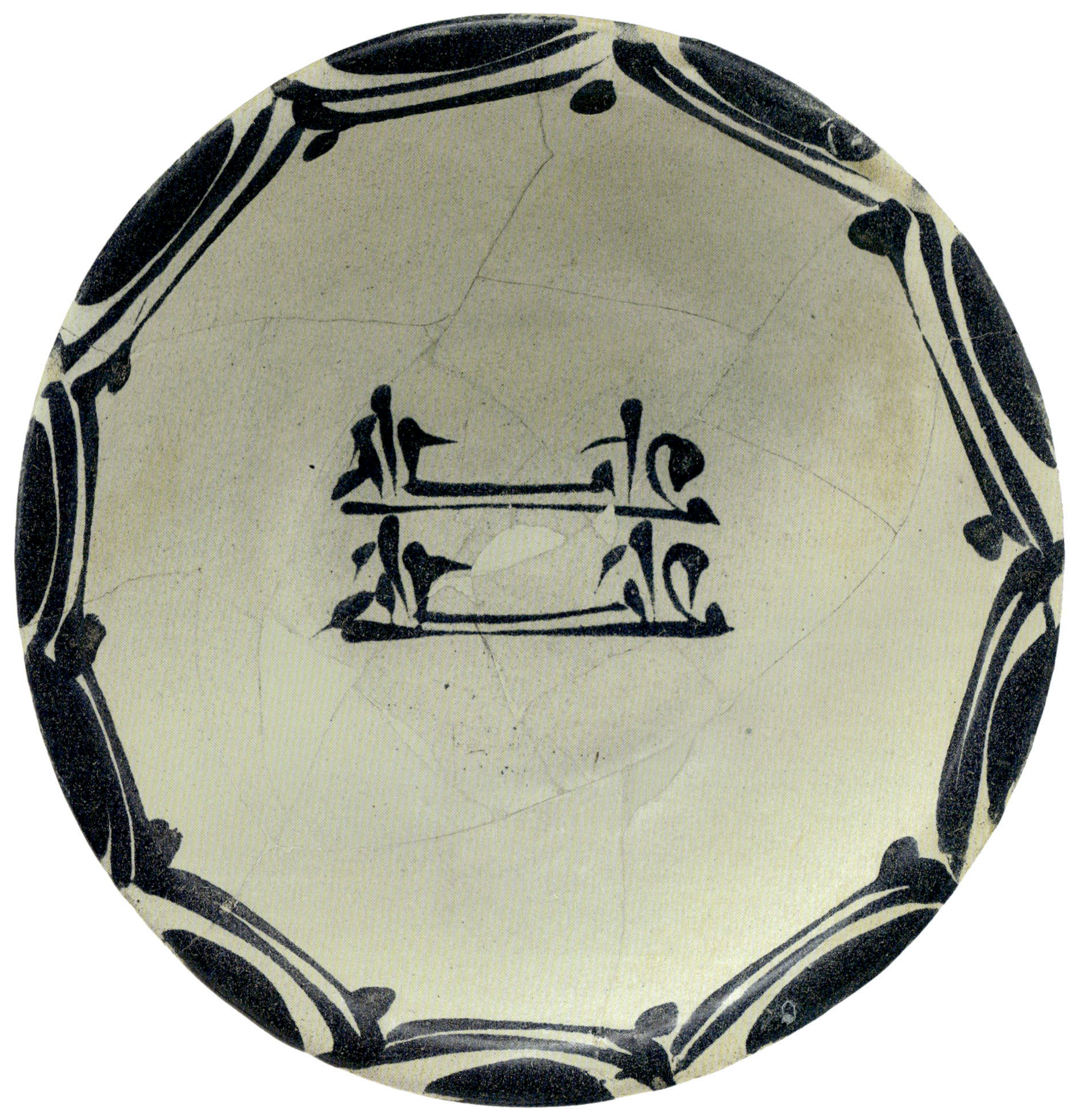

Elegantly proportioned, the bowl is decorated with a *kufic* inscription in cobalt blue against an opaque white ground. Like others of its type, it is one of the first examples of pottery in the early Islamic period to incorporate Arabic calligraphy as the main element of decoration. Not entirely legible, the inscription appears to be the Arabic word *ghibta* (felicity), which is repeated twice at the center.[2] Many of these bowls include calligraphic designs with messages of good fortune or the name of the potter, although some also feature vegetal and green splash designs. The tin-opacified wares of Iraq were also the first to incorporate blue designs on a white surface, a striking combination adapted by Chinese potters of the Yuan (1271–1368), Ming (1368–1644), and Qing periods (1644–1911) and later used extensively in Europe.[3]

Here the calligraphic composition and overall visual effect take priority over legibility. The striking contrast between the cobalt blue of the calligraphy and the white opaque ground creates a visual impression that resembles blotted ink, while the garland-like motifs decorating the rim combine with the central inscriptions to establish a balanced composition. ME

1. Allan 1991a, p. 6.
2. There is an almost identical bowl with an identical inscription in the Harvey B. Plotnick collection in Chicago. See Chicago 2007, p. 42.
3. Ibid. See also Watson 2004, pp. 171–80.

PROVENANCE: [Nasli Heeramaneck, New York, until 1963; sold to MMA]

11. Bowl

Iraq, probably Basra, first half of 9th century
Earthenware; polychrome luster-painted on opaque white glaze
H. 2 3/8 in. (6 cm); Diam. 7 3/4 in. (19.7 cm)
Rogers Fund, 1952 52.114

12. Bowl

Iraq, probably Basra, second to third quarter of 10th century
Earthenware; luster-painted on opaque white glaze
H. 3 3/4 in. (9.5 cm); Diam. 12 in. (30.5 cm)
Fletcher Fund, 1964 64.134

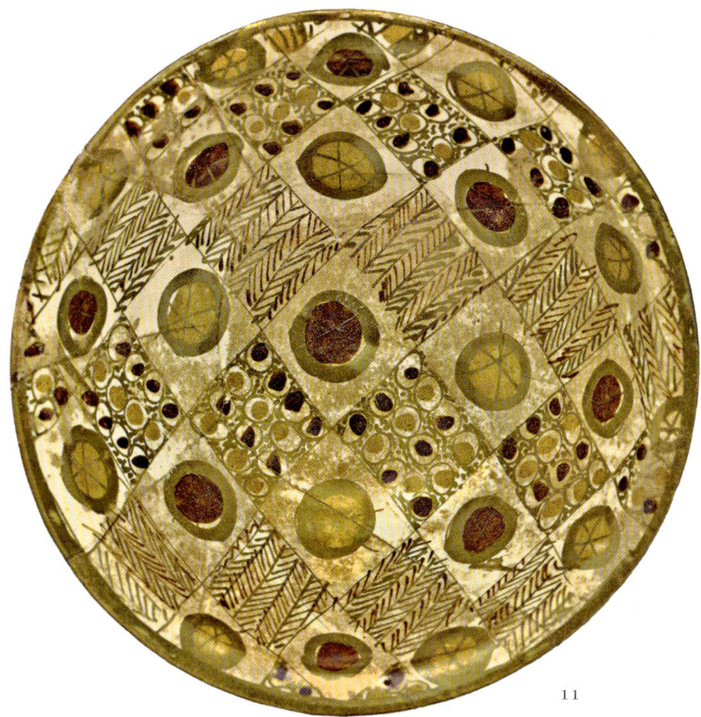

11

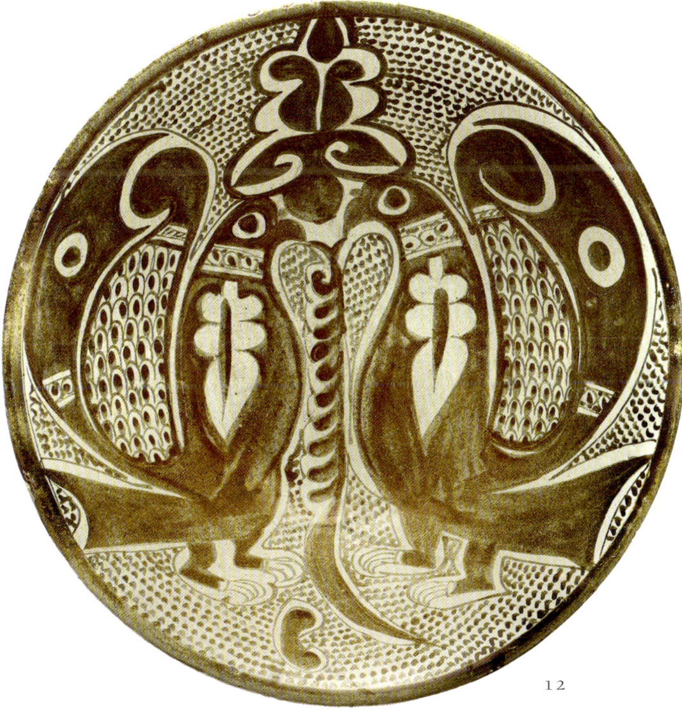

12

While both bowls share the creamy yellow body fabric so characteristic of Basra pottery, they represent two very different approaches to luster painting and design, reflecting discrete phases in the history of Abbasid lusterware.[1] The first bowl (cat. 11) belongs to the early phase, associated with the first half of the ninth century. Standing on a low foot, its curved sides terminate in an everted lip. Polychrome painting, a distinctive feature of early Abbasid lusterware, decorates both the interior and the exterior; here, the potters used three colors—olive green, yellow gold, and copper red. Most of the luster ceramics dating to this early period bear nonfigural designs that explore pattern and texture within a rubric of stylized vegetal motifs or geometric frameworks. On this bowl, the tension between the structure of the checkerboard format, the variety of patterns within its compartments, and the painterly freedom with which they are executed is particularly successful. Reminiscent of a pattern sampler, the decoration includes herringbone designs, "peacock-eye" motifs, and rows of dots and stipples probably inspired by *millefiori* glass.[2] The variety and dynamism of early lusterware design correspond to the expansive and vibrant time of al-Mu'tasim (r. 833–42) and his foundation of Samarra, where luster tiles decorated the new palaces, and a period when the distribution of Basra ceramics reached far and wide.[3]

The second bowl (cat. 12) represents Basra lusterware roughly a century later. The bowl profile now has a straighter wall and lip. More significant is the new approach to painting and design. The densely patterned backgrounds and the continued use of certain motifs, such as the "peacock eye," provide continuity with early Abbasid lusterware. By this time, however, potters had abandoned polychrome painting in favor of monochrome decoration. Their designs are often figural, with central human or animal forms, alone or in symmetrical pairs. This bowl depicts confronted peacocks flanking a plant, against a ground filled with a repeated V-shape. This shift in decoration may reflect the taste of a new elite, since the period coincides with the arrival of the Buyids in Iraq.[4]

EK

1. Ernst Kühnel's identification of three phases of Abbasid lusterware is more or less supported by recent petrographic analysis; see Kühnel 1934 and Mason 2004. Mason has sampled and analyzed the petrography of both of these bowls and has published their profile drawings, ibid., pp. 192–93.
2. The exterior of the bowl bears the "dash-circle" motif diagnostic of early Basra production.

3. One fragment of a luster tile excavated from Samarra is in the Metropolitan's collection (acc. no. 23.75.25); for others, see Sarre et al. 1925, pls. 21, 22; Porter, V. 1995, pp. 24–27, figs. 10, 12; and Watson 2004, p. 184, no. E.1 (LNS 1057 C). On the wide distribution of early Basra lusterware, see Mason 2004, p. 44.
4. Mason 2004, pp. 159–60.

Provenance
Cat. 11: [E. Safani, New York, until 1952; sold to MMA]
Cat. 12: [Khalil Rabenou, New York, until 1964; sold to MMA]

13. Bottle

Egypt or Syria, 7th–early 8th century
Glass, bluish; blown, applied blue decoration
H. 7 7/8 in. (20.1 cm); Diam. 3 1/4 in. (8.2 cm)
Museum Accession x.21.210

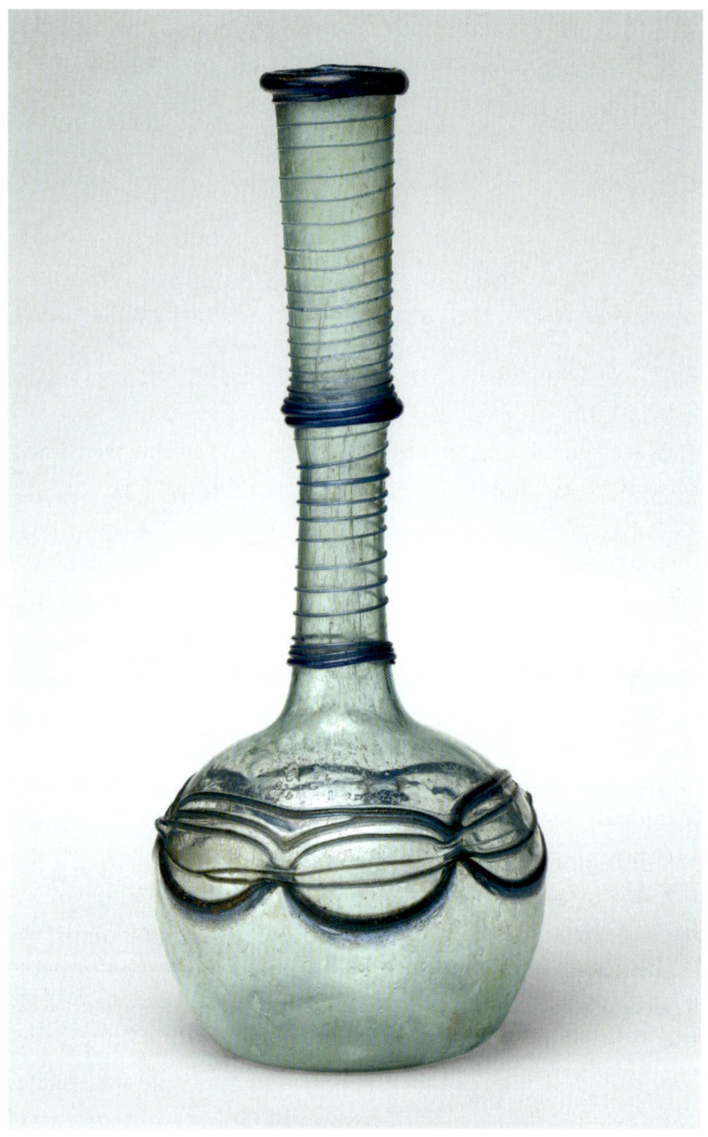

This bottle clearly illustrates the transitional phase of development between Late Antique and early Islamic period artifacts. Of all the crafts, glassmaking was perhaps the most conservative in terms of both artistic continuity over time and the transfer of skills and ideas from one generation to another. Since the revolutionary discovery of glassblowing during the first century B.C. in the Roman-controlled areas of the eastern Mediterranean, the enormous possibilities linked to this practice had allowed glassmakers to expand dramatically their creative horizons, in particular to increase the variety of shapes and decorative techniques.

With elegant proportions and a long, narrow neck, this pale blue bottle is decorated with dark blue trails applied in a spiraling motion around the entire neck as well as in a wide band on its body. The thickening of the pattern around the neck divides it evenly into two sections, while the "spectacle" design around the body—created by pinching the trails together at regular intervals—gives the vessel a dynamic appearance. The shape, the trailed decoration, and the spectacle pattern of applied decoration had become well established in the fourth to fifth centuries A.D. but continued to be used at least into the eighth century.[1] The base of this bottle shows no evidence of the use of the pontil; this technical feature would suggest a pre-Islamic date. Around the advent of Islam, glassmakers universally adopted the use of the pontil (a short metal rod that was attached under the base of the vessel before detaching the blowpipe) to facilitate both handling and the application of decorative techniques.

These considerations demonstrate how difficult it is to differentiate between objects produced before or after the advent of Islam because of the strong continuity in production over centuries. The history of this bottle within the Museum is instructive in this respect as well: acquired at an unknown time and under unknown circumstances, it was accessioned initially by the Department of Greek and Roman Art, then eventually transferred to the Department of Near Eastern Art (subsequently divided into the departments of Ancient Near Eastern and Islamic Art) in 1960.

While it could be argued that this bottle does not belong to the Islamic period, its importance lies in the fact that it symbolizes the transition between two historical eras. Thus, it finds its rightful place in the galleries of early Islamic art. SC

1. This continued use was evidenced particularly in the Egyptian region but also found as far away as eastern Iran; see Ann Arbor 1978, no. 34; Kröger 1995, no. 151; Scanlon and Pinder-Wilson 2001, p. 65, pl. 32i. The last reference relates to a conical lamp found in Fustat (Old Cairo) in a 750–800 archaeological context.

Provenance: Accessioned by the Metropolitan Museum in 1921; provenance unknown

14A, B. Two Zoomorphic Bottles

A. Probably Syria, late 7th–8th century
Glass, amber-colored; blown, applied decoration
4⅜ × 3¼ in. (11.1 × 8.3 cm)
Gift of Mrs. Charles S. Payson, 1969 69.153

B. Probably Syria, late 7th–8th century
Glass, yellowish and pinkish; blown, applied decoration
3⅜ × 3½ in. (8.6 × 8.8 cm)
Purchase, Friends of Islamic Art Gifts, 1999 1999.145

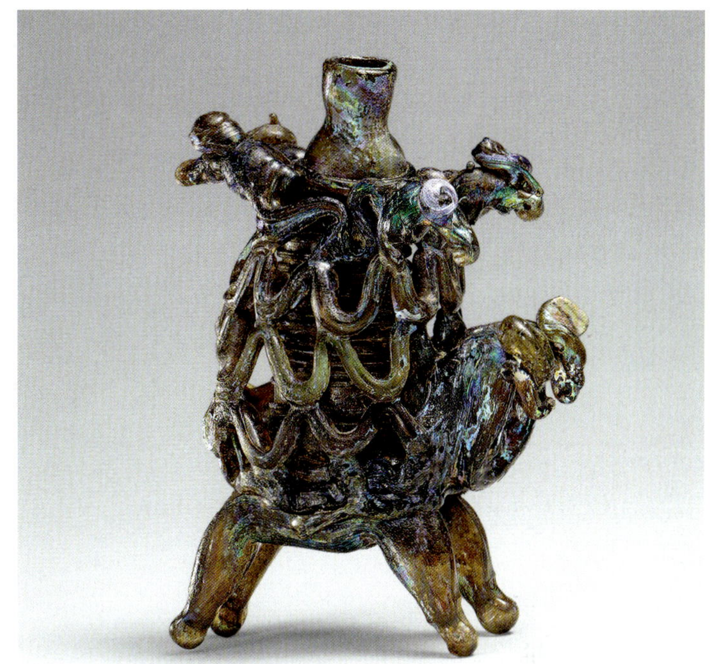

A

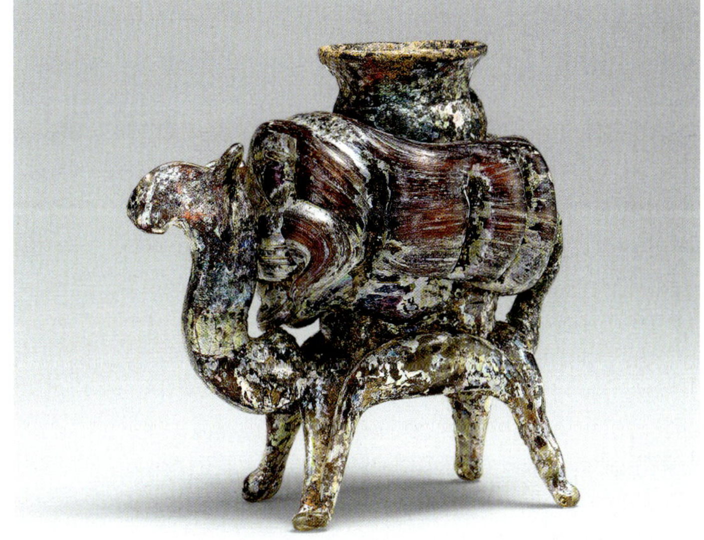

B

Like the blue bottle decorated with applied threads of blue glass (cat. 13), these playful utilitarian objects testify to the transition between two glassmaking traditions, the Roman and the Islamic, along the coastal zone of the Mediterranean region. They are also examples of the versatility and flexibility of glass as a medium, which poses no restrictions on the creativity of the glassmaker. Here, two simple vessels, small bottles for ointments or valuable liquids such as essences and perfumes, are transformed into zoomorphic figurines that "carry" the container as part of their burden.

Once a bottle had been blown and shaped, the rest of the figure was constructed around it from trails and blobs of hot glass, forming the stylized body, legs, head, and burden surrounding the functional vessel. The quadruped with a bottle (cat. 14A) is typical of early Islamic production and is probably slightly earlier than the camel (cat. 14B) because it follows more closely the Late Antique, eastern Roman tradition. It combines a figure that supports a slender tubular flask known as *balsamarium* (container for balm) and is in turn encased in a cage. This latter feature evolved from extremely accomplished third- to fourth-century bowls known as *vasa diatreta*, in which vessels encased in open cages were produced by cutting the glass when cold. In their imitations (known as *pseudodiatreta*) produced in Alexandria on the Egyptian coast, the cage was constructed from hot-worked glass trails.[1] Evidently the idea of constructing a cage around a vessel was adopted by the early Islamic glassmakers and fused with features of a *balsamarium* container.

The bottle of cat. 14A was built entirely with one batch of amber-colored glass whose surface has taken on an iridescent hue due to weathering. Many of these animal-shaped bottles, now preserved in various collections around the world, carry a cage made of different trails from two contrasting colors—usually nearly colorless and dark blue glass[2]—thus also offering a pleasant chromatic variety. In this example, the figure is given a more whimsical appearance by its double head and by the addition of four protruding stylized heads atop the cage, almost as if it is meant to represent an entire caravan of horses, donkeys, or camels carrying their precious goods.

On the other hand, figurine cat. 14B is atypical for this group because the burden that surrounds the bottle is solid. The surface of the glass is entirely weathered from long burial in the ground, but when viewed through transmitted light the object is revealed to have been made of two different colors. Unmistakably a camel, feet well planted on the ground and ostensibly conscious of its mission, this lively piece is evocative of the vital role played by these animals along the caravan trade routes of western Asia in a time of transition between two empires. SC

1. For the *diatreta*, see Corning, London, and Cologne 1987, nos. 134–39. For the *pseudodiatreta*, see Bussagli and Chiappori 1991, fig. p. 65.
2. See Corning, New York, and Athens 2001–2, pp. 112–14, nos. 29, 30.

PROVENANCE
Cat. 14A: Mrs. Charles S. Payson, New York (until 1969)
Cat. 14B: [Art market, Israel]; [Taiyo Ltd., Tokyo, until 1999; sold to MMA]

15. Bowl

Probably Iraq, 9th century
Glass, green, opaque yellow, and opaque red mosaic; fused, slumped, ground, and polished, applied foot
H. 2 in. (5.1 cm); Diam. 5⅝ in. (14.3 cm)
Rogers Fund, 2001 2001.266

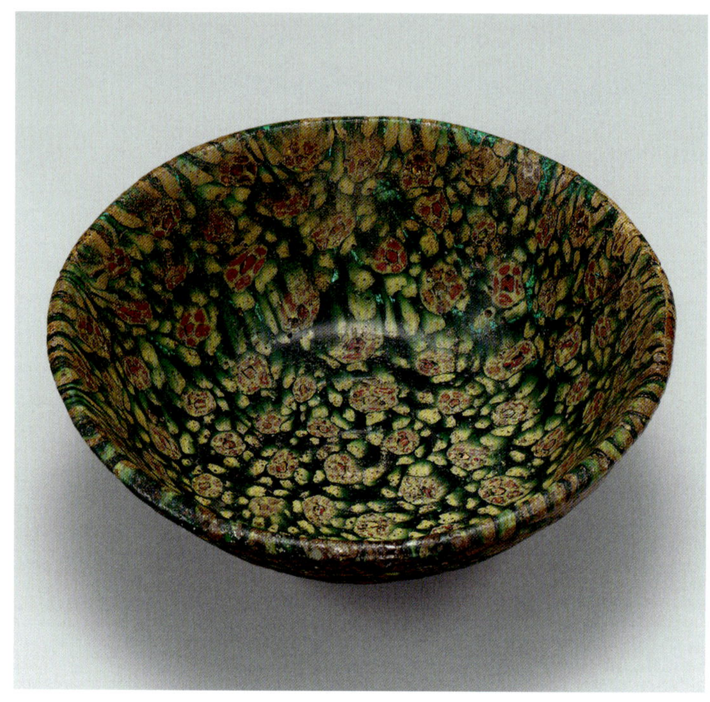

The final stage of mosaic-glass production is relatively simple: the tiny tesserae are arranged according to a desired pattern one by one over a heat-resistant form that gives shape to the object. It is then placed in a kiln at high temperature to fuse their edges, thus creating a single piece, and left to cool down slowly. After polishing, the work is complete.[1]

The preparatory stage, however, is extremely time-consuming because each tessera represents a diminutive slice from a long and narrow glass cane that was originally formed by wrapping layers of different-colored glass around its core until the desired combination was achieved. The finished cane probably had a diameter of three to four inches (7.5–10 cm) and was at least fifteen to twenty inches long (35–50 cm). In order to reduce it to the desired diameter of about one-tenth of an inch (2.5 mm), the cane was softened and pulled from both ends, maintaining the original cross-section pattern; once the cane had cooled, it was cut into thin slices. Initially made of simple patterns of concentric circles or bicolored spirals, by late Roman times canes began to include more complex and ambitious designs. Islamic glassmakers inherited the canemaking technique, improving upon it in late eighth- or early ninth-century Abbasid Iraq.

Inevitably, glass-mosaic vessels were destined to be small in size with simple open shapes not only due to the complexity of the technique but also because they were slumped over a mold and could not be blown to a larger size. The present bowl, with a diameter of almost six inches (15 cm), seems to represent the largest intact work in this technique. When viewed through transmitted light, the bowl comes alive because the fused outer edge of each slice is a translucent emerald green.

First created in imitation of variegated stones such as agates, mosaic glass acquired a more ornamental function in the Islamic period. We know, for example, that the floor in front of the throne of the Abbasid caliph in Samarra was composed of multicolored, flowerlike mosaic tiles.[2] Venetian glassmakers, who revived the technique, which became known as *millefiori* or "a thousand flowers" in Europe during the fifteenth century, were able to use it to create blown vessels. SC

1. A photographic demonstration of the various phases of canemaking, fusing, and slumping performed by William Gudenrath of the Corning Museum of Glass can be found in Corning, New York, and Athens 2001–2, pp. 58–59.
2. The largest surviving fragment of these tiles is in the Museum für Islamische Kunst, Staatliche Museen zu Berlin. For a color image that fully suggests the original dazzling effect of mosaic glass, see ibid., p. 148, no. 61.

Provenance: [Mansour Gallery, London, until 2001; sold to MMA]

16. Goblet

Probably Syria or Iraq, 8th–9th century
Glass, bluish green; blown, applied solid stem and blown foot; scratch-engraved
H. 4⅝ in. (11.7 cm); Diam. 3½ in. (9 cm)
Purchase, Joseph Pulitzer Bequest, 1965 65.173.1

Inscription in Arabic in *kufic* script:
اشرب بركة من الله لصاحب الكأس
Drink! Blessings from God to the owner of the goblet.

The decorative technique employed on this elegant and unusual goblet, with its flat base, solid yet segmented stem, flaring cup of aquamarine or pale blue color, and Arabic inscription, is usually known as "scratched" or "engraved." Although distinctive, the goblet relates to a varied group of vessels and shards that employ the same engraved technique, which have been found east of Egypt and as far away as China. Their dating has never been questioned: archaeological finds have situated these works firmly in eighth- and ninth-century contexts because the first fragments were excavated in places like Samarra in Iraq, Fustat in Egypt, and, more recently, in the crypt of a Buddhist temple sealed in 874 A.D. in the Shaanxi province of northwestern China.[1] While their wide distribution has puzzled scholars over the decades, a fragmentary plate in dark blue glass found in the 1930s on the site of Nishapur in eastern Iran,[2] which for many years was regarded as the key example of the group, tipped the balance in favor of an Iranian origin. The extraordinary discovery in the 1980s of six intact plates in the Chinese temple, however, together with dozens of additional archaeological and other new finds, has forced scholars to study this material in a more systematic fashion. The present writer has suggested a Syrian or Iraqi origin for the bulk of this group (rejecting an Iranian provenance), a conclusion that has also been reached by Jens Kröger.[3]

This goblet represents one of the most memorable demonstrations of this decorative technique due to its rare shape, enviable state of preservation, and subtle pale blue color (80 percent of these engraved works are made from dark blue glass). Exceptional as well is the presence of a legible inscription, "Drink! Blessings from God to the owner of the goblet." The patterns drawn within horizontal bands (from top to bottom: a saw-tooth band just below the rim; the inscription; a band of small circles enclosed in rectangular sections; and a row of diamond-shaped designs) may not be as sophisticated and precisely executed as those of many other works belonging to this group. Yet this goblet remains an outstanding example of a short-lived but sought-after production that reached the farthest corners of the Asian routes through trade and gift exchange. SC

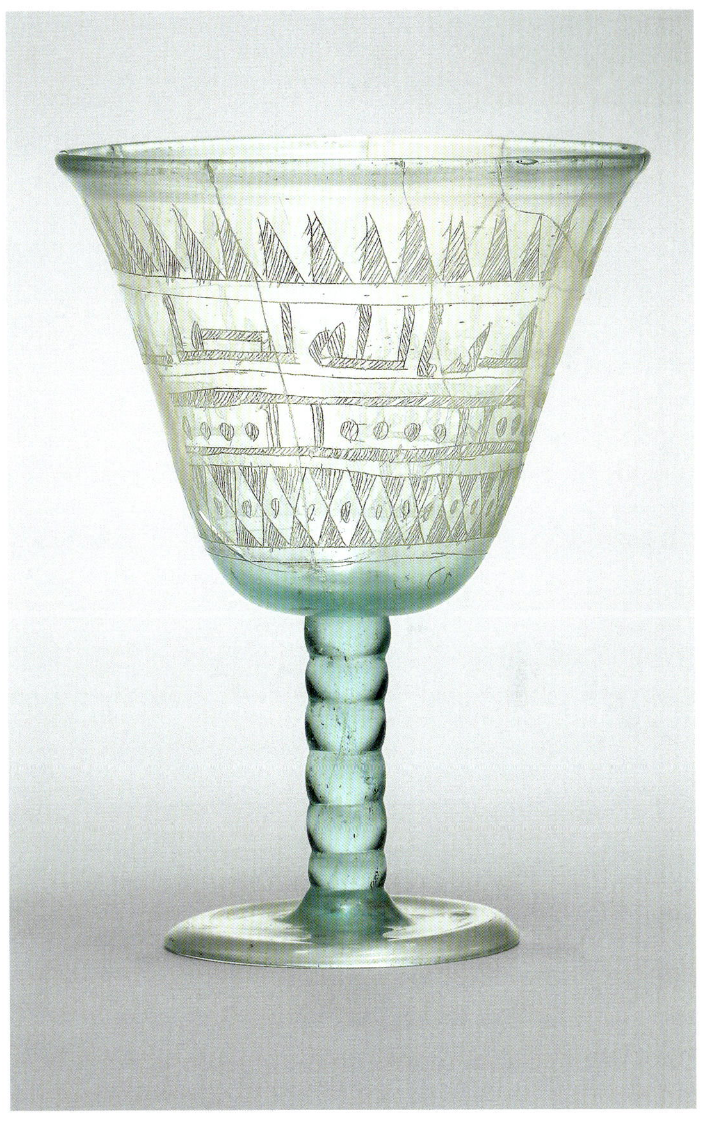

1. For the finds in Samarra, see Lamm 1928, pp. 79–82, nos. 251–59, figs. 51–52, pl. 8. For Fustat, see, most recently, Scanlon and Pinder-Wilson 2001, pp. 82, 83, fig. 39, pl. 39a. For China, see An 1991.
2. Also in the Metropolitan Museum (acc. no. 40.170.131).
3. Carboni 2001, pp. 76–81, no. 17; Kröger 2005.

PROVENANCE: [Mohammad Yeganeh, Frankfurt, until 1965; sold to MMA]

17. Cup

Iran, 8th–9th century
Glass, colorless with a green tinge; blown, cut
H. 2¾ in. (7 cm); Diam. 3⅝ in. (9.2 cm)
Purchase, Joseph Pulitzer Bequest, 1965 65.172.1

18. Beaker

Iran, 9th–10th century
Glass, colorless; blown, cut
H. 5⅜ in. (13.6 cm); Diam. 5⅝ in. (14.3 cm)
Purchase, Rogers Fund, and Jack A. Josephson, Dr. and Mrs. Lewis Balamuth, and Mr. and Mrs. Alvin W. Pearson Gifts, 1974 1974.45

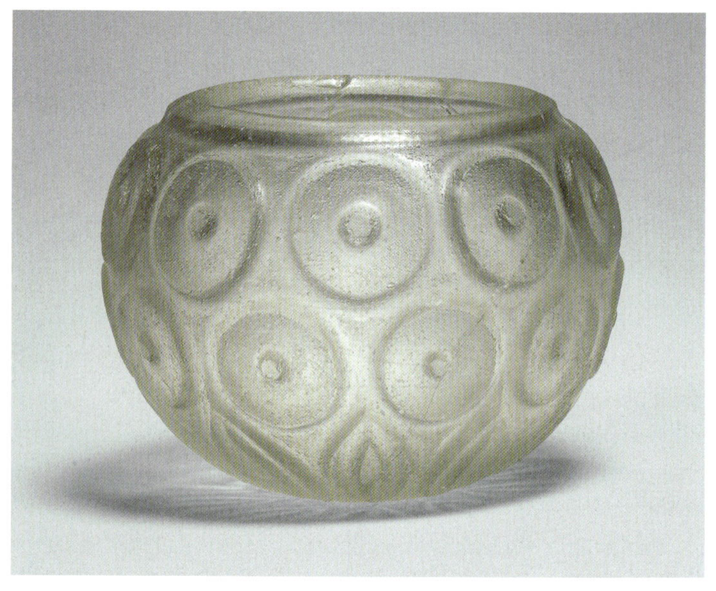

17

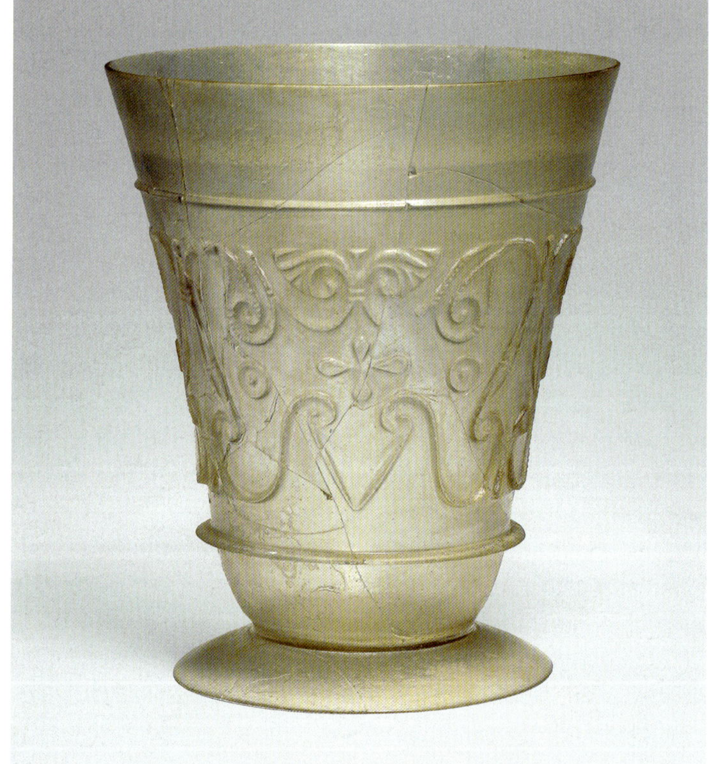

18

Inevitably, the immediate models used by Iranian glassmakers following the advent of Islam came from their Sasanian heritage, which in turn had developed from a centuries-long distinctive and individual artistic tradition in the geographical area of Greater Iran. Under Islam, this approach was raised to new heights with the production of transparent, almost colorless cut glass, which was decorated with the aid of a rotating wheel, thereby treating the material more like stone instead of taking advantage of its great malleability when hot. Once a colorless batch had been created (by decolorizing the glass with the appropriate oxide of manganese), a thick-walled "blank," roughly in the shape of the required vessel (usually either an open bowl or cup or a globular bottle with a narrow elongated neck), was blown either freely on a blowpipe or into a dip mold. After it cooled down to room temperature, the blank was transferred to another area of the glass workshop or, more likely, to an entirely different workshop that specialized in glass- as well as stonecutting.

For both objects presented here, this was the common origin. The artistic intent and therefore the final results, however, appear to be very different when the two works are compared.

The small cup (cat. 17) is solid, perfectly balanced in the distribution of its weight and its decoration, and sits comfortably in the hand. Its pattern is executed in high relief and looks decidedly to earlier models: the pointed petals or leaves that arise from the center of the base are strongly reminiscent of designs used in Iran during Achaemenid times (sixth–fourth centuries B.C.). The so-called *omphalos* disks (Greek for "navel," thus termed because of the central protuberance), arranged into two staggered bands, represent one of the most popular and successful patterns from Late Antiquity through the early Islamic period. Clearly this object was a valuable drinking vessel made in imitation of the more precious and expensive rock crystal. Once the cup was empty, the drinker would place it upside down to rest on its flat rim, revealing the attractive floral pattern around the base.

When handled, the beaker (cat. 18) creates almost an opposite effect: it is weightless and appears to be very fragile. Its decoration is dynamic and light, and the beaker itself seems insubstantial to the point of creating a sense of trepidation in the person who holds it. Indeed, it is almost a miracle that, though broken and repaired, it has survived virtually complete to this day. The skill of the glasscutter who was able to create patterns on its surface is astonishing. He not only reduced the thickness of the walls to about 3/64 inch (about 1 mm) while avoiding breakage, but also produced the relief decoration with a thickness of less than approximately 5⁄64 inch (2 mm). An ideal point of reference for the viewer is provided by the lower ridge, which protrudes for 3⁄32 inch (about 2 mm). Combined with the excellence of its cut decoration—a six-unit repeat design of palmettes, half palmettes, and calyx motifs, linked with a scroll arranged horizontally around the circumference—these qualities establish this drinking vessel as one of the very few surviving masterpieces of relief-cut glass from the first millennium A.D. Although it has been attributed to both Iran and Egypt (the latter particularly because of strong connections in technique and design with celebrated Egyptian rock-crystal vessels),[1] there is little doubt that the beaker represents one of the highest points of Iranian glasscutting. The identification of rock-crystal cutting traditions in the eastern lands of the Islamic world, which is corroborated by the appearance on the market in recent times of objects with an Iranian or Central Asian provenance, further validates the Iranian origin of this splendid beaker.[2] SC

1. Most recently, by David Whitehouse in Corning, New York, and Athens 2001–2, pp. 172–73, no. 79.
2. See, for example, Kröger 1993. To my knowledge, no specific study has been published on the subject; the largest number of rock-crystal objects of eastern Islamic origin is in the Dar al-Athar al-Islamiyya, al-Sabah Collection, in Kuwait City.

PROVENANCE
Cat. 17: [Saeed Motamed, Frankfurt, until 1965; sold to MMA]
Cat. 18: [Saeed Motamed, Frankfurt, until 1974; sold to MMA]

19. Bottle

Probably Iran, 10th–11th century
Glass, greenish yellow; blown in two parts, impressed with tongs, applied blue rim
H. 7¼ in. (18.5 cm); Diam. 3⅜ in. (8.7 cm)
Purchase, Rogers Fund, Louis E. and Theresa S. Seley Purchase Fund for Islamic Art, and Mrs. Charles D. Kelekian Gift, 1994 1994.211

A less time-consuming and inexpensive alternative to cold relief-cut vessels (see cats. 17, 18) was provided by objects whose surface decoration was created by using either molds or tonglike tools that made permanent impressions in the fabric of the glass. Unlike the process of cutting the glass when cold, these techniques were applied when the glass was hot, and the entire object was fashioned before it cooled down. Rather than having been created in two distinct phases that involved different skills and possibly different workshops, the final product therefore depended entirely on the concept and skill of the glassblower. Neither as sophisticated nor as detailed as their relief-cut counterparts, these hot-worked objects nonetheless find a merited place in the annals of Islamic glass production for their variety of shape, color, and decoration—as well as for the often fanciful creativity of their makers.

The decorative pattern on this bottle, whose profile and shape are strongly reminiscent of eastern Islamic metal vessels, is related to the *omphalos* (navel) design previously noticed on the bowl (cat. 17) and represents a survival of this popular ornamental type well into the turn of the millennium. The angularity of the cut relief is here replaced by the softer lines and curves achieved through inflating and tooling the glass, offering a different overall effect.

Most bottles—a closed shape with an elongated neck and a narrow mouth—were produced quickly with the aid of a bronze mold that carried in reverse the desired pattern: the glass gather on the blowpipe was inserted into the mold, slightly inflated to impress the pattern, extracted from the mold, and subsequently reinflated and tooled. The entire operation would have taken just a few minutes. However, in this case—and this is what makes the present object more valuable—the glassmaker deliberately complicated his task: the bottle is composed of two units (the

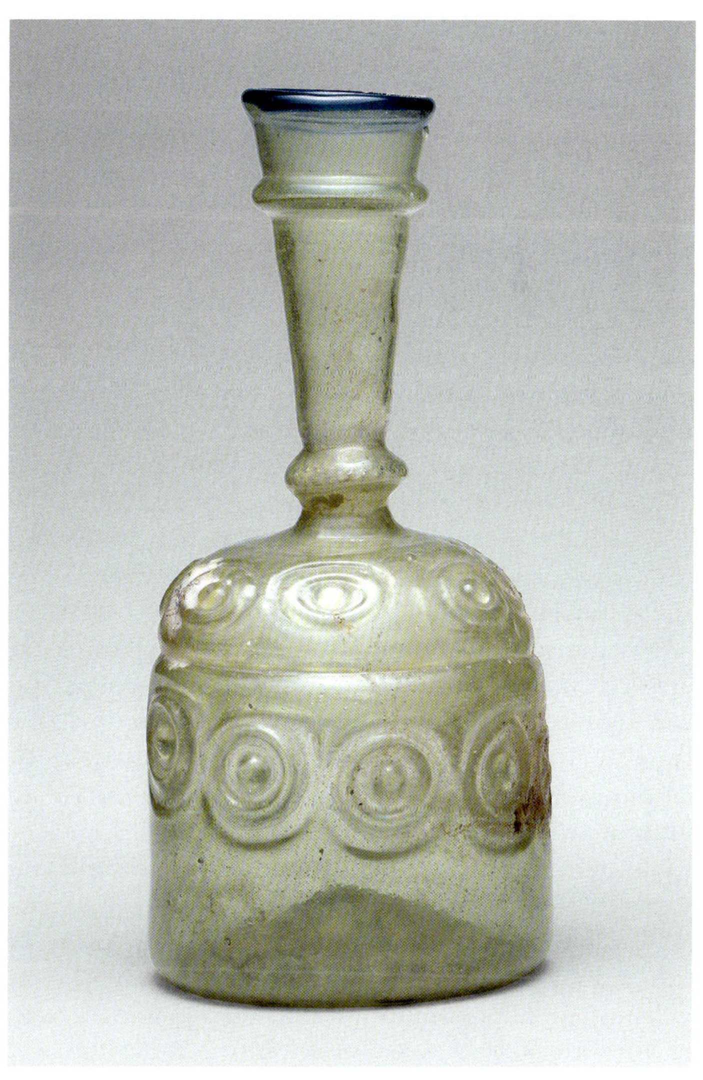

horizontal seam between them is evident between the two *omphalos* rows); the decoration was created from repeated applications by tongs carrying the "navel" pattern before the two halves had been fused. The joining technique itself, known in Italian as *incalmo*, is deceptively simple but would have required great skill to ensure that the two halves fit together.

The end result, an elegant bottle with a strong profile softened by the dark blue rim and the understated decoration, has a spontaneous feeling to it that does not reveal the complexity of its creation. SC

PROVENANCE: [Phoenix Ancient Art, Geneva, until 1994; sold to MMA]

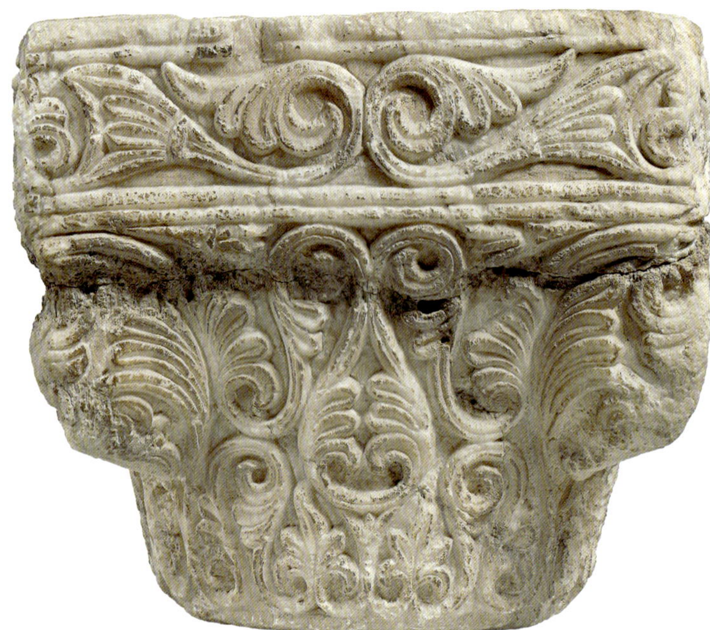

20. *Capital*

Syria, probably Raqqa, late 8th century
Alabaster, gypsum; carved
11 1/4 × 12 1/4 in. (28.6 × 31.1 cm)
Samuel D. Lee Fund, 1936 36.68.3

This capital probably comes from the site of Raqqa on the middle Euphrates in Syria. The Abbasid caliph al-Mansur (r. 754–75) built a new settlement, al-Rafiqa, alongside the antique city of Raqqa in 772, but it was twenty-four years later that the new city reached its apogee, when Harun al-Rashid (r. 786–809) established his caliphal residence there, spurring a huge building initiative.[1] Among the remains of more than twenty palatial complexes, nineteenth-century visitors found similar capitals and, more recently, excavators have recovered panels of carved stucco bearing related designs.[2] Several comparable capitals now dispersed in various collections reportedly originated from this site as well.[3] This evidence, together with the ornate design and refined workmanship of the carving, suggests that the capital was created for a monumental building such as a palace or mosque.

The alabaster capitals in this group probably belong to the period of Harun al-Rashid's residence in Raqqa between 795 and 808.[4] Despite this narrow time range, the capitals vary widely in style. Some, like this example, are inspired by a type of vegetal ornament found in Late Antique architectural decoration at Palmyra, situated about seventy-five miles (120 km) south of Raqqa.[5] Its form is distantly reminiscent of acanthus capitals, but the leaf motifs are less three-dimensional than their classical antecedents, and the foliate elements are more stylized. Around all four sides the design consists of two registers of half palmettes within a symmetrical scroll pattern filled with small trefoil sprigs. In the abacus zone atop the capital, paired winglike palmettes with blossoms adorn two of the sides, and vegetal scrolls encircle rows of blossoms on the other two. Prominent acanthus-leaf bosses articulate the four corners. Other alabaster capitals in this group, among them a contemporaneous example at the Metropolitan Museum and another in the David Collection, Copenhagen, display a beveled style associated with stucco carvings from the Abbasid palaces at Samarra built about thirty years later.[6] These capitals and the related wall decoration suggest, as has been argued, that the "Samarra" stucco styles developed in Syria.[7] EK

1. For an overview of these developments, see Heidemann 2003.
2. Sarre and Herzfeld 1911–20, vol. 2, p. 352, fig. 321; vol. 4, pl. 140. Another similar capital is reproduced in Heidemann and Becker, eds. 2003, p. 275, pl. 17.2, below, and in situ carved stucco panels with related designs are illustrated in Daiber and Becker, eds. 2004, pls. 40, 41, and 73.
3. The Metropolitan Museum holds two related capitals (acc. nos. 36.68.1, 36.68.2). See Dimand 1936, p. 155. A nearly identical alabaster capital is in the collection of the Museum für Islamische Kunst, Staatliche Museen zu Berlin (no. I. 2195), and another is published in Kühnel 1938, pl. 5, upper left; related examples include two in the David Collection, Copenhagen: nos. 35/1986 (illustrated in Folsach 2001, p. 242, no. 384), and 2/2001 (published in Boston and Chicago 2006–7, p. 156, no. 81).
4. Dimand 1936, p. 157.
5. For a discussion of parallels between the architectural ornament at these two sites, see Meinecke and Schmidt-Colinet 1993 and Meinecke 1999.
6. Metropolitan Museum (acc. no. 36.68.1); David Collection, Copenhagen (no. 2/2001). See note 3 above.
7. Meinecke 1998. See also Haase 2007.

PROVENANCE: [Eustache de Lorey, Paris, until 1936; sold to MMA]

21. Panel (Lid from a Chest?)

Probably Egypt, second half of 8th century
Wood (fig); mosaic with bone and four different types of wood
18¾ × 76½ in. (47.6 × 194.3 cm)
Samuel D. Lee Fund, 1937 37.103

One of the most fascinating and mysterious objects of early Islamic art in the Museum's collection, this wood panel was acquired in 1937 from the dealer Paul Mallon in Paris. It is the largest and most complete of a small group of similar panels that can be found today in the Museum für Islamische Kunst, Staatliche Museen zu Berlin; the Museum of Islamic Art, Cairo; the Museum of Archaeology of Cairo University; and the Musée du Louvre, Paris.[1] Their hearsay provenance—unconfirmed—is that they were found in the cemetery of 'Ain al-Sira near Fustat (Old Cairo).[2] For this reason, the most common identification of their function has been that they are fragments from a cenotaph. This is a possible option considering the over-six-foot length (nearly two meters) of the complete panel in the Museum. Various other considerations, however, can be put forward that question such an interpretation. First, had it been a cenotaph (*tabut*, in Arabic),[3] this decorated wooden box would have been placed at the center of a small room within a mausoleum dedicated to a high-ranking individual. While little is known of burial practices during the first two to three centuries of Islam when these panels were undoubtedly created, it is unlikely, given the lack of both archaeological and literary evidence, that the cemetery of 'Ain al-Sira would have hosted a sophisticated architectural structure that included this cenotaph.

In addition, close inspection of the Museum's panel in the Department of Objects Conservation indicates that the metal pins in the top edge may have originally been used to secure hinges; their location suggests that the panel functioned as the lid of a chest. If this was the case, the dimensions of the panel correspond to the width and length of the box (rather than the height and length of a side panel), making it a cenotaph of odd proportions if it was meant to suggest the perimeter of the body beneath.

An alternative possibility put forward in the past that has now gained support is that the chest might instead have been a container for an early copy of the Qur'an. Frequently written on thick parchment and produced in bound, multivolume sets, early Qur'ans were not only sacred but also precious and expensive manuscripts. The text of the Qur'an was divided into thirty established parts at an early stage, and it is likely that sets of even larger divisions were made. The dimensions of extant individual folios suggest that volumes of a height of about 16–18 inches (40–45 cm) would have been relatively common and would have fit nicely inside this chest arranged one next to another and stacked vertically in a few rows.[4] As demonstrated by late seventh- to early eighth-century Qur'an folios found inside the ceiling of the Great Mosque of Sana'a, Yemen, a few decades ago, early illuminated manuscripts of the Qur'an included both architectural arcades and geometric patterns similar to the central design of this panel, providing a direct link between the illumination of Qur'an manuscripts and the exterior decoration of Qur'an chests.[5]

From the technical as well as the art-historical point of view, this panel is a rare early example of wood-mosaic decoration, notable for the high quality of its execution. A single panel of fig wood

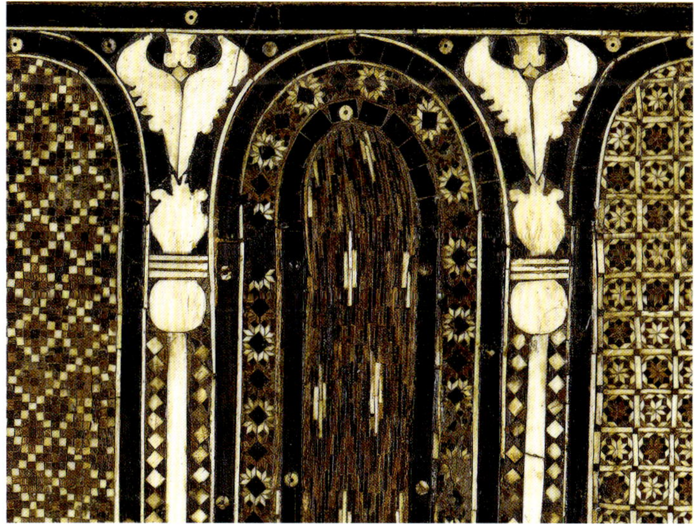

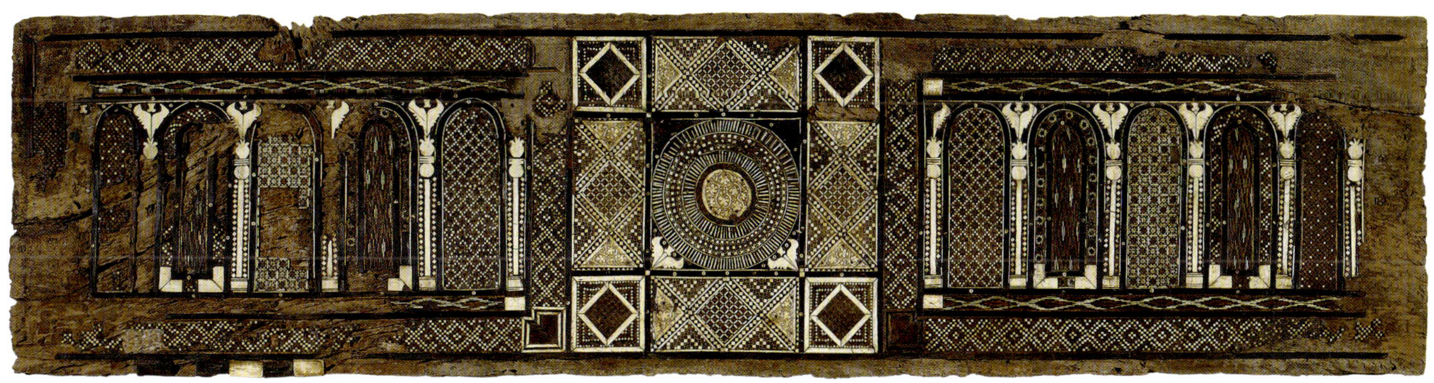

(*ficus* sp.) served as the substrate. Ebony (*Diospyros*) or granadilla (*Dalbergia melanoxylon*), European yew (*Taxus baccata*), an unknown wood from the family *Rutaceae*, and bone (not ivory, as one might think) were applied to produce the complex geometric decoration. The diminutive triangular, square, rectangular, and diamond shapes were cut from wood rods in six different sizes and subsequently individually glued in place according to the desired patterns. Tool marks on the bone elements indicate the use of a saw, a knife, a rasp, and shaped carving tools with triangular-section blades. Holes were made using a bow drill. X-radiography reveals the metal pins in the top edge of the panel to be the only joining hardware; similar metal pins or corresponding holes in analogous locations have been observed in the closely related wooden panels in the other institutions in Berlin and Cairo mentioned above.

The composition is symmetrical with a central composite square that is strongly reminiscent of Roman stone-mosaic floors. Each of the two sides includes a series of five narrow arches separated by stylized columns (see detail, p. 43). There is no sense of architectural depth in the design as the interior of each arch is filled with a dense, sometimes complex and sophisticated mosaic pattern. The prominent columns emphasize the decorative aspect of the panel especially at their top ends, which recall the crowns of Sasanian rulers. This use of elements from the artistic languages of the two great traditions inherited by the early Islamic artists, Roman on the Mediterranean coasts and Sasanian in the Greater Iranian region, makes this panel an intriguing work to study. It also helps to date it in the first two—unlikely the third—centuries after the advent of Islam. SC/DH

1. Museum für Islamische Kunst, Staatliche Museen zu Berlin (no. I. 5684 a-b); Museum of Islamic Art, Cairo (nos. 9518, 11636); Museum of Archaeology of Cairo University (no. 58); and Musée du Louvre, Paris (no. AA 201).
2. New Cairo, or al-Qahira, was founded by the Fatimids in 969, and nearby Fustat lost its political importance while maintaining a lively society and busy trading and commercial activities. Related panels in carved wood, now at the Louvre, have also been reported to come from 'Ain al-Sira: see Anglade 1988, pp. 23–26, figs. 8–10a.
3. According to Muslim burial practice, the body of the deceased is wrapped in a simple cloth and placed in the ground. A cenotaph is therefore a sumptuous but empty grave marker placed on the ground directly above the burial place.
4. A cursory review of the recent George 2010, pp. 45 and 92 (fig. 61), for example, shows that a Qur'an in the Bibliothèque Nationale de France, Paris (no. Arabe 331), measures 16¼ by 13¾ inches (41.3 × 34.8 cm), and one in the Khalili Collection, London (no. KFQ 27), is 18½ by 13 inches (47 × 33 cm). George also observes (p. 44) that "the dimensions of preserved Hijazi fragments are consistently large (typically 33 × 24 cm and above . . .)" and shows the image (p. 87, fig. 57) of a folio from a "Giant Qur'an" in style C.Ia (also in the Bibliothèque Nationale, no. Arabe 324c) that measures 21⅛ by 24⅜ inches (53.7 × 62 cm).
5. Ibid., pp. 79–86, figs. 53–56.

PROVENANCE: [Paul Mallon, Paris, until 1937; sold to MMA]

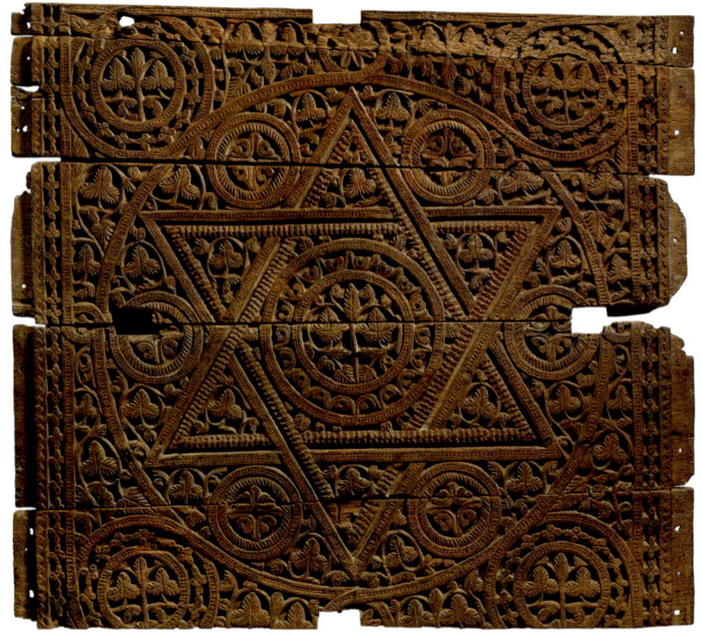

22. Panel

Iraq, probably Baghdad, early 9th century
Wood (teak); carved
29½ × 33½ in. (74.9 × 85.1 cm)
Rogers Fund, 1933 33.41.1a–e

This panel is one of fourteen carved wooden elements acquired as a group, all reportedly found in the ruins of Takrit, in Iraq.[1] Made of teak, it appears to be a fragment of a larger piece, perhaps a door or a piece of furniture. Interlacing bands frame its design within a square, of which the two lateral sides and part of the top remain, surrounding a large central circle with smaller circular loops around its circumference. Inside the large circle, an interlaced six-pointed star encloses another circle. A dense, crisply carved vine scroll, with striated trefoil sprigs, lancet leafs, and split-palmette motifs, fills the square framework.

Both the iconography and the style of this panel recall the stone-carved facade of the eighth-century palace of Mshatta (from present-day Jordan, now in the Museum für Islamische Kunst, Staatliche Museen zu Berlin) though with less variety and greater stylization.[2] Yet the motifs here are not as repetitive and abstract as the carving in wood and stucco associated with the ninth-century palaces at Samarra; even the so-called Samarra Style A is more regularized in its imagery and less varied in the manner of its carving. Perhaps the closest parallel from a dated context—albeit physically the farthest afield—is the wood *minbar* of the Great Mosque of Qairawan, in Tunisia, produced between 856 and 863. Whether these *minbar* panels were carved in Baghdad, as previously believed, or sent as raw material to North Africa and carved there according to early Abbasid models, they share with the

Metropolitan Museum's panel its motifs and compositional approach.[3] A design almost identical to that found on this panel decorates a pair of doors in the Benaki Museum, Athens. There, an eight-pointed interlaced star within a circle framed in a square makes up the central part of the rectangular door leaves, enclosing similar vegetal elements.[4] The Benaki doors have been attributed to late eighth- or early ninth-century Baghdad, and it is likely that this panel originally comes from that milieu as well.[5] EK

1. Dimand 1933b.
2. For a discussion of the development of this carving, see Dimand 1937. See also Ettinghausen 1979, p. 20.
3. Ettinghausen, Grabar, and Jenkins-Madina 2001, p. 94.
4. For a recent succinct discussion of the "Solomon's-Seal" motif, see Hasson 1998.
5. Pauty 1931b, pp. 77 and 81. Cf. Moraitou 2001, which demonstrates the continuity of Umayyad-style ornamentation and compositions into the Abbasid period, and proposes a mid-eighth-century date for the Benaki doors.

PROVENANCE: Sidney Burney, London (until 1933; sold to MMA)

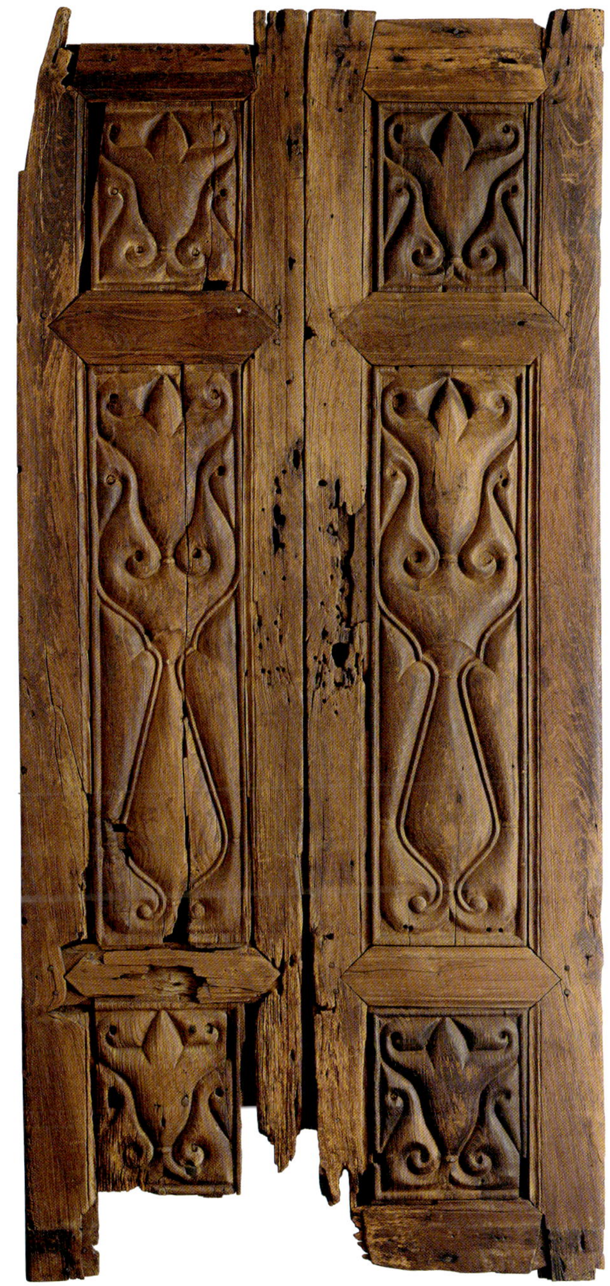

23. *Pair of Doors*

Iraq, probably Samarra, 9th century
Wood (teak); carved
31.119.1: 87 × 20¼ × 1½ in. (221 × 51.4 × 3.8 cm)
31.119.2: 87¾ × 21 × 1½ in. (222.9 × 53.3 × 3.8 cm)
Fletcher Fund, 1931 31.119.1 and 31.119.2

According to Museum files, the findspot for these doors was the town of Takrit in north-central Iraq. Researchers, however, have deduced that local residents in modern times had brought them there for reuse from the ruins of Samarra, a site located on the east bank of the Tigris, about seventy-eight miles (125 km) north of Baghdad.[1] It was at Samarra, in 836, that the Abbasid caliph al-Mu'tasim (r. 833–42) established a new administrative and military center, the ruins of which cover over fifty square miles (80 square km). Excavations at Samarra have revealed a series of sprawling palace complexes, constructed of fired and unfired brick as well as pisé (mud or clay applied in courses);[2] the walls were decorated with dadoes of carved or molded stucco panels, wall paintings, ceramic tiles, and glass mosaics.[3] The Museum's doors resemble the finds from Samarra so closely that they probably originated there as well.

Wood was not an abundant resource in this region, and at Samarra it seems to have been used sparingly in building interiors, primarily for doors, soffits, and jambs. The Museum's doors are made of teak, a highly prized material shipped from Southeast Asia.[4] Each leaf consists of a rectangular panel between two square panels, arranged vertically and set within a plain framework. The six inset panels embellished with symmetrical designs represent quintessential examples of the so-called beveled style of ornament that developed under the Abbasids, characterized by the slanted profile of its carving and the rhythmic undulation of its surfaces.[5] Typical of beveled-style ornament, the designs on these doors vaguely suggest vegetation, with palmette-like forms and tendril-like spirals, while retaining their abstract nature. Here a raised ridge accentuates the outlines, and it is likely that brightly colored paint and gilding once highlighted the carved designs, as is the case on most of the wood fragments associated with the Samarra palaces.[6] EK

1. Dimand 1932a, p. 135.
2. Samarra was first excavated by Ernst Herzfeld between 1911 and 1914. His endeavors are fully explored in Gunter and Hauser, eds. 2004; see also Leisten 2003. Iraqi excavations took place at Samarra in 1936–39 and 1979–82 (see al-Janabi 1983). For a more recent analysis of Abbasid Samarra, see Northedge 2005.
3. Herzfeld 1923.
4. Milwright 2001, pp. 86–87.
5. This style is also known as Samarra Style C, after Herzfeld 1923. See also "Beveled Style," in Bloom and Blair, eds. 2009, vol. 1, pp. 280–81.
6. Among the close parallels in other collections are examples in the Benaki Museum, Athens (no. GE 9128); Musée du Louvre, Paris (no. AA 267), which came in as a gift in 1938 and may be a "mate" of the Benaki panel (the attribution to Jawsaq al-Khaqani is actually based on its similarity to the stucco found there; see Anglade 1988, pp. 18–20); and the British Museum, London (no. 1944, 0513.1–2), a frieze and door purchased from a private collector in 1944. See also Canby 2000, pp. 132–35, for a discussion of the dispersal of the Samarra finds.

PROVENANCE: B. Cooke, Harrow on the Hill, England (until 1931; sold to MMA)

24. Cover Fragment

Egypt, 5th century
Wool, linen; plain weave, tapestry weave
$25\frac{1}{2} \times 38\frac{1}{4}$ in. (64.9 × 97 cm)
Gift of George F. Baker, 1890 90.5.807

Finely woven, this light green and purple fabric fragment has an intricate pattern of vine scrolls and geometric interlace patterns, motifs prevalent in all media from monumental floor mosaics to textiles during Byzantine rule of the eastern Mediterranean. Here grapevines emerge from small, ornate pots at each side of the fabric to fill two large canted squares and extend on to join in a small grape-leaf-filled medallion at the center of the field. The grape-vine-filled squares are each overlaid with a square and a medallion filled with geometric interlace to form two eight-pointed stars. Both the elaborate pattern and the thin red border at the fringed end of the fragment were probably repeated at the other end of the textile; fringe also appears along one side of the fabric. While the scale of this fragment suggests that it may have been a domestic covering, a similar eight-pointed star in Berlin has been described as part of a tunic.[1] Grapevines were popular symbols of fertility and productivity; the intricate patterns of the two stars may have been meant to protect by diverting the evil eye.[2]

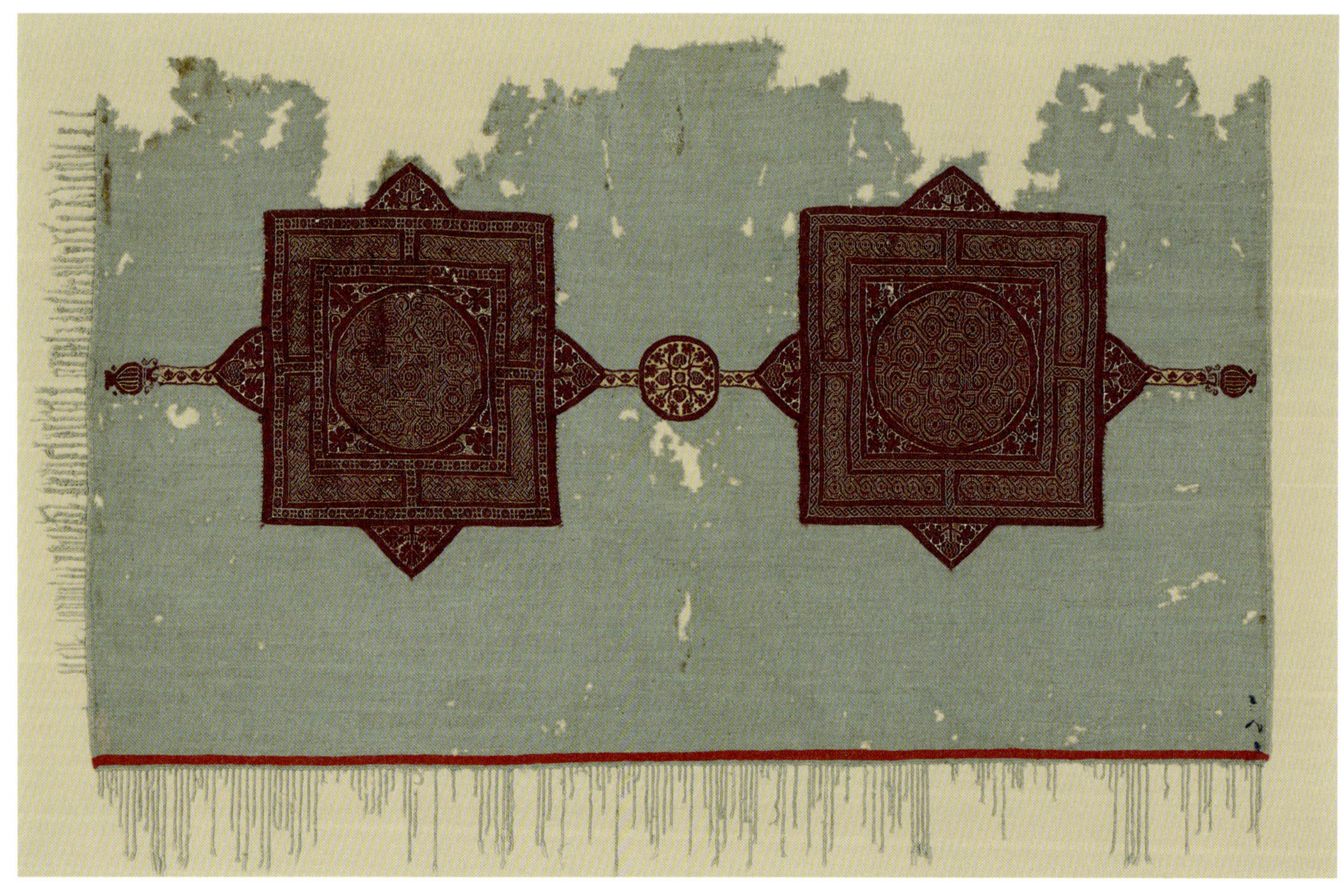

Like most textiles from Egypt of the Byzantine era, this piece of fabric was probably used for the wrapping of a body for burial; both clothing and domestic furnishings were employed in the process. The term *Coptic* was long applied to these works, as the textiles were thought to have all been woven by native Egyptians who were members of the Coptic Church, the Egyptian Christian church. It is now recognized that these textiles include many imported works and reflect patterns popular throughout the Byzantine Empire.[3] The exceptional quality of this fragment suggests an awareness of the luxury goods produced north of Egypt in Syria.[4] In later centuries, eight-pointed stars would be a motif widely used in Islamic art. HCE

1. Museum für Spätantike und Byzantinische Kunst, Staatliche Museen zu Berlin (no. 9239a). See Hamm and other cities 1996–98, pp. 346–47, no. 395c.
2. Hoskins 2004, pp. 101–2; New York 1995–96, pp. 13–14; Maguire 1990, pp. 215–17.
3. Thomas 2007; New York 1995–96, pp. 5–15; Gonosová 1989.
4. New York 1995–96, p. 9.

PROVENANCE: Emil Brugsch Bey, Cairo (until 1890); George F. Baker, New York (1890)

25. Textile Fragment

Iran, Iraq, or Egypt, mid-8th century
Wool; tapestry weave
12 × 18¾ in. (30.5 × 47.6 cm)
Rogers Fund, 1950 50.83

Opulent silks with bold patterns were appreciated by the Sasanian ruling elite in the centuries preceding the advent of Islam in Iran. Rock carvings at royal tombs and other important Sasanian dynastic sites display carefully executed depictions of figures wearing garments cut from such cloth.[1] These carvings, along with rare surviving textiles, offer a glimpse into the sartorial taste of the period, which tended toward costume featuring staggered rows of large pearl-bordered roundels, multipetaled rosettes, and sprouting floral medallions. At the time, fabrics bearing these motifs were widely traded from China to the Mediterranean, as attested by excavated examples.[2] The international exchange of such cloths along the Silk Road and beyond gave rise to locally woven variations;[3] weavers active in the early centuries of Islamic expansion were no doubt familiar with these luxury trade goods—and, perhaps, looked to them for inspiration.

Sasanian silks often were created using drawloom technology, in which the design was "programmed" into the loom in advance, permitting a more rapid replication of the pattern during the weaving process. The present textile, however, was produced in the more time-consuming tapestry-weave technique. And, unlike the lightweight silks that probably served as its models, this textile has a heavier texture that suggests it was intended to serve as a floor covering or as furnishing fabric.

While the design of the present piece may emulate patterns favored by Sasanian weavers, the Museum's textile has been dated to the early period of Islamic expansion. Comparing it to a group of related silk textiles with inscriptions dating to the reign of the Umayyad ruler Marwan II (744–50), scholars have attributed the Metropolitan's fragment to the mid-eighth century.[4] Other wool tapestry-woven fragments, exhibiting nearly identical floral forms, color palette, and weave technique, also have been dated to the eighth century.[5] Many of these early pieces are attributed to Iran or Iraq, yet the presence of S-spun wool in some examples has led scholars to posit a third possible production site—Egypt, where

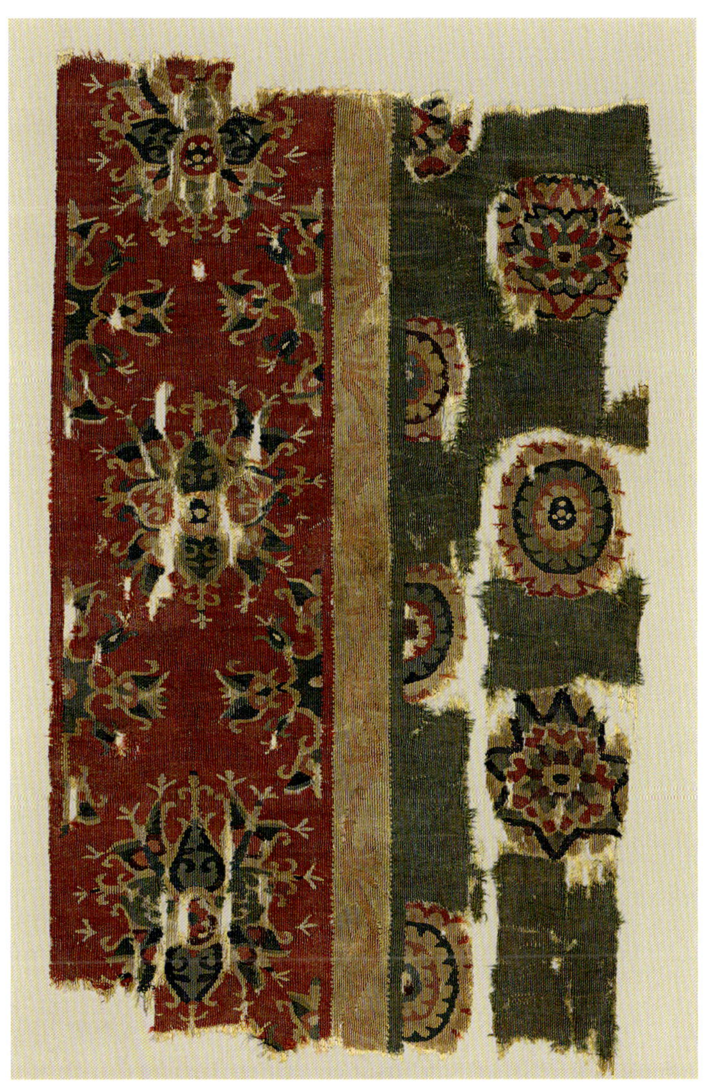

the utilization of counterclockwise spun wool was a characteristic of textile production for centuries.[6] Regardless of their place of production, these skillfully woven fragments are a testament to the continuity and adaptability of the tapestry weavers' art during the early centuries of Islamic expansion in these regions. DMT

1. New York 1978, pp. 119ff. Also Fukai and Horiuchi 1984, esp. pp. 80ff. and related plates.
2. For a discussion of the spread of motifs and weaving techniques along the "Silk Road," see Cleveland and New York 1997–98, esp. Chapter 1: "Early Exchanges: Silks from the Eighth through the Eleventh Century," pp. 20–51; and also Feng 2004–5.
3. For example, see the overall designs of a silk samite textile excavated in Qinghai Province and attributed to the eighth–ninth century (Feng 2004–5, p. 75, fig. 74) and that of a tapestry-woven fragment attributed to eighth-century Iran or Iraq (New York 1978, p. 138, no. 62).
4. See Walker, D. 1995–96. For the entry on the present fragment, see pp. 14, 28. Early writings on the Marwan silks include Guest and Kendrick 1932, and Day 1952 (Day argues for an even earlier dating, assigning it to the reign of Marwan I). For color reproduction of some of the pieces, see Baker, P. 1995, p. 39.
5. Some are published in Geneva and Paris 1993–94; see esp. p. 51, no. 6.
6. See ibid.

PROVENANCE: [J. Acheroff, Paris, until 1950; sold to MMA]

26. *Tiraz Textile Fragment*

Iran, Khurasan, dated A.H. 266/879–80 A.D.
Silk, cotton: plain weave, embroidered
6¼ × 12 in. (15.9 × 30.5 cm)
Gift of George D. Pratt, 1931 31.106.27

Inscription in Arabic in *kufic* script, embroidered in red silk:
[. . . اميرالــ]مؤمنين ايد[ه] الله مما امرابو احمد اخو اميرالمؤمنين في طراز نيشابور
سنة ست ستن [؟] مئتين أبي عبدالله الخامس
[. . . commander of the] faithful, may God strengthen [him],
of what Abu Ahmad, the brother of the commander of the faithful,
ordered [in the] *tiraz* of Nishapur, year two hundred sixty-six
(879–80 A.D.). –Abu 'Abd Allah al-Khamis

A unique specimen of historic importance, this *tiraz* fragment incorporates a pattern of blue and tan stripes woven in silk and cotton.[1] To allow for the later insertion of an inscription, the weaver created a plain band entirely woven of silk. This text, embroidered on the obverse of the fabric with red silk, provides the name of a commissioner along with a date and place of production. Its date of A.H. 266/879–80 A.D. falls within the reign of the Abbasid caliph al-Mu'tamid (r. 870–92), and its patron can be identified as his brother, Abu Ahmad al-Muwaffaq, who served as al-Mu'tamid's viceroy of the east, with its capital at Merv.

Although in 875 al-Mu'tamid had designated his own son Ja'far al-Mufawwad as his heir and viceroy of the west, the latter had little real power. It was the caliph's brother, al-Muwaffaq, who commanded the Turkish military during the years marked by the

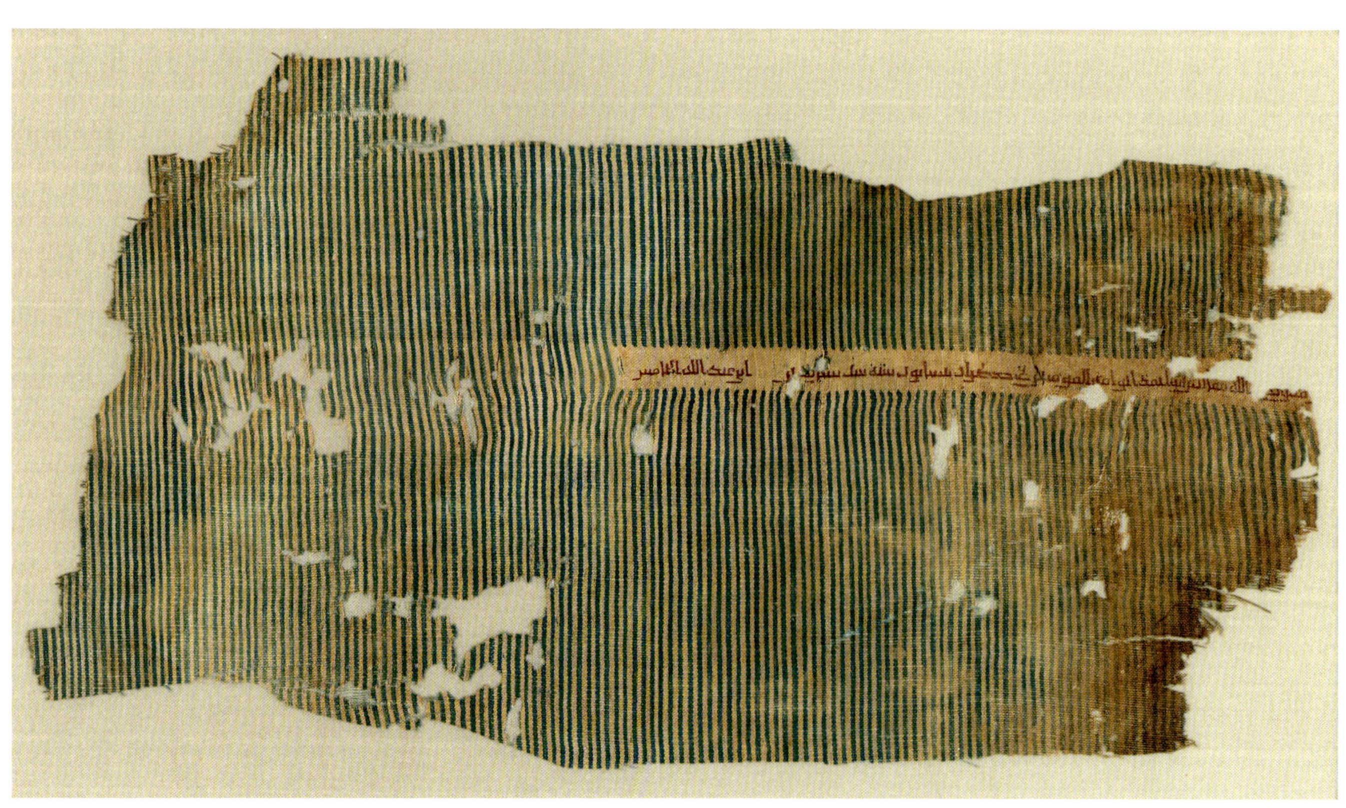

Zanj rebellion in Iraq (869–83) and the rise of the Saffarids in Iran.[2] Two textiles commissioned by al-Muwaffaq in Merv are known; one is dated to A.H. 260/873–74 A.D.,[3] the other to A.H. 277/890–91 A.D.[4] The fact that al-Muwaffaq was in effective control of Khurasan for nearly twenty years may help to identify the place of production mentioned in this textile's inscription, which could be read as either "Bishapur," in the province of Fars, or "Nishapur," situated in Khurasan.

The evidence of Islamic postreform coinage tells us that Bishapur, known in Arabic as *Sabur*, had a mint more active under the Umayyads than under the early Abbasids. On the other hand, as the Metropolitan Museum's excavations in the 1930s under Charles K. Wilkinson have shown, in the Abbasid period Nishapur was a thriving commercial center with a mint. Abbasid literary sources mention that Nishapur was famous for its textiles, particularly its silk and *mulhams* (see cat. 27). It is no surprise that the twelfth-century geographer al-Idrisi actually reports that it had a *tiraz* workshop.[5]

Given the survival of two textiles from Merv inscribed with al-Muwaffaq's name, as well as numismatic, archaeological, and literary evidence concerning Nishapur's importance as a textile center, it is appropriate to attribute the present textile to Nishapur. Furthermore, the traditional attribution of other textiles to Bishapur should be reconsidered. JS

1. To the present piece can be compared a striped *mulham tiraz* fragment in the Metropolitan Museum (acc. no. 31.106.41), which may have come from an eastern workshop.
2. Kennedy 1993.
3. Kühnel and Bellinger 1952, p. 10, pl. 5.
4. *Répertoire chronologique d'épigraphie arabe* 1932, p. 246, no. 753.
5. Jaubert, ed. 1936–40, vol. 1, pp. 352–53.

PROVENANCE: George D. Pratt, New York (until 1931)

27. Tiraz Textile Fragment

Eastern Iran or Khurasan, ca. 892–902
Silk warp and cotton weft (*mulham*); plain weave, embroidered
14¾ × 14 in. (37.5 × 35.6 cm)
Gift of George D. Pratt, 1931 31.19.2

Inscription in Arabic in *kufic* script, embroidered in chain stitch in red silk:
بسم الله الرحمن الرحيم الحمد لله الملك الحق المبين وحمل [*sic*] الله على محمد النبي نعم الله
للخليفة أبي العباس الإمام المعتضد بالله (. . .)
In the name of God, the Merciful, the Compassionate. Praise be to God, the King, the pure Truth, and may God praise Muhammad the Prophet, may God delight in the Caliph Abu l-'Abbas al-Imam al-Mu'tadid billah [. . .]

On right margin in tiny stitch:
بن الخشوعي [أ] عانه [؟]
Ibn al-Khushu'i, may [God] help him(?)

This textile is inscribed with a protocol in the name of the Abbasid caliph al-Mu'tadid (r. 892–902). The inscription begins with a religious formula containing benedictory phrases alluding to the Prophet Muhammad and to the person of the caliph, the leader of the early Islamic empire and community. It is very likely that the inscription would have mentioned a place, possibly a workshop and date of production, unfortunately lost here. A tiny inscription in the right margin contains the name *Ibn Khushu'i*, possibly a refernce to the weaver of the textile.

Especially notable on this textile are the style and execution of the inscription and the material of the ground fabric. Characterized

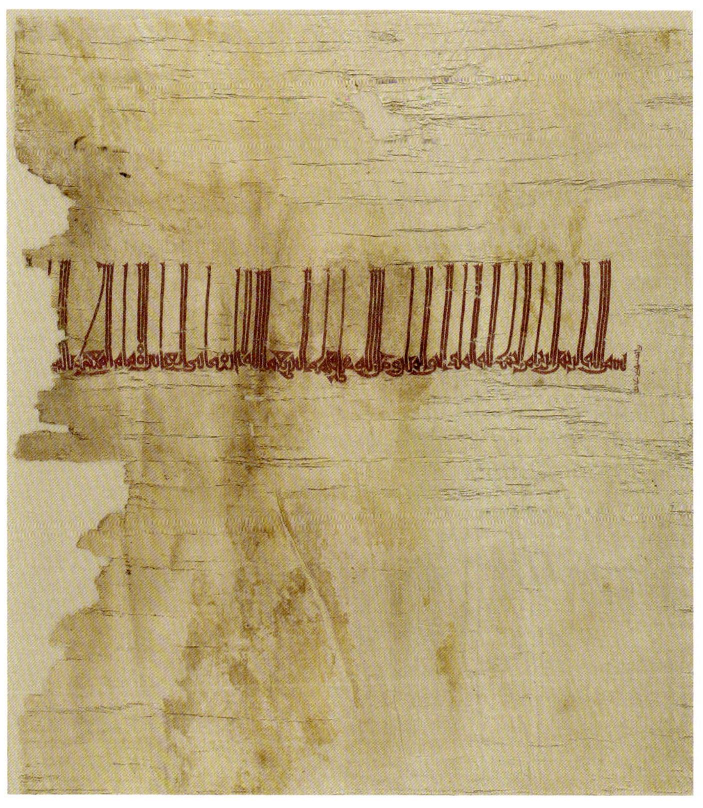

by the calligraphic treatment of individual letter forms and the ratio between low-lying letters and high letter stems, as well as their rhythm, the line of inscription in *kufic* script comprises an even thickness with pronounced, wedgelike letter ends that are embroidered in chain stitch with red silk. The ground fabric is composed of silk warps and cotton wefts, a mix that is referred to in the contemporary Arabic literature as *mulham*. A *tiraz* fragment in the Textile Museum in Washington, D.C., bears an inscription dated to A.H. 283/896–97 A.D. in the name of al-Mu'tadid and has a comparable calligraphic style on a *mulham* ground fabric.[1] Medieval Arabic sources tell us that the production of *mulham* was a particular specialty of Merv, the capital of the Abbasid province of Khurasan,[2] and several *mulham tiraz* fragments have survived that, according to their inscriptions, were produced in Merv.[3]

One of these, a piece in the Museum für Islamische Kunst, Staatliche Museen zu Berlin, is significant as it was produced in Merv in the year A.H. 287/899–90 A.D., and thus during al-Mu'tadid's reign.[4] Although the style and execution of the inscription on the Berlin fragment are not as refined as those of the present textile, both share significant epigraphic details, among them the wedge-shaped pointed letter terminals and triangular and circular letter shapes, executed in chain-stitch embroidery. It is thus very likely that the present piece too was produced in Khurasan, possibly in Merv itself. JS

1. Kühnel and Bellinger 1952, pp. 14–15, pl. 6.
2. Lamm 1937, pp. 105–6; Serjeant 1972, pp. 89–92, also p. 15 n. 32.
3. Sokoly 2002, nos. 83, 122, 171, and 190.
4. Ibid., no. 122; Kühnel 1952, p. 166, no. J 6412, fig. 3.

PROVENANCE: George D. Pratt, New York (until 1931)

28. Prayer Mat

Tiberias (present-day Israel), first half of 10th century
Hemp (warp), straw (weft); weft-faced plain weave, brocaded
63⅜ × 33⅞ in. (161 × 86 cm)
Purchase, Joseph Pulitzer Bequest, 1939 39.113

Inscription in Arabic in *kufic* script:
بركة كاملة و نعمة شاملة و سعادة متواصلة و غبطة و سرور لصاحبه
Complete blessing and universal prosperity and continued happiness and joy to its owner

Floor coverings like this one were once highly esteemed, as the historical writings of medieval Islamic authors—among them al-Muqaddasi (before 985–86), the eleventh-century Persian traveller Nasir al-Din Khusrau, and the twelfth-century geographer al-Idrisi—tell us.[1] Perhaps most notable is al-Idrisi's remark that Tiberias produced widely praised mats, called *al-samaniyya*, that were made only in Palestine, thus establishing Tiberias as a noteworthy center of production from which the mats were exported to a variety of locations.

An inscribed mat from Tiberias, now in the Benaki Museum, Athens, survives complete. Its inscription, which contains a number of benedictions conferred on its owner (*li-sahibihi*), records that it had been ordered from the private *tiraz* workshop in Tabariyya, or Tiberias (*mimma umira bi-'amalihi fi tiraz al-khassa bi-Tabariyya*).[2] This mat and the Metropolitan Museum example are related, sharing rough dimensions, weave structure, extraordinary quality, minimalist aesthetic, and style of *kufic* inscription. The ground fabric of both consists of hemp warps into which a double weft of fine flattened reed strands has been woven. The use of spun textile yarns, rather than reed, for the warp, as well as the presence of a fringe and carefully executed selvages, suggests that these mats were woven on conventional looms. The rather angular script of the inscriptions, with wedge-shaped letter ends and reversing *ya'*, as well as the large size of the letters, recalls the style of Egyptian *tiraz* textile inscriptions from the reigns of the tenth-century Abbasid caliphs al-Mustakfi and al-Muti'. Furthermore, the dimensions of the mats, combined with a sparing use of ornament and single lines of inscription, bring to mind linen shawls or turban cloths of the period, of which only fragments have survived in Egypt. Several other fragments of similar mats are in the Dar al-Athar al-Islamiyya, al-Sabah Collection, Kuwait City; the Bouvier Collection, Geneva; and the Biblioteca Apostolica Vaticana, Vatican City.[3]

Such mats were used within the Fatimid court in Egypt, as documented by a passage in the *Sirat al-Ustadh Jawdhar*, an account of the life of one of the caliph al-Mu'izz's most important secretaries, Jawdhar, written by his assistant, Abu 'Ali Mansur al-'Azizi al-Jawdhari. It describes how al-Mu'izz (r. 975–96) asked Jawdhar to order reed prayer mats from Mahdiya, which were to be inscribed with a text chosen by al-Mu'izz himself.[4] Further references to reed mats at the Fatimid court can be found in the historian al-Maqrizi's description of the contents of the *khaza'in al-farsh*, a treasury of furnishings that contained tents and their contents as well as reed mats (*husur*).[5]

Recent controlled excavation of the funerary complex at Istabl 'Antar in the Southern Cemetery of Cairo has shown that mats were used in several tombs to wrap an enshrouded corpse and to provide a supplementary layer between corpse and ground.[6] This may explain the rather fragmentary nature of most surviving examples. The mat pieces at Istabl 'Antar, however, seem to have survived almost complete, as did the present example and the mat in the Benaki Museum. The *Kitab dhikr al-mawt wa-ma ba'dahu* (Book of the Remembrance of Death and the Afterlife) of the imam Abu

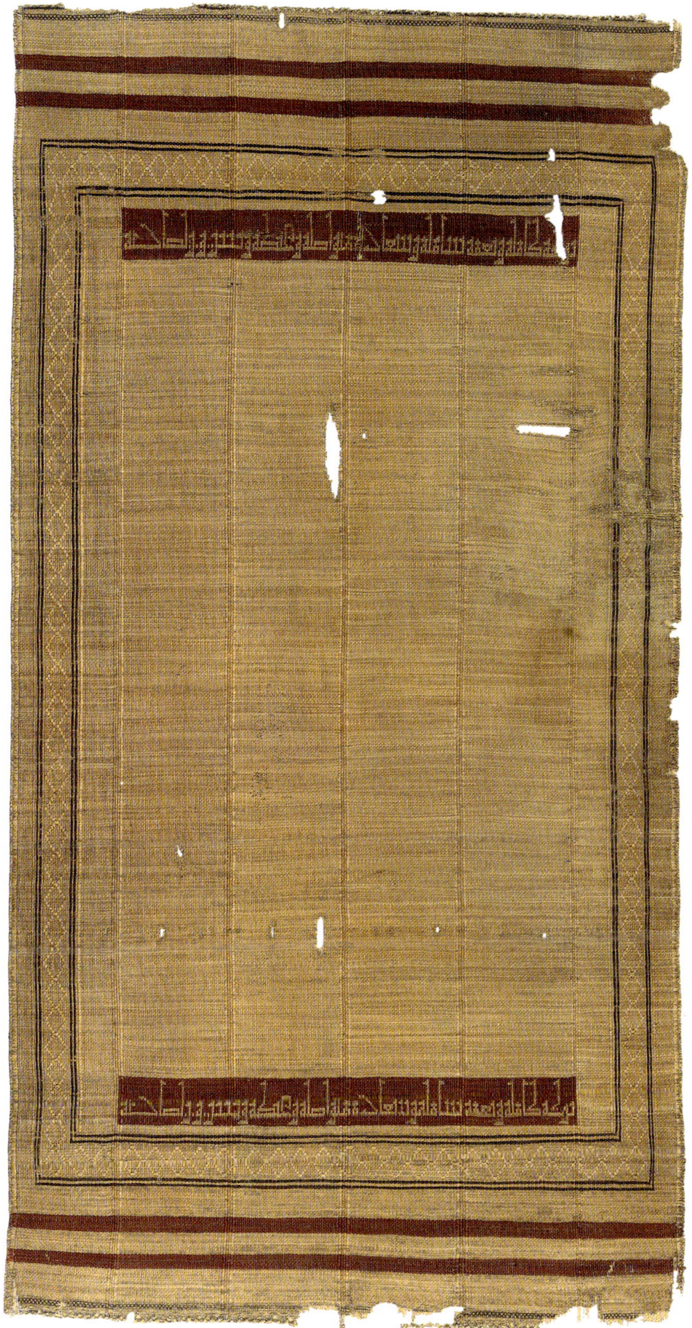

Hamid Muhammad ibn Muhammad al-Ghazali (died 1111), the famous Shafi'ite theologian active under the Seljuq vizier Nizam al-Mulk, describes in one chapter the death of the Prophet Muhammad and his interment: after the Prophet had been washed by members of his family and clothed in his designated burial outfit, he was laid on a mat that was covered with some of his garments from life.[7] It is difficult to deduce from this account alone that there existed a tradition in Islam to deposit the dead on a mat. Yet the fact that such mats were sometimes used by the living as prayer mats, as the account in the biography of al-Mu'izz's secretary Jawdhar tells us, might also explain why the deceased were sometimes buried with them: perhaps they were thought to carry *baraka* (blessing) that would thus be transmitted to the deceased.

JS

1. Al-Muqaddasi 1906, p. 180; Nasir al-Din Khusrau 1881, vol. 1, p. 58; Gildemeister 1885, text n.p. [10] and trans. p. 128.
2. Combe 1939.
3. Al-Sabah Collection, Kuwait City, no. LNS 54 T. Bouvier Collection, Geneva, no. JFB I 45 (Geneva and Paris 1993–94, pp. 130–31, no. 65); no. JFB I 46 (ibid., pp. 131–32, no. 66). Biblioteca Apostolica Vaticana, Vatican City, no. 6940 (Cornu et al. 1992, p. 60). Fiber analysis on no. JFB I 45 in the Bouvier Collection has shown that the materials used were hemp for the warp and esparto grass, often referred to as reed or rushes, for the weft.
4. Al-Jawhari 1954, p. 88; al-Jawhari 1957, pp. 129–30.
5. Al-Maqrizi 1853–54, vol. 1, pp. 416–17; translated in Serjeant 1972, p. 159.
6. Tombs nos. 49, 15, and 10; Gayraud 1995, esp. p. 8, figs. 16–17.
7. Al-Ghazali 1989, pp. 73–74.

PROVENANCE: [Maurice Nahman, Cairo, until 1939; sold to MMA]

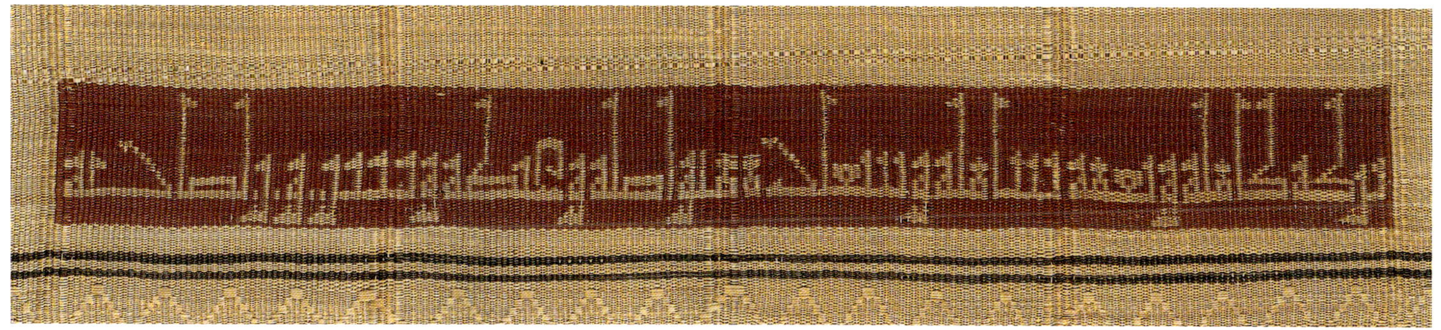

29. Tiraz Textile Fragment

Yemen, late 9th–early 10th century
Cotton, ink, and gold; plain weave, resist-dyed (*ikat*), painted
23 × 16 in. (58.4 × 40.6 cm)
Gift of George D. Pratt, 1929 29.179.9

Band of pseudo-*kufic* characters outlined in ink and gilded
Inscribed in Arabic above band:
الملك له
Dominion belongs to Him [God]

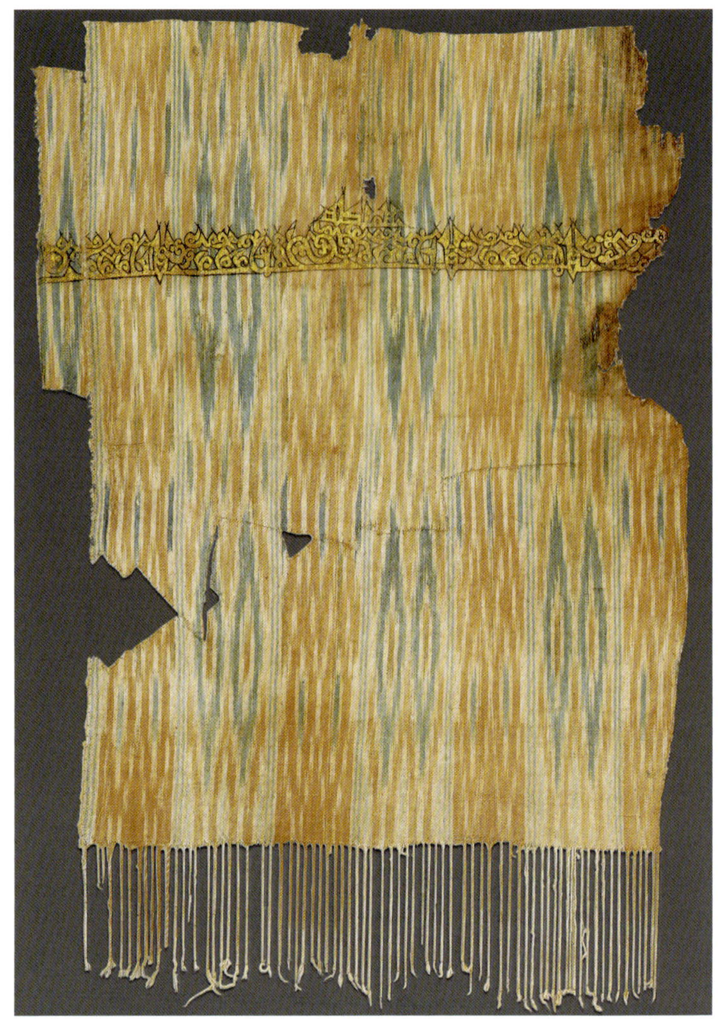

Ikat, a technique that involves using individually resist- or tie-dyed cotton warp threads, was a specialty of Yemen during the early Islamic period, attested in the literary sources of the period. The Arabic term for this type of cloth is *'asb*, the root of which means to bind or tie. *Ikats* were also produced in other locations throughout the Indian Ocean region. The piece seen here is a magnificent example of this type of textile, in both its manufacture—the fineness of the cotton threads, the regularity of the weave with its pattern, and the delicately twisted fringe—and its gilded benedictory inscription in ornamental *kufic* characters. While several *ikats* with embroidered personalized inscriptions in the names of Abbasid caliphs have survived, some of which attest the Yemeni capital Sana'a as a place of production, only two have caliphal inscriptions outlined in ink and gilded.[1] Both refer to a son of the Abbasid caliph al-Muntasir, the amir Abu Ibrahim. Al-Muntasir ruled from 861 to 863 and before that held governorships of several Arab provinces, possibly including Yemen. These two inscriptions share with the present piece a style of *kufic* inscription with pronounced hooklike letter ends as well as an interlaced *lam-alif* with small foliations that are typical of various regions of the Abbasid Empire during the late ninth and early tenth centuries. Textiles such as this inscribed *ikat* are testimony to the importance of Yemen as a center for the production of Abbasid luxury goods, linking the trade routes of the Red Sea and the Indian Ocean.

JS

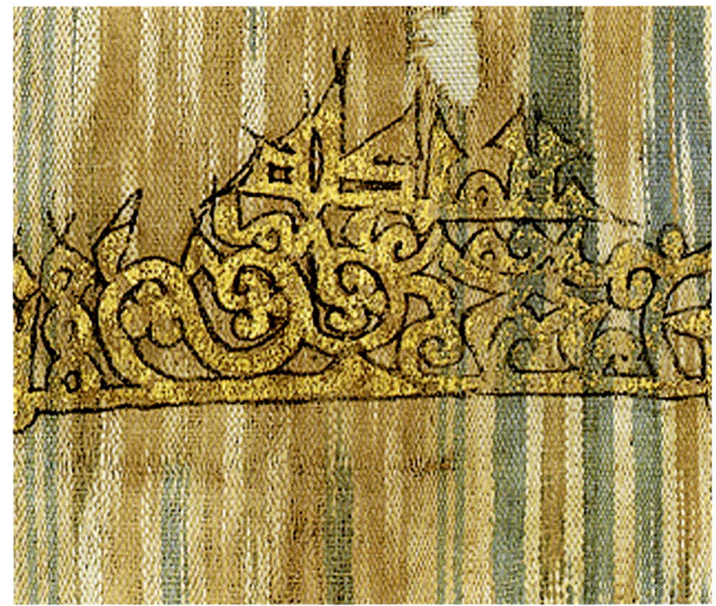

1. Biblioteca Apostolica Vaticana, Vatican City, no. 6744 (Cornu et al. 1992, pp. 63–65); Dumbarton Oaks Research Library and Collection, Washington, D.C., no. 33.37 (Glidden and Thompson 1989, pp. 89–91, no. 12).

PROVENANCE: George D. Pratt, New York (until 1929)

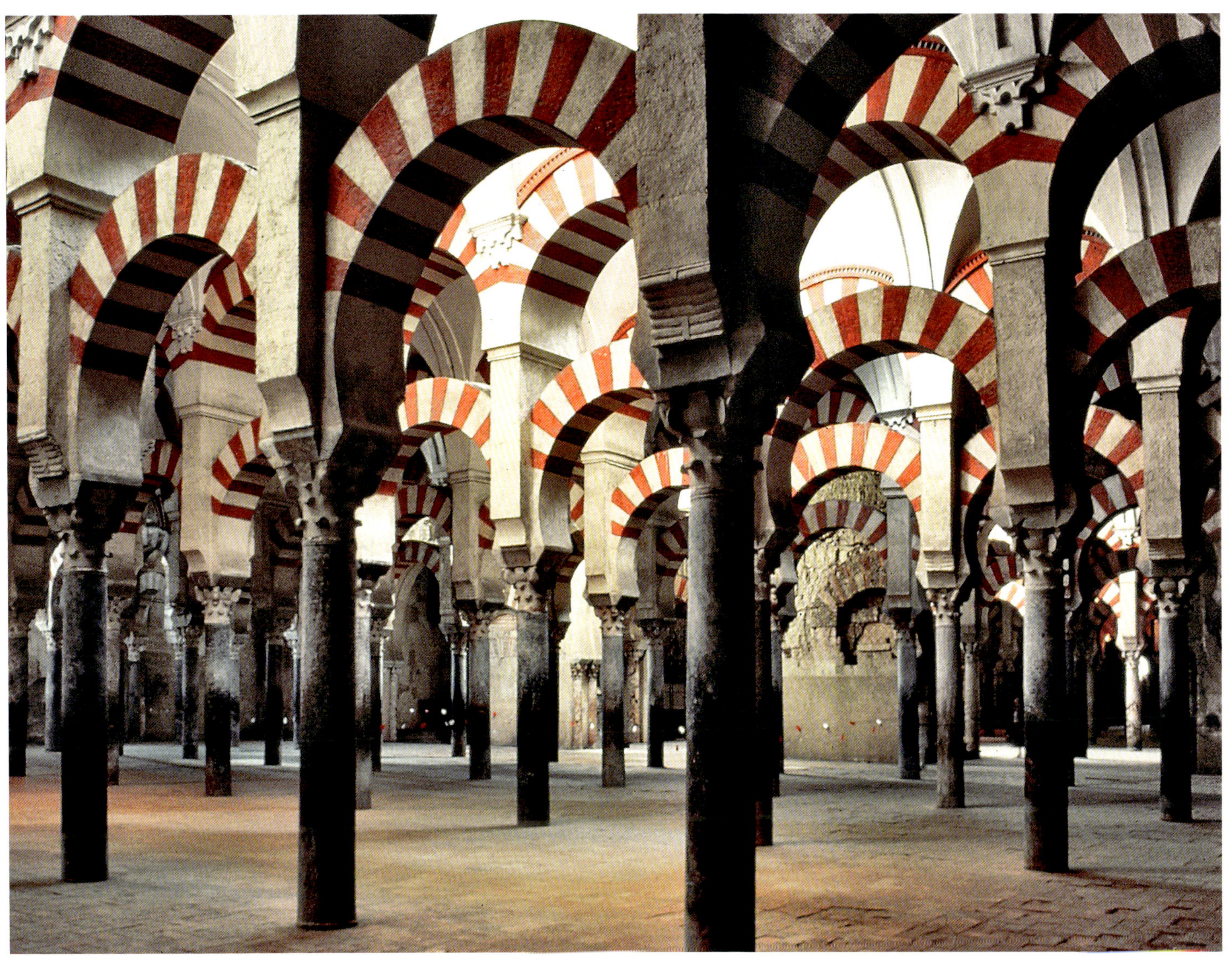

Art of Spain, North Africa, and the Western Mediterranean

OLGA BUSH

In the first century after the *hijra*, as Islamic faith and power quickly spread, the Iberian Peninsula (reached by Berber armies in 711) appeared to be land's end. But by the time the Umayyad ruler of al-Andalus, 'Abd al-Rahman III (r. 912–61), had adopted the title of caliph in 929, Cordoba was a capital city with some four hundred neighborhood mosques, seventy libraries, thousands of shops, a mint, and a royal workshop for the manufacture of luxury textiles. Its population of three hundred thousand religiously, linguistically, and ethnically diverse inhabitants comprised Muslims—including Arabs from Syria, North African Berbers, and Muwallads (Christian converts to Islam)—and *dhimmis* (protected subjects), both Jews and Christians, who lived in designated neighborhoods and practiced their religions in return for payment of a special tax. Cordoba was one of the largest cities on earth.[1] The map of the medieval world had been redrawn.

An apt guide for reading that new map is provided by an anonymous text from the fourteenth or fifteenth century describing Madinat al-Zahra (the City Most Splendid), 'Abd al-Rahman III's opulent palace-city on the outskirts of Cordoba. It relates that, in the center of the sumptuously decorated Majlis al-Khilafa (Hall of the Caliphs), there hung a gift from the Byzantine emperor: a pearl of unmatched size and brilliant luster, which had been identified by the eleventh-century Cordoban historian Ibn Hayyan as *al-Yatima* (the Orphan or the Unique).[2] The central position chosen for this gift reflects a world that was oriented visually and culturally around points of contact in a complex network of exchange rather than around a set of fixed geopolitical borders and stable, bounded identities. In light of current scholarship, which favors a view in which the frontier is everywhere—and everywhere permeable—the arts of Western Islam may be mapped as what Oleg Grabar has called a "shared culture of objects." The geographic reach of this culture is at least pan-Mediterranean, if not considerably broader; its chief binding mechanism, at the level of court culture, is a gift economy; and its ideological foundation is the concept of monarchy.[3]

The history of *al-Yatima* sheds further light on this view.[4] When the Umayyads ruled in the East as the first Muslim dynasty, the pearl was displayed in the Dome of the Rock in Jerusalem. It was later sent to the Ka'ba in Mecca by the Abbasid caliphs, who came to power after annihilating all but one member of the Umayyad royal family in Damascus in 750. That survivor fled across North Africa and reestablished the Umayyad dynasty in Cordoba as 'Abd al-Rahman I (r. 756–88). Sanctified by its association with the two most sacred shrines of Islam, *al-Yatima* accrued symbolic capital as the bearer of collective memories. The pearl spoke for the continuity of legitimate succession in the language of the gift. Hanging at Madinat al-Zahra, it communicated Byzantium's recognition of 'Abd al-Rahman III as "the Unique," the one true ruler of *Dar al-Islam* (the Muslim world) at a time when the Abbasids, as well as the Fatimids in North Africa, also laid claim to the caliphate. But balancing such shared understandings, luxury objects could further acquire more local meanings: as the Orphan, *al-Yatima* would also recall the Umayyad forebear 'Abd al-Rahman I, the lone survivor.

Examining some exemplary objects in various media and following a historical trajectory will clarify certain aspects of the culture of the pan-Mediterranean contact zone, and especially its microcosm in al-Andalus. The all but inevitable starting point is the Great Mosque of Cordoba, with its hypostyle sanctuary of marble columns supporting two-tiered horseshoe arches, which has come to be the very icon of medieval art in Western Islam.[5] The architectural and decorative forms of the mosque express the Umayyad claim to legitimate succession by forging artistic links to the Great Mosque of Damascus and the Dome of the Rock of the Umayyads of Syria. At the same time, however, they augment the tradition by their recourse to the more local vocabulary of Roman and Visigothic architecture on the Iberian Peninsula.[6] The grandeur of the Cordoba mosque further communicates the political power and triumph of Islam: after its fourth expansion, in 981, it became the second largest mosque in *Dar al-Islam* after the Abbasid mosque in Samarra (present-day Iraq). Thus, in addition to the work of skilled craftsmen, both Christian and Muslim, on the masonry of the interior, mosaicists and tesserae were sent to Cordoba by the Byzantine emperor upon the request of al-Hakam II (r. 961–76) to embellish the *mihrab* of the mosque and the dome in front of it. Qur'anic verses inscribed in gold script against a blue ground in the area of the *maqsura* reinforced the association with the Dome of the Rock, where the same colors and technique were employed for Qur'anic inscriptions as well. Such colors also recall those of the Blue Qur'an (cat. 30), which was executed in gold script on blue-dyed parchment, most likely in modern-day Tunisia around the middle of the tenth century under Fatimid patronage. In addition, the luxury manuscript evokes Byzantine imperial documents written with gold and silver on purple-dyed parchment and sent by envoy to Muslim rulers.[7] Parallels such as these illustrate the multidirectional, transcultural, and intermedial circuit of pan-Mediterranean aesthetics.

This movement of architectural and decorative vocabularies communicated shared understandings—principal among them, ideological presuppositions concerning monarchy—through the use of recognizable visual tropes. Royal attributes of strength and magnificence were conveyed through an iconography that dated back to the Sasanian period and even earlier, as seen, for instance, in the many carved ivory boxes made in Madinat al-Zahra that show eagles, lions, peacocks, and griffins, often bearing an enthroned ruler (cats. 36, 37). As early as the tenth century, elephants were added to that panoply in a garden sculpture in Madinat al-Zahra, and they later appeared more prominently in southern Italy and Sicily, which were wrested from the Fatimids by the Normans in 1091. Sculpted elephants adorn the facade of the Cathedral of San Nicola Pellegrino in Trani (commissioned 1159–86), while, in a veritable anthology of royal motifs, the bishop's throne in the Cathedral of San Sabino in Canosa (commissioned 1078–89) is supported by sculptures of elephants, lions, griffins, and splayed eagles.[8]

As the elephant's most martial part, the tusk could represent the animal as a whole and was often given to rulers at medieval courts in Byzantium and the Christian and Muslim West as a tribute payment and symbol of allegiance.[9] It was also fashioned as a finished luxury object, the oliphant, a carved horn that could function either as a drinking vessel that imparted magic powers to its contents or as a wind instrument employed in ceremonials or hunting (cat. 38). The primary ideological import is inscribed succinctly on one such object as *al-mulk* (kingship/dominion).[10] In the Christian West, the oliphant is famously associated with the *Chanson de Roland*, but considered within the context of a shared culture of objects, the epic hero Roland may be seen not only as a defender of Christendom *against* Islam but also as a participant in a gift economy *with* Islam. The instability of borders, identities, and allegiances is even more apparent in the Castilian epic of El Cid.

In this unstable cultural geography, crossed by "pathways of portability," locating centers of production (or even the traditional assignment of styles and objects to particular dynasties) can be uncertain.[11] For instance, seventy-five oliphants and numerous ivory boxes (cat. 39) dated to the period between the tenth century and the end of the twelfth have traditionally been associated with the Fatimid dynasty. Yet they could have been made under various patrons in any of the Mediterranean cultural centers—Egypt, Syria, southern Italy, Sicily, al-Andalus, Byzantium—a fact that attests to an "international" style as well as to shared meanings.[12] These objects were also often encoded with additional meanings spawned by local circumstance. In the political environment of al-Andalus, for example, the iconography of royal power on one ivory pyxis has been interpreted as a specific warning to a lesser potentate to forgo his aspirations to the caliphal throne.[13] Another ivory pyxis, in the shape of a cylindrical box with a domical lid and inscribed with erotic verses proclaiming, "The sight I offer is of the fairest, the firm breast of a delicate maiden,"[14] has prompted discussion of issues relating to sexuality and gender.[15] Recent studies illuminate the role of court women in al-Andalus as patrons and recipients in the gift economy[16] and also as donors and founders of monumental works and public institutions.[17] Findings are also emerging with regard to the participation of women as an artisanal workforce in the production of luxury objects and, no doubt, of more common domestic objects as well.[18] And scholars are now attending to the role of women as preservers and transmitters of culture, especially in those complex households in which ethnic and religious origins were mixed.[19]

Even when sites of production can be determined, the results may reflect a shared culture of objects rather than constitute a map of discrete points and impermeable borders. Two examples may suffice as illustrations. First, a wood-and-ivory *minbar*, or preacher's pulpit, most likely commissioned by an Almoravid sultan for his mosque in Marrakesh about 1120, bears an inscription stating that it was produced in Cordoba.[20] This declaration of portability is reinforced by evidence of Umayyad craftsmanship in the carved and inlaid surfaces and in the embellishment with geometric strapwork interspersed with dense vegetal arabesques reminiscent of Cordoban ivories and metalwork. The *minbar* was later brought to the Kutubiyya Mosque in Marrakesh by the ruler of the Almohad dynasty (1130–1269), which supplanted the Almoravids both in the Maghrib and in al-Andalus.

A second example, a textile known as the Chasuble of San Juan de Ortega, confounds the assumptions raised by the first. The weaving technique, colors, and script of its *tiraz* (inscribed band) indicate that it was made in al-Andalus; however, its large medallions with paired lions and harpies are inscribed with the phrase, "This was made in Baghdad. May God watch over it."[21] The inscription, then, would seem a bald-faced deception, perhaps aimed at fetching a better price. Yet, at an extreme, it may also suggest a certain truth: the movement of objects and styles hints at a reconfiguration of cultural identity based more on incorporation (of Baghdad in Cordoba, for instance) than on provenance. That this textile was used as part of a liturgical garment is also noteworthy: in Iberia particularly, many of the extant textiles customarily associated with Muslim dynasties have been preserved in church treasuries or recovered from Christian tombs (cat. 46A–C).[22]

The crossing of boundaries may, of course, reinforce the distinctive identities of self and other. The capture of the Almohad banner at the decisive battle of Las Navas de Tolosa in 1212 represented the defeat of the Muslim enemy by the Christian armies, not the end of enmity. Indeed, the annual parading, even today, of a replica of the banner through the streets of Burgos, where the original is housed, gives evidence of the ways in which contemporary Spanish national identity is still articulated as the triumph of a Christian "us" over a Muslim "them."[23] Nevertheless, the politics of modern nationalism do not necessarily reflect the complexities of the medieval period. To cite another example, Don Rodrigo Jiménez de Rada (d. 1247), archbishop of Toledo, an ardent promoter of the crusade against the Almohads and spiritual guide of the Christian forces at Las Navas de Tolosa, was buried in a silk tunic embellished with gold and silver brocade and decorated with a *tiraz* that repeats the word *prosperity* in Arabic. This garment appears to have been the posthumous gift of King Ferdinand III of Castile and Leon (r. 1217–52), who received it from his vassal Muhammad ibn Yusuf ibn Nasr ibn al-Ahmar (r. 1232–73), the founder of the Nasrid dynasty, which ruled al-Andalus from its capital in Granada.[24] It is a fitting gift, not so much as another commemoration of reconquest, but because it is of a piece with the two dozen ecclesiastical copes made of sumptuous textiles woven in al-Andalus that Jiménez de Rada amassed during his lifetime. The burial tunic, like the other textiles that he collected, forms part of a field of cultural production in which the self and the other are intimately interrelated on an overlapping frontier.[25]

An emblem of the mixed, pan-Iberian culture (a microcosm of the pan-Mediterranean culture) is offered by the doors to the Hall of the Ambassadors in the Alcazar of Seville. Built by Pedro I of Castile and Leon (r. 1350–69), this palace became home to his vassal the Nasrid king Muhammad V (r. 1354–59, 1362–91) when the latter returned from his exile at the Marinid court in Fez (Morocco) in 1362. On the interior of the wooden

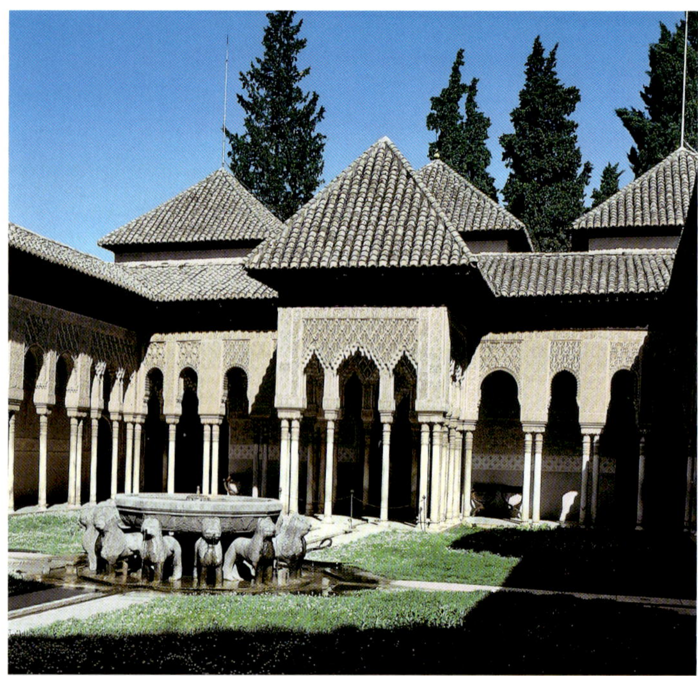

Fig. 29 Court of the Lions in the Alhambra, Granada, mid-13th–late 14th century. Photo: Walter B. Denny

doors, passages from Psalm 53 are inscribed in Castilian; on the exterior, Pedro I is lauded in Arabic as "Our exalted lord the sultan."[26] Rather than a border strictly dividing insiders from outsiders, the doors are bilingual, as were many of those who crossed the threshold. There is even a "trilingual" parallel in the contemporaneous Tránsito Synagogue in Toledo, built by Samuel Halevi, Pedro I's treasurer, in which inscriptions in Hebrew and Arabic are combined with the lions and castles of the Castilian coat of arms.[27] Extending the metaphor, multiple languages are also found in the ceiling paintings in the Hall of Justice in the Palace of the Lions in the Alhambra (Madinat al-Hamra), built under Muhammad V when he regained his throne in Granada with the support of Pedro I.[28]

Overlooking the Nasrid capital of Granada, the Alhambra is the best-preserved palatial complex from the medieval Muslim world. Its architecture and decoration have been studied from many perspectives.[29] In this brief survey, in which inscriptions have frequently been key, the Alhambra may be cited for its abundant parietal epigraphy and especially for the distinctive use in its inscriptions of prosopopeia, the poetic device that allows inanimate objects to speak in the first person. Verses by Ibn Zamrak inscribed in the Hall of Two Sisters (al-Qubba al-Kubra) declare, for instance, "I am the garden appearing every morning adorned with beauty; contemplate my beauty and you will be penetrated with understanding."[30] Muhammad V is extolled in the following verses, for one of the primary functions of the epigraphy and other aspects of the architectural design is to reinforce the ideology of monarchy. But, given the opportunity to speak for themselves, the walls make two other statements characteristic of the Alhambra: an intermedial translation—here likening architecture to gardens but elsewhere comparing it to textiles—and an instruction to the beholder to undertake a certain aesthetic exercise.[31] The two points intersect. The textile metaphors suggest an integrative aesthetic, both in al-Andalus and in the pan-Mediterranean culture of which it is a part. In this light, large-scale textile furnishings, such as the double-panel curtains associated with the Nasrids, may be viewed as temporary, textile architecture, actively reconfiguring multiuse spaces, as did smaller textiles (cat. 48) and portable objects in other media.

With the fall of the Nasrid dynasty in 1492, Western Islam came definitively under the hegemony of the East. Exiled from Christian Iberia, resettled artisans continued to practice the crafts of al-Andalus, most notably in the architecture and decoration of the *madrasas* built under the Marinid dynasty (1269–1541) in present-day Morocco. But in the following centuries, no site of political and artistic prestige arose in Western Islam to rival the supremacy of the Ottoman dynasty (1299–1923). And while the relationship between waxing Christian and waning Muslim power maintained certain aspects of the pan-Mediterranean medieval map from the sixteenth to the eighteenth century, European colonialism was changing the larger world and would transform North Africa as well. In consequence, the arts of Western Islam are now commonly known through the avatars of Orientalism, those exoticizing appropriations of Islamic art that spread through Europe and the United States in the nineteenth century.[32] The map is changing again, however, and a Friday mosque now crowns the Albaicin Hill in Granada, facing the Alhambra, after a hiatus of some five centuries.

I am grateful to the late Oleg Grabar for his comments on a draft of this essay.

1. Hillenbrand, R. 1992, and the exhibition catalogue Madinat al-Zahra' 2001. Among studies on the literary production of the Cordoban court, see Menocal 2002.
2. For the complete passage from the *Dikr bilad al-Andalus*, see Fierro 2004, p. 312. The remark from Ibn Hayyan's *Muqtabis* is discussed by Labarta and Barceló 1987, p. 102. For an examination of textual sources on that artifact as well as its history and significance, see Rabbat 1993, pp. 71–73; and Shalem 1997. For another description of *al-Yatima*, in an eleventh-century anonymous text, see al-Qaddumi, ed. 1996, pp. 181 and 353.
3. Grabar 1998. On the medieval gift economy and the monetary value of luxury goods, see Cutler 2001 and numerous examples in al-Qaddumi, ed. 1996, as well as Hoffman 2001. For a comprehensive theoretical discussion of gift exchange and an analysis of the

corresponding cultural networks in the context of medieval South Asia, see Flood 2009.

4. See Avinoam Shalem's development of Grabar's concept of the "shared culture of objects" in Shalem 2004a. See also the related theoretical conceptualization in Nora 1989.
5. An extensive list of studies on various aspects of the archaeology, architecture, and decoration of the Great Mosque of Cordoba can be found in Souto 2007.
6. For a summary of Roman and Visigothic forms adapted in the architecture of al-Andalus, see Dodds 1992, as well as Dodds 1990.
7. Bloom 2007, pp. 42–44.
8. See Cilento and Vanoli 2007, pp. 222–25. Textual sources speak of an elephant in 'Abd al-Rahman III's zoo in Madinat al-Zahra and of one given by the Abbasid caliph Harun al-Rashid to Charlemagne about 801 (see Shalem 2004b, p. 102).
9. Ibn Hayyan recorded, for instance, that in 991 the Cordoban caliph Hisham II received "eight thousand pounds of the most pure ivory" in addition to numerous other gifts from a North African Berber prince. See de Gayangos 1840–43, vol. 2, pp. 190–91, a version of *The History of Muhammedan Dynasties in Spain* adapted from al-Maqqari, *Nafh al-tib*.
10. Shalem 2004b, p. 67. In the Umayyad context, the word *al-mulk* is found on the earthenware ceramics produced in Madinat al-Zahra; more important, it recalls *Dar al-Mulk* (the House of Kingship/Dominion), the name of 'Abd al-Rahman III's palace there. The word *al-mulk* is inscribed on objects that can be traced to other areas in the Mediterranean, but more immediately, in the context of al-Andalus, it should be noted that the term appears on a Nasrid lusterware "Alhambra" vase, found at the excavations at Mazara del Vallo in Sicily (now in the Galleria Regionale della Sicilia, Palermo). See Guillermo Rosselló Bordoy in Granada and New York 1992, p. 354, no. 110. The export of the Nasrid luxury lusterware once again reflects shared meanings in the pan-Mediterranean context.
11. Hoffman 2001. For trade routes, seafaring, commerce, and consular networks in the Mediterranean from the thirteenth through the fifteenth century, see Barcelona 2004.
12. Priscilla Soucek has made a related point about the similarities between the decorative motifs of Byzantine textiles and Umayyad ivories made in Cordoba. See Soucek 1997, pp. 409–10, 517. For a comprehensive discussion of ivory sources, trade routes, and cutting and carving techniques during the medieval period in the Mediterranean, see Cutler 1994 and Shalem 2004b, pp. 50–79. For a compendium and related bibliography of medieval ivories made in Muslim lands, see Galán y Galindo 2005.
13. Prado-Vilar 2005. The entire issue of the *Journal of the David Collection* in which Prado-Vilar's work appears is dedicated to papers from a symposium entitled "The Ivories of Muslim Spain," held in Copenhagen, November 18–20, 2003 (Folsach and Meyer, eds. 2005).
14. Ettinghausen, Grabar, and Jenkins-Madina 2001, p. 95, based on Kühnel 1971, pp. 43–44. For an interpretation of the erotic aspect of the verses, see Washington, D.C. 2004, pp. 125–26.
15. For the most recent bibliography on women in al-Andalus, see Anderson forthcoming. I wish to thank the author for sharing her essay manuscript with me.
16. For the association of foliate decoration with the fecundity of royal concubines and, by implication, with women's role in the legitimate succession to the throne, see Holod 1992, p. 43; Prado-Vilar 1997; and Blair 2005.
17. On the architectural patronage of mosques, cemeteries, and other pious foundations by Umayyad court women, see Anderson forthcoming. Anderson rightly remarks that the only monograph to date on women's patronage during the caliphal period (660–1236) is Cortese and Calderini 2006.
18. For instances of women employed at the Umayyad court—as cooks and servants but also as a treasurer of luxury textiles—and of women of other social classes working as weavers, embroiderers, and vendors, see Marín 2000, pp. 270–72, 283–91. On women poets, calligraphers, and copyists, see Ávila 1989 and Ávila 2002.
19. On the construction of the hybrid genealogies of the Umayyads of Cordoba and the impact of non-Arab and non-Muslim mothers on the cultural identities of the rulers, see Ruggles 2004a. An expansion of this discussion to include the Christian kings of the Iberian Peninsula can be found in Dodds, Menocal, and Krasner Balbale 2008, pp. 22–28. On women as "defenders of the cultural identity of their communities" in the later medieval period, see Jesús Fuente 2009.
20. See Jonathan M. Bloom in Granada and New York 1992, pp. 362–67, no. 115.
21. Shepherd 1957 and Partearroyo Lacaba 1992, p. 106. It is possible that the chasuble was made in Almeria, a thriving center of textile production and a commercial port, since the inscription on the *tiraz* of a similar textile, the Chasuble of Saint Thomas Becket, refers to that city. See Simon-Cahn 1993. For a recent overview of textiles made in al-Andalus, see Partearroyo Lacaba 2005.
22. For a catalogue of objects preserved in church treasuries but associated with the patronage of medieval Muslim dynasties, as well as a discussion of their function and meaning in the context of the Christian West, see Shalem 1998.
23. For the most recent study of this banner, see Ali-de-Unzaga 2007 and Antonio Fernández-Puertas in Madrid 2005, pp. 262–69, no. 66.
24. For a discussion of mortuary vestments of Iberian Christian kings, nobles, and churchmen, including those of Jiménez de Rada, in the context of an argument for a pan-Iberian aesthetics, see Feliciano 2005. See also Madrid 2005. Despite the shared taste for luxury textiles, not only did the dress of Christian nobles differ in cut from that of Muslims, but specific decorative motifs were preferred by Christians. See Fernández González 2007.
25. Dodds, Menocal, and Krasner Balbale 2008 posited the concept of "intimacy" as an alternative to the notion of *convivencia* (coexistence). In connection with that important revision of prevalent notions of cultural interrelationship in al-Andalus, the term *mudéjar style*, coined by José Amador de los Rios in 1859 and a mainstay of the study of Iberian art history ever since, has also come under new critical consideration. Common to both terms—*convivencia* and *mudéjar style*—is the presupposition of clearly identifiable borders between self and other; moreover, they reflect a tendency to map the movement of culture in a single direction, as part of the history of Christian Spain. In addition to Dodds, Menocal, and Krasner Balbale 2008, see the essays in the following volumes for a critique of these terms, which is central to new developments in the study of Western Islam: Robinson, C., and Rouhi, eds. 2005; Feliciano, Rouhi, and Robinson, eds. 2006; Robinson, C., and Pinet, eds. 2008; and Valdés Fernández, ed. 2007. See also Robinson, C. 2003; Ruiz Souza 2004; and Ruiz Souza 1998.

26. Iberian architecture from the twelfth through the fourteenth century contains many examples of monumental inscriptions combining phrases in Arabic and Latin. With regard to the inscriptions in Latin, Hebrew, Arabic, and Castilian on the tomb of Ferdinand III, Dodds, Menocal, and Krasner Balbale argued that they "provide particularly striking markers of the Castilian intimacy with the communities they represent" (2008, p. 199). Recent studies of Pedro I's palace in the Alcazar of Seville include Almagro Gorbea 2007 and Ruggles 2004b.
27. On Iberian synagogues, see Ben-Dov 2009. Among recent studies in Sephardic art history, see Kogman-Appel 2004 and Harris 2005.
28. For interpretations of the visual narratives of the ceiling paintings in the Hall of Justice, see Robinson, C., and Pinet, eds. 2008.
29. Much of this research agenda was set in Grabar 1978. See Orihuela Uzal 1995, Fernández-Puertas 1997, and Angustias Cabrera et al. 2007.
30. Among studies on the poetry in the Alhambra, see García Gómez 1996, Puerta Vílchez 1990, Puerta Vílchez 2007, Jarrar 1999, Robinson, C. 2008, Bush 2009, Rubiera Mata 1970, Rubiera Mata 1981, Rubiera Mata 1994, and Sumi 2004, pp. 155–93.
31. On the relationship between the architecture of the Alhambra and the gardens and landscape evoked in the verses of its parietal epigraphy, see Ruggles 2000, pp. 199–208; Ruggles 1997; and Bush 2006.
32. For a recent discussion of Orientalism with respect to the legacy of al-Andalus, see Rosser-Owen 2010, pp. 109–45.

30. Folio from the Blue Qur'an

Probably Tunisia, Qairawan, second half of 9th–mid-10th century
Gold and silver on indigo-dyed parchment
12 × 15⅞ in. (30.4 × 40.2 cm)
Purchase, Lila Acheson Wallace Gift, 2004 2004.88

From the Blue Qur'an, one of the most lavish Qur'an manuscripts ever produced, this double-sided leaf contains fifteen lines of *kufic* script in gold ink on indigo-dyed parchment. Like most Qur'ans from the eighth through the tenth century, it is distinguished by a horizontal format, use of parchment, and *kufic* script. On the two sides of this leaf, as with all the pages from the Blue Qur'an, the voweling and diacritical marks are omitted, and ornamentation is kept to a minimum. The only decoration found on many of these pages consists of the circular silver marks, now almost entirely oxidized and faded, that separate each verse. The sparse ornamentation allows for an uninterrupted progression and bold movement of the letters from right to left. The text on the two sides here is from Sura 30:24–32 (*al-Rum*, "The Byzantine Empire").

Firm evidence is lacking regarding the origin, exact date, and patron of this manuscript, although all of the thirty-seven extant pages, now scattered in museum and private collections throughout the world, probably come from one manuscript preserved at the Institut National d'Archéologie et d'Art in Tunis.[1] Several scholars have suggested dates for the Blue Qur'an, ranging from the ninth to the mid-tenth century, and attributed it to either Qairawan in present-day Tunisia or Cordoba in Umayyad Spain.[2] Some have posited a date on the basis of stylistic affinities between the Blue Qur'an illuminated folios in Qairawan and Raqqada and the palmette trees and vegetal designs on the *minbar* and *mihrab* of the Great Mosque of Qairawan.[3] Jonathan Bloom's attribution of the manuscript to Qairawan derives from a particular system of *abjad* numbering in the manuscript that is specific to the Islamic West.[4] In addition, a description of a manuscript having the same specifications was found in an inventory in the Mosque of Qairawan in A.H. 693/1293 A.D. This implies that at the end of the thirteenth century, the work was still in the city in which it was probably produced.[5]

Very few Qur'ans on colored parchment are known. The majority of early Qur'an manuscripts are executed in brown or black ink with red voweling and diacritical marks against a white ground. The use of gold lettering makes this manuscript an especially rare and luxurious example. It could have been commissioned by the caliph himself or by a wealthy, pious patron such as a governor. The practice of writing in gold or silver ink on blue or purple vellum or parchment most likely came from the Christian Byzantine Empire, where official documents and manuscripts were often executed in this manner. ME

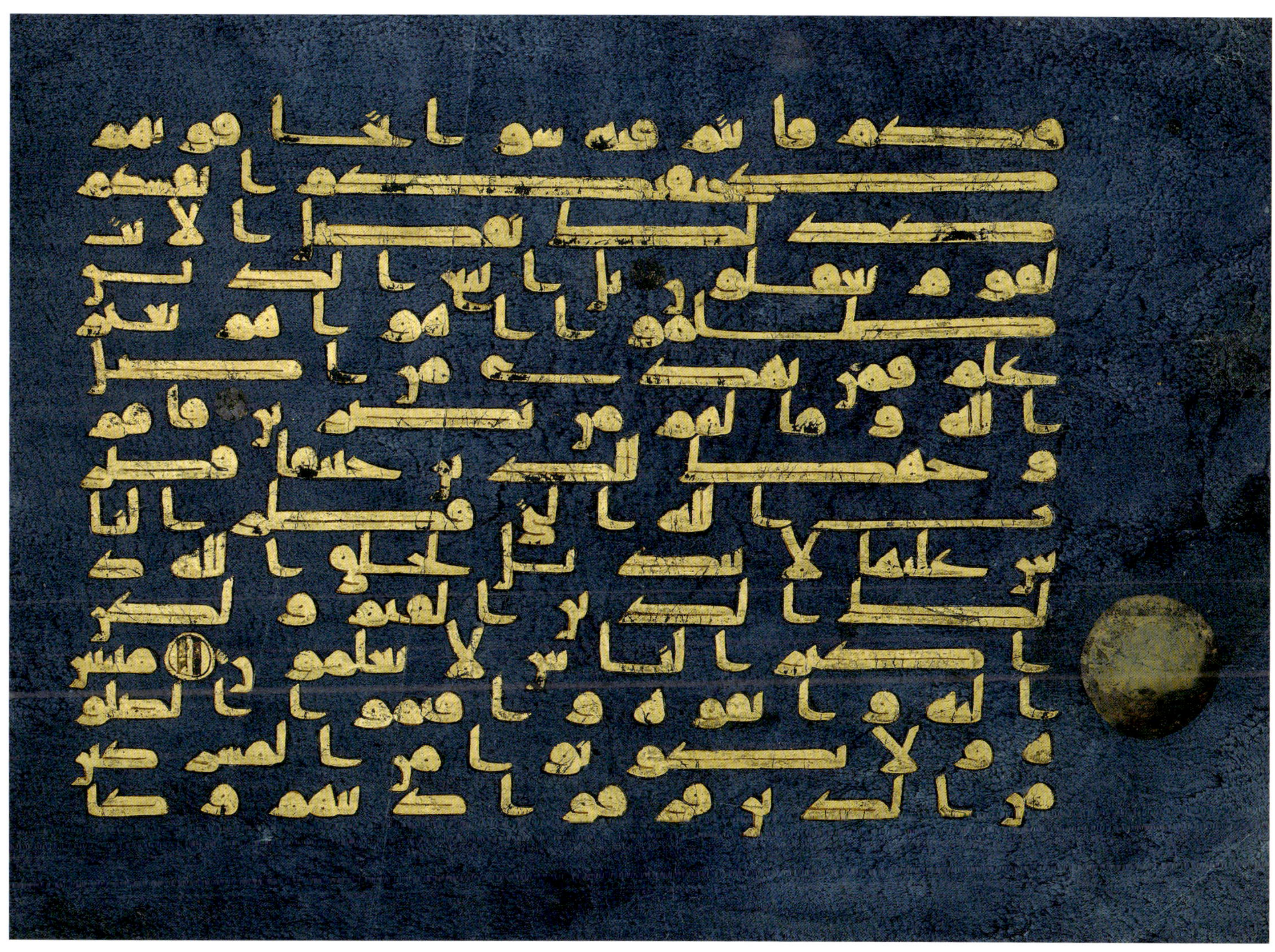

1. The Bibliothèque Nationale de Tunisie in Tunis and the Musée National d'Art Islamique in Raqqada have the greatest share of the pages. The equivalent of a *juz'* is presently in the Musée National d'Art Islamique de Raqqada. See Ettinghausen, Grabar, and Jenkins-Madina 2001, pp. 98–99, 312.
2. Bloom 1989. See also Ettinghausen, Grabar, and Jenkins-Madina 2001, pp. 98–99.
3. Ettinghausen, Grabar, and Jenkins-Madina 2001, p. 98.
4. Bloom observed that calligraphers from the Maghrib or western Islamic lands, comprising Spain and North Africa, sometimes used different letters than their Muslim counterparts in the east to represent numbers in the *abjad* system. He based his argument upon the differences between markings on Iraqi and Andalusian astrolabes made around the same time. See Bloom 1989.
5. London 1980, p. 22. This connection was made by the scholar Ibrahim Shabbuh in 1956. See Neumeier 2006, p. 13.

PROVENANCE: Probably Great Mosque of Qairawan, Tunisia (from about 900); [Sam Fogg, London, by 2002–4; sold to MMA]

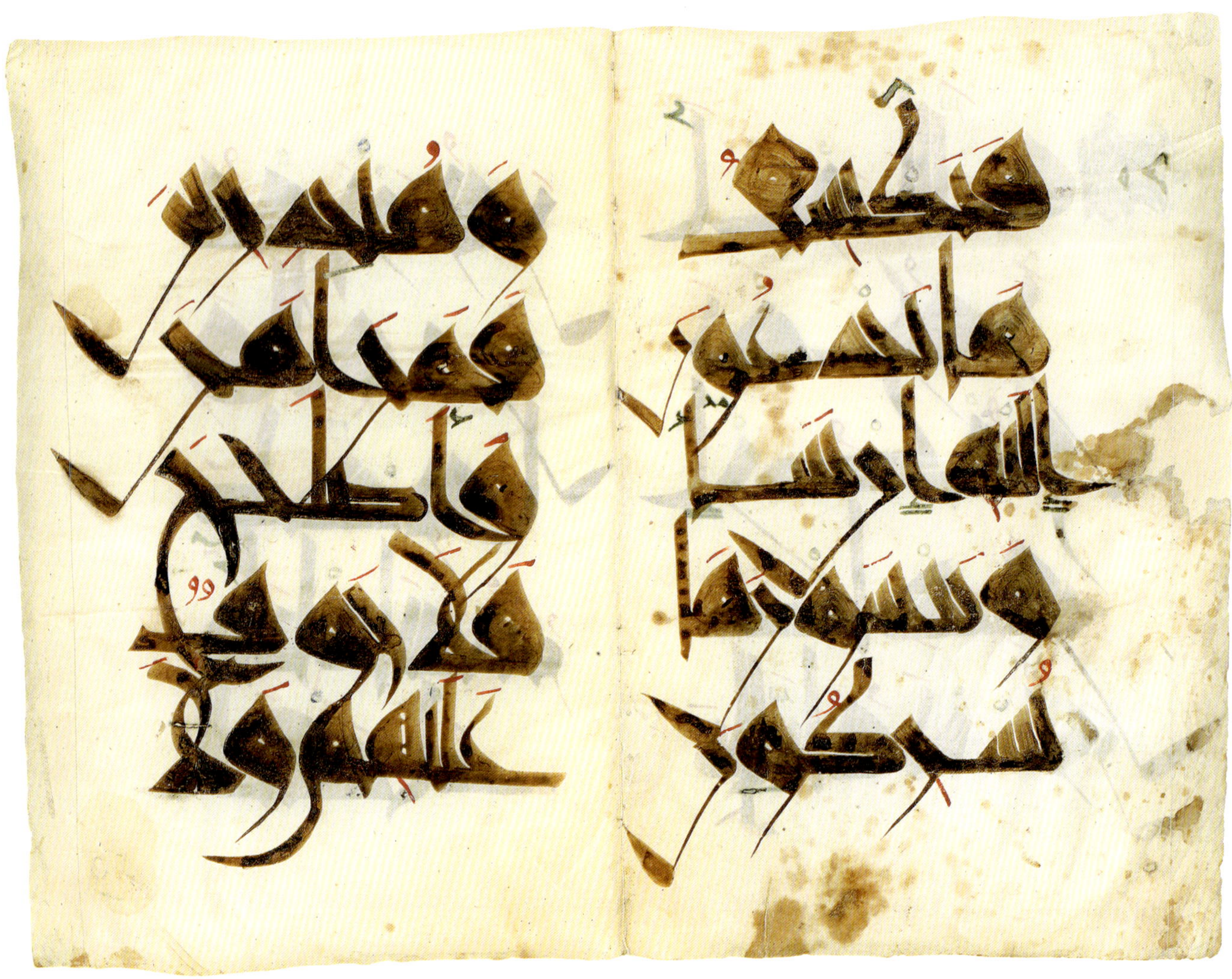

31. Bifolio from the Mushaf al-hadina (Nurse's Qur'an)

Calligrapher: ʿAli ibn Ahmad al-Warraq
Probably Tunisia, Qairawan, ca. A.H. 410 / 1019–20 A.D.
Ink, opaque watercolor, and gold on parchment
17½ × 23⅝ in. (44.5 × 60 cm)
Purchase, James and Diane Burke Gift, in honor of Dr. Marilyn Jenkins-Madina, 2007 2007.191

This bifolio comes from one of the most impressive manuscripts of the Qur'an, the *Mushaf al-hadina* or Nurse's Qur'an, which was produced in North Africa. Among the best-preserved extant leaves of the manuscript,[1] it features calligraphy executed on parchment in brown ink, with diacritical marks in red, blue, and green. Each page contains only five lines, and great attention has been devoted to the contrast between the thick, rounded forms and the thin verticals so characteristic of this distinct "new-style" script. This manuscript is also one of the few indicating that the "new-style" script, traditionally associated with the eastern realms, had spread farther west in the Islamic world than had previously been known. The text, written on both sides, is taken from Sura 6:40–41, 48–49 (*al-Anʿam*, "The Cattle").

Producing a volume as monumental in size as the *Mushaf al-hadina* would have required a fully staffed workshop of talented calligraphers, illuminators, and binders. That no one calligrapher could have undertaken all the work accounts for the variations in the calligraphy in the Qur'an.[2]

This is an unusually well-documented bifolio. A series of colophons[3] written in cursive *maghribi* on the original manuscript, part of which is now in the Musée National d'Art Islamique de Raqqada in Tunisia, state that the work was commissioned by Fatima, the nursemaid (*al-hadina*) of one of the Zirid rulers. The Zirids were Berbers who governed territories in central North Africa (Ifriqiya) on behalf of the Fatimid dynasty, whose capital was Cairo. Since the manuscript is not dated, it is not entirely clear under which Zirid prince it was commissioned. However, the inclusion of A.H. Ramadan 410 / January 1019–20 A.D. as the date when the manuscript was dedicated to the Great Mosque of Qairawan has anchored its current attribution and its association with al-Mu'izz ibn Badis, the fourth Zirid ruler of Ifriqiya (r. 1016–62).[4] The colophon further notes that the entire manuscript, including its binding, was vocalized, illuminated, and gilded by 'Ali ibn Ahmad al-Warraq (the papermaker), a renowned calligrapher and artist of the period who was supervised by Durrah al-Katiba (Durrah, the lady scribe).[5]

A number of the surviving Qur'an manuscripts commissioned by Zirid princesses and other powerful women at the Zirid court were dedicated to the Great Mosque of Qairawan. Among them are Umm Milal's Qur'an and that of Umm 'Ulu, the sister of al-Mu'izz ibn Badis.[6] But the *Mushaf al-Hadina* is probably the best-known and important extant manuscript commissioned by a North African female patron.[7] It serves as a testament to the generosity, faith, and influence of women patrons at the Zirid court. ME

1. It is estimated that the original manuscript had approximately 3,200 folios, or 1,600 bifolios, and was divided into sixty sections (departmental curatorial files, Department of Islamic Art, Metropolitan Museum).
2. Roxburgh 2007.
3. *Discover Islamic Art*: http://www.discoverislamicart.org.
4. Ettinghausen, Grabar, and Jenkins-Madina 2001, pp. 285–86.
5. Blair 2006, p. 155. See also Paris 1982–83, pp. 272–73.
6. Paris 1982–83, pp. 272–73. See also: http://www.discoverislamicart.org.
7. Sections of this Qur'an containing illuminated folios are in the Musée National d'Art Islamique de Raqqada, the Musée d'Art Islamique in Qairawan, and the Musée National du Bardo in Tunis. Other dispersed folios are in the Khalili Collection, London, the David Collection, Copenhagen, and in private collections in Riyadh and Houston.

PROVENANCE: Fatima al-Hadina, Tunisia (until 1019–20); Great Mosque of Qairawan, Tunisia (from 1019–20); [Charif Fine Arts, Dubai, sold to Fogg]; [Sam Fogg, London, until 2007; sold to MMA]

32. Folio from a Qur'an Manuscript

Spain, late 13th–early 14th century
Ink, opaque watercolor, and gold on parchment
21 1/8 × 22 in. (53.5 × 55.9 cm)
Rogers Fund, 1942 42.63

Few luxury Qur'ans from thirteenth- and fourteenth-century Spain and North Africa exceeded twenty inches (approximately half a meter) in width and height, and even fewer of that size on parchment have survived. It seems that these two characteristics were combined in only one example, to which this individual folio originally belonged. The most distinctive qualities of Spanish and Moroccan Qur'an manuscripts were established in the Almoravid and Almohad periods and are still evident in this manuscript page: a roughly square format, the archaic use of parchment at a time when paper had become the most common support, and a spidery calligraphy known as *maghribi* (Western Islamic) script.

This folio therefore belonged to one of the most ambitious and largest (if not the largest) parchment Qur'an manuscripts ever produced in the medieval Maghrib. A two-volume Qur'an now in the Museum of Turkish and Islamic Art in Istanbul seems to provide a good match for the dimensions, calligraphic style, and illumination of the Museum's folio.[1] Copied on both sides (recto and verso), this folio contains the first four verses and most of verse 5 of Sura 39 (*al-Zumur*, "Of the Crowds"), which was revealed in Mecca and includes a total of seventy-five verses.[2] The recto is particularly notable. Its first line, which gives the heading for the Sura, is copied in an intricate, dramatic *kufic* gold script outlined in red and ending in an impressive circular pendant; the pendant itself is outlined in blue and filled with a densely illuminated but perfectly balanced scrolling composition in red and gold. The end of each verse is highlighted by a small but prominent circular medallion including a white interlacing geometric motif and the

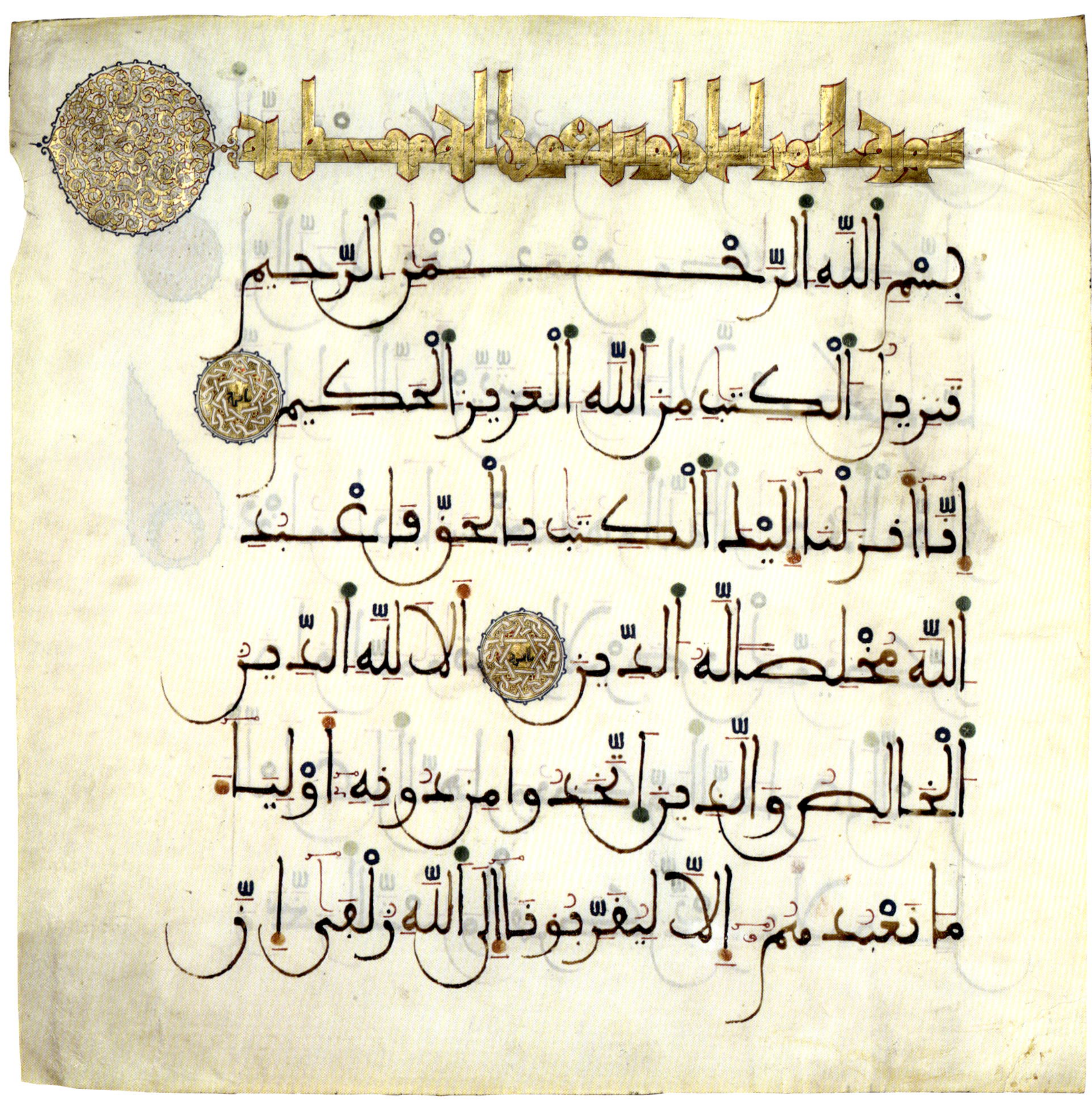

word *aya* (verse) in blue; on the verso, the fifth verse is emphasized in the margins of the page with a larger pointed medallion including the word *khamsa* (five) in white.

The seven amply spaced lines of text on each page were copied in black ink that has subsequently turned brownish against the slippery surface of the parchment. Diacritical and reading marks were added in blue, orange, and green pigments. Although the overall effect of the calligraphy is squarish, uniform, and balanced, the deep, curving, almost semicircular endings of some of the letters brilliantly tie the text together and punctuate its rhythm, not unlike the notes in a musical score. Considering that *Qur'an* means "recitation," this monumental *maghribi* calligraphy splendidly illustrates how writing, reading, and reciting can coalesce in a truly superb combination.

SC

1. Şahin 2009, pp. 86–89, and Lings 2005, p. 52, pls. 166–69.
2. The heading states that the number of verses is seventy-two, which may correspond to a specific division of the text used in the Maghrib.

Provenance: [Mrs. Kamer Aga-Oğlu, Ann Arbor, Michigan, until 1942; sold to MMA]

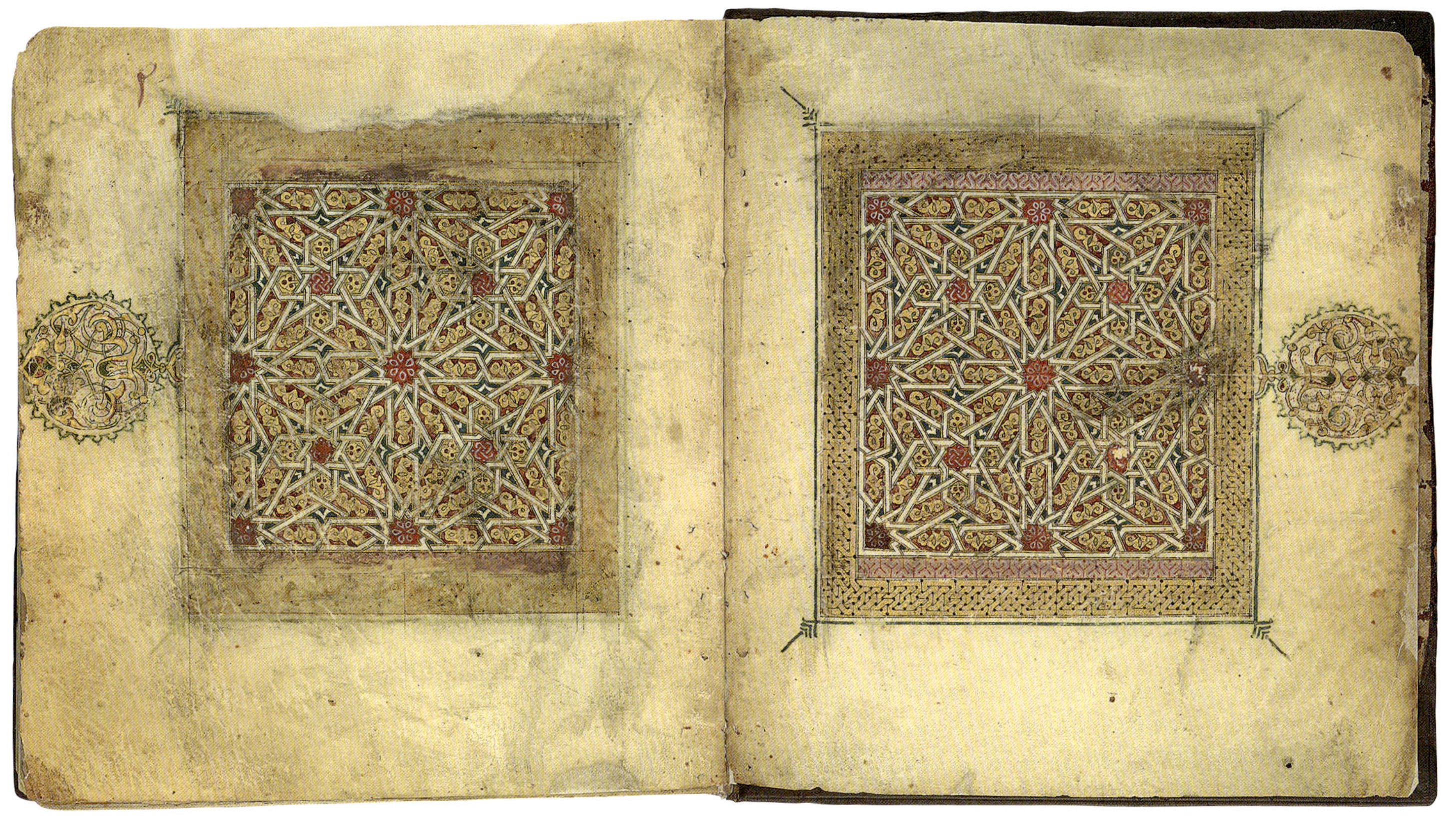

33. Segment of a Qur'an Manuscript

Morocco or southern Spain, ca. 1300
Ink, gold, and opaque watercolor on parchment
8 × 7½ in. (20.2 × 19.2 cm)
Purchase, Lila Acheson Wallace Gift, 2004 2004.90

Containing Suras 5 through 9, this codex represents the second volume of a seven-volume Qur'an.[1] As a medial volume, it has no colophon, but a few of the pages bear *waqf* inscriptions that indicate its endowment to a *ribat* in Medina known as the Ribat Sayyidna 'Uthman.[2] In the holy cities of Mecca and Medina, *ribats* generally functioned as accommodations for indigent Muslims, sufis, or travelers. Most were founded by individuals from other regions whose endowments often specified their own compatriots as eligible residents.[3] Such was the case with the Ribat Sayyidna 'Uthman, which was dedicated to Maghribi residents.[4] Undoubtedly, it is through this connection that the library of the *ribat* obtained this manuscript, which was probably made in Morocco.

In most respects, the manuscript exhibits the highly traditional approach typical of Qur'an production in the Maghrib.[5] Although paper had been introduced to the region well before this volume was made, parchment was favored there for Qur'ans and other religious texts through the fourteenth century. The square format of the text block here is another characteristic feature. The two opening pages are written entirely in black-contoured lettering infilled with gold, but most of the others are executed in thick brown ink, in the *maghribi* script.[6] When no illuminated heading is present, both the incipit pages and the continuing pages bear eleven lines of text. Characteristically, *qaf* is indicated by one dot above the grapheme, and *fa'* by one dot below it; green dots are used for *hamzat al-wasl*, yellow dots for *hamzat al-qat*, blue-green ink for *shadda* and *sukun*, and red lines for vowel markers. The graphemes combine features of the two subtypes of *maghribi* calligraphy: the compact, rhythmic scroll of the *andalusi*-type lettering and the sinuous, sprawling flourishes of the *fasi* script.[7] Another singular feature of this manuscript appears on the pages with gold lettering: the looped letter forms—such as *sad*, *dad*, and *ta*—are filled with pigment.

The manuscript opens with an illuminated double page that features a design of gold-bordered white strapwork enclosing gold palmettes against a blue ground. Every fifth verse is marked by gold trefoil motifs embellished with red and blue dots, and every tenth verse by gold disks supplemented by marginal roundels containing the word *'ashara*. Large circular devices in gold and pigments signal *hizb* divisions. Most of the Sura headings are distinguished by gold *kufic* letters with marginal split-palmette medallions. The heading on the opening page, however, is set within an illuminated panel against a blue ground within a pearl border, flanked by knotted interlace and surrounded by a gold braid with a circular-palmette medallion in the margin. Similar compositions surround the text on the bottom half of the penultimate page (folio 88v) and all of the final page (folio 89r).

EK

1. The eighty-nine folios of this volume have been rebound, as indicated by the modern spine and trimmed pages. Although the front and back covers, lined in dark brown leather blind-tooled with an allover pattern of rosettes around a floral cluster, may be historical, they are not original; their association with these pages probably dates to the time of its rebinding.
2. Formerly, the manuscript was understood to be endowed to an institution in Rabat, Morocco (Fendall 2003, pp. 62–63). I am grateful to Priscilla Soucek, Abdullah Ghouchani, Stefan Heidemann, and Werner Ende for their assistance with this research.
3. Mortel 1998.
4. The Ribat Sayyidna 'Uthman reportedly stood in the vicinity of the Great Mosque of Medina until at least 1951 (Ansari 1985, p. 30). For further reference to this *ribat*, see Ibn Silm 1993, pp. 39–40, and Badr 1993, vol. 3, pp. 111–12.
5. Baker, C. 2007, pp. 28–29.
6. Blair 2006, pp. 221–29, 392–99.
7. Fendall 2003, pp. 62–63; Blair 2006, p. 392.

PROVENANCE: Ribat Sayyidna 'Uthman, Medina, Saudi Arabia, sale, Sotheby's London, October 12, 2000, lot 39; [art market, from 2000]; [Sam Fogg, London, until 2004; sold to MMA]

34. *Qur'an Manuscript*

Morocco or Tunisia, 18th century
Ink, opaque watercolor, and gold on paper; leather binding, stamped and gilded
8 × 6 in. (20.3 × 15.2 cm)
Purchase, Gift of George Blumenthal, by exchange, 1982 1982.120.2

This Qur'an belongs to a group of late North African manuscripts noted for their use of a wide range of vibrant colors, a feature that sets them apart from earlier manuscripts of the same region (see, for example, cat. 33). Deeply saturated tones of orange, red, yellow, green, pink, and blue not only dominate the frontispiece and finispiece but also highlight the Sura and verse markers throughout the text. These bright compositions are illuminated with gold and intricately patterned in scrolling arabesques and stylized floral motifs.

Although this manuscript has been dated to the period when the arts flowered under the patronage of the Alawi sultans in eighteenth-century Morocco, a Turkish seal on the flyleaf suggests that it may have been created in Ottoman-controlled Tunisia. Morocco, though culturally and geographically linked to Tunisia, was never under the control of the Ottoman Empire. Supporting this alternate attribution is the presence of Ottoman-style "forked" tulips on the frontispiece, the doublure, and the inside of the doublure flap.

The manuscript contains the last five *juz'* (sections 26 through 30) of the Qur'an in forty folios. The text, in black ink, is executed in horizontally elongated *maghribi* script that creates a visually dramatic calligraphic composition.[1] Further enlivening the text are red, yellow, and blue diacritical marks. The verse markers, in the form of gold, blue, and red trefoil and winged vegetal motifs, are traditional in North African Qur'ans, which display similar markers as early as the thirteenth century.[2] *Maghribi*, an early cursive script that probably developed out of the more angular *kufic*, was the primary calligraphic style of North Africa and remained relatively unchanged in the region from the twelfth century onward.[3] This Qur'an, like others of the eighteenth century, trades the traditional brown ink of earlier North African Qur'ans for the more ubiquitous black ink. The text frames are also not characteristically

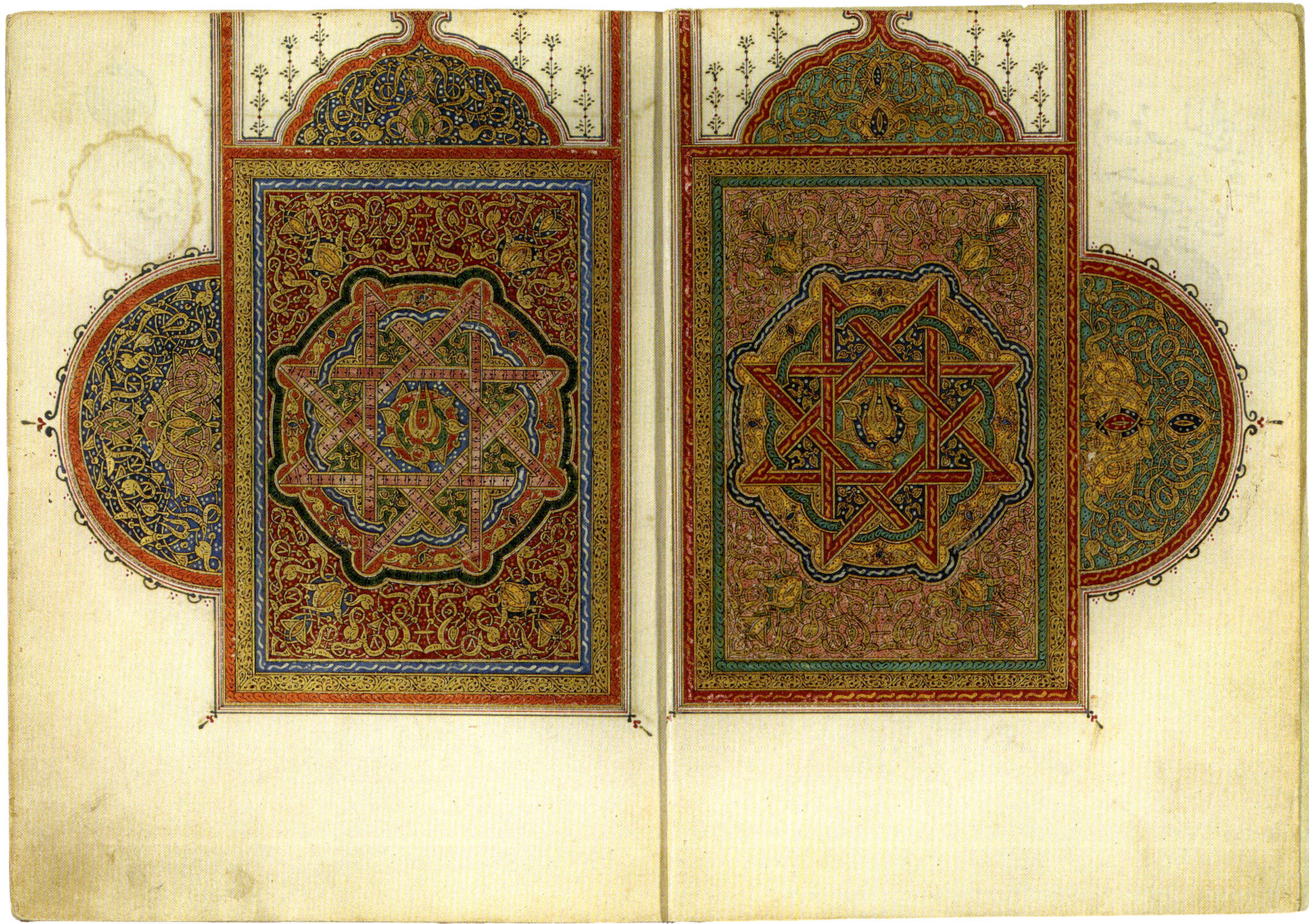

Moroccan, and it has been suggested that they were adopted in conscious emulation of Ottoman manuscripts.[4] This Qur'an thus represents both a continuation of traditional North African elements, such as the *maghribi* script and ornamental verse markers, and a breaking away from earlier regional prototypes in the use of black ink, text frames, and bold colors. ME/KW

1. This type of elongation, in which individual letters are stretched horizontally, is called *mashq* in Arabic and appears in early *kufic* texts as well. See Roxburgh 2007, pp. 8–10.
2. The trefoil motifs (essentially three conjoined gold circles tipped in polychrome) can in fact be seen in earlier manuscripts, such as a twelfth-century Qur'an from Spain in the collection of the Cleveland Museum of Art (no. 1993.440.a), but they do not seem to be paired with the winged vegetal motif until the thirteenth century (see, for example, a Qur'an from Marrakesh in the Topkapı Palace Library, Istanbul [no. R.33]).
3. Roxburgh 2007, p. 35.
4. Stanley 1999, p. 42. This feature was probably introduced in the early eighteenth century, around the same time that Qur'ans and other manuscripts of North Africa began to take on a vertical format instead of the traditional square/oblong *maghribi* format.

Provenance: Hajji Ahmed, Turkey; Philip Hofer, Cambridge, Mass. (until 1982; sold to MMA)

35. Qur'an Case

Spain, possibly Granada, second half of 15th century
Leather embroidered with gilt-silver wire
$4^{1/4} \times 4^{7/8}$ in. (10.8 × 12.4 cm)
Rogers Fund, 1904 04.3.458

Inscription in Arabic in *naskhi* script, repeated on front and back:
لا غالب إلا الله
There is no Victor but God

Of the few embroidered leather objects that have survived from the Nasrid period, this pouch is a rare and fine example. Square in format with a shield-shaped opening flap, it contains vegetal interlacing scrolls on the front as well as the Nasrid dynastic motto, all embroidered in gilt-silver wire. Similar foliate designs also surround the silver crescents that flank the inscription. On the back, there are interlacing star and curvilinear motifs and a repetition of the motto. Pouches such as this were likely made to hold segments of the Qur'an, possibly a *juz'* (the Qur'an is typically divided into thirty parts, or *juz'*, one for each day of the month).[1] The small size and square shape are typical of Spanish Qur'ans from the twelfth century onward.

The embroidered motifs on this Qur'an case belong to the larger decorative repertoire associated with Nasrid Granada. Metal embroidery on leather appears on the surfaces of Nasrid armor coverings such as scabbards, shields, and other ceremonial objects. The scabbards of two Nasrid *jineta* swords bear embroidered interlacing ornamentation and decorative heraldic shields with epigraphy similar to that on the present Qur'an case.[2]

The Nasrid dynastic shield is found on objects as varied as silk textiles and architectural tilework. With their fanning terminals, vertical ascenders, and blocklike lettering, the boxlike Arabic inscriptions combine here with the dynastic motto and the use of gilt-metal wires to suggest a royal provenance. Such richly embroidered objects reflect the refinement and opulence of the Nasrid court. In fact, a piece of paper found inside the pouch at the time of purchase states that it once belonged to the last Islamic ruler of Granada, Muhammad XII (Boabdil, r. 1482–83, 1487–92). PC

1. James 1988, p. 266.
2. The scabbards are in the Bibliothèque Nationale de France, Cabinet des Médailles, Paris (no. 959). See Granada and New York 1992, pp. 284–86, no. 61.

PROVENANCE: Marquis de Dos Aguas, Valencia; [Duc de Dino, Paris, until 1904; sold to MMA]

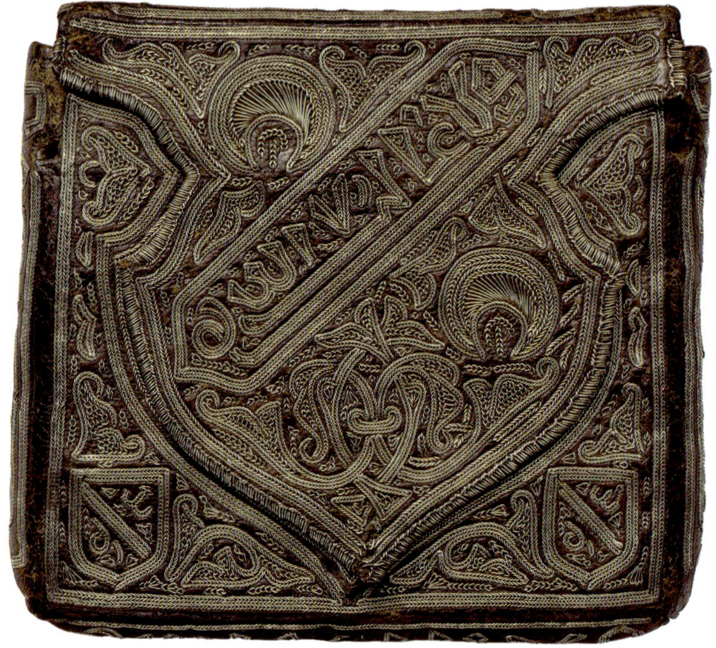

Front

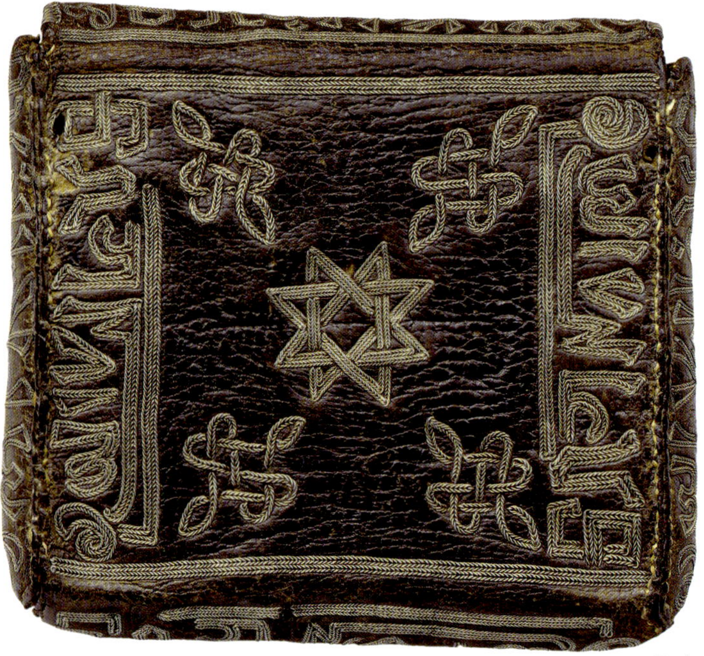

Back

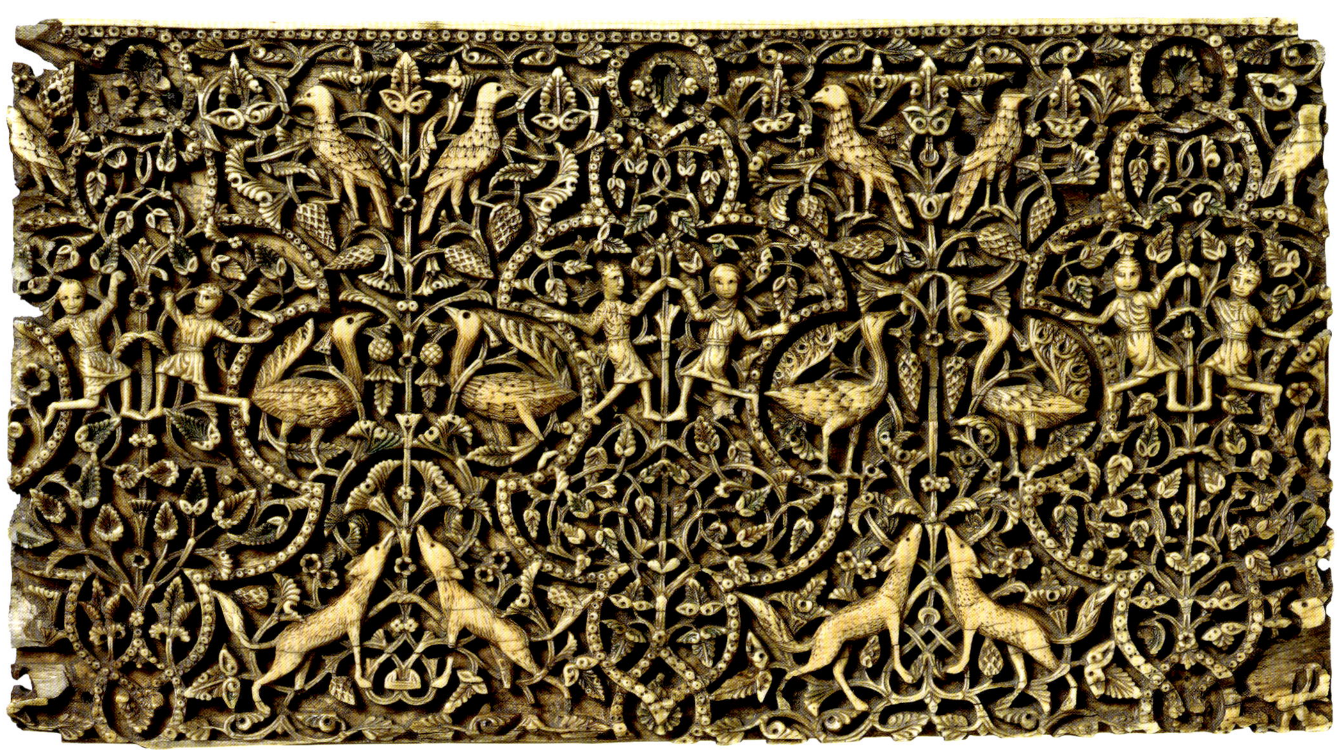

36. Panel

Spain, probably Cordoba, 10th–early 11th century
Ivory; carved, inlaid with stone with traces of pigment
$4\frac{1}{4} \times 8 \times \frac{3}{8}$ in. (10.8 × 20.3 × 1 cm)
John Stewart Kennedy Fund, 1913 13.141

In their time, the royal quarters at Madinat al-Zahra, the caliphal court in al-Andalus, must have been a spectacular sight, with lavish architectural decoration; luxuriant curtains, textiles, and furnishings; and sumptuous objects. Elephant ivory, one of the favorite materials, was used mostly to create objects of small size that were made with painstaking attention to the details and quality of the carvings. In caliphal Spain, as far as is known, entire elephant tusks were not kept as trophies or symbols of power, nor were they turned into oliphants (see cat. 38).

The most common small ivory object was the cylindrical box with a domed lid that is usually referred to as a pyxis (see cat. 37).[1] Such boxes were carved from a piece of solid ivory taken from a section of the tusk that could be made into a container with straight walls. To create a square box—four sides plus a bottom and a lid—the panels of solid ivory needed to be flat; even larger tusks that would offer a usable cross section were then required.

At roughly four by eight inches (11 by 20 cm) and one half inch (1 cm) thick, this relief-carved flat panel may seem diminutive, but a wide portion of a tusk would have been needed for its production. It originally belonged to one of the panels of a square or rectangular casket, and the quality of its carving is nothing short of superb. The precision of detail, paired with the careful planning of the design, places the work among those few that continue to appear sharp and delicate under significant magnification. Features such as the minuscule shiny quartz stones embedded in the eyes of the figures and the red, green, and blue pigments highlighting the carved elements only increase one's appreciation for this extraordinary work.

It has been suggested that the decoration of the plaque was inspired by contemporary textiles,[2] and indeed the repeated units and density of its design recall patterns found in woven textiles and embroidery. The main features of the composition—the playful paired dancing figures facing each other on either side of a stylized tree and the paired predatory birds, peacocks, and jackals—strongly recall older traditions from Late Antiquity as well as contemporaneous ones from early medieval southern Europe. The general pattern, however, is quintessentially Islamic: allover decoration and harmonious symmetry within a subtle geometric division of the space. The excellent parallels it finds in the carved-stucco and stone architectural decorations from Madinat al-Zahra testify to the current decorative taste at the caliphal court.[3] SC

1. The most celebrated of these objects is the so-called al-Mughira Pyxis in the Musée du Louvre, Paris (no. OA 4068); see multiple color views in Paris 2000, pp. 120–21, no. 103. Many such boxes are reproduced in Folsach and Meyer, eds. 2005, pt. 2, pp. 314–25, 330, 332, 336–37, 339.
2. Granada and New York 1992, p. 203, no. 6.
3. See Rosser-Owen 2010.

Provenance: [Jacques Seligmann, Paris, until 1913; sold to MMA]

37. Box (Pyxis)

Spain, 10th century
Ivory; carved
H. 2⅝ in. (6.7 cm); Diam. 3¼ in. (8.3 cm)
Theodore M. Davis Collection,
Bequest of Theodore M. Davis, 1915 30.95.175

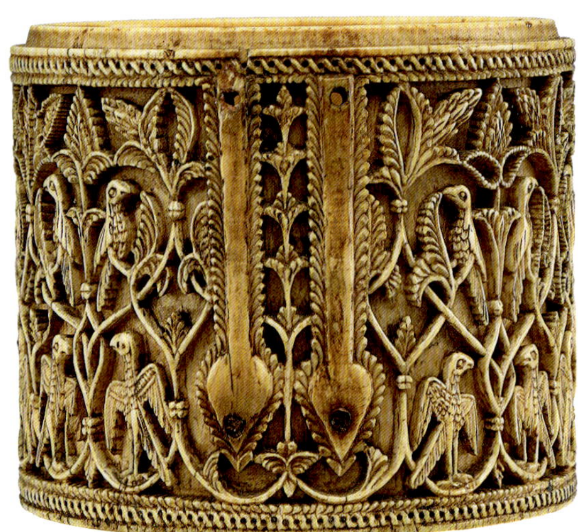

This pyxis, or cylindrical box, belongs to a group of ivory boxes and caskets that became synonymous with the artistic production of luxury objects under the caliphate of the Umayyad dynasty of Cordoba. Skillfully carved and often gilded or painted with colored pigments,[1] such objects were often presented as gifts to commemorate an event or occasion and were sometimes inscribed with the name of the recipient.[2] These elaborately decorated pyxides served both as carriers of multivalent social and political meanings, encoded in their iconography,[3] and as objects of aesthetic delectation. They frequently contained precious aromatic substances, such as ambergris, musk, and camphor, as recorded in the poetic inscriptions on one example.[4] The inscriptions commonly found on the lids of pyxides give the names and titles of the patrons, blessings and good wishes for the owner, and even the signatures of craftsmen. In this incomplete example, however, the knobbed lid and the metal fittings that originally held the lid in place are missing.

The body of this pyxis displays a deeply carved decoration composed of intertwined vines forming two rows of heart-shaped compartments that enclose birds of prey. These addorsed birds are depicted either perched on a branch or standing with outspread wings. The delicate stems of the vines terminate in the large, luxuriant leaves at the top, recalling the crown of a tree, under which the birds are sheltered. A narrow interlace border, typical of such ivory boxes, frames the composition.

Caliphal ivories produced in the royal workshops at the same time as this example show a complex iconographic decorative program that includes human and animal figures set against a dense and varied foliate decoration.[5] However, the simplified composition and sparse vegetation of this pyxis have led to the suggestion that it was made in a secondary workshop.[6] OB

1. A panel from a casket in the Metropolitan Museum (acc. no. 13.141) retains traces of red and green pigments. See Daniel Walker in Granada and New York 1992, p. 203, no. 6.
2. For instance, the inscriptions on a casket in the Victoria and Albert Museum, London (no. 301-1866), record that it was made for the daughter of the Cordoban caliph 'Abd al-Rahman III (r. 912–61). A reference to the caliph as deceased made it possible to date the casket to after 961. See Renata Holod in Granada and New York 1992, p. 192, no. 2.
3. Prado-Vilar 2005; Prado-Vilar 1997.
4. Hispanic Society of America, New York (no. D 752).
5. Prado-Vilar 2005.
6. Galán y Galindo 2005, p. 44. Stylistically, this pyxis is most closely associated with two other examples, one in the Hispanic Society of America, New York (no. D 752), and another in The Metropolitan Museum of Art, The Cloisters (acc. no. 1970.234.5).

Provenance: Theodore M. Davis, New York (until d. 1915); on loan from his estate during settlement of estate (1915–30)

38. Signal Horn (Oliphant)

Southern Italy, 11th–13th century
Ivory; carved
L. 22 in. (55.9 cm); Diam. at opening 4⅞ in. (12.4 cm)
Rogers Fund, 1904 04.3.177a

The use of animal horns or shells both to produce sounds and to communicate is common to many ancient cultures and societies, and it precedes the development of sophisticated musical instruments. Elegantly curved elephant tusks, cut down to a manageable length of about twenty inches (approximately half a meter) and capable of emitting a single note, became popular in medieval Europe from about the eighth century to at least the thirteenth.[1] The exoticism linked to the importation of ivory, its high cost, its perceived magical properties, and the ancient and timeless fascination with the "mysterious" African continent created a special aura around these objects. They were especially coveted as hunting horns by European noblemen, most notably in areas influenced by France. Islamic society, which does not seem to have used such horns, played a part in their diffusion throughout Europe by participating in the ivory trade.

A sizable number of these horns have survived[2]—and only in Europe, none in the Islamic world—because they were prized objects that were often deposited in church treasuries and other institutions, where they were sometimes turned into reliquaries or displayed during festivities.[3] In addition to their original functional use as signal horns, it seems that such objects were also symbols of land tenure: the two metal rings here could have been attached to a metal chain in order to suspend the object from the arched entrance to an estate.

This horn apparently belonged to a Benedictine monastery in Dijon and subsequently passed through the collections of various owners in France before it was acquired by the Museum in 1904. Exceptionally, its leather traveling case has also survived.[4]

Scholars agree that such ivory horns were produced in southern Italy[5] for the Normans between the eleventh and thirteenth centuries. Nevertheless, they "look" Islamic, to such an extent that it has been suggested they were carved by Muslim craftsmen who worked under Christian rule or even by Muslims who had converted to Christianity. The simple explanation is that Sicily and southern Italy under the Normans were still at the artistic and intellectual intersection of Islamic, Latin, and Greek cultures. Whether the makers were Muslim or Christian is relatively unimportant: it was the shared southern Mediterranean artistic language that enabled fabulous and real beasts and birds, grotesque figures, and turbaned warriors to inhabit vine and acanthus scrolls on these remarkable objects. SC

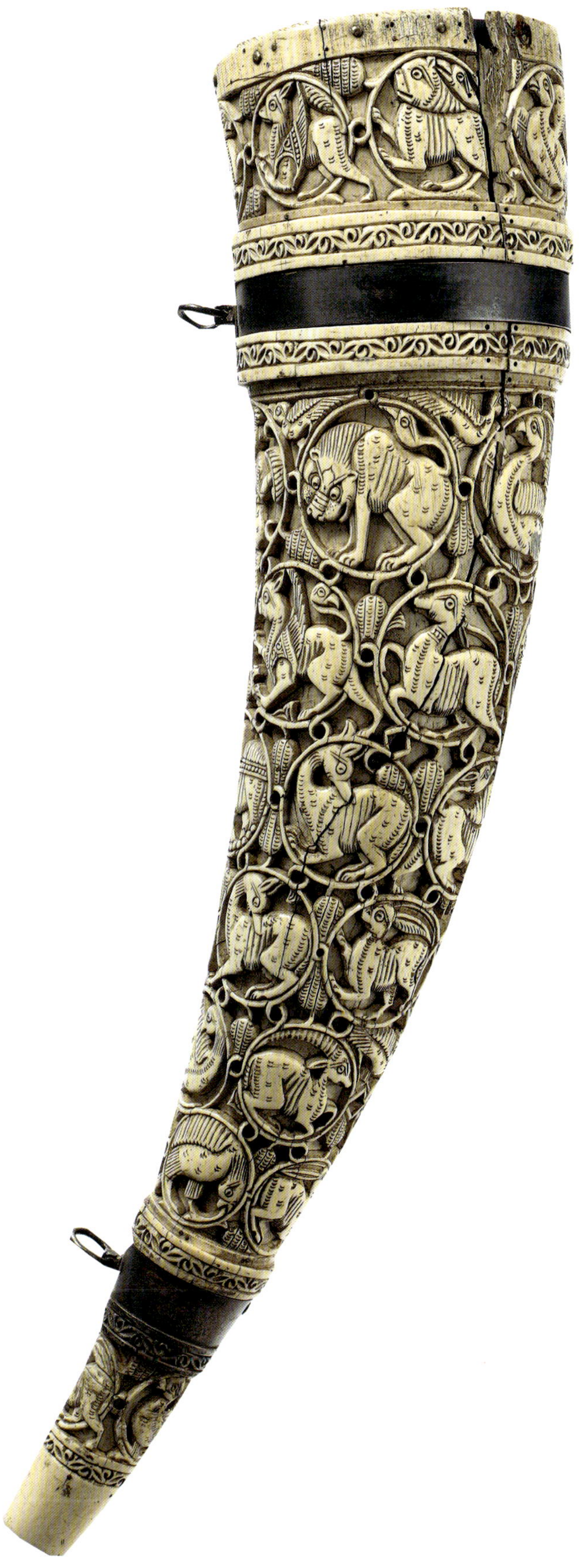

1. They are often associated in early European literature with celebrated and semilegendary figures such as Charlemagne, Roland, and El Cid Campeador.
2. The most recent and comprehensive study is Shalem 2004b.
3. It seems that they were also played liturgically during Holy Week, when the sound of bells was forbidden. On the use of oliphants in Christian churches, see in particular Chapter 7: "Oliphants in Church Treasuries, III: How Were They Used and Displayed?" in Shalem 2004b, pp. 125–30.
4. Metropolitan Museum (acc. no 04.3.177b).
5. Amalfi, one of the Italian maritime republics south of Naples, was apparently a center of ivory carving, although several places in Sicily, starting with the capital, Palermo, must have been equally active.

PROVENANCE: Henri Baudot, Dijon, France; Maurice de Talleyrand-Périgord, Paris; [Duc de Dino, Paris, until 1904; sold to MMA]

39. The Morgan Casket

Southern Italy, 11th–12th century
Ivory; carved
8¾ × 15¼ × 7⅞ in. (22.3 × 38.6 × 20 cm)
Gift of J. Pierpont Morgan, 1917 17.190.241

One of the most accomplished and yet most understudied objects of carved ivory from the Norman-ruled areas of southern Italy is the so-called Morgan Casket. These ivories were created in an extraordinary milieu that linked Fatimid traditions (filtered through the Islamic community of the southern Italian peninsula) with new artistic approaches that arose in France, northern Italy, and the Germanic world. All this occurred in a region that had witnessed a productive medley of Roman and Greek-Byzantine cultures for many centuries before the arrival of either the Muslims or the Normans.

This large box was made by joining nine decorated panels, four for the body and five for the lid. The structure was completed with four narrow strips attached to the bottom of the lid. These strips were necessary because, unlike the great majority of ivory boxes with four vertical panels joined at the sides, the panels on this lid are slanted and form a truncated pyramid. This casket also displays an unusual design for its corners. On each, a pair of stern-looking, bearded men wearing tunics and carrying straight swords stand on a pedestal, as if they were guardians of the precious contents of the box. The four corner units were first carved as single

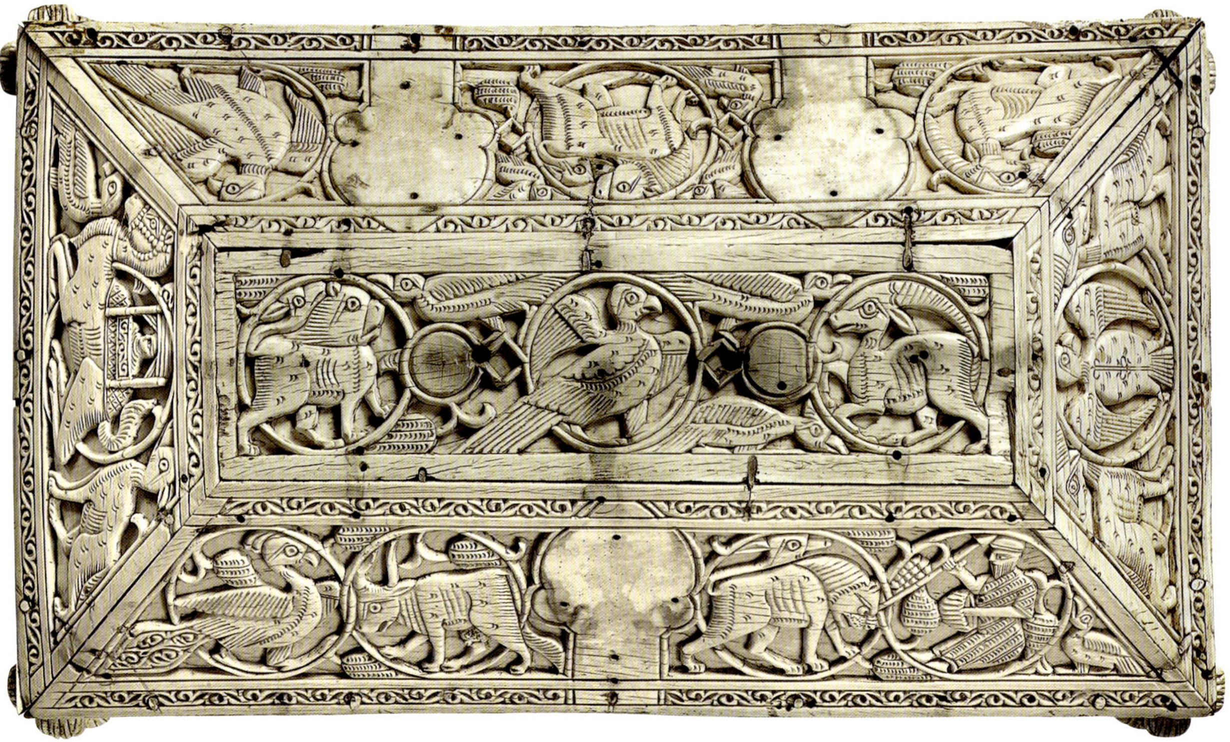

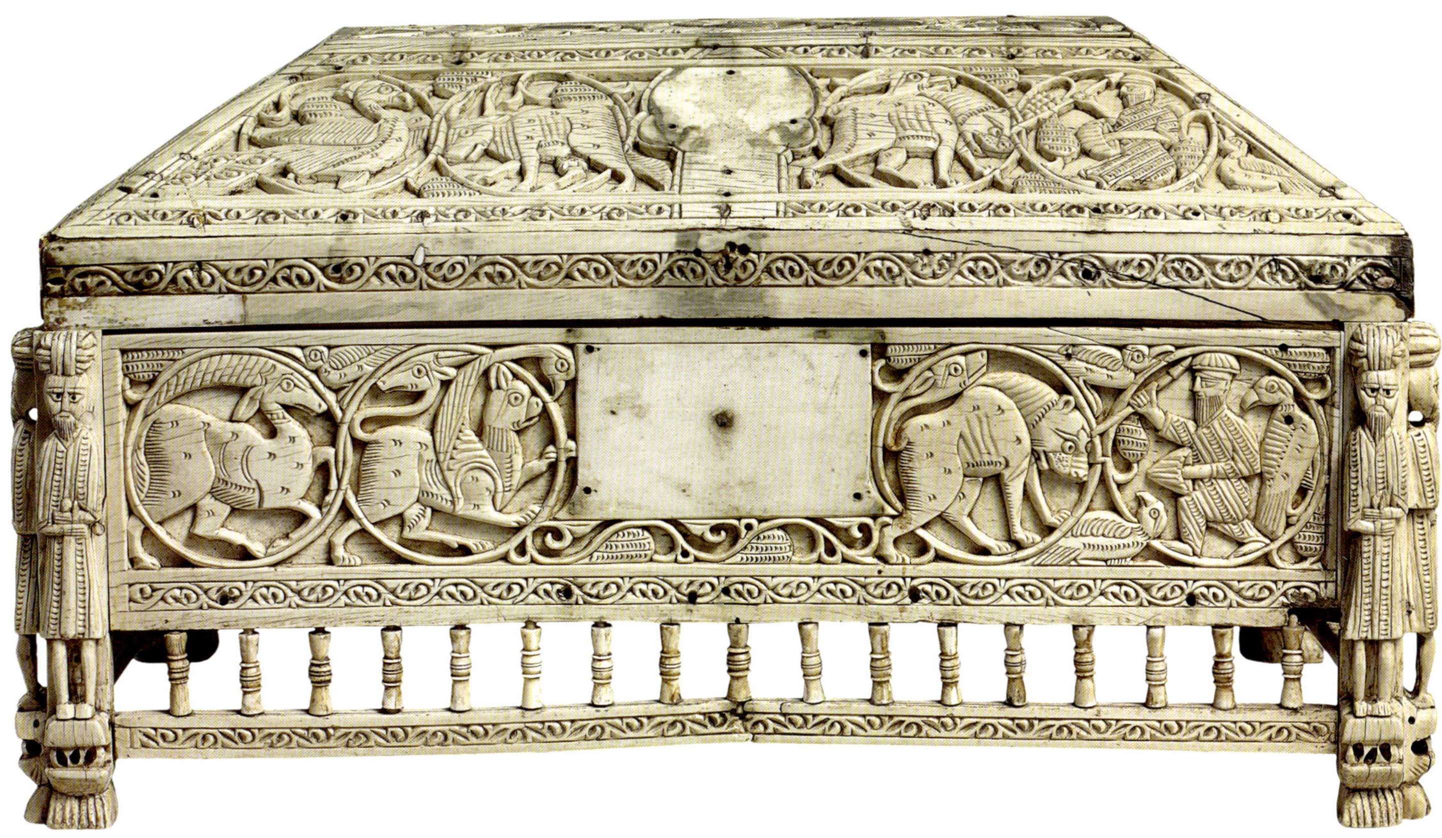

blocks, then the two figures in relief were arranged at a ninety-degree angle facing away from the box and protruding from its perimeter. Because of the corner units, the panels of the body are shorter than the sides of the lid, with the narrow strips facilitating the transition between both sections.

The box gives the impression of being uncommonly delicate and lightweight because of the openwork on the body: four narrow strips are connected vertically to the lower edges of the panels through cylindrical pegs spaced at regular intervals.[1] Metal fasteners, now lost, added significantly to the original appearance of the casket. A single clasp and a rectangular locking plate appeared on the front, and two large hinges on the back; their locations are still evident. Attachments for a handle are also visible on the top of the lid.

Carved in low relief, the figural decoration on all the panels is standard for such ivories and does not have a specific narrative. The larger individual animals and human figures are encircled by continuous vegetal scrolls, while small birds and leaves fill the other available spaces. Symmetry predominates, with pairs of animals facing each other or a man with a spear attacking a feline head-on, although the frontal panel shows an antelope and a gryphonlike quadruped both facing right. The overall quality of the carving is exceptional when compared to that of similar works. A few vignettes stand out, including a veiled woman sitting inside a howdah atop an imposing kneeling camel, carved on one side of the lid; this motif is also the most reminiscent of the Fatimid, North African Islamic models for these works.

J. P. Morgan acquired this splendid casket from the Galerie Imbert in Rome in 1910, but the object had been known since it was exhibited in Brussels in 1880, when it belonged to G. Vermeersch.[2] SC

1. There were originally seventeen pegs along the longer sides and eight along the shorter ones; many of these have now been replaced.
2. Vermeersch was a member of the Musée Royal d'Antiquités de Bruxelles. See de Roddaz 1882, p. 196, fig. 2, for the earliest drawing and reference to this casket.

PROVENANCE: G. Vermeersch, Brussels (in 1880); [Bourgeois Frères, Cologne, until 1904; sale, Krings and Lempertz, Cologne, October 27–29, 1904, lot 1055]; [Galerie A. Imbert, Rome, until 1910; sold to Morgan]; J. Pierpont Morgan, New York (1910–17)

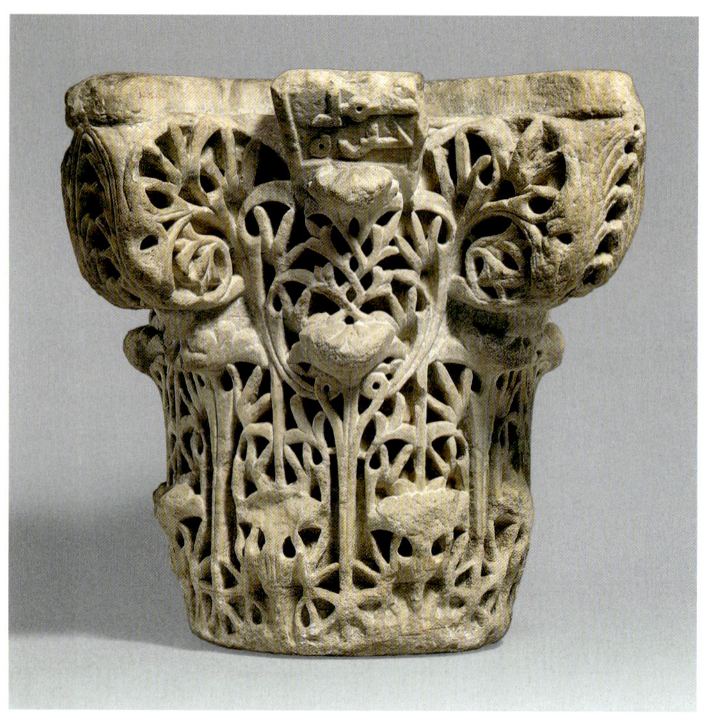

40. Capital

Spain, probably Cordoba, 10th century
Marble; carved
14½ in. × 13½ in. (36.8 × 34.3 cm)
Theodore M. Davis Collection,
Bequest of Theodore M. Davis, 1915 30.95.134

Inscription in Arabic in cursive script on boss at one side of capital:
عمل خبرة
Made by Khabara[?]

Masterfully carved, this Corinthian-style capital must have originally decorated a colonnaded hall or courtyard arcade in one of the lavishly embellished palaces erected during the tenth century under the patronage of the Umayyad dynasty in and around Cordoba, its capital. Three crowns of thick, fleshy acanthus leaves, springing from graceful stems with delicate foliage, form its main decorative elements; the curved finials of the leaves have been lost. The effect of the richly carved surface is rendered through the vigorous stems of the plant, which intertwine, branch out, and enclose the leaves and the other foliate motifs. As it fans out onto the surfaces of the corner volutes, the fine foliate spray emphasizes the volume of the capital, the complexity of the design, and the skillfulness of the workmanship. Executed in deep relief, the carving is crisply and distinctly articulated against the background. The name of the craftsman responsible for the carving appears in the partially preserved inscription on a boss at the top and center of one side of the capital.[1]

The harmonious dimensions, refined decoration, carving technique and style, and content and placement of the inscription indicate that the capital was most likely made in the royal workshops for Madinat al-Zahra.[2] This palatial city was begun by the Umayyad caliph ʿAbd al-Rahman III (r. 912–61) in 936 on the outskirts of Cordoba and continued by his son and heir, al-Hakam II (r. 961–76). The palaces of Madinat al-Zahra, their reception halls lavishly adorned with carved and painted stone capitals, arcades, and wall panels—all set within verdant gardens, open courtyards, and reflecting pools—are a testament to the wealth, power, and artistic accomplishments of the Umayyad caliphs at the height of their rule. OB

1. The inscription could be interpreted as عمل خبرة (made by Khabara), although other readings of the name are possible. Many craftsmen in the royal workshop during the Umayyad caliphate are known by their names, which they inscribed on architectural elements in the royal constructions. For identification of craftsmen who worked on one of the reception halls of Madinat al-Zahra, see Martínez Núñez 1995.
2. Similar capitals are extant in situ in one of the reception halls at Madinat al-Zahra, as well as in the museum on site. See Cressier 1995. Among the examples closest to this capital stylistically are those in the Museo Arqueológico Provincial, Cordoba (no. 28.609), and in the Dar al-Athar al-Islamiyya, al-Sabah Collection, Kuwait City (no. LNS 1 S).

Provenance: Theodore M. Davis, New York (until d. 1915); on loan from his estate during settlement of estate (1915–30)

41. Panel

Morocco, 14th century
Wood (cedar); carved and painted
19 in. × 10 ft. 1 in. × 2¾ in. (48.3 × 307.3 × 7 cm)
Mr. and Mrs. Isaac D. Fletcher Collection,
Bequest of Isaac D. Fletcher and Rogers Fund, by exchange, 1985 1985.241

Inscription in Arabic in cursive script is written nine times, four of which appear in mirror image:
يمن
Good luck

This monumental wood panel embellished with carved decoration served as an architectural element. Such carved-wood panels, along with carved and molded stucco on the upper walls and dadoes of ceramic-tile mosaic on the lower ones, formed the rich architectural decoration of the buildings erected in Morocco during the Marinid period. For instance, the interior courtyards of two *madrasas* in Fez, Bu ʿInaniyya and al-ʿAttarin, are embellished with similar carved-wood panels, which are placed above an

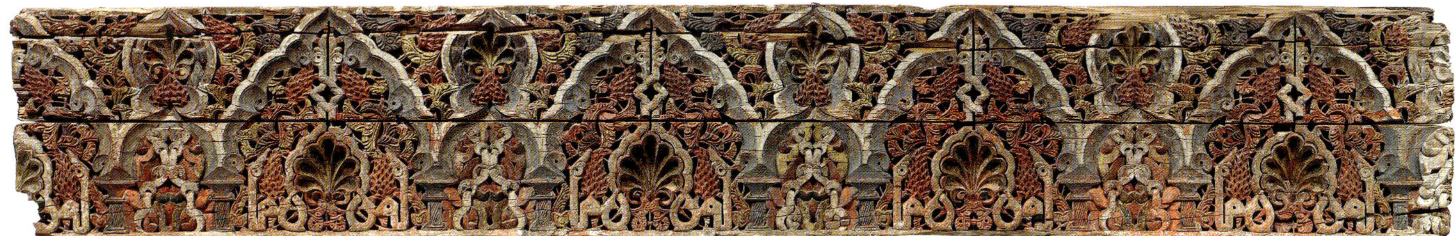

inscribed wooden lintel that spans the openings of the ground arcade. The dadoes of ceramic-tile mosaic and panels of carved and molded stucco complete the architectural decoration of the space.

Assembled from two long boards, the present panel retains multiple layers of polychromy. Its carved decoration is composed of an arcade of tall cusped arches, each of which encloses under its apex a seven-lobed scallop-shell motif flanked by an inscription that reads "good luck." The interstices of the large arches are filled with a smaller, five-lobed shell motif similar to the element under the cusped arcade. The background of the panel is carved with densely packed, varied vegetal decoration that includes pinecones, split palmettes, and other foliate motifs.

The architectural and decorative forms and materials prevalent during the Marinid period exhibit clear affinities with the architecture and arts of the Nasrid dynasty of Iberia and reflect the contribution of craftsmen who emigrated to Morocco under the advancing reconquest of the peninsula by Christian monarchs.

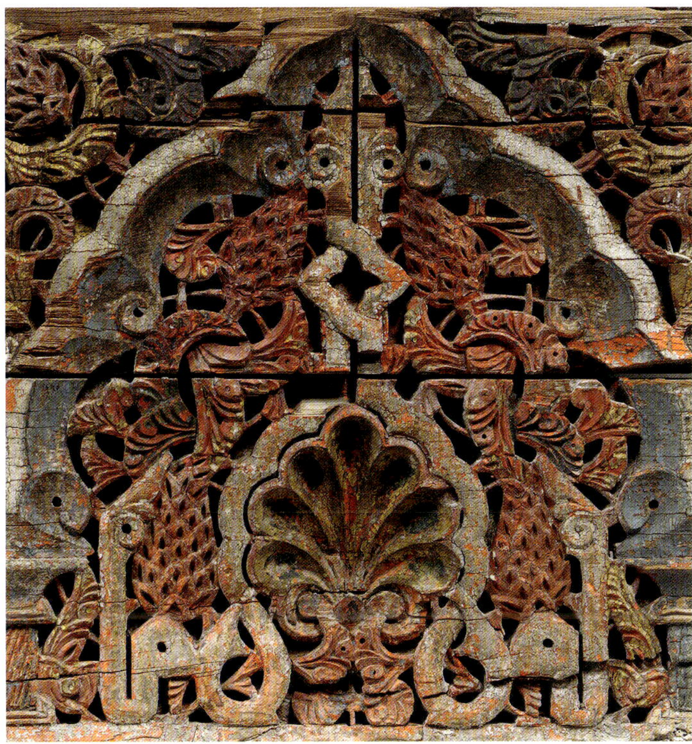

Much of the currently visible polychrome surface decoration of this panel made of cedar (*cedrus* spp.)—red, yellow, blue, green, white, and black paints bound in a protein-based medium, probably animal glue—actually represents a later painting campaign. The pigments in these layers include orpiment, red lead, vermilion, white lead, and indigo, all traditional pigments that do not allow for any specific dating of this campaign. Areas of the earlier, original painted surface are also visible within losses to the later layers. The original surface decoration began with overall preparatory layers of red lead or orpiment applied beneath the arches and in the spandrels, respectively. Though the complete original decoration scheme is as yet unclear, some well-preserved areas show bright red and blue backgrounds embellished with dots and outlines in black and white. In the spandrels, the original surface of certain areas is composed of an orange-pigmented glaze applied over the yellow preparation layer, which resulted in a deep yellow-orange color. The binding medium in the original red-lead paint layer was identified as egg tempera.[1]

The two long, parallel cedar boards of which the panel is constructed were originally connected to each other with five hand-wrought iron spikes that were tapered at both ends; two of the spikes are now broken, with half of each missing, indicating that the panels were detached at one time. Additional spikes along the top and bottom edges, as well as empty holes in the same areas, demonstrate that similar hardware was used to attach the panel to adjacent architectural elements. At the top, these iron spikes almost certainly held a narrow carved and painted floral border, as seen in a matching panel in the al-Sabah Collection.[2] The remains of both a tenon and a mortise on the proper right end indicate the original joinery with the architectural woodwork. OB/BE/KrW

1. Pigments and media analyses were carried out in the Metropolitan Museum's Department of Scientific Research by scientists Adriana Rizzo, Mark T. Wypyski, and Tony Frantz. Egg tempera was identified by Daniel P. Kirby at the Straus Center for Conservation, Harvard Art Museums, Harvard University, Cambridge, Massachusetts.
2. Dar al-Athar al-Islamiyya, al-Sabah Collection, Kuwait City, Kuwait (no. LNS 62W).

Provenance: [Spink & Son Ltd., London, by 1978–79; sold to Homaizi]; Jasim Homaizi, Kuwait (1979–85; to MMA by exchange)

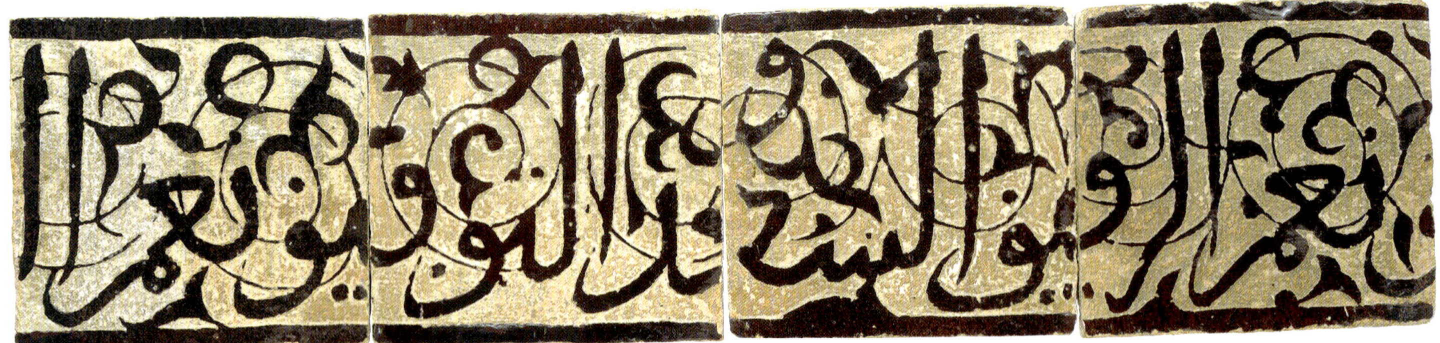

42. Panel of Four Calligraphic Tiles

Morocco, 14th–early 15th century
Stonepaste; glazed and carved
4⅞ × 22¼ in. (12.4 × 56.6 cm)
Purchase, Leon B. Polsky and Cynthia Hazen Polsky Gift, in honor of Patti Cadby Birch, 1999 1999.146

Inscription in Arabic in *thuluth* script:
نعم الرفيق السعد والتوفيق
What excellent companions are happiness and good fortune

Panels of ceramic tiles, embellished with inscriptions and employed as a frieze, formed an integral part of the architectural decoration of buildings in Morocco from the fourteenth century onward. Placed on the walls slightly below eye level and thus accessible for reading, these friezes were combined with mosaic, stucco, and carved-wood panels to create colorful, textured surfaces of interior rooms and courtyards alike. Bu 'Inaniyya and al-'Attarin, two *madrasas*, or religious schools, constructed in Fez under royal patronage in 1323–25 and 1350–55, respectively, are the most representative examples of fourteenth-century Marinid architecture. Architectural and decorative forms of this period were inspired by the arts and architecture of the Nasrid dynasty of Spain, as exemplified by the palaces of the Alhambra in Granada. Close political and cultural ties between the dynasties facilitated the transmission of artistic ideas when builders and craftsmen from Muslim Iberia emigrated to Morocco as the reconquest of the peninsula progressed under the Christian kings.

Composed of four rectangular ceramic tiles, the present panel is decorated in the intaglio technique, called *zilij* in Morocco, in which the entire surface is covered with a purplish black glaze and then carved away to leave the inscription and the foliate scroll of the background in relief. The auspicious content of the repeated phrase in the inscription suggests that the panel was originally part of a frieze of much greater length that was used to decorate a secular building.[1] Completing the decorative composition are a delicate spiraling scroll with foliate motifs and a border that frames the inscription at the top and bottom. OB

1. Carboni 2000.

PROVENANCE: [Spink & Son Ltd., London, until 1999; sold to MMA]

43A, B. Two Star-Shaped Tiles

A. Spain, probably Malaga, first half of 15th century
Earthenware; luster-painted on opaque white glaze
W. 9¼ in. (23.5 cm)
H. O. Havemeyer Collection, Gift of H. O. Havemeyer, 1941 41.165.40

Inscription in Arabic in *naskhi* script on lower border:
[. . .]ولاول [*sic*] [والاول؟] ان كان الغرض منه الاحتراز عن الخطأ في تأدية الفن المراد فهو
الفن الاول و إلا فهو مايع فيـه وجوه التحسين و هو الفن الثالث و عليه ميغ ظاهر يدمع بالكـ
. . . بعد ما اعرق و قيل رتبه على مقـ[ـاطع][. . .]
[. . .] and first is the intention to avoid making mistakes and that is the highest art; if not, there is a liquid for correcting [mistakes] that is the third art . . . it creates a cloudy film [that once applied] runs down like tears [. . .]

B. Spain, probably Malaga, first half of 15th century
Earthenware; luster-painted on opaque white glaze
W. 9¾ in. (24.8 cm)
H. O. Havemeyer Collection, Gift of H. O. Havemeyer, 1941 41.165.41

Malaga, on the southern coast of Spain, was one of the principal manufacturing centers of lusterware in the Nasrid kingdom.[1] These two eight-pointed star-shaped tiles featuring copper-toned luster-painted designs were probably produced there. One tile (cat. 43A) bears a pattern of serrated leaves and flowers and an Arabic inscription on its lower border, while the other (cat. 43B) is covered in fruit-bearing scrolling vines that radiate out from a central floral medallion.

Though the use of luster tiling was not unusual in the decoration of Nasrid architecture, few eight-pointed star-shaped luster tiles survive. The scrolling-vine-and-branch and the radiating floral motifs seen here belong to the artistic vocabulary of the period. It has been suggested that tiles of this type once covered the walls of Granadine palaces such as the Alixares and the Alhambra.[2] Two other examples resembling our tiles in technique and ornamentation are a contemporary Malagan tile in the collection of the Musée des Arts Décoratifs, Paris,[3] and the famed "Fortuny" plaque in the Instituto de Valencia de Don Juan, Madrid.[4] The Paris tile, dated to the early fifteenth century, bears a grapevine with naturalistic leaves and bunches of fruit framed within an eight-pointed star; the foliage outside the frame is typical of that seen on Malagan lusterware. The large plaque that once belonged to the artist Fortuny is among the luster-painted grave markers that have been instrumental in dating tiles of this period. Its long inscription includes a dedication to the Nasrid sultan of Granada Yusuf III (r. 1408–17). Another luster-painted grave marker, from Huelva, with similar vegetal decoration is dated A.H. Du'l Qa'da 811/ March 1409 A.D.[5]

The charming lightness and freedom of execution of the scrolling vines and naturalistic plant forms on these two tiles recall contemporary Gothic manuscript illumination in Spain. These vegetal designs may, however, present an even closer affinity with the fourteenth-century tilework of the Hall of the Ambassadors in the Seville Alcazar, which was produced by Christian craftsmen from the eastern coast of the Iberian Peninsula working for King Pedro I of Castile and Leon (r. 1350–69). Such itinerant craftsmen may have actually been responsible for the Gothic designs seen in numerous pieces of lusterware from the late fourteenth and the fifteenth century.[6]

Although previously the subject of much discussion, the impetus for the arrival of the luster-painting technique in Islamic Spain is now thought to have most likely come from the Egyptian Fatimid craftsmen who moved to the Malagan coast after the fall of the Fatimid Empire in 1171.[7] By the time the Nasrids came to power in 1232, a rich repertoire of designs from North Africa and the Western Islamic world had permeated Andalusian arts.

The inscription on the lower border of one of these tiles (cat. 43A) is especially unusual. Though sections of the writing are no longer decipherable, what remains is an Arabic text enumerating the skills required by the ceramic artist to glaze and decorate luster tiles. Such references, which are virtually unknown in Andalusian art, offer insight into the technique of luster tile making in Nasrid Spain. ME/RV

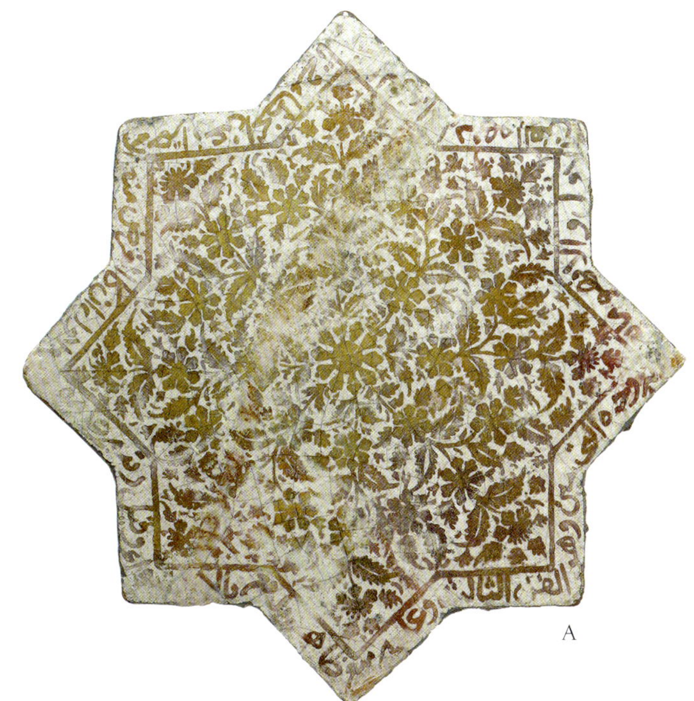

A

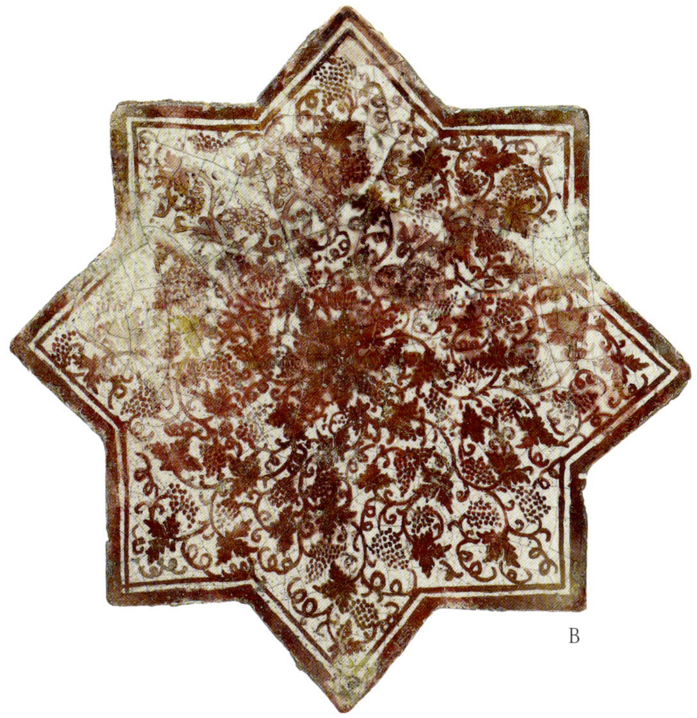

B

1. Scholars have also suggested that Granada may have been a major center of luster ceramic production, but little documentary or literary evidence supporting this theory has come to light. See Frothingham 1951, pp. 21–27.
2. Ibid., p. 66.
3. See Degeorge and Porter 2002, p. 64.
4. See Granada and New York 1992, pp. 360–61, no. 113.
5. Ibid., p. 72.
6. Ibid., p.73.
7. Frothingham suggested that the luster technique arrived in Spain as the result of Persian craftsmen's having fled the Mongol invasions of the early thirteenth century. Sheila Blair and Jonathan Bloom, however, argued that differences in the composition of Andalusian and Iranian wares preclude such a theory. See Frothingham 1951, pp. 21–27; Rosser-Owen 2010, pp. 66–70; and Blair and Bloom 1995, pp. 129–31.

PROVENANCE: H. O. Havemeyer Collection, New York (until 1941)

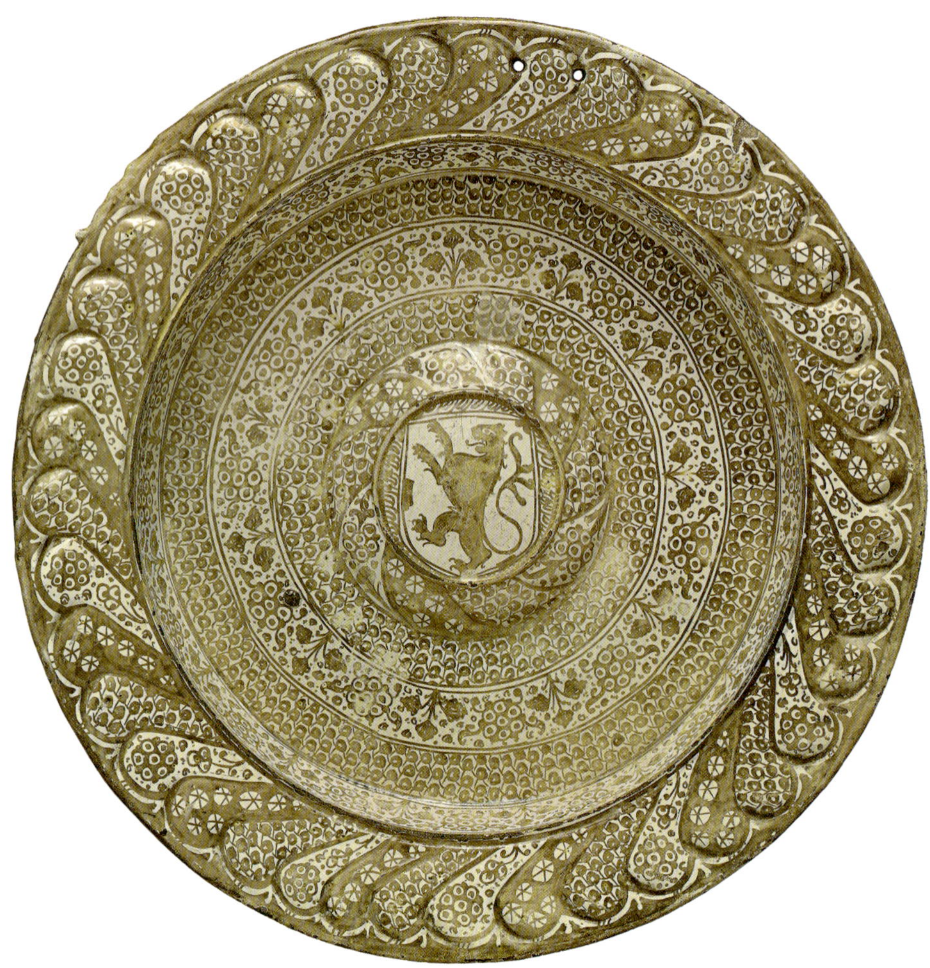

44. Dish (Brasero)

Spain, Manises (Valencia), late 15th–early 16th century
Earthenware; molded and luster-painted on opaque white glaze
Diam. 18 1/4 in. (46.4 cm)
Edward C. Moore Collection, Bequest of Edward C. Moore, 1891 91.1.427a

At the center of this luster-painted *brasero*, or deep bowl, is a rampant lion in a heraldic shield, surrounded in the cavetto by concentric bands with alternating designs of fish-scale and floral motifs. The same designs alternate on the slanted, wheel-like gadroons molded in relief that cover the broad, everted rim.

The *brasero* is representative of ceramic wares produced in Manises, Valencia, in the final decades of the fifteenth century. Many luster-painted *braseros* of this period contain heraldic blazons of rampant lions. Yet in most cases the patron is unknown, since by that time such blazons were frequently used as decorative emblems of prestige and luxury rather than as identifiers. Since the lion here has been removed from the context of a coat of arms, it cannot be connected with a particular family.

The rampant lion and decorative program on this *brasero* are reminiscent of those found on the Coello Plate (ca. 1480–99) in the collection of the Hispanic Society of America, New York, which bears a leonine coat of arms as well as nearly identical designs of gadroons, fish scales, and floral patterns.[1] As one of the earliest examples of so-called gadrooned ware, the Coello Plate has helped to establish the last quarter of the fifteenth century as the earliest use of this decorative device.[2] Several other Valencian luster ceramics dating from the fifteenth century onward—in the Metropolitan Museum, the Hispanic Society of America, and elsewhere—show the repeated use of the designs found on this *brasero* and the Coello Plate.

The technique of luster-painting was probably first brought to Malaga and Murcia in southern Spain by Fatimid potters from Egypt in the late twelfth century.[3] It is believed that the technique made its way to Manises in the early fourteenth century.[4] The appearance of the heraldic device on so many examples affirms that luster-painted ceramics were regarded as precious luxury objects by the Valencian nobility in the fourteenth and fifteenth centuries and that they were highly coveted in, and exported to, places as far away as Egypt, Algeria, and Sicily.[5] PC

1. Heather Ecker in Washington, D.C. 2004, no. 77. The Coello Plate bears the coat of arms of Joan Payo Coello, a member of a noble Portuguese family and abbot of Poblet.
2. Ibid.
3. Lane 1946, p. 252; Rosser-Owen 2010, pp. 66–67.
4. Rosser-Owen 2010, pp. 66–67.
5. Frothingham 1951, p. xlviii. See also Rosser-Owen 2010 and Washington, D.C., and other cities 2004–6, pp. 120–21.

PROVENANCE: Edward C. Moore, New York (until d. 1891)

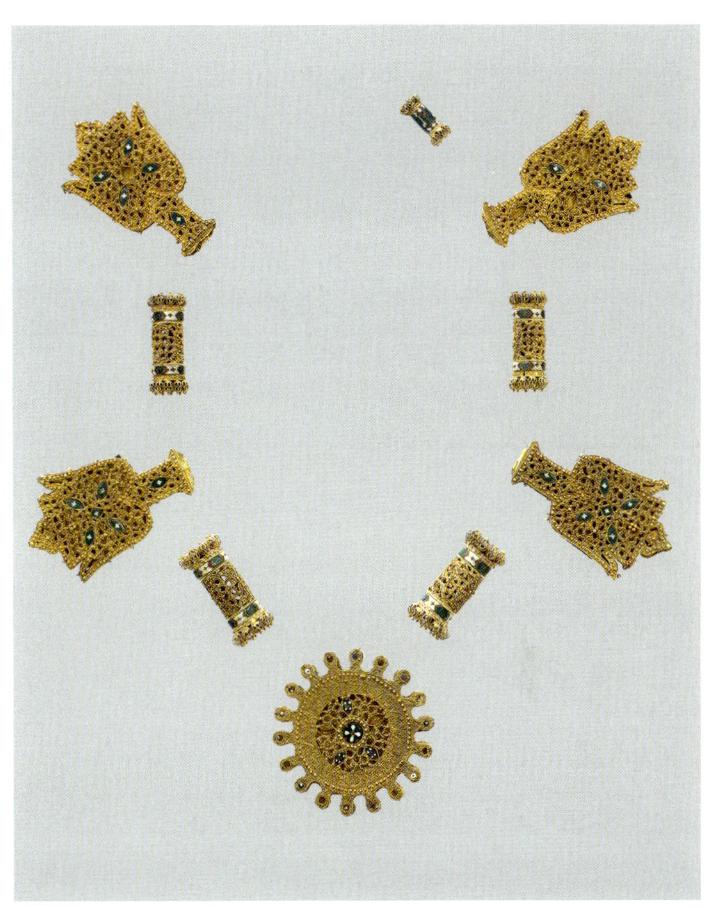

45. *Necklace Elements*

Spain, probably 15th century
Gold; cloisonné enamel; filigree; granulation
Circular pendant: Diam. 3 in. (7.6 cm)
Pendants: L. 3 1/4 in. (8.3 cm)
Beads: L. 2 in. (5.1 cm); 1 1/2 in. (3.8 cm); 1 in. (2.5 cm)
Gift of J. Pierpont Morgan, 1917 17.190.161

Inscription in Latin on circular pendant:
AVE MARIA GRACIA PLEN[A]
Hail Mary, full of grace

A large circular pendant, four pendants in the shape of stylized palmettes, and five cylindrical beads of three different sizes most probably formed the main elements of an elaborate necklace made during the late Nasrid period in al-Andalus. The richness of their delicate, colorful surfaces is achieved through a combination of goldsmithing techniques. Gold sheet is pierced to create the openwork of the overall background pattern, while the band framing the pendants is executed in repoussé. The surfaces are elaborated in filigree and in cloisonné techniques; in the latter, cells formed by soldered wire are filled with colored enamels. Green, white, and dark red enamels accentuate the floral motifs in the center of the pendants, and the cylindrical beads are embellished with a colored enamel band at each end, crowned by a row of hollow filigree spheres. Tiny clusters of gold balls produced by granulation technique add texture throughout. The small loops around the perimeter of the palmettes originally held wire on which pearls or stones would have been strung. In contrast, the circumference of the circular pendant was finished with circular finials decorated with enamel that is now mostly lost.

The combination of various goldsmithing techniques is characteristic of medieval jewelry making from western Europe to China.[1] The present necklace elements display strong affinities to the jewelry made under the Fatimid dynasty.[2] Stylistically, both the cylindrical beads and the four palmette-shaped pendants can be related to Nasrid necklace elements found in Bentarique (Almeria, Spain);[3] the circular pendant can be associated with two other examples.[4]

An inscription on the circular pendant speaks to the complexities of the culture of al-Andalus. The broad band around the central rosette contains the opening words of the "Hail Mary"[5] in large letters outlined by a granulated border, and the phrase is preceded by a cross executed in repoussé. This inscription, often found on other portable objects from the early sixteenth century onward,[6] indicates that the necklace was made for a Christian patron and thus that aesthetic values were shared across religious boundaries. OB

1. The dissemination of artistic styles and techniques, especially during the medieval period, is ubiquitously attributed to the portability of objects. Precious materials, elaborate techniques, and complex decorative compositions—as carriers of aesthetic and social meaning—contribute to the desirability of luxury objects and their adaptation by other cultures.

2. New York 1983, pp. 92–93.
3. Juan Zozaya pointed out that the pendants from the Bentarique hoard (Museo Arqueológico Nacional, Madrid) have a curvilinear profile resembling that of their Ilkhanid prototypes; see Zozaya in Granada and New York 1992, pp. 302–3, no. 73. The pendants from Bentarique further support Jenkins's proposition that Ilkhanid stylistic features were transmitted to Mamluk jewelry, which in turn was adapted by jewelers in al-Andalus during the Nasrid period; see Jenkins 1988, p. 37.
4. Museum für Islamische Kunst, Staatliche Museen zu Berlin (no. I. 4940); Benaki Museum, Athens (no. 1856).
5. It should be noted that the cartouches in the bands of the cylindrical beads are embellished with a detail, executed in gold wire of cloisonné technique, that may be a poorly executed inscription of the word *Allah*.
6. Zozaya in Granada and New York 1992, p. 302, no. 73.

PROVENANCE: J. Pierpont Morgan, New York (until 1917)

46A–C. Textile Fragments: Vestments of Saint Valerius

Spain, 13th century

A. Fragment of a Dalmatic with Tapestry
Silk, gilt animal substrate around a silk core; tapestry weave
3⅛ × 8¼ in. (8 cm × 21 cm)
Fletcher Fund, 1946 46.156.10

Inscription in Arabic in *naskhi* script, repeated twice:
اليمن والعز والرفعة والعظمة
Good luck and glory and exaltedness and magnificence

B. Fragment of a Dalmatic
Silk, gilt animal substrate around a silk core; lampas with separable layers in the ground weave
3 × 4¾ in. (7.6 × 12.1 cm)
Fletcher Fund, 1946 46.156.4

C. Fragment of a Chasuble
Silk, gilt animal substrate around a silk core; *taqueté*
6 × 5¼ in. (15.2 × 13.3 cm)
Fletcher Fund, 1946 46.156.3

These fragments belong to a once-complete set of liturgical vestments that consisted of a chasuble, two dalmatics, and a pluvial cope.[1] Fashioned in the thirteenth century at the Cathedral of Roda de Isabena (Huesca), the vestments have been attributed to the cult of Saint Valerius, bishop of Saragossa, Spain, from 290 until his death in 315 under the Roman emperor Diocletian. They were made to venerate the saint's relics and were especially prominent in celebrations of his feast day.[2]

In the eleventh century Saint Valerius's relics were translated to the Church of San Vicente in Roda, and some relics were later sent from there to other churches.[3] It is uncertain when the vestments themselves were brought to the cathedral of Lerida, where they remained until 1922. However, a document from the cathedral chapter dated 1498 states that the chapter intended to repair the garments.[4] As a result of alterations undertaken at various times from that date to 1851, none of the vestments, now housed in the Museu Tèxtil i d'Indumentària in Barcelona, is in its original state.[5] Many fragments cut from these vestments are preserved in various museums in the United States and Europe, and most of them have been published.

All three fragments shown here, with their patterns of small-scale motifs, are characteristic of the thirteenth-century luxury

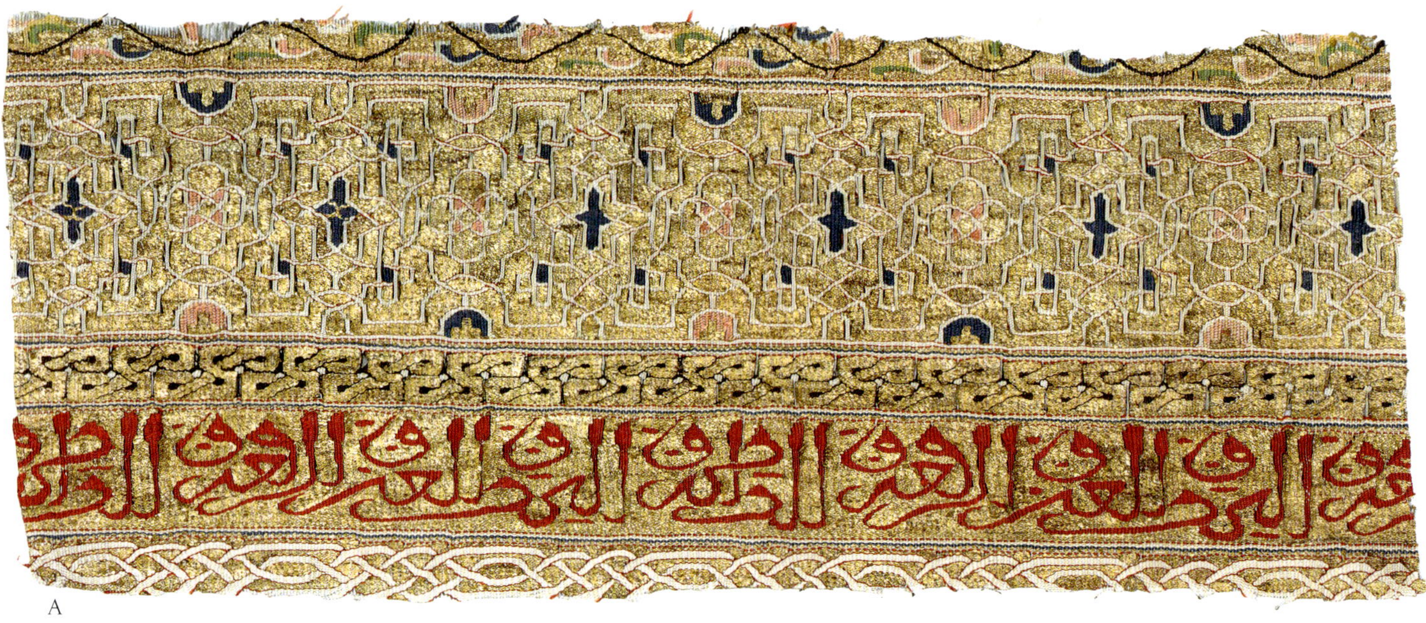
A

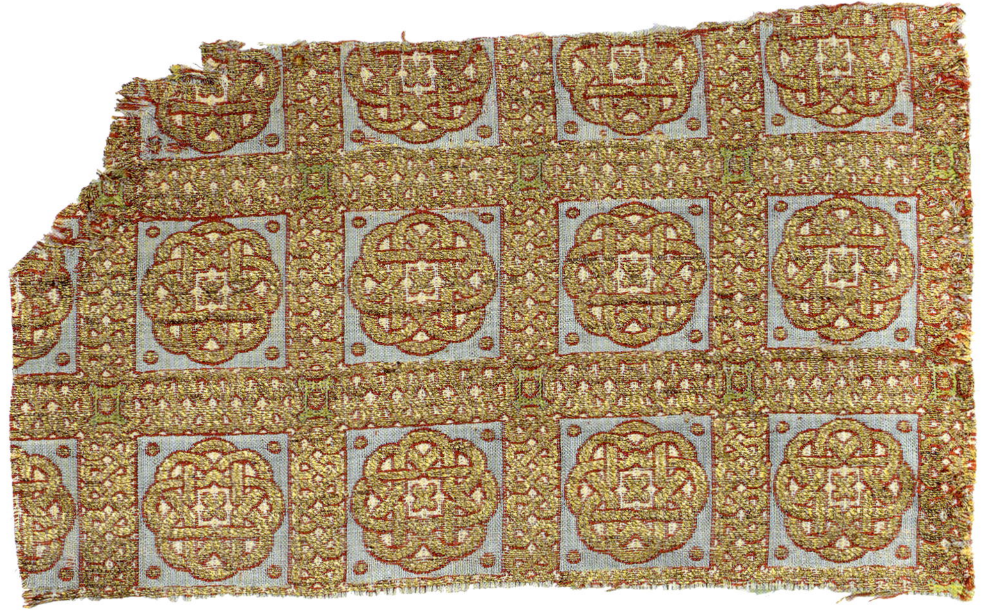

B

silk textiles woven in al-Andalus. In the tapestry-woven fragment of the dalmatic (cat. 46A), the delicate geometric interlace is created by fine lines of white silk. The simple, minute secondary motifs—executed in brilliant blue, green, and pink threads and embedded in the interstices of the interlace against the shimmering gold brocade—recall the jewel-encrusted surfaces of goldwork. An epigraphic band in vivid red against the gold ground repeats an auspicious phrase.

The decoration of the second fragment of the dalmatic (cat. 46B) consists of a square grid formed by an interlace of gold brocade on a light blue background. Each square of the grid contains a small rosette of gold interlace in the center and minute gold dots in the corners. Bright red silk outlines all the elements. The fragment of the chasuble (cat. 46C) is decorated with alternating rows of eight-pointed stars and crosses. The stars contain a pair of addorsed rampant lions, while the crosses are filled with profuse foliate motifs. All the decorative elements are executed in gold brocade on a dark blue ground, with pink employed as an outlining device.

On the Iberian Peninsula, opulent silk textiles lavishly embellished with gold brocade were eagerly sought after by Muslims, Christians, and Jews alike as signs of wealth, power, and aesthetic sophistication. Fashioned into sumptuous dress for court ceremonials, they were also used in religious rituals, although sometimes they had originally been made for different purposes. Textiles produced in al-Andalus during the thirteenth century are known today largely from their discovery in the tombs of Christian kings, nobles, and churchmen, where they were found as mortuary vestments and as coffin linings.[6]

OB

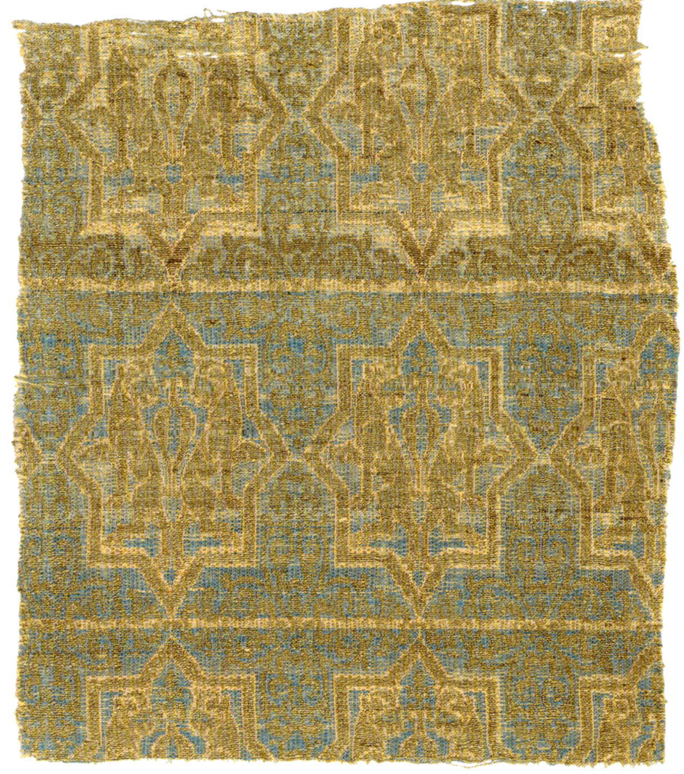

C

1. For technical analysis of the weaving structures of the vestment fragments preserved in the Instituto de Valencia de Don Juan, Madrid, see Borrego Díaz 2005, pp. 102–5 and 111–15.
2. Partearroyo Lacaba 2005, p. 58.
3. May 1957, p. 75.
4. While Partearroyo Lacaba suggests that the vestments were brought to Lerida in the fifteenth century for repair, Rosa M. Martín i Ros cites a

document indicating that they might have been brought there not long after 1275. See Martin i Ros in Granada and New York 1992, p. 332, no. 95.

5. May 1957, p. 75, and Martin i Ros in Granada and New York 1992, pp. 332–33, no. 95. It should be noted that fragments from the chasuble were reused for the sleeves in one of the dalmatics. Another group of small fragments, all from the pluvial cope of Saint Valerius, is also extant in the collection of the Metropolitan Museum (acc. nos. 46.156.2 and 27.52).
6. In her discussion of the use of luxury textiles on the Iberian Peninsula during the twelfth and thirteenth centuries, María Judith Feliciano argued persuasively for the shared aesthetics of the Muslim and Christian elite. Instead of ascribing a textile to a ruling Muslim dynasty, she proposed that much can be gained from denoting it as "Andalusi," which would take into account a much broader view and reflect the actual practices of Iberian society. See Feliciano 2005.

Provenance

Cat. 46a: [Giorgio Sangiorgi, Rome, by 1920–46; to Loewi]; [Adolph Loewi, Venice and Los Angeles, 1946; sold to MMA]

Cat. 46b: [Giorgio Sangiorgi, Rome, until 1946; to Loewi]; [Adolph Loewi, Venice and Los Angeles, 1946; sold to MMA]

Cat. 46c: [Giorgio Sangiorgi, Rome, by 1920–46; to Loewi]; [Adolph Loewi, Venice and Los Angeles, 1946; sold to MMA]

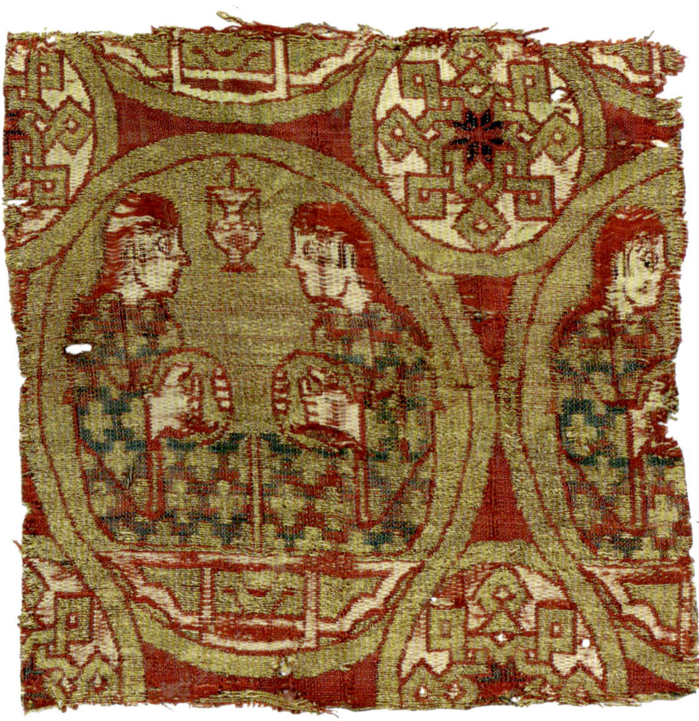

47. Textile Fragment

Spain, 13th century
Silk; gilt animal substrate around a silk core; lampas
4 × 4¼ in. (10.3 × 10.8 cm)
Rogers Fund, 1928 28.194

Esteemed for their expensive materials, refined design, and craftsmanship, luxury textiles manufactured in al-Andalus were admired and coveted by rulers, nobles, and ecclesiastics alike.[1] They were considered among the most valuable commodities in the medieval economy, were collected in royal treasuries, and often served as ambassadorial gifts. In addition, elaborate, if somewhat less opulent, textiles appeared in more modest settings, for example, as part of a bridal trousseau or as valued items in a family inheritance. Silk textiles produced in Muslim royal workshops (*tiraz*) were found in Christian lands in medieval Iberia, whether created for Christian patrons or cut and refashioned for entirely new uses. By one means or another, these textiles were often employed in ecclesiastic vestments or church furnishings, such as altar cloths and reliquary linings. As a result, many examples have been preserved in church treasuries.[2]

This silk fragment embellished with gold brocade is decorated with a row of large roundels enclosing two seated female musicians.[3] Dressed in robes of patterned design, the figures are depicted playing tambourines. The lamp hanging between the figures suggests a luxurious interior setting. These roundels are interlaced with a row of smaller ones containing stars. A rich, shimmering effect is produced by the juxtaposition of the vivid reds and the lavish gold brocading. The circular shapes of the roundels and the gold brocade used for the interlace and stars are characteristic of the luxury silks of the thirteenth century.[4] This fragment along with fourteen others (some cut in a circular shape to fit under the metal bosses of choir books) belonged originally to the same textile. The fragments were discovered between the pages of a thirteenth-century manuscript in the cathedral of Vich in Spain.[5]

OB

1. María Judith Feliciano provided a cogent argument for an aesthetic shared by Muslim and Christian elites in medieval Iberia and so proposed the designation "Andalusi" in place of the prior scholarly practice of ascribing a given textile to a particular ruling Muslim dynasty. The new designation allowed her to take into account a more complex—and a more convincing—view of medieval Iberian society. See Feliciano 2005.
2. Sustained research on this topic was first conducted and published in May 1957.
3. May examined fragments with similar designs, which she dated to the fourteenth century; see ibid., pp. 134–41.
4. Cristina Partearroyo Lacaba in Madrid 2005, p. 248.
5. May 1957, p. 139. Most of these fragments are now in the Archivo Episcopal of the cathedral of Vich; see Partearroyo Lacaba in Madrid 2005, p. 249. For technical analysis of the weaving structure of the fragment preserved in the Instituto de Valencia de Don Juan, Madrid, see Borrego Díaz 2005, pp. 107–8.

Provenance: H. A. Elsberg, New York (until 1928; sold to MMA)

48. Textile Fragment

Spain, 14th century
Silk; lampas
40 1/8 × 14 3/4 in. (102 × 36.3 cm)
Fletcher Fund, 1929 29.22

Inscription in Arabic in *kufic* script, written twice
on a band (once in mirror image):
الغبطة
Felicity

Second Arabic inscription in *naskhi* script in cartouches:
واليمن والإقبال
Good luck and prosperity

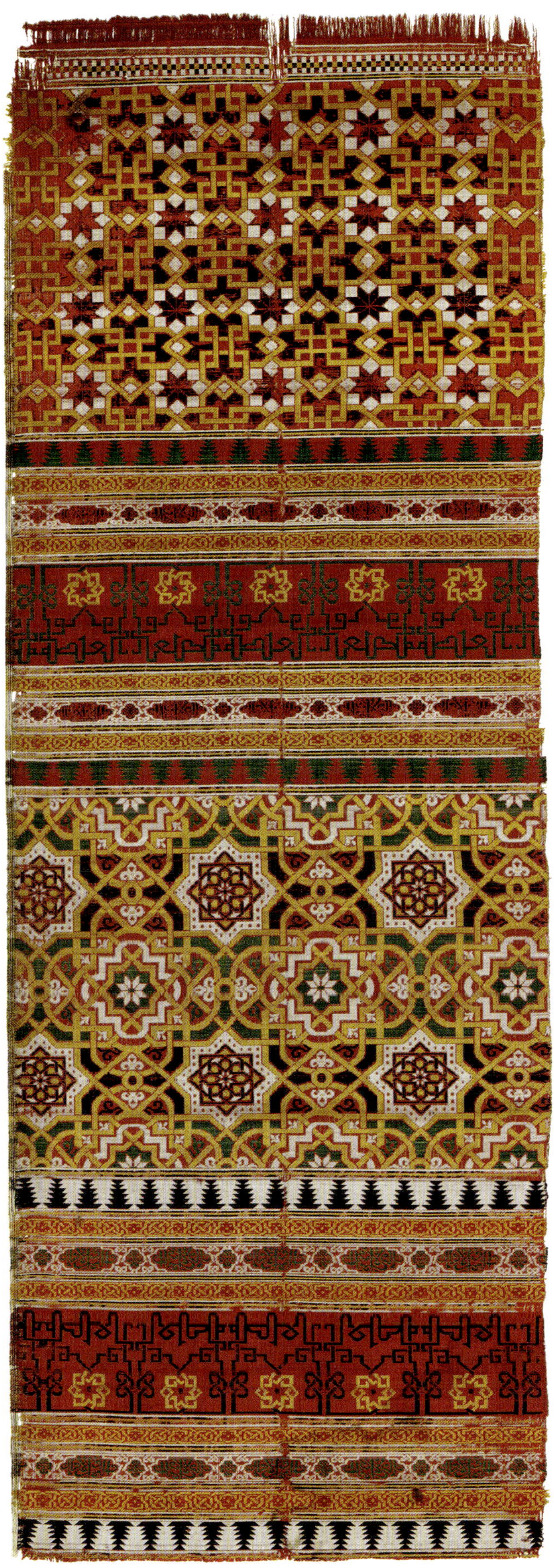

The royal textile factories of al-Andalus were famous throughout the medieval world in a period when luxury textiles constituted one of the most valuable possessions in a ruler's treasury as well as in the trousseaux of wealthy brides.[1] Wall hangings, curtains, mattresses, cushions, and pillows made from silk and embellished with gold and silver brocade were assembled in the halls and open courtyards of well-to-do homes and palaces. Medieval textual sources give evidence of these abundant textile furnishings and of the political, economic, and aesthetic meanings that they conveyed in court ceremonials.[2]

This silk fragment woven in bright colors and richly decorated with geometric and epigraphic motifs could have been made for such a ceremonial purpose. The large dimensions of the fragment, with the selvage preserved on one side and the fringe on the bottom, suggest that it would have served as a furnishing, not a garment. This supposition is supported by the size of many similar extant fragments, none of them complete, but many of nearly identical dimensions.

The design of this textile is composed of broad and narrow bands. The two widest contain a geometric interlace based on eight-pointed radiating stars, while other, narrower bands are embellished with a repeated, knotted *kufic* inscription and small cartouches with a phrase in cursive *naskhi* script. Additional bands with merlons and small-scale interlace motifs complete the composition. The similarity in design of the upper interlace band to carved-stucco panels in the Alhambra, the palaces of the Nasrid dynasty in Granada, and of the lower interlace band to dadoes of ceramic-tile mosaics on the Alhambra's walls, has led scholars to conclude that this and similar textiles belong to the milieu of the Nasrid court at the height of its artistic production.[3] OB

1. Although little textual evidence is available with regard to the employment of textile furnishings in the ruling courts of al-Andalus, and at the Nasrid court in particular, more is known with respect to other medieval Muslim dynasties. For instance, the Fatimid dynasty, centered in Egypt, had stores for upholstery and furnishings in its treasury with an inventory of thousands of textiles. On the Fatimid treasury, see al-Qaddumi, ed. 1996, p. 237; and Serjeant 1972, pp. 157–60. On the

significance of textiles in the households of the medieval elite during the Fatimid period, see Goitein 1983a, pp. 328–31.

2. Among the most famed accounts is one concerning the reception of the Byzantine ambassadors at the Abbasid court in Baghdad in 917, when sixty thousand textiles were employed to adorn numerous palaces of the caliph. For the description of this reception, see al-Qaddumi, ed. 1996, pp. 148–50.

3. May 1957, pp. 118–70; Shepherd 1943, p. 389; Fernández-Puertas 1973; Wardwell 1983; Partearroyo Lacaba 1995; and Cristina Partearroyo Lacaba in Granada and New York 1992, p. 335, no. 97.

PROVENANCE: [Adolph Loewi, Venice, until 1929; sold to MMA]

49. Textile Fragment

Spain, late 14th–early 15th century
Silk; lampas
10⅝ × 21¼ in. (27 × 54 cm)
Rogers Fund, 1918 18.31

Inscription in Arabic in *thuluth* script on central band, repeated:
[السـ]ـطان عز لمولانا السلطان عز لمولانا الـ[ـسلطان]
Glory to our lord the Sultan

This textile fragment woven in vibrantly colored silk is organized in bands. Its main decorative motif is a phrase in Arabic inscribed in cursive *thuluth* script of Andalusian form on the widest, central band.[1] The laudatory inscription, repeated within the band throughout the width of the cloth, is executed in yellow thread against the red background; the finials of the letters and the spaces between them are embellished with foliate elements. Palmettes, split palmettes, and other foliations repeated in the manner of a frieze in the narrower bands echo the foliate elements in the inscribed band. Yet they also contrast effectively with that central band through the use of bright colors: yellow, cream, and red on a blue ground. The design is completed by a very narrow band with an interlace motif executed in cream color on a darker ground of the same hue.

The phrase glorifying the sultan was often employed in the embellishment of the arts and architecture of the Nasrid period, especially in the fourteenth and fifteenth centuries. Carved in wood and stucco in the decoration of the palaces in the Alhambra, the dynastic seat of the Nasrids in Granada, it also appeared on luxury objects, especially textiles. Silk textiles made in al-Andalus for sumptuous attire and costly furnishings were among the luxury commodities sought after by the Muslim and Christian elites on the Iberian Peninsula and far beyond its borders.

Many examples of Nasrid textiles inscribed with the same phrase as this example, and similar in decoration, survive today as

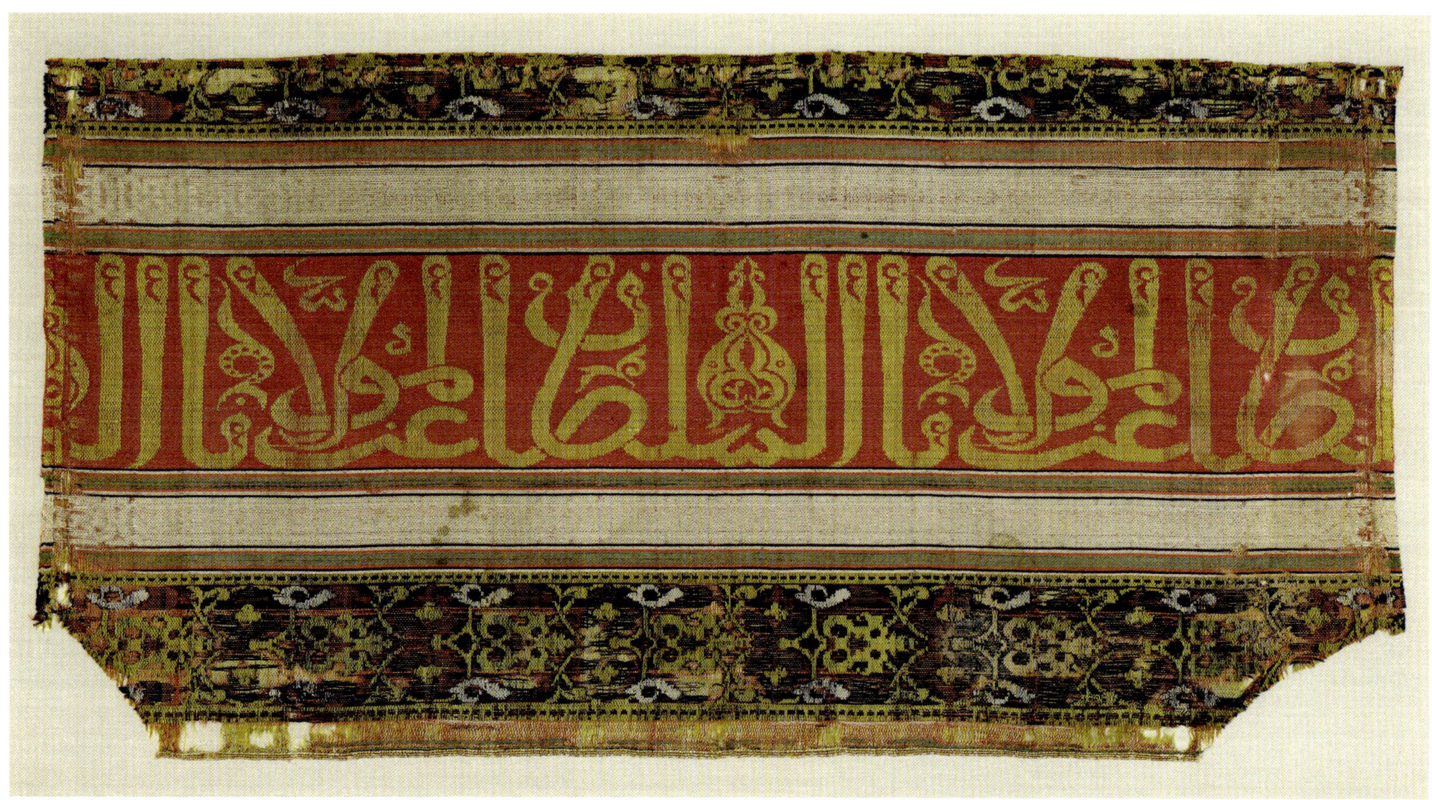

fragments. Their original function remains obscure, since they were cut and reused in later times. The most splendid of these fragments, which are housed today in various collections,[2] is a pluvial (ecclesiastic vestment) preserved in the treasury of the cathedral of Burgos in Spain. OB

1. One selvage on this fragment has been preserved.
2. Among the collections with similar fragments are the Victoria and Albert Museum, London; the Museo Lázaro Galdiano, Madrid; the Cooper-Hewitt, National Design Museum, New York; and the Museo Nazionale del Bargello, Florence. It has been proposed that an inscription on the second, additional band on a similar fragment in the Instituto de Valencia de Don Juan, Madrid, may refer to the sultan Muhammad V (r. 1354–59, 1362–91). The reference would give grounds for dating that fragment and the present one to the second half of the fourteenth century. See Partearroyo Lacaba 1995, p. 126. For technical analysis of the woven structure of the fragment preserved in the Instituto de Valencia de Don Juan, see Borrego Díaz 2005, pp. 118–19.

PROVENANCE: [Dikran G. Kelekian, New York, until 1918; sold to MMA]

50. *Hanging (Arid)*

Chefchaouen, Morocco, ca. 1800
Linen, silk; plain weave, embroidered
8 ft. 10½ in. × 31¾ in. (270.5 × 80.6 cm)
Purchase, Everfast Fabrics Inc. Gift, 1970 1970.272

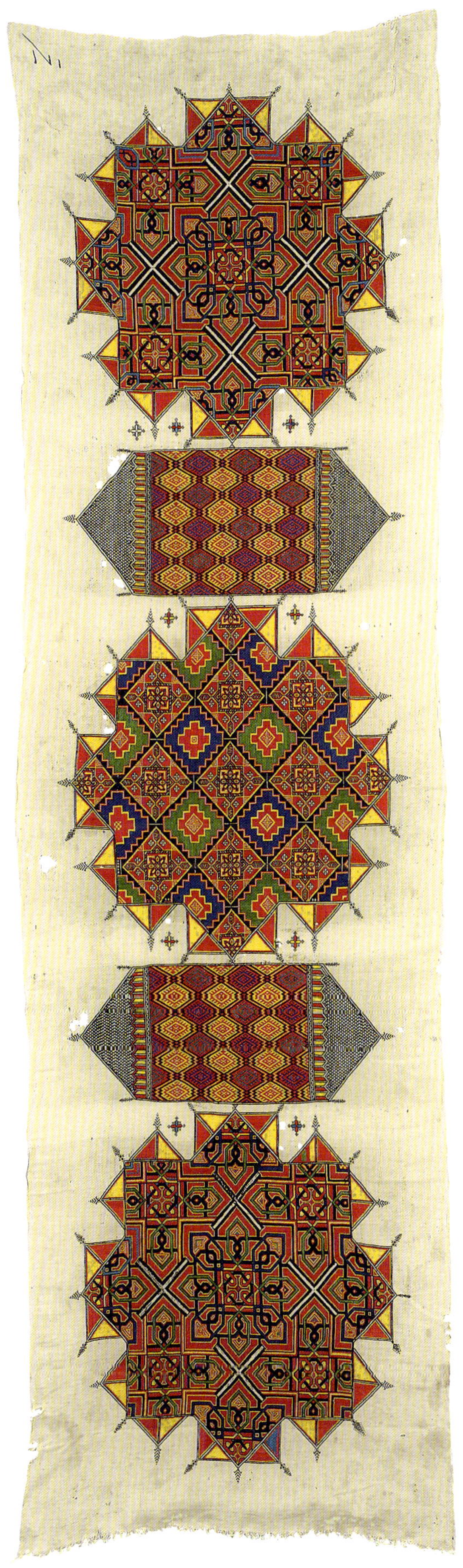

An example of North African embroidery traditionally associated with the cities of Chefchaouen and Tetouan, near the north coast of Morocco,[1] this textile is identified by its format and scale as an *arid*, or wall hanging. Such embroideries were created by women and, in their original contexts, likely decorated the home during ceremonial occasions and festivities.[2] Though it is unclear exactly where *arids* were displayed within the domestic interior, they were probably secured flat against a wall (rather than hanging loose) and could be arranged either vertically or horizontally.[3] Interestingly, this particular *arid* may have been repurposed for use as an altar curtain in a Nestorian church in Jerusalem.[4]

The work is executed in polychrome silk thread on white linen. In technique and general scale, it resembles a larger group of North Moroccan embroideries, but the latter works display different patterns and formats.[5] While the distinction is not often made between the type of embroidery represented by the present example and those of the larger group, the color palette and patterns of this *arid* place it in a subset of Chefchaouen embroidery of which only a few related examples exist.[6] The rarity of the type presents problems in dating: the only known examples belong to the eighteenth and nineteenth centuries, but it is likely that the type has a longer history.

As a group, the textiles in this subset exhibit an alternating cartouche-and-star pattern in a long, narrow format. The interiors of the cartouches and stars are filled with geometric patterns in bright shades of red, blue, green, and yellow. The repeating motifs inscribed within the larger stars and cartouches bear a resemblance to patterns seen in Andalusian tilework, woodcarving, and early textiles.[7] This stylistic relationship may be attributed in part to the settlement in the region of Spanish Muslims fleeing the *reconquista*.[8] The overall alternating cartouche-and-star pattern here has parallels in both Moroccan architectural decoration and woodwork, and the origins of the design may perhaps be found in these earlier artistic traditions.[9] Much remains to be learned about these remarkable embroideries, of which the Metropolitan's *arid* represents a rare type within the rich and varied North Moroccan textile tradition. ME/KW

1. The style originated in Chefchaouen but was eventually transmitted to Tetouan, and it is therefore impossible to determine where any specific *arid* was made. For more on the connection between these two cities, see Denamur 2003, p. 75.
2. Guérard 1974, p. 229.
3. For a helpful image of such textiles in situ, see Denamur 2003, p. 53.
4. This information, provided at the time of acquisition but unconfirmed, is taken from a catalogue card in the Department of Islamic Art at the Metropolitan Museum.
5. For examples of the more common type, see Vivier 2002–3, pp. 64–65.
6. Similar pieces can be found in the collection of Eliza M. and Sarah L. Niblack, published in Vivier 2002–3, pp. 62–63; unknown collection, published in de la Nézière 1924, pl. 46; and private collection, published in Denamur 2003, pp. 88–90, and foldout. See also Guérard 1974, pp. 236–38 and figs. 156–60. Another example was recently published in Denamur 2010, p. 57.
7. Stone 1985, p. 19; Guérard 1974, p. 226. In addition to Andalusian influence, there may also be some degree of Turkish influence in Moroccan art, especially in the embroideries of Tetouan (a neighbor of Chefchaouen). See Olagnier Bey 1961. This is an especially tempting hypothesis in light of the almost Holbeinesque center motifs of the two flanking stars in the present example.
8. Vivier 2002–3, p. 62; Denamur 2003, p. 75.
9. For the cartouche-and-star design in tilework, see, for example, the Royal Palace at Rabat (Castéra 1999, p. 58). In woodwork, but not in the embroideries, the cartouche is often larger than the star; see, for example, the Metropolitan Museum's wood screens from Morocco (acc. no. 2008.567a,b) or pl. 73 in de la Nézière 1921.

PROVENANCE: Mrs. Benjamin Ginsburg, Tarrytown, N.Y. (until 1970; sold to MMA)

51. Lattice-Design Carpet

Southern Spain, possibly Alcaraz, late 15th century
Wool (warp, weft, and pile); single-warp (Spanish) knotted pile
8 ft. 11 5/8 in. × 54 in. (273.5 × 137.1 cm)
The James F. Ballard Collection, Gift of James F. Ballard, 1922 22.100.124

The carpets of Islamic Spain have a peculiar relationship to those of the rest of the Islamic world. Many of the earliest surviving examples, from the fourteenth and fifteenth centuries, in fact take major aspects of their design from the Anatolian carpets of Turkey. Some Spanish carpets thus probably constituted Iberian "knock-offs" of expensive Anatolian originals, which were much in demand in Spain at the time.[1] Others were apparently woven by Muslim artists known as *mudejares* under Spanish Christian patronage, as Castile, Aragon, and Leon gradually extended their reconquest of Spain from the Christian north to the Muslim south. Such works, including the Metropolitan's carpet from the Ballard collection, often utilized designs adapted from silk textiles. However, all Spanish pile carpets do share one unusual characteristic: the pile is woven in a "Spanish knot" tied on a single warp, with multiple parallel shoots of weft between each row of knots.[2]

Dominated by hues of red and blue, the Ballard carpet has an attractive repeating design: floral sprays are outlined by long leaves that form an ogival layout of small, repeating medallion-like compartments. This pattern most likely originated in silk textiles produced in Spain under the Nasrid dynasty,[3] whose small principality was centered in Granada in the fourteenth and fifteenth centuries. The Nasrids continued to make luxury silk textiles of high quality during the twilight of Muslim rule in southern Spain, and their art had an enormous influence on that of the Christian kingdoms steadily encroaching from the north. Just as the Alcazar, the palace of the Castilian kings in Seville, was built by Muslim artists in the style of the Nasrids' Alhambra, so carpets such as this, made by Muslim artists for Christian patrons, reflect the designs, genres, and styles of the once-dominant Muslim culture of Iberia.[4] WBD

1. See Sherrill 1996, pp. 28–55.
2. Kühnel and Bellinger 1953.
3. See Partearroyo Lacaba 1992 and Granada and New York 1992, pp. 342–45, nos. 101, 102.
4. The Ballard Spanish carpet in the Metropolitan is in the care of the Department of Medieval Art.

PROVENANCE: James F. Ballard, St. Louis, Mo. (until 1922)

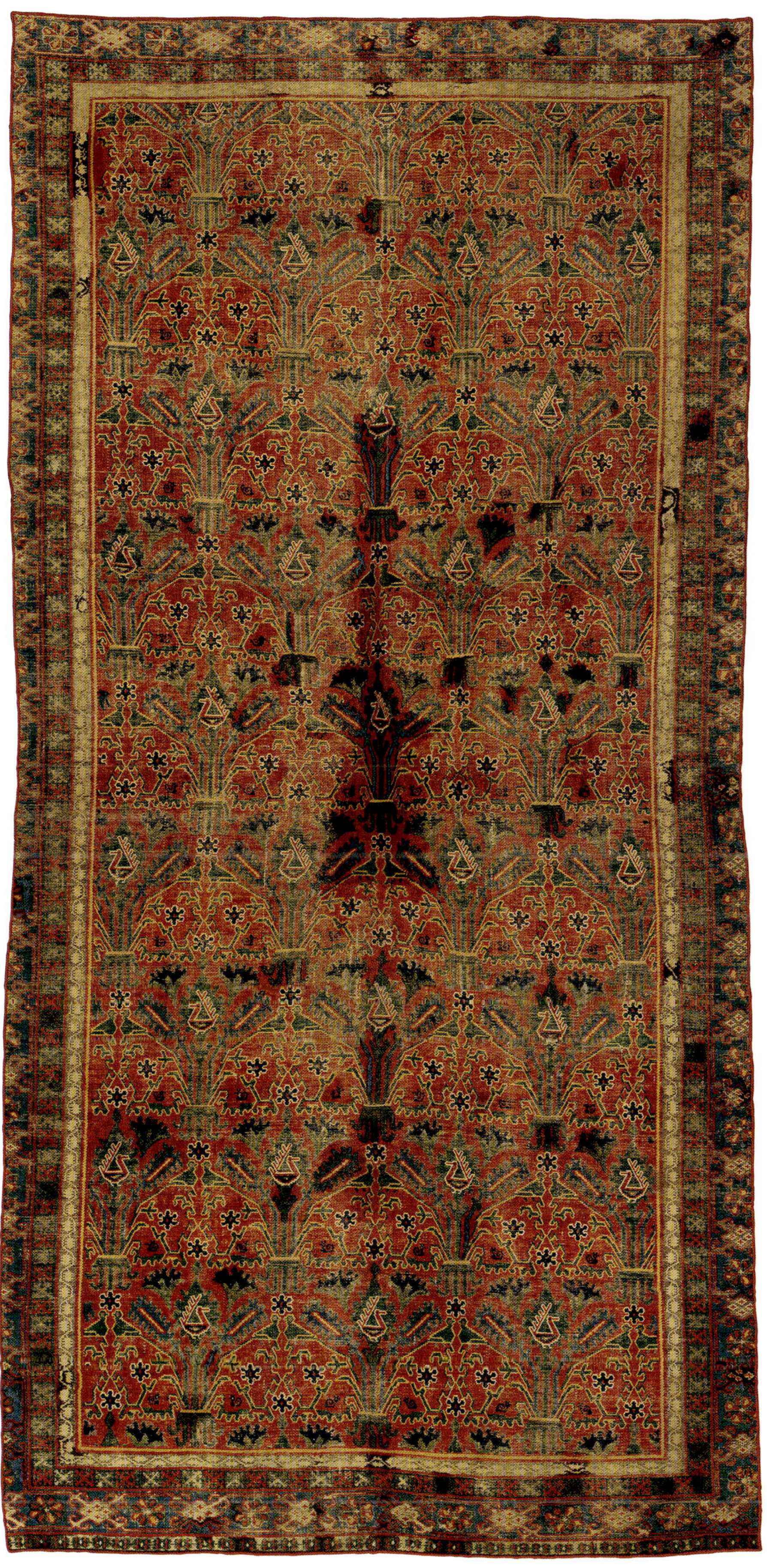

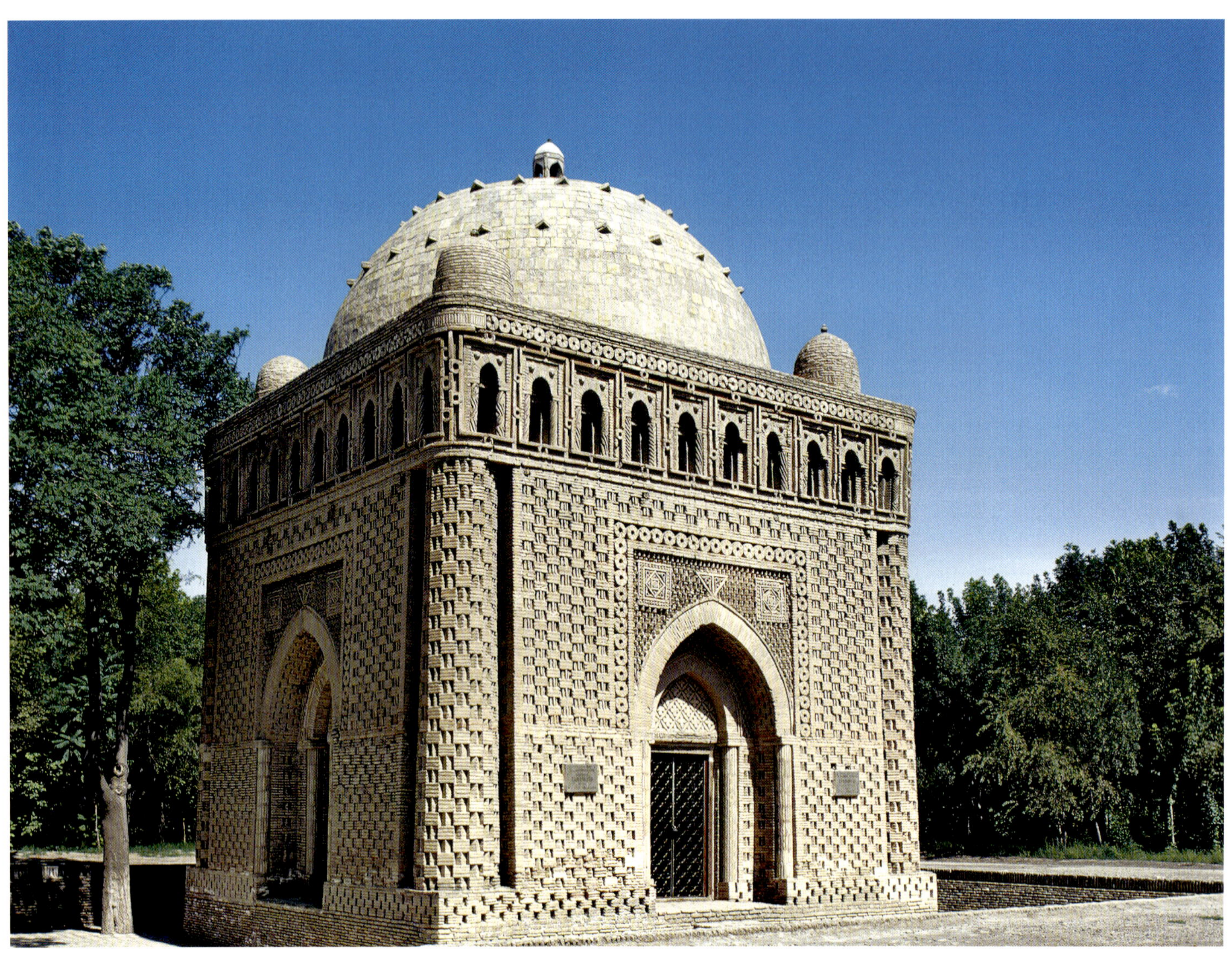

Art of the Eastern Islamic Lands (9th to 14th Centuries)

PRISCILLA P. SOUCEK

Although artistic accomplishment and innovation were often supported by the patronage of a particular dynasty or ruling group, in the period that stretched from the ninth to the fifteenth century—one of the high points of artistic production in the Near East under Islam—standards of creative excellence appear to have derived from the craftsmen themselves. In dynastic terms, the five-hundred-year period represented by the objects discussed here can be divided into two periods of unequal length. The longer, from 900 to 1258, coincides with the rule of the Abbasid caliphate (750–1258), whereas the subsequent one hundred fifty years were shaped by the presence of the Ilkhanid Mongols (1256–1353) and the various local dynasties that succeeded them in the areas of Iran, Iraq, and Central Asia that they had dominated.[1]

While Abbasid caliphs in Baghdad may have been the titular leaders of the Muslim community, in practice they were obliged to recognize that actual power resided with regional authorities, including the Samanids of eastern Iran and Central Asia, the Buyid amirs of Iran and Iraq, the Ghaznavids of Afghanistan and western India, and the Seljuqs—who at one point controlled a vast area stretching from modern Uzbekistan to Iran, Iraq, Syria, and Turkey. Such proliferation of competing regional political centers was often reflected in the parallel creation of regional artistic traditions. This is particularly evident in the diverse techniques exhibited by the ceramics and metalwork of these centuries.[2]

The fragility of the Abbasid state as a military and governmental power, however, does not negate the importance of the ties that arose from the economic and commercial networks that developed within their dominion, which facilitated the movement of ideas and techniques over substantial distances. Indeed, the distinctive character of the Abbasid period for the visual arts resulted more from such interchanges between the empire's center and its periphery than from any cultural stewardship exercised in Iraq.[3]

Yet Baghdad's role as an intellectual center stimulated artistic developments, and caliphal initiative was important in certain areas. The translation of texts from Greek into Arabic between the eighth and tenth centuries was encouraged and supported by some of the caliphs and was a catalyst for the development of scientific knowledge in the Abbasid Empire.[4] A few luxury copies of such translations were even embellished with pictures. The page from an Arabic translation of the *De Materia Medica* of Dioscorides dated to 1224 that illustrates the preparation of a medical potion from honey (cat. 55) provides a rare glimpse of daily life in thirteenth-century Iraq.

The prestige of the Abbasid caliphs rested on their position as interpreters of traditions ascribed to the Prophet, which was most evident in their role as arbitrators of religious disputes—a role that also gave special prominence to the forms of calligraphy they favored. Qur'an manuscripts produced in Abbasid Iraq were thus endowed with a particular status, and this, in turn, encouraged their use as models in other regions. Manuscripts of the Qur'an were often copied in the most precise hands used in a given period and region, with its text given a full range of diacritical marks to eliminate any ambiguities in meaning or pronunciation. The Metropolitan Museum is fortunate to have in its collection pages from well-known Qur'an manuscripts linked to the Abbasid Empire, some of which were even produced in Baghdad. All were written on paper, though their script and decorative headings vary in appearance. Among these are a page from a manuscript dated to 993 that was copied in Isfahan and folios from manuscripts copied in Baghdad in 1192 and 1307 (for the latter, see cat. 54B).[5]

This sequence of pages provides a sampling of the broader history of calligraphy and manuscript production. While the Isfahan folio of 993 displays an innovative script, its dimensions and format replicate the appearance of earlier Qur'ans written on parchment. From the eleventh century onward, Iraqi scribes favored the use of a geometrically proportioned script in which individual letters have a consistent size and shape, replacing the more idiosyncratic variants found in earlier hands in which certain letters could be expanded or contracted to suit the available space.[6] The regularity of later manuscripts even extended to their dimensions. Both the Qur'an of 1192 and the one from 1307 were designed to have seven lines of text per page, but the later example is approximately twice the size of the earlier one, a difference that reflects the standardization of paper sizes.[7] It is worth noting that the 1307 Qur'an was produced nearly fifty years after the official demise of the Abbasid dynasty and is thus indicative that the importance of Baghdad as a center for bookmaking and calligraphy continued after the caliphs themselves had been removed.

During the eleventh and twelfth centuries portions of the Qur'an were also inscribed on objects that served a religious purpose. Two such examples—of nearly identical date and produced in the same place, the central Iranian city of Yazd—are in the Museum's collection: a stone tombstone dated to 1150 (cat. 64) and sections of a wooden pulpit or *minbar* from a local mosque that bear the date of 1151 (cat. 65A). The striking similarities between the calligraphic and ornamental repertoire of these objects demonstrate that craftsmen skilled in these two media worked closely together.

For millennia, monumental architecture in Iran and Iraq had been constructed from bricks, both sun-dried and kiln-baked. To enliven the surfaces, local builders developed decorative techniques that could lend color and texture to otherwise monotonous stretches of wall. In turn, decorative techniques established in one region spread easily to other areas where brick was also the favored material for construction. Thus it was that carved-and-painted stucco emerged as a major artistic medium in buildings erected under Abbasid patronage in Iraq, and its use spread rapidly through various centers in Iran and Central Asia. The Abbasids or their builders favored abstract patterns that often had a vegetal origin, and the popularity of such designs in Iran and Central Asia appears to reflect cultural ties with the Abbasid domains. The Iranian city of Nishapur exemplified these trends, as can be seen from architectural decoration excavated there that is now on view in New York (cats. 60, 61). Abstract patterns inspired by Abbasid-period architectural ornament were even replicated on ceramic vessels from eastern Iran or Central Asia.[8]

One of the special features of artistic production in areas under Muslim domination is the care and attention devoted to the creation of patterns on works made from simple materials, such as ceramic vessels or objects of base metal. The credit for the varied ways in which this practice stimulated artistic innovation lies with the craftsmen themselves. Humble ceramic vessels for everyday use were widely produced, with important regional variations in the subtle and creative manipulation of this material to create objects of arresting beauty. Potters active in eastern Iran and adjacent regions of Central Asia used slip painting to produce calligraphy of a high order (cat. 69).[9] Sometimes these inscriptions offer prosperity and good health to the user and sometimes they carry aphorisms of a more pious flavor.[10] We know little about the individuals who created these ceramic masterpieces during the ninth and tenth centuries.

Fortunately, we are better informed about the identity and personal history of the potters active in the central Iranian city of Kashan during the twelfth to the fourteenth century because a number of objects that they produced bear both signatures and dates.[11] This knowledge is further amplified by a treatise on ceramic production written by a member of this workshop during the fourteenth century. His text allows us to follow the workshop's production both before and after the mid-thirteenth-century Mongol invasions.[12]

The international reputation of this workshop was bolstered by the ability of its craftsmen to use metallic oxides to create objects that had the optical qualities of precious metals but were produced in ceramic kilns. Some of the pieces they manufactured were of considerable size, such as luster-painted *mihrabs* for use in mosques or shrines. Their most widely distributed lusterwares, however, were probably sets of tiles used for wall revetments in both religious and secular structures.[13]

Another distinctive accomplishment of the Kashan ceramic workshop was the ability to paint pictures on ceramic surfaces, thereby producing images as rich and subtle as those created on a sheet of paper. At times, these objects even depict stories taken from Persian literature, hinting at the social setting in which such works were used and enjoyed.[14] The skills required for this exacting form of ceramic decoration appear to have been lost by the middle decades of the thirteenth century, perhaps due to the disruption and loss of life associated with the Mongol conquests.

Regional specialization and individual creativity also underlie the accomplishments of metalworkers active during the tenth to the fifteenth century. Artisans in the city of Herat in present-day Afghanistan refined the technique of inlaying metal objects with contrasting substances to create ornamental surfaces that expanded the significance of the objects.[15] Often such inlay included texts that alluded to an object's function or identified the person for whom it was made.[16] Wares made of silver were inlaid with substances that darkened with time, so that the added design was clearly visible. The text inlaid into the small silver cup with flaring sides (cat. 83), for example, suggests that it was to be used as a wine cup, confirming the popularity of wine drinking within courtly circles despite religious strictures discouraging it.

Base metals such as bronze or brass were also treated in novel ways through the use of intricate inlays cut from thin sheets of silver or gold and held in place by the crimping of the vessel's surface. Here too the decorative themes employed inform us about an object's function or meaning. The most common inscriptions offer benedictions and praises to the work's owner, making it a bearer of good fortune. Inkwells served a practical purpose and were emblems of office for scribes. In addition, circular vessels like the museum's inkwell (cat. 86) could be embellished with symbols of the zodiac or other heavenly bodies, suggesting an analogy between their shape and the design of the heavenly spheres.[17]

Although metalwork objects and ceramic vessels used in a secular context might feature figural decoration, such depictions were usually executed in two dimensions. Wall paintings, for example, sometimes portrayed nearly lifesize figures, as at the Lashkari Bazaar in Afghanistan.[18] More unusual are three-dimensional figures of people or animals. The Museum owns a pair of lifesize sculptures with elaborate costumes and weapons (cats. 62, 63) as well as a carved-stone head of a youth.[19] More research is needed to properly situate these figures within their original contexts.

The invasion of Central Asia and the Near East by the Mongol armies between 1218 and 1220 had a devastating impact on the cities of those regions. However, the Mongol habit of enslaving craftsmen and moving them to new locations did ensure that some artistic skills were transferred from one area to another. While a second phase of the Mongol conquest in the 1250s was less brutal than the first, it did result in the 1258 extinction of the Abbasid caliphate. Despite these traumatic events, by the 1260s some places in the Near East had begun to revive, and the vast Mongol Empire facilitated long-distance communication between previously distinct regions.[20]

The empire controlled by the Genghizid Mongols did not long endure, but certain aspects of their legacy informed the artistic patronage of the successor states that came to power in sections of their dominion. Economic ties that resulted from long-distance travel and trade between regions appear to have had a more lasting impact than did the political and military ideology directly associated with Mongol rule. The production of and trade in luxury textiles is one such area. Textiles embellished with gold held a high artistic and economic value for the Mongols, perhaps due to their peripatetic lifestyle. Because of this, textile production in eastern and western Asia grew closer together in both design and technique in the late thirteenth and early fourteenth centuries. The vigorous trade networks of the period also contributed to the wide distribution of these fabrics, which are now preserved in European churches as well as various museum collections around the world.[21]

Several objects in the Metropolitan Museum exemplify the post-Mongol revival of the arts. The potters of Kashan seem to have been well treated by the Mongols, and tiles made there from the 1260s onward employed a new artistic vocabulary of

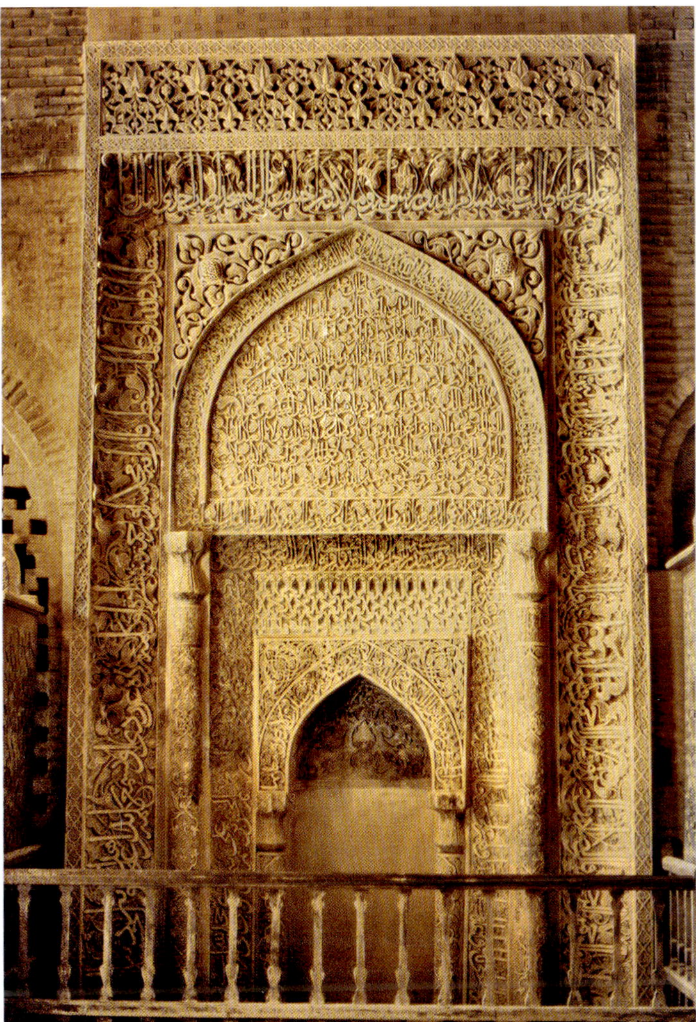

Fig. 30 Interior view of the Sanctuary of Uljaytu, Great Mosque of Isfahan, installed 1310. Photo: Walter B. Denny

East Asian origin.[22] Among these is a molded, luster-painted tile bearing lotus blossoms and a bird with elaborate plumage (cat. 78). This same repertoire is evident in other media, including a page from an illustrated manuscript that depicts a pair of birds (cat. 56).

In the 1290s the conversion of the Mongols to Islam, along with a gradual economic revival of Iran and Central Asia, stimulated the construction or redecoration of shrines, mosques, and tombs with glazed-ceramic revetments. The most laborious variant of this decoration featured complex designs composed of several colors of glazed ceramics that were cut to a pattern and fitted together to create a unified surface. Typically this technique was used to accent key parts of a structure, such as the *mihrab* of a mosque or the portal of a building.[23] The *mihrab* dated to 1354 from a religious school, or *madrasa*, in Isfahan (cat. 81) demonstrates the strong visual impact of this technique.[24] Although the origin of this technique is difficult to pinpoint, it may have developed in western Iran, whence it spread to other regions.

The illustration of secular manuscripts with pictures acquired new prominence in the period following the Mongol invasion. Most striking were the changes in the illustration of texts written in Persian, particularly those of the long epic poem of Persian dynastic history, the *Shahnama* (Book of Kings). This text had been composed about the year 1000 by the eastern Iranian poet Firdausi of Tus, but few traces survive of manuscripts produced before the second half of the thirteenth century. From the late thirteenth century onward, however, the number and variety of illustrated versions proliferated.[25]

Pictures included in manuscripts became more varied during the fourteenth century. Some copies, such as the page from a *Shahnama* dated to 1341 (cat. 58), have simple, striplike images filled with human figures that show little if any attention to the setting of events.[26] At about the same time, another copy of this text contained illustrations that focus on the depiction of emotion, as seen in the funeral scene (cat. 57) in which grief is expressed with emotional and graphic immediacy.

Some innovations appear to reflect the creativity of the painters, whereas others may be due to requests made by patrons. One combination featured picture riddles in which words and pictures were used together to complete the verses of a poem; the Museum owns a page of this type from a manuscript produced in Isfahan in the 1340s (cat. 59).[27] Adding to the variety, some fourteenth-century paintings included the new visual repertoire brought by the Mongols; others illustrated narratives that may have carried personal meanings for a patron.[28] During the course of the fourteenth century, painters experimented with new ways of telling stories by integrating figures into lavish landscapes or by situating them in elaborately decorated buildings, approaches that would be exploited by artists working in Iran during the fifteenth and sixteenth centuries.

1. Bosworth 1996, pp. 6–10, 250–51, 264–68.
2. London 1976a, pp. 23–35, 54–77, 136–52; Watson 2004, pp. 45–61.
3. Grabar 1975, pp. 349–51.
4. Gutas 1998.
5. On the Isfahan Qur'an of 993 (Metropolitan Museum, acc. no. 40.164), see Déroche 1992, pp. 154–55, no. 83; for cat. 54B, see also James 1988, pp. 77, 81, 83, 235, no. 39. The folio from the 1192 manuscript is in the collection of the Metropolitan Museum (acc. no. 2004.89).
6. Blair 2006, pp. 157–78.
7. Ibid., pp. 247–51.
8. Wilkinson 1986, pp. 229–42.
9. Compare Wilkinson 1973, pp. 96–104, 113–22, and the slip-painted earthenware bowl (cat. 69).
10. Pancaroğlu 2002; Ghouchani 1986.

11. Ettinghausen 1936; Watson 1985, pp. 176–82.
12. Allan 1973.
13. Watson 1985, pp. 22–140.
14. Simpson 1981; Watson 2004, pp. 363–71.
15. Barrett 1949, pp. ix–x; Baer 1983, pp. 4–5, 71, 102.
16. Melikian-Chirvani 1973, pp. 70–91.
17. London 1976a, pp. 69–70, 123–24.
18. Schlumberger 1952.
19. On the carved-stone head (acc. no. 33.111), see Riefstahl 1931.
20. Masuya 2002–3.
21. Watt and Wardwell 1997–98.
22. Masuya 2002–3; Watson 2006.
23. Wilber 1939.
24. Crane 1940; Wilber 1955, pp. 103, 183–84, no. 100.
25. Simpson 1979, pp. 1–40.
26. Swietochowski 1994.
27. Carboni 1994.
28. Grabar and Blair 1980, pp. 13–28; Soudavar 1996, pp. 97–101.

52. *Bifolio from a Qur'an Manuscript*

Iran, Isfahan, A.H. Ramadan 383 / October–November 993 A.D.
Ink and gold on paper, 9 1/2 × 13 7/8 in. (24 × 35.1 cm)
Rogers Fund, 1940 40.164.5a, b

53. *Folio from a Qur'an Manuscript*

Eastern Iran or Afghanistan, ca. 1180
Ink, opaque watercolor, and gold on paper, 11 3/4 × 8 3/4 in. (29.8 × 22.2 cm)
H. O. Havemeyer Collection, Gift of Horace Havemeyer, 1929 29.160.23

Some of the new scripts developed from the tenth to the twelfth century in the Near East were employed primarily for religious texts. The earlier of these leaves (cat. 52) belongs to a manuscript that was conservative in its use of the horizontal format characteristic of Qur'an copies on parchment from the ninth century, but innovative in the script it adopts to transcribe that text. It belongs to the last volume of a four-part Qur'an manuscript, other folios of which (in the Museum of Turkish and Islamic Art, Istanbul), provide the date of A.H. Ramadan 383 / October–November 993 A.D. and indicate that it was copied in the Iranian city of Isfahan.[1] The text on the Metropolitan Museum's bifolio, from Sura 54 (*al-Qamar*, "The Moon"), is discontinuous—one leaf (a) contains verses 6–13, while the other leaf (b) bears verses 31–39—indicating that another bifolio once separated the two. A folio now in the Khalili Collection, London, that contains the end of Sura 53 (*al-Najm*, "The Star") along with the chapter heading and first five verses of Sura 54 must have preceded the Metropolitan Museum folios.[2]

Knowing the precise date and place of origin of this manuscript gives it a special importance. Its calligraphy occupies an intermediate zone between the angular script of the earliest Qur'an manuscripts, used here for the heading of Sura 53, and the fluid, more cursive book hands that have been in vogue since the twelfth century. This variant, sometimes called the "new script" or "broken cursive," shows considerable variety in the size of its letters and width of its strokes. The letters that fall below the baseline are unusually long and create a visual rhythm that propels the eye forward through the text. Another notable stylistic feature is the difference in the sizes of the letters in the word *Allah*, which appears in both the final verse of Sura 53 and the first line of Sura 54. In both cases, the initial *alif* is more than twice the height of the others, a contrast that serves to emphasize the word.

Certain features of the "new script" have been exaggerated in the other page presented here (cat. 53), which contains Qur'an 5:20–21 from a widely dispersed Qur'an. Among these are the height of its vertical letters and a similar visual emphasis on the word *Allah*. Each page contains only four lines of text because of the large scale of its writing; the manuscript is also distinctive in that the spaces between its letters are embellished with a background of foliate scrolls. B. Saint Laurent, who has collated the surviving fragments of this copy, estimated that when complete it would have contained 2,250 folios. Aside from its background decoration, the manuscript resembles those in a group produced in

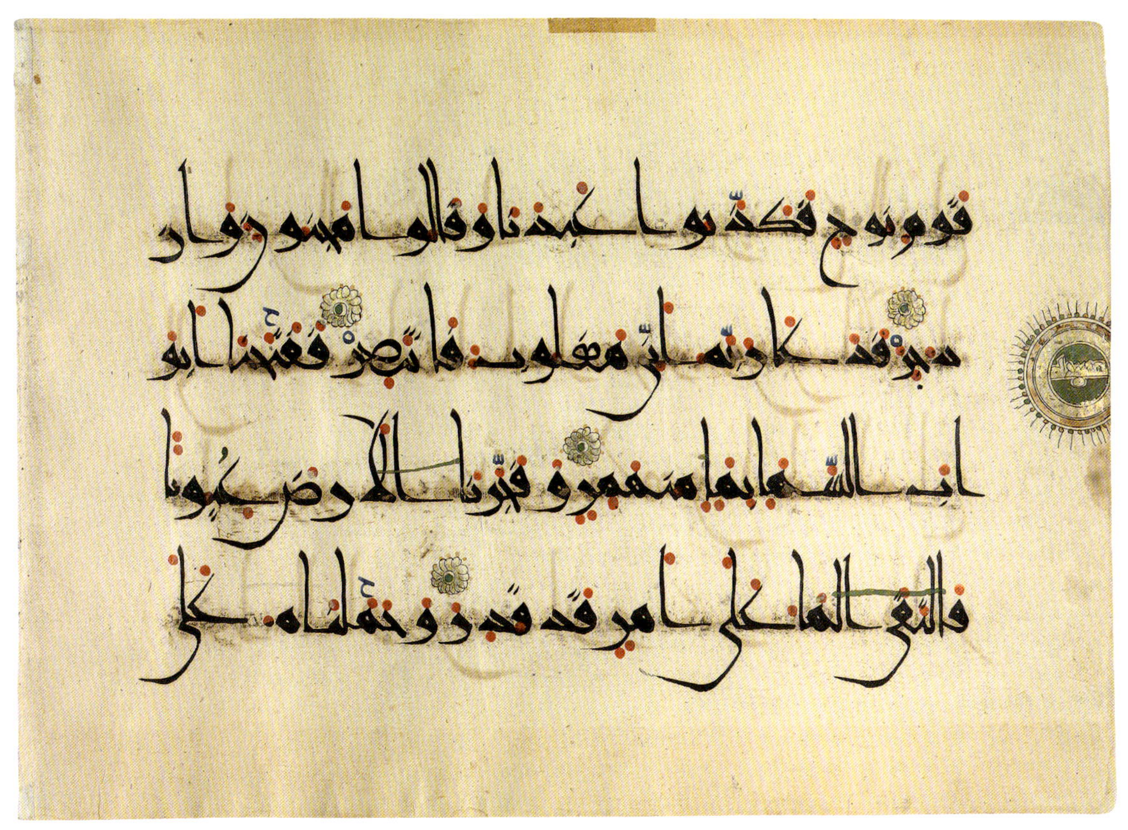

52

eastern Iran or Afghanistan between the late eleventh and late twelfth centuries, including one dated to 1092, formerly in the collection of Aqa Mahdi Kashani, and another in the Topkapı Palace Library, Istanbul, copied in 1177 by a scribe of Afghan origin. These two examples help to establish the approximate date and place of production for the page and for the other leaves from this volume.[3] PS

1. Déroche 1992, pp. 154–55, no. 83.
2. Déroche 1988–89, pp. 24–27, fig. 6; Sotheby's London, October 13, 1989, lot 76; Déroche 1992, pp. 154–55, no. 83.
3. Saint Laurent 1989; Lings 2005, pp. 57–59 and pls. 14–15, 20–21, 24.

Provenance
Cat. 52: [Mrs. Kamer Aga-Oğlu, Ann Arbor, Mich., until 1940; sold to MMA]
Cat. 53: H. O. Havemeyer Collection, New York (until 1929)

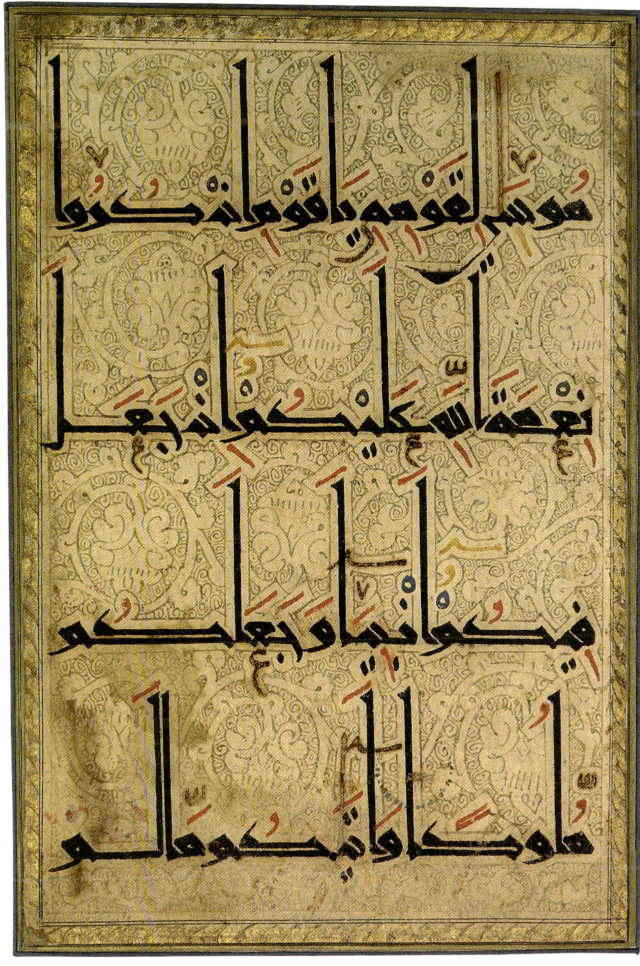

53

54A, B. Two Folios from the Anonymous Baghdad Qur'an

A. Frontispiece, Right Side, Vol. 26
Calligrapher: Ibn al-Suhrawardi
Illuminator: Muhammad ibn Aibak ibn 'Abdallah
Iraq, Baghdad, A.H. 706/1306–7 A.D.
Ink, opaque watercolor, and gold on paper
17 × 13⅞ in. (43.2 × 35.2 cm)
Rogers Fund, 1950 50.12

B. Colophon, Left Side, Vol. 30
Calligrapher: Ibn al-Suhrawardi
Illuminator: Muhammad ibn Aibak ibn 'Abdallah
Iraq, Baghdad, dated A.H. 707/1307–8 A.D.
Ink, opaque watercolor, and gold on paper
20¼ × 14½ in. (51.3 × 36.8 cm)
Rogers Fund, 1955 55.44

Cat. 54A
Inscription in Arabic in "new-style" script in borders at top and bottom:
وإنه لكتاب عزيز لا يأتيه/الباطل من بين يديه [ولا من خلفه]
[. . .] and surely it is a Book Sublime; falsehood comes not to it, from before it, [nor from behind it] (Qur'an 41:41–42)

Cat. 54B
Inscription in Arabic in "new-style" script in borders at top and bottom:
بغداد حماها الله تعالى في شهور/سنة سبع وسبعمائة هلالية
Baghdad, may God, the exalted, protect her, in the months of the year A.H. 707 [1307–8 A.D.] *hilali* [calendar]

Inscription in Arabic in *muhaqqaq* script at center:
احمد بن السهروردي البكري/حامداً ومصلياً على نبيه/محمد وآله وصحبه مسلماً
Ahmad ibn Suhrawardi al-Bakri praises God and prays for His messenger Muhammad, his family, and his companions and salutes.

These two illuminated pages come from different sections of one of the acknowledged masterpieces of calligraphy and book production in the Islamic world. The so-called Anonymous Baghdad Qur'an was created under Ilkhanid patronage in the first decade of the fourteenth century, specifically between late 1301 (or very early 1302) and 1308.[1] Under the Ilkhanid rulers, who converted to Islam in the late thirteenth century, several luxury copies of the Qur'an were commissioned with the aim of distributing them across the country, either as endowments to major mosques or for placement in mausoleums that were built while the patrons were still alive. Crucial to this was the guidance of the Ilkhanid vizier Rashid al-Din (d. 1318), a converted Persian Jew who created in the capital of Tabriz an atelier for copying and distributing literary texts. In addition to that scriptorium, several other important Ilkhanid cities had long-standing traditions of book production, foremost among which was Baghdad, the former capital of the Abbasids, which had been captured by the Ilkhanids in 1258.

While we know that the thirty-part manuscript to which these two pages once belonged was produced in Baghdad, we do not know the name of its patron or its intended destination. Possible candidates have included Sultan Ghazan (r. 1295–1304); his successor, Sultan Uljaitu (r. 1304–16); or one of their powerful viziers, perhaps Rashid al-Din or Sa'd al-Din Savaji. It may have been made for deposit in the mausoleum of Sultan Ghazan, which was completed in 1301.

However, we do know the names of both the calligrapher and the illuminator of this splendid codex: not surprisingly, they were among the most celebrated and prolific artists at the court of the Ilkhanids. The calligrapher, Ibn al-Suhrawardi, may have been the grandson of a well-known sufi from the small town of Suhraward in northwestern Iran. A pupil of Yaqut al-Musta'simi (d. 1298), the most renowned calligrapher of his time, he may well have surpassed his master while copying this Qur'an. Ibn al-Suhrawardi is credited with designing inscriptions for a number of buildings in Baghdad and with the production of thirty-three complete Qur'an manuscripts. Unfortunately, few of his works survive. The illuminator, Muhammad ibn Aibak ibn 'Abdallah, signed his name several times throughout the present manuscript, adding that he was working in the City of Peace, Baghdad; although Ibn Aibak's signatures appear in a few other manuscripts as well, little is known about his life.[2] The dates provided by the calligrapher and the illuminator throughout the surviving sections of this codex

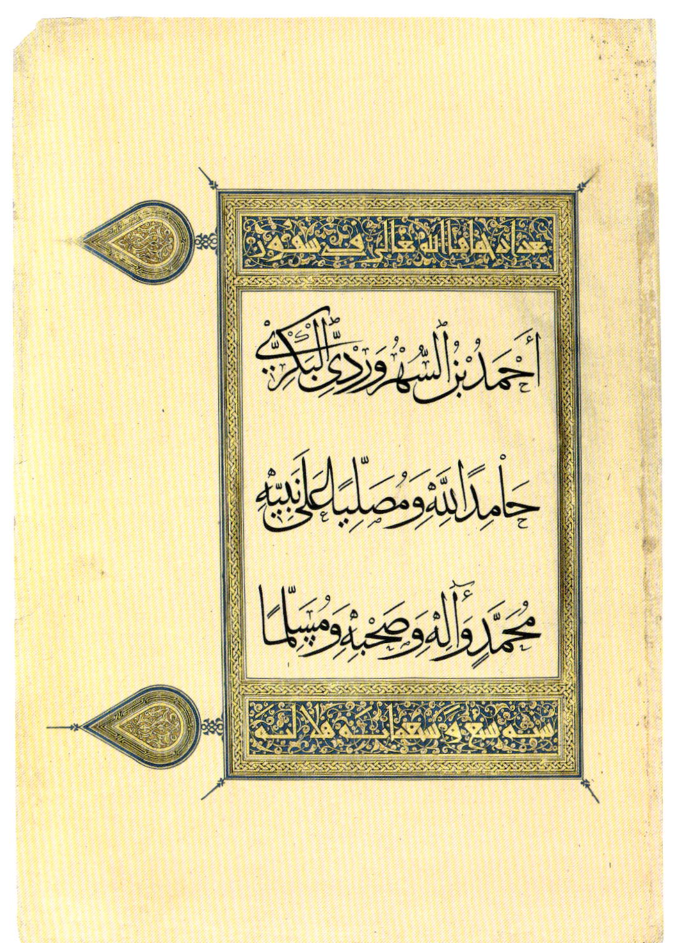
B

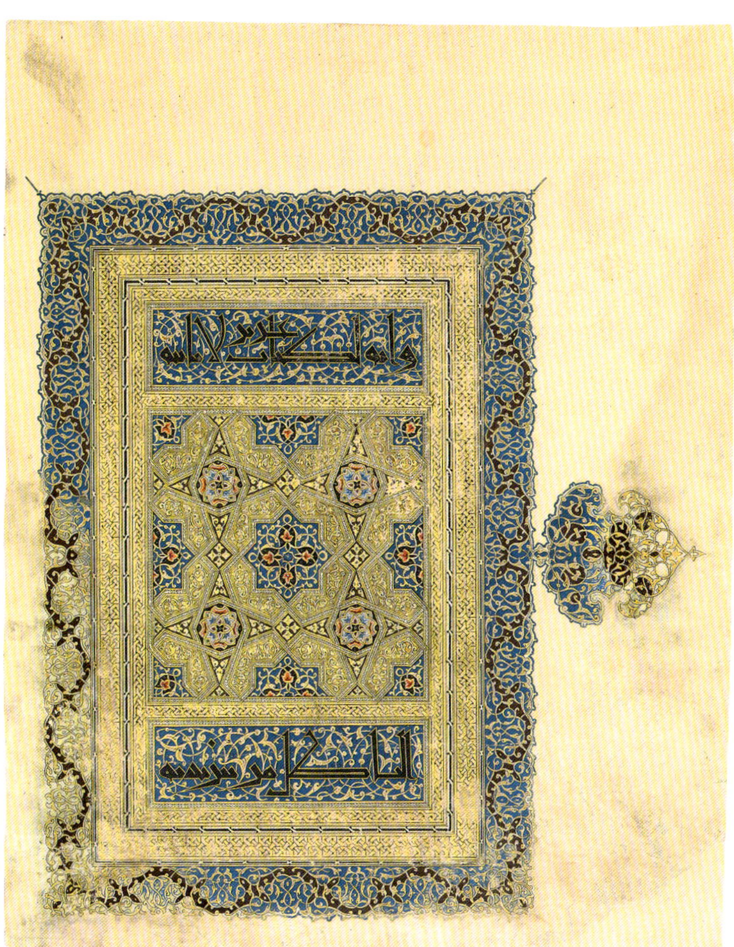
A

document the different paces at which they worked: Ibn Suhrawardi was able to copy approximately eight volumes each year, while Ibn Aibak managed to illuminate only four of them.[3]

Catalogue 54A is the right-hand side of the two-page frontispiece for the twenty-sixth *juz'*, or part, of this Qur'an.[4] According to the colophon for this section, now in the Iran Bastan Museum in Tehran, it was finished by Ibn Suhrawardi in A.H. 706/1306–7 A.D. The quality of Ibn Aibak's illumination here is nothing short of superb: the central eight-pointed star set against a lapis blue background is duplicated within an ever-expanding pattern that is interrupted by the square framing, thus allowing the view of half stars in the center of the four sides and quarter stars at the corners. The complex gold geometric interlacing that separates the stars becomes the dominant pattern and creates space for four small polychrome "flowers." The elegant inscription in black outlined in gold represents half of the text originally copied on this double-sided frontispiece.[5] The outer border, although slightly discolored due to damage, is also spectacular, with an undulating brown band contrasting against the blue background and a large pendant off to the right side.[6]

The two illuminated sections of catalogue 54B are in Aibak's hand; the text contains the second half of the colophon, possibly of the thirtieth and last *juz'* of the Qur'an.[7] The most prominent feature of this folio is the three lines of text set against the polished white paper, copied by Ibn Suhrawardi in a most accomplished, artistic, balanced, and flowing *muhaqqaq* cursive calligraphy. The magnificent achievement of this artist enables even those viewers who cannot read Arabic to have an emotive appreciation for it. In possibly the very last written words of the last volume of this extraordinary manuscript, the calligrapher offers his name to posterity: Ahmad ibn Suhrawardi al-Bakri.[8] SC

1. Due to the fact that none of the surviving volumes or individual folios contains a *waqfiyya* (official endowment) or a record of commission, this manuscript has been referred to as the Anonymous Baghdad Qur'an. See James 1988, pp. 78–92.
2. Ibid., pp. 89–92.
3. Ibid., p. 90.
4. Published in ibid., fig. 58.
5. See the translation above. The full verse would have ended on the other side with ". . . nor from behind it. A revelation from the Wise the Praised One."

6. One has to keep in mind that a mirror-illuminated page once faced the present one, thus balancing the pattern and doubling the pleasure to the eye. This page seems to have been lost.
7. Published in James 1988, fig. 47; Schimmel and Rivolta 1992, p. 16; New York and Los Angeles 2002–3, pp. 204, 258–59, no. 64, fig. 245; Blair 2006, p. 252.
8. To my knowledge, Ibn al-Suhrawardi added the word *al-Bakri* to his name only on this page, making it particularly significant. It confirms that he belonged to the Suhrawardi order of sufis.

Provenance
Cat. 54a: [J. Acheroff, Paris, until 1950; sold to MMA]
Cat. 54b: [Khalil Rabenou, New York, until 1955; sold to MMA]

55. Folio from the De Materia Medica of Dioscorides

"Preparation of Medicine from Honey"
Calligrapher: 'Abdullah ibn al-Fadl
Possibly Baghdad, Iraq, or Northern Jazira,
dated a.h. Rajab 621/ June–July 1224 a.d.
Ink, opaque watercolor, and gold on paper
12⅜ × 9 in. (31.4 × 22.9 cm)
Bequest of Cora Timken Burnett, 1956 57.51.21

This illustrated folio is from an Arabic manuscript of Dioscorides' *De Materia Medica (Kitab al-Khawass al-Ashjar)* probably produced in Baghdad and dated a.h. 621/1224 a.d. The painting depicts the interior of a two-storied house in which two male figures stand at either side of a large caldron over a burning fire, one mixing a medicine made of honey called *abuma'ali*, prescribed to cure weakness; another figure on the second story transfers the concoction into large jugs. A row of vessels, which were probably used to preserve the medicine, can be seen at the center of the top floor.

De Materia Medica was one of the most popular Greek scientific manuscripts translated into Arabic. The author, Dioscorides, was a physician from Asia Minor who served in the Roman army in the first century b.c. Translated in Baghdad in the mid-ninth century, the treatise describes ways to prepare medicines from up to five hundred plants. Developed in the fourth century b.c. and continuing in the Byzantine period, the Greek tradition of herbals provided the model for Islamic herbals and pharmacological texts.[1]

The illustration of Islamic herbal manuscripts developed in two directions: pictures of plants alone or vignettes including human figures, as in this example.[2] Characteristic of the Baghdad School in the mid-thirteenth century are the two-dimensionality of the painting, the bright colors, the sprightly figures in contemporary local garb with halos crowning their heads, and the bilateral symmetry of the composition. Representing a skillful blend of Persian, Byzantine, and Arab features typical of the Baghdad School,[3] the paintings are compositionally and stylistically akin to those in a manuscript of the *Maqamat* by al-Hariri produced in Baghdad and dated a.h. 634/1237 a.d., now in the Bibliothèque Nationale de France, Paris.[4]

This folio is from a manuscript dated a.h. Rajab 621/June–July 1224 a.d., the bulk of which is presently in the Süleymaniye Library, Istanbul.[5] The text, which is in *naskhi* script, is by the calligrapher 'Abdullah ibn al-Fadl. Additional folios from the same manuscript are preserved in the Arthur M. Sackler Gallery in Washington, D.C., the David Collection in Copenhagen, and the British Museum in London, among other collections.[6] ME

1. Hoffman 2000.
2. James and Ettinghausen 1977, p. 88.
3. Ibid., p. 87.
4. Bibliothèque Nationale de France, Paris (ms. Arabe 5847). Ibid., p. 121.
5. Süleymaniye Library, Istanbul (Aya Sophia no. 3703).
6. See London 2009, p. 204.

Provenance: Frederik R. Martin, Stockholm (by 1910); V. Everit Macy, New York; Cora Timken Burnett, Alpine, N.J. (until d. 1956)

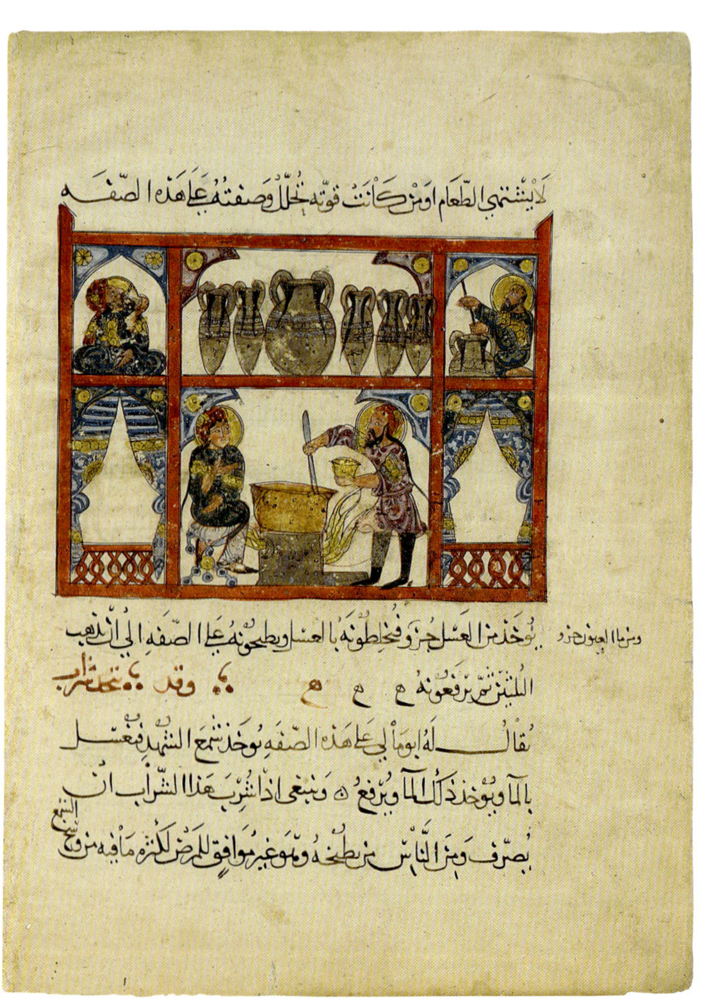

56. *Folio from the Manafi' al-hayawan (On the Usefulness of Animals) of Ibn Bakhtishu*

Iran, ca. 1300
Ink, opaque watercolor, and gold on paper
Image: 5¾ × 6⅛ in. (14.6 × 15.7 cm); page: 15⅞ × 12½ in. (40.3 × 31.8 cm)
Rogers Fund, 1918 18.26.2

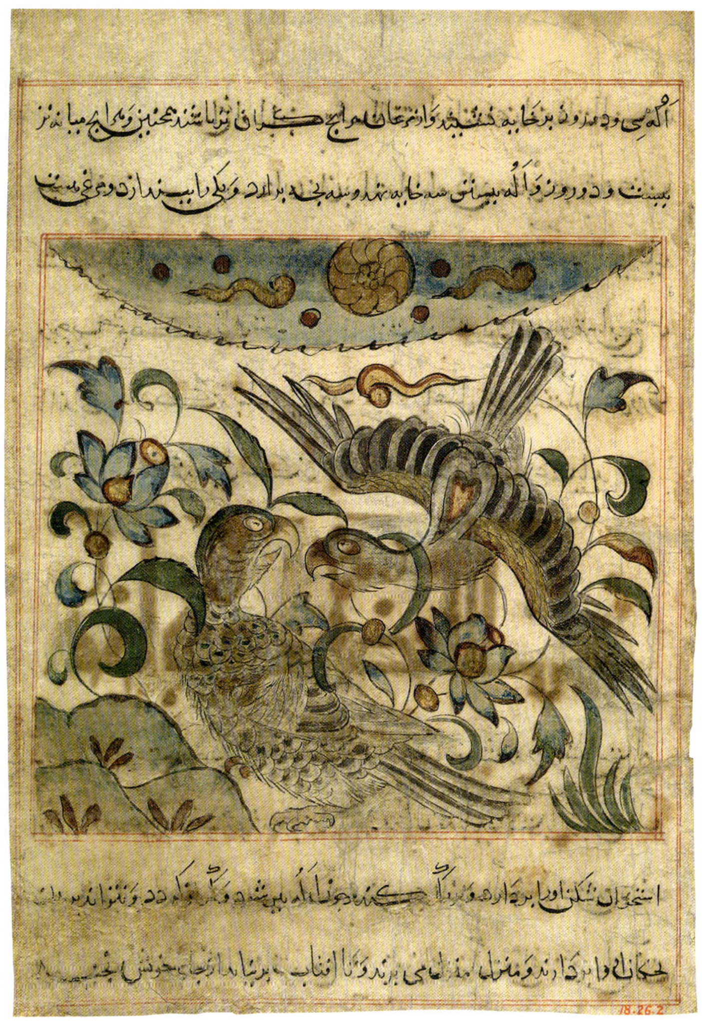

This folio was once part of a manuscript of the *Manafi' al-hayawan* (On the Usefulness of Animals), a bestiary composed in the tenth century by Abu Sa'id ibn Bakhtishu for the Abbasid caliph al-Muttaqi (r. 940–44).[1] The text was especially popular during the thirteenth century; three of the earliest surviving manuscripts of this text were produced at that time, including the first Persian edition[2] and the dispersed manuscript to which this folio belonged.[3] The page is dominated by a bold illustration of two eagles with rich plumage; the first bird rests on the ground with his head turned back toward his mate, who is flying in his direction. The illustration is framed by a few lines of text that discuss the attributes of eagles, specifically the gestation period of the eagles' eggs and the conditions under which they will hatch.

Created during the transformative phase of pictorial production that occurred during the rule of the Mongol Ilkhanids, this illustration fuses features of Arab painting with Chinese elements. The influence of Arab painting can be seen in the essentially decorative and two-dimensional quality of the landscape, especially in the canopy-like sky and the stylized stems and flowers. These characteristically Arab elements are combined with such Chinese influences as the strong, almost calligraphic, line, the delicate palette, and the concern for spatial relationships. The illustration also responds to the text, specifically in its inclusion of a stylized golden sun, which is described in the lines of script below the two eagles.

The cultural and political exchange between the new rulers of Iran, the Ilkhanids, and the Yuan dynasty in China, of whom the Ilkhanids were vassals, was largely responsible for the incorporation of Chinese motifs into the Ilkhanid artistic repertoire. Along with other motifs of Chinese inspiration, peonies, swirling cloud bands, and fantastic beasts like the phoenix—whose classical iconography with stretched wings appears to have inspired the shape of one of the birds in this composition—became part of the Ilkhanid and Islamic decorative repertoire at this time. FL

1. The text's original Arabic title is *Kitab na't al-hayawan wa manafi'ihi* (Book of the Identification and Benefits of Animals).
2. The manuscript, now in the Morgan Library and Museum, New York (MS. M. 500), bears the date 1297–98 and was made during the reign of the Ilkhanid Ghazan Khan (1295–1304).
3. A second page from the same manuscript is also in the collection of the Metropolitan Museum (acc. no. 57.51.31).

Provenance: [Hagop Kevorkian, New York, by 1914–18; sold to MMA]

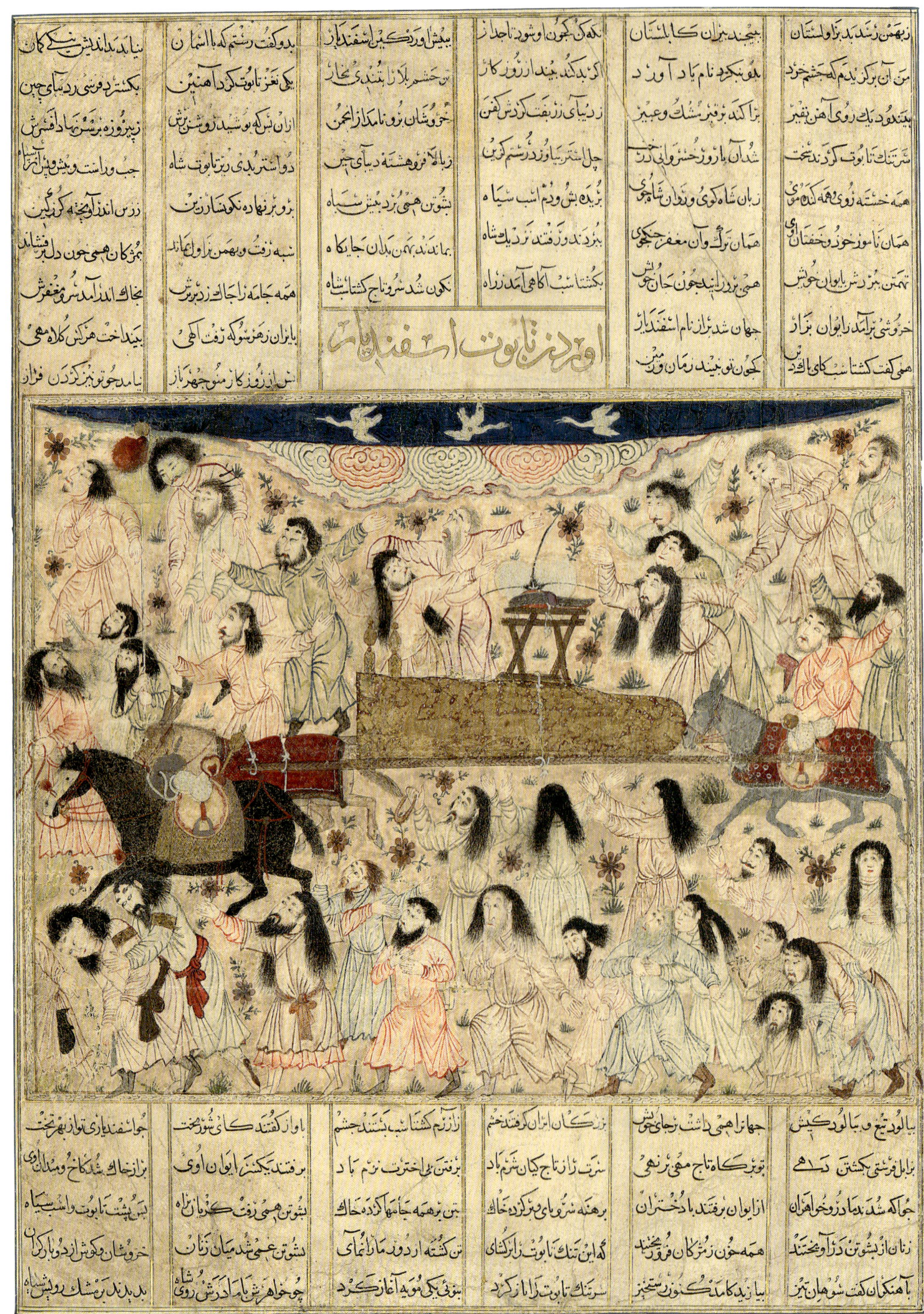
اوردن تابوت اسفندیار

57. *Folio from the Shahnama (Book of Kings) of Firdausi*

"The Funeral of Isfandiyar"
Iran, Tabriz, 1330s
Ink, opaque watercolor, and gold on paper
$22\frac{7}{8} \times 15\frac{3}{4}$ in. (58×40 cm)
Purchase, Joseph Pulitzer Bequest, 1933 33.70

Blending Iranian myth, Mongol traditions, and Chinese motifs, this folio bears witness to the rich artistic and cultural exchanges that occurred in Iran under the Ilkhanid dynasty. It comes from a dispersed copy of the *Shahnama* (Book of Kings) known as the Great Mongol *Shahnama*, and illustrates the funeral procession of Isfandiyar, one of the central characters of the epic. King Gushtasp ordered Isfandiyar to bring the hero Rustam to his court in chains (with the promise of making him king). Reluctant to do this because of Rustam's long-standing loyalty to the crown of Iran, Isfandiyar attempted to convince him to return to Iran. Rustam's refusal to comply with the royal order led to a fight that ended in the death of Isfandiyar.

As in other paintings in this manuscript, the illustration closely follows the narrative, but it is also infused with details taken from contemporary Mongol mourning customs.[1] Mongol historical sources have noted that funerary processions were opened by the horse of the deceased with the saddle placed in reverse. Fittingly, the image shows Isfandiyar's black horse in front of the cortege, with his tail cut and the saddle upturned to signal mourning. The coffin, said to have been wrapped in Chinese silk and carried by mules, is accordingly depicted, escorted by a large group of mourners whose animated gestures and unbalanced postures effectively communicate the profound grief caused by the prince's death. The monochromatic palette of the scene further draws the viewer's attention to the individual expressions of the participants, enhancing the dramatic quality of the representation.

The Great Mongol *Shahnama* was commissioned by the Ilkhanid ruler Abu Sa'id (r. 1317–35) toward the end of his reign. The codex was never completed, but in its final version it would have been in two volumes and contained some 280 folios and between 180 and 200 illustrations,[2] making it one of the most richly illustrated codices in the history of the Persianate arts of the book.[3] Some of the paintings in the manuscript and their association with contemporary Mongol practices have led scholars to identify it with the *Abu Sa'idnama*, a saga about the reign of the Ilkhanid ruler that is mentioned in later sources but is now lost.[4] Although intriguing, this interpretation is not universally accepted.[5]

It has been suggested that the Ilkhanids' interest in the Persian epic tradition was a way for them to assimilate local culture into their own and to reinforce their claim as the legitimate rulers of Iran. Only a few decades after the Ilkhanids' accession, scenes and verses from the *Shahnama* were being used on luster tiles to decorate the Ilkhanid summer residence at Takht-i Sulaiman, in northwestern Iran. At the same time, through the adoption of the local epic tradition, the Ilkhanids embraced a practice that is attested in earlier times and that linked power to myth.[6] The recurrence of the *Shahnama* in their cultural production ultimately demonstrates how the epic offered a formula for idealized kingship that articulated the aspirations of many generations of rulers. FL

1. As first noted by Grabar and Blair 1980, p. 100.
2. Blair 1989.
3. Another profusely illustrated version of the *Shahnama* was produced for Shah Tahmasp (r. 1524–76) starting in the 1520s. Seventy-seven folios of this manuscript are currently in the Metropolitan Museum (acc. nos. 1970.301.01–77). See, for example, cat. 138A–G.
4. In the preface for the album assembled for the Safavid prince Bahram Mirza in 1544, the *Abu Sa'idnama* is mentioned by Dust Muhammad in relation to the painter Ahmad Musa; see Thackston 2001, p. 12. The interpretation of the Great Mongol *Shahnama* as *Abu Sa'idnama* was proposed in Soudavar 1996.
5. Among the various critiques of this interpretation, see Blair 2004, esp. pp. 46–47.
6. According to the thirteenth-century historian Ibn Bibi, 'Ala' al-Din Kai Qubad I had quotations from the *Shahnama* on the walls of his palaces in Konya and Sivas (New York and Los Angeles 2002–3, p. 102).

PROVENANCE: [Demotte, Inc., New York, by 1926–33; sold to MMA]

58. *Folio from the Shahnama (Book of Kings) of Firdausi*

"Bizhan Slaughtering the Wild Boars of Irman"
Iran, Shiraz, dated A.H. 741/1341 A.D.
Ink, opaque watercolor, and gold on paper
Image: $3\frac{1}{2} \times 9\frac{1}{2}$ in. (8.9×24 cm); page: $14\frac{3}{8} \times 11\frac{7}{8}$ in. (36.5×30.3 cm)
H. O. Havemeyer Collection, Gift of Horace Havemeyer, 1929 29.160.22

This folio illustrates the culminating moment in the tale of Bizhan and the boars of Irman, one of the many stories of heroic exploits contained in the *Shahnama* (Book of Kings). In this tale, Bizhan offers his help to the tribe of Irman—a region lying on the border between Iran and Turan—when a delegation from that land asks for Kai Khusrau's assistance against the hordes of ferocious boars plaguing their forests. The illustration is a faithful rendition of the verses preceding it, which describe how an armor-clad and mounted Bizhan pursues and slays the wild boars. In spite of the illustration's loose style and simple layout, the painting eloquently conveys the magnitude of Bizhan's task by minimizing the landscape and multiplying the number and size of the boars that the hero must slaughter.

This succinct, incisive pictorial style distinguishes the earliest surviving illustrated versions of the *Shahnama*, which date from the

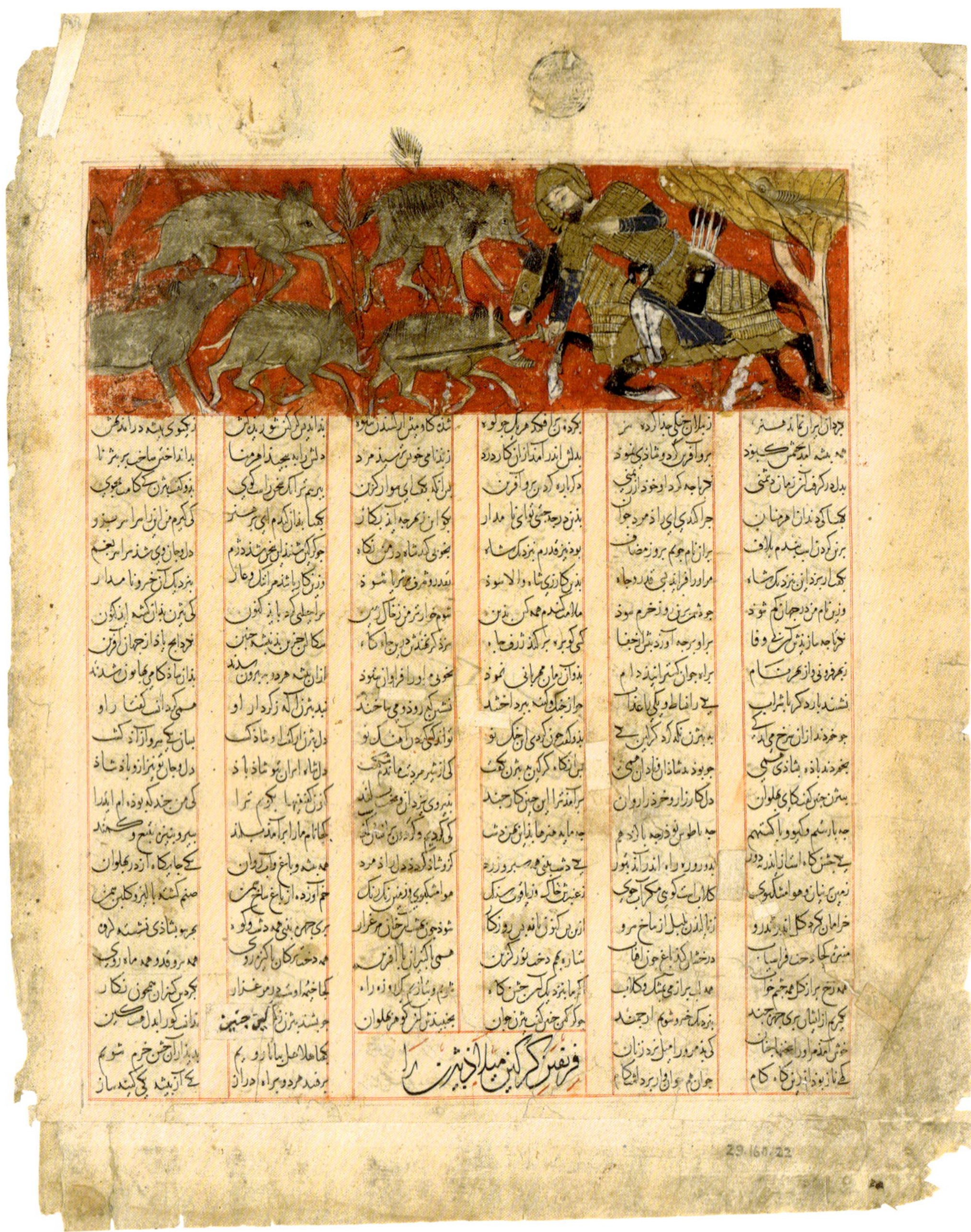

beginning of the fourteenth century. The manuscript from which this page derives is now dispersed, but its colophon bears the date A.H. 741/1341 A.D., with a dedication to Qiwam al-Daula wa'l-Din Hasan.[1] Qiwam al-Daula (ca. 1303–1357) was the vizier of the Injuids, who emerged as more or less independent rulers of the Iranian province of Fars in the decades preceding and immediately following the fall of the Ilkhanid dynasty.[2] The surviving folios from this codex shed light on the sophisticated nature of the original manuscript, which is, however, not comparable in quality or complexity to the almost contemporary illustrated version of the same text commissioned by the Ilkhanid Abu Sa'id (r. 1317–35), known as the Great Mongol *Shahnama*.[3] At the same time, the fact that an increasing number of officials decided to commission illustrated copies of the Persian epic testifies to the growing interest in the ancient royal traditions of Iran.[4] FL

1. Lowry et al., 1988, pp. 69–70.
2. Eighty illustrated pages are currently scattered among private and public collections. Seven are in the Metropolitan Museum (in addition to cat. 58, acc. nos. 29.160.21, 36.113.1–3, 57.51.35, and 57.51.36), while the dedication page is in the Arthur M. Sackler Gallery, Smithsonian Institution, Washington, D.C. (no. S86.0110).
3. See cat. 57.
4. At least seven manuscripts can be attributed to the Injuids, and four of them are copies of the *Shahnama* (New York and Los Angeles 2002–3, p. 217). A list of these manuscripts is provided in Grube 1978, pp. 15–16 and n. 43.

PROVENANCE: H. O. Havemeyer Collection, New York (until 1929)

59. Folio from the *Mu'nis al-ahrar fi daqa'iq al-ash'ar* (Free Man's Companion to the Subtleties of Poems) of Muhammad ibn Badr al-Din Jajarmi

Iran, Isfahan, A.H. 741/1340–41 A.D.
Ink, opaque watercolor, and gold on paper
9 1/8 × 6 5/8 in. (23.2 × 16.8 cm)
Cora Timken Burnett Collection of Persian Miniatures and Other Persian Art Objects,
Bequest of Cora Timken Burnett, 1956 57.51.25

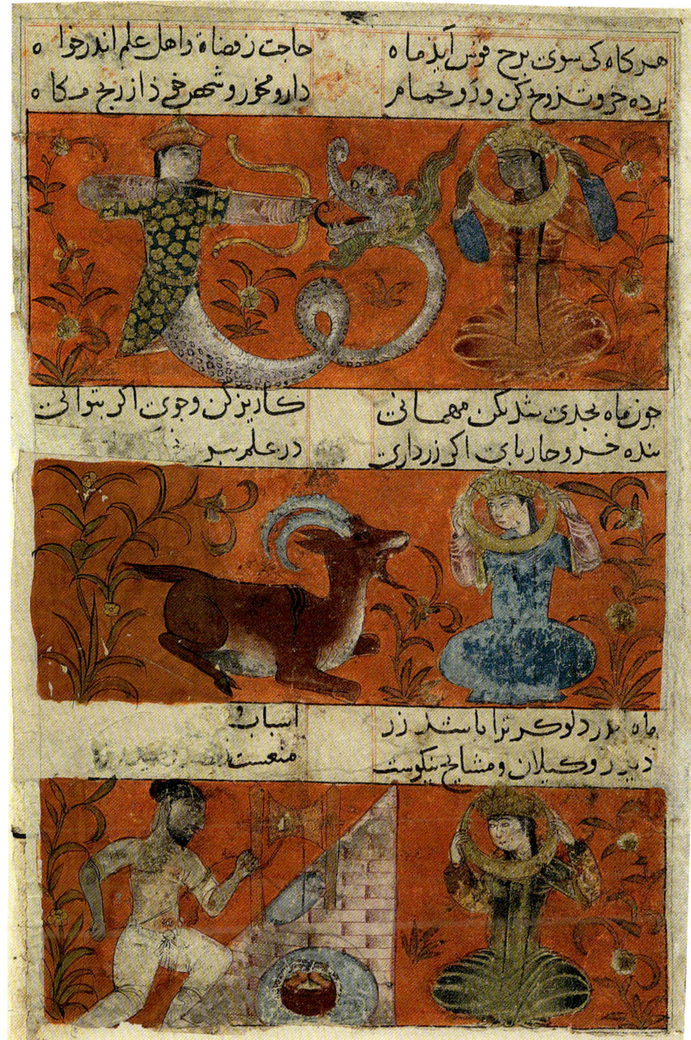

This illustrated page was originally part of a compilation of poems assembled by the Persian intellectual and poet Muhammad ibn Badr al-Din Jajarmi and titled *Mu'nis al-ahrar fi daqa'iq al-ash'ar* (Free Man's Companion to the Subtleties of Poems).

Internal evidence in the manuscript[1] strongly suggests that Jajarmi was in Isfahan when he copied the text, and its colophon states that he finished it in Ramadan A.H. 741/February–March 1341 A.D. It is therefore one of the few dated illustrated texts from the Ilkhanid period and the only surviving one that can be attributed to Isfahan. The codex, known to scholars since 1914, was in the Kevorkian Foundation, New York, until the Dar al-Athar al-Islamiyya, al-Sabah Collection, in Kuwait City acquired it through Sotheby's London in 1979.

The manuscript currently contains a double-page figural frontispiece showing a princely couple in a mature though provincial Ilkhanid style. However, the six pages that once formed chapter 29 of this poetic anthology—the only other illustrated folios in an otherwise strictly textual work—were detached early in the twentieth century and purchased by five different institutions in the United States.[2]

Once reconstructed,[3] chapter 29 includes a fascinating and rare example of pictorial poetry,[4] an astrological poem, and a final *ruba'i* (quatrain).[5] The two folios in the Metropolitan Museum (acquired in 1919 and 1957)[6] cover almost the entire astrological poem,[7] which explains in rhyme the most appropriate things to do when the Moon is in conjunction with each of the twelve signs of the zodiac.

Illustrated here is the verso of the folio that includes the text and images of Sagittarius, Capricorn, and Aquarius. Didactically arranged on the left facing a female figure who holds a crescent around her head to represent the Moon, the three signs are easy to identify, respectively, as an archer who shoots an arrow against his own dragonlike tail, a kid with long curved horns, and the planet Saturn (the water carrier) lifting a bucket from a well. Each rectangular vignette is set against a red background sparsely filled with large plants. As an example, the poet says: "When the Moon is in Aquarius, if you have money / Buy furnishings and goods and Indian slaves. / To see agents and sheikhs is good. / There is a ban on bleeding, hunting, marriage, and travel."[8] SC

1. Alexander Morton's analysis of the text convinced him that the author was writing in Isfahan. See New York 1994, p. 51.
2. These are the Arthur M. Sackler Museum, Cambridge, Mass.; the Cleveland Museum of Art; the Princeton University Library, Robert Garrett Collection; the Freer Gallery of Art, Smithsonian Institution, Washington, D.C.; and the Metropolitan Museum, the only institution owning two pages.
3. Five of the six folios as well as the manuscript in Kuwait were reunited in the Museum as part of the 1994 exhibition "Illustrated Poetry and Epic Images: Persian Painting of the 1330s and 1340s," organized by Marie Lukens Swietochowski and myself. The accompanying book with the same title (New York 1994) fully addresses the literary and art-historical aspects of the manuscript.
4. Attributed to the poet al-Rawandi, the first half of each verse of the poem is written in words whereas the second half is in the form of an illustrated riddle or rebus. See New York 1994, pp. 26–37, nos. 2–4.
5. The last two poems are attributed by Jajarmi to his father, also a well-known poet.
6. The folio purchased in 1919 is acc. no. 19.68.1.
7. Not included are the last two verses and illustration, which shows the Moon in Pisces.
8. In the translation of Alexander Morton in New York 1994, p. 44.

PROVENANCE: Cora Timken Burnett, Alpine, N.J. (by 1933–d. 1956)

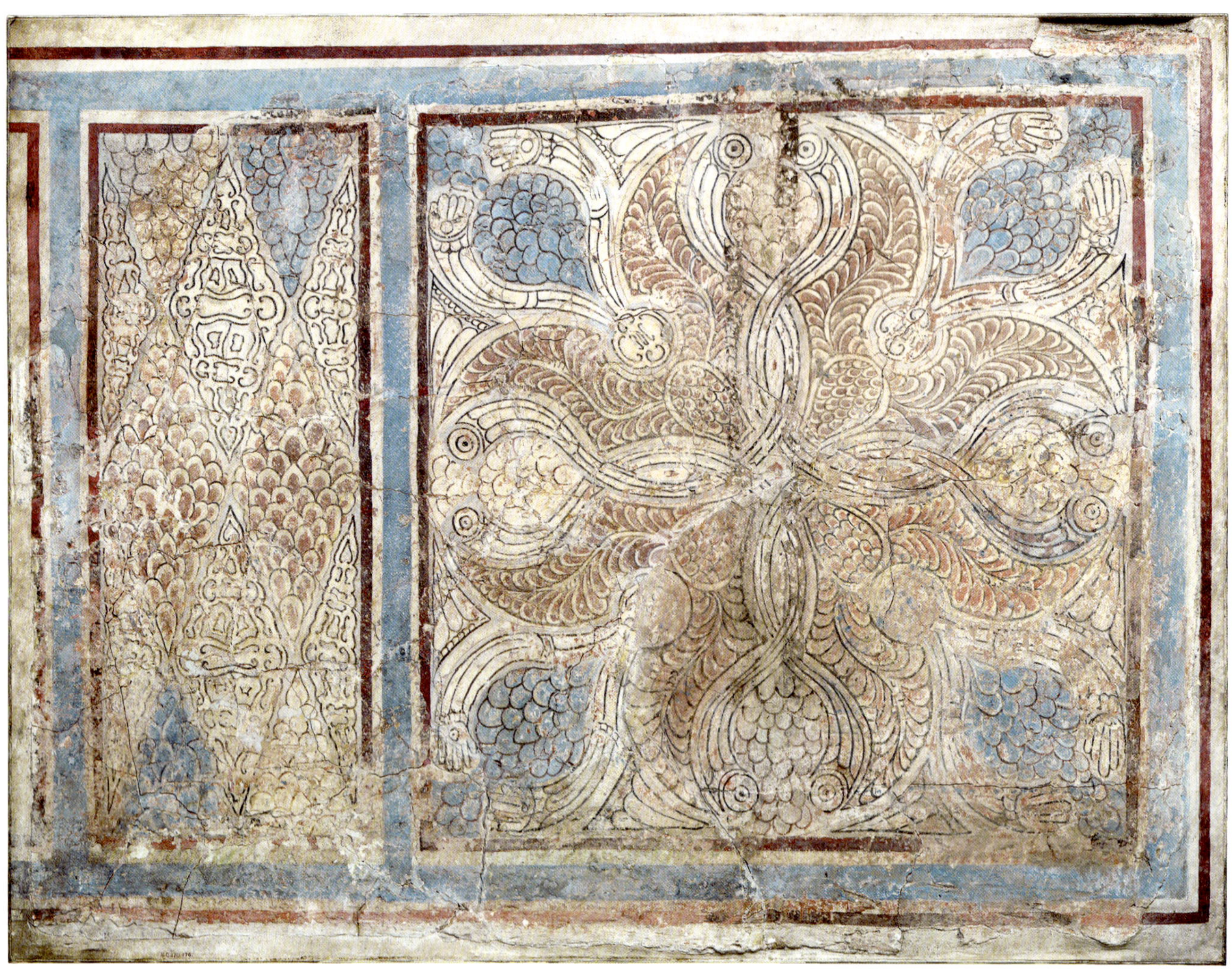

60. Dado Panel

Iran, 9th century
Excavated at Tepe Madrasa, Nishapur
Stucco; painted
40⅜ × 53½ × 2 in. (102.6 × 135.9 × 5.1 cm)
Rogers Fund, 1940 40.170.176

The room in Nishapur, Iran, from which this dado panel was excavated once had a lively scheme of painted decoration. The upper section of the wall was colored a deep red, beneath which was a short horizontal frieze of hexagons and diamonds, and a four-foot-high dado with alternating rectangular and square panels. Each dado panel was framed with red, blue, and white lines; the rectangular panels contained a diamond or lozenge-shaped pattern filled with a design akin to quarter-sawn marble or fish scales, and the square panels featured a motif composed of a variety of feathery shapes, scale-covered elements, and interlaced ribbons ending in stylized eyes and hands. These patterns were executed in shades of blue, red, yellow, and brown.[1]

The section of Nishapur where this panel was found was known locally as Tepe Madrasa; judging from its modern name, the Metropolitan Museum's archaeologists had hoped to find one of Nishapur's famed institutions of learning, or *madrasas*. During the excavations of 1938–40, they instead uncovered a large residential area with a mosque that had been developed and rebuilt in several phases between the ninth and twelfth centuries. It is within one of the residences in this area that this panel was discovered, inside a room measuring approximately sixteen by nineteen feet (roughly five by six meters).

The excavators later determined that the building from which the painted dadoes were extracted dated to the ninth century, and suggested that the room was once part of the Tahirid-period palaces mentioned in historical sources.[2] The panel here and the numerous other examples found at Nishapur, all in different styles, are the earliest known examples of wall painting from the Islamic period in Iran.

While the meaning of this panel's decoration remains an enigma, most scholars believe that its imagery had an apotropaic function. One hypothesis is that the eye and hand symbols derived from representations of the "hand of God," but it has also been argued that the iconography should be linked to pre-Islamic bird-snake motifs that were believed to represent the souls of the deceased.[3] Either of these interpretations makes it unlikely that the room containing these panels was part of a palace, although so far there are no other indications of its function, as the excavators suggested. MS

1. Of the dado surface that the excavators uncovered, it was possible to preserve only two square and two rectangular panels; one set went to the Iran Bastan Museum, Tehran, and one set came to the Metropolitan Museum. See Wilkinson 1986, pp. 159–84. The structure where these panels were found is labeled "W20."
2. For an evolving discussion and identification of the site, see Hauser and Wilkinson 1942, pp. 97–100; Bulliet 1976, p. 75; Wilkinson 1986, p. 181; and Sims, Marshak, and Grube 2002, p. 28.
3. Wilkinson 1986, p. 173; and Rührdanz 1995, p. 593.

PROVENANCE: 1939, discovered at Tepe Madrasa, Nishapur, Iran, by the Metropolitan Museum's expedition under a concession granted by the Council of Ministers, Iran, upon the recommendation of the Ministry of Education of Iran; title transferred to The Metropolitan Museum of Art pursuant to the concession

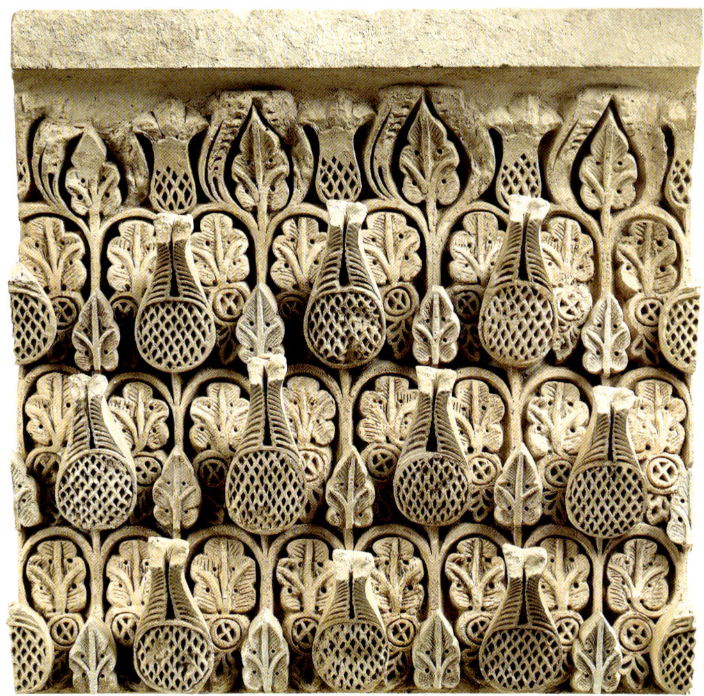

61. Cornice Panel

Iran, 10th century
Excavated at Tepe Madrasa, Nishapur
Stucco; molded, applied, carved
28⅛ × 29⅜ × 6⅞ in. (71.3 × 74.5 × 17.5 cm)
Rogers Fund, 1940 40.170.441

Found at Tepe Madrasa, Nishapur, this panel with vine leaves and projecting pineapple-shaped bosses was located among many other stucco fragments that had once decorated a group of buildings northwest of this area's mosque. As these fragments were piled among the remains of destroyed structures, with little in situ, it was impossible to determine where this particular panel originally appeared, or even to know the type of room to which it belonged. Nevertheless, its curved upper margin led the excavators to conclude that it had once formed part of a cornice.[1]

The panel's decoration is quite different from the stuccowork found at other parts of Nishapur, such as that excavated at the part of the site known as Sabz Pushan, or even in adjacent buildings at Tepe Madrasa. However, its design can be favorably compared to stuccowork with similar motifs found at Merv and at the Samanid palace of Afrasiyab (modern Samarqand), both thought to be of the ninth century,[2] and at Hira, possibly of the eighth century.[3]

The finds from these sites elucidate the use of stucco in the medieval Islamic world, testifying to this medium's widespread popularity during the ninth and tenth centuries, especially in the Samanid realms of northeastern Iran, which included Nishapur. Although scholars have tended to credit the use of stucco at the Abbasid capital of Samarra to the prevalence of stucco throughout the Abbasid cultural sphere, remains from earlier periods at Afrasiyab, Merv, Rayy, and other late Sasanian sites in Iran seem to suggest a long local history for the stucco patterns found in Islamic-period buildings, indicating that the Samanid-era stuccowork may have had an indigenous source. The finds from Iran also provide evidence for the simultaneous use of many styles of carving at a single site. Reconstructions made by the excavators of Afrasiyab suggest that the buildings had entire walls and ceilings covered with stucco panels, each with a different design. These panels were often colored bright blue, yellow, and red, and traces of such pigments were found on this panel as well. MS

1. These fragments were found in the structure C2; see Wilkinson 1986, pp. 116–36. The panel as shown here has been restored; for the fragments as excavated, see ibid., p. 133, fig. 1.142.
2. Akhrarov and Rempel 1971, p. 45, fig. 22.
3. Rice, D. T. 1934, p. 63, fig. 14.

PROVENANCE: 1938, discovered at Tepe Madrasa, Nishapur, Iran, by the Metropolitan Museum's expedition under a concession granted by the Council of Ministers, Iran, upon the recommendation of the Ministry of Education of Iran; title transferred to The Metropolitan Museum of Art pursuant to the concession

62. Princely Figure with Winged Crown

Iran, mid-11th–mid-12th century
Stucco; modeled, carved, polychrome-painted, gilded
H. 47 in. (119.4 cm)
Cora Timken Burnett Collection of Persian Miniatures and Other Persian Art Objects,
Bequest of Cora Timken Burnett, 1956 57.51.18

63. Princely Figure with Jeweled Crown

Iran, mid-11th–mid-12th century
Stucco; modeled, carved, polychrome-painted, gilded
H. 56¾ in. (144.1 cm)
Gift of Mr. and Mrs. Lester Wolfe, 1967 67.119

Cat. 62
Inscription in Arabic in *kufic* script on *tiraz* band, left sleeve:
عليک [ـم] بالـ

On *tiraz* band, right sleeve:
ـمؤمنين
[Anxious is he] over you, [gentle] to the believers.
(most likely from Qur'an 9:128)

Cat. 63
Inscription in Arabic in *kufic* script on *tiraz* band with cartouches, on right and left sleeves:
الملك
Dominion [belongs to God]

Nearly lifesize, these two stately figures with Turkic "moon faces" wear embroidered and highly embellished coats or kaftans over an undergarment and pants. The kaftans' upper sleeves are embroidered with *tiraz* bands whose inscriptions are only partially visible. Both figures have long, flowing hair and wear elaborate crowns; one is adorned with a winged palmette (cat. 62), while the other (cat. 63) is richly decorated with jewels. In addition, each figure's right hand firmly grips the hilt of a slightly curved sword or saber. Although their posture recalls standing Sasanian royal and Umayyad caliphal figures, it was also typical at a later date for images of palace guards.[1] A symbol of royalty, the *mandil* or the royal napkin, can be seen in the right hand of the second figure and may have been held in the right hand of the first one, although it is missing now. The plaster figures were highlighted in different colors, among them ultramarine, red, orange, and black; minute traces of gold foil remain on such raised elements as the flowers, jewelry, and headdresses. Even though these figures arrived at the Metropolitan Museum at different times, their technique, style, size, and decoration suggest that they once belonged to the decorative program of the same palace complex, which has yet to be identified.

Initially dated to the later Seljuq period, about the twelfth and thirteenth centuries,[2] these carvings have several features that suggest an earlier dating between the mid-eleventh and mid-twelfth century. After the decline of the Abbasid Empire in the early tenth century, Iran saw a revival of pre-Islamic, Sasanian, and even Soghdian forms and images of royalty. These images were intended to shed a favorable light on new dynasties of Iranian and Turkish origin as revivers of past glory. Images of winged crowns, such as the one seen on cat. 62, are markers for this revival style.

The calligraphic design, especially with respect to the *tiraz* brassards of cat. 63, allows an approximate dating. Beginning in the early tenth century, the pointed triangular fins of the short vertical letters of such inscriptions evolved to reach the height of the long vertical shafts of the letters, as seen here. This style was popular from the eleventh century until the middle decades of the twelfth century.[3] A *minbar* panel in the Metropolitan Museum dated A.H. 546/1151 A.D. (cat. 65B) displays a fine example of this calligraphic style.

Several similar but much smaller figures, which presumably came from western Iran, were acquired by a number of museums prior to World War I. In northern Mesopotamia and Seljuq Asia Minor, large reliefs of humans and princely figures were made of stone rather than stucco, and differed in style. The closest parallels in terms of imagery are offered by frescoes in Central Asian palaces in Bust (present-day Afghanistan) and Samarqand. The fresco murals in Bust at the Lashkari Bazaar palace complex are dated to the reign of the Ghaznavid ruler Mas'ud I (r. 1031–41).

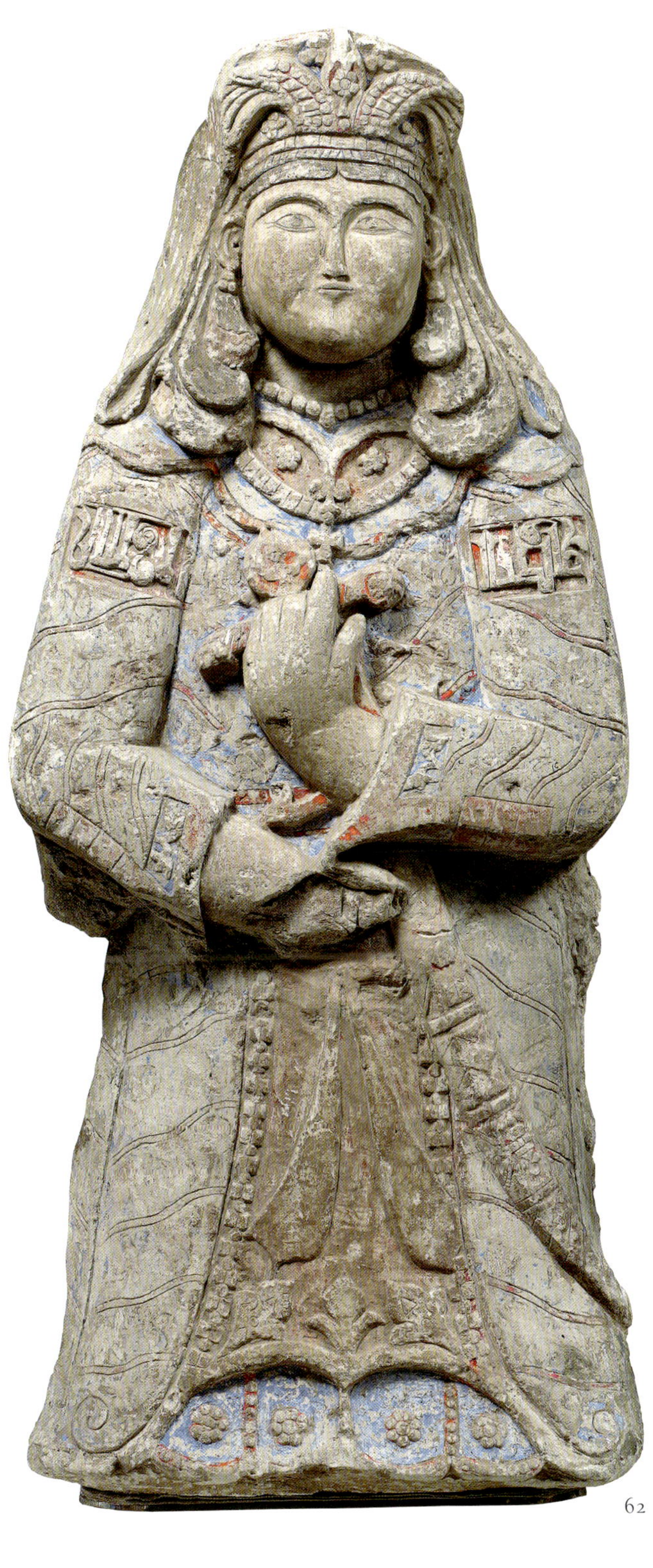

62

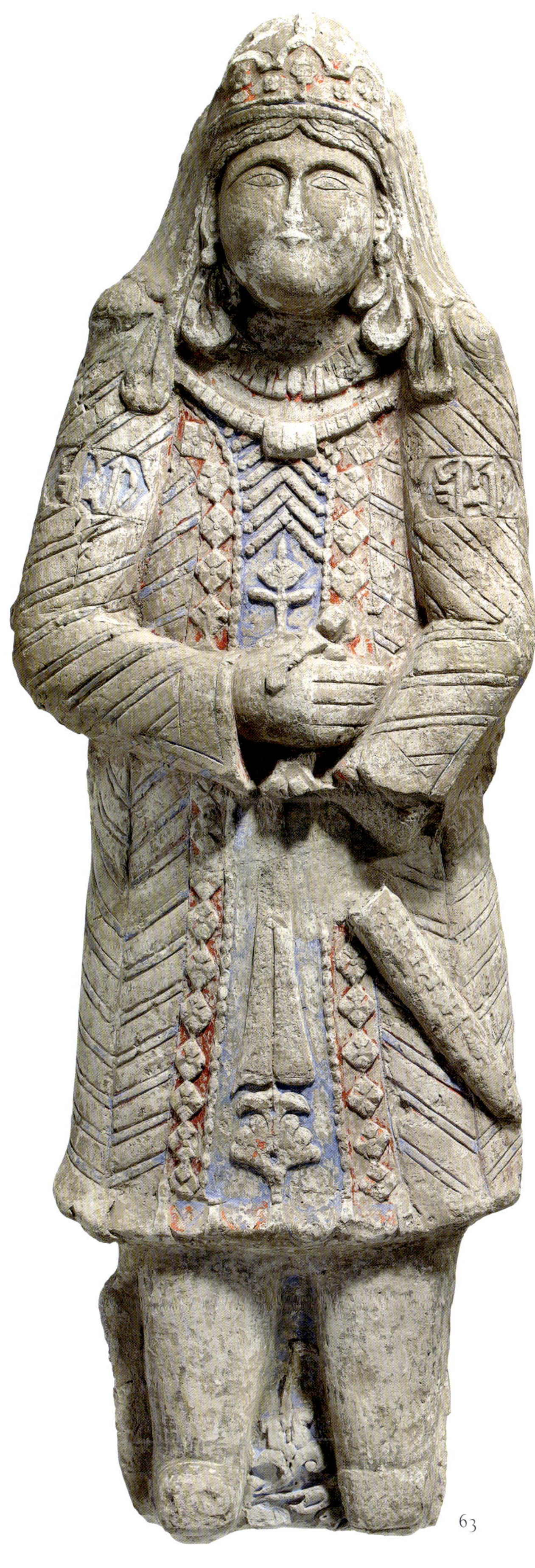

63

Depicted are forty-four standing courtly figures in three-quarter view, all with Turkish Asiatic "moon-face" features and clothed in kaftans of blue and red. The scene appears to be a royal audience, in which courtiers or guards turn to a central figure that is now missing.[4] Quite similar are the murals in a pavilion in Samarqand from the Qarakhanid period (992–1212), dated to the mid-twelfth century.[5]

The Metropolitan's two extraordinary, large polychrome stucco sculptures of princely figures probably once served as centerpieces of a larger courtly scene of stucco revetments that complemented a palace complex in Iran about 1050 to 1150. SH

1. Gibson forthcoming.
2. Riefstahl 1931.
3. Sourdel-Thomine 1978. For Ghaznavid inscriptions, see Flury 1925, esp. pp. 83–84, no. 12, for the tomb of a certain As'ad ibn 'Ali, which Flury dated to the early twelfth century.
4. Casal 1978. Some of the figures carry a kind of rod or mace over the right shoulder.
5. Karev 2005.

Provenance
Cat. 62: Cora Timkin Burnett, Alpine, N.J. (by 1940–d. 1956)
Cat. 63: Mr. and Mrs. Lester Wolfe, New York (by 1966–67)

64. *Tombstone of Abu Sa'd ibn Muhammad ibn Ahmad ibn al-Hasan Karwaih*

Carver: Ahmad ibn Muhammad Astak
Iran, Yazd, dated A.H. Muharram 545/April–May 1150 A.D.
Marble; carved, painted
22¼ × 14⅝ × 2⅞ in. (56.5 × 37.1 × 7.3 cm)
Rogers Fund, 1933 33.118

Inscription in Arabic in *kufic* script on outer border:
بسم الله الرحمن الرحيم إن الذين قالوا ربنا الله/ثم إستقاموا تتنزل عليهم
الملا/ئكة ألا تخافوا و لا تحزنوا و أبشروا بالجنة التي كنتم [توعدون]
In the name of God, the Merciful, the Compassionate.
Those who have said, "Our Lord is God," then have gone straight, upon them the angels descend, saying, "Fear not, neither sorrow; rejoice in Paradise that you were promised." (Qur'an 41:30)

Inscription in Arabic in *thuluth* script on inner border:
بسم الله الرحمن الرحيم شهد الله أنه لا إله إلا هو/ و الملائكة و أولوا
العلم قا/ ئماً بالقسط لا إله إلا هو العزيز الحكيم
In the name of God, the Merciful, the Compassionate.
God bears witness that there is no God but He—and the angels, and men possessed of knowledge—upholding justice; there is no god but He, the All-Mighty, the All-Wise. (Qur'an 3:18)

Inscription in Arabic in *kufic* script on band at top (between borders):
لا إله إلا الله محمد رسول الله
There is no god but God and Muhammad is the Messenger of God.

Signature in Arabic in *kufic* script on band at bottom (between borders):
عمل احمد بن محمد استك
Work of Ahmad son of Muhammad Astak

Inscription in Arabic in *kufic* script on central panel:
هذا قبر/ابي سعد بن/ محمد بن احمد/ بن الحسن كا/ رويه توفي/ في
محرم سنة/ خمس و اربعين/ و خمس مائة
This is the grave of Abu Sa'd son of Muhammad son of Ahmad son of al-Hasan Karwaih, he died in the month of Muharram of the year five hundred and forty five.

One of the few surviving examples of tenth- to twelfth-century tombstones from Yazd (a city southeast of Isfahan in central Iran) in museum collections, this piece is carved from beige (*gandumi*) marble and contains a central prayer niche framed by Qur'anic inscriptions.[1] The outer border, which is the widest, contains verses from *Surat al-Fussilat* (Sura 41:30) while the inner border contains verses from *Surat al-Imran* (Sura 3:18). Two registers between the inner and the outer borders on the top and bottom

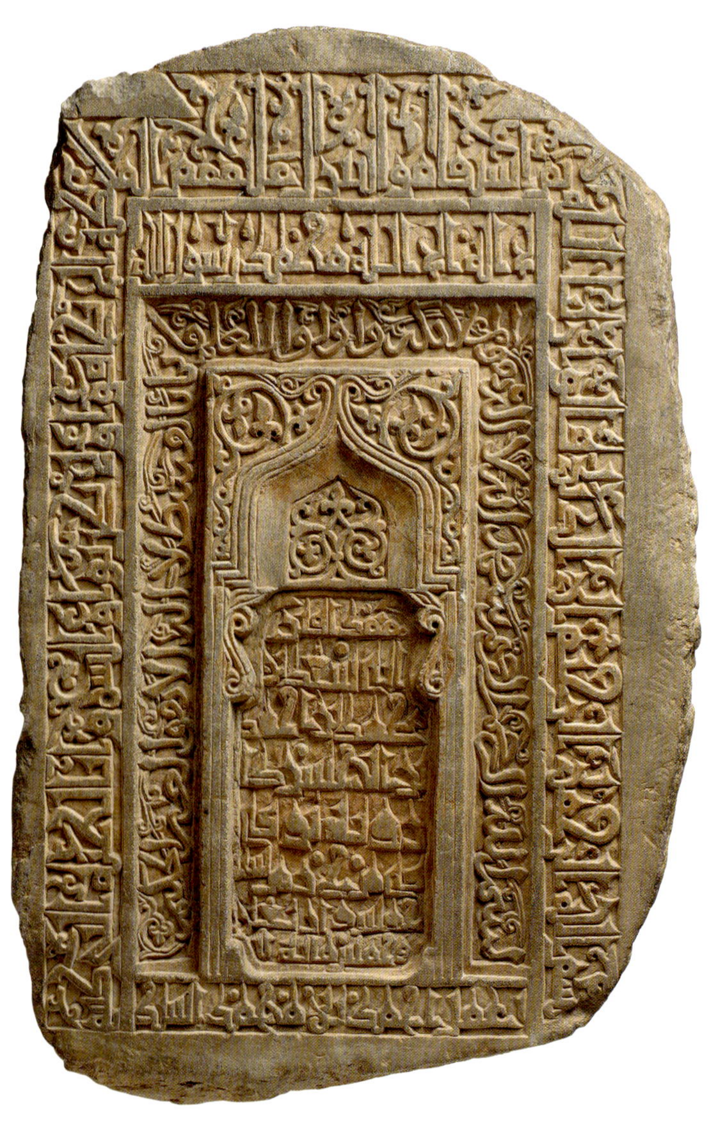

feature the *shahada* (the profession of the faith) and the signature of the carver, "Ahmad son of Muhammad Astak."[2]

The central panel includes an arched prayer niche with the name of the deceased, Abu Sa'd son of Muhammad son of Ahmad son of al-Hasan Karwaih, and his death date, A.H. Muharram 545/ April–May 1150 A.D. Traces of red and black paint suggest that segments of the tombstone were originally painted, perhaps to highlight the inscriptions.[3] The upper part of the niche is decorated with curvilinear vegetal motifs with spiral ends.

Most significant for this tombstone is its prayer niche (*mihrab*). The evolution of *mihrabs*—and the relationship between contemporaneous *mihrabs* and these tombstones—has engendered much discussion among scholars. Although similar *mihrab* designs were used in the local production of Asia Minor, Spain, and North Africa, the complexity of Iranian examples, which bear several bands of inscriptions, sets them apart them from tombstones of other regions.[4]

A very similar style of *kufic* script and vegetal designs can be seen on two fragments from a twelfth-century *minbar* in the Museum's collection (cat. 65A, B), suggesting that this form of *kufic* was prevalent in Iran in the twelfth century and was used across media in Seljuq art.[5] Another, almost identical twelfth-century tombstone in situ in Yazd dates to nine years before the Metropolitan's example[6] and is signed by the same carver, Ahmad son of Muhammad. Other examples in the Museum of Fine Arts, Boston,[7] the Arthur M. Sackler Museum, Cambridge, Massachusetts,[8] and the Cleveland Museum of Art[9] have a similar composition, surface ornament, and style of script. Ideally, further paleographic studies will identify other objects produced by the same stone carver in Yazd. AG/PG

1. These beige-colored *gandumi* stones and similar tombstones are found in Maibud, Tabas, Qaznaviyya, and Bafq in the Yazd region. For a survey of tombstones in Yazd and more information on this type of composition, see Afshar 1969 and Afshar 1973, pl. 42.
2. For more information on the inscription, see Cairo 1931, p. 27, no. 22.
3. Technical examinations determined the traces of red (iron oxide) and black (amorphous carbon-based black).
4. Fehérvári 1972, p. 241; Whelan 1986; Khoury 1992; Khoury 1998; Hanover and other cities 1991–92, p. 96, no. 32.
5. For more information, see Dimand 1944a, pp. 91–97.
6. The tombstone is published in Pope, A.U., and Ackerman, eds. 1938–39, vol.5, pt. 1, pl. 519E.
7. Museum of Fine Arts, Boston (no. 31.711), published in "Acquisitions [MFA]" 1931, p. 95.
8. Arthur M. Sackler Museum, Cambridge, Mass. (no. 1963.18), published in Hanover and other cities 1991–92, p. 79, fig. 14.
9. Cleveland Museum of Art (no. 1950.9), published in Binghamton 1975, fig. 18. The tombstone is dated A.H. 545/1150 A.D., and the inner inscription from Qur'an 41:30 is the same as the outer inscription of the Metropolitan's tombstone.

PROVENANCE: [A. Rabenou, Paris, by 1931–33; sold to MMA]

65A, B. Two Fragments of a Minbar

Iran, Yazd, dated A.H. 546/1151 A.D.
Wood (teak); carved and painted

A. Vertical Pulpit Fragment
47½ × 12⅜ × 3¼ in. (120.7 × 31.4 × 8.3 cm)
Fletcher Fund, 1934 34.150.1

B. Horizontal Fragment
18¼ × 30⅛ × 2½ in. (46.4 × 76.5 × 6.4 cm)
Fletcher Fund, 1934 34.150.2

Inscription in Arabic in *kufic* script on vertical fragment (A):
[. . . تفا]وت فارجع البصر هل ترى من فطور ثم أرجع البصر كرتين ينقلب
/ إليك الـ(ـبـ)ـصر خـ/
[ـاسئاً و]هو حسير و لقد زينا السماء الدنيا بمصابيح وجعلناها رجوماً للشـ[ـياطين]
[. . .] Return your gaze; seest thou any fissure? Then return again, and again, and thy gaze comes back to thee dazzled, aweary. And we adorned the lower heaven with lamps, and made them things to stone Satans. . . . (Qur'an 67:3–5)

Inscription in Arabic in *kufic* script on horizontal panel (B):
أمر هذا/
المنبر عبد مذنب/
أبو بكر بن محمد بن أحمد كلاى/
ثمانة (؟) تقرباً إلى الله و رجاء إلى رحمة الله/
في زمن الأمير الأجل السيد المؤيد المظفر/
المنصور عضد الدين شمس الملوك/
و السلاطين علاء الدولة گرشاسب/
بن علي بن فرامرز بن علاء الدولة حسام أمير/
المؤمنين في جمادى الأولى سنة ست وأربعين وخمس مائة
This *minbar* was ordered by a sinful slave, Abu Bakr ibn Muhammad ibn Ahmad Kalai [. . .], to be closer to God and in hope of God's mercy. In the time of the most exalted commander, the Lord, the God-aided, the Vanquisher, the Victorious, 'Adud al-Din Shams al-Muluk wal-Salatin 'Ala' al-Daula Garshasp ibn 'Ali ibn Faramurz ibn 'Ala' al-Daula, Husam Amir a-Mu'minin, in Jumada I, in the year A.H. 546 [August / September 1151 A.D]

Inscription in Arabic in *kufic* script on upper right and left of horizontal panel (B):
لا إله إلا الله/ محمد رسول الله
There is no god but God and Muhammad is the Messenger of God

These two wood fragments, which served both structural and decorative functions, belong to a *minbar* (pulpit) from a mosque at Yazd in central Iran. The horizontal fragment (cat. 65B) once crowned the tall vertical panel on the back of the *minbar* where the imam would sit, while the vertical fragment (cat. 65A) formed the lower side section, possibly carrying the fourth step.[1] Both fragments are carved with Arabic inscriptions in *kufic* script.

The horizontal fragment contains the foundation inscription stating that the *minbar* was commissioned by Abu Bakr ibn Muhammad in the time of 'Ala' al-Din Garshasp, a governor of Yazd under the Seljuqs; it also bears the date A.H. 546/1151 A.D. The angularity of the letters is typical of the archaic styles of late tenth- and eleventh-century Iranian carved tombstones, *mihrabs* (prayer niches), and *minbars*. (For an example of tenth- to twelfth-century tombstones from Yazd with a similar style of calligraphy, see cat. 64.)[2]

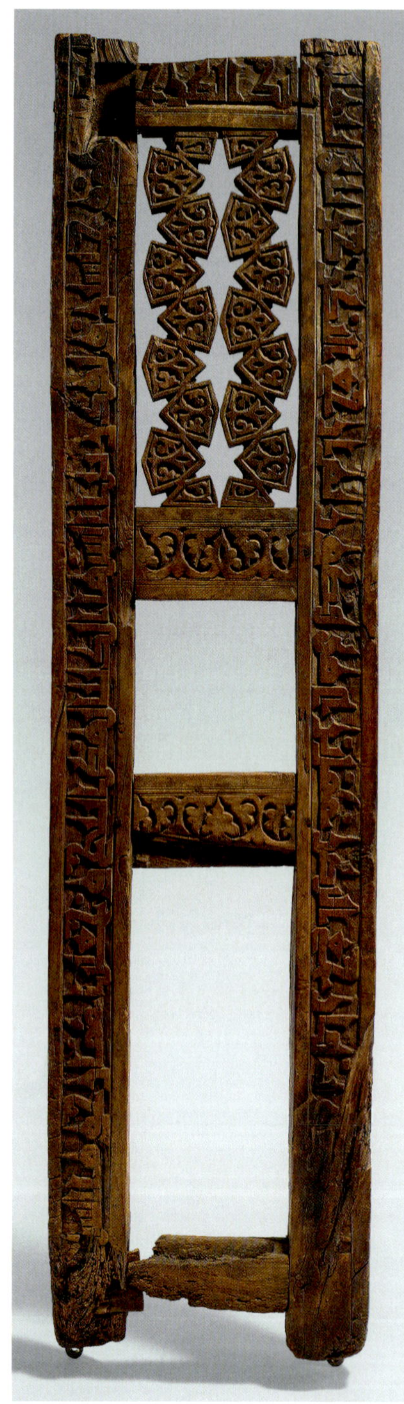

A

The deeply carved scrolling vegetal pattern seen here is also a characteristic feature of the tombstones of Yazd.

The vertical fragment is composed of six pieces of wood fastened with mortise-and-tenon joints. A Qur'anic inscription from Sura 67 (*al-Mulk*, "Dominion") runs along the uprights as well as the top crosspiece.[3] As a central axis between the two upper crosspieces, two lines of vertically arranged hexagonal forms create a repeating pattern of six-pointed stars in negative space. Both fragments contain traces of red, indigo, and white paint on the surface, suggesting that they were once painted to highlight inscriptions and ornament.[4]

Vegetal motifs on the two fragments are typical of those found on twelfth-century Iranian carved wood, although their origins can be traced to the ninth century. By the end of the eleventh century, this motif had evolved into a more naturalistic and curvilinear style with spiral ends, and by the twelfth century it came to include elaborate floral and geometric forms of vine scrolls, seen here in the two middle crosspieces of the vertical fragment.[5]

A tombstone in Farasha in Yazd[6] displays an almost identical scrolling vegetal design. This style of ornamentation is also found on a wood *minbar* of the Great Mosque of Abiyana, Isfahan province, Iran, dated 1073.[7] Similar vegetal motifs embellish Seljuq carved woodwork of Konya and Ankara in the twelfth and thirteenth centuries,[8] suggesting the wide dissemination of these motifs during this period. AG/PG

1. A very similar wooden construction can be found in the Nadushan Friday Mosque in Yazd. See Afshar 1975 and Ghouchani 2004. Technical analyses of these two fragments were carried out by Daniel Hausdorf, Assistant Conservator, The Metropolitan Museum of Art, The Sherman Fairchild Center for Objects Conservation.

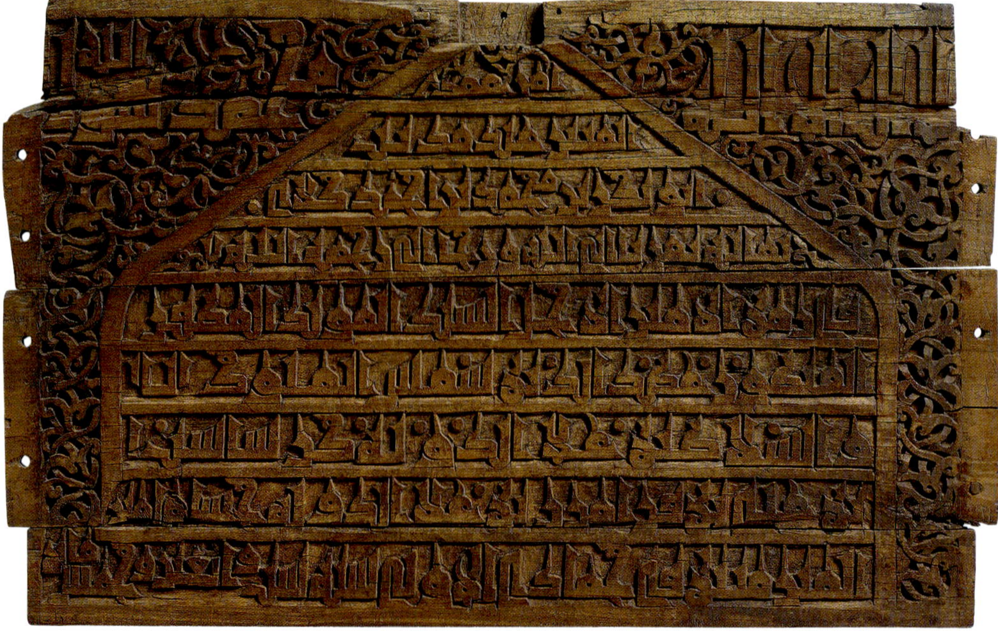

B

2. Another related piece in the Museum (acc. no. 34.152) is a tenth-century alabaster tombstone from Iran, carved in *kufic* script with the name *Yusuf*, the profession of faith, and prayers for the deceased.
3. The inscription starts from the second half of Qur'an 67:3, continues through 67:4, and ends at the first half of 67:5. Some of the missing verses may have originally been carved on the lower crosspiece. For more information on the inscription, see Ghouchani 2004.
4. Technical analysis was carried out by the Metropolitan Museum's wood conservators Daniel Hausdorf and Mechthild Baumeister.
5. Ettinghausen, Grabar, and Jenkins-Madina 2001, p. 213, and also Chapters 2 and 4: "Central Islamic Lands" and "Eastern Islamic Lands."
6. See Afshar 1973, pl. 42.
7. Also see an example in the David Collection, Copenhagen (no. 11/1977), attributed to eastern Iran and dated 1109. For bibliography, see Schimmel and Rivolta 1992 and Ettinghausen 1952, pp. 76–81. Also see Afshar 1973.
8. The panel mounted above the main door of a *minbar* in a Seljuq mosque in Konya is dated to 1155, and the *minbar* of Arslanhane Mosque in Ankara is dated to 1290.

PROVENANCE: [A. Rabenou, Paris, until 1934; sold to MMA]

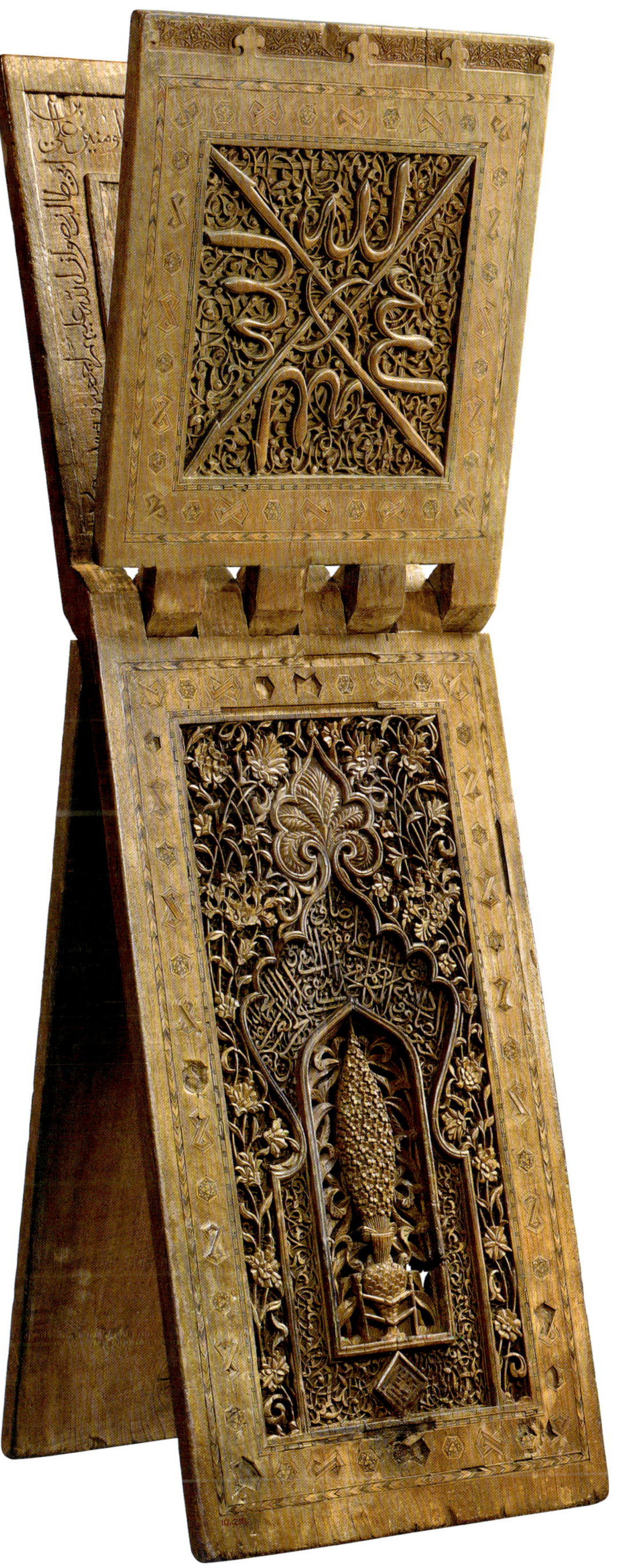

66. *Stand for a Qur'an Manuscript (Rahla)*

Maker: Zain(?) Hasan Sulaiman Isfahani
Iran, dated A.H. 761 / 1360 A.D.
Wood (teak); carved, painted, inlaid
Closed 51¼ × 16⅛ in. (130.2 × 41 cm); open 45 × 50 × 16½ in. (114.3 × 127 × 41.9 cm)
Rogers Fund, 1910 10.218

Inscribed in Arabic in *thuluth* script on inner face of stand in six segments, three of which are missing:

اللهم صلّ على محمد و على آل محمد سلّم و [. . .]
[. . .] و أمير المؤمنين علي بن . .
ابي طالب رضوان الله عليهم اجمعين
وقف مدرسة صدر آباد انار صانها الله عن الآفات—في ذي الحجة حجة إحدى و ستين
و سبعمائة

May God bless Muhammad and his family and [. . .] and the commander of the faithful 'Ali son of Abi Talib, may God's good favor be upon all of them! Endowed to the Madrasa Sadrabad in Anar, may God protect and preserve it from disaster! In the month of Dhu l-Hijja of the year A.H. 761 [October–November 1360 A.D.][1]

On top square panel outside (in each side), four times in square *thuluth* script:
الله
Allah

On bottom panels in *thuluth* script:
[Shi'i prayers for the Prophet Muhammad and the Twelve Imams (on one side up to *Muhammad Baqir*, on other up to *al-Mahdi*)]

On bottom panel under flower vase in angular *kufic* script:
الملك لله
Dominion [belongs to] God

On other side:
الشكر لله
Gratitude is to God

On two corners of one side, signature in *naskhi* script:
عمل زين؟ حسن سليمان اصفهانى
The work of Zain[?] Hasan Sulaiman Isfahani

A masterpiece of design, this carved book stand, or *rahla,* is made from a single slab of teak and is framed by inlays composed of various woods in shades of brown and black. Its several inscriptions signal its sacred function and provide information about its origin. When closed, the stand is flat; when open, it forms an X-shape in which the upper portion is about half the height of the lower one. The upper arms once served to support a book, probably a Qur'an.

The majority of the inscriptions are prayers, with the texts on the outside of the panels carved in high relief and surrounded by decoration, while those on the inside are unornamented and incised. A network of vegetal scrolls, divided into four quadrants by diagonal lines, covers the outer faces of the upper arms of the X; in each of these quadrants the word *Allah* appears in high relief. The decoration on the lower panels, which also serve as the supports for the *rahla,* has three concentric zones. The outermost is filled with a sinuous plant springing from a baseline and bearing blossoms of various sizes that twist and turn as they rise toward the upper frame. Some of the plants resemble peonies, others lotuses: the plant was obviously imagined rather than observed.

The central zone of the lower panel is designed as a pair of niches filled with, and separated by, carved ornament that is largely symmetrical around the central axis. At the center, a heart-shaped vase with a pointed base rests on a low hexagonal support. Covered with overlapping scales, the vase holds a bouquet of flowers that has a well-defined, treelike contour. Two concentric frames separate the vase from the "peony-vines." The inner one is ogival, while the outer expands into seven lobes and is crowned by five palmlike fronds. Between these frames a prayer is carved in high relief that invokes blessings on the Prophet, 'Ali, and the Twelve Imams, each of whom is identified by name and epithet. The first five are mentioned on one side and the sixth through twelfth on the other. The maker, Zain(?) Hasan Sulaiman Isfahani, has carved his name on the outer surface, just above the foot, an appropriately modest location.

An incised peripheral inscription appears on the inner surface of the upper arms and was probably intended to be visible even when a book had been placed on the *rahla.* It originally carried blessings on the Prophet and his immediate successors, but it has been crudely mutilated, probably to excise portions that praised the caliphs Abu Bakr, 'Umar, and 'Uthman. Only the name and titles of the fourth caliph, 'Ali, are preserved. The same inscription also states that the *rahla* was made in A.H. 761 / 1360 A.D. for the Sadrabad Madrasa in Anar. Although the precise location of this village is unknown, the same combination of prayers for the Twelve Imams with occluded inscriptions for Abu Bakr, 'Umar, and 'Uthman was found in the inscriptions of the Masjid-i Jami' at Ashtarjan, near Isfahan, which was dated to 1315. The existence of texts praising the Orthodox caliphs was revealed only by restorations carried out in the twentieth century.[2] In Iran, inscriptions praising both the first four caliphs and the Twelve Imams are characteristic of the fourteenth century. From the sixteenth century onward, the increasing polarization of the Sunni and Shi'a communities led to the concealment or mutilation of earlier texts, such as the ones carved on this *rahla,* that extolled the Orthodox caliphs. PS

1. The beginning of the inscription, defaced, may have included the names of the first three caliphs. The designs on the exterior bearing the names of the twelve Shi'a imams must have been carved later than the date of the stand.
2. On the condition of the Ashtarjan inscriptions before restoration, see Miles 1974, esp. p. 92 and pl. Ia-c; for their restored state, see Hunarfar 1971, pp. 269–71.

PROVENANCE: Sadrabad Madrasa, Anar, Iran; [Tabbagh Frères, Paris and New York, until 1910; sold to MMA]

67. Bowl

Iran, Nishapur, 10th century
Earthenware; white slip with black-slip decoration under transparent glaze
H. 7 in. (17.8 cm); Diam. 18 in. (45.7 cm)
Rogers Fund, 1965 65.106.2

Arabic inscription in "new-style" script around the inner rim:
التدبير قبل العمل يؤمنك من الندم اليمن والسلامه
Planning before work protects you from regret; good luck and well-being

Produced in northeastern Iran, in the province of Khurasan during the Samanid period, this large bowl with its high, flaring sides and bold, rhythmically spaced inscription in "new-style" script exemplifies the elegance and perfect harmony of the "black-on-white wares" unearthed in the cities of Nishapur and Samarqand. The most important contribution of Samanid potters was the invention and perfection of slip-painted ware. Clarity of design is achieved through the use of a white engobe (a thin wash of slip, or fluid clay, and pigment used as a ground) to cover the red earthenware, on which the inscription is painted in brownish pigment mixed with slip. By adding slip to the pigments, the potters prevented inscriptions and designs from running into one another.

Since this bowl was not among the objects unearthed in Nishapur at the time of the Metropolitan Museum excavations, its attribution is based entirely on visual analysis. It is a superb example of the

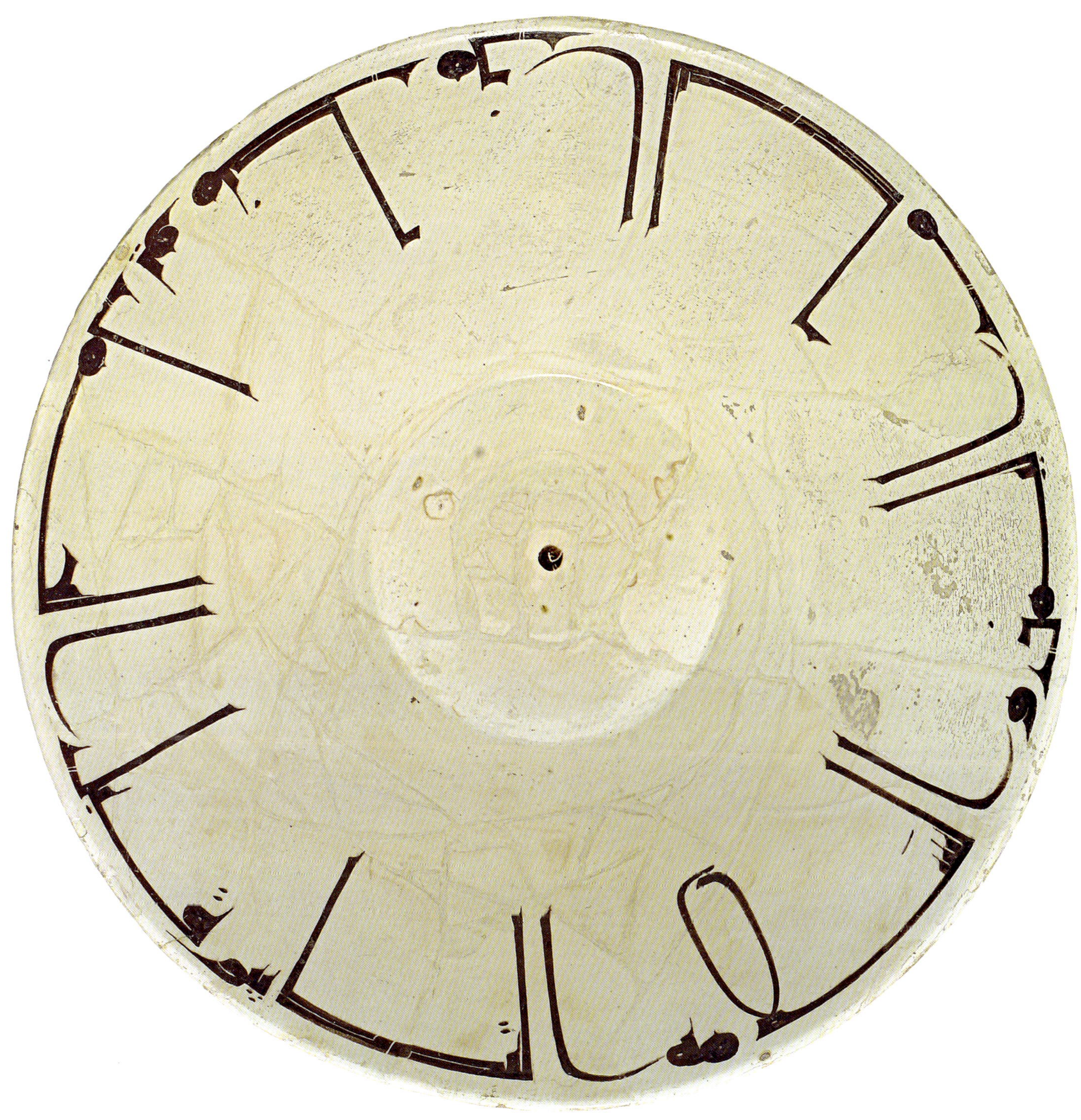

most common type of black-on-white ware associated with that center. The style of the calligraphy, which is characterized by tall, slender vertical shafts and angular letters, is probably among the earliest versions of "new-style" script. Later adaptations of this script include floriated and plaited variations. The elegance and sophistication of the calligraphy demonstrate a particularly close kinship between calligrapher and potter.

By 875 the Samanids had established an autonomous state, controlling a vast and important area of the eastern Islamic world. In 900 they were granted the governorship of Khurasan by the Abbasid caliph in Baghdad. Although the Samanids often looked to their imperial past for inspiration, it is unlikely that this bowl was produced for a royal patron. In fact, the inscription suggests that it was probably made for a humbler individual. Inscriptions such as this one and others on similar vessels constitute the first extant examples of Arabic proverbs and adages to appear in the Islamic world.[1] Many make reference to the social codes and high standards of moral etiquette held by the denizens of Samanid Nishapur at a time when hospitality and generosity were deeply valued.[2] This particular saying belongs to the hadith of the Prophet Muhammad transmitted by 'Ali.[3] Aphoristic in nature, it advises the owner against harmful or impetuous actions and decisions.

ME

1. Ettinghausen and Grabar 1987, p. 230.
2. Chicago 2007.
3. Ghouchani 1986, p. 80.

Provenance: [E. Safani, New York, until 1965; sold to MMA]

68. Bowl

Present-day Uzbekistan, probably Samarqand, late 10th–11th century
Excavated at Tepe Madrasa, Nishapur, Iran
Earthenware; white slip with polychrome-slip decoration under transparent glaze
H. 4¼ in. (10.8 cm), Diam. 14 in. (35.6 cm)
Rogers Fund, 1940 40.170.15

Inscription in Arabic in "new-style" script around rim:
البركة و الغبطة و النعمة و السلامة و السعادة الـ
Blessing, felicity, prosperity, well-being, happiness [. . .]

This bowl exemplifies the distinctive group of Samanid-era ceramics, known as epigraphic wares, which have calligraphy as their major form of decoration. The texts on these objects tend to be either proverbs or general blessings, and while the inscription on this bowl falls into the latter category, its particular phrasing appears to be unique.[1]

Unlike many of the known epigraphic objects with stark white or black slip backgrounds, the walls of this bowl are covered by alternating red and black strokes, and the base of its interior has a motif of interlacing straps on a stippled ground. Because of these features, the bowl has been attributed to Samarqand, although it was found at Nishapur, during the Metropolitan Museum's excavations at this site.[2] The evidence of metalwork seems to support this attribution, because the use of its strapwork motif and stippled ground can be related to the decoration of metalwares from Transoxiana, the region of Samarqand, rather than Khurasan, the region of Nishapur.[3]

Another distinctive feature of the bowl that may point to its place of origin is the way in which the tips of the tall vertical letters in the inscription bend forward. While it has been suggested that the letters have been elongated to evoke the head of a bird,[4] no study has thus far attempted to tie the use of certain scripts or their decorative modifications to a particular place of production.

The flourishing of epigraphic wares, so specific to the Samanid realms, has yet to be explained. Perhaps there was a tradition of making inscribed metalware in this region, comparable to the silver objects from the Hamadan hoard of western Iran, to which the inscribed ceramics can be related.[5]

MS

1. The extensive bibliography on this group includes Krachovskaya 1949 and Krachovskaya 1955; Bol'shakov 1958–66; Davidovich 1960; Volov 1966; Ventrone 1974; Ghouchani 1986; Paris, Caen, and Toulouse 1992–93, pp. 54–58, 90–92, 96, 103–4; Grube et al. 1994, pp. 51–53, 76–91, 94–105; and Pancaroğlu 2002.
2. See Wilkinson 1973, pp. 130–31 and p. 146, pl. 1. This bowl was found at Tepe Madrasa in a well with another similarly decorated bowl that is now in the Iran Bastan Museum, Tehran. For more information on the attribution, see ibid.
3. Raby 1985, pp. 198–99.
4. Grube et al. 1994, pp. 55, 98, 102, 105.
5. Raby 1985, p. 190.

Provenance: 1939, discovered at Tepe Madrasa, Nishapur, Iran, by the Metropolitan Museum's expedition under a concession granted by the Council of Ministers, Iran, upon the recommendation of the Ministry of Education of Iran; title transferred to The Metropolitan Museum of Art pursuant to the concession

69. Bowl

Present-day Uzbekistan, Samarqand, 10th century
Earthenware; white slip with polychrome-slip decoration under transparent glaze
H. 2¼ in. (5.7 cm), Diam. 10½ in. (26.7 cm)
Rogers Fund, 1928 28.82

Although the decoration of this bowl is typical of a style that was used in the Abbasid heartland in the ninth century, aspects of its manufacture suggest that the bowl was made far to the east, near Samarqand, during the tenth century. This duality can be explained by the connections between Transoxiana and Iraq that arose as the Abbasid Empire came to rule over this entire area, fostering the spread of this type of ornament, known as the beveled style, throughout its lands. The popularity of this style in Transoxiana is reflected not only in the decoration of this bowl, but also in the design of stucco panels in the Samanid palaces in Afrasiyab (modern Samarqand).[1]

From its place of invention at Samarra, and the medium of stucco in which it was initially employed, the beveled style eventually appeared in many media, from Egypt to Iran.[2] When applied to wood panels or stone capitals, the style was quite easily transferred because it was possible to copy both the characteristic motifs—curved lines ending in spirals surrounded by dots, notches, and slits, with no clear foreground or background—and the method of carving, which utilized an angled, or beveled, cut.

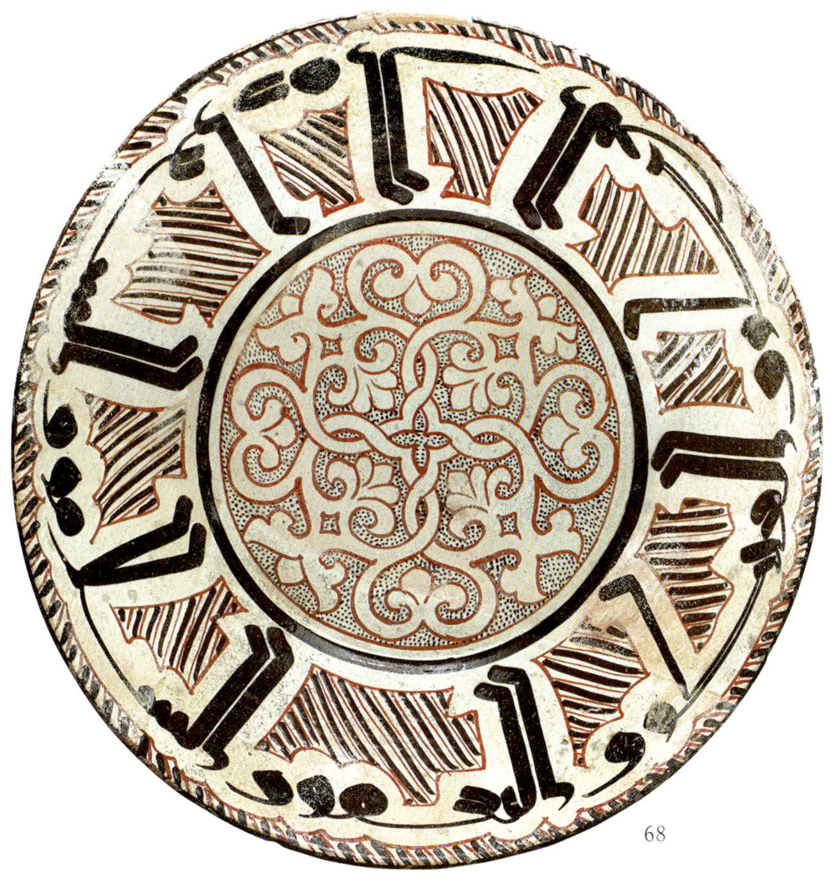

68

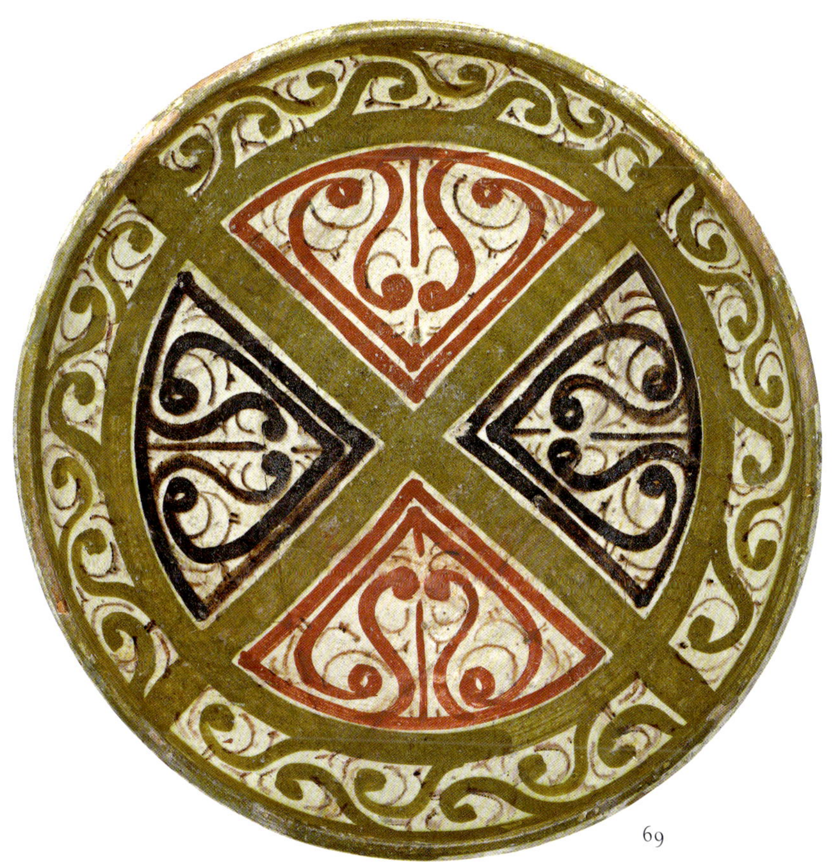

69

In the case of other objects, however, the transfer was less straightforward. This potter from Samarqand has captured the essence of the style's main motif and has tried to re-create the beveled profile of the shapes by using lines of varying thickness. Yet the decision to fit the decoration into four quadrants created by strong diagonal lines and the palette of olive green, brick red, and manganese purple reflect local practice. Samarqand was an important center of ceramic production for several centuries, and local potters created three major types of glazed ceramics: calligraphic wares, red and black slip-painted wares, and three-color splashwares, each with its own distinctive decoration. Although only a very small number of bowls with this beveled decoration are known,[3] the style of painting and compartmentalization of the design can be seen on other examples of ceramics from this area.

MS

1. Illustrated in Akhrarov and Rempel 1971.
2. Richard Ettinghausen was the first to trace the spread of the beveled style (Ettinghausen 1952).
3. For three other examples, see Paris, Caen, and Toulouse 1992–93, p. 98.

PROVENANCE: [Charles Vignier, Paris, until 1928; sold to MMA]

70. Chess Set

Iran, attributed to Nishapur, 12th century
Stonepaste; molded and glazed
Largest piece (king): H. 2 1/8 in. (5.5 cm); Diam. 1 3/4 in. (4.4 cm)
Smallest piece (pawn): H. 1 1/4 in. (3.2 cm); Diam. 1 1/8 in. (2.9 cm)
Pfeiffer Fund, 1971 1971.193a–ff

Literary tradition attributes the origin of chess to northern India.[1] By the late Sasanian period the game had been introduced into Iran. One of the tales preserved in the Persian national epic, the *Shahnama* (Book of Kings), explains the invention of chess as a way of demonstrating to a grieving queen the battle in which one of her sons died opposing his brother. Another recounts how the game was introduced to Iran: the ruler of India sent a set of chess pieces with an envoy as a challenge, declaring that his continued payment of tribute depended on the ability of the Iranian king to decode the point of the game.[2] While these legends underscore the courtly roots of chess, other sources demonstrate that the game gained popularity at all levels of society in the medieval Islamic world.[3]

This is one of the earliest extant chess sets, and it is nearly complete.[4] The pieces are molded of stonepaste and finished by hand. Seventeen of them are coated with the turquoise glaze

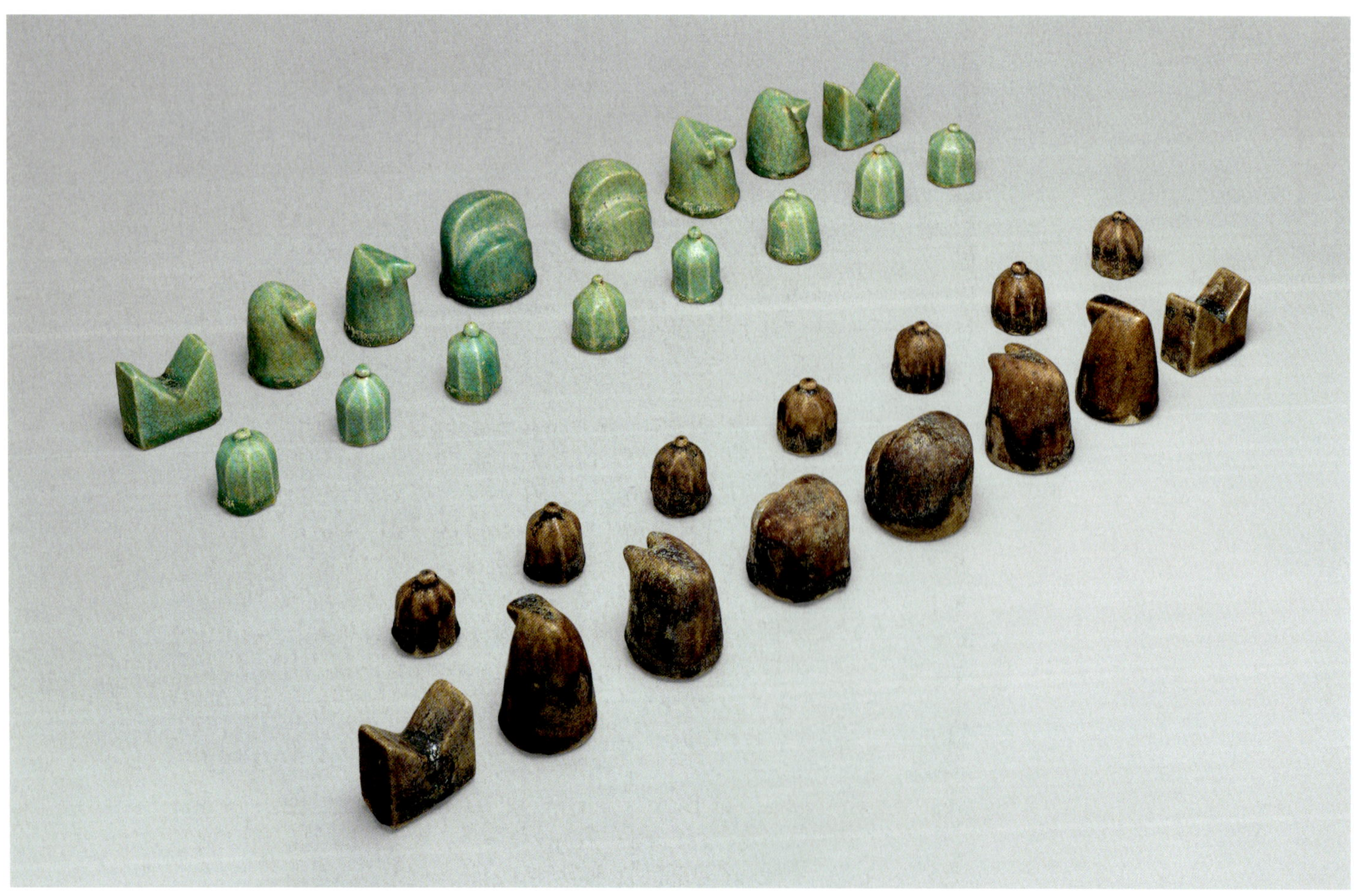

frequently employed in monochrome-glazed ceramics of Seljuq Iran; the other fifteen pieces are glazed with manganese.[5] The individual pieces are highly abstracted versions of the figures to which they refer.[6] The *shah* (king) is represented as a large throne and the *firzan* or vizier (in European chess, the queen) as a smaller throne. The *fil* (elephant, which became the bishop) has a circular base and a flattened top from which two protrusions recall the animal's tusks. The *faras* (horse, the knight) has a circular base with a triangular knob representing the head. The *rukh* (chariot, the equivalent of the rook or castle) has a rectangular base with an inverted wedge at the top. The pawns are faceted domical forms surmounted by small knobs. The near-abstraction of these forms was not a recent development, as it is evident in the earliest dated chess pieces firmly attributed to the Islamic world, a group of similarly shaped ivory examples excavated at Nishapur, dating as early as the ninth century.[7] EK

1. Rosenthal 1997, p. 366.
2. Gunter 2004–5, pp. 139–48. She illustrates two fourteenth-century paintings from Iran in the Metropolitan Museum collection (acc. nos. 34.24.1, 1974.290.39) in which the transmission episode is depicted, and summarizes other creation stories for the game of chess as well.
3. On the popularity of chess, see Cassavoy 2004; on the permissibility of the game, see Rosenthal 1975, pp. 37–40. For a more cross-cultural perspective, see Wilkinson 1943.
4. Thermoluminescence testing carried out by the Research Laboratory for Archaeology and the History of Art at Oxford University on two pieces of this set determined that they were manufactured some time between ca. 1080 and ca. 1530 (curatorial files, Metropolitan Museum, Department of Islamic Art). See also New York and Washington, D.C. 2004–5, pp. 150–51.
5. On the use of manganese in glaze, see Watson 2004, p. 305.
6. They correlate to the type that Anna Contadini terms "Style A," most examples of which date to the eleventh to thirteenth centuries (Contadini 1995, p. 121).
7. The previously asserted explanation that the abstraction of the forms had to do with Islamic religious prohibitions of figuration has been largely set aside (Contadini 1995, p. 143 n. 4; however, see Cassavoy 2004, p. 331).

PROVENANCE: [Saeed Motamed, Frankfurt, until 1971; sold to MMA]

71. Cup

Iran, probably Rayy, second half of 12th century
Stonepaste; incised decoration through black-slip ground under turquoise glaze (silhouette ware)
H. 5 in. (12.7 cm); Diam. 5⅝ in. (14.3 cm)
Purchase, Joseph Pulitzer Bequest, 1967 67.104

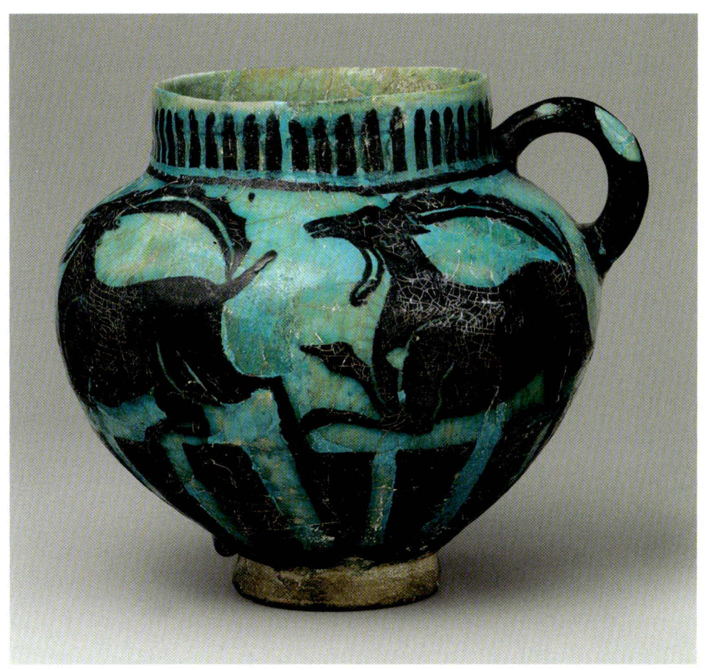

"Silhouette ware" is a technique that developed shortly after the introduction of stonepaste in Iran about the twelfth century; this small cup is among the finest examples of its type. Bulbous in profile, it has a rounded handle and a body glazed in transparent turquoise with a row of black ibexes running across the belly. The treatment and rendition of the ibexes across the body, the rays radiating from the foot, and the black stripes on the rim stand in relief, exhibiting affinities to metal vessels, which may have inspired the potter.

Silhouette ware technically involved the application of black-colored underglaze and stonepaste to the body of the vessel, which was then carved to reveal a design rendered in relief. A transparent turquoise glaze was subsequently applied to the vessel, creating the black-against-turquoise silhouette effect seen in this cup. In some examples a transparent rather than a turquoise glaze was applied, resulting in a black design on a creamy white background.[1] This technique may have been a modification of a technique of ceramic decoration used in Nishapur and Samarqand in the ninth and tenth centuries, in which colored slip was painted over a white engobe ground.[2] The transition to the relief technique may have been related to a new type of body imported to Iran from western Islamic lands in the early twelfth century, called stonepaste or frit. Composed of glass, clay, and quartz, this material allowed for a thin white body, as well as for greater experimentation with color and design than was possible in earlier Iranian pottery. No dated examples of silhouette ware survive, but according to scholars, it may have come into use in Iran about the year 1200.[3]

Although this technique was used on vessels of different shapes and sizes, such as bowls, jars, ewers, beakers, and cups, the most common seems to have been the cup. These wares featured a wide array of motifs ranging from humans, animals, and mythological creatures to calligraphic and abstract vegetal friezes, in keeping with the proliferation of animal and human figural imagery in a variety of media, including painted manuscripts and metalwork, during the Seljuq period. While the reasons for this tendency are not fully understood, it has been proposed that the representation of animals such as gazelles or ibexes may have held apotropaic qualities, offering protection and luck to the vessels' owners.[4]

ME/RV

1. Grube et al. 1994, nos. 198–99.
2. Watson 2004, p. 188.
3. Ibid., pp. 333–45. See also Fehérvári 2000, pp. 107–8.
4. Ettinghausen 1970b.

Provenance: Mousa Settareh Shenas, New York (until 1967; sold to MMA)

72. Bowl Depicting Bahram Gur and Azada Hunting

Iran, Kashan, 12th–13th century
Stonepaste; polychrome in-glaze and overglaze-painted and gilded on opaque monochrome glaze (*mina'i*)
H. 3 3/8 in. (8.7 cm); Diam: 8 3/4 in. (22.1 cm)
Purchase, Rogers Fund, and Gift of The Schiff Foundation, 1957 57.36.2

Among the most technically complex and luxurious glazed wares produced in the Seljuq period was a type known as *mina'i* (the Persian word for enamel). Incorporating a range of colors and intricate compositions and renditions, much of the painting found on *mina'i* wares recalls manuscript illustrations. As with Seljuq lusterware, many of these vessels portray visual and poetic themes derived from Persian literature, such as the *Shahnama* (Book of

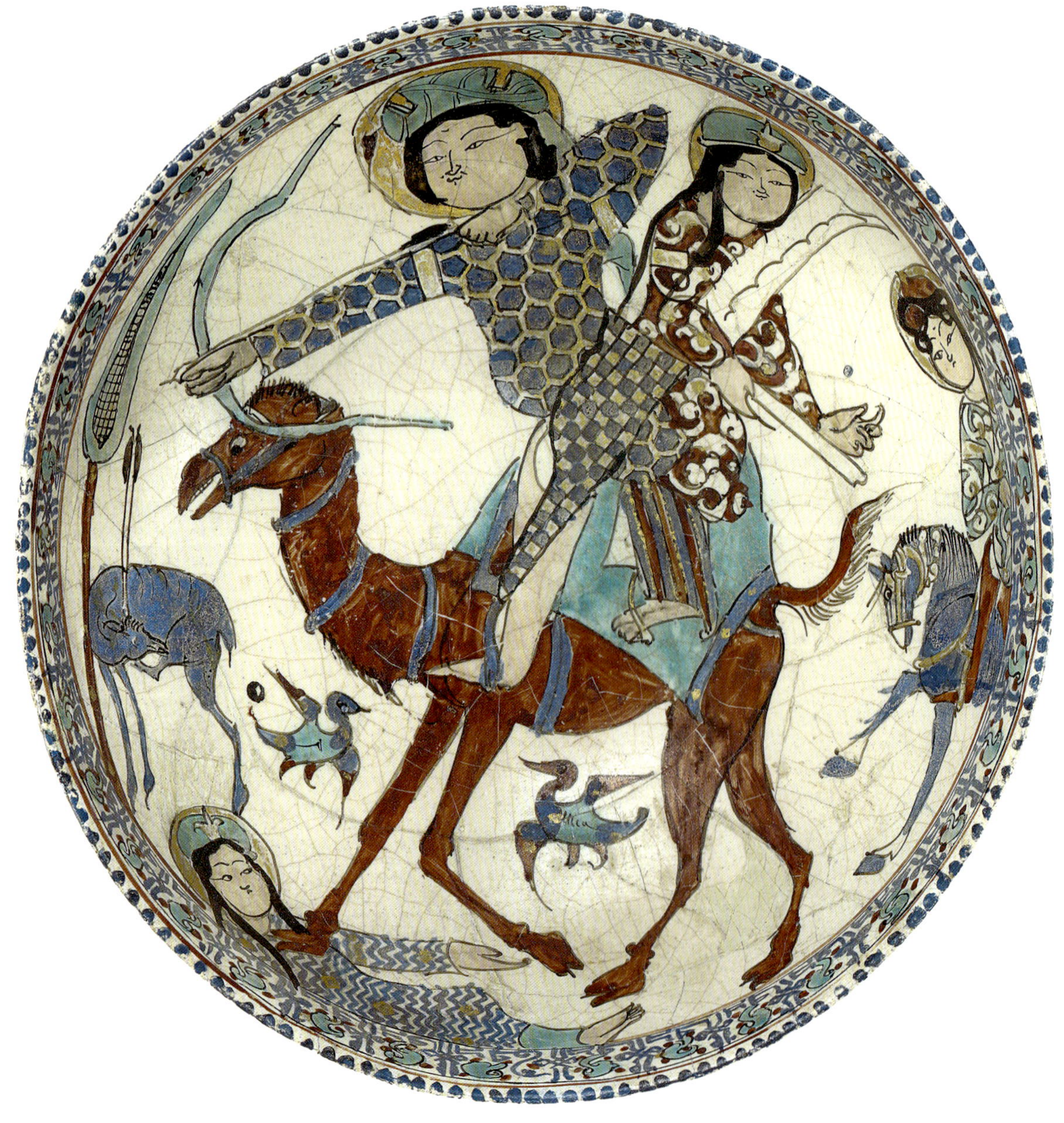

Kings), depicting heroes, warriors, lovers, and fantastic beasts. Kashan, also the site of production of lusterwares, appears to have been the main production center for *mina'i* ceramics, providing vessels in an array of forms such as bowls, ewers, and flasks.

This bowl is a fine example of *mina'i* and depicts one of the cherished tales from the *Shahnama* of Firdausi—that of Bahram Gur and Azada mounted on a camel, hunting. The story is as follows: Azada, Bahram Gur's concubine, entertains the ruler by playing a harp, and challenges him to a hunting feat. When he succeeds, however, she pities the slain animal and reproaches him for being coldhearted and vain. In anger, he tramples her under the camel's feet. Here, two moments in the story are conflated into one scene, both rendered with extraordinary charm and immediacy.

This tale has great longevity and dates back to the pre-Islamic period. A number of Sasanian silver plates, including one in the Metropolitan Museum,[1] illustrate the same story, although in most of those examples the hunting couple are mounted on a horse rather than a camel. The inscriptions around the rim on the exterior of the bowl contain messages of good fortune and well-being to the owner. ME

1. Metropolitan Museum (acc. no. 1994.402), formerly in the Guennol Collection. See also New York 1978, p. 48.

PROVENANCE: Mortimer L. Schiff, New York (until d. 1931); his son, John M. Schiff (by 1940–1957; gift and sale to MMA)

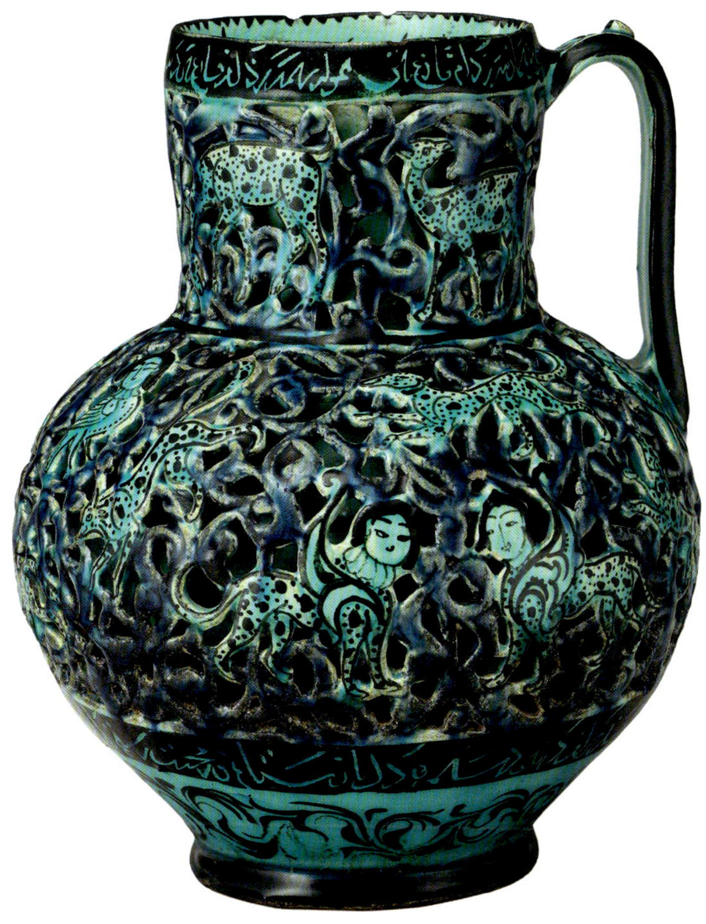

73. Reticulated Jug

Iran, probably Kashan, dated A.H. 612/1215–16 A.D.
Stonepaste; openwork decoration, polychrome-painted under turquoise glaze
H. 8 1/4 in. (20.8 cm); Diam. 6 7/8 in. (16.8 cm)
Fletcher Fund, 1932 32.52.1

Inscription around mouth of jug, a Persian *ruba'i* (quatrain)
by Rukn al-Din Da'vidar Qummi:
من بی تو همان سر زده ام فارغ باش
همواره بهم بر زده ام فارغ باش
دست از تو بمهر دیگری از سر تو
بیزار شدم گر زده ام فارغ باش
Without you, I am depraved; Be free from care.
Ceaselessly, I am unsettled; Be free from care.
[Turning] from you, I reach for the kindness of another, because of you.
Although I have done so, I despised it; Be free from care.[1]

Inscription around base of jug, a Persian *ruba'i* by an as-yet-unidentified poet:
گفتم چو رسد بزلف دانی دستم
دل باز ستانم وز محنت رستم
یک لحظه چو در پیش رخش بنشتم
جان نیز چو دل در سر زلفش بستم
I said, "[Do] you know, if my hand reaches her tresses,
I [could] reclaim my heart and be free from suffering."
One moment, while sitting face-to-face with her,
I tied my soul, like my heart, to the end of her curls.[2]

Inscription following the above:
في شهور سنة إثني عشر و ستمائة
In the months of the year A.H. 612 [1215–16 A.D.]

Fanciful winged griffins, human-headed harpies, and lithesome speckled quadrupeds leap and cavort within the tangle of vine scrolls on this finely worked reticulated jug. Its free-flowing, animated drawing in black slip against a vivid turquoise- and cobalt-glazed ground offers a striking combination of color and design. While its contrasting glazes and lively imagery are exceptional, it is the skillful execution of its delicate, weblike reticulation that ranks this piece among the finest of all surviving Persian ceramics.

A tour de force of construction and technique, it has a pierced double-walled structure that only an extremely skilled potter could have created. Considering the intricate and time-consuming nature of the production process, coupled with the difficulties involved in firing, this type of ceramic was undoubtedly extremely costly to make and thus available only to a wealthy clientele. Despite their fragility and the passing of centuries, a surprising number of reticulated ceramics of this type have survived.[3]

Given the challenging nature of producing such a vessel in clay, it is unlikely that the shape and construction embodied by this piece originated in the ceramic arts. Rather, this vessel type likely emulates metalwork forms, as a number of Persian metal jugs exhibiting this overall profile have survived.[4] Further underscoring its debt to a metal prototype, this jug retains the small knop at the top of its handle, common to many metalwork examples. A large number of these metal jugs display inscriptions, often in narrow bands among multiple registers of decoration. This ceramic piece exhibits similar inscriptional decoration—around the top rim and foot of the jug, executed in turquoise on a black ground. These inscriptions comprise two *ruba'is*, or quatrains, both voicing a lover's lament. At the end of one of the poems, near the base of the jug, the artist has included the date of A.H. 612/1215–16 A.D., enabling us to attribute this exceptional jug, and others of its type, securely to the early thirteenth century. DMT

1. The Persian text appears in Da'vadar Qummi 1986.
2. My thanks to Sina Goudarzi for kindly assisting me in the translation of these two *ruba'is*.
3. For related pieces, see Grube et al. 1994, p. 197, no. 212, with color plate on p. 196. Grube states, on p. 151, that at least twenty-one pieces utilizing this technique are known. See his n. 14, p. 153, for more bibliography on these other openwork pieces. The two that appear from published photos to be most closely related to our jug include one in the Khalili Collection, London; see Grube et al. 1994, no. 212; and another formerly in the Mahboubian Collection, today in the Reza 'Abbasi Museum, Tehran; see Austin 1970, no. and pl. 211.
4. For a related profile, see also cat. 132.

PROVENANCE: V. Everit Macy, New York (by 1923–d. 1930; his estate, until 1932; sold to MMA)

74. Bowl

Iran, late 12th century
Stonepaste; luster-painted on opaque monochrome glaze
H. 3 1/4 in. (8.3 cm); Diam. 8 in. (20.3 cm)
Rogers Fund, 1916 16.87

As the Fatimid dynasty in Egypt declined and finally fell to Salah al-Din in 1171, its skilled craftsmen sought new markets for their wares. Some of them, like the makers of lusterware ceramics, emigrated to Syria and Iran. The creation of lusterware pottery

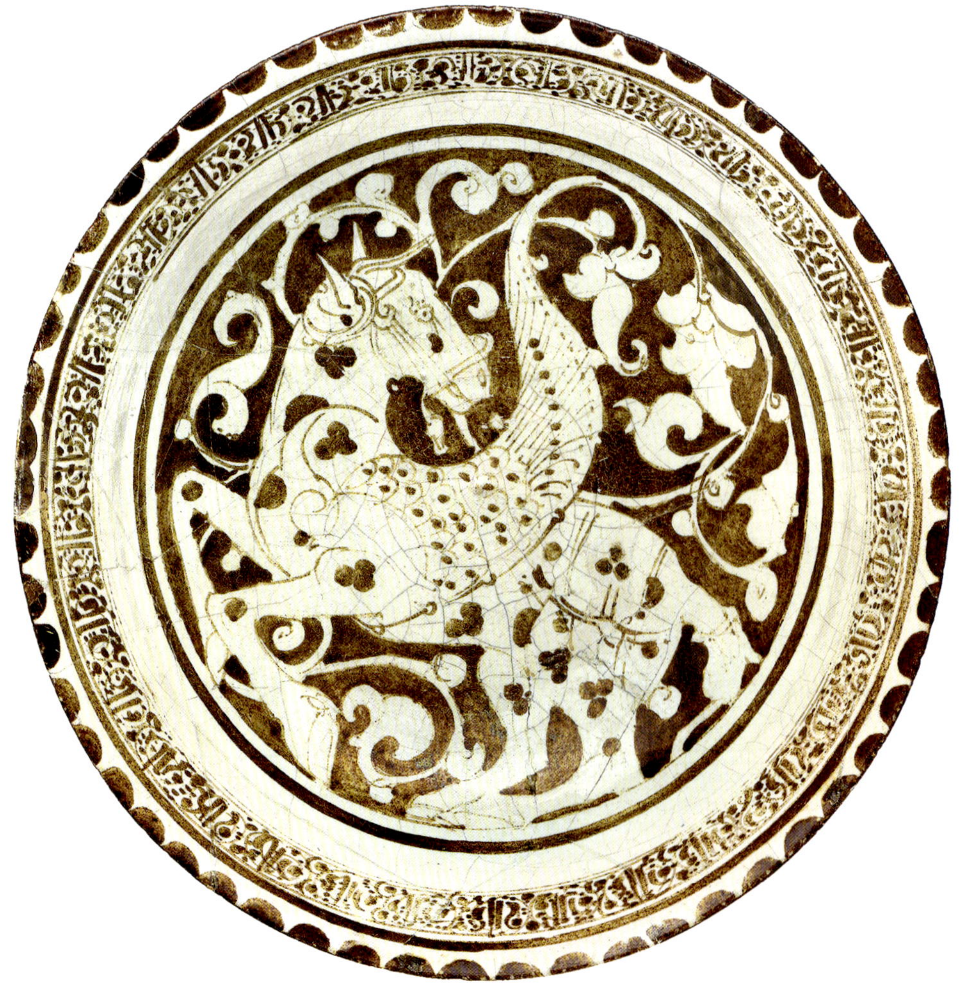

required special knowledge and technical skill, which, apparently, were closely guarded secrets; thus it was not produced simultaneously in different centers in the Islamic world during the eleventh century. Instead, the technique of lusterware passed from Abbasid Iraq to Fatimid Egypt, and then in the twelfth century from Egypt to Syria and Iran. In the earliest Iranian lusterwares the stylistic influence of Fatimid antecedents is particularly marked.[1]

As on one distinct group of Fatimid lusterwares, the main motif of this bowl, a winged horse, appears reserved on a luster ground. A lively vine scroll terminating in split leaves and trefoil shapes weaves through the space around the horse. The animal's slightly rearing pose, the backward swing of its head, and the dramatic S-curve of its wing all complement the circular shape of the bowl. On the interior walls, above a plain band of white glaze, a repeating but illegible *kufic* inscription appears in a band of small vegetal elements. The small scale and density of the comma-shaped vegetal motifs anticipate the so-called Kashan style of Persian lusterware that matured around 1200. However, the luster-painted gadrooning around the inner rim of the bowl, along with the single large image of the winged horse, strongly relates to Fatimid lusterware and suggests that this piece was made between 1180 and 1200.

Although Buraq, the human-headed horse that Muhammad rode on his night journey to heaven (*mi'raj*) is also winged, the horse in this bowl is more likely derived from Pegasus, the winged horse of Greek myth. Whether the ancient iconography of Pegasus as the bearer of Zeus's thunderbolts was understood by its maker or owner is unclear. However, medieval Iranians certainly would have been familiar with the constellation named after Pegasus, *Faras al-'Azam*. While the clusters of three dots that decorate the horse's body are found in many lusterwares and in the earlier ceramics of Nishapur, they also suggest the stars one would see in a drawn depiction of the constellation of Pegasus.[2] In a society in which astrology and astronomy played an important role, a bowl containing a winged horse would certainly have had positive connotations for its owner.

SRC

1. Watson 1985, pp. 48–52.
2. Wellesz 1959, fig. 30.

PROVENANCE: [Georges Tabbagh, New York, until 1916; sold to MMA]

75. Bowl (Charger)

Iran, Kashan, mid-13th century
Stonepaste; luster-painted on opaque monochrome glaze
H: 4 3/8 in. (11.1 cm); Diam. 19 5/8 in. (49.8 cm)
Fletcher Fund, 1932 32.52.2

76. Tile

Iran, Varamin, dated A.H. 661/1262–63 A.D.
Stonepaste; luster-painted on opaque white glaze
H. 12 1/4 in. (31.1 cm)
Edward C. Moore Collection, Bequest of Edward C. Moore, 1891 91.1.100

Cat. 75
Inscriptions divided into four registers, starting on outer rim and moving inward
First register, Arabic in *naskhi* script:
والعز والاقبال والدولة والسعادة والسلامة والكرامة والغالب والدولة والسلامة
والغالب والدولة والعز والاقبال والدولة والسعادة والكرامة والنعمة والبركة
والتأييد والكرامة والسعادة والسلامة والعز
Glory, prosperity, dominion, happiness, well-being, generosity,
victory, dominion, well-being, victory, dominion, glory, prosperity,
dominion, happiness, generosity, prosperity, blessing, support,
generosity, happiness, well-being, and glory

Second register, four *ruba'is* (quatrains) in Persian
and two blessings in Arabic, all in *naskhi* script:
First *ruba'i*:
دیدار توأم همیشه در دیده بود   آن کن صنما کز تو پسندیده بود
ای جان جهان دلم بدان خرسند است   گواهم که او ترا دیده بود
Your beautiful countenance is forever [captured] in my eyes,
O beloved, do what you prefer.
O life of creation, my heart is joyful; I can swear that
[it is] because I caught a glimpse of you.
Blessings:
عز اقبال دولة سلامة بقاء . . . لصاحبه
Glory, prosperity, dominion, well-being and long life . . . to its owner

Second *ruba'i*:
گفتم که مگر آن صنم نیک اندیش   رحمی آرد . . . با دل ریش
کی دانستم که آن کافر کیش   کارد سر مارا بدامن و گردن خویش
I said: "Won't that virtuous beloved with a broken heart forgive you?"
How did I know that the heretic would hold our knife against your body and neck?

Third *ruba'i*, attributed to Sadr al-Din Khujandi:[1]
مقصود بیافت هر آنچ با غم یار بساخت   در کام رسید هرچ با کار بساخت
مه نور بدان یافت کز شب نرمید   گل بوی بدان گرفت که با خار بساخت
Whoever endures living with the sorrow of the beloved
will find happiness and purpose.
The moon is luminous because it did not escape the night;
the flower is fragrant because it lives with the thorn.

Fourth *ruba'i*:
آنی که درین جهان خسته جانی   بر لشکرخوبان جهان سلطانی
این آب دو چشم بنده ضایع مگذار   آخر بزمینی بر اگر دهقانی
He whose soul is tired in this world, is the king of the virtuous.
Do not waste my tears, for the farmer can rejuvenate the earth with them.

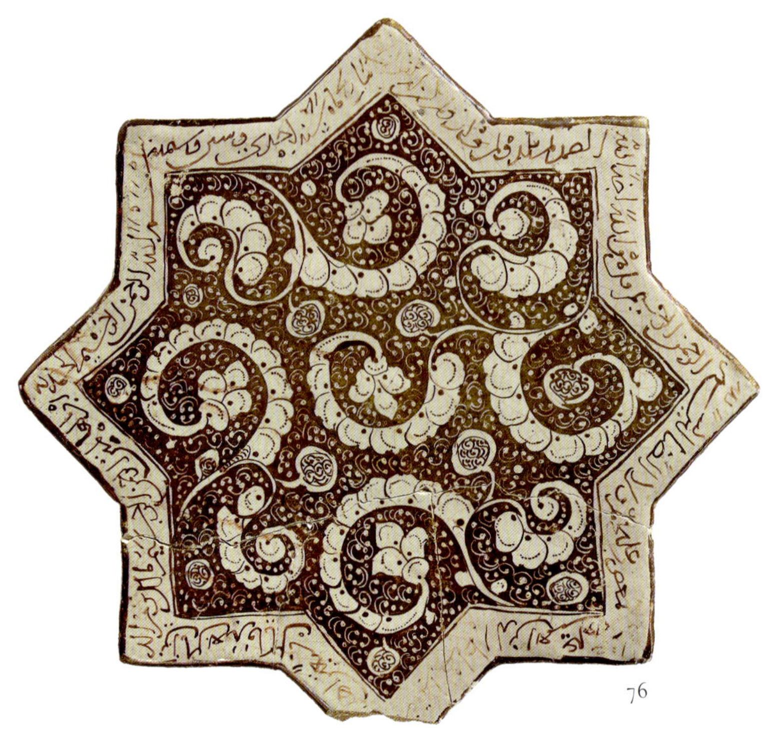

76

Blessings:

عز اقبال دولة سلامة بقاء عز اقبال دولة سلامة عز اقبال دولة سلامة

Glory, prosperity, dominion, well-being, long life, glory, prosperity, dominion, well-being; glory, prosperity, dominion and well-being

Third register, Arabic inscription in ornamental *kufic* on cavetto: [illegible]

Fourth register, Persian verses by the mystical poet Sana'i,[2] followed by blessings in Arabic:

ای مه نو بروی تو دیده   و اندر تو ماه نو بخندیده
تو نیز ز بیم خصم اندر من   از دور نگاه کرده دزدیده
بنموده فلک مه نو و خود را   در زیر سیاه ابر پوشیده
تو نیز مه چهارده بنمای   بردار ز سر خلق شوریده
کی باشد کی که در تو آویزم   چون در زر و سیم مرد نادیده
تو روی مرا بناخنان خسته   من دو لب تو ببوسه خاییده

The full moon looked at you and smiled
And you fearing hostility in me, glanced at me secretly from a distance.
The sky has hidden itself and the full moon under dark clouds.
Be like the half-moon and keep unhappy dispositions away.
When will I be able to hang upon you like gold and silver?
You stroke my face with your tired nails while I shower your lips with kisses.

Blessings:

عز اقبال دولة سلامة بقاء . . . لصاحبه

Glory, prosperity, dominion, well-being and long life . . . to its owner

Some of the finest Persian lusterware was produced in the city of Kashan during the thirteenth and fourteenth centuries. This charger (cat. 75), covered in brownish luster, is a refined example of a type known as Kashan-style lusterware.[3] Inscriptions arranged in four concentric bands cover most of its interior, surrounding a medallion in which two musicians—one playing a lute while the other holds castanets—are seated against a background of vegetal scrolls.

The bowl exemplifies the artist's attention to surface pattern, leaving only select areas in reserve.[4] Its verses, each including blessings, are largely mystical in nature. The text on the outer rim, in *naskhi* script, is executed in reserve and consists of blessings and good wishes for the owner. The next zone, also inscribed in *naskhi*, contains four *ruba'is* (quatrains), also followed by blessings and good wishes for the owner.[5] The striking decoration of the bowl's cavetto consists of a wide band of illegible plaited *kufic* set against a stippled ground with vegetal scrolls. The innermost inscription band that frames the pair of musicians contains verses by the mystical poet Sana'i (d. ca. 1131) and is also followed by blessings to the owner.

In its architectural quality, the "new-style" plaited *kufic* calligraphy in the cavetto resembles the inscriptions on the facades of Seljuq and Ilkhanid tomb towers, including Pir-i 'Alamdar in Damghan and the Imamzada Yahya in Varamin. The distinct treatment of the vegetal scrolls against a stippled background is closely related to that seen on luster tiles from the Imamzada Yahya in Varamin, a large group of which is in the collection of the Victoria and Albert Museum in London and bears the dates A.H. 661–63/1262–64 A.D. Similar tiles from a *mihrab* of 1264, signed by the famous Kashan potter 'Ali ibn Muhammad ibn Abi Tahir, and this tile in the Metropolitan Museum dated A.H. 661/1262–63 A.D. (cat. 76) have also been linked to the Imamzada in Varamin.[6]

After the Mongol destruction of Rayy in 1222, that city's potters ceased to play a significant role in Iranian ceramic production. By contrast, the potters of Kashan, who produced tiles for the buildings and mosques of other cities, including Qum, Varamin, Mashhad, and Baku, expanded their existing production of lusterware and other classes of ceramics.[7] The increasing production of fine pottery during this period has been linked to expanding mercantile activity and the rise of an urban bourgeoisie.[8]

The Museum's charger has a lyrical quality. Its central image of musicians is an allusion to a princely feast (*bazm*) at which people gathered, recited love poetry, and were entertained by musicians. The fact that nearly all its inscriptions include blessings and good wishes for an owner suggest that it was intended as a gift for a celebration, such as a wedding or Nauruz (Persian New Year); its texts personalize and enliven the object. The inclusion of the same verses on a range of luster objects indicates that the potters had a repertoire from which they selected verses for specific objects.[9] With its calligraphic ornament, mystical verses, and performing musicians, the charger would have made a sophisticated and desirable gift.

ME

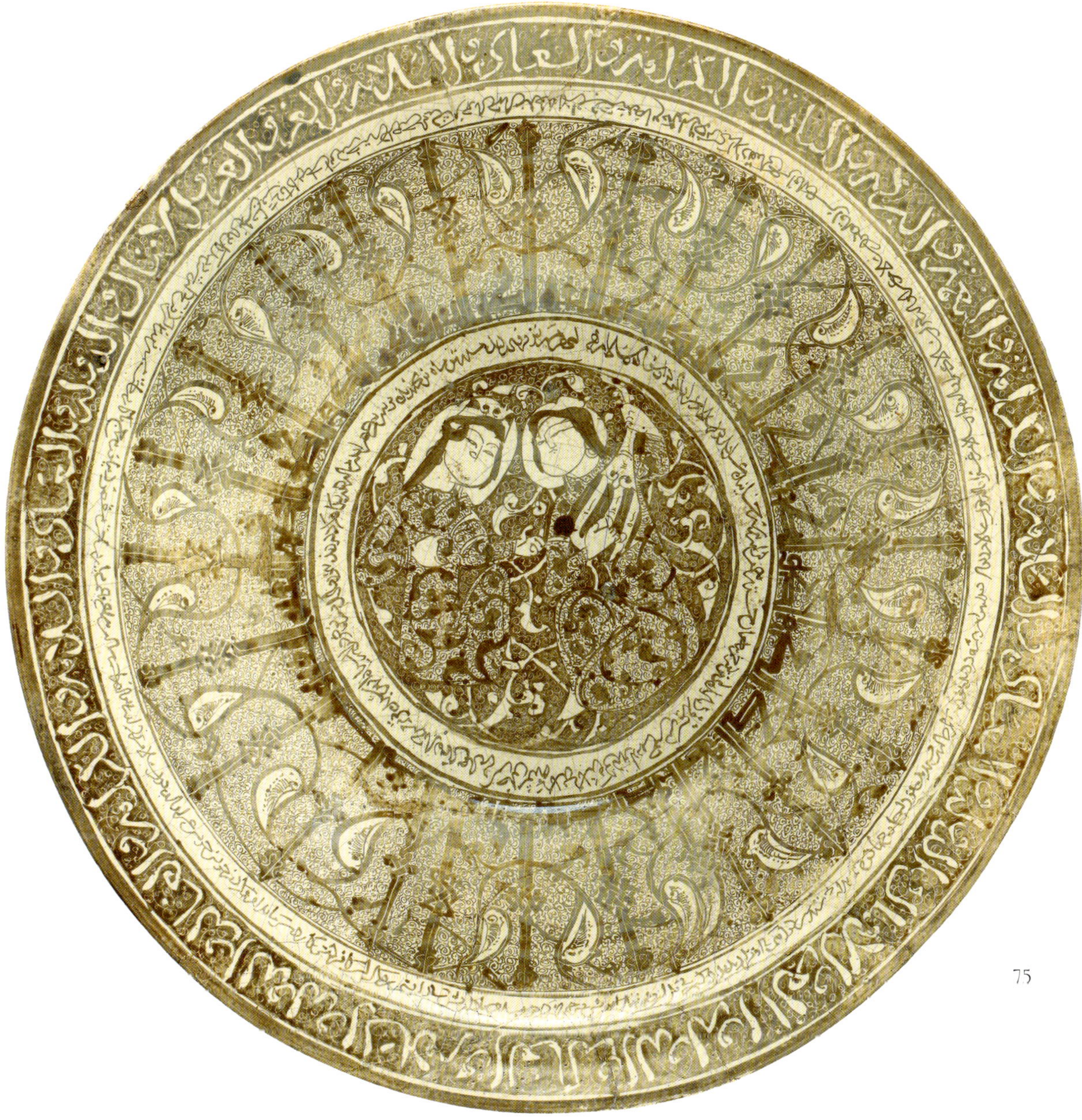

75

1. This *ruba'i*, with some different words, appears to be by Shams Tabrizi, in Rumi 1984, p. 1334. It is also attributed to Sadr al-Din Khujandi and appears in Shirvani 1987, p. 208, no. 767. I would like to thank Abdullah Ghouchani for reading the inscriptions and identifying the poets.
2. Sana'i 1983–84, p. 1010. Sana'i (d. 1131) was a Persian mystical poet who lived in Ghazna, in present-day Afghanistan, and served at the Ghaznavid court of Bahramshah (r. 1118–52).
3. Watson 1985, pp. 90, 93, 104, fig. 65.
4. Ibid., p. 90, and Dimand 1944a, p. 199.
5. The poets of three of the four *ruba'is* have been identified as Maulana Rumi (1207–1273), Sadr al-Din Khujandi (d. ca. 1200), and Khwarazmshah Abu al-Faraj Runi (d. ca. 1200).
6. Other examples are in the collections of the British Museum, London, and the Musée du Louvre, Paris.
7. Dimand 1944a, p. 199. In fact, the same potter who produced the Varamin *mihrab* was also responsible for the Qum *mihrab* of 1264, now in the Museum für Islamische Kunst, Staatliche Museen zu Berlin.
8. Ettinghausen 1970b, pp. 113, 115.
9. In research conducted at the Metropolitan Museum in 1998, Abdullah Ghouchani found that a number of objects in other collections contained the same verses.

Provenance

Cat. 75: V. Everit Macy, New York (until d. 1930; his estate, until 1932; sold to MMA)

Cat. 76: Edward C. Moore, New York (until d. 1891)

77. Tile

Iran, probably Natanz, from the Shrine of 'Abd al-Samad, dated [Shawwa]l A.H. 707/March 24–April 22, 1308 A.D.[1]
Stonepaste; modeled, underglaze-painted in blue, luster-painted on opaque white ground
15 × 15 in. (38.1 × 38.1 cm)
Gift of Émile Rey, 1912 12.44

Inscription in Arabic in *thuluth* script:
[شوا]ل سنة سبع وسبعماية
[Shawwa]l of the year A.H. 707 [March 24–April 22, 1308 A.D.][2]

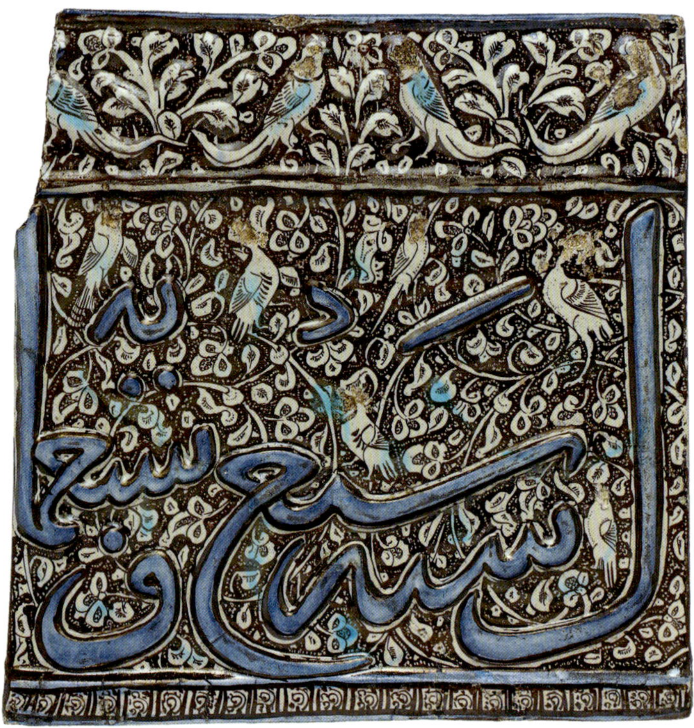

Elegant calligraphy in *thuluth* script graces the central band of this large, intricately decorated tile. Executed in low relief, the cobalt-blue glazed inscription is set against a field of scrolling vines, where tiny birds perch among leafy foliage—some alighting upon the letters themselves.

The theme of birds in vegetation is continued in the smaller band above, which contains a series of confronted birds between small plantings.[3] Appreciable both from a distance and upon closer examination, the bold, sweeping lines of calligraphy stand in sharp contrast to the detailed rendering of the inhabited background, finished in a gold luster glaze with touches of turquoise.

This tile was probably one in a series that formed a glittering inscriptional frieze encircling the interior walls of a fourteenth-century tomb pavilion located in Natanz, Iran.[4] The frieze sat close to eye level, crowning a dado of equally opulent star- and cross-shaped tiles.[5] This tomb pavilion was erected in honor of Nur al-Din 'Abd al-Samad, a shaikh of the Suhrawardiyya sufi order. Shortly after 'Abd al-Samad's death in about 1300 construction began on a tomb complex in his honor in Natanz, a city located a few miles north of Isfahan.[6] The complex soon became a shrine that pilgrims visited to pay homage to the shaikh.[7]

Upon entering the tomb, a visitor would have encountered walls covered with carved stuccowork and luster-painted tiles, including this piece. Other similarly inscribed and decorated tiles, also attributed to 'Abd al-Samad's tomb pavilion, contain Qur'anic verses from Sura 76, passages that describe the rewards awaiting the worthy in Paradise.[8] This tile, however, contains an Arabic inscription with the date A.H. 707, said to mark the year in which work was completed on the tomb. DMT

1. It has been suggested that the letter *lam*, positioned at the beginning of the text, likely represents the last letter of the month *Shawwal*, allowing us to more precisely date the tile to March 24 to April 22 of 1308. See New York 1993, p. 25, no. 20.
2. The spelling of سبعماية is provided as it appears on the tile.
3. The heads of the birds on the Metropolitan's tile, as well as those on many other tiles also said to be from the shrine, appear to have been intentionally defaced, likely due to iconoclastic sentiment.
4. For comparable pieces, see Ettinghausen 1938–39 and Blair 1986b, pp. 100–101 and n. 23. Blair, p. 64, states that about twenty such tiles are known. She reproduces the Museum's piece on p. 137, pl. 53. See also Blair 2002–3, pp. 126–28 and fig. 149, no. 114. For information on the movement of tiles from Natanz into private and public collections, see Masuya 2000, esp. pp. 41–44.
5. Blair 1986b, p. 134, pl. 47, shows a section of where the cross- and star-shaped tile dado and related luster frieze once were installed. On ibid., p. 64, Blair states that this dado measures about sixty-five inches (165 cm) high. See also pp. 50, 64, where she discusses the placement of the Metropolitan's tile with respect to the dado.
6. Ibid., p. 5. The shaikh is said to have died in about A.H. 699/1299–1300 A.D. For more on the dating of the different parts of the complex, see ibid., pp. 17, and 20ff.
7. Ibid., p. 21.
8. On ibid., p. 64, Blair states that other tiles in the group contain portions of verses 76:1–7.

PROVENANCE: Shrine of 'Abu al-Samad, Natanz, Iran (from 1307); Émile Rey, New York (until 1912)

78. Tile

Iran, probably Takht-i Sulaiman, late 13th century
Stonepaste; modeled, underglaze-painted in blue and turquoise, luster-painted on opaque white ground
$14\frac{3}{4} \times 14\frac{1}{4}$ in. (37.5 × 36.2 cm)
Rogers Fund, 1912 12.49.4

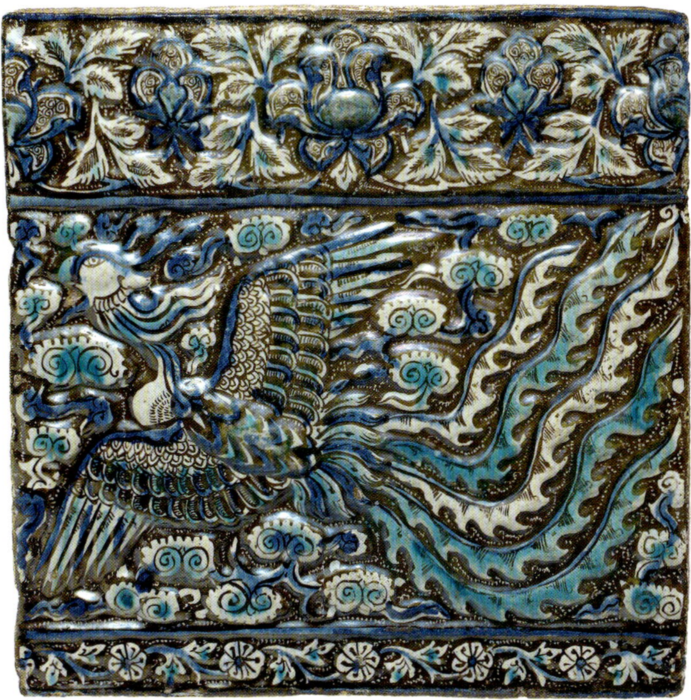

This image of a soaring phoenix with crested head and elaborate plumage, surrounded by swirling clouds, is a striking example of the adaptation of Chinese imagery by Persian artists.

With ancestry that included Genghis Khan and the Great Khans of China, the Mongol Ilkhanid rulers had strong ties with eastern Asia, facilitating the movement of people and goods across the continent. As a result, Persian art produced under Ilkhanid rule exhibits an infusion of new motifs—including depictions of the *feng* (phoenix) and *long* (dragon), both traditional Chinese symbols of imperial sovereignty.[1] The affinity between this new Persian iconography and that of contemporary Yuan China strongly suggests that Ilkhanid artists were aware of Chinese models.[2]

Excavation evidence indicates that this tile once graced the walls of a late thirteenth-century Ilkhanid palace known as Takht-i Sulaiman, located in a mountainous region southeast of Tabriz. Built on the shores of a small lake during the reign of Abaqa (d. 1282), the palace served as a seasonal camp, its location and elevation allowing the ruler and his court to escape the summer heat.[3] Many of its rooms were lavishly decorated with stuccowork and ceramic tiles in a rich variety of techniques, including the combination of cobalt and luster glazes seen on this molded tile.[4]

The appearance of motifs such as the dragon and phoenix within the context of this Ilkhanid royal palace may reflect a dual iconographic system. As traditional Chinese symbols of royalty, these images were well understood by the recently arrived Mongol Ilkhanid rulers and their court. At the same time, Persian artists began to adopt Chinese *feng* imagery as a way to visualize the Persian mythical bird known as the *simurgh*.[5] The possibility of two simultaneous readings for this tile's iconography underscores the cosmopolitan and hybrid nature of the arts produced for the Ilkhanid court.[6] DMT

1. Masuya 1997; see pp. 564ff. for her discussion of these motifs and their associated meanings. Also see Masuya 2002–3, esp. pp. 96–97.
2. Masuya 1997, p. 577, states "Characteristics shared by the *feng* motifs during the Yuan period and the phoenixes on the Takht-i Sulaiman tiles include the pair of long crests flowing from its forehead, a long comb under its beak, long hair-like feathers flowing from the neck, zigzag patterns in the body feathers, and long tail feathers." For more on the relationship between Persian and Chinese arts in this period, see Soucek 1999.
3. Masuya 2002–3, pp. 84ff.
4. Ibid., p. 96, and Masuya 1997, pp. 128–34, 577, 597, and 621. See ibid., pp. 514ff., for a description of tile type 6-2-2-b, findspots in the excavation, further references, and comparanda. Also see Masuya 2002–3, p. 89, for a plan of the palace complex.
5. See Masuya 1997, pp. 580–81. She states that as early as the 1290s the *simurgh* began to be depicted by Persian artists using the Chinese *feng* iconography.
6. As Masuya points out, however, it is unclear if the image of the *feng* would have been immediately recognized by the local population as representative of the *simurgh*. See ibid., p. 578. For another theory of how such imagery may have been perceived, see Melikian-Chirvani 1984, especially his discussion of the *simurgh* motif at Takht-i Sulaiman beginning on p. 317. See also Melikian-Chirvani 1991, esp. pp. 102ff.

PROVENANCE: [Indjoudjian Frères, Paris, until 1912; sold to MMA]

79. Storage Jar (Albarello)

Iran, second half of 13th–14th century
Stonepaste; overglaze-painted and leaf-gilded (so-called *lajvardina*)
H. 14¾ in. (37.5 cm)
Henry G. Leberthon Collection, Gift of Mr. and Mrs. A. Wallace Chauncey, 1957 57.61.12a, b

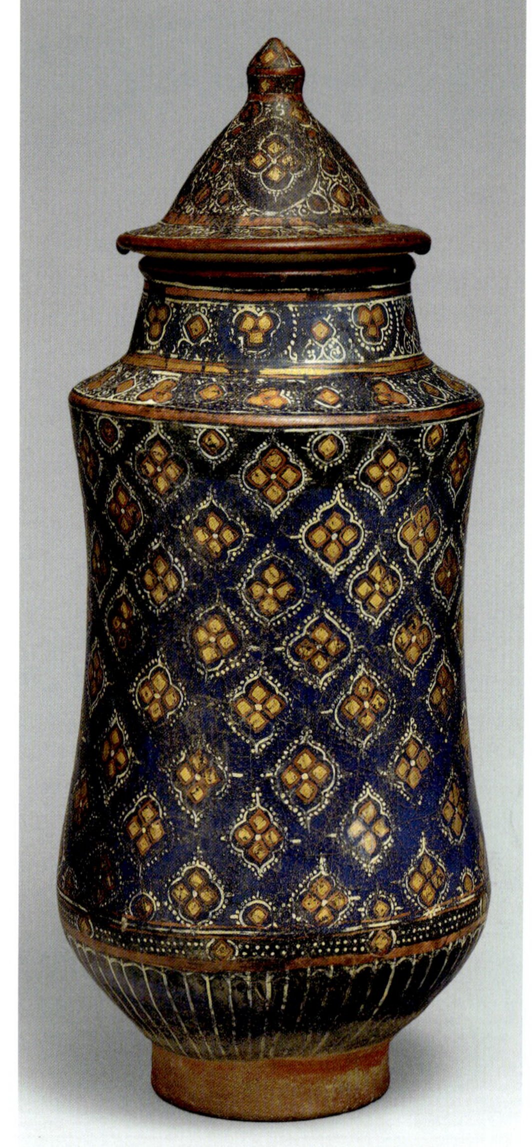

Jars exhibiting this distinctive shape—an elongated cylinder with a concave waist—are often referred to as *albarelli* (singular, *albarello*). The application of this Italian term is likely due to the popularity of such vessels in Italy beginning in the fifteenth century, where they were used to store pharmaceuticals, medicinal plants, and other natural remedies.[1] Their functional shape allowed for easy handling and arrangement on shelves.

Origins of the form lie outside of Europe, however, as ceramics of this shape are known from earlier periods in Syria, Egypt, and other parts of the Islamic world. This well-preserved and sumptuous example—with its repeating quatrefoil medallion pattern in gold, white, and red on a deep blue ground—was produced in Iran during the reign of the Ilkhanid dynasty. It exhibits a rare glaze type referred to as *lajvardina*, from the Persian word for lapis lazuli (*lajvard*).[2]

The elegant, curving profile of this jar is complemented by its vivid blue glaze and glittering gold-leaf patterning. The design is composed of tiny squares of gold leaf arranged in diamond-shaped patterns over the surface. Each square is carefully outlined in red glaze and enclosed within a white medallion. A time-consuming and costly technique, the application of gold leaf to ceramics is described in an early fourteenth-century treatise written by the Persian author Abu al-Qasim ʻAbdallah al-Kashani.[3] A member of an illustrious multigenerational family of potters from Kashan, he relates that such ceramics were subject to two firings—the first to establish the dark blue background glaze, the second to set the overpainted red and white enamels as well as the gold leaf.[4]

While overpainting can also be seen in earlier Persian ceramics known as *mina'i* (enameled wares), the combination of intense blue underglaze with predominantly gold overpainting is characteristic of the Ilkhanid era. It was a relatively short-lived phenomenon, and *lajvardina* ceramics are known to survive in only limited numbers.[5] These surviving vessels, along with *lajvardina* tiles found in the excavations of the Ilkhanid royal palace known as Takht-i Sulaiman, attest to the luxurious and precious nature of this class of ceramics—perhaps considered fit for royalty alone.[6] DMT

1. Wallis 1904. See his "Introduction" for more on the form.
2. See the entry for this piece in New York and Los Angeles 2002–3, p. 271, no. 131, image on p. 200, fig. 241. Description of the *lajvardina* glaze technique on pp. 201–2.
3. Allan 1973, esp. pp. 114–15. See also the Persian edition mentioned by Allan (ibid., p. 120): *ʻArayis al-Jawahir wa Nafayis al-Atayib* (Tehran, 1345). Two manuscript copies of the treatise are known, one dated A.H. 700/1301 A.D.
4. See Allan 1973; Masuya 2002–3, pp. 92ff.
5. Other examples in the Metropolitan Museum include acc. nos. 91.1.1529; 20.120.73; 34.151; 40.181.16; 66.95.8; 1975.30; 1976.245; and 1991.224.1.
6. See Masuya 2002–3, pp. 96ff.; and Carboni 2002–3, pp. 201–2.

PROVENANCE: Henry G. Leberthon, New York (by 1931–d. 1939); Mrs. Louise Ruxton Chauncey, New York (1939–57)

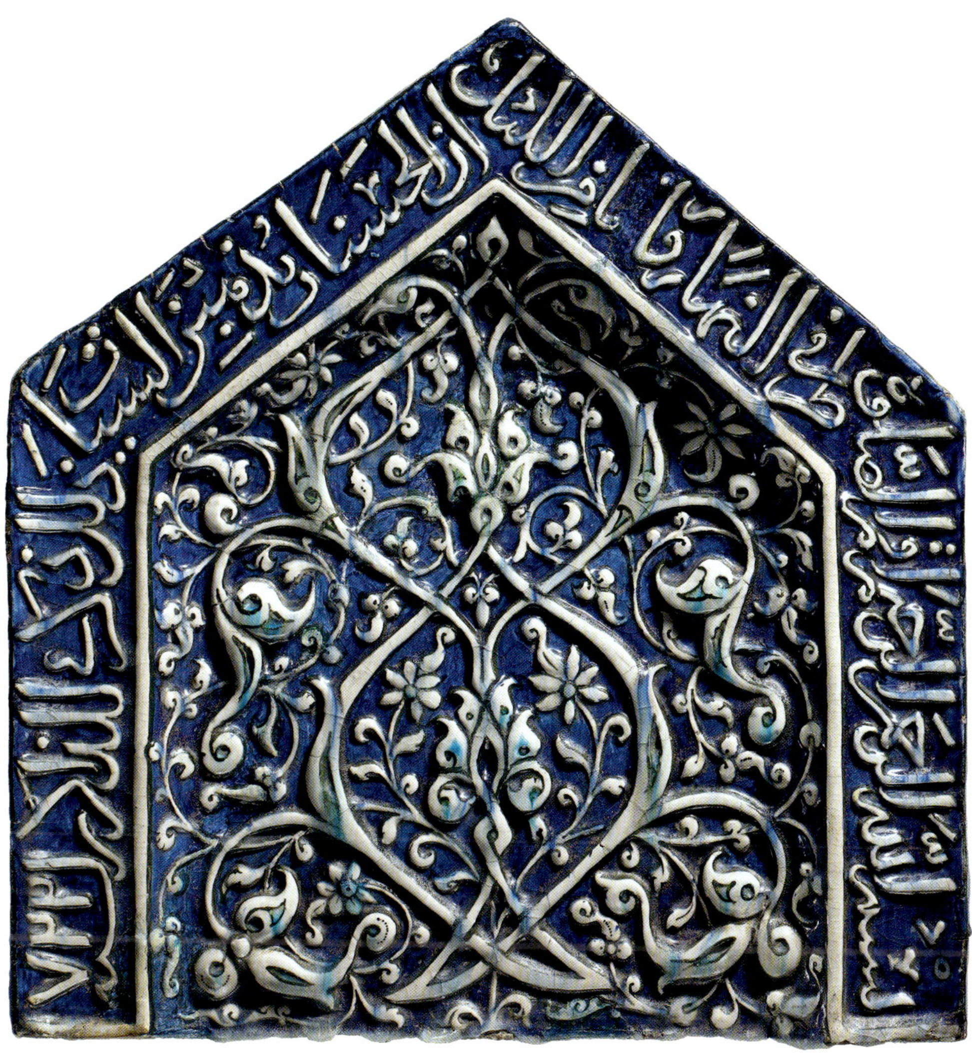

80. Tile from a Mihrab

Iran, dated A.H. 722/1322–23 A.D.
Stonepaste; modeled, painted under transparent glaze[1]
27 ⅜ × 26 in. (69.5 × 66 cm)
Gift of William Mandel, 1983 1983.345

Inscription in Arabic in ornamental *naskhi* script:
بسم الله الرحمن الرحيم
أقم الصلوة طرفي النهار وزلفا من الليل إن الحسنات يذهبن السيئات ذلك ذكرى للذاكر[ين]
لسنة ٧٢٢
In the name of God, the Merciful, the Compassionate.
And perform the prayer at the two ends of the day and nigh of the night;
Surely the good deeds will drive away evil deeds.
That is a remembrance unto the mindful (Qur'an 11:114).[2]
A.H. 722 [1322–33 A.D.]

With its unusual pointed arch shape and Qur'anic inscription, this large-scale tile with interlacing vegetal decoration likely formed part of a *mihrab*—a niche indicating the direction of prayer within mosques and other sacred structures.[3] Surviving *mihrab* assemblages incorporating similarly shaped tiles are found in museum collections throughout the world; still others remain in their original architectural context. Complex, puzzlelike configurations, these tile panels were specially designed commissioned works, carefully fitted for installation into specific locations.

Many extant tile panels of this type were produced by a family of potters sharing the *nisba* Kashani, indicating their origins in the city of Kashan—a traditional center for Persian ceramic production. From the early thirteenth to early fourteenth century, the patriarch of this family, Abu Tahir, and his descendants produced several *mihrab* tile groupings for mosques and major shrines in the region.[4] In form and content, some of the individual tiles in these assemblages are analogous to the Museum's example.

While the tiles that this family produced were almost without exception luster-glazed,[5] this one is not. Rather, it is one of the few extant underglaze-painted *mihrab* tiles. With its simple, fresh palette of bright cobalt blue and white with touches of turquoise, its closest parallel is a tile in the Museum of Islamic Art, Cairo, also executed in an underglaze technique.[6] Roughly the same size and shape as the Metropolitan's piece, the Cairo tile displays a somewhat similar vine scroll design and calligraphic script.[7] The Cairo niche tile is joined to two other panels, one containing an inscription referring to the grouping as a *mihrab*, and stating that it was ordered (*'amara*) by 'Ali ibn Abi Talib ibn Abi Nas[r] in A.H. 719/1319–20 A.D.[8] The Metropolitan's tile, displaying a date of A.H. 722/1322–23 A.D., was produced shortly thereafter. While neither the Cairo group nor the Metropolitan's tile can be securely attributed to the Abu Tahir family of artists, both survive as testaments to the long-lived tilework *mihrab* tradition established in the region by this multigenerational line of potters. DMT

1. My thanks to Abdullah Ghouchani for his valuable insights on this piece and to Jean-François de Lapérouse (Department of Objects Conservation, The Metropolitan Museum of Art) for ascertaining that portions of this tile were modeled, and not molded, as previously thought.
2. Translation after Arberry 1955, pp. 252–53. The transcription presented here reflects the calligraphy as it appears on the tile. Because of damage to the inscription near the top of the tile, the letter ف is missing from the phrase وزلفا من. It also appears that the letters و and ل in the same phrase may have been joined in the course of an earlier phase of restoration. My thanks to Stefan Heidemann for his assistance in reviewing the inscription and its transcription.
3. See New York and Los Angeles 2002–3, pp. 199, 270, no. 125, and p. 128, fig. 152.
4. For more on the family and the various works that they produced, see Watson 1983 and Watson 1985, esp. Chapter 10: "Tiles," pp. 122ff., and Appendix I: "Lustre Potters and Their Works," pp. 176ff. More recently, Sheila Blair discusses the Abu Tahir family in relation to other families of Kashani potters in Blair 2008.
5. Only one potter in this family, Yusuf ibn 'Ali ibn Muhammad ibn Abi Tahir, is known to have worked in the underglaze technique. See Watson 1983.
6. See Cairo 1931, pp. 134–35, no. 719, and pl. 2. It is published more recently in full color (with restoration) in O'Kane, ed. 2006, pp. 274–75, no. 236. Museum of Islamic Art, Cairo (no. 3745).
7. New York and Los Angeles 2002–3, p. 270 n. 2, no. 125, provides the dimensions of the Cairo tile group.
8. See Cairo 1931, p. 135.

PROVENANCE: William Mandel, New York (by 1967–83)

81. *Mihrab (Prayer Niche)*

Iran, Isfahan, A.H. 755/1354–55 A.D.
Mosaic of polychrome-glazed cut tiles on stonepaste body; set in mortar
11 ft. 3 in. × 9 ft. 5⅝ in. (3.43 × 2.88 m)
Harris Brisbane Dick Fund, 1939 39.20

Large inscription in Arabic in *muhaqqaq* script on outer border: (Qur'an.9:18–22)

Inscription in Arabic in *kufic* script framing the niche:
قال عليه الصلوة والسلام بنى الاسلام على خمس شهادة ان لا إله إلا الله وأن محمداً رسول الله
واقام الصلوة وإيتاء الزكوة و الحج و صوم رمضان وقال عليه الصلوة و السلام من بنى لله
مسجداً ولو بمفحص قطاة على التقوى
He [the Prophet], blessings and peace be upon him, said: "Islam is built on five attestations: there is no god but God and Muhammad is the Messenger of God, he established prayer and the giving of alms and the pilgrimage and fasting of [the month of] Ramadan." And he [the Prophet], blessings and peace be upon him, said: "Whoever builds a mosque for God, even the size of a sand-grouse nest, based on piety, [God will build for him a palace in Paradise]."[1]

Inscription in Arabic in *kufic* and *thuluth* scripts at center of niche:
قال النبي عليه الصلوة والسلام/المسجد بيت كل تقي
The Prophet, blessings and peace be upon him, said:
"The mosque is the abode of the pious."

This prayer niche, or *mihrab*, was originally an architectural element in a theological school (*madrasa*) in the city of Isfahan. An inscription in the courtyard of this former school, now known as Madrasa Imami, is dated to the year A.H. 754/1354–55 A.D. The *madrasa* was built shortly after the collapse of the Ilkhanid dynasty, when rival Injuids and Muzaffarid leaders competed for control over Isfahan. The *qibla* wall, which is now whitewashed, was originally graced with this monumental and impressive *mihrab*. It was produced by joining together a myriad of cut-to-size glazed tiles to produce the intricate arabesque and calligraphic designs.

Created predominantly with tiles of contrasting dark blue and milky white glazes, the *mihrab* has additional turquoise, ocher-yellow, and dark green colors that enrich the complex geometric, vegetal, and calligraphic patterns. The decorative achievement, combined with the challenge of creating a three-dimensional work that includes a deep, rounded niche with pointed vault, makes this one of the earliest and finest examples of mosaic tilework to survive. Inscriptional bands reflect the careful planning of the decorative program: the outer frame bears a Qur'anic inscription in white *muhaqqaq* script, in which words and letters progress in two superimposed lines from the bottom right to the bottom left (Qur'an 9:18–22), while an inscription in *kufic* script containing sayings of the Prophet Muhammad (hadith) frames the pointed arch of the niche and is set in blue against a white background, rhythmically punctuated by continuous vertical letter endings. The most legible words are inside the rectangular cartouche at the center of the niche: ocher-yellow inscriptions in *kufic* script mentioning the prophet are followed by a clear, larger, cursive white reference to the function of the mosque.

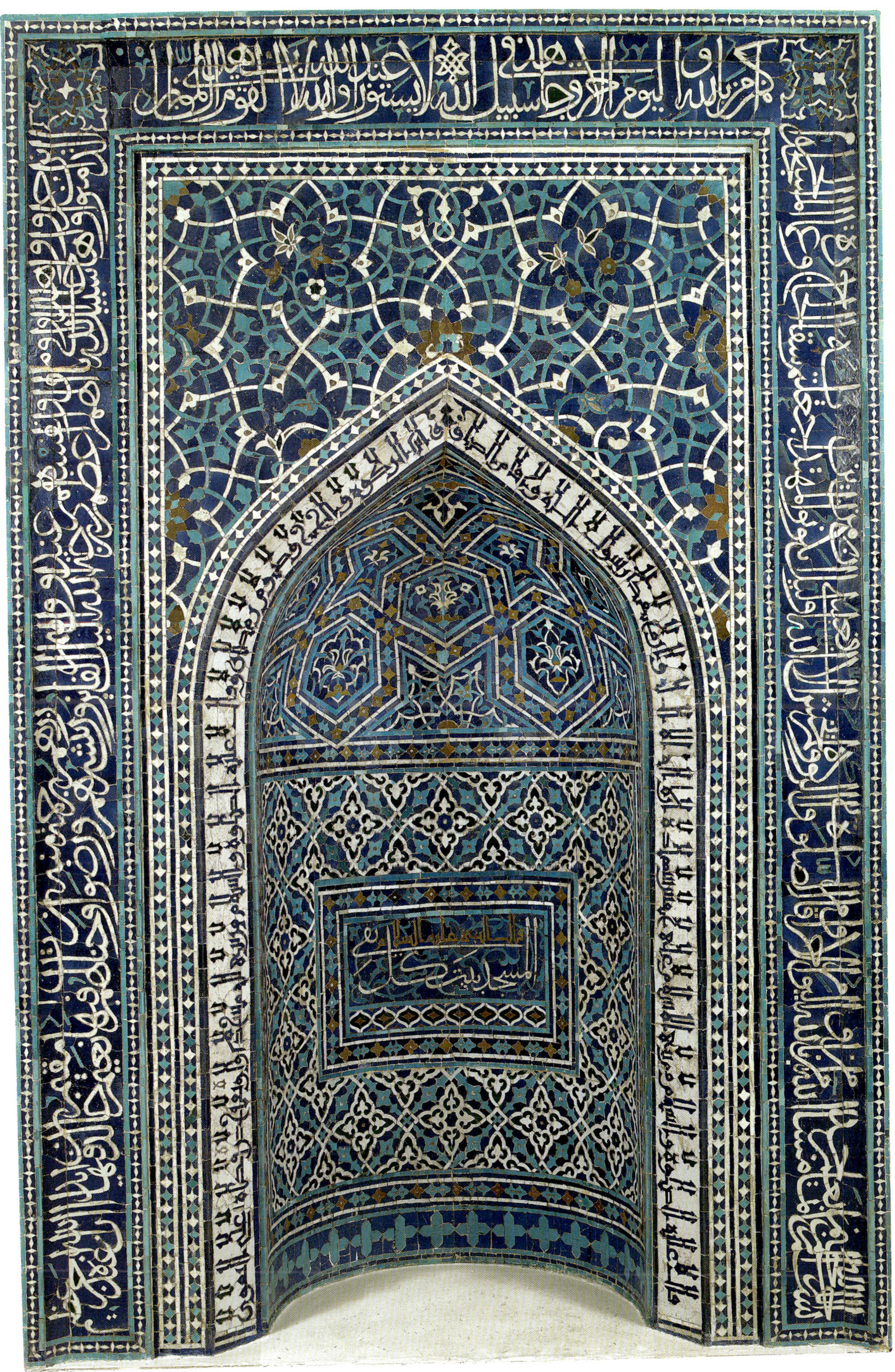

This prayer niche underwent a series of restorations and relocations before it was acquired by the Metropolitan Museum.[2] The *mihrab* was removed from the Madrasa Imami in the late 1920s, after skillful local potters had provided extensive (and almost undetectable) restoration in the area below the central inscription. Shipped to Philadelphia and stored in the University Museum there, it also spent some time in London, where it was shown at a legendary exhibition of Persian art at Burlington House in 1931. The Metropolitan eventually purchased it in 1939.

Now displayed as a splendid example of religious architectural decoration of Iranian Islamic art, the *mihrab* of the Madrasa Imami is one of the most significant and noteworthy works in the Museum's collection. SC

1. The Muslim reader can complete the phrase with the latter part of the sentence.
2. For a summary of the *mihrab*'s history, see New York 1993, p. 36, no. 31.

PROVENANCE: Madrasa Imami, Isfahan, Iran (1354–late 1920s); [A.Rabenou, Paris, by 1931–39; sold to Arthur U. Pope for MMA]

82. *Jug*

Probably Iran, 10th century
Excavated at Tepe Madrasa, Nishapur
Glass, colorless; blown, folded foot, applied handle, cut
H. 5¾ in. (14.5 cm); Diam. 4 in. (10.2 cm)
Rogers Fund, 1939 39.40.101

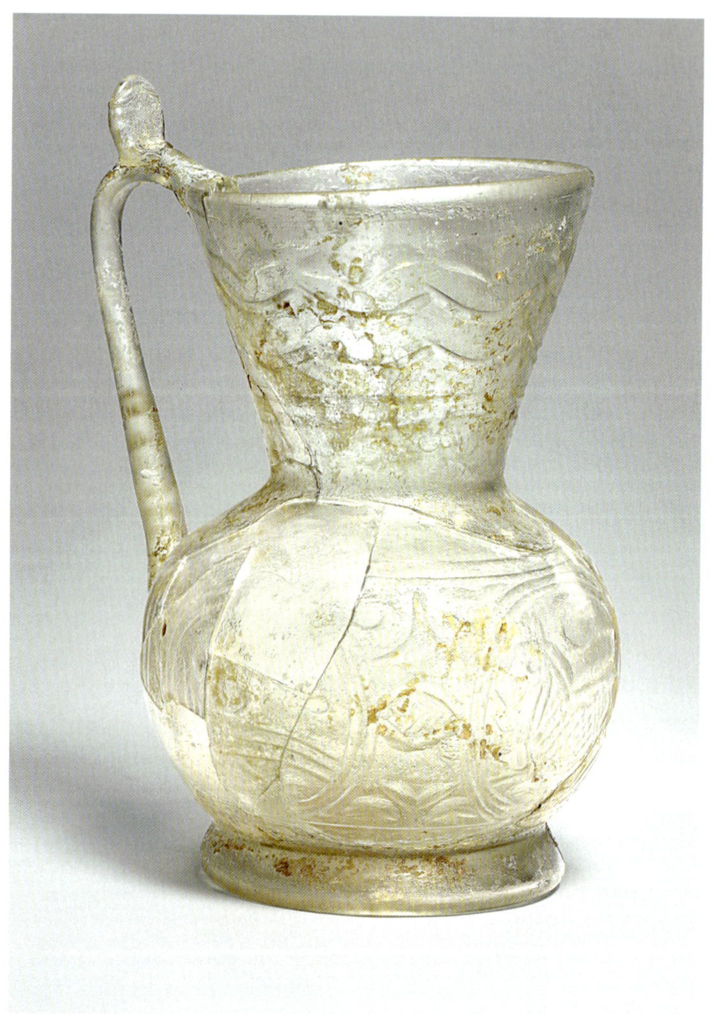

Made from transparent yellowish colorless glass, this jug has a rounded body narrowed at the base of the neck and a flared opening. It stands on a low foot ring with a pontil mark at the base, and a handle with a thumb rest is attached at the rim and body. Broken when excavated, it has been reassembled from approximately twenty pieces, and its surface retains slight traces of iridescence. The entire surface is decorated with wheel-cut motifs that stand in relief against the ground and provide the principal decoration on the body—three roundels separated by geometric and vegetal designs. The two roundels on either side of the handle show long-tailed birds, and the third bears a crouching lion, all facing left. This was the only glass vessel found at Nishapur with a pattern of roundels around its body, a type of decoration known from other examples of Sasanian and Islamic metalwork, textiles, ceramics, and glass.[1]

In addition to carved stucco architectural elements, extensive wall paintings, coins, high-quality ceramics, and metalwork, a total of 115 glass vessels or fragments were found at the site of Tepe Madrasa.[2] None of the glass finds were from the mosque itself; many were from rooms in different parts of the complex, with a concentration in what may have been a residential quarter, and many others came from the wells, drains, and latrines, indicating that they had probably been discarded. This jug was in a drain on the lower level of the site. Although no glassmaking kilns were found at Nishapur, the number and range of finds point to a flourishing and highly developed industry in the ninth and tenth centuries. QA

1. See Kröger 1995 and Corning, New York, and Athens 2001–2, p. 157, for a detailed list of comparative examples.
2. Kröger 1995, p. 14.

PROVENANCE: 1938–39, discovered at Tepe Madrasa, Nishapur, Iran, by The Metropolitan Museum of Art's expedition under a concession granted by the Council of Ministers, Iran, upon the recommendation of the Ministry of Education of Iran; title transferred to The Metropolitan Museum of Art pursuant to the concession

83. Cup

Iran, 10th–12th century
Silver; fire-gilded, hammered, and chased
H. 3¼ in. (8.3 cm); Diam. 5 in. (12.7 cm)
Harris Brisbane Dick Fund, 1964 64.133.2

Inscription in Arabic in *kufic* script below the rim:

اشرب فلليوم فضل لو علمت به	بادرت باللهو واستعجلت بالطرب
[ورد الخدود، وورد الوض قد جمعا	والغيم مبتسم، والشمس في الحجب]
لاتحبس الكاس واشربها مشعشعة	حتى تموت بها موتاً بلا سبب

Drink! For this day has a special boon, which if you had known about it
[You would have hurried up with entertainment and hastened with rapture!]
Don't hold the cup back, but drink it diluted, until you die from it without reason[1]
(The couplet in the brackets above does not appear on the cup)

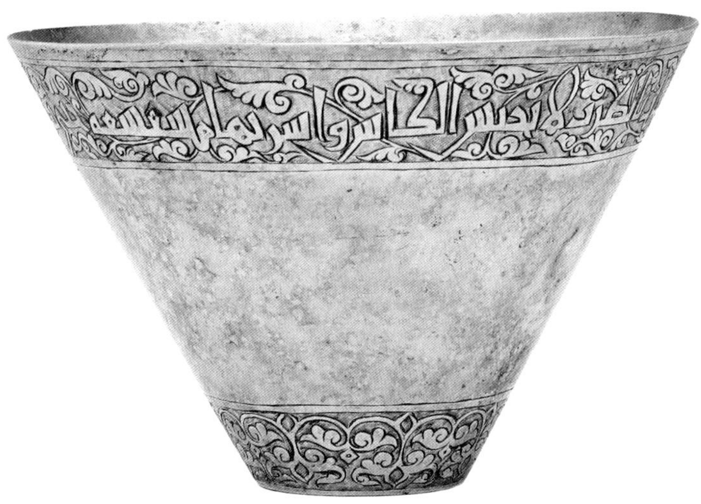

This cup belongs to a group of silver vessels whose production peaked in Iran under the Buyids and the Seljuqs.[2] Used by nobles at court, or carried by high-rank militaries during their campaigns,[3] vessels like this were often part of larger sets of tableware. This cup shares several features with a silverware set, now in Tehran, that bears the name of the amir Abu'l 'Abbas Valkin ibn Harun, and may once have been part of a similar group.[4] In addition to the shape—characterized by straight, flaring sides and a narrow base—the cup shares these vessels' decoration, which consists of an epigraphic band located right beneath the rim. In the present example the inscription is engraved on the exterior in foliated *kufic*, a style that also appears on a group of epigraphic ceramic wares produced in northeastern Iran between the tenth and eleventh centuries.[5] Vessels of this type are distinguished by inscriptions framed by black paste, which serves to outline the inscriptions as well as to create a bolder aesthetic. Here a second, narrower band with vegetal arabesques runs around the base, also outlined in black.

The verses implicitly suggest that the cup was used for wine. Bacchic-style verses like these are also found on a golden bowl that was part of a hoard found near Hamadan,[6] indicating that the practice of drinking wine from precious vessels, which was common in pre-Islamic times, continued in the Islamic period.

According to a prophetic tradition, Muslims are forbidden to use gold and silver vessels for eating and drinking, a prohibition that is further confirmed in a twelfth-century encyclopedic work that devotes an entire chapter to licit and illicit uses of gold and silver wares.[7] Yet the material evidence provided by this and other vessels, along with many references contained in sources,[8] demonstrate that actual practice often contradicted well-established prescriptions.

FL

1. The poem, by Ibn Sukkara al-Hashimi (d. 995–96 A.D.), is found in the *Yatimat al-dahr fi mahasin ahl al-'asr*, an anthology by Abu Mansur al-Tha'alibi (d. 1038 A.D.). See Abu Mansur al-Tha'alibi 1956, vol. 3, p. 19.
2. Superb examples produced under these dynasties include a gold jug with repoussé decoration inscribed with the name of the Buyid ruler 'Izz al-Daula Bakhtiyar ibn Mu'izz al-Daula (r. 967–78), now in the Freer Gallery of Art and Arthur M. Sackler Gallery, Washington, D.C. (no. 43.1); reproduced in Pope, A. U., and Ackerman, eds. 1938–39, vol. 6, pl. 1343. See also Marshak 1986, pl. 146.
3. Ferrier, ed. 1989, p. 171.
4. The objects, currently held in the Iran Bastan Museum, Tehran, are reproduced in Pope, A. U., and Ackerman, eds. 1938–39, vol. 6, pls 1345–46. This and other hoards are discussed in Ferrier, ed. 1989, pp. 171–74, figs. 1–2 and 6–7, and Ward 1993, pp. 53–55
5. Baer 1983, p. 191.
6. British Museum, London (no. 1939.11-12). See Ward 1993, p. 54, and fig. 38.
7. Quoted in Melikian-Chirvani 1982a, esp. pp. 158–59.
8. The *Kitab al-Aghani* refers to the gold cups used by the Umayyad al-Walid II in his drinking parties (quoted in Baer 1983, p. 103 n. 235). In his *Siyasatnama*, the Seljuk vizier Nizam al-Mulk records their use during a banquet of military officials (Nizam al-Mulk 1891–97, vol. 3, p. 190).

PROVENANCE: [Nasli Heeramaneck, New York, until 1964; sold to MMA]

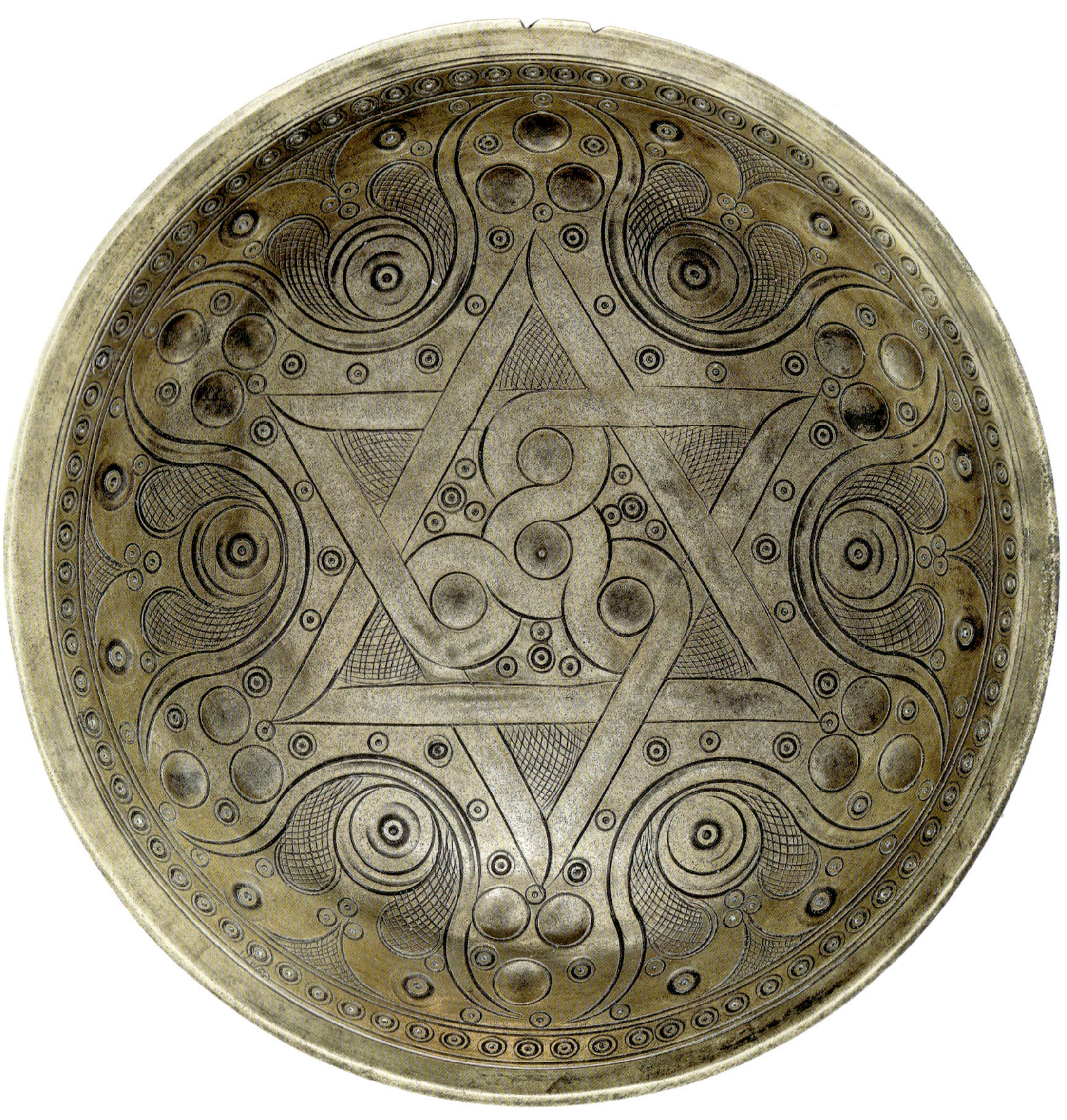

84. Bowl

Afghanistan, 12th century
High-tin bronze; cast, chased, punched, engraved
H. 1 5/8 in. (4 cm); Diam. 7 in. (17.9 cm)
Louis E. and Theresa S. Seley Purchase Fund for Islamic Art and Rogers Fund, 2000 2000.57

An example of medieval Islamic high-tin bronze ware, this metal bowl features a central six-pointed star with intertwined sides surrounded by stylized flowers and smaller motifs—in effect, minimal decoration applied only to the interior of the vessel. The bowl belongs to a group of objects associated with the metalwork production of the eastern Islamic world, characterized by a preference for open forms, the use of engraved or punched decorative motifs, and a silver color.[1]

These features are the result of the alloy used in the casting, called high-tin bronze, also known in the Islamic tradition as "white bronze" (*safid ruy*). The minimal decorative repertoire found here is partly the result of the medium's limitations. The high percentage of tin in the alloy produced a shiny and highly malleable metal. As a result, traditional working methods such as hammering were not adaptable to high-tin bronze, and artisans instead used chasing, engraving, and punching, as seen on this example.

The production of this alloy is first mentioned by the eleventh-century scholar al-Biruni, who documents the causes that presumably led to its introduction.[2] Following a Qur'anic prohibition, the Umayyad governor of Iraq and Iran al-Hajjaj (r. 694–714) outlawed gold and silver vessels, the use of which had been popular in the Middle East since pre-Islamic times. Although high-tin bronzes predate this prohibition, their precious appearance did make them an appealing substitute for gold and silver vessels, satisfying the taste for luxury objects while adhering to the governor's new decree. In addition, the tin component of the alloy prevents the high-tin vessels from developing the poisonous green patina known as verdigris, thus in part accounting for the popularity and longevity of the technique.[3]

Although the production of high-tin bronze peaked in medieval Iran, the metal was in use in India from the third century A.D. as well as in China, before being adopted under the Parthian Empire (238 B.C.–226 A.D.) in Sistan and Sogdiana. Hence, Muslim craftsmen rehabilitated an old technology in order to meet new requirements. FL

1. Two related high-tin bowls can be found in the Metropolitan's collection, one with figural decoration (acc. no. 1971.42) and one with geometric designs (acc. no. 1973.338.8).
2. Al-Biruni 1936, esp. pp. 264–66; Nasir al-Din Tusi 1969, p. 228, quoted in Allan et al. 1979, pp. 47ff.; al-Kashani 1966, quoted in Allan et al. 1979, pp. 47ff.
3. Ward 1993, p. 30.

PROVENANCE: Sale, Christie's London, April 26, 1994, lot 310; [Momtaz Islamic Art, London, until 2000; sold to MMA]

85. Incense Burner

Maker: Ja'far ibn Muhammad ibn 'Ali
Iran, dated A.H. 577 / 1181–82 A.D.
Bronze; cast, engraved, chased, pierced
Overall 33½ × 9 in. (85.1 × 22.9 cm); length 32½ in. (82.6 cm)
Rogers Fund, 1951 51.56

Inscription in Arabic in *kufic* script around neck and continued on chest:
امر به الامير العادل العالم/سيف الدنيا والدين بن محمد/الماوردي
Ordered by the just and wise prince Saif al-Dunya wa'l-Din ibn Muhammad al-Mawardi[1]

Inscription in Arabic in *kufic* script on left and right bosses and boss on chest:
السعادة الاقبال السلامة
Happiness, prosperity, well-being

Signature in Arabic in *kufic* script at left, on chest, and on right foot:
عمل جعفر بن محمد بن علي سنة سبع وسبعين وخمسمائة
Work of Ja'far son of Muhammad son of 'Ali in the year A.H. 577 [1181–82 A.D.]

Each element of this monumental incense burner, a demonstration of the excellence achieved in metalwork under the Seljuqs, was cast individually and then attached with solder; the head remained removable so that incense could be inserted and lit, then waft from the figure, perfuming the air. This piece, and others like it, would have probably been used in domestic, secular settings, as their zoomorphic and aromatic attributes would have made them unsuitable in a religious context.[2]

The object exhibits an elaborate decorative program that combines openwork patterns and epigraphic bands. The neck, body, and upper part of the thighs are pierced with trefoils, creating a latticelike design. The scrolling vine motifs that mark the ears of the animal are mirrored in the upturning of the corners of the eyes, and the snout is incised with stylized whiskers. Epigraphic bands in foliated *kufic* script run along the base of the neck and the chest, giving the name of the patron, Saif al-Dunya wa'l-Din Muhammad al-Mawardi; of the artist, Ja'far ibn Muhammad ibn 'Ali; and the date, A.H. 577/1181–82 A.D. In addition, the words *happiness, prosperity,* and *well-being* appear on the three round bosses located on the chest and on the two sides of the lion's front paws.

Zoomorphic vessels gained popularity in the medieval period, and lion-shaped incense burners were especially common in the eleventh and twelfth centuries, though this example is larger than most of them and belongs to a small group of related works.[3] The group shares common features, including openwork decoration on the body, stylized facial features, incised eyes and whiskers, and upturned tails. The related examples differ most dramatically in their scale, in the pattern of openwork, and in the modeling of the body. The Metropolitan's example is the largest of this group and exhibits robust modeling and smooth joinery

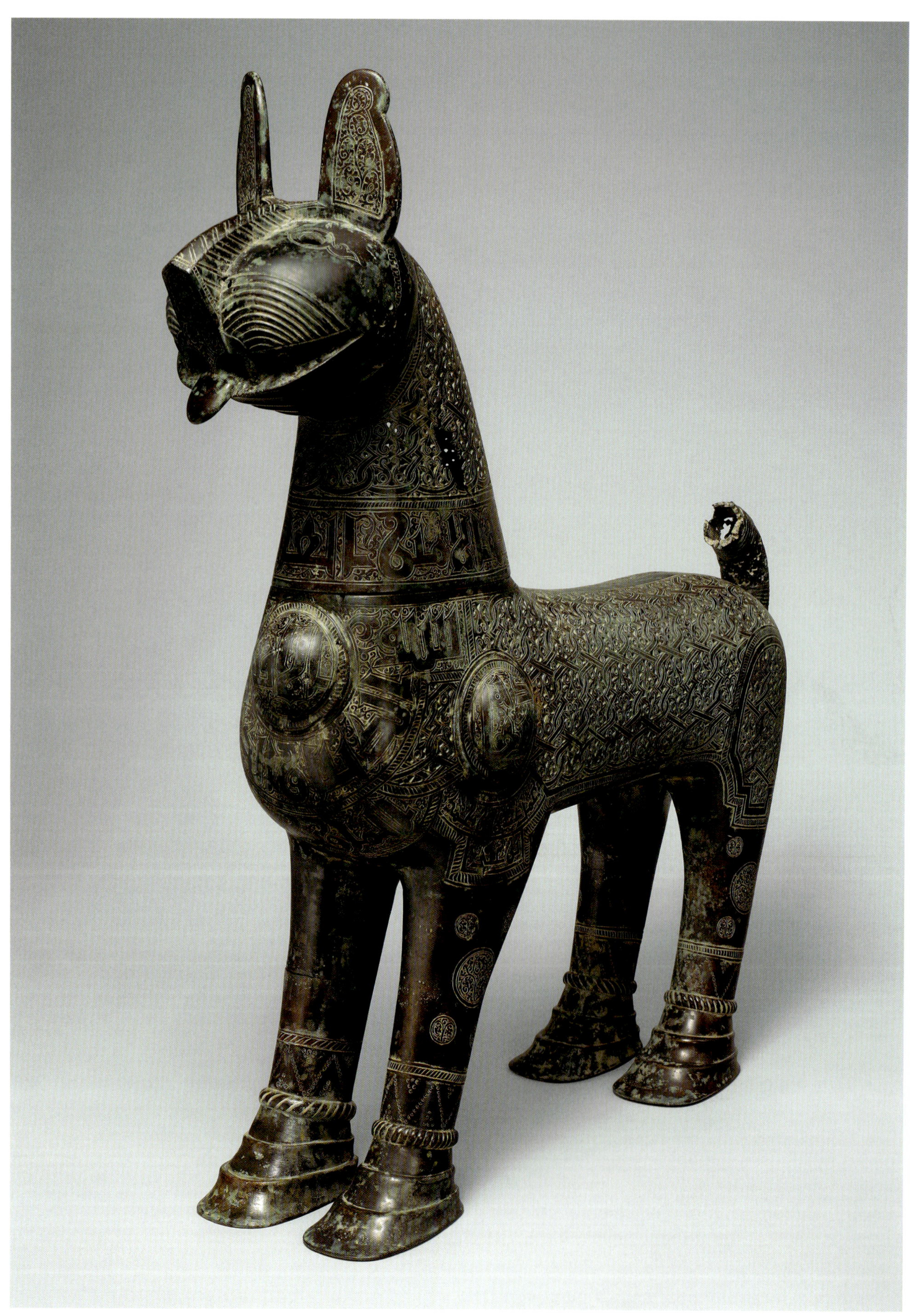

that together convey a sense of musculature. Another example, in the Cleveland Museum of Art, while much smaller in scale and lacking the copious inscriptions of the Metropolitan's lion, has a similar robustness and comparable features, and its long curving tail provides a sense of how the Metropolitan's burner may have looked when intact.[4] FL

1. The family name *Mawardi* is written on the chest between the name of the metalworker and under the name of the prince, so it is not clear to which one of them it applies. Although the word *al-Mawardi* means "the rosewater-seller," the size of the inscription corresponds to that of the prince and not that of the maker, which is considerably smaller.
2. Boston and Chicago 2006–7, p. 197.
3. Other examples can be found at the Cleveland Museum of Art (no. 1948.308.a), in the State Hermitage Museum, St. Petersburg (no. IR-1565), and in the David Collection, Copenhagen (no. 48/1981). A list of the examples is given in Baer 1983, p. 58 n. 114. To them a further example in the Museum of Fine Arts, Houston (no. 2007.1301.A,.B) should be added.
4. See n. 3 above.

PROVENANCE: [Khalil Rabenou, New York, until 1951; sold to MMA]

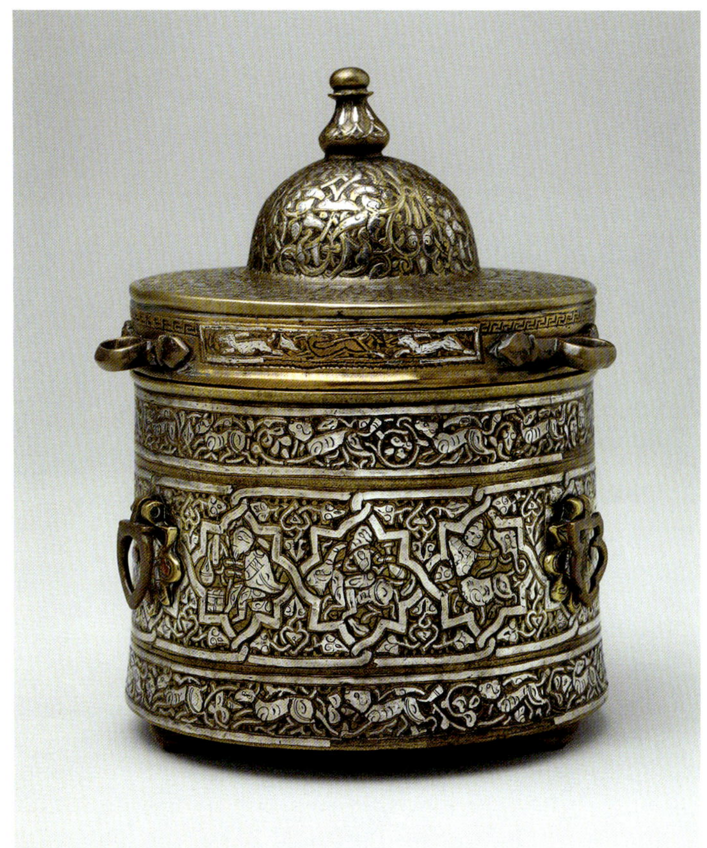

86. Inkwell

Probably Iran, early 13th century
Brass; cast, inlaid with silver, copper, and black compound
H. 5⅞ in. (14.9 cm); Diam. 4⅝ in. (11.6 cm)
Harris Brisbane Dick Fund, 1959 59.69.2a, b

Remarkably well preserved, this inkwell is a fine example of the elaborate embellishment applied to utilitarian objects in the medieval Islamic world. Calligraphic tools and implements were particularly ornate, often made of brass or other copper alloys and decorated with elaborate openwork or inlaid designs.[1] It bears a rich decorative program of benedictory Arabic inscriptions in animated *naskhi* script, animal motifs, and zodiac signs. The body is divided into three registers; the middle one is the widest and is decorated with the twelve signs of the zodiac inscribed in interlocked star-shaped medallions. Above and below this wide middle band run two thinner registers with the secondary design of animals set against a background of scrolling vines. The motif of running animals is mirrored on the lid, despite the fact that the base and lid originally belonged to separate objects.

Cylindrical inkwells similar to this one were produced in Greater Iran during the eleventh century under the Seljuq dynasty and continued to be produced in Iran through the thirteenth century. The popularity and often lavish ornamentation of inkwells in this period speak to the cultural importance attached to the art of writing.[2] The choice of astrological signs as the primary decorative theme also reflects contemporary taste, and similar designs can be seen on numerous examples in the Metropolitan Museum and other collections.[3] First introduced into the Islamic world through Greek texts, the art of astrology was considered integral to the science of astronomy.[4] The depiction of the zodiac on precious objects such tions in the medieval Islamic world. Moreover, the presence of such imagery on these objects was thought to invest them with cosmological and talismanic properties, thereby placing their owners under the auspicious influence of the stars. FL

1. See, for example, a thirteenth-century pen box also in the Department of Islamic Art at the Metropolitan Museum (acc. no. 89.2.194). See New York 1997a, p. 18, no. 6.
2. Ibid., p. 30.
3. Another inkwell, deprived of its lid but also decorated with the zodiac, is housed in the Metropolitan Museum (acc. no. 44.131). In addition, astrological themes decorate two of the Museum's ewers (acc. nos. 44.15 and 91.1.530) and a mortar (acc. no. 91.1.527a), all of which are associated with the twelfth- and thirteenth-century metalwork production of central or eastern Iran (ibid., p. 16, no. 5; p. 22, no. 8; and p. 24, no. 9).
4. Ibid., p. 3.

PROVENANCE: Charles Mège, Paris (by 1903); [Brimo de Laroussilhe, Paris, until 1959; sold to MMA]

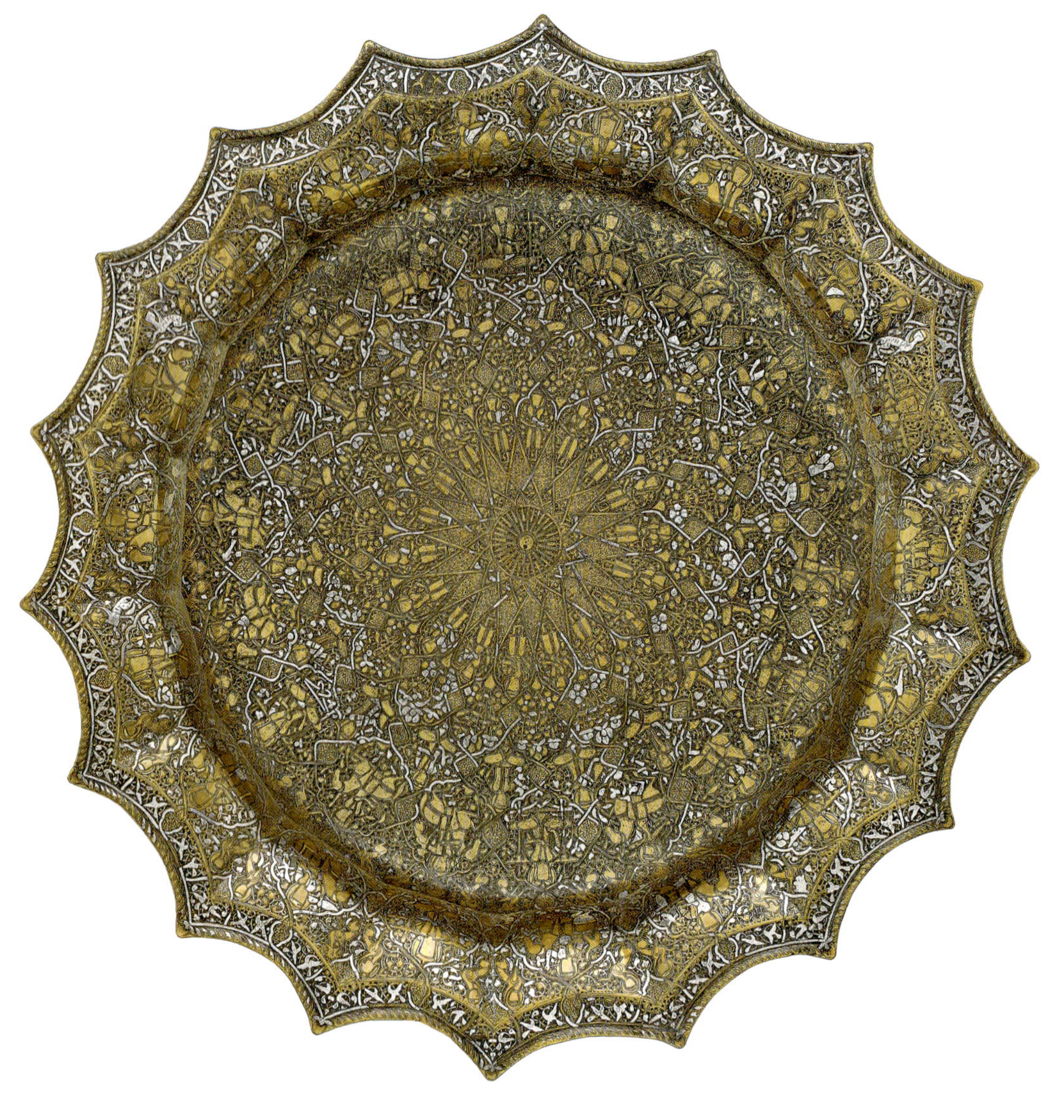

87. Basin

Probably Iran, early 14th century
Brass; raised, engraved, inlaid with silver and gold
H. 5⅛ in. (13 cm); Diam. 20⅛ in. (51.1 cm)
Edward C. Moore Collection, Bequest of Edward C. Moore, 1891 91.1.521

Called *tasht* or *lagan*, large hand basins such as this are documented in the eastern Islamic world from the late twelfth century onward.[1] Yet the distinctive scalloped form of this basin appears to have been specifically produced under the Ilkhanid dynasty, as seen in a similar example datable to about 1300–1320, now in the collection of the Victoria and Albert Museum, London.[2]

The decoration, which was once entirely inlaid with gold and silver, covers the interior of the basin and is organized in concentric bands. Radiating from a central sun-shaped medallion, the registers contain depictions of servants, seated musicians playing instruments, courtiers and attendants, and five enthroned figures flanked by hunters and polo players (a motif that appears twice, once on the base and once on the wall of the basin). Additional details include images of birds on the crenellated border, addorsed griffins and human-headed winged animals, and high-stem flowers distributed in the interstitial spaces created by an intricate geometric grid used to frame the decoration.

Although inscribed in separate registers and medallions, and thus used as individual decorative units, the characters are thematically related. They all belong to the princely cycle, a group of themes illustrating royal life and pastimes. Courtly subjects were recurrent motifs on sumptuous inlaid brasses and ceramic vessels produced for aristocratic patrons.[3] In a few instances, the objects employ motifs directly inspired by literary texts that celebrated

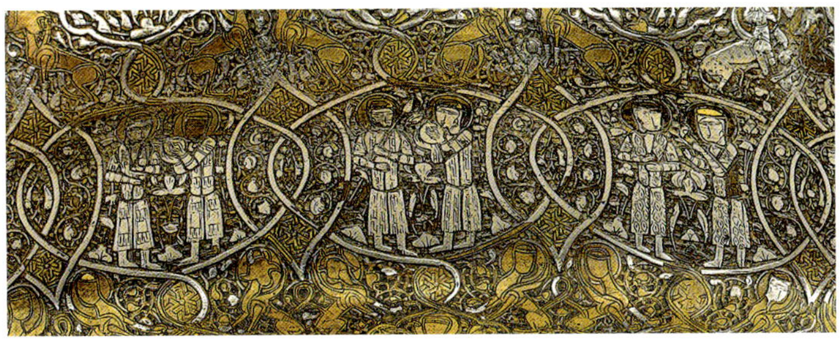

royalty, as in the case of the Victoria and Albert's basin, which is decorated with scenes from the story of Bahram Gur, narrated in both Firdausi's *Shahnama* (Book of Kings) and Nizami's *Khamsa* (Quintet). In most instances, however, the decoration consists of standardized formulas such as enthronement scenes, musical entertainments, and outdoor activities comparable to those ingeniously combined in the present vessel. The choice of these motifs, their detailed execution, and the use of fine materials indicate that this object was probably produced in a royal workshop. FL

1. An example from Ghazni is discussed in Melikian-Chirvani 1982b, pp. 61–63.
2. Victoria and Albert Museum, London (no. 546-1905), published in ibid., pp. 202–7, no. 93, in New York and Los Angeles 2002–3, pp. 179–80, and p. 280, no. 169, and in Ward 1993, p. 87, pl. 66.
3. See, for example, the late thirteenth-century brass basin signed by ʿAli ibn ʿAbdallah al-ʿAlawi al-Naqqash al-Mawsili currently in the Museum für Islamische Kunst, Staatliche Museen zu Berlin (no. I-6581), or the fourteenth-century tray now in the Museum of Fine Arts, Tbilisi (no. 48/I). Both are discussed and reproduced in Komaroff 1992b, pp. 10–11, figs. 2 and 4.

PROVENANCE: Edward C. Moore, New York (until d. 1891)

88. Necklace Elements

Iran or Central Asia, late 14th–16th century
Gold sheet; worked, chased, and set with turquoise, gray chalcedony, and glass
Large medallion: 2⅞ × 2¾ in. (7.3 × 7 cm)
Half medallion: 1¾ × 2¾ in. (4.4 × 7 cm)
Cartouches: ¾ × ½ in. (1.9 × 1.3 cm)
Purchase, Rogers Fund and Habib Anavian Gift, 1989 1989.87a–l

The dating and attribution of gold jewelry from the Islamic world presents numerous challenges to scholars and art historians. Hardly any of the extant examples are dated or bear inscriptions. Furthermore, because of their inherent value, gold and other precious metals were melted down and reused in times of economic crisis. As a result, few examples survive, complicating research and comparative analysis, as in the case of these necklace elements. The basic form and arrangement of similar necklaces are, however, depicted in paintings of women from the late fourteenth to the late sixteenth century in Iran and Central Asia.[1]

Two medallions in the necklace—one a large circular medallion pendant with lobes, and the other a smaller fan-shaped piece—are both of box construction. The large central pendant is inset with a cartouche of gray chalcedony with a turquoise bead at its center, surrounded by turquoise, chalcedony, and glass beads of different sizes and shapes. The fan-shaped element, also inset with a variety of gems and glass, lacks a large cartouche. The two are joined by ten small cartouche-shaped elements, each with a central turquoise. The backs of both of the larger elements are chased and punched with animal motifs of Far Eastern inspiration, including gazelles and quadrupeds attacked by lions, while the fan-shaped medallion has a number of small loops, presumably to hold a delicate string of pearls.

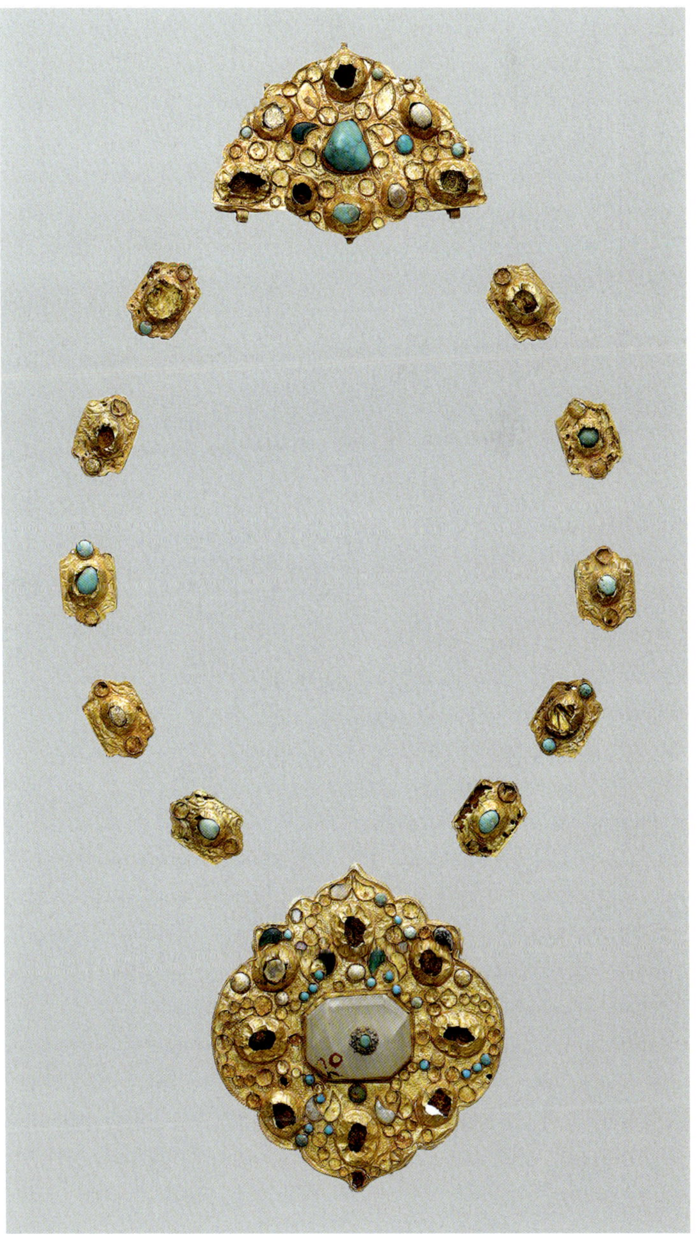

A close look at paintings of women, ranging from an illustrated folio in the Great Mongol *Shahnama* of about 1330 to fifteenth- and sixteenth-century images from Bukhara, shows that comparable gold necklaces were indeed worn by women.[2] The pendants in these representations are all in the shape of half medallions with lobes (rather than full medallions), similar to the one in the scene of "Rudaba Chastised by Her Mother" from the Great Mongol *Shahnama*.[3] The paintings also show cartouche-shaped elements alternating with other shapes, but these connecting pieces are missing from the Metropolitan Museum's assemblage. Lisa Golombek, who has studied the Metropolitan's necklace in great detail, has reproduced a number of these paintings; her survey, however, does not extend beyond the fifteenth century, mentioning the sixteenth century only in passing. She assigns the Museum's necklace elements to late fourteenth- or early fifteenth-century Iran or Central Asia on the basis of their relationship to paintings, cartoons, and preparatory sketches in one of the Timurid albums in the Topkapı Palace Library (H.2152), which was used by artists and craftsmen to replicate patterns in a variety of media. A close stylistic resemblance between the chased motifs on the back of the large elements of this work and those in the Topkapı cartoons is evident, and this association is corroborated by Ruy Gonzalez de Clavijo in a vivid account of the Spanish envoy to the Timurid court in 1405–6.[4]

However, it is not entirely clear that these jewelry elements belong to a single ensemble. The large lobed central medallion, in fact, more closely resembles elements of men's belts seen in paintings. This type of element is almost never shown as the central pendant in a necklace, and when it is represented, it appears on the back of the neck of the female wearing it. The absence of holes for stringing the elements complicates matters further. Upon close inspection, these elements appear to have been produced in the same workshop, but they raise unanswered questions. Until a painting appears with an identical configuration of elements, it can be said only that individual elements of this so-called necklace attest to the popularity and longevity of tastes, forms, and techniques of jewelry making in Iran and Central Asia from the fourteenth through the sixteenth century. ME

1. See Golombek 1991.
2. See, for example, the image of a young women from an anthology painted by Mahmud (Bukhara, ca. 1550) in the Topkapı Palace Museum, Istanbul (Revan 1964, fol. 2a; Titley 1983, p. 90), and a folio from an album dated Dhu'l Qa'da 935 [July 1529] produced in Bukhara (Russian Academy of Sciences, St. Petersburg, no. c-860).
3. Arthur M. Sackler Gallery, Smithsonian Institution, Washington, D.C. (no. S1986.0102). Golombek 1991, p. 66; New York and Los Angeles 2002–3, pp. 86–87.
4. Golombek 1991, p. 65.

PROVENANCE: [Habib Anavian, New York, until 1989; sold to MMA]

89. Textile Fragment

Eastern Islamic Lands, second half of 13th–14th century
Silk, silvered(?) animal substrate around cotton core; lampas[1]
Purchase, Friends of Islamic Art Gifts, 1996 1996.286

Opulent textiles woven of silk and gold threads referred to as *nasij al-dhahab al-harir* (cloth of gold and silk) were treasured fabrics among the Mongol ruling elite and subsequent Ilkhanid dynasty rulers.[2] The most luxurious surviving examples are gold-on-gold fabrics in which both pattern and background are executed in differing types of gold thread.[3] This textile fragment—with a pattern of confronted birds and pinecone medallions against a blue silk background—is only slightly less ornate and ranks among the most lavish textiles of its day.

After the Mongol conquest of Persia in the thirteenth century, an extensive trade network opened from China to the Mediterranean, allowing goods to move more easily than ever before. Luxury textiles traveled along this route, and as they moved, their motifs were widely copied and dispersed by weavers seeking to emulate their sumptuous effect.[4] The achievements of these weavers make it difficult to identify textile origins based on surface pattern alone. As a result, this textile and others like it have been variously attributed over the years to Italy, Mamluk Egypt and Syria, Iran, and China.[5]

Anne Wardwell and other textile scholars have demonstrated that comparisons of structure and weave can aid in delineating the origins of some of these pieces.[6] Among the many factors to be considered is the composition of their gold threads.[7] During the Ilkhanid period, such thread was made in different ways in various regions along the Silk Road. In contemporary Chinese textiles, for example, long narrow strips of gilded paper were wrapped around a silk core to create a golden thread suitable for weaving.[8] In the Metropolitan's example, however, gilded animal skin replaces the paper, and cotton forms the core of the wrapped threads.

Only a very small group of related textiles shares this unusual combination of structure and materials.[9] While their precise place of production remains unknown, Wardwell argues for their

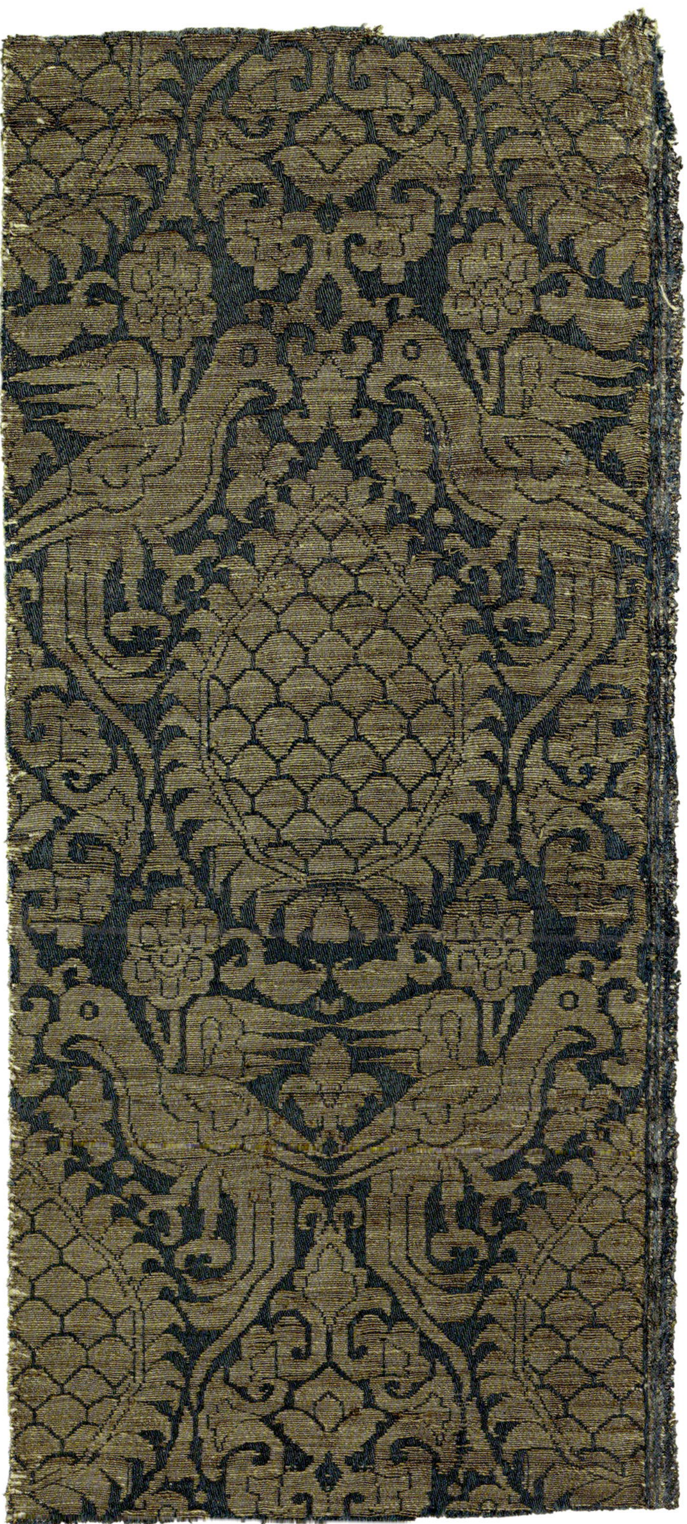

origins in Khurasan, in eastern Iran. Many publications, however, attribute them more generally to the "Eastern Islamic Lands" of this period. Whatever their specific origins, these luxurious fabrics were most likely woven by artists seeking to emulate the splendid gold-on-gold textiles of the Ilkhanid court. DMT

1. During microscopic examination of this textile in consultation with the Museum's textile conservator Janina Poskrobko, only the presence of a silver-colored metal (not gold) on the animal substrate was noted, despite the overall golden appearance of this fabric. It is possible that the brownish-beige color of the underlying substrate now lends this piece its golden hue. Further scientific analysis would need to be conducted to identify the metal used here. The same examination also observed the presence of hair-follicle pockets on the substrate, confirming it as animal skin.
2. Allsen 1997, pp. 2–3. For more on types and terminologies, see pp. 11ff.
3. See the discussion of textiles of this type in Wardwell 1992, Folsach 1993, and Watt and Wardwell 1997–98, esp. pp. 132–38.
4. Wardwell 1987. See also Watt and Wardwell 1997–98, pp. 127ff., and Komaroff 2002–3, esp. pp. 171ff.
5. Wardwell 1988–89, pp. 95ff., and Copenhagen 1993, pp. 100–101, no. 12. For attributions of textile fragments similar to the Metropolitan's piece, see Mayer, C. 1969, p. 55, pl. 34 (attributed to Italy); and Lafontaine-Dosogne 1981, p. 14, fig. 4 (attributed to Iran).
6. Wardwell 1988–89 examines differences in the formation of selvages, the combinations of fibers, and the composition of metal threads in order to delineate the various groups and to propose possible regions of production for these textiles.
7. Indictor, Koestler, Blair, and Wardwell 1988 (fig. 1, no. 2) analyze a piece very similar to the Museum's textile, in Vienna's Kunsthistorisches Museum.
8. Wardwell 1988–89, pp. 99ff. Exceptions are noted in Folsach 1993, esp. pp. 44–61.
9. Wardwell 1988–89, "Category V," pp. 106–8, and "Appendix I," figs. 36–37, for comparable pieces. Pieces of similar textiles are said to be in the Musées Royaux d'Art et d'Histoire, Brussels, no. 554 (published recently in Raemdonck 2006, p. 78); Musée Historique des Tissus, Lyon, no. 22.724; Art Institute of Chicago, no. 61.1196; Kunstgewerbemuseum, Staatliche Museen zu Berlin, no. 80,257; and the Museum of Decorative Art, Copenhagen, no. B 19/1931 (published in Copenhagen 1993, pp. 100–101, no. 12).

PROVENANCE: Iklé Collection, St. Gallen, Switzerland (until 1989; sale, Christie's South Kensington, November 7, 1989, no. 90); [The Textile Gallery, London, until 1996; sold to MMA]

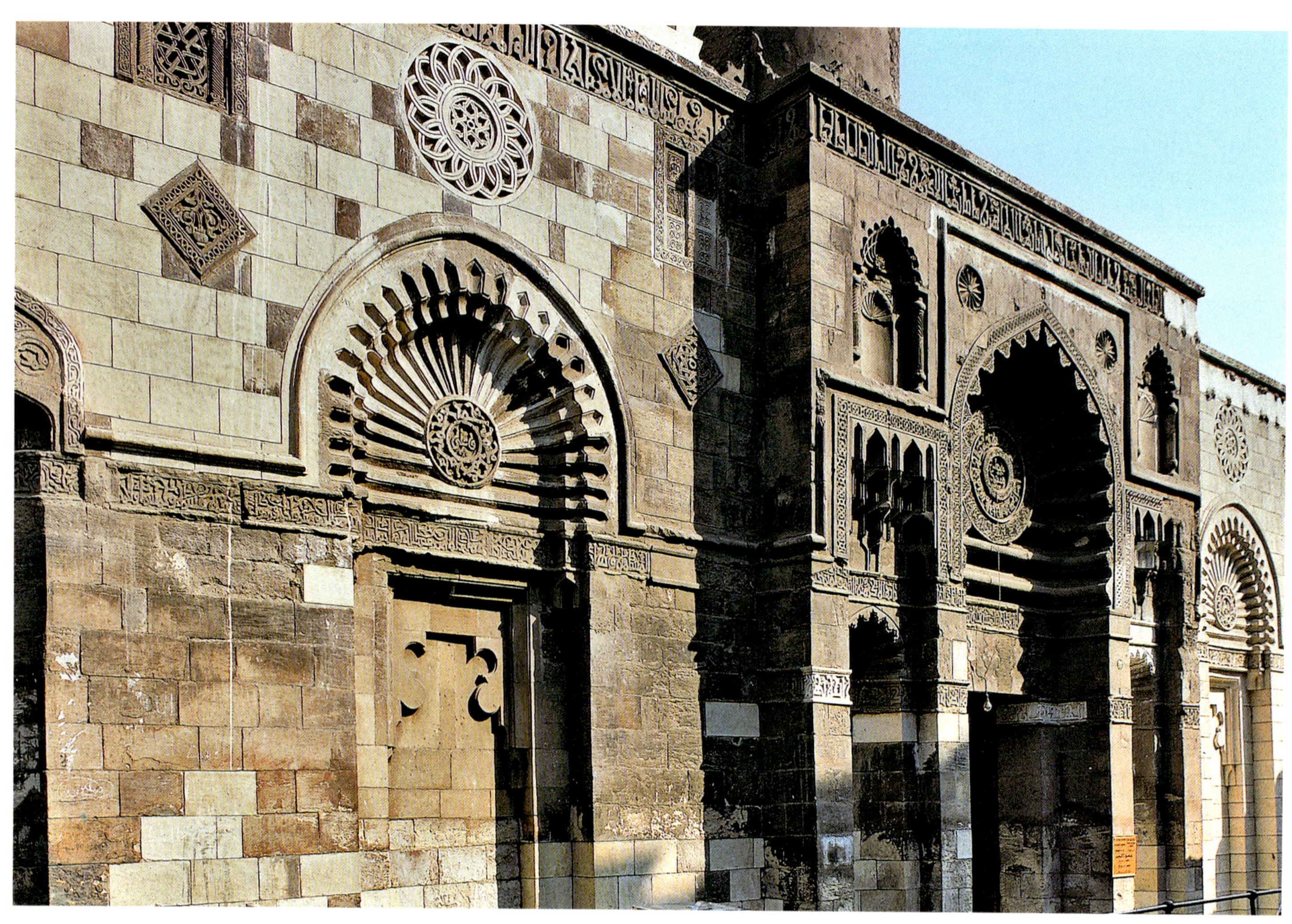

Art of Egypt and Syria (10th to 16th Centuries)

STEFANO CARBONI

The Metropolitan's vibrant carved wooden panel showing the heads of two horses (cat. 112) exemplifies the visual compositions created by artists in eleventh-century Egypt at a time when the city of Cairo (*al-Qahira*, the Victorious, founded by the Fatimids in 969) had recently become one of the great world capitals. Symmetry, repetition, overall patterning, and abstraction:[1] these were the patterns that had been established in Abbasid Iraq in the ninth century, and they would reverberate across the entire Islamic world. Symmetry and repetition are evident in the Museum's panel through the vertical division of the space into two almost identical, mirror-reverse patterns. Overall patterning is manifest in the creator's reluctance to leave undecorated areas anywhere on the surface. Abstraction—intended here as a transformation of naturalistic forms into nonrepresentational shapes for decorative purposes—could in this instance more appropriately be termed ambiguity, meaning the tendency of Fatimid artists to hark back to the figurative tradition without negating two centuries of steady movement toward abstraction. The horses' heads are clearly defined, but their bodies dissolve into semipalmettes and curls that form the vertical axis of the composition, while their ears evolve into large spiraling scrolls. These seahorse-like creatures are part of a remarkable work of early Fatimid art. Originally set into the door of a Fatimid palace, the panel belonged to a large composition that included its companion[2] and a number of other similarly paired panels, forming a triumphant and public display of symmetry, overall patterning, and ambiguity—our starting place in discussing the development of the portable arts in Egypt and Syria from the advent of the Fatimids (909–1171) to the demise of the Mamluks (1250–1517).

The Fatimids had their origins in North Africa and traced their descent from the Prophet Muhammad through his daughter Fatima (hence the name) as well as from the seventh imam, Isma'il.[3] They were therefore fervent Isma'ili Shi'is,[4] and their expansionist goals were fed by their assumed right of rule over the Muslims after they became a powerful dynasty. The occupation of Egypt and the transfer of power to Cairo were conscious decisions to position themselves in an important geographic and political area. Their eastward expansion briefly included Baghdad, the seat of the rival Abbasid caliphate, and Jerusalem and Damascus for somewhat longer periods. But Cairo became the heart and soul of the Fatimids, and it quickly grew into a cosmopolitan and economic hub where goods from northern Europe and the Indian Ocean were exchanged; where the social fabric was complex and varied (a tiny portion of the Muslim population became Isma'ili, and Copts and Jews were well represented); and where public buildings, magnificent ceremonials, and the creation of luxury products were highly encouraged.[5]

Today we can afford only a partial glimpse into the dynastic arts of the Fatimids. Cairo, with its innumerable sumptuous buildings, mosques, and mausoleums, was transformed by successive dynasties and had already become a "dream from the past" in the historian al-Maqrizi's description of the early fifteenth century.[6] In the mid-eleventh century the treasures of the court were looted and dispersed during a severe political crisis. Described in the *Book of Gifts and Rarities*,[7] many objects found their way into ecclesiastic treasuries in Europe or the palaces of the Byzantine emperor in Constantinople before these too were looted during the infamous Fourth Crusade of 1204.[8]

Striving to imitate their Byzantine counterparts, members of the Fatimid court were particularly fond of objects carved from semiprecious stones, especially transparent rock crystal. Less expensive (but equally impressive and sophisticated) relief-cut glass works in imitation of turquoise, emerald, ruby, and rock crystal were also in great demand.[9] Unfortunately, only a handful of rock-crystal ewers carved in relief with well-executed designs of confronted animals, vegetal patterns, and inscriptions mentioning the caliph's name provide direct links to the Fatimid court.[10] The Museum's collection can offer a hint of how the taste for carved rock crystal percolated to different levels of the Fatimid elite through a thriving production of small objects, in particular perfume flasks.[11]

The textile industry was under the control of the Fatimid establishment. High-quality linens with tapestry-woven bands of figural designs and inscriptions produced in *tiraz* factories in Cairo and the Nile delta were destined for the court or tagged as gifts for the court entourage and visiting delegations. They were also used for burial purposes. Although their fragility, function, and age allow today only a partial understanding of the sumptuousness and significance of these textiles, the weaving and the bold inscriptions carrying the names of the caliphs are impressive.

Fatimid artists, as mentioned above, often made use of figural imagery in their works. The high-end media for such expressions were carved ivory and precious rock crystal, though little has survived.[12] Exported north, these objects found fertile ground in southern Italy under the rule of the Normans; the spectacular results of this cross-fertilization are exemplified in the Metropolitan's collection by the Morgan Casket (cat. 39) and the signal horn or oliphant (cat. 38).

Ceramic production—in particular popular monochrome luster-painted pottery produced also for the lower classes of patronage—demonstrates how the new Fatimid figural style had soon filtered through all levels of artistic production from the court to the bazaars. A fine example depicting a heraldic eagle, renowned also because it carries the signature of Muslim, one of the earliest known potters (or pottery production centers), is in the Museum's collection (cat. 93).

While the Fatimids survived the eleventh-century crisis, they could not prevail against their vizier Salah al-Din Ayyub (d. 1193), who had the ambition, ability, and opportunity to overthrow his masters. Known in the West as Saladin, he proclaimed himself ruler of Egypt upon the death of the Fatimid caliph al-'Adid in 1171. Within fifteen years the new rulers, the Ayyubids, had entirely replaced the Fatimids, and their territory extended from Tunisia to northern Iraq and to Yemen. In 1187 Saladin's army defeated the Crusaders at the celebrated battle of Hattin.[13]

Unlike the Fatimids, the Ayyubids were organized into a collective government through an association of principalities bound by family rule. Saladin became the "Great Sultan" (*al-sultan al-mu'azzam*), whereas family members were semi-independent "petty sultans." This type of government inevitably created rivalry for succession and weakened the sultanate. Although Cairo remained the economic engine of the realm and the preferred residence of the Ayyubid rulers, the strategic political focus shifted east. Damascus was central to the control of the Crusaders and the ambitious principalities of Syria and the Jazira.[14]

Despite their relatively short rule (1169–1250 in Cairo, until 1260 in Damascus and Aleppo), the Ayyubids had a lasting impact as great builders of military architecture (the Citadels of Cairo and Aleppo provide splendid examples) and as patrons of educational and Sunni religious institutions.[15]

Under the Ayyubids, Syria became the leader in the manufacture of both luxury objects and the less expensive and sophisticated works made for the middle class and the bazaars. Metalwork, glass, and ceramics—the three principal media—

were all produced there; under Ayyubid patronage, the Fatimid luxury Cairene works in carved rock crystal, ivory, and colored glass seem to have all but disappeared.

Metalwork production, at least at court level, provides some perspective on the interconnections of this era. Stimulated by the transfer to Syria of specialized metalworkers from Mosul in Iraq, splendid objects with silver and gold inlays made a triumphant appearance in the Ayyubid-dominated regions, perpetuating a tradition well established east of Syria. This, combined with the influential presence in Greater Syria of eastern Christian communities and monasteries as well as the constant interaction—not exclusively confrontational but also commercial and economic—with the Crusaders, resulted in the creation of distinctive and highly accomplished inlaid-metal objects that depict Christian themes and/or figures.[16] As some of these outstanding thirteenth-century works are unquestionably dedicated to Muslim rulers, it cannot be established with certainty why the Ayyubid court would have taken an interest in Christian scenes or if the Syrian Christian community and the bordering Crusaders provided a broader patronage. The Metropolitan owns a relatively minor yet significant work from this distinctive group, a cylindrical box that depicts the entrance of Jesus into Jerusalem (cat. 102).

Enameling and gilding on glass had its first great flowering in the Ayyubid period, when Syrian glassmakers were able to bring their experimentation with these techniques to successful results and thus pave the way for future developments. The most distinctive of these objects are elongated beakers with small circular bases and flaring curved walls. Among these, the earliest datable example carries a dedication to the ruler of Mosul, Sanjar Shah (r. 1180–1209).[17]

Several Syrian ceramic centers, Raqqa in particular, enjoyed a renaissance under the Ayyubids. They became extremely productive and served the market across a broad geographic area, overshadowing Egyptian output. Syrian pottery in this period is characterized by dark brown luster decoration (cat. 96) and by the technique, relatively new to the west of Iran, of underglaze painting, which resulted in objects decorated either with black under a blue glaze or with several colors with a clear glaze (cat. 97).[18]

As with the Fatimids, the brief rule of the Ayyubids collapsed under internal pressure, in this case at the hands of their own corps of Mamluks. Originally military slaves of Turkish descent (hence *mamluk*, "owned"), the Mamluks steadily rose in the ranks, obtained freedom and power over time, and became an essential part of security and defense under the Ayyubids. When the sultan al-Salih Najm al-Din Ayyub died in Cairo in 1249, his personal corps of Bahri Mamluks (*bahr* being the Nile, where they had their headquarters) supported the installation on the throne of his widow, Shajar al-Durr. The chief of the Mamluks, 'Izz al-Din Aybak, installed himself at the head of the Ayyubid army; three months later he married al-Salih's widow and seized power.[19] Thus began the long reign of the Mamluk dynasty (or *Daulat al-turk*, the Turkish state), which put an end to Mongol expansion in western Asia as well as to the Crusaders' campaigns in the Holy Land. This powerful political entity endured until the Ottoman conquest in 1517.[20]

The trading and commercial roles that the dynasty played between the Mediterranean Sea and the Indian Ocean for over 250 years in the late medieval, precolonial European world should not be underestimated. Their outreach, resources, power, and political influence successfully allowed the Mamluks to thrive in an increasingly competitive world. In addition, their complex hierarchical, nonhereditary, and military structure seems to have worked to their advantage both in Cairo and in the provincial cities. The status of the capital as the new seat of the caliphate combined with control over the three holiest cities—Mecca, Medina, and Jerusalem—made the Mamluks the undisputed champions of Islam.

Not surprisingly, the dynasty's best contributions to the arts coincide with the period of their greatest political and economic fortune. In 1340 Cairo was the largest city west of China, with an estimated half million people,[21] and the religious university of Al-Azhar had become one of the preeminent centers of learning in the world. Today, what remains of Mamluk Cairo still offers a sense of the grandeur of a medieval metropolis with its urban structure and staggering number of architectural gems, such as the complex of Sultan Qalawun, the Blue Mosque of Aqsunqur, the gigantic mosque of Sultan Hasan, and the mausoleums in the Eastern Cemetery.[22]

Most visible among the developments in the arts in the Mamluk period is the progressive disappearance of figural decoration and an increasing predominance of inscriptions and vegetal backgrounds. The continuation of Ayyubid imagery, which had a strong figurative component, was relatively brief. Nonetheless, specific motifs originating from the regions east of Syria controlled by the rival Mongol Ilkhanids, such as the *simurgh* or phoenix (cat. 111), provided intriguing additions to the diminishing figural repertory.

This change in taste occurred during the long reign of Sultan al-Nasir Muhammad (1294–1340, with brief interruptions) and was probably encouraged by the Mamluks' strong focus on religious buildings and their patronage of aniconic architectural decoration, furnishings, Qur'an manuscripts, and portable objects destined for religious establishments. Such patronage trickled down to the sultanate's administration—virtually every amir who could afford it would sponsor and endow his own buildings.[23] Gradually, the only figurative decoration encountered in a secular context became the amir's emblem of office as a

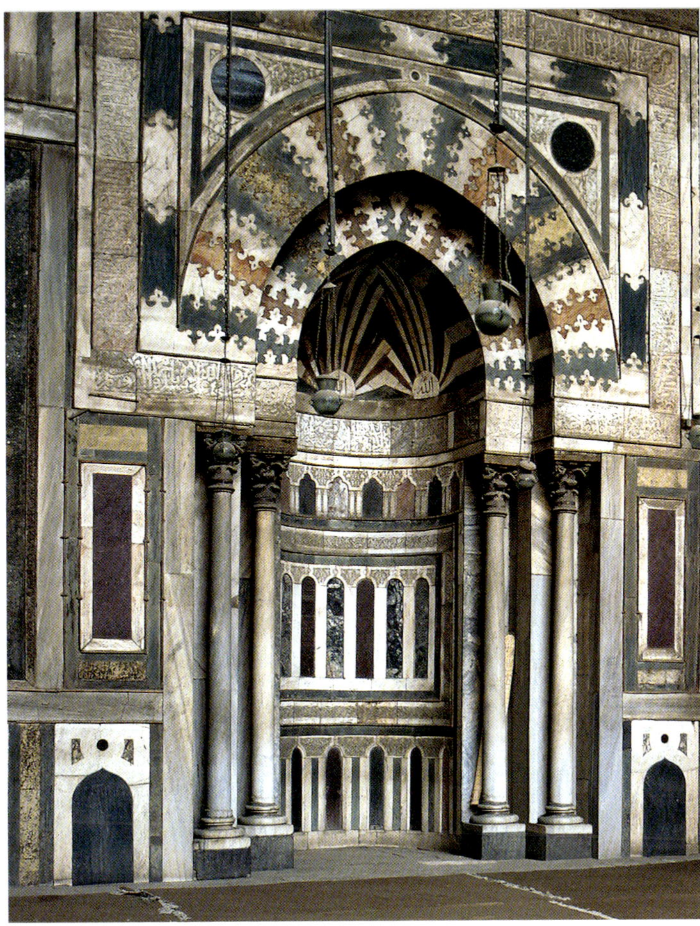

Fig. 31 *Mihrab*, or prayer niche, Complex of Sultan Hasan, Cairo, 1356–63. Photo: Walter B. Denny

symbol of ownership, identification, and acknowledgment of rank, such as a footed cup, polo sticks, pen box, and crossbow (see, for example, the emblem on cat. 109).[24]

Doors from the *minbar* of the Mosque of Amir Qawsun in Cairo (cat. 113) splendidly illustrate the essential aspects of Mamluk art. Here, a virtuoso designer planned a geometric pattern of stars within polygonal compositions so that the two larger patterns are split symmetrically along the outer edges of the two doors and meet seamlessly in the middle once they are closed; half stars and quarter stars complete a composition that could equally have been designed for Qur'anic illumination, marble mosaic, stained glass, or the dome of a mosque. The technical skills required to execute the details of the individual wood and ivory sections that constitute the whole are stunning. Symmetry, repetition, and overall patterning have here lost the "ambiguous" aspect of earlier Fatimid works and have evolved into full geometric abstraction.

The greatest accomplishments, both artistic and technical, of Mamluk craftsmen in the portable arts include large enameled-and-gilded glass mosque lamps and bottles as well as silver-inlaid metal basins, ewers, and trays. The Museum's collection includes the largest group of mosque lamps outside of Egypt (cat. 109)[25] and a remarkable selection of richly inlaid metalwork from the first century of Mamluk rule (cats. 103, 105, and 106). Glass enameling—a technique that required extraordinary skill to ensure that the enamel adhered to the glass surface during a second firing, without damage to the object—was perfected in the second half of the thirteenth century, resulting in a variety of shapes and decorations that would become prized examples in faraway European church treasuries and Chinese palaces.[26] Works such as the magnificent footed *tazza* (cat. 110) and bottle (cat. 111) offer a hint of this superb production that, as a measure of its achievement, would be understood, imitated, and improved upon only after the industrial revolution in Europe in the late nineteenth century.[27]

The brass and silver brazier (cat. 104), a masterpiece of Mamluk inlaid metalwork, is a powerful "architectural" piece with the relatively humble function, perhaps only symbolic, of a heater or grill. Its silver-inlaid decoration is dominated by a large inscription, but the lively sequence of running animals along the narrow upper bands and the menacing, dynamic looped dragon heads confer a sculptural and animated appearance to this object. The inscription and the five-petaled rosette—the dynastic emblem of the Rasulids (the dynasty that ruled Yemen from 1229 to 1454, and with whom the Mamluks shared control of trade from the Indian Ocean into the Red Sea)—also indicate that the brazier falls into a special category of metalwork production created for export, in this case most likely as a diplomatic gift from the sultan in Cairo to a key political ally, or to the Rasulid court in Yemen.[28] Enameled glass was similarly produced and exported.

The slow decline of Mamluk power and influence—due to economic changes, internal struggles, and the growing confidence of the Ottomans—began shortly after the establishment of the Burji branch of the Mamluks (*burji*, "of the tower," refers to the Citadel in Cairo, from which they ruled from 1390 to 1517).[29] Patronage declined, with architecture remaining the favored type of sponsorship. This is not to say that workshops entirely disappeared, but demand dwindled, and almost all glass factories were forced to close.[30] Here and there we have evidence that inlaid metalwork continued to be commissioned at high standards, like a box made for the keeper of hours of prayer in Damascus.[31] Only under the rule of the last great sultan of the Mamluk dynasty, Qaitbay (r. 1468–96), did court patronage have a period of resurgence, although by then the level of execution in most crafts had dropped off.

The Ottomans completed their conquest of the Mamluk sultanate in 1517. Cairo lost its status as a great capital and became instead an important albeit provincial town of the longest-lasting empire in the history of Islam. Since its foundation in 969, Cairo of the Fatimid, Ayyubid, and Mamluk dynasties had been a beacon of thriving humanity, architecture and urban sprawl, learning, wealth, commercial power, and political intrigue. While all this diminished dramatically after the arrival of the Ottomans, at least one craft marks a bright passage between the Mamluk and the Ottoman periods. Possibly made in Ottoman Cairo, the Simonetti Carpet (cat. 116), which with its nearly thirty feet (almost nine meters) of length and five brilliant medallions dominates the room it shares with the Spanish ceiling in the new galleries, is celebrated as one of the most beautiful and accomplished Mamluk rugs.[32] These precious and extraordinary carpets, which began to be woven in a limited palette of three to four colors in fifteenth-century Cairo, have all the hallmarks of Mamluk compositions, bringing forward in time the illustrious artistic traditions of the great capital that for over half a millennium was Cairo.

1. With special reference to Samarra, see Ettinghausen and Grabar 1987, p. 104.
2. An almost identical panel is in the Museum of Islamic Art in Cairo (no. 3391).
3. One of the best historical surveys on the Fatimids is Walker, P. 2002.
4. The Isma'ilis are still today a well-established community throughout the world under the spiritual leadership of the Aga Khan.
5. On Cairo and the role played by the Fatimids in the Mediterranean area, see among others Goitein 1967–93 and Sanders 1994.
6. Two works by Taqi al-Din Ahmad al-Maqrizi (1364–1442) are relevant to the history of the Fatimids: *Al-mawa'iz wa al-i'tibar bi-dhikr al-khitat wa al-athar* (Exhortations and Instructions on the Districts and Antiquities; al-Maqrizi 1853–54), now in a critical edition by Ayman Fu'ad Sayyid (al-Maqrizi 1995); and *Itti'az al-hunafa' bi-akhbar al-a'imma al-fatimiyyin al-khulafa'* (Admonitions of the Orthodox on the Most Important Information about the Fatimid Caliphate; al-Maqrizi 1967–73). The most significant and best-preserved Fatimid monument in Cairo is the small Mosque of al-Aqmar.
7. An English translation of this eleventh-century work by Ibn al-Zubayr is available, al-Qaddumi, ed. 1996.
8. Among many others, see Phillips 2004 and Lace 2006.
9. See Erdmann, with Grabar and Hahnloser 1971, pp. 103–8, nos. 117–20, pls. 89–94; and Corning, New York, and Athens 2001–2, pp. 176–79, 187–88, nos. 83–84, 92.
10. Two rock-crystal objects are linked directly to the caliphs al-'Aziz (r. 975–96) and al-Zahir (r. 1021–36): a ewer in the Treasury of San Marco, Venice (no. 80), and a crescent-shaped ornament in the Germanisches Nationalmuseum, Nuremberg (no. KG 695). Another ewer is dedicated to the general Husain ibn Jawhar (ca. 1000–1008), now in the Palazzo Pitti, Florence (no. 1917). The three objects were published most recently in color in Bloom 2007, pls. 72–74. A survey of Fatimid rock crystal as a medium is in Contadini 1998, pp. 16–38, where the three objects mentioned above are figs. 15–17.
11. Two such examples in the Museum's collection are acc. nos. 31.18.1 and 31.125.
12. For rock crystal, see above, note 10. The most important examples in ivory are four plaques assembled as a frame in the Museum für Islamische Kunst, Staatliche Museen zu Berlin (no. I 6375), and six plaques in the Museo Nazionale del Bargello in Florence (no. 800 and Solenne 460, legato Carrand 1094). See Hoffman 1999 and Venice 1993–94, no. 63. All figural ivories can be found in Kühnel 1971, pp. 68–73, nos. 88–101, pls. 97–100.
13. A basic bibliography on the history and social history of the Ayyubids includes Humphreys 1977, MacKenzie 1992, Chamberlain 1994, Tabbaa 1997, Lev 1999, and Hillenbrand, C. 2000.
14. The Jazira (literally, island) is a geographic area that includes modern-day northeastern Syria, northern Iraq, and southeastern Turkey.
15. The Ayyubids adhered to the Shafi'i legal system. The other three major Sunni juridical-religious systems are the Hanafi, Hanbali, and Maliki. For a good survey of the arts of the Ayyubids, see the exhibition catalogue *L'orient de Saladin: L'art des Ayyoubides* (Paris 2001b).
16. See, among others, Schneider 1973, Katzenstein and Lowry 1983, and Baer 1989.
17. Carboni 1999, esp. pp. 173–74 and fig. 3.
18. See among others Grube and Tonghini 1988–89, Tonghini 1994, and Jenkins-Madina 2006.
19. Court intrigues, treason, and tragedy inevitably followed, and by 1257 both Aybak and Shajar al-Durr had died. The latter had her husband killed while taking a bath, the plot was revealed, and she was subsequently arrested and beaten to death with a clog; her body was found near the Citadel.
20. The *Mamluk Studies Review* is a periodical dedicated to various aspects of the history of the Mamluk dynasty. Significant recent studies for various aspects of Mamluk history and historiography in relation to the arts are Behrens-Abouseif, ed. 2000, Kennedy, ed. 2001, and Alsayyad, Bierman, and Rabbat, eds. 2005.
21. Shillington, ed. 2005, vol. 1, p. 342.
22. A large body of literature is available on Mamluk architecture. See, for example, Creswell 1959, Meinecke 1992, Rabbat 1995, Behrens-Abouseif 2007, Warner 2005, Kahil 2008, and Kenney 2004.
23. *Amir* is a military rank and title that was conferred on powerful ministers, army chiefs, and provincial governors.
24. This statement is challenged by a few scholars who date a few key pieces, such as the so-called Baptistère de Saint Louis in the Louvre, to the mid-fourteenth century, thus implying that figural decoration was still strong at that time. On the emblems of the amirs, the standard work remains Mayer, L. 1933; see also Meinecke 1972.
25. The largest number is in the Museum of Islamic Art, Cairo. See Wiet 1929.
26. For example, two works now in the Cathedral and Diocesan Museum, Vienna, recently published in Corning, New York, and Athens 2001–2, pp. 249–53, nos. 124–25. For exports to China, see Hardie 1998.
27. An introduction to the subject is offered in Whitehouse 2001–2, pp. 297–301.
28. Porter, V. 1987–88, pp. 232–40; Porter, V. 1998. Mamluk art made for the Rasulids was also the subject of a departmental exhibition in the Hagop Kevorkian Special Exhibitions Gallery of the Metropolitan Museum in 1995 titled "The Five-Petaled Rosette: Mamluk Art for the Sultans of Yemen."
29. The first ruler of the Burji Mamluks had declared himself sultan in 1382 but was expelled and recaptured Cairo only in 1390.
30. Carboni 2004.
31. Lidded box of Muhammad al-Hamawi, timekeeper at the Umayyad Mosque, Damascus (Metropolitan Museum, acc. no. 91.1.538).
32. Shtrum et al. 2010.

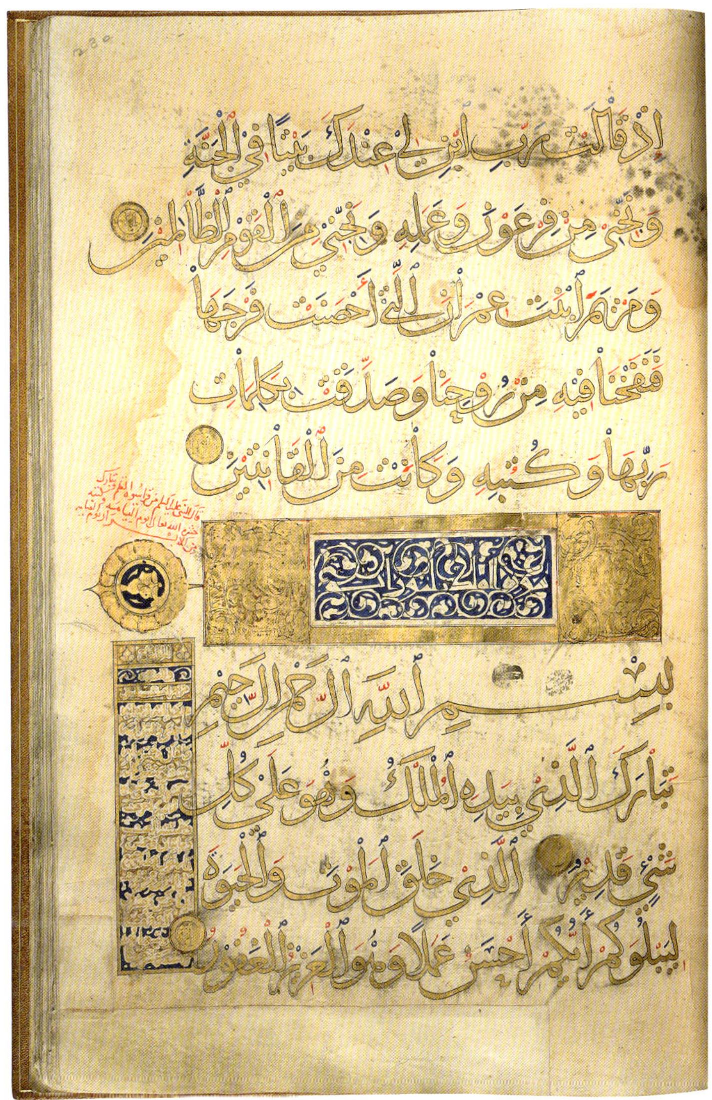

Fol. 230r

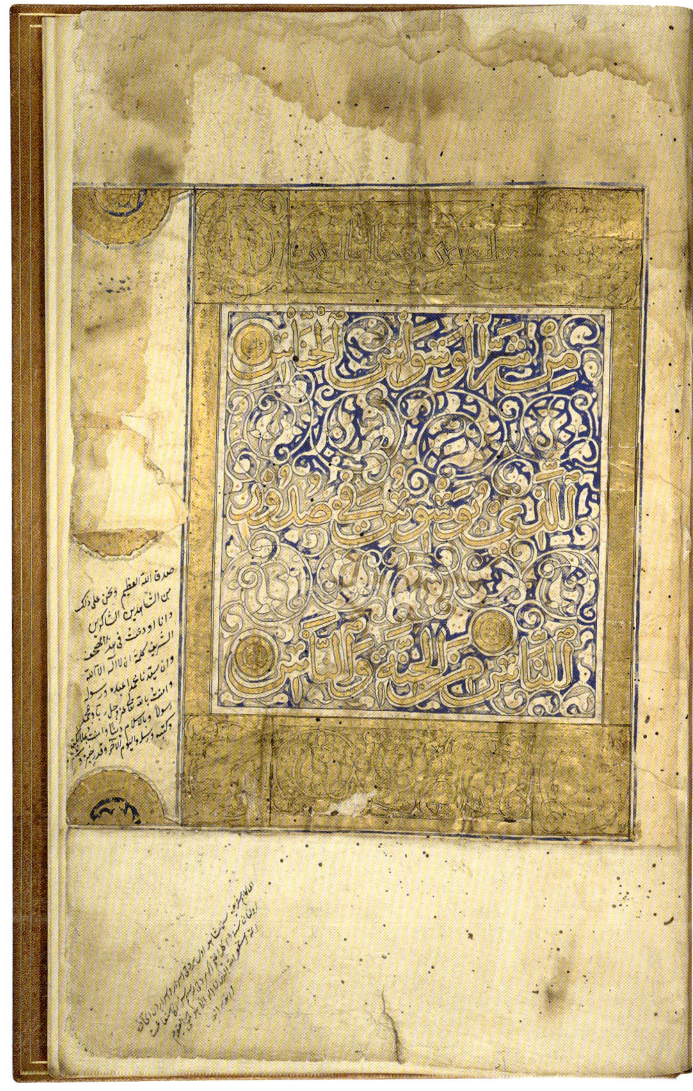

Fol. 274r

90. Segment of a Qur'an Manuscript

Syria or Egypt, 13th century
Ink, opaque watercolor, and gold on paper
20 × 13¼ in. (50.8 × 33.7 cm)
Fletcher Fund, 1924 24.146.1

The 274 folios of this manuscript comprise the second half of a large Qur'an, extensively illuminated and inscribed throughout in gold.[1] The thick, creamy-white paper has been extensively consolidated, trimmed (sometimes grazing the text block), remargined, and rebound. As no colophon survives and no signatures have been detected, the date and attribution of this Qur'an rest on stylistic and technical evidence.

This luxurious manuscript preserves three of its fully illuminated text pages.[2] On each, a square panel with three lines of text over densely swirling vegetal scrolls is set within a gold frame, also decorated with vegetal scrolls and headings in "new-style" script. The final folio consists of the right half of a double page decorated with a rectangular panel of gold with large-scale vegetal scrolls, around which a gold-on-blue calligraphy border proclaims the ritual purity required for handling the Qur'an—an excerpt of Sura 56 frequently employed on Qur'an frontis- and finispieces.

Illuminated bands on the other folios contain Sura headings, most also in "new-style" script against a background of vegetal scrolls (above, left). For each heading, a palmette extends into the margin and red annotation provides a related hadith.[3] The text, generally eleven lines per page, is entirely gold outlined with black, in a script corresponding to what medieval sources classified as *ash'ar* or *thuluth ash'ar*.[4] Diacritical marks are also gold, while vowels and orthoepic signs are in alternating red and blue. Illuminated disks, inscribed with the word *aya*, indicate verse endings, and marginal disks or teardrop shapes surrounded with colorful petal-like borders highlight the fifth and tenth verses—as well as prostration points. Each section is announced by a rectangular margin table—also written in gold—providing its number, a count of the verses, words, letters, and diacriticals in it, and a count for the entire text of one letter of the alphabet. Two annotations are inked on the penultimate page of the manuscript: one, in Arabic, an attestation of faith; the other, in Turkish, a sacred oath (p. 141, right).[5]

While the all-gold calligraphy and the absence of text-block borders recall the 1304–6 Qur'an of Baybars al-Jashnagir at the British Library in London as well as other luxury manuscripts attributed to Mamluk Cairo, some aspects of the script and ornament correspond more closely to Damascene Qur'ans, such as that made (ca. 1330–40) for the Umayyad Mosque, now in the Khalili Collection, London.[6] Futhermore, the illumination of the present Qur'an appears archaic in comparison to both of these examples and contains none of the geometric compositions or interlacing cartouche frameworks so characteristic of fourteenth-century Mamluk manuscripts. A number of the illuminated devices, the flowing calligraphic hand, and certain letter forms compare with much earlier examples, among them the Zangid Qur'an dated 1199–1219 and attributed to Sinjar or Nisibin.[7] For these reasons, the attribution of this Qur'an has been broadened to include a possible Syrian place of production and a thirteenth-century date. EK

1. The first folio begins partway through the third verse of Sura 19 (*Maryam*), and the continuing text is complete except for four points where replacement pages substitute for originals (fols. 61–64, 98–99, 267, and 269).
2. These are the first folio, which is the left half of a double page, and the penultimate and final folios, bearing the last Sura (114, *al-Nas*, "Mankind") on a double page.
3. One of these hadith annotations is done in gold *ash'ar* script (fol. 8r, next to the heading for Sura 20, *Taha*).
4. James 1999, pp. 18–19; and James 2009, p. 351. However, some aspects of the script relate better to *tawqi'* and *tumar*, especially the way the final letter of *Allah* is open, and the tail of the *mim* is relatively short and hooks upward (Safwat and Zakariya 1996, pp. 74, 234; Blair 2006, pp. 318, 345–49).
5. We are very grateful to Abdullah Ghouchani and Rifat Günalan for their assistance with these readings.
6. British Library, London, Add. 22406-13 (James 1999, p. 220, no. 1; James 1992b, p. 176, no. 43).
7. James 1992b, p. 44, no. 7.

PROVENANCE: [Maggs Bros., London, until about 1914]; Vladimir G. Simkhovitch, New York (from ca. 1914); [Brummer Gallery, Inc., New York, until 1924; sold to MMA]

91. Folio from the Mantiq al-wahsh (Speech of the Wild Animal) of Ka'b al-Ahbar

Egypt, probably Fustat, 11th–12th century
Opaque watercolor on paper
$6\frac{1}{8} \times 4\frac{3}{4}$ in. (15.7 × 12.1 cm)
Rogers Fund, 1954 54.108.3

Verso: Inscription in Arabic in *naskhi* script at top and bottom of page:
كتاب فيه منطق الوحش/بأمر مليح مصور
This book includes *Mantiq al-wahsh* by the order of Malih, the illustrator

Recto: Inscription in Arabic in *naskhi* script at top of page:
بسم الله الرحمن الرحيم/ذكر . . . قال كعب الأحبار عن منطق الوحش فقال نعم إنه
إذا . . . /ضياع ا الأسد يقول
In the Name of God, the Merciful, the Compassionate. Mention [. . .]
Ka'b al-Ahbar said about *Mantiq al-Wahsh*. He says yes
it is if [. . .] the realms of the lion who says [. . .]

This fragmentary folio was originally part of a zoological treatise with strong roots in the classical tradition. It belongs to a group that is considered to be among the earliest Arabic illustrated manuscripts to survive.[1] The verso features the image of a lion outlined in black ink with touches of red and pink and a few lines of text. The inscription identifies the animal and gives the text's title, *Mantiq al-wahsh* (Speech of the Wild Animal), as well as the name of its author, Ka'b al-Ahbar (d. 652/53), who was among the first Jews to convert to Islam. The title is repeated on the recto, where the image of a hare is painted in the same style and palette.

Although little is known about the *Mantiq al-wahsh* in particular, the text is part of a group of Arabic sources that are connected to the classical tradition of scientific handbooks, which were copied and expanded by Muslim scholars for centuries. The ninth-century encyclopedic work of al-Jahiz (d. 868/69) titled *Kitab al-hayawan* (Book of Animals) and the later *Kitab na't al-hayawan wa-manafi'ihi* (Book of the Identification and the Benefits of Animals) by Ibn Bakhtishu are two of the best-known bestiaries based on Greek texts, which were translated in the late eighth and ninth centuries.[2]

This folio was probably executed during the Fatimid dynasty, whose rulers were avid collectors of illustrated codices.[3] Lions and hares similar to those on this page are seen in Coptic textiles and abound in Fatimid ivories and woodcarvings. In addition, paleographic comparison of the text to other Fatimid works reveals close affinities. The folio was found with hundreds of other paper fragments in the course of early twentieth-century excavations at Fustat, a garrison built in 641 for the armies leading the first phase of the Arab conquest and later incorporated by the Fatimids in their new foundation for *al-Qahira* (the Victorious), present-day Cairo. The fact that the folio was found in Egypt reinforces its Fatimid attribution. FL

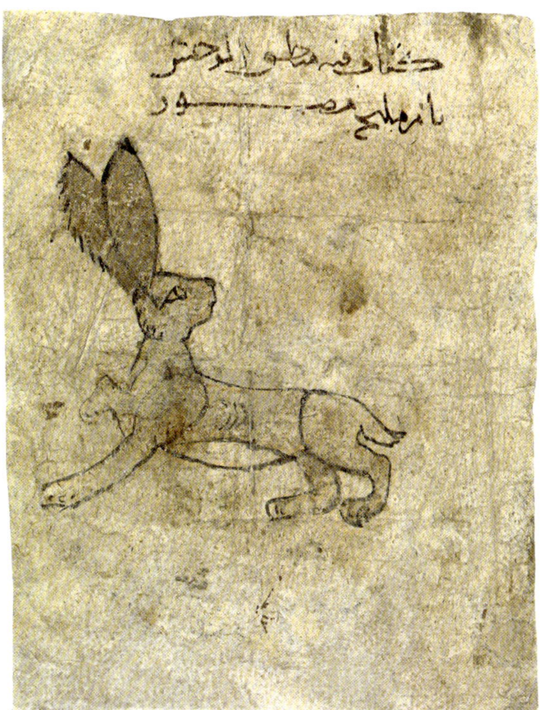

recto

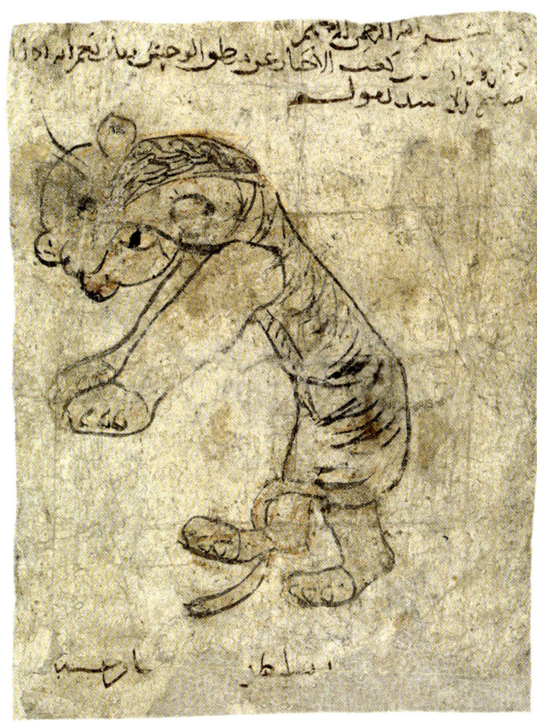

verso

1. Hoffman 2000, p. 38. See also Grube 1963c.
2. Two pages from a thirteenth-century copy of the work by Ibn Bakhtishu are also in the Metropolitan Museum (acc. nos. 18.26.2, 57.51.31).
3. No single, intact illustrated book survives from this period; see Bloom 2007, p. 109.

PROVENANCE: [Michel Abemayor, New York, until 1954; sold to MMA]

92. Folio from the Kitab fi ma'rifat al-hiyal al-handasiyya (Book of Knowledge of Ingenious Objects) of al-Jazari

"The Elephant Clock"
Syria, dated A.H. 715/1315 A.D.
Ink, opaque watercolor, and gold on paper
11 7/8 × 7 3/4 in. (30 × 19.7 cm)
Bequest of Cora Timken Burnett, 1956 57.51.23

Inscription in Arabic in *naskhi* script at lower left:
الفصل الثاني صح فصل
The second chapter is the correct chapter

One of the finest surviving examples of Mamluk painting, this manuscript page belongs to a dispersed copy of the *Kitab fi ma'rifat al-hiyal al-handasiyya* (Book of Knowledge of Ingenious Mechanical Devices) transcribed by Farrukh ibn 'Abd al-Latif in A.H. 715/1315 A.D.[1] Originally composed at the beginning of the thirteenth century by Badi' al-Zaman ibn al-Razzaz al-Jazari (1136–1206) for the Artuqid ruler of Amid (present-day Diyarbakir), Nasir al-Din Mahmud (r. 1201–22), the treatise discusses fifty mechanical devices used for princely entertainment.[2] In addition to clocks, the text mentions drinking vessels, fountains, automated devices for hand-washing and bloodletting, and other machines activated by heat or hydraulic mechanisms.

The spectacular automated clock illustrated here is the subject of one chapter, which includes detailed instructions for its assembly. Every half hour, the rider would hit the elephant with his pickax and the bird would turn, allowing the falcon to release a pellet into the dragon's mouth. The dragon would next drop the ball into a pot, where it hit a gong before ending up in a bowl at the bottom of the pot. The time would then be determined by counting the balls gathered in the bowl.

The illustration reflects the impact of the Arab style of manuscript painting developed in Iraq and Syria during the thirteenth century. In particular, features such as the rider's halo, the robe with *tiraz* bands, and the turban with loose ends appear in thirteenth-century copies of Dioscorides' *De Materia Medica* and al-Hariri's *Maqamat*.[3] At the same time, the conservative nature of the illustrations accompanying scientific manuscripts accounts for the representation of the dragons as open-mouthed serpents with coiled and scaled bodies, a formula that occurs in the oldest known copy of al-Jazari's treatise, made in 1206.[4] In acknowledging the achievements of Jaziran artistic centers while finely reinterpreting the contents of the treatise, the 1315 manuscript remains one of the most accomplished copies of al-Jazari's work.[5] FL

1. The intact codex contained 150 folios and was accompanied by nine diagrams and ninety-eight paintings. See Washington, D.C., and other cities 1981–82, p. 255.

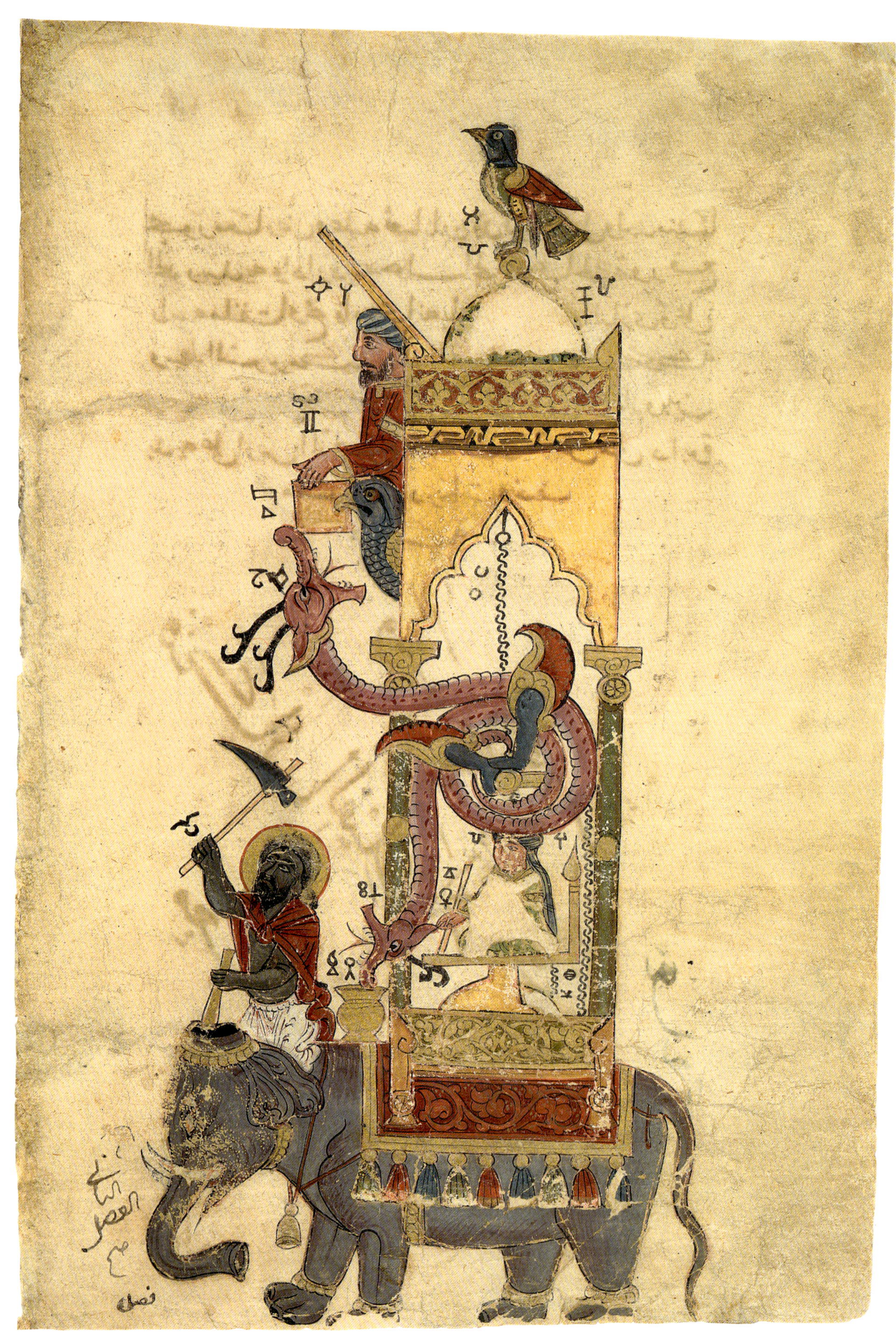

2. At least fourteen copies of al-Jazari's text have survived. See Washington, D.C. 1975, p. 102 n. 12. See also al-Jazari 1974.
3. Washington, D.C. 1975, esp. pp. 53–60.
4. London 2005, p. 113, fig. 33.
5. Eight folios from this manuscript in the Freer and Sackler Galleries, Smithsonian Institution (nos. 30.71r, 30.72r, 30.73r, 30.74v, 30.75r, 30.76r, 30.77r, and 42.10v), are discussed in ibid., pp. 102–10.

PROVENANCE: Cora Timken Burnett, Alpine, N.J. (by 1932–d. 1956)

93. *Bowl with Eagle*

Signature by Muslim
Egypt, ca. 1000
Earthenware; luster-painted on opaque white glaze
H. 2⅞ in. (7.3 cm); Diam. 10 in. (25.4 cm)
Gift of Charles K. and Irma B. Wilkinson, 1963 63.178.1

Inscription in Arabic in *kufic* script on interior, below eagle's claw, and on base:
مسلم
Muslim[1]

94. *Bowl with Hare*

Egypt, first quarter of 11th century
Earthenware; luster-painted on opaque white glaze
H. 3 in. (7.6 cm); Diam. 10¼ in. (26 cm)
Purchase, Joseph Pulitzer Bequest, 1964 64.261

The tenth and eleventh centuries under the Fatimid caliphate were times of prosperity in Egypt and the neighboring lands, when a burgeoning class of wealthy consumers emerged. The luster potteries recently established in Cairo by émigré specialists from Basra offered exactly the kind of luxury products this new elite demanded. In such an atmosphere, it is not surprising that makers' marks are often found on Fatimid-period lusterware. One such instance is that of *Muslim*, a name that appears in two places on the bowl decorated with an eagle (cat. 93).[2] More than forty known Fatimid-period ceramic objects or fragments and at least one luster-painted glass piece bear some version of this signature.[3]

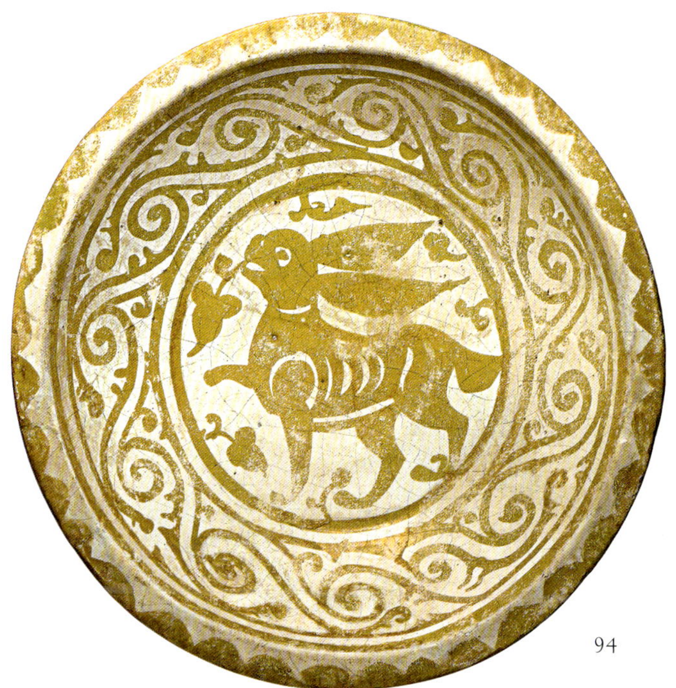
94

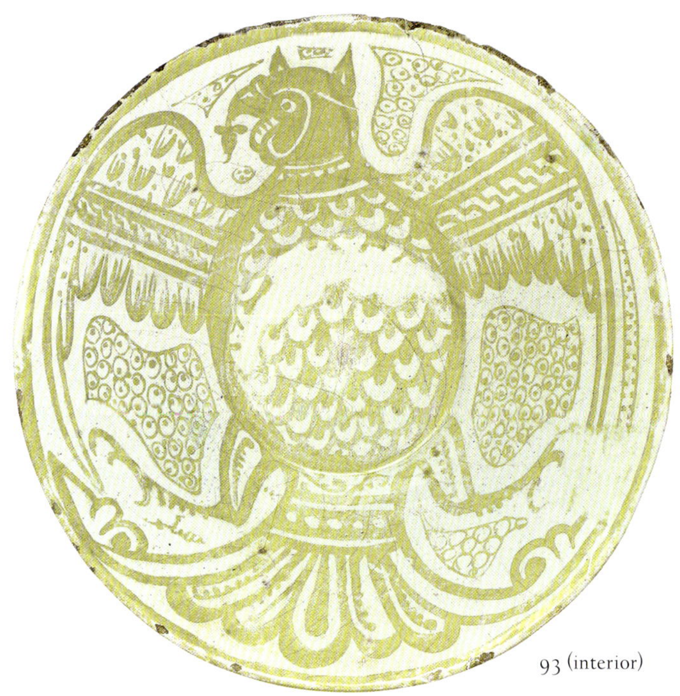
93 (interior)

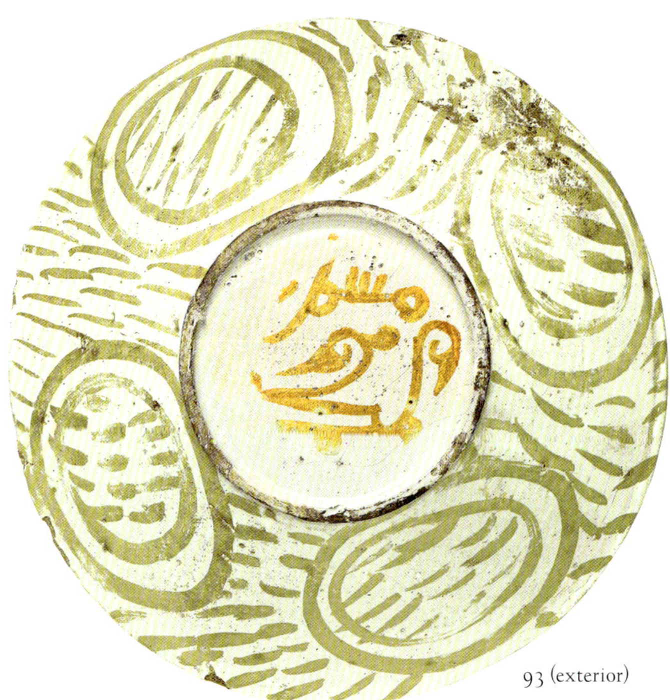
93 (exterior)

A more complete rendering of the name, *Muslim ibn al-Dahhan* (Muslim son of the painter), appears on one of these fragments in the Benaki Museum, Athens, along with the name of the patron, whose *nisba* suggests that he was associated with the court of Caliph al-Hakim (r. 996–1021). This inscription dates the ceramist's production to the time of that reign.[4] Because these works vary considerably in quality and style, it has been argued that the word *Muslim* must be a workshop trademark rather than the signature of an individual artist.[5] However, elsewhere such variability is explained by the suggestion that Muslim was both a master ceramist and the head of a workshop that used his name on its ware.[6]

This straight-sided, low-footed bowl is one of the few signed *Muslim* works that is complete. Its decoration provides a prime example of the vitality characteristic of Fatimid painting, which is quite distinct from the rigidity of late Abbasid lusterware. The monumental eagle, painted in a greenish-yellow luster against a white ground, occupies the entire interior of the bowl. Even though the artist has adopted an age-old, heraldic pose and embellished the creature improbably with strings of pearls and *tiraz*-like bands, his painterly execution breathes life into the eagle. A similar depiction of an eagle with spread wings may once have decorated the center of the previously mentioned Benaki fragment.[7]

The same sense of dynamism enlivens the second bowl, depicting a hare (cat. 94), which shares many features with the "Muslim" bowl but bears no signature. The hare strikes an especially lively pose: it raises its front leg playfully, in an animated version of the heraldic "passant" position, and—like the eagle above—grasps in its mouth a sprig of clover. Its figure is executed in yellow-colored luster pigment. As is typical of most of the "Muslim" examples, the details of its eyes and the articulation of its body parts are reserved in white. The hare was a particularly popular motif in the art of the Fatimid period in Egypt, where it may have been associated with good fortune.[8] A number of similar hares decorate objects and fragments in other collections.[9] Surrounding the hare, trefoils and sprigs sprout from a circular border that is itself enclosed by a slanted vine scroll repeated in a wavelike pattern. Both bowls carry over features from the Basran phase of luster-painted ceramic production, including the interstitial "peacock eye" filler on the eagle bowl, the festoon border on the hare bowl, and the circle-and-dash motifs on the outer walls of both.[10]

EK

1. Abdullah Ghouchani suggests that the birdlike form below the word *Muslim* on the base of this bowl may be a floriated version of the word *Muhammad* (personal communication, 2011).
2. Jenkins 1968a. As Jenkins pointed out, it was not that uncommon for Fatimid-period ceramics to bear signatures of some kind, but Muslim's is the only one so far that can be assigned dates on an inscriptional basis.
3. Jenkins listed twenty in her appendix (ibid., pp. 366–69). Helen Philon published another eleven (Philon 1980, pp. 167–78, 197–201), and noted further examples (ibid., p. 168 n. 53). A shard published in Watson 2004 (p. 280, cat. Ja.8, no. LNS 975 C e) can be added to this list. On the glass object, see Contadini 1998, p. 82.
4. Jenkins 1968a, p. 361.
5. Watson 2004, p. 280.
6. This explanation, first suggested by Marilyn Jenkins (1968a), was supported by Robert Mason's petrographic analysis pointing out the shared attributes among these works, which belong to a technical group that he dated between 975 and 1025 (Mason 2004, p. 65). Mason sampled and analyzed the petrography of both the bowls presented here and published their profile drawings (ibid., p. 83, fig. 4.4, and p. 193).
7. Philon 1980, p. 198. Jonathan M. Bloom demonstrated Philon's proposition with superimposed images in Bloom 2007, p. 95, fig. 3. For another similar eagle bowl, see O'Kane, ed. 2006, pp. 80–81, no. 73.
8. For publications on the symbolism of the hare in the Fatimid context, see Dodd 1972 and Daneshvari 1981.
9. For examples, see Benaki Museum, nos. 19447 (Philon 1980, p. 206, fig. 425), 207 (ibid., p. 202, fig. 414), and 19599a [signed "Muslim"] (ibid., p. 199, fig. 408); O'Kane, ed. 2006, pp. 80–81, no. 72.
10. Mason 2004, p. 63.

PROVENANCE
Cat. 93: Walter Hauser (by 1938); Charles and Irma Wilkinson, Sharon, Conn. (by 1961–63)
Cat. 94: [Charles D. Kelekian, New York, until 1964; sold to MMA]

95. *Pyxis*

Syria, late 11th–early 12th century
Stonepaste; luster-painted on incised, opaque white glaze
H. 8 in. (20.3 cm); Diam. 5½ in. (14 cm)
Purchase, Lila Acheson Wallace Gift, Harvey and Elizabeth Plotnick Gift, and Louis E. and Theresa S. Seley Purchase Fund for Islamic Art, 1998 1998.298a, b

Inscription in Arabic in *kufic* script, on exterior of body:
توكل يكفا (!) الصبر عز من صبر قدر
Trust [in God] suffices. Perseverance becomes glory.
[He] who is patient possesses strength.

By the late eleventh century, a new type of ware had emerged in Syria that represented the transfer of two technologies pivotal for ceramic development in the region: stonepaste and overglaze luster-painting.[1] These ceramics relate so closely to the lusterware produced in Fatimid Egypt that they have often been misclassified. Only gradually, over the course of the first half of the last century, was the group identified as a type distinct both from the Egyptian material and from the Syrian material classified as Raqqa ware. This type has come to be known as Tell Minis ware, based on the putative findspot of a cache in the eponymous village, located between Hama and Aleppo. However, there is no evidence to

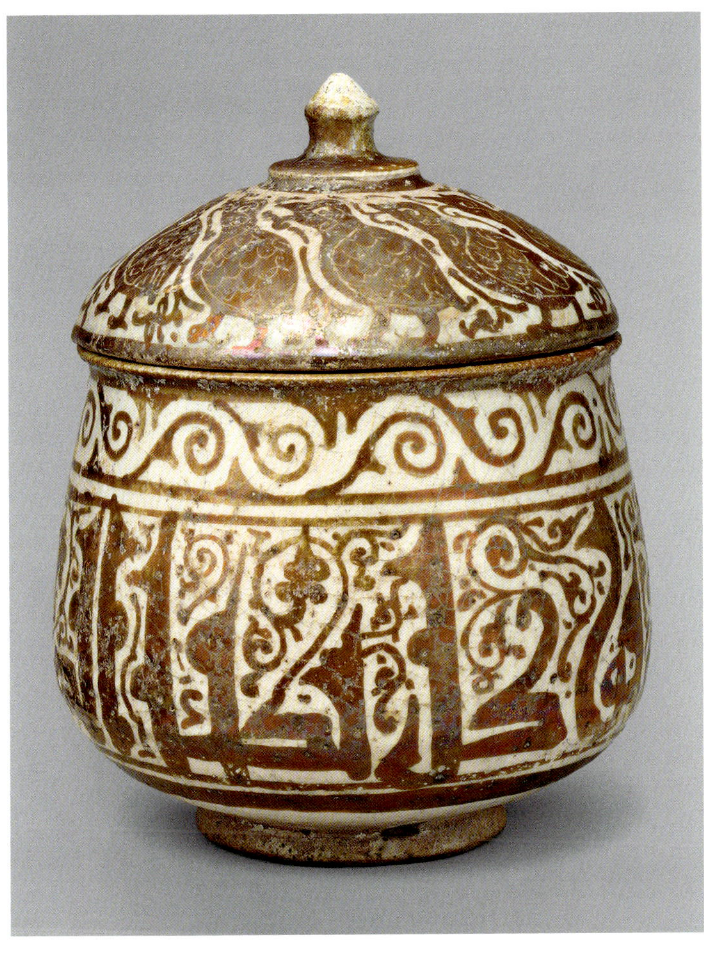

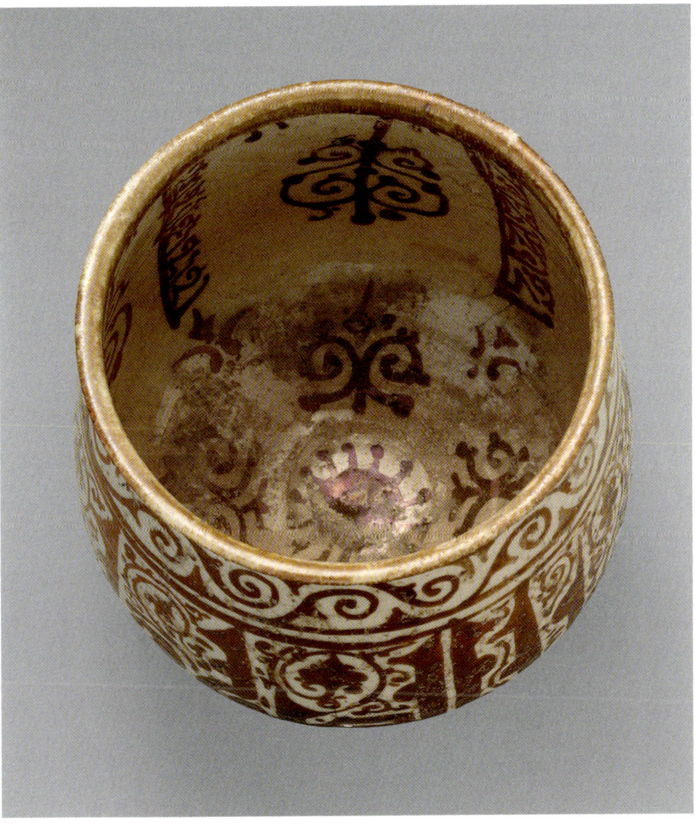

suggest that it was manufactured in that village, and the exact place of production is still undetermined.[2] In fact, recent analyses suggest that this type of ware was produced in multiple centers in Syria rather than in a single workshop or town.[3]

The body of this container is composed of the fine white stonepaste typical of Tell Minis ware and distinguishable from the coarser, darker fabric of Raqqa ware. It also has the characteristic thin walls, chiseled foot, crackling glaze, and copper-red monochrome luster paint with a tendency to iridesce.[4] Two registers decorate the exterior: above, a narrow band with a thick white scrolling motif created in reserve; below, a broad calligraphic band of *kufic* lettering interspersed with slender vine scrolls, all luster painted against white. On the lid is a row of partridges, with the details etched through the luster to reveal the white of the stonepaste beneath. The inner surface is also glazed and luster-painted, with a starburst motif on the bottom and alternating pseudo-calligraphic panels and composite scrolls on the sides.

The pyxis shares a number of specific characteristics with pieces in other collections. For example, the decoration on a bowl in the Robert Mouawad Private Museum, Beirut, corresponds to that on the calligraphic band here, with similar proportions expressed between the *kufic* lettering and surrounding scrolls.[5] The reserve painting employed in the upper register of the pyxis and the etched details found on its lid compare closely with the decoration on a bowl in the David Collection, Copenhagen.[6] However, in one respect, this pyxis is unique: its form does not appear among other Tell Minis pieces, which most often take the shape of conical bowls. EK

1. For nearly a century after Basran lusterware ceramists retrenched to Egypt, their specialized technique was employed exclusively there, but in the late eleventh century these ceramists began to disperse, eventually taking up their specialization again in different regions. On the transmission to Syria, see Mason 2004, pp. 160–61.
2. Porter, V., and Watson 1987. Similar material was excavated at Hama and published in Riis and Pousen 1957, pp. 132–40.
3. Until recently, Tell Minis ware was usually dated either around the mid-twelfth or simply twelfth century (see Porter, V., and Watson 1987). Marilyn Jenkins argued for an earlier date, partly on the basis of the presence of luster pieces embedded in the walls of eleventh-century buildings in Italy (Jenkins 1992), which, however, provides only a terminus ante quem. More accurate evidence, emerging from archaeological contexts and petrographic analysis, suggests that production began in the last quarter of the eleventh century (Mason 2004, p. 97).
4. The copper-rich luster of Tell Minis ware may have been the result of a shortage of silver in the region (Mason, lecture, Metropolitan Museum, December 2009).
5. No. 0776, illustrated in Mouawad and Carswell 2004, p. 125, no. 47.
6. No. Isl. 196, illustrated in Boston and Chicago 2006–7, p. 121, no. 51.

Provenance: [Phoenix Ancient Art, Geneva, Switzerland, until 1998; sold to MMA]

96. Lantern

Syria, probably Raqqa, early 13th century
Stonepaste; underglaze-painted in blue, luster-painted on transparent glaze
9 1/8 × 5 3/4 in. (23.2 x 14.6 cm)
Edward C. Moore Collection, Bequest of Edward C. Moore, 1891 91.1.138

Recent studies point to the production of glazed ceramics in twelfth- and thirteenth-century Syria at multiple locations and indicate that several types were produced at each of the various centers.[1] One type from this period, a group of underglaze- and luster-painted stonepaste ware, is associated mainly with Raqqa, a site on the middle Euphrates.[2] The Ayyubid prince al-Malik al-Ashraf Musa lived in this city from 1201 to 1229, during which time ceramic production is thought to have thrived there; it tapered off toward the middle of the thirteenth century and ended with the Mongol invasion in 1258. This ware belongs to a larger class of ceramics referred to as Raqqa ware, which shares the same body fabric and glaze composition.

While this lantern represents a classic example of Raqqa lusterware in its stonepaste composition, overglaze luster-painting technique, and decorative motifs, its form is unusual. Modeled from slabs and rolls, its shape resembles a square-domed building, articulated at each corner by a column and finial.[3] On two opposing sides, the walls of this "building" are pierced with eight-petaled rose windows. The other two sides are open and surmounted by lobed arches. The dome is also pierced, with small openings on its sides.[4]

The decoration of the lantern highlights its architectonic elements. A sketchy vegetal scroll with dots, executed in brown luster against a white ground, meanders across the dome and the walls. The columns are painted entirely in luster, which is now rather abraded. Concentric outlines of blue and luster paint accentuate the piercings of the dome as well as the four rectangular wall panels and their openings. Surmounting the arches is interlace ornament that mimics a decorative device frequently found in Syrian buildings of the Ayyubid and Mamluk periods.

Two similar ceramic lanterns are known, both roughly contemporaneous examples of the same technique attributed to Raqqa: one, slightly larger, has corner columns and finials but is open on all four sides;[5] the other, like the Museum's lantern, has alternating rose windows and openings.[6] EK

1. See, for example, Watson 2004, p. 289.
2. This is a subgroup that has been identified through petrographic analysis (Mason 2004, pp. 91–120). The attribution of this group of Raqqa ware is explored in Jenkins-Madina 2006.
3. Three of the existing finials are modern reconstructions based on the fragmentary remains of the fourth.
4. The original summit of the dome is lost. A pierced spherical knob that was formerly applied to the dome was identified as a modern reconstruction and removed in a 1975 restoration.
5. Sotheby's London 1986, p. 47, lot 157. These references come from a report by Annie-Christine Daskalakis in the Department of Islamic Art files, Metropolitan Museum, New York.
6. Dumbarton Oaks (no. D.O. 50.39).

PROVENANCE: M. Albert Goupil, Paris (until d. 1884; sale Hôtel Drouot, Paris, April 23–27, 1888; Edward C. Moore, New York (probably 1888–d. 1891)

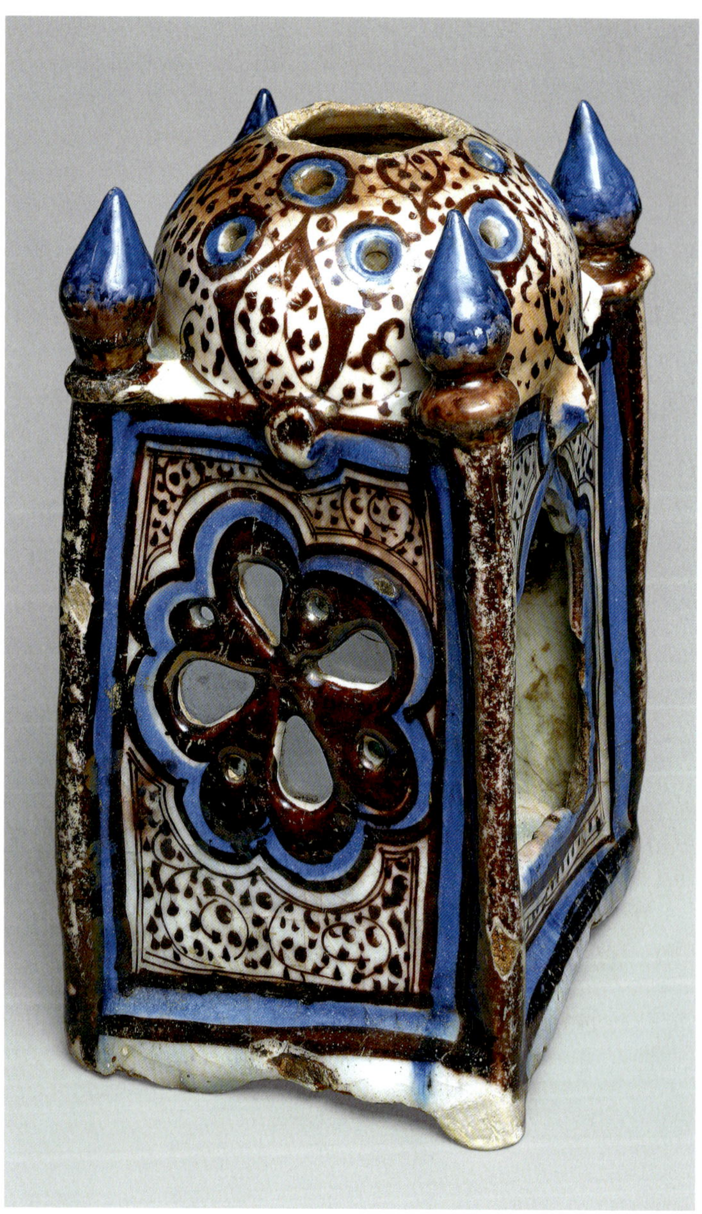

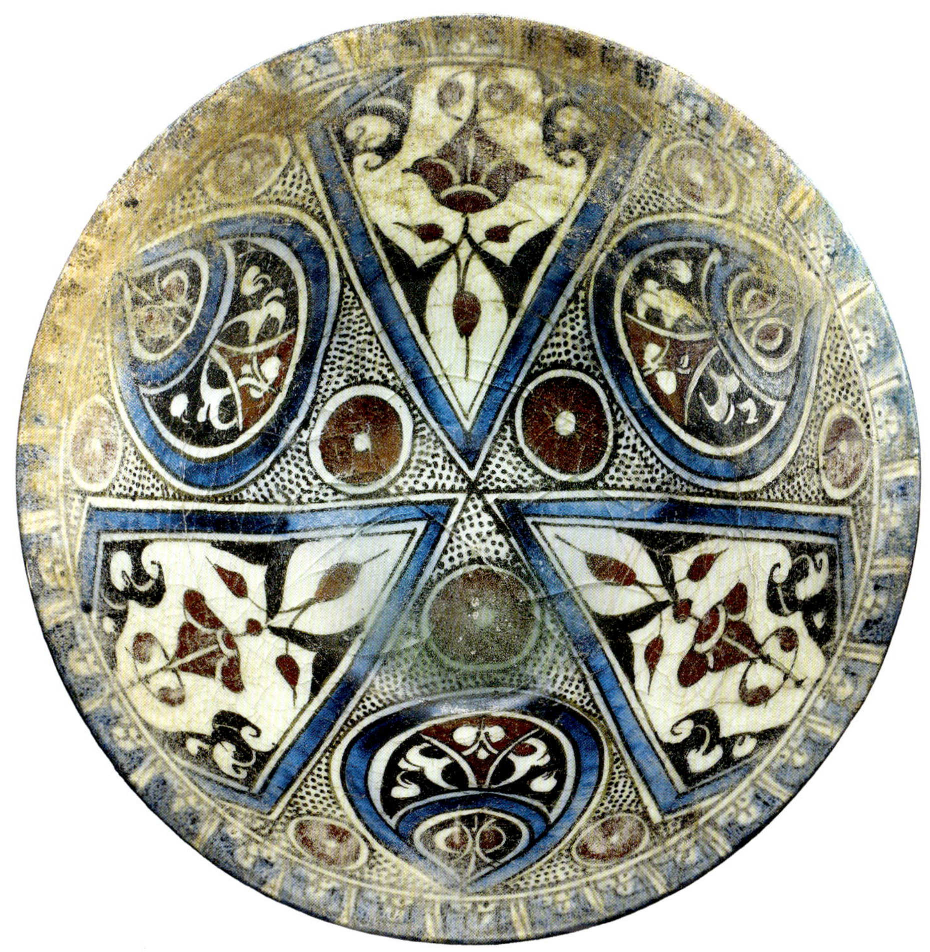

97. Bowl

Syria, probably Damascus, late 12th–early 13th century
Stonepaste; polychrome-painted under transparent glaze
H. 4⅛ in. (10.5 cm); Diam. 8⅞ in. (22.5 cm)
H. O. Havemeyer Collection, Gift of Horace Havemeyer, 1941 41.165.2

It has been difficult to pin down the attribution of the ceramic type to which this handsome polychrome bowl belongs. Found at sites throughout Syria, such bowls were formerly classed with ceramics attributed to Rusafa. Later, they came to be grouped with Raqqa ware. One theory—that they were made not only at multiple centers in Syria but also in Egypt—is based on shards found at Fustat "in quantities and of a quality that show it [Egypt] was an important producer."[1] Another, based on recent petrographic analysis and supported by a study of archaeological evidence, suggests Damascus as the main center of production for this ware.[2]

To create the design on this bowl, the ceramist painted directly on the white stonepaste body with three pigments—chromium black, cobalt blue, and bole red—over which he applied a transparent alkali glaze. The interior design consists of a band of pseudo-inscription around the rim, surrounding a framework of radial panels with alternating designs of bold, crisply drawn palmettes, split palmettes, crescents, "big-eye" motifs, and trefoils against either white or stippled grounds. The outer walls are painted with loosely drawn arc motifs, another diagnostic indicator for this pottery group.

Similarities in technique, form, and design clearly suggest a relationship between this group of Syrian underglaze-painted pottery and comparable material from Iran. This ware may have appeared in Syria and Egypt as an attempt at imitating the colorful Iranian *mina'i* ware, a development linked with the east-to-west transfer of the conical bowl form around 1200.[3] Another chronology for medieval Syrian ceramics, however, dates the appearance in Syria of polychrome underglaze-painted ware as early as about 1125, preceding *mina'i* production by about fifty years.[4] The technical, formal, and stylistic ceramic relationships between Syria and Iran in the twelfth and early thirteenth centuries appear to be more complex than previously thought and warrant further consideration.[5] EK

1. Watson 2004, p. 296; Tonghini 1994, p. 255. I am grateful to Rosalind Wade-Haddon for her assistance and bibliographic suggestions.
2. Mason 2004, pp. 106, 108.
3. Watson 2004, p. 294. See also Porter, V. 1981, pp. 30–33.
4. Mason 2004, pp. 108–9 (where he also points out the technical dissimilarity between *mina'i* and "true under-glaze painting"), and p. 178.
5. Chicago 2007, pp. 96, 101, and 107, no. 65. The relationship between the ceramics of Iran and Syria in earlier phases is discussed in Allan and Roberts, eds. 1987.

PROVENANCE: H.O. Havemeyer Collection, New York (by 1931–41)

98. Tile Panel

Syria, Damascus, ca. 1430
Stonepaste; modeled, polychrome-painted under transparent glaze
45 × 45 in. (114.3 × 114.3 cm)
Gift of Prof. Maan Z. Madina and
Dr. Marilyn Jenkins-Madina, 2009 2009.59.2a–p
Gift of Ralph Minasian, 2011 2011.156a, b

In the first half of the fifteenth century, a ceramics workshop headed by the master Ghaybi al-Tawrizi flourished in Mamluk Syria and Egypt, producing more than a dozen known tile panels or revetments for architectural contexts as well as portable objects.[1] As the *nisba* "al-Tawrizi" indicates, Ghaybi probably emigrated

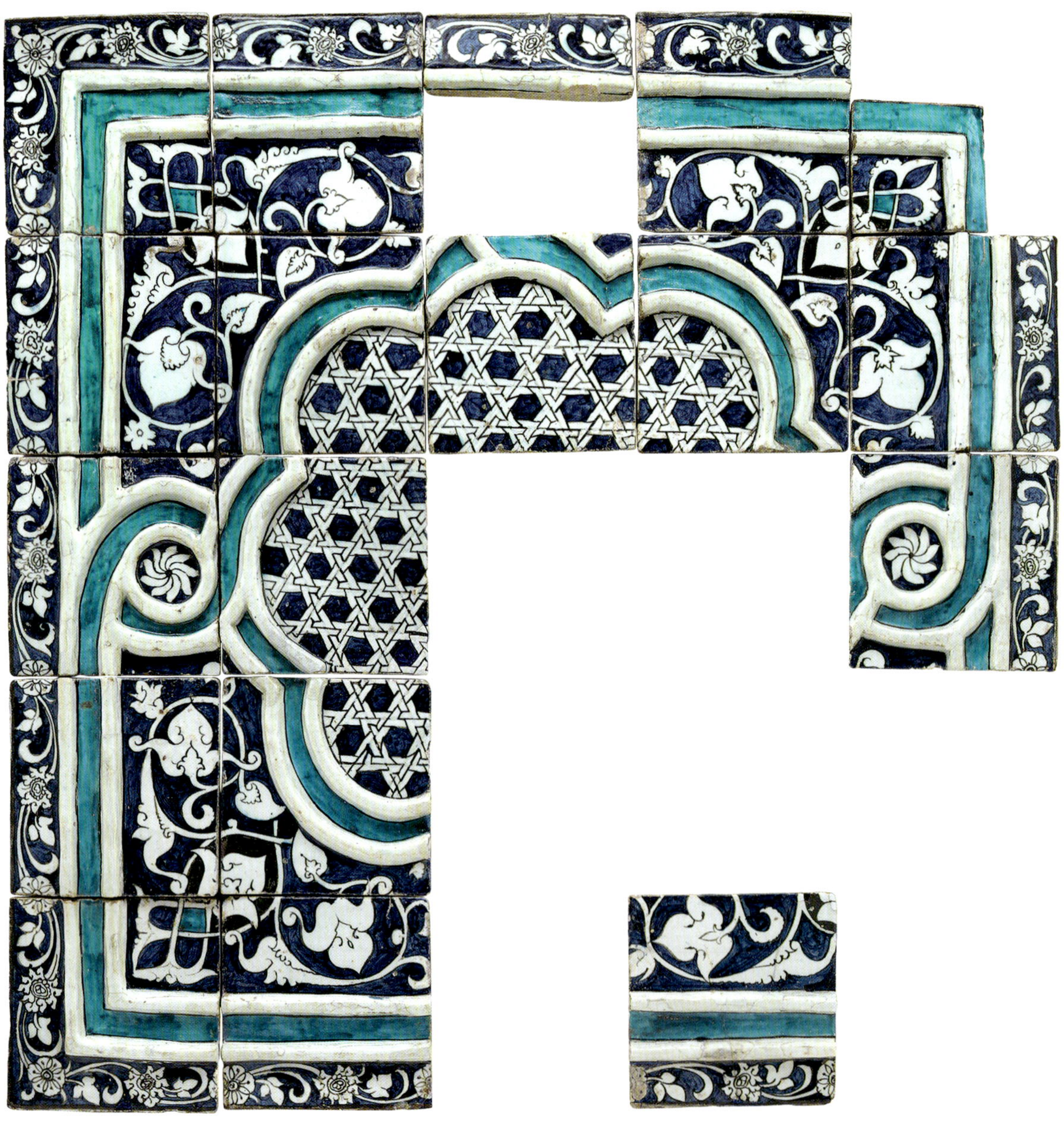

from the Iranian city of Tabriz to Syria.[2] This set of eighteen tiles, which originally belonged to a panel consisting of twenty-five, is so similar in technique, composition, and style to revetments signed by Ghaybi that it most probably can be attributed to his workshop. A report that the panel was acquired in Damascus in the early decades of the twentieth century suggests that it came from one of several buildings in that city decorated in the early fifteenth century with ceramic tiles.[3]

The best known of these Ghaybi revetments in Damascus survives in an incomplete state in the funerary complex of Ghars al-Din al-Tawrizi (d. 1430).[4] While the majority of revetments associated with the Ghaybi workshop are composed of hexagonal tiles, a few are made up of square or rectangular ones. At Ghars al-Din's complex, in addition to the hexagonal and triangular tiles lining the walls of the mausoleum, there are two rectangular panels composed of square tiles located in the prayer hall. One of these compares quite closely with the present panel, which may well come from the same building—especially in light of the fact that only part of the revetment in the mosque building survives in situ.[5] Both panels are decorated in reserve, the designs standing out in white, outlined with thin black lines, against a cobalt ground. Both bear medallions filled with a distinctive basket-weave motif, which is also found on signed Ghaybi shards in the Museum's collection.[6] On the other hand, a number of Damascus buildings were once decorated in this manner as well, including sections of the Umayyad Mosque *riwaq*, which appears to have been partially tiled in connection with an early fifteenth-century restoration.[7] EK

1. A survey of these revetments is published in Meinecke 1988. The Museum has more than a dozen shards bearing the signature of this workshop, as well as a ceramic mosque lamp signed "Ibn Ghaybi" (acc. no. 91.1.95).
2. Marilyn Jenkins-Madina has argued that the artisan settled in Syria before moving to Cairo (Jenkins 1984, pp. 112 and 113 n. 20), but Meinecke—while allowing for that possibility—believed Ghaybi executed the Ghars al-Din revetment in Damascus after already establishing himself in Cairo (Meinecke 1988, p. 211 n. 29).
3. According to a communication from the donor in the files of the Department of Islamic Art, Metropolitan Museum.
4. Interestingly, both the patron of the building and the master ceramist who decorated it appear to have come from Tabriz (Degeorge and Porter 2002, p. 188).
5. Carswell 1972b, p. 117, pl. 8, left.
6. Acc. nos. 08.184.53 and 08.256.113.
7. Meinecke 1988, pp. 210–11.

Provenance

Acc. no. 2009.59.2a–p: [Hagop Kevorkian, New York]; Dr. Maan Madina and Dr. Marilyn Jenkins-Madina, New York (until 2009)
Acc. no. 2011.156a, b: [Hagop Kevorkian, New York]; Dr. Maan Madina and Dr. Marilyn Jenkins-Madina, New York; Ralph Minasian, New Hyde Park, New York (until 2011)

99. Biconical Bead

Egypt or Syria, 11th century
Gold; filigree and granulation
2 × 3/4 in. (5.1 × 1.9 cm)
Purchase, Sheikh Nasser Sabah al-Ahmed al-Sabah Gift, in memory of Richard Ettinghausen, 1980 1980.456

100. Spherical Bead

Egypt or Syria, 11th century
Gold; filigree and granulation
Diam. 7/8 in. (2.1 cm)
Purchase, Mobil Foundation Inc. Gift, 1980 1980.457

101. Pendant

Egypt, 11th century
Gold, cloisonné enamel, turquoise; filigree
1 3/4 × 1 3/8 in. (4.5 × 3.5 cm)
Theodore M. Davis Collection, Bequest of Theodore M. Davis, 1915 30.95.37

Among the luxury arts that flourished under the Fatimid caliphs, gold jewelry stands out for its innovation and complexity. According to literary sources, prodigious amounts of such jewelry were manufactured for both royal and patrician patrons; most of

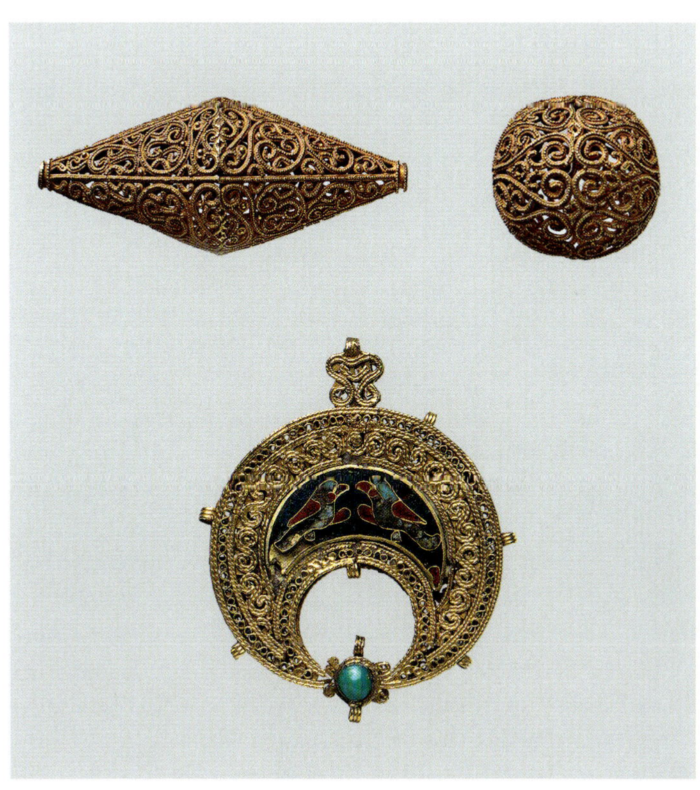

these items were later melted down for currency or refashioned into newer pieces. Gold jewelry elements of the Fatimid period share several distinct characteristics, including box construction, rings for stringing, filigree openwork with S-curve decoration, and, at least until the later period, granulation. The three pieces here—two beads and a pendant—demonstrate all these characteristics.

Both beads exemplify the distinctive Fatimid tradition of filigree openwork with granulation. The biconical bead (cat. 99) is divided into five sections by strips decorated with granulation along the body, creating an allover design of scrolls and S-curves. A nearly identical bead is found in the Khalili Collection, London.[1] The spherical bead (cat. 100) is composed of two hemispheres of curling scrolls that form heart-shaped units. Two eleventh-century gold rings from Fatimid Egypt in the Khalili Collection bear the same scrolled-heart motif on the bezels, shanks, and sides; this motif can also be seen in a drawing of a woman in the Israel Museum, Jerusalem, dating from the Fatimid period.[2]

Practically all the published Fatimid beads are independent, unattached to any larger piece of jewelry, but one exception shows how these beads might have been incorporated into a larger jewelry setting. A necklace in the collection of the Israel Antiquities Authority, part of a hoard excavated at Caesarea, consists of several beads, the most important of which are one biconical and two spherical beads that form the centerpiece of the necklace. All three are constructed of openwork filigree and decorated with granulation.[3] Because the necklace had been preserved in a vessel with other objects, it remained intact and presumably in its original form.

The pendant (cat. 101) employs the typical Fatimid box construction and filigree technique, using straight and twisted gold wire. The points of the crescent terminate in a turquoise bead, and several loops around its perimeter suggest that a string of gems originally embellished the border. At the center, a pair of confronted birds is depicted in polychrome cloisonné enamel, a technique more closely associated with Byzantine production in Constantinople than with the eastern Mediterranean during the Fatimid period. However, enamel work (known in the medieval Arabic literature as *mina*) clearly had appeal in Fatimid Egypt as well. One eleventh-century source mentions a gift from a Byzantine king to the Fatimid court that included five bracelets and three saddles, all encrusted with polychrome enamel.[4] Another source includes jewelry with enameled elements in trousseau lists.[5] The cloisonné enamel inserts on this pendant may have been purchased ready-made, perhaps imported from the Byzantine world, and then incorporated into the locally made gold setting, a theory supported by the construction of the setting and the apparent use of adhesive to fix the enameled plaque in place.[6] A similar polychrome-enameled crescent medallion, which was excavated at Fustat, is in the collection of the Museum of Islamic Art in Cairo. It, too, bears a confronted-bird motif.[7]

EK/KZ

1. Another biconical bead is in the collection of the L. A. Mayer Institute for Islamic Art, Jerusalem, but it is not openwork. Rather, it is made of a flat sheet in the form of two attached cones, with decoration in wire filigree possibly covered by granulation (Jerusalem 1987, p. 89, no. 119). The National Museum of Damascus has a necklace composed of gold beads, both spherical and biconical, along with pearls and other round beads (see Amsterdam 1999–2000, p. 272, no. 266).
2. Amsterdam 1999–2000, p. 268, nos. 257, 258. For the drawing, see Rosen-Ayalon 1991, p. 15.
3. Weyl et al. 1995, p. 90.
4. Al-Qaddumi, ed. 1996, pp. 113–14, and see also note on p. 302 explaining the translation of the term *dusut* as "bracelet" rather than "chest" (cf. al-Qaddumi 1990, p. 90, cited in an essay on this pendant by Marilyn Jenkins in New York 1997c, p. 420).
5. Goitein 1983b, pp. 200–26, esp. p. 208.
6. Jenkins in New York 1997c, p. 421. Other enameled pieces of the period bearing inscriptions correctly rendered in Arabic suggest that Fatimid jewelers eventually adopted this technique; see Gonzalez 1999.
7. O'Kane, ed. 2006, p. 61.

Provenance

Cat. 99: [Art dealer, Jerusalem, until about 1977–78]; [Derek J. Content, England, from about 1978]; [Khalili Gallery, London, until 1980; sold to MMA]

Cat. 100: [Art dealer, Jerusalem, until about 1977–78]; [Derek J. Content, England, from about 1978]; [Khalili Gallery, London, until 1980; sold to MMA]

Cat. 101: Theodore M. Davis, New York (until d. 1915); on loan from his estate during settlement of estate (1915–30)

102. *Pyxis*

Syria, mid-13th century
Brass; hammered, chased, inlaid with silver and black compound
H. 4 1/8 in. (10.5 cm); Diam. 4 in. (10.3 cm)
Rogers Fund, 1971 1971.39a, b

This pyxis is one of a group of inlaid brass pieces, dated around the thirteenth century, that technically and stylistically belong to the Islamic metalwork tradition but are decorated with scenes related to the life of Christ, certain Christian saints, and ecclesiastical figures.[1] Most of these objects, including the present work, are anepigraphic and thus yield little documentary information. Their visual sources, patronage, attribution, and authorship have been discussed in several studies.[2] Scholars generally attribute most of them to Ayyubid Syria and concur that different examples from the group were made for a variety of reasons and patrons.[3] Some may have been ordered by local Christian patrons, others for crusader knights who wished for Holy Land souvenirs, and still others for Muslim patrons who wanted them as diplomatic gifts

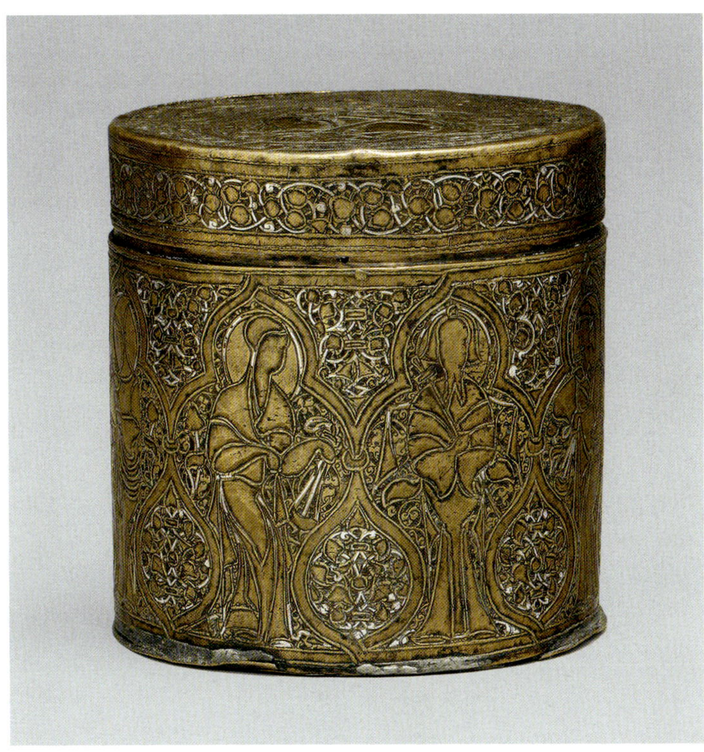

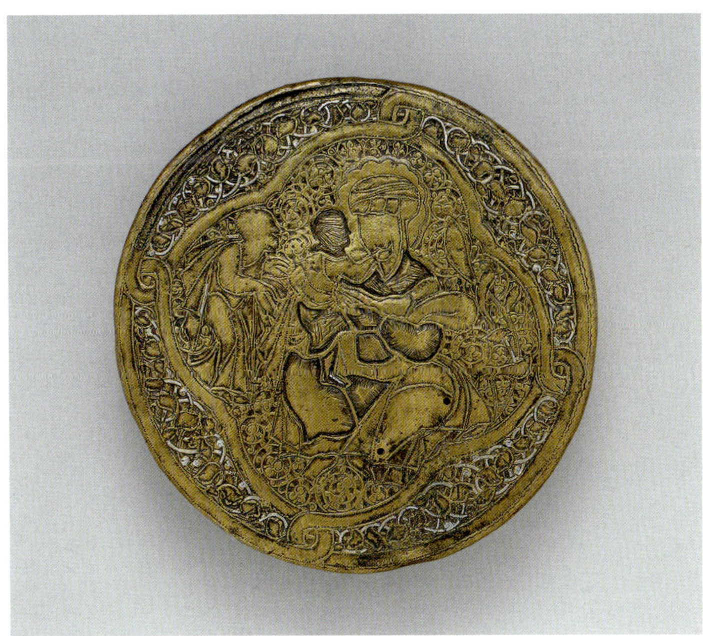

to crusader representatives or European potentates or even for their own appreciation.[4]

Here, eight trilobed arches contain figures against a background filled with tightly interwoven vegetal scrolls, which also decorate the interstices between the arches. One arch represents a compressed version of the Entry into Jerusalem, with Christ shown seated upon a donkey; two figures below the donkey spread garments while another couple behind it holds branches. At the apex of this vignette, two angels support a canopy over Christ.[5] The other arches contain single standing figures, and the lid represents a scene of the Madonna and Child. The absence in this decorative program of any of the geometric interlace, T- or Y-fret patterns, or plaited bands so frequently encountered in inlaid metalwork of the period is striking. The only exception occurs on the underside of the pyxis, where one small, central roundel bearing a six-pointed star composed of centrifugal Y-frets appears amid dense vegetal scrolls.

Even though the pyxis is missing most of the inlay that would have provided design details, the figures are unusually expressive in their gestures, poses, and sense of movement. The two to the right of the Entry scene both turn in the direction of Christ. To the left of that scene, a male extends his hands in supplication toward Christ, and a female twists in his direction as her feet face away. Only the figure positioned opposite the Entry scene stands frontally, while those flanking him signal his importance by turning in his direction. This personage has been tentatively identified as Saint Andrew on the basis of his forked beard, an attribute found in other representations of the apostle.[6] Since Andrew was the patron saint of an eponymous crusader fraternity founded in the 1230s and based in Acre, it is tempting to associate his representation here with crusader patronage.[7] The iconography of the Madonna and Child scene is especially intriguing. Whereas the other figures are haloed, the Christ Child is not, the Madonna's halo is lobed in an atypical fashion, and her headgear—a turban more suitable to a man than to a woman—is curious.[8] Unlike most eastern Madonnas, she sits on the ground, not a throne.[9] Here again, gesture performs an important role: the mother tilts her head toward the infant, who reaches up to her face tenderly. EK

1. Eva Baer surveyed eighteen of these objects (Baer 1989).
2. Katzenstein and Lowry 1983; Washington, D.C. 1985–86, pp. 124–46; Baer 1989, pp. 41–49; Ward 1993, pp. 84–85; Hoffman 2004; Ward 2005; Auld 2009.
3. Indeed, as Rachel Ward recently concluded, "The provenance, patronage and meaning of each . . . should be reassessed individually" (Ward 2005, p. 321). For a broader perspective on the question of Christian imagery and iconographic intent, see Snelders 2010.
4. Stefano Carboni in New York 1997c, p. 427, no. 285.
5. Auld 2009, p. 50.
6. Baer 1989, p. 38.
7. On the Brotherhood of Saint Andrew, see Setton et al. 1985, pp. 167–68. On the other hand, Saint Andrew is also connected with the foundation of the See of Constantinople, and it is conceivable that his representation here relates to that role.
8. For further discussion of the unusual iconography of the lid, see the catalogue entry by Carboni in New York 1997c, pp. 426–27, no. 285. The lid displays evidence of reworking.
9. Auld observes that this was a convention of European representations of the Madonna only from the fourteenth century and later (Auld 2009, p. 68).

PROVENANCE: Hagop Kevorkian, New York (until d. 1962); Kevorkian Foundation, New York (1962–70); Kevorkian sale, Sotheby's London, December 8, 1970, lot 73, to MMA

103. Spherical Incense Burner

Syria, Damascus, late 13th–early 14th century
Brass; spun and turned, pierced, chased, inlaid with gold, silver, and black compound
H. 6¼ in. (15.9 cm); Diam. 6¼ in. (15.9 cm)
Gift of J. Pierpont Morgan, 1917 17.190.2095 a, b

Inscription in Arabic in *thuluth* script, at top and bottom:
عز لمولانا الملك المالك العا / لم العادل المؤيد المظفر المنصور / المجاهد المرابط المثاغر الغازي
Glory to our lord, the king, the master, the wise / the just, the supported [by God], the triumphant, the victorious, the defender [of the faith], the warrior [at the frontiers], the warden [of the marches], the vanquisher

On top hemisphere, central band (same as above, but with the following added after الغازي):
ركن الاسلام والمسلمين
pillar of Islam and the Muslims

On lower hemisphere, central band (same as above, with the following added after المسلمين):
والملوك والسلاطين قاتل الكفر[ة] داو[د؟]
the kings and the sultans, slayer of the infidels, Dawu[d?]

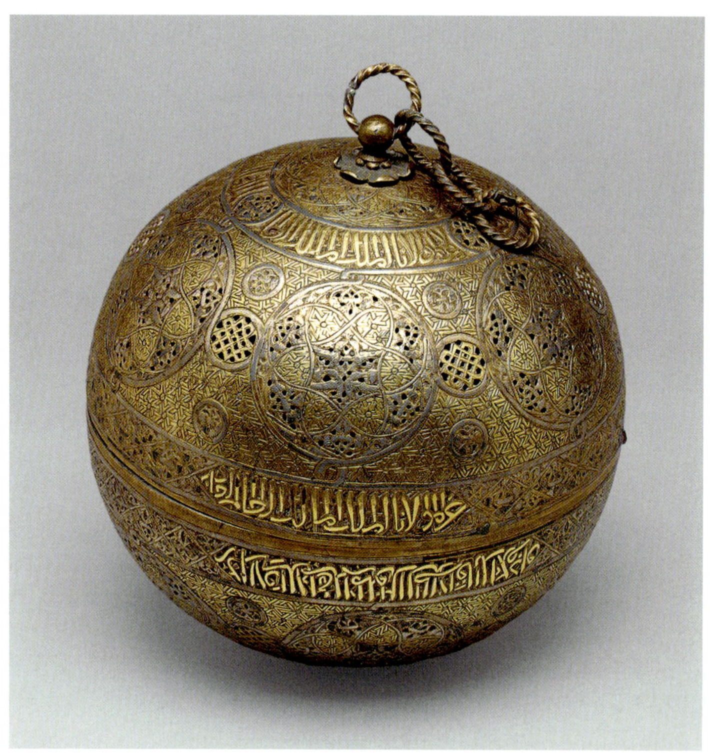

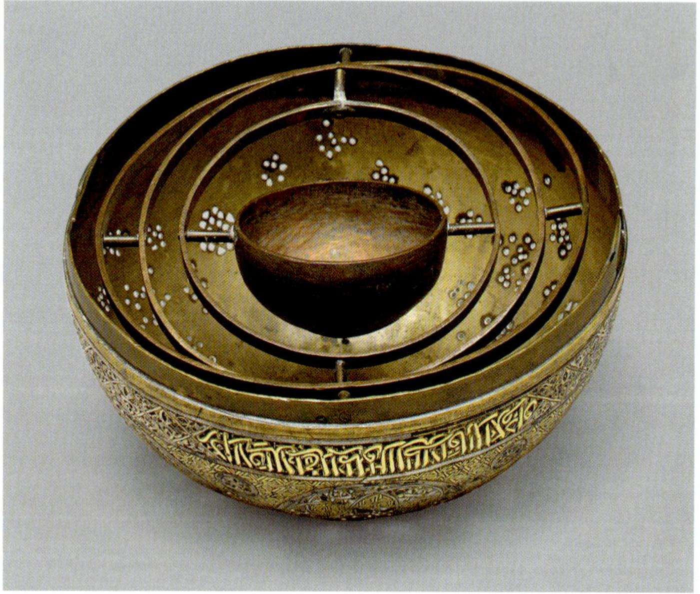

A large number of medieval Islamic pierced-brass globes survive.[1] Like the present example, the globes in this group are composed of two hemispheres. The walls of the hemispheres are usually decorated with inlays of metal or a black compound and perforated with small holes, usually arranged decoratively in groups corresponding to the inlaid design. Most of the globes were fitted inside with a small metal bowl attached to a set of gyroscopic rings that kept the bowl upright, whatever the position of the globe.[2] The function of pierced globes has been the subject of some debate, and it is possible that not all of these objects had the same purpose. The smaller examples—some of which are only a few inches in diameter—may have been carried as hand warmers, with burning coal in the cup, or worn as pomanders containing perfumed substances.[3] Larger globes, such as this one, are generally classified as incense burners, with the cup considered a receptacle for an aromatic substance.[4] It has been argued compellingly that the cups may have held perfumed candles, which would have not only emitted a pleasing scent but also illuminated the perforations.[5]

The designs on the two hemispheres of this globe mirror each other almost exactly. Around the rim of each, epigraphic bands alternate with sets of diamond-shaped cartouches filled with stylized vegetal motifs. A wide register of interlaced large and small circular medallions frames a Z-fret background and pierced sections with knotted openwork, vegetal motifs, or groups of confronted ducks. A smaller epigraphic band circles each hemisphere near its apex. This globe is fitted with a knob and suspension ring, but similar examples were designed without suspension fixtures so that they could roll freely on a surface.[6] Inside, a cup is supported on gimbals, three concentric rings that pivot from their attachment point.

EK

1. Sylvia Auld has catalogued sixty-four of them (Auld 2004, pp. 116–40).
2. Baer 1983, pp. 60–61.
3. Washington, D.C., and other cities 1981–82, p. 58.
4. On thurification in early and medieval Islamic contexts, see Aga-Oğlu 1945, pp. 28–29.
5. Ward 1990–91, pp. 67–82.
6. Ibid., pp. 69, 78; Baer 1983, p. 60.

Provenance: J. Pierpont Morgan, New York (until 1917)

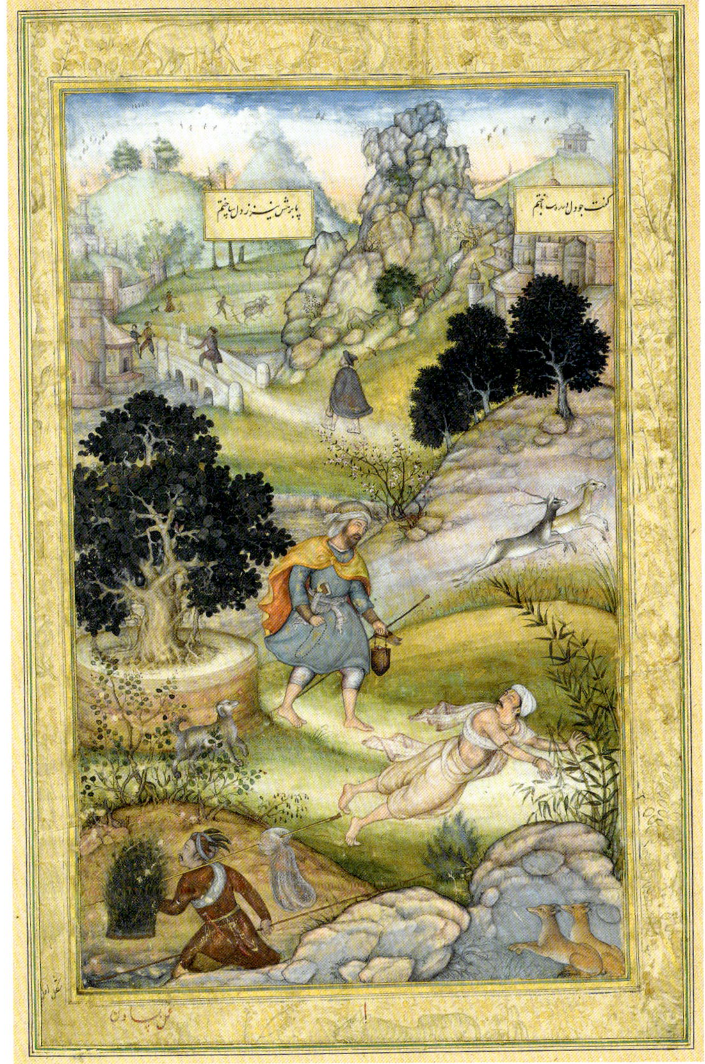

A

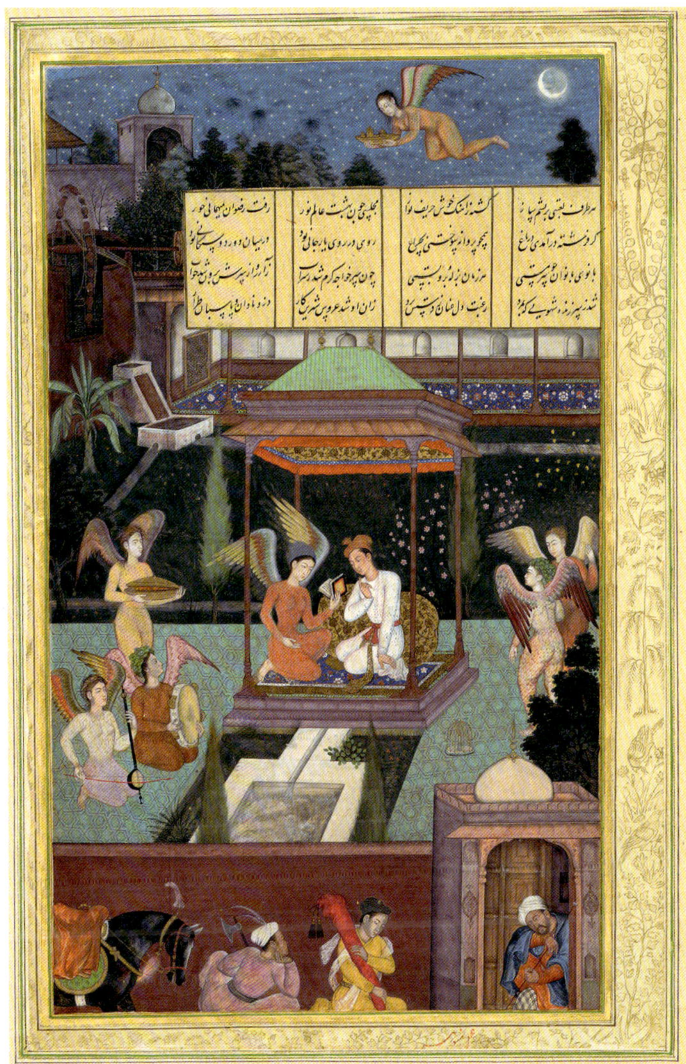

B

several inscribed by leading court artists of the period, are now shared between the Metropolitan Museum and the Walters Art Gallery, Baltimore; the bulk of the text block and the painted lacquer binding are also in Baltimore. The flawless *nasta'liq* calligraphy is by the hand of Muhammad Husain Kashmiri, whom Akbar titled Zarin Qalam (Golden Pen) and who wrote out the text at the rate of sixteen and a half lines per day.[1] The luxurious illustrations, some signed, are surrounded by richly decorated borders, with figures, plants, animals, and birds outlined in gold.[2]

While modeled on the *Khamsa* of Nizami (d. 1209) and thus paying homage to the Persian master's classic text, Amir Khusrau's quintet thoroughly localizes the form by rooting several of the stories in an Indian idiom. This illustration, taken from the *Matla' al-anwar* (Rising of the Luminaries) section, depicts one such tale, that of a meeting between a Muslim pilgrim and a Brahman devotee. Here, the pilgrim, on his way to Mecca, meets the prostrate Brahman, clad in a simple white *dhoti* (draped garment) and traveling to a Hindu temple inch by inch along the ground. When asked the reason for his actions, the Brahman replies that he has turned his heart into a symbolic foot on which he makes his way to his idol. Impressed by this religious zeal, the Muslim removes his own shoes and continues his pilgrimage barefoot.

In the hands of the Mughal master Basawan, the subject is executed with the virtuosity of a painter in his prime. From the multilayered landscape setting, filled with observed and imagined vignettes, to the convincing manner (despite the unusual pose) in which the tensed toes of the Brahman are drawn, Basawan's skill in rendering both composition and detail is manifest.[3] His interest in Europeanizing elements can be seen in the modeling of the tree, the depiction of the architecture, and the Portuguese-style figures in the distance. The palette of pale, melting colors is another hallmark.

Taken from the *Hasht bihisht* (Eight Paradises) section of Amir Khusrau's *Khamsa*, the painting by Basawan's son Manohar illustrates a variation on the well-known allegorical tale of the Persian hero Bahram Gur, who makes a nighttime visit to a garden pavilion where he is entertained by a lovely fairy princess and her attendants. The couple are shown here resting against a brocade bolster rendered in two shades of gold, while, all around, winged creatures play musical instruments and present platters of delicacies. In the starry sky above, a figure covered in delicate feathers descends bearing a golden tray, and in the foreground, outside the garden walls, the prince's attendants slumber beside a wakeful horse.

Manohar, a far greater conservative than his father, imbues the scene with all the traditional sweetness of the Indo-Persian tradition while retaining the formal reason of Mughal painting. The poetic, blooming night garden, enchanting fairies, and carefully observed waterwheel combine to create a Mughal vision of Amir Khusrau's celebrated mystical verses. NNH

1. Baltimore 2001, pp. 39–40, suggests that the writing must have begun in early 1596 and been completed by regnal year 42 (March 1597–March 1598). Most scholars use the colophon date (1597–98), but the total production time would be 1596–98.
2. The manuscript contains the names of twelve artists and four illuminators, with further attributions. The inscribed names are those of the painters Basawan, Narsingh, Lal, Manohar, Sanwala, Farrukh Chela, 'Ali Quli, Dharamdas, Farrukh, Jagannath, Mukund, Miskin, Madhav, and Surdas Gujarati and of the illuminators Mansur *Naqqash*, Khwaja Jan Shirazi, Lutfullah *Muzahhib*, and Husain *Naqqash*.
3. Brend 1988–89, p. 283, points out that the Brahman's pose here may have been adapted from a standing figure, accounting for the stiffness of the knees.

PROVENANCE: Alexander Smith Cochran, Yonkers, N.Y. (until 1913)

248. Buffaloes in Combat

Attributed to Miskin (active ca. 1570–1604)
India, late 16th century
Ink, watercolor, and gold on paper
6⅞ × 9½ in. (17.5 × 24.1 cm)
Harris Brisbane Dick Fund, 1983 1983.258

Muscles straining as they propel themselves against one another, the hulking masses of two bulls fill the center of this drawing, while a group of men, caught up in the action, swirl around the perimeter of the composition.

The drawing has been completed in the *nim qalam* style, in which elements are outlined in black and highlighted in certain areas with thin washes of color—here, white for the *jamas* and turbans and tiny dashes of red for lips and the ends of *patkas* and turban sashes. This style enjoyed popularity in the Mughal court in the late sixteenth century, when it was used for single-page works, for various illustrations in an *Akbarnama* of about 1596–97 (Chester Beatty Library, Dublin), a *Tutinama* (Beatty Library), *Darabnama* (British Library, London), *Baburnama* (Victoria and Albert Museum, London), *Anvar-i suhaili* (Bharat Kala Bhavan Museum, Varanasi), and the dispersed 1598–1600 *Razmnama*.[1] The *nim qalam* drawings have been characterized as an approximation of the European grisaille paintings and drawings brought to India in the sixteenth century, but this type of drawing has more in common with examples produced in Iran at about the same time, particularly from Khurasan in the work of Muhammadi of Herat, which in turn may have been inspired by Chinese works.

This drawing has been attributed to the Mughal artist Miskin,[2] whose father, Mahesh, and brother Asi also worked for Emperor Akbar on several of the royal manuscript projects of the 1580s. At first Miskin was a colorist (a junior position in the hierarchy of the Mughal workshop), but by the end of the decade he had risen to the position of designer. In this role he created several famed animal compositions,[3] including another animal combat depicting a bull and a lion,[4] on the basis of which the present drawing has been assigned to him. Although this attribution is still debated, various aspects of the drawing tie it to Miskin's known works: a certain amount of space separates the buffaloes from the rest of the otherwise full composition, and the outthrust arms of the figures accentuate the action. In addition, several *nim qalam* works are attributed to Miskin, who appears to have been particularly interested in the expressive possibilities of this technique.[5]

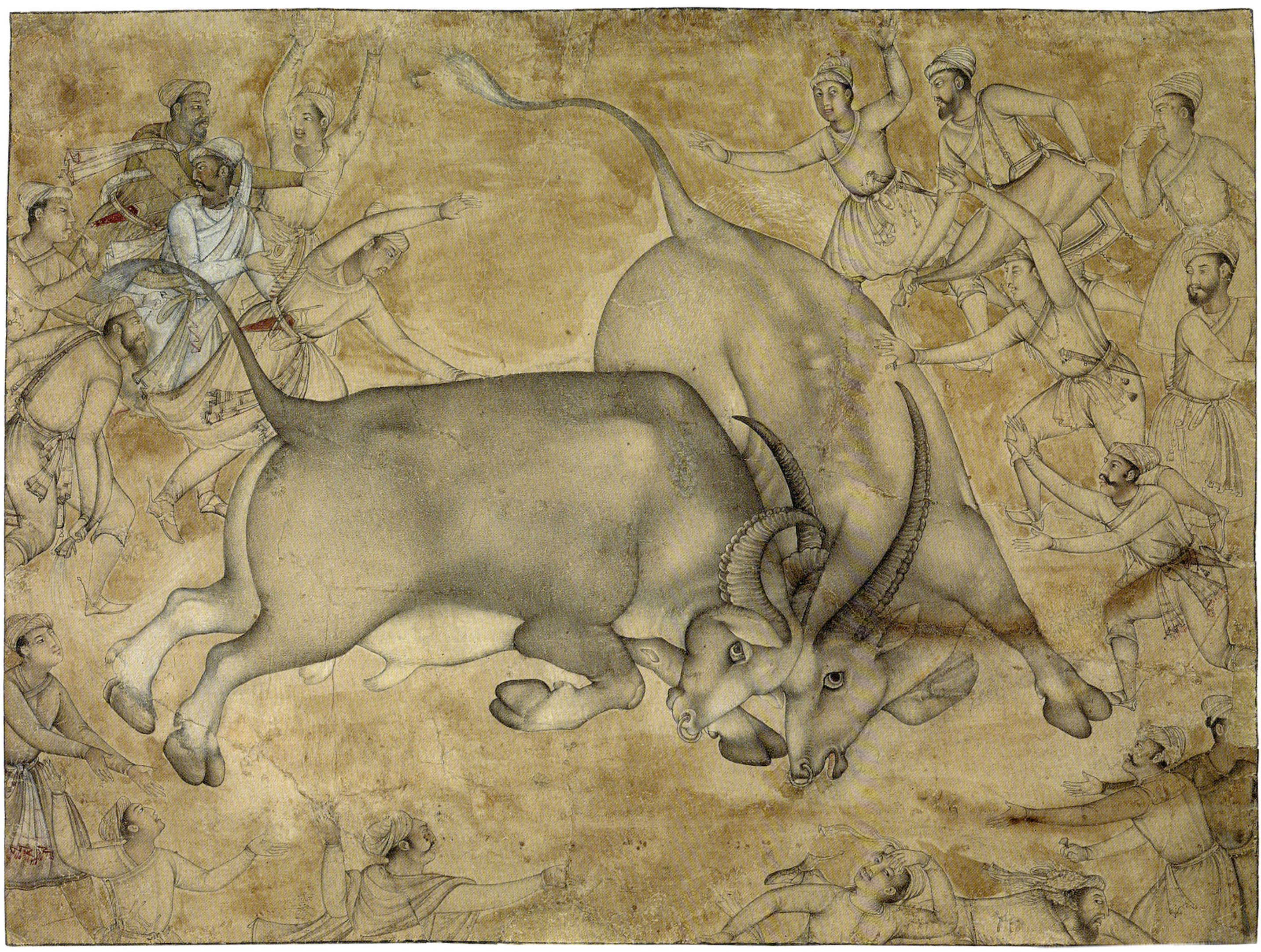

The size and shape of the drawing, as well as the abbreviation of the figures along the edges, indicate that it was probably part of a larger composition. Miskin's bull and lion combat includes several other elements around the two central animals—a group of spectators, a rocky landscape with a city in the distance, and a group of Hindu ascetics in the woods. Similarly, the *Buffaloes in Combat* may have been surrounded by additional vignettes. MS

1. Listed in Seyller 1985.
2. Stuart Cary Welch in Welch, S. C., Jenkins, and Kane 1983–84, pp. 6–7. When sold earlier, the drawing had been identified as "Indian School, 17–18th century" (Sotheby's New York, December 15, 1962, lot 285) or attributed to Farrukh Chela (Sotheby's London, June 20, 1983, lot 143).
3. Miskin's other animal compositions are a double-page hunting scene in the *Akbarnama* (Victoria and Albert Museum, London, no. IS. 2-1986, fols. 55, 56), two paintings in the *Anvar-i Suhayli* (Bharat Kala Bhavan Museum, Varanasi, no. 9069), and the detached folio, *The Raven Addressing the Assembled Animals* (British Museum, London, no. 1920, 0917, 0.5).
4. First illustrated in Welch, S. C. 1963, p. 224 and fig. 7 (now Harvard Art Museums, Cambridge, Mass., no. 1999.297). See San Francisco and Cambridge, Mass. 2004–5, pp. 86–87.
5. These include *Prince Salim Being Attacked by a Wounded Lion*, which is signed by Miskin (discussed in Welch, S. C. 1963, p. 224), and two others attributed to him: *Beasts, Real and Mythological on a Rocky Hillside* (Chester Beatty Library, Dublin, Ms. 73 [I]) and *The World of Animals* (Freer Gallery of Art, Washington, D.C., no. 45.29).

PROVENANCE: Lt.-Col. Wingate Wemyss-Muir (until 1952; sale, Sotheby's London, November 24, 1952, lot 107); Hagop Kevorkian, New York (until d. 1962; sale, Sotheby's New York, December 15, 1962, lot 285, to Heeramaneck); [Nasli and Alice Heeramaneck, New York, from 1962; sold to Humann]; Christian Humann (Panasian Collection), New York (until 1983; sale, Sotheby's London, June 20, 1983, lot 143, to MMA)

249A–D. Four Folios from the Ramayana

A. "Rama Receives Sugriva and Jambavat, the Monkey and Bear Kings"
Reverse: Four lines of Sanskrit and one line of Bundeli Hindi; evidence of a red ink seal or stamp (reportedly the Datia Palace imprint)
India, ca. 1605
Ink, opaque watercolor, and gold on paper
11 1/8 × 7 1/2 in. (28.2 × 19.1 cm)
Cynthia Hazen Polsky and Leon B. Polsky Fund, 2002 2002.503

B. "The Death of King Dasharatha, the Father of Rama"
Reverse: Eight lines of Sanskrit text; four lines of Sanskrit and one line of Bundeli Hindi
India, ca. 1605
Opaque watercolor and gold on paper
11 1/2 × 7 1/2 in. (29.2 × 19.1 cm)
Cynthia Hazen Polsky and Leon B. Polsky Fund, 2002 2002.506

C. "The Court of Ravana"
Reverse: Eight lines of Sanskrit text.
India, ca. 1605
Opaque watercolor and gold on paper
10 7/8 × 7 1/2 in. (27.6 × 18.9 cm)
Cynthia Hazen Polsky and Leon B. Polsky Fund, 2002 2002.505

D. "The Awakening of Kumbhakarna in the Golden City of Lanka"
Reverse: Twelve lines of Sanskrit text and one further, extensively damaged, line at bottom of page; ink stamp reading: *tasvir-khana datia* [state 48?]
India, ca. 1605
Opaque watercolor and gold on paper
10 7/8 × 7 1/2 in. (27.6 × 18.9 cm)
Cynthia Hazen Polsky and Leon B. Polsky Fund, 2002 2002.504

The Indian epic poem *Ramayana* recounts the tale of the legendary prince Rama and his battle against Ravana, the king of the demons, which Rama fought and won with the aid of the monkey and bear armies. In contrast to other *Ramayana* manuscripts of this period, which were translated into Persian at the order of the Mughal emperor Akbar (r. 1556–1605), this particular series retains its original Sanskrit text, an indication that it was probably made for a Hindu patron.[1] Its provenance from the Datia collection and the existence of pale traces of drawings on the reverse in a Datia style suggest that the patron may have been the wealthy Bundela Rajput noble Bir Singh Deo Bundela (d. 1627). Bir Singh was prominent at the Mughal court, supporting Prince Salim in his rebellion against Akbar and infamously remembered as the assassin of Abu'l Fazl. As a court noble he was able to patronize Mughal-trained artists (although ones of lesser fame than those in the employ of the emperor) in the practice known as subimperial patronage, which is confirmed here by the characteristic simplified Mughal style of these paintings.

These painted folios were never bound with a continuous text; rather each illustrated leaf had selected passages written on the reverse. Damage from a fire soon after the completion of the series explains the irregular shape of the pages, but their essential compositions and palpable liveliness still survive. The series contained an unknown number of painted folios executed by a group of minor artists, who have been associated with other subimperial projects and who may have been dismissed from the imperial atelier at the end of Akbar's reign.[2] The multiple hands involved drew upon a variety of sources—both from the imperial Mughal style and from farther afield—and contributed an inventive approach to pattern and space. As a result, the manuscript has a richly flavored character, which is reflected in the Metropolitan's folios, some of which show influences from Persian models as well as Indian styles.

The brilliant red color and oversized Chinese ribbon cloud seen in "Rama Receives Sugriva and Jambavat" (cat. 249A) reflect the strong palette and forms of Rajput painting and contrast with the more classically restrained Mughal approach in "Kumbhakarna in the Golden City of Lanka" (cat. 249D). Understated emotion is conveyed in "The Death of King Dasharatha" (cat. 249B), which shows the blind king's three wives pulling their hair loose in an expression of grief. Also seen on other folios, the juxtaposition of patterns here appears to be a throwback to Mughal projects of an earlier period such as the *Hamzanama*.[3] Oversized clouds and the employment of the figure style suggest that the artist might have been the same as in the previous folio depicting Rama. "The Court of Ravana" (cat. 249C), which shows the ten-headed demon and his son Indrajit holding *durbar*, is the most unusual in style, with a bolder, less refined handling of the demons, who are nonetheless appealingly characterized. The Persianate *div* models upon which the demons are ultimately based, the blue-and-white-tiled *iwan* arch in the background, and, more remotely, the tiered composition indicate that the artist was aware of Shiraz and other Persian painting styles. In the folio depicting Ravana's brother, the giant Kumbhkarna, being awakened by demons, similar *div* figures are treated in a far more refined manner. NNH

1. All four folios here are published: Navina Haidar in New York 2004–5, pp. 360, 367, figs 159–62. Further pages from the same series are on pp. 354–55, figs. 157–58. Further leaves from the same series are illustrated in the following: Chandra, P. 1957–59; Chandra, P. 1960, fig. 16; Gairola 1970, no. 8; Portland and other cities 1973–74, nos. 24, 34; Washington, D.C. 1981–82, p. 130, fig. 18; London 1982a, nos. 6–7; London 1982b, pp. 82–83, 205, no. 382; New York and other cities 1984–87, no. 15; London, Washington, D.C., Zurich, and Oxford 1991–93, no. 4; Pal 1993, nos. 83 a-b; Pal 1997, no. 38; Goswamy and Bhatia 1999, pp. 46–47, no. 36 and front cover ill.; Seyller 1999, figs. 12–13; Philadelphia 2001, no. 16; Turin 2010, p. 156, no. 142.
2. John Seyller in Philadelphia 2001, no. 16, discusses this series and speculates on artists.
3. Seyller, ibid., points this out.

PROVENANCE: Datia Royal Collection; private collection, Calcutta (from 1947); private collection, Europe; [Terence McInerney, New York, until 2002; sold to MMA]

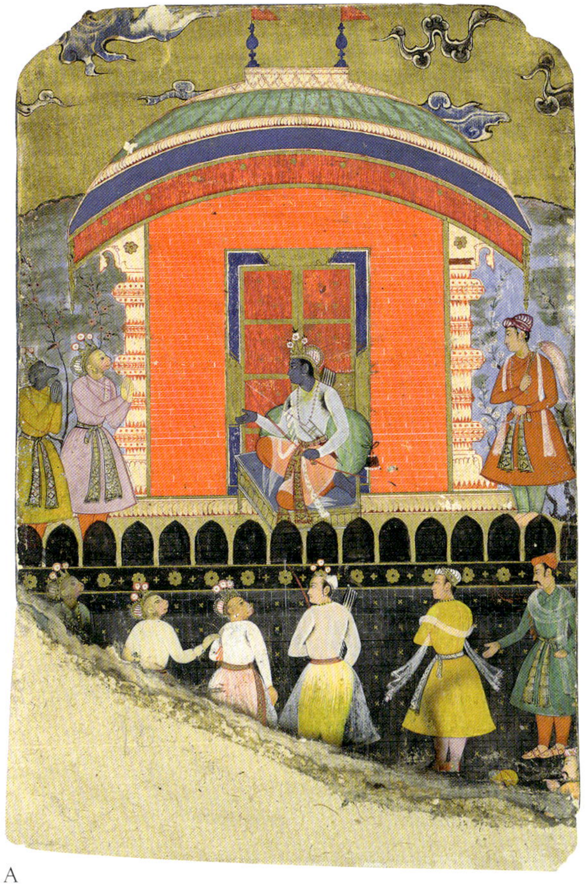

A

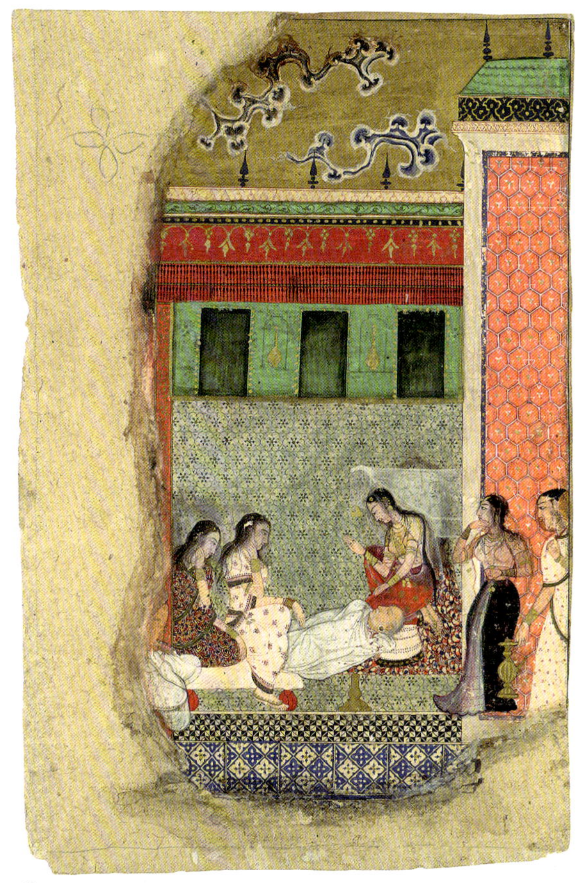

B

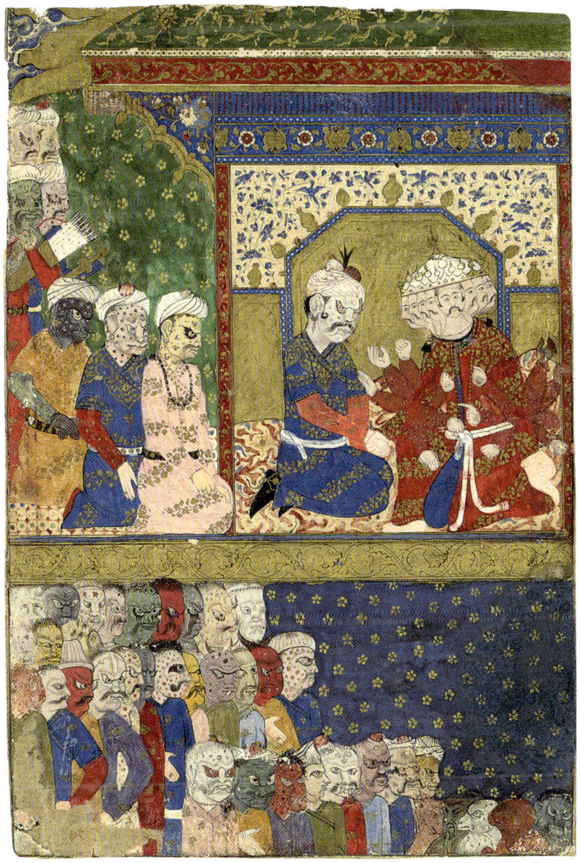

C

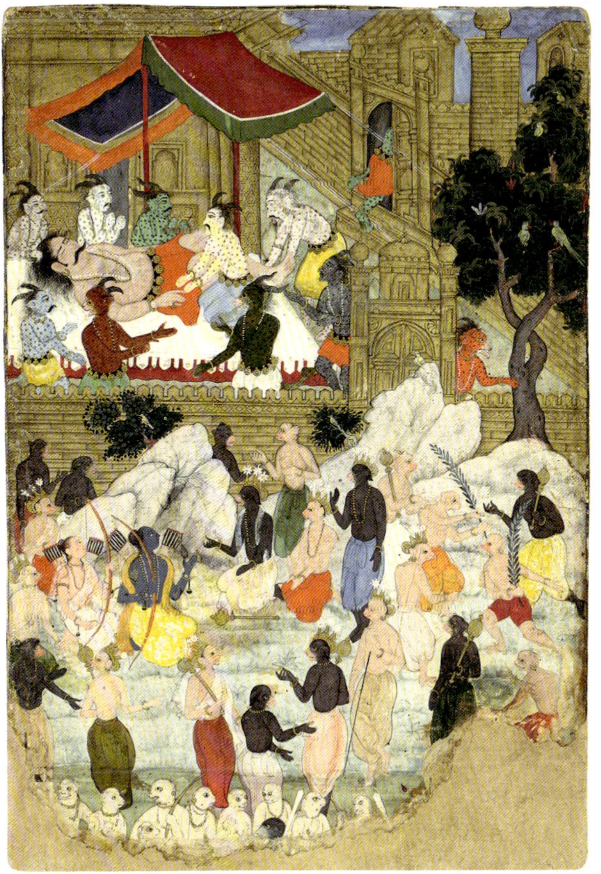

D

250A–D. Four Folios from the Emperors' Album

A. Rosette Bearing the Names and Titles of Shah Jahan
India, ca. 1645
Ink, opaque watercolor, and gold on paper
15¼ × 10⅜ in. (38.6 × 26.5 cm)
Purchase, Rogers Fund and The Kevorkian Foundation Gift, 1955 55.121.10.39

Inscription in Arabic in *tughra* script at center:
حضرت شهاب الدين محمد شاه جهان پادشاه غازى خلد الله ملكه و سلطانه
His Majesty Shihab al-Din Muhammad Shah Jahan, the king, the vanquisher, may God perpetuate his dominion and sovereignty.

B. "Study of a Nilgai (Blue Bull)"
Painter: Mansur (active ca. 1589–1626)
Calligrapher: Mir 'Ali Haravi (d. ca. 1550)
India, ca. 1620
Ink, opaque watercolor, and gold on paper
10⅛ × 15¼ in. (25.6 × 38.9 cm)
Purchase, Rogers Fund and The Kevorkian Foundation Gift, 1955 55.121.10.13

Inscription in Persian in *nasta'liq* script at top:
جهانگيرشاهى
From the reign of Emperor Jahangir

In front of animal's leg:
عمل بنده درگاه منصور نا در العصر
Work of the servant of the palace, Mansur, "Wonder of the Age"

C. "Shah Jahan on Horseback"
Painter: Payag (active ca. 1591–1658)
India, ca. 1630
Ink, opaque watercolor, and gold on paper
15¼ × 10⅛ in. (38.9 × 25.7 cm)
Purchase, Rogers Fund and The Kevorkian Foundation Gift, 1955 55.121.10.21

Inscription in Persian in *nasta'liq* script:
عمل پاياگ
Work of Payag

D. Page of Calligraphy Illuminated with Animals and Plants in a Field of Flowers
Calligrapher: Mir 'Ali Haravi (d. ca. 1550)
Calligraphy: Iran, 16th century
Illumination: India, 17th century
Ink, opaque watercolor, and gold on paper
15⅛ × 10¼ in. (38.3 × 26.2 cm)
Purchase, Rogers Fund and The Kevorkian Foundation Gift, 1955 55.121.10.4r

Inscription in Persian in fine *nasta'liq* scriptscript, three couplets by Ibn Yaqmin:
مرد بايد كه هر كجا باشد — عــزت خويشتـــن نگهـــدارد
خود پسندى و ابلهى نكند — هر چه كبر و منيست بگذارد
بطريقى رود كه مردم را — سـر مويـــى ز خـــود نيـــازارد
A true man should, wherever he is / Preserve his honor well;
Show no conceit or foolishness / Or selfish pride in life
And act so that nobody's hair / Is touched or hurt by him
Mir 'Ali

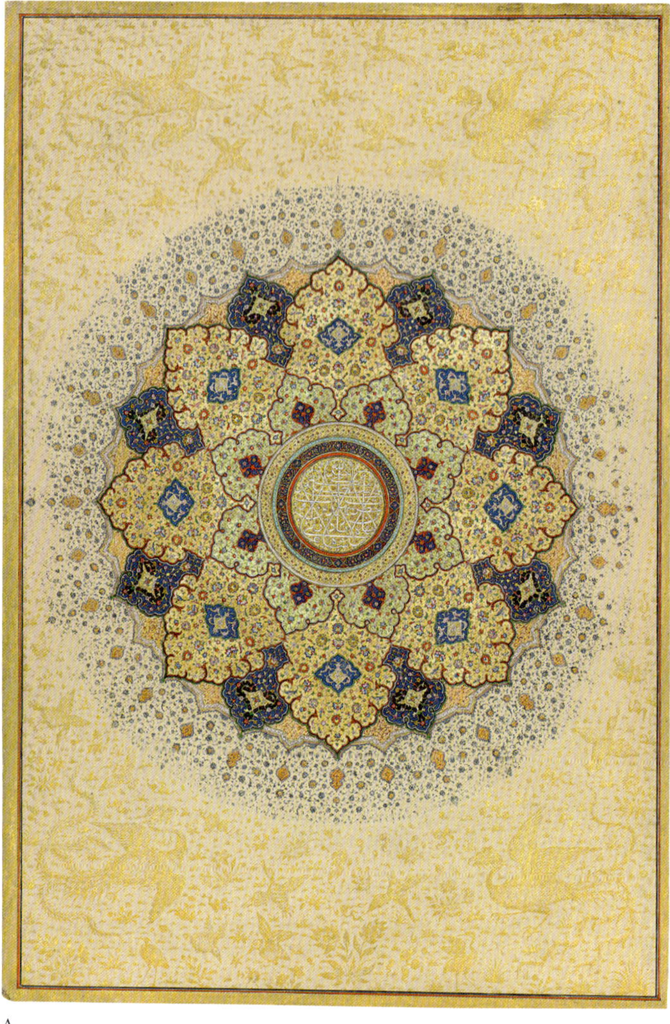
A

This celebrated imperial Mughal album (*muraqqa'*), known as the Shah Jahan, or Emperors', Album originally consisted of fifty leaves containing paintings, illuminated pages, and calligraphy. Thirty-nine of these date from the seventeenth century, while the remaining eleven date from the early nineteenth century. Of the earlier folios, the first few were commissioned by Emperor Jahangir (r. 1605–27), but it was under the patronage of his son Shah Jahan (r. 1627–58) that most of the leaves were added. The nineteenth-century folios contain copies of the earlier subjects as well as some new compositions. This album belongs to a family of related imperial albums that share similar formats and subject matter, most notably the so-called Wantage and Minto albums in British collections, particularly the Victoria and Albert Museum, London, and the Chester Beatty Library, Dublin.

Most of the calligraphic panels in the Shah Jahan Album were executed by the sixteenth-century Persian master Mir 'Ali Haravi, who first practiced his art at Herat and later at Bukhara. His writing was so prized in Mughal India that it was collected, mounted in albums, and illuminated. Here (cat. 250D), the illumination

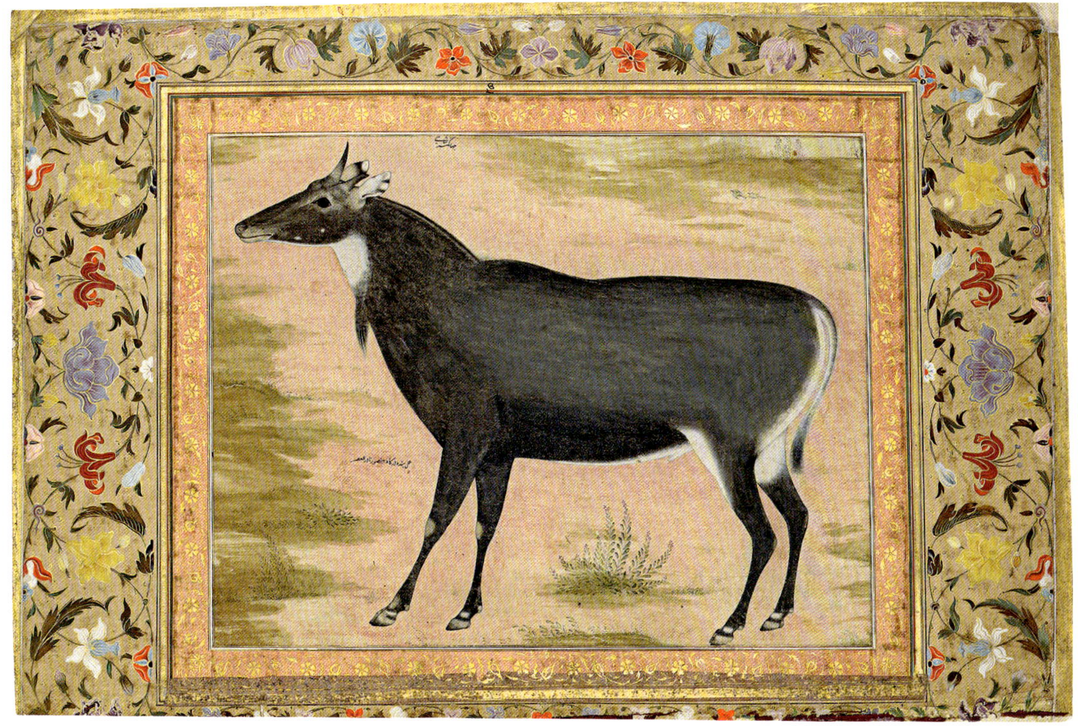

B

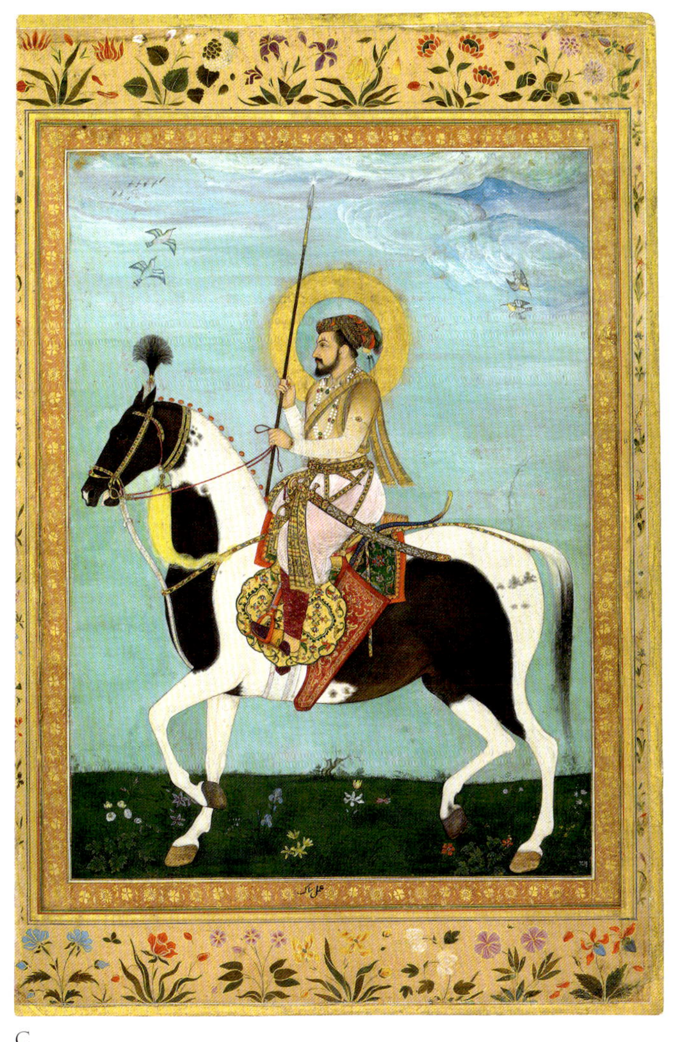

C

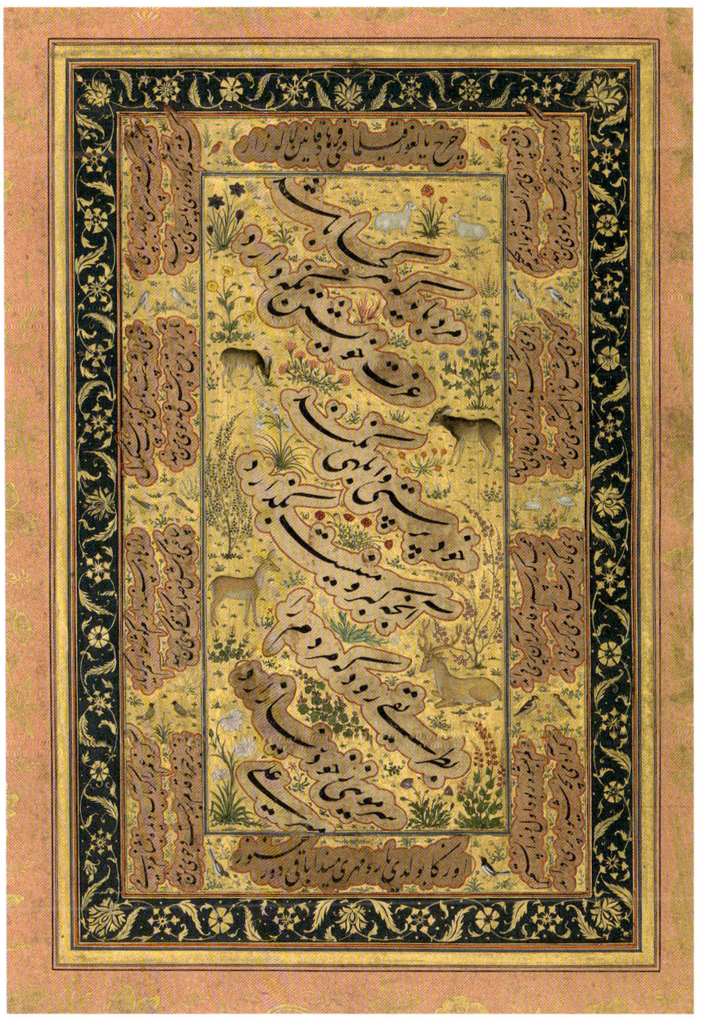

D

takes on a special character, departing from the more usual arabesque-based motifs seen in Indo-Persian ornament and moving toward a naturalism typical of Mughal painting.[1] The inclusion of natural life as part of the decoration of text pages is also seen in an earlier Mughal *Gulistan* of Sa'di in the Royal Asiatic Society of Great Britain and Ireland, London, which contains over two thousand bird images.[2] In the Museum's folio, six lines of Persian poetry written out by Mir 'Ali in *nasta'liq* script are set against a burnished gold ground that contains landscape features as well as various animals and birds, including a pair of sambar deer, nilgai antelope, white goats, mynah birds, robins, starlings, egrets, and shrikes. The lyrical poetry framing the composition is by the poet Hilali Chughata'i (two couplets are in Chagatai Turkish).

Recorded observations of the emperors Babur (r. 1526–30) and Jahangir reflect the Mughal interest in the natural world; indeed, modern science has recognized the latter as having made at least two original contributions to zoology.[3] Jahangir's remarkably acute interests in the flora and fauna of India are expressed in the sensitive natural studies produced by his leading artist, Mansur, as demonstrated in this album by the nilgai, or blue bull (cat. 250B), one of several such works therein.[4] This beast may have roamed in Jahangir's zoological garden, where Mansur, a multifaceted artist who earlier in his career had been trained in the art of illumination, would have been able to record details such as the broken horn and the whorl of hair at the base of the animal's neck (the slightly less detailed brushwork on the body of the beast, however, may indicate the hand of an assistant). While this natural study depicts a relatively humble subject, a local animal, other works by Mansur portray more exotic creatures, including a zebra (which arrived at court as a gift in 1616), a turkey-cock (arriving in 1612), and a chameleon.[5] Although Mansur was not the only artist who addressed such natural themes, he was an acknowledged master of the genre, gaining mention in Jahangir's memoirs and earning the title Nadir al-'Asr, Wonder of the Age.

Grand compositions such as cat. 250C, which shows a bejeweled Shah Jahan with a radiating nimbus astride a magnificent piebald stallion, were part of the imperial Mughal image disseminated around the world.[6] The ruler's firm black ink inscription names the artist as Payag, further confirmed by a recently discovered artist's signature in a minuscule inscription located on the extension of the saddle.[7] In many ways the hard-edged formality of this composition epitomizes the Shah Jahan painting style, yet demonstrated equally is Payag's facility with royal portraiture, a somewhat rare genre for him. This crystalline imperial likeness and the layering of patterns and shapes in the area of the saddlecloth stand in contrast to the artist's use of smoky landscapes, dark tones, and washy colors in the *Padshahnama* (Royal Library, Windsor).[8] Of note is the subtle radiance around the point of the emperor's spear. Also appearing in folios of that royal manuscript is the emperor's same piebald steed.[9] This particular formula of Shah Jahan in equestrian mode proved to have lasting popularity, judging from the number of later copies made, including one in the Emperors' Album itself.[10]

A *shamsa* (sun or sunburst in Arabic) traditionally opened or closed imperial Mughal albums. Worked in bright color, predominantly lapis, and several tones of gold, this meticulously designed and unerringly precise radiating medallion from the Shah Jahan Album (cat. 250D) is enriched by painted arabesques, fantastic flowers, cloud bands, birds, and insects. The Emperors' Album contains two such masterpieces, this one centered around the name of Shah Jahan written in an elaborate *tughra* (cipher) style and its companion containing the seal imprint of his successor and later owner of the album, Aurangzeb (r. 1658–1707). Specifically trained masters of ornament painted such illuminations. Although many Iranian prototypes for this rosette can be cited, the Mughal *shamsa* differs from them in its heightened three-dimensionality and warm coloring.[11] The importance of solar symbolism in many aspects of Indian and Islamic visual representation and courtly life made such radiating motifs particularly meaningful to their royal patrons.[12]

NNH

1. New York 1987–88, pp. 124–25, no. 22.
2. London 1982c, p. 87, no. 58.
3. Alvi and Rahman 1968, p. 5.
4. Published in New York 1987–88, pp. 178–81, no. 47; New York 1985–86, p. 216, no. 142; Welch, S. C., et al. 1987, p. 145, no. 111.
5. Williamstown, Mass., Baltimore, Boston, and New York 1978–79, pp. 137–43, provides a list of the artist's major works; see also Blunt 1948.
6. Published in New York 1987–88, pp. 202–3, no. 59.
7. A recent examination of the painting by Robert Elgood resulted in this new discovery.
8. See Welch, S. C. 1995 for a discussion of Payag's style.
9. New Delhi and other cities 1997–98, p. 52, no. 17, pp. 72–75, no. 29.
10. New York 1987–88, p. 257, no. 86.
11. Ibid., pp. 80–81, no. 1; Welch, S. C., et al. 1987, p. 149, no. 114; New York 1985–86, pp. 236–37, no. 156.
12. Skelton 1988, pp. 181–82.

PROVENANCE: Jack S. Rofe, Scotland (1929; sale, Sotheby's, London, December 12, 1929, to Kevorkian); [Hagop Kevorkian, New York, 1929–55; gift and sale to MMA]

251. *Portrait of the Elephant 'Alam Kaman*

Painter: Attributed to Bichitr (active ca. 1610–60)
India, ca. 1640
Opaque watercolor and gold on paper
11 7/8 × 17 3/8 in. (30.2 × 44.1 cm)
Harris Brisbane Dick Fund, 1996 1996.98a

Inscription in Persian in *naskhi* script in gold cartouche:
شبیه عالم کمان کجراج / قیمت یک لک روپیه
Likeness of 'Alam Kaman Gajraj (the arrogant one of the earth, king of elephants), whose value is one *lakh* [100,000 rupees]

The famous elephant immortalized here fell into the hands of the army led by Prince Khurram, the future Shah Jahan (r. 1627–58), during the Mughal campaign to annex the maharana of Mewar's territories. Along with seventeen other elephants from Mewar, 'Alam Kaman was presented to Emperor Jahangir (r. 1605–27) on March 21, 1614, during the celebration marking the commencement of the ninth year of his reign. In his memoirs, the emperor makes mention of his pleasure: "On the second day of the New Year, knowing it propitious for a ride, I mounted ['Alam Kaman] and scattered about much money."[1]

Another portrait of 'Alam Kaman in the National Museum, New Delhi, depicts him on cloth, with a number of his calves.[2] The more informal presentation suggests an earlier date in the Jahangir period, although the practice of identifying the subject with an inscription between its legs, characteristic of Shah Jahan–period elephant portraits, is already in place.[3] An image of the royal elephant Mahabir Deb is similar in pose and layout to this work and bears an inscription comparable in style and formula, which has been attributed to Shah Jahan, and on the basis of which this inscription, in its gold cartouche, is also believed to be by the emperor's hand.[4]

The present portrait conveys the monumentality of the animal both in the contrasting size of its rider and in the sober coloring of its dark body. The face and trunk are sensitively handled, and particular attention is paid to the luxurious trappings, which are typical on formal portraits of royal elephants; here, they include medallion- and leaf-shaped pendentives, a jeweled headdress, tusk bands, and a bell on a heavy chain of long, closely set links affixed around the elephant's middle. Bichitr is best known for his portraits of human royals dating to the 1630s, but he also captured animal likenesses on paper.[5] Among his works from that period is one showing Prince Dara Shikuh on an albino elephant.[6]

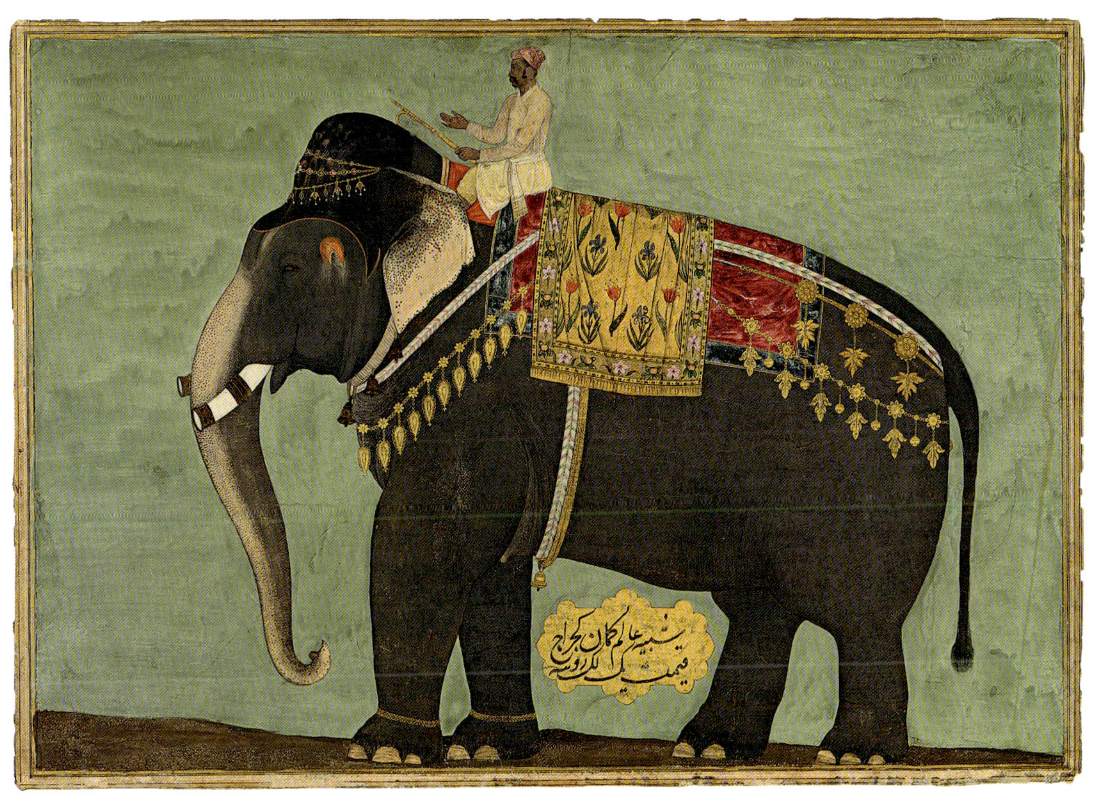

Elephants were among the most prized possession of the Mughal, Deccani, and Rajput courts and were central to Indian culture. While portraits of individual elephants were known from the period of Akbar (r. 1556–1605), it was under Shah Jahan's patronage that a formula for elephant portraits was established, in which the beast, sometimes shown with rider, dominates the composition, filling the picture space, and in which an accompanying inscription gives its name, its value, and, occasionally, how it was acquired.[7] These images may have served as a visual inventory of the elephant stables, but their production also falls into the broader Mughal practice of meticulously recording the treasures of the court. The enduring popularity of the genre is demonstrated by the rich range of elephant portraits that continued to be produced in the post-Mughal period in almost every major Indian painting tradition.[8] NNH

1. Jahangir 1909–14, vol. 1, p. 260; Jahangir 1999, pp. 156–57.
2. New York 1963–64, p. 36.
3. Das 1999 discusses this subject and also illustrates the National Museum's portrait of 'Alam Kaman (p. 46, fig. 10).
4. London and other cities 1983, fig. 17.
5. Williamstown, Mass., Baltimore, Boston, and New York 1978–79, pp. 101–2, for a discussion of Bichitr.
6. Ibid., fig. 33.
7. London, Washington, D.C., Zurich, and Oxford 1991–93, p. 36 n. 4, for a list of related important imperial Mughal elephants; Williamstown, Mass., Baltimore, Boston, and New York 1978–79, p. 105 n. 4.
8. Sotheby's New York, September 20, 2005, p. 88, lot 101, attributed to Mihr Chand or Bahadur Singh at Lucknow, ca. 1770, shows an elephant wearing very similar jewelry.

PROVENANCE: [Terence McInerney, New York, until 1996; sold to MMA]

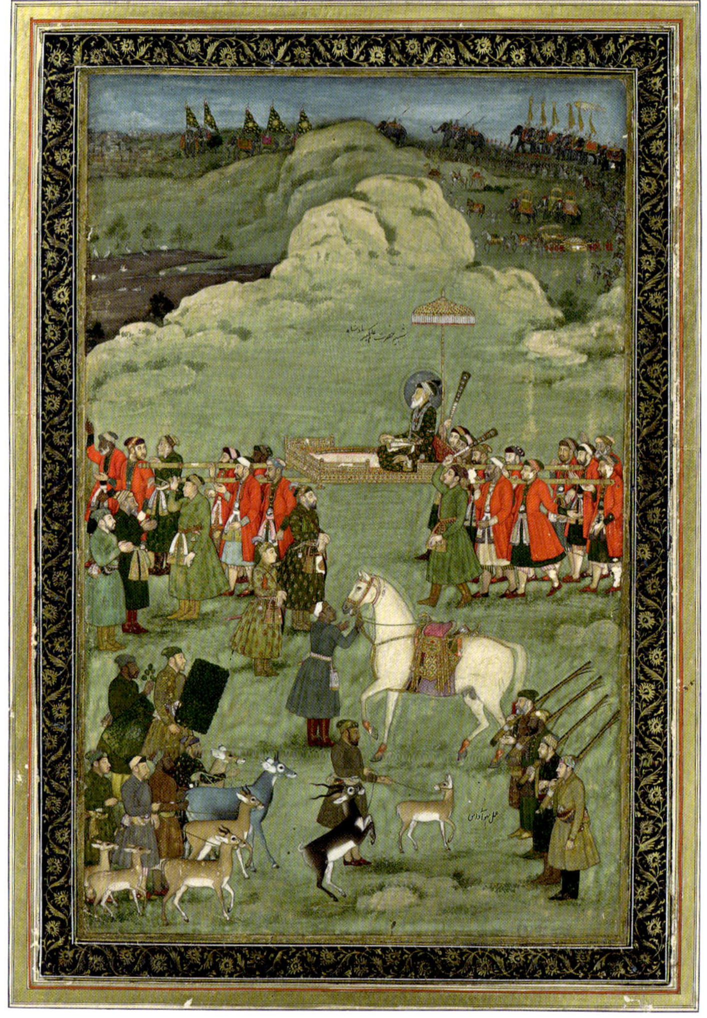

252. The Emperor Aurangzeb Carried on a Palanquin

Painter: Bhavanidas (active ca. 1700–48)
India, ca. 1705–20
Opaque watercolor and gold on paper
22⅞ × 15⅛ in. (58.1 × 38.4 cm)
Louis V. Bell Fund, 2003 2003.430

Inscriptions in Persian in *nasta'liq* script at center:
شبیه حضرت عالم گیر پادشاه
The likeness of his majesty the Emperor 'Alamgir

Below horse:
عمل بهوانی داس
Work of Bhavanidas

In faint gold in front of first four attendants carrying imperial palanquin:
عمل بهوانی داس
Work of Bhavanidas

This elaborate hunting scene depicting the emperor Aurangzeb (r. 1658–1707) and his hunting party is among the last imperial subjects of such grandeur created at the close of the age of the great Mughals. The artist is the master Bhavanidas, who spent his early career at the Mughal court and moved to the Rajput court of Kishangarh in 1719.[1] The inscription in black ink identifies the subject and the artist; there is also a hidden signature in pale gold against the green middle ground.[2]

The multitiered composition shows the Mughal emperor seated on a gilded palanquin held aloft by numerous red-coated attendants, among whom are two noblemen in green (whose similar beardless faces suggest a familial relationship) serving as symbolic bearers in a show of respect. All the figures are treated with great individualism, and the lavish background parade includes a *mahi-o-maratib*, or fish ensign, held up high—a signature detail that Bhavanidas included in several other works.[3] Standing before the emperor are a Mughal prince (possibly his son and successor, Bahadur Shah I; r. 1707–12) and the prince's son, while the foreground contains a line of readied hunters and deer. Bhavanidas's sensitive handling of the ethereal white horse in the middle ground heralds his interest in equine subjects, which became a particular specialty of his at Kishangarh. The painting is notable for its degree of detail and observation, expressed, for example, in the costumes and weapons, facial characterizations, and richly filled background. The dramatic rocky landscape indicates that the scene is likely to have been set in some part of the Deccan, where the emperor devoted the last twenty-six years of his life to the pursuit of regional conquests.

Although treating a Mughal subject, the painting relates more closely to Bhavanidas's later work at Kishangarh in terms of its greater naturalism, softer palette, smaller figures, and more sensitive detailing, as seen particularly in comparison with an illustration of the *Rukmini mangala* of about 1720–25.[4] The hunting scene also relates to a posthumous portrait of Maharaja Sahasmal of Kishangarh (r. 1615–18) that has been attributed to Bhavanidas, in which a similar composition shows rows of hunters in the foreground, a comparable palette, and an elaborate background.[5] The figure style here, however, is markedly different, with more stylized and attenuated forms. The present work may have been made at the very end of Aurangzeb's life or during the brief reign of Bahadur Shah I, perhaps for Raj Singh of Kishangarh (r. 1706–48) while the artist was still in service at the Mughal court; therefore, the span of possible dates for its execution could range from about 1705 to 1720. NNH

1. The artist and his career are discussed in more detail by the author in Haidar 1995 and in Beach, Fischer, and Goswamy, eds. 2011.
2. The presence of this signature was first noted by John Seyller (personal communication). See also Haidar in Beach, Fischer, and Goswamy, eds. 2011, vol. 2, p. 537.
3. Irvine 1903, pp. 31–33. The term is translatable as "fish and dignities." The ensign is usually made in the shape of a fish, four feet in length, and fixed horizontally on a pole. It can be accompanied by gilded balls, silk trimmings, or the image of a man's head.
4. Archer, W. 1960, pl. 59; Dickinson 1949, p. 35; Sumahendra 1995, among endplates.
5. Dickinson and Khandalavala 1959, p. 35, pl. 8.

PROVENANCE: Ardeshir family, Mumbai, India, and London, England; [Terence McInerney, New York, until 2003; sold to MMA]

253. *A Gathering of Holy Men of Different Faiths*

Painter: Mir Kalan Khan (active ca. 1730–80)
India, Lucknow, ca. 1770–75
Opaque watercolor and gold on paper
10½ × 7½ in. (26.7 × 19.1 cm)
Purchase, Friends of Islamic Art Gifts, 2009 2009.318

Inscription in Persian in *nasta'liq* script in front of central figure:
عمل میر میران
Work of the Lord of Lords

Based on a well-known work of about 1655 in the Victoria and Albert Museum, London, this painting presents an established theme in Mughal painting: a mystical gathering of holy men of different faiths.[1] In the present composition, most of the figures were copied directly from the London painting and, on the basis of inscriptions on the earlier work, they can be identified as (from left to right) Kabir, the great early fifteenth-century mystic, poet, and social reformer; Kamal, the son of Kabir; Aughar, a follower of Gorakhnath; Namdev, a late fourteenth-century devotee of Vitobha from Maharashtra; Sena, a barber who performed menial tasks for holy men; and Ravidas (active ca. 1470), a cobbler from Varanasi and the guru of Mirabai. The saints are accompanied by

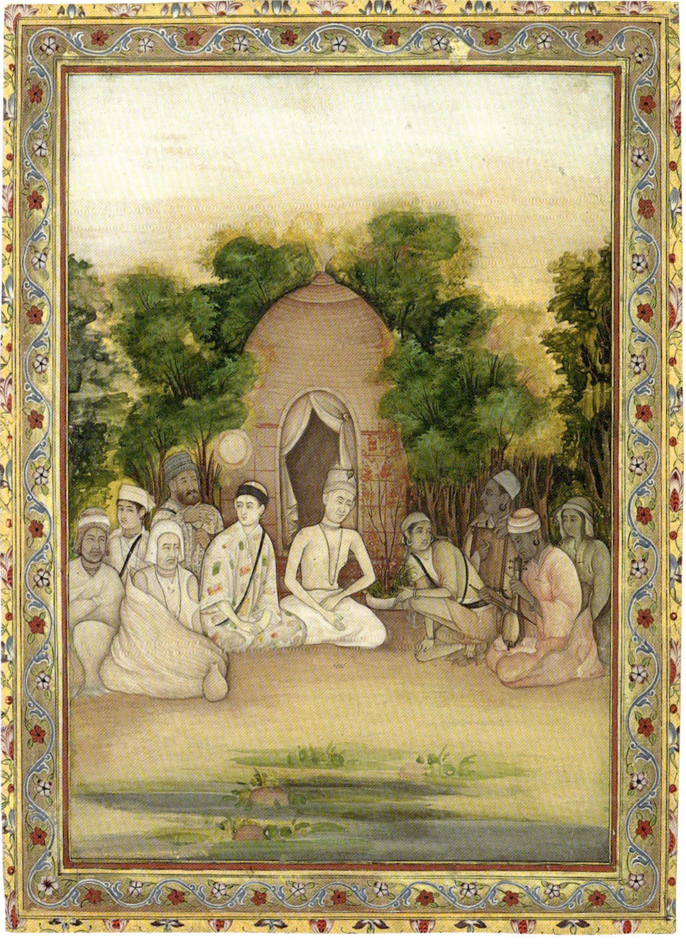

four *chelas* (followers) playing musical instruments (these figures are based only loosely on the earlier painting).

Among the most influential and individualistic painters of the eighteenth century, Mir Kalan Khan first came to prominence in the 1730s as one of the painters in the employ of Muhammad Shah at Delhi (r. 1719–48). The disarray in the Mughal capital after the invasion of Nadir Shah in 1739 compelled many artists to abandon the court; evidence shows that Mir Kalan Khan left Delhi for Lucknow, although the exact date of his departure is not known.[2] At Faizabad and Lucknow, he became the leading court painter of the nawabs Shuja' al-Daula (r. 1754–75) and Asaf al-Daula (r. 1775–97), producing a substantial body of work in an eclectic style that was widely imitated.

Mir Kalan Khan incorporated Europeanizing elements into both his motifs and his technique, as is apparent here in the washy watercolor background. His distinctive handling of foliage and light effects may be seen in the softly rendered trees and the golden sky behind them. His subjects range from gatherings in bucolic settings to copies of Deccani paintings and elements from European prints, sometimes with his own additions, as in this case.[3] The title "Lord of Lords" was likely awarded to him late in his career; its inclusion here, probably by a court scribe, is a sign of distinction for the work.

NNH

1. Gadon 1986, pp. 155–57.
2. Leach 1998, pp. 168–69.
3. R. W. Skelton, personal communication: judging by Mir Kalan's interest in and access to Deccani works, his father may have been a Deccani artist.

PROVENANCE: Private collection, England (ca. 1960); [Terence McInerney, New York, until 2009; sold to MMA]

254. *Princesses Gather at a Fountain*

India, Farrukhabad, ca. 1770
Opaque watercolor and gold on paper
9 × 13⅝ in. (22.9 × 34.6 cm)
Cynthia Hazen Polsky and Leon B. Polsky Fund, 2001 2001.421

Scenes of courtly pleasure, garden settings, and long-legged female figures dressed in high-waisted, flowing *angarkhas* typify paintings attributed to the northern Indian court of Farrukhabad. A cultural satellite of Lucknow, Farukkhabad, under the rule of the Rohilla chieftains of the Bangash tribe, developed the influential Avadhi idiom into its own stylistic expression, which flourished during the later part of the eighteenth century. The painting style at Farrukhabad essentially grew from the distinctive hands of Muhammad Faqirullah Khan and Faizullah Khan, who painted at Lucknow and Faizabad in the third quarter of the eighteenth century.[1]

The present work depicts twelve courtly ladies and a child gathered around a fountain. A partial view of a palace is seen at the left, with a canopy extending over the fountain and some of the figures. The principal woman seems to have been introduced into the painting from a model in which the figure would have been seated on a chair, but little care was taken to adapt it to its present use. She therefore rests somewhat awkwardly on the edge of the fountain, with a hand and a foot extended into the water. An open background of rolling hills, trees, and a lake contains numerous birds and animals, mostly in pairs, as is typical in Indian painting. The necks of the swans are looped around each other in a feature that is sometimes seen in Deccani painting.[2] The

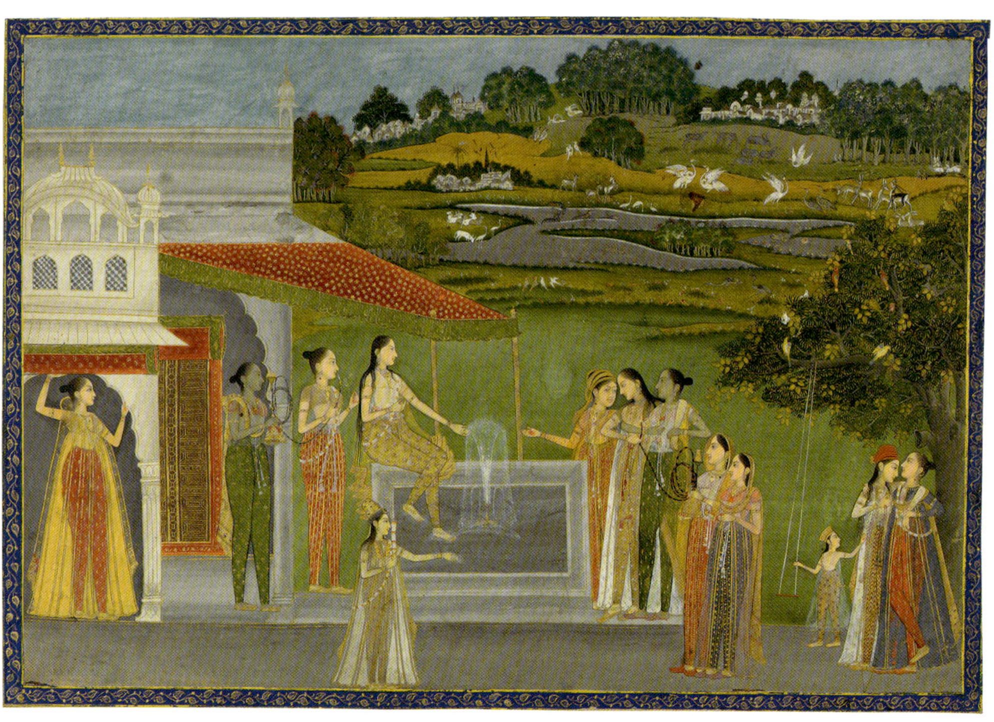

composition may be connected to a larger group that includes a similar painting in the India Office Library (now in the British Library, London) and another in the Los Angeles County Museum of Art.[3] The India Office Library folio has been identified as part of a *ragamala* (musical modes) series. That classification is, however, less suited to the present work, which, although stylistically similar, does not bear inscribed or obvious iconographical evidence of being such an illustration. NNH

1. Leach 1995, pp. 618–19, fig. 6.354.
2. This feature can apply to trees as well as birds, as seen in a *Futuh al-haramain* manuscript in the Metropolitan Museum (acc. no. 2008.251), in which the imagery is probably connected to descriptions in the text.
3. Falk and Archer 1981, no. 362, pl. 11; Los Angeles County Museum of Art painting (no. M.87.278.9), published on that museum's website.

PROVENANCE: [Natesan Galleries Ltd., London, until 2001; sold to MMA]

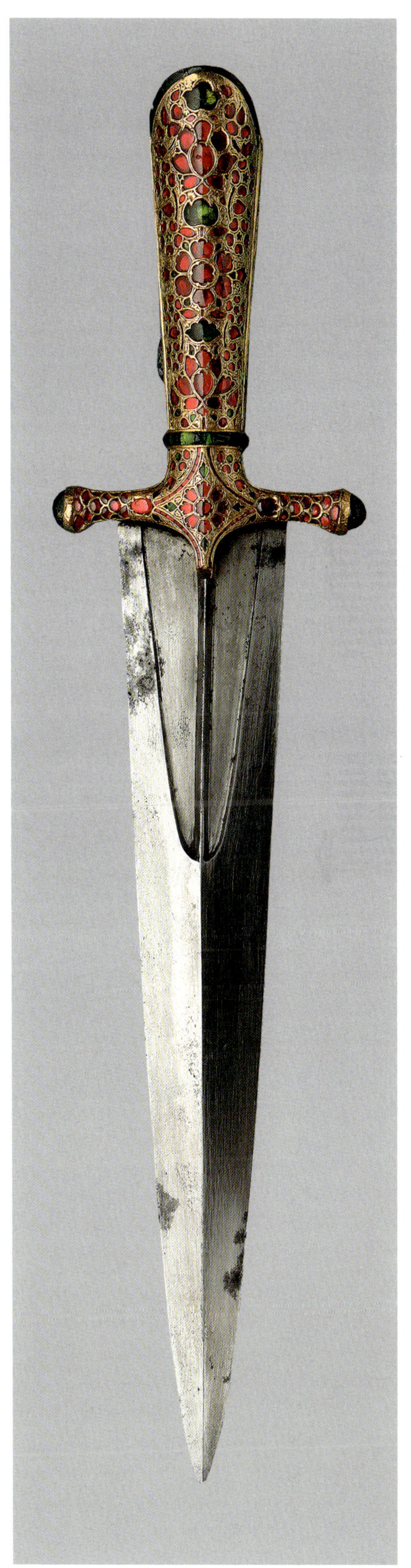

255. *Dagger*

Northern India, ca. 1605–27
Blade: crucible steel; hilt: gold, rubies, colored glass
Length overall: 14 in. (35.4 cm); blade: 9⅛ in. (23.2 cm)
Purchase, Harris Brisbane Dick Fund and The Vincent Astor Foundation Gift, 1984 1984.332

Dagger hilts such as this one, in the form of a split pommel, first appear in imperial Mughal painting of the early seventeenth century and are also seen in Deccani painting by the end of that century.[1] The motifs in the hilt of the dagger and in the chape of the scabbard include stylized lotuses and medallion blossoms, with scale-like elements along the quillon. Slender lines of green and red gems in channel settings along the edges, borders, and in the field are among the distinguishing features of the ornamentation.

This jeweled dagger belongs to a group of objects attributed to the workshops of the Mughal emperors Jahangir (r. 1605–27) and Shah Jahan (r. 1627–58). These pieces are characterized by the distinctive style and technique of the *kundan* setting of the gems, whereby their flattened surface is flush on all sides with the surrounding gold ground.[2] In this technique gold is purified until it becomes malleable at room temperature, at which point the gemstones can be pushed into place relatively easily. Also, as is typical of this style, the surface gold between the stones is incised with scrolls, foliate ornament, and the figures of birds and animals.

The group includes a ceremonial spoon and an archer's thumb ring in the Victoria and Albert Museum, London, and a dagger with jeweled hilt in the Dar al-Athar al-Islamiyya, al-Sabah Collection, Kuwait City, among others.[3]

A portrait of Jahangir of about 1615 wearing a similar, if not the same, dagger as the example in the Kuwait collection provides evidence for dating this group of jeweled works to his period.[5] Given its technique and high quality, it seems most likely that the present dagger is also from his royal workshop.[6] DGA/NNH

1. See, for example, daggers of this type in a miniature painting of about 1680 from Bijapur in the Deccan; New York 1985–86, p. 310, no. 208 (acc. no. 1982.213).
2. Described by Manuel Keene in London and other cities 2001, p. 18; see also Keene 2004.
3. The daggers include one each in the Dar al-Athar al-Islamiyya, Kuwait City, al-Sabah Collection (no. LNS 25 J; see New York 1985–86, p. 198, no. 127; and London and other cities 2001, pp. 56–57, fig. 5.2), the Wallace Collection, London (no. OA 1409; see Norman 1982, p. 12, no. 2), and the British Museum, London; the locket from the scabbard of a punch dagger, also in the al-Sabah Collection (no. LNS XIX SH; see London and other cities 2001, pp. 56–57, fig. 5.1); and the spoon and thumb ring in the Victoria and Albert Museum, London (nos. I.M. 173.1910 and I.M. 207-1920; see New York 1985–86, pp. 200–201, nos. 128–29; and Bradford and London 1988–89, no. 93). A related but probably slightly later piece is a pendant in the British Museum (no. OA. 14178; see ibid., no. 63). Also related are another dagger (with associated scabbard) in the State Hermitage Museum, St. Petersburg (no. OR-452), recorded in the Treasury of Peter I in 1730, and a bracelet and an archer's ring (nos. VZ-720 and VZ-703) presented as gifts from Nadir Shah in 1741 and certainly booty from his conquest of Delhi in 1739 (see Kuwait 1990, nos. 112, 95, and 93, respectively). Manuel Keene (London and other cities 2001, p. 56) attributed the group to the early seventeenth century by comparison with an archer's ring.
4. London and other cities 2001, pp. 56–57.
5. New York 1987–88, p. 110, no. 16.
6. See, for example, the *Padshahnama* of Jahangir in New Delhi and other cities 1997–98, pls. 12, 24, 37, 39.

PROVENANCE: Private sale, Sotheby Parke-Bernet, New York, 1984; to David Wille for MMA

256A–E. Coins with Signs of the Zodiac

India, Agra, 1619–25
Gold
Diam. ca. 7/8 in. (21 mm)
Bequest of Joseph H. Durkee, 1898

A. Taurus, dated A.H. 1028, 14th regnal year (April 20–May 20, 1619) 99.35.7402

B. Leo, dated A.H. 1033, 19th regnal year (July 23–August 22, 1624) 99.35.7403

C. Libra, dated A.H. 1034, 19th regnal year (September 23–October 22, 1625) 99.35.6552

D. Capricorn, dated A.H. 1031, 16th regnal year (December 22, 1621–January 19, 1622)[1] 99.35.7401

E. Pisces, dated A.H. 1028, 13th regnal year (February 19–March 20, 1619) 99.35.2391

Inscription in Persian in *nasta'liq* script on obverse of each coin:
یافت در اگره روی زر زیور از جهانگیر شاه، شاه اکبر
The face of gold was decorated in Agra by Jahangir Shah, [son of] Shah Akbar.[1]

These gold coins were minted in India during the reign of the Mughal emperor Jahangir (r. 1605–27). On the reverse of each there is an image of the constellation corresponding to the month of issue, and on the obverse a poetic inscription, a number for the year of Jahangir's reign, and the corresponding year in the *hijra* calendar.[2] The Metropolitan Museum owns ten of these rare coins, five gold and five silver; shown here are the gold *mohurs* corresponding to the months Urdibihisht (Taurus), Murdad (Leo), Mihr (Libra), Day (Capricorn), and Isfand (Pisces).[3]

Jahangir took a strong interest in the coins to be minted during his reign, specifying their names, denominations, weights, and inscriptions. In his memoirs, one can find mention of several decrees he issued regarding the designs of new coins,[4] including the following, which relates to his decision in April 1618 to create this unique issue:

> Prior to this, it has been the rule that on one side of gold coins my name has been engraved, and on the other side the name of the minting place, the month, and the regnal year. Around this time it occurred to me that instead of the month a figure of the constellation representing the month should be depicted. For example, for the month of Farvardin a figure of Aries could be made, and for the month of Urdibihisht the figure of Taurus, and so on for every month in which a coin was minted, one side would bear a picture of the constellation in which the sun rose. This method is peculiarly my own and has never been used before.[5]

There are slight variations in the zodiac coins issued between 1618 and 1625 (when production stopped), which indicates that different dies were used to strike them.

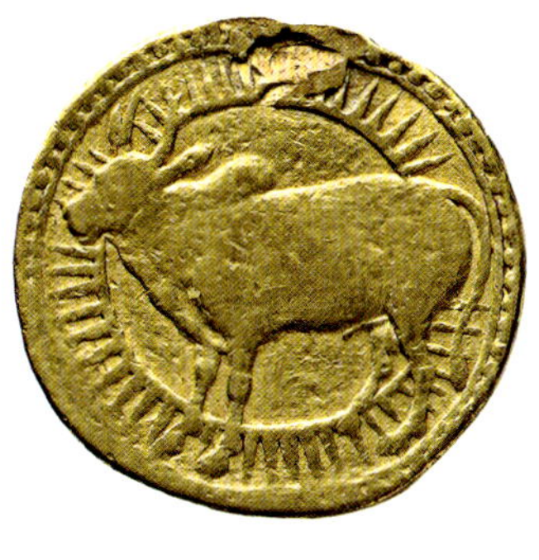

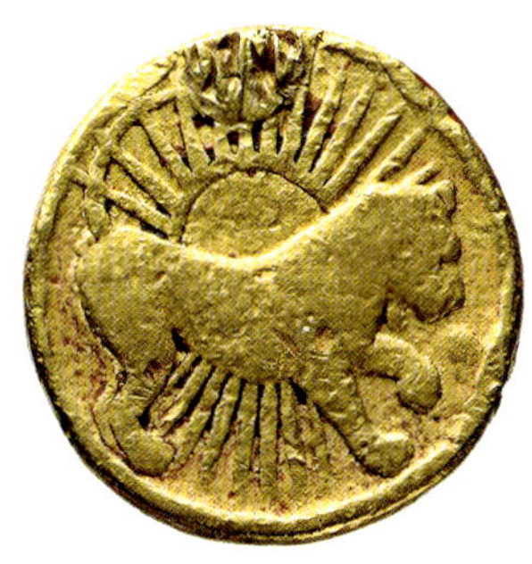

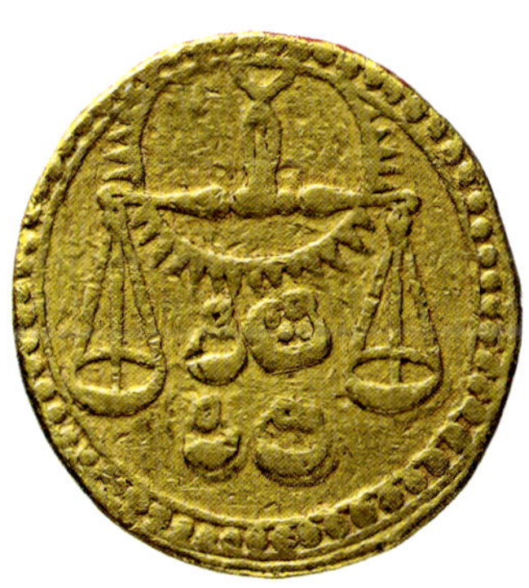

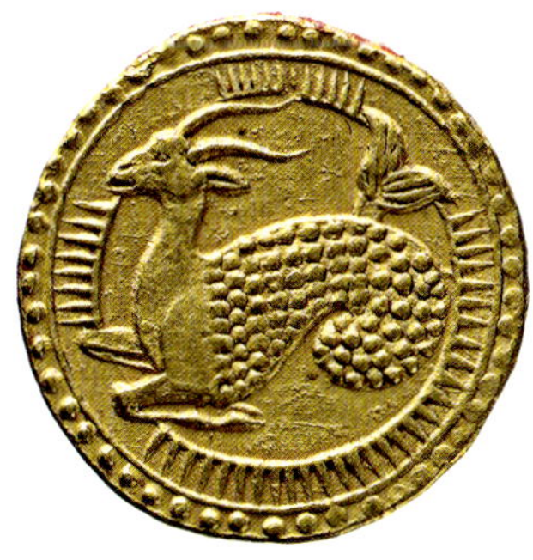

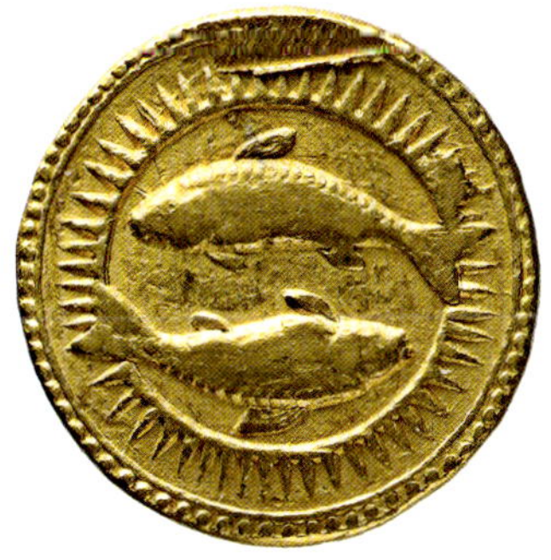

These coins are quite unusual in the context of both Indian and Islamic numismatics because those issued by Muslim rulers tend to have no figural decoration, and no other Indian coins have astrological imagery. Together with the portrait and figural coins issued during Jahangir's reign, these specimens provide a fascinating complement to the other works of art related to this emperor's exacting patronage. MS

1. Translation from Codrington 1904, p. 108.
2. The dates provided here differ slightly from those given in earlier publications because determining exact Gregorian equivalents for the dates that appear on Jahangir's zodiac coins is complicated by several factors. The dies used to create them were reused over several years, and the regnal and *hijra* years were not always accurately or identically updated. In addition, the coins appear to have been minted in each city only when Jahangir was present; therefore the obverse and reverse dies were sometime incorrectly matched to keep up with his itinerant schedule. See Kulkarni 2004.
3. Other examples are held by the British Museum, London; the Nationalmuseet, Copenhagen; the National Museum, New Delhi; the Indian Museum, Kolkata; and the State Museum, Lucknow.
4. See, for instance, Jahangir 1999, pp. 27, 123–24, 241.
5. Ibid., p. 260.

Provenance: Joseph H. Durkee, New York (until d. 1898)

257. Mango-Shaped Flask

India, mid-17th century
Rock crystal; set with gold, enamel, rubies, and emeralds
H. 2 1/2 in. (6.5 cm)
Purchase, Mrs. Charles Wrightsman Gift, 1993 1993.18

During India's Mughal period, the jeweled arts were greatly patronized by the ruling family and nobility who often appear in paintings holding or handling precious objects. Various exquisite rock-crystal inlaid objects were created for courtly use, with a notable group surviving in a private collection in Kuwait.[1] Mughal taste for such treasures had deep roots: in India, carved and polished rock crystal had been used from ancient times to create Buddhist and Hindu religious artifacts. Within an Islamic context, hardstone carving of vessels and luxury items also had a long tradition in parts of the Near East.

This diminutive curved flask is created by two halves of rock crystal fitted together to form its body and held in place in part by a cage of meandering scrolls in gold wire.[2] The finely balanced, elegantly drawn arabesques, inset with rubies and emeralds in gold mounts, recall the Mughal debt to Safavid Iran, where similar networks of scrolling vines with palmettes, blossoms, and

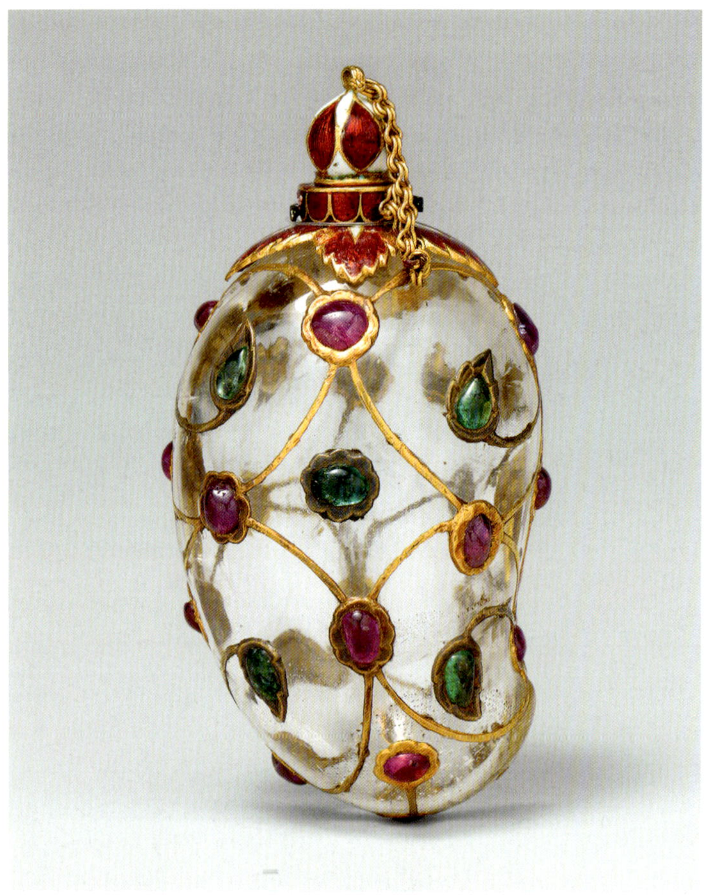

leaves were in vogue in the sixteenth century, although in different media, including tilework and illumination. The Mughal penchant for natural shapes is demonstrated in the mango-shaped profile of the bottle and in the bud form of the enamel stopper. Red leaves on a white background create the decoration on the stopper, and a delicate gold chain connects it to the collar.

The bottle may have been meant to hold lime, an ingredient of *pan*, a mildly intoxicating narcotic popularly used in India. Alternatively, this object may have been used as a container for perfume, which was worn by both men and women in the Mughal period. Two other rock-crystal flasks (one recorded in 1690) of this shape and size are known in European collections.[3] In other media, a mango-shaped *bidri*-ware flagon and a silver flask are comparable vessels.[4] The gently curving mango shape also appears widely as a repeating motif in textile patterns. NNH

1. London and other cities 2001, pp. 32–33, nos. 2.5–2.8.
2. Published: Walker, D. 1993; Mexico City 1994–95, pp. 240–41.
3. Folsach 2011, p. 238, fig. 370, p. 332, fig. 537; also in Boston and Chicago 2006–7, p. 171, no. 96; Leatham 2000, p.170, recorded in 1690.
4. New York 2004–5, p. 239 and n. 2, no. 99, for a silver and fabric example; Folsach 2011, p. 332, fig. 537.

PROVENANCE: [Spink & Son Ltd., London, until 1993; sold to MMA]

258. Bowl with Bud Handles

Central Asia, second half of 18th century
Nephrite; carved
H. 2⅝ in. (6.7 cm); W. at handles 8½ in. (21.6 cm); Diam. of rim 6¾ in. (17.1 cm), of foot 2¾ in. (7 cm)
Gift of Heber R. Bishop, 1902 02.18.762

This cup is carved from translucent green jade (nephrite) in what is generally known as the Mughal style. Each of its lobed sides bears a leaf (a simplified version of the acanthus) at the bottom. Two of the leaves, at opposite sides, rise to meet hanging buds that form lugs for the cup. The carved decoration on the base is in the shape of a chrysanthemum. On the upper part of the exterior is inscribed a poem, dated 1771, by the Qianlong emperor (r. 1736–95) of the Qing dynasty of China, that may be translated as follows:

This bowl of chrysanthemum pattern from Hindustan,[1] measuring
about a foot across and more than three feet around,[2]
Is fashioned in a style different from that of our ancient work.[3]
The handles hang down suspended like two swelling buds
And the foot is carved beneath with serried ranks of petals.
Such offerings come to us not only as tribute from Yülong,[4]
There is constant traffic along Quxu [or Qu and Xu].[5]
The chrysanthemum is still, as of old, the flower of the autumn holiday.
And this is a fitting gift for Yuanming[6] in his five-willow retreat.

In 1755 the Qianlong emperor initiated a series of military campaigns in eastern Turkestan, first in Ili, north of the Tianshan Mountains, and later in the Muslim region of Kashgaria.[7] The territories newly gained for the Qing empire included the cities of Yarkand and Khotan, each by a river running down the northern slope of the Kunlun Mountains, the chief sources of jade for all of Asia. In these areas there was also a tradition of jade working that can be traced ultimately to Iranian and Chinese origins. For want of archaeological evidence, it is not known when this tradition started. In more recent centuries, the craft of jade working, or the craftsmen themselves, migrated to serve the Timurids and afterward the Mughals of India. And it was at the Mughal court in the seventeenth century that the tradition of Central Asian jade carving reached its highest artistic and technical expression. When the Mughal court rapidly declined in the second half of the eighteenth century, the Central Asian jade carvers found new customers—the Chinese, and the Chinese emperor in particular.

From 1756, a year after the beginning of Qianlong's campaigns in Central Asia, large quantities of jade boulders and pebbles began to arrive in interior China together with a number of carved jades, most of which entered the emperor's collection as tribute. This would continue through the reign of Jiaqing (1796–1820). The present cup is among the most common types of jade objects sent as tribute to the Qing court. About a dozen pieces of this type are known from publications, and all can be ascribed to the

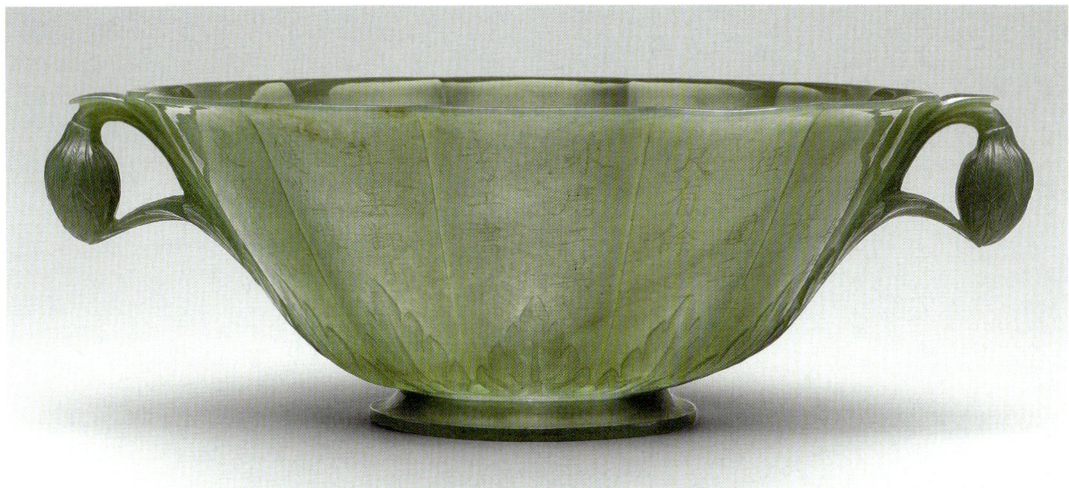

Mughal style, as the craftsmen continued to work in the fashion favored by Mughal rulers of the previous century. Pieces that arrived later at the Qing court, during the Jiaqing reign, would show some Chinese influence.

After about 1820, tributes of jades ceased to arrive at the Qing court, mainly because of political and economic developments in Central Asia but also because of the impoverishment of the Qing court. There remain a total of about eight hundred jades from Central Asia in the Palace Museum, including pieces in Beijing and Taiwan. This collection provides a unique and well-documented record of jade carving in Central Asia for a seventy-year period, from about 1750 to 1820.[8]

Nearly all Mughal-style jade carvings are ornamented with vegetal motifs, of which the acanthus and the "chrysanthemum" are among the commonest. Jade craftsmen in India, particularly those working for the imperial Mughal court, were masters at exploiting the translucency of jade to special effect. This element remained a characteristic of jade working in Muslim Central Asia even after the decline of Mughal patronage, as can be seen in the present example. JCYW

1. Transcribed phonetically by the four characters *Hen du si tan*.
2. This poem might have been originally written for another, much larger piece that also bore the "chrysanthemum" motif on the base, as commonly seen on Mughal-style jade cups.
3. Literally, "from that of the Kao gongji," the name of the ancient book on handicrafts of the late Zhou dynasty (ca. fifth–third century B.C.).
4. Contraction of Y'urung Kash, a river of Khotan in Chinese Turkestan.
5. In Qianlong's own annotation, this is a reference to "Hindustan, beyond the Hindu Kush."
6. Tao Yuanming (365–427), a Chinese pastoral poet known for his love of chrysanthemums.
7. For a brief account of Qianlong's campaigns in eastern Turkestan, see Fletcher 1968, pp. 218–24, 358–68.
8. For a detailed study of the Islamic jade collection in these museums, see see Teng 2004.

PROVENANCE: Heber R. Bishop, New York (until 1902)

259. Pair of Flower-Style Doors

Northern India, second half of 17th century
Wood; carved with residues of paint
73 × 30 × 3 in. (185.4 × 76.2 × 7.6 cm)
Gift of Harvey and Elizabeth Plotnick, 2009 2009.376a, b

The flower style associated with the height of Mughal taste finds expression in this pair of carved-wood doors with alternating square and rectangular panels that have cusped cartouches enclosing flowering plants. A frieze of stylized leaf motifs borders the top and outer edges of the doors, and individual floral medallions decorate the astragal(?) that covers their junction. The doors turn on hooks that extend from iron straps attached across each leaf and fit into sockets on the surrounding frame; they probably also had pivots at the bottom, now missing.

The use of complete flowering plants as a decorative motif appears to have had its genesis in works on paper produced during the reign of Jahangir (r. 1605–27). In 1620 the emperor requested that his artist Mansur paint the many types of flowers he observed in Kashmir (see also cat. 264). The three surviving studies by Mansur show such strong affinities with European botanical studies that it is very likely that he and the other Mughal artists who later took up this theme were using them as a model. Herbals known to have been presented by European visitors to the Mughal court are usually identified as the source of inspiration.[1] Flowering plants were also used to decorate the borders of album pages—and for these another source has been recently suggested, namely, royal English charters, which were also decorated with flowering plants.[2]

Sometime during the reign of Jahangir's son Shah Jahan (r. 1627–58), the plant studies were transformed into decorative motifs and arranged in rows to cover textiles, carpets, luxury objects, and architectural spaces.[3] Individual plants carved in low relief are found in several buildings at the Agra Fort (such as the

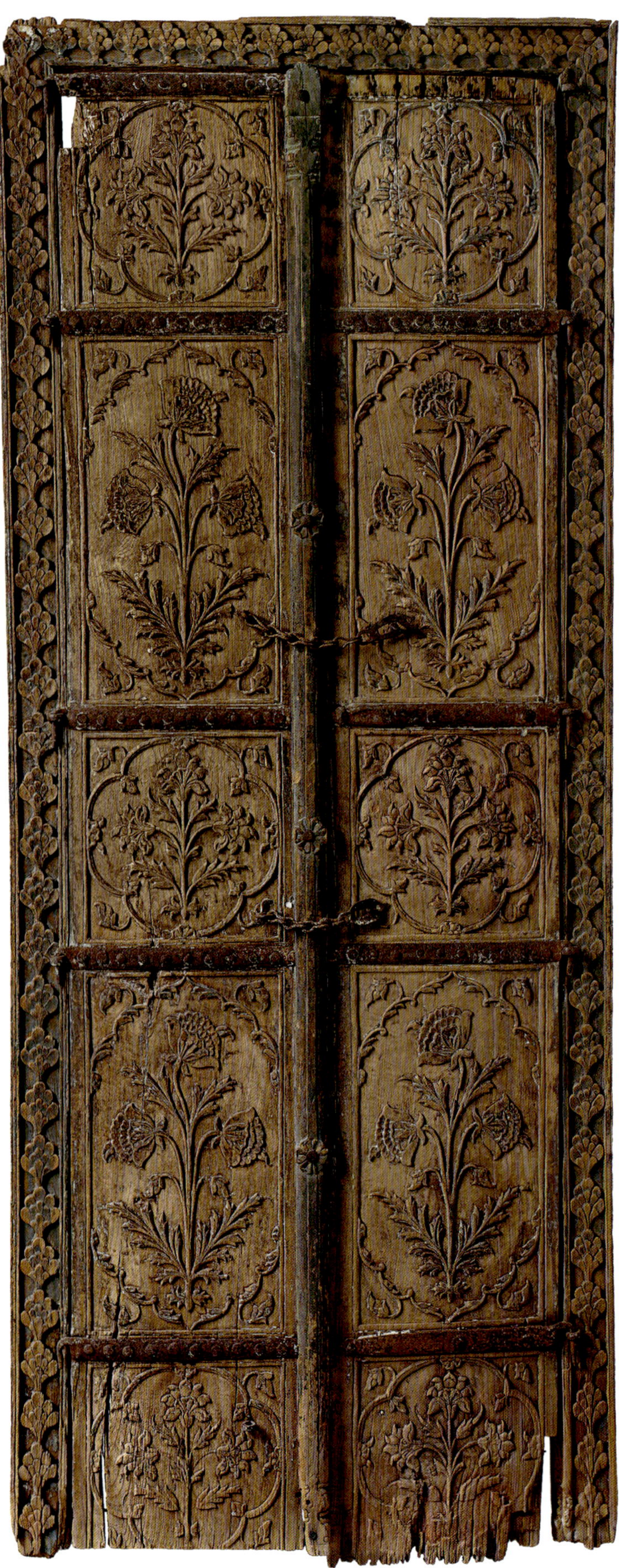

Mussaman Burj, the Shah Burj, the Diwan-i Khas, and on the *jharoka* of the Diwan-i 'Am) as well as in the tomb, mosque, and Mihman Khana of the Taj Mahal complex.[4] Such features were also found at the contemporary palaces of the Rajput royal families, including the Shish Mahal at the Amber Fort. Doors with this motif are rare, however, perhaps known only from one other example in the David Collection, Copenhagen.[5] MS

1. This connection was first made in Skelton 1972a, pp. 147–52. Vivian Rich later identified the European books known to be in India during the period of Jahangir in Rich 1987.
2. Brend 2004.
3. Veronica Murphy, however, has suggested that the use of the flowering-plant motif on textiles may have been fashionable from the time of Jahangir, if not earlier (Murphy 1987). For a discussion in relation to carpet design, see New York 1997–98, pp. 87–117.
4. For the transfer of this motif to architecture, see Koch 2006, pp. 218–19.
5. David Collection, no. 15/1987.

PROVENANCE: Dr. William K. Ehrenfeld, San Francisco (until about 2002, to McInerney); [Terence McInerney, New York, about 2002–4; sold to Plotnick]; Elizabeth and Harvey Plotnick, Chicago (2004–9)

260. Panel with Rows of Flowers

India, mid-17th century
Silk, cut and voided velvet, with continuous floats of flat metal thread
65⅞ × 29⅞ in. (167.4 × 76 cm) overall
Rogers Fund, 1930 30.18 (upper fragment)
The Alice and Nasli Heeramaneck Collection, Gift of Alice Heeramaneck, 1991 1991.347.2 (lower fragment)

Velvets patterned with rows of flowers were employed in India from about 1630 on in the context of palace interiors, where blossoms were seen virtually everywhere—in wall paintings, marble panels and other elements decorated with *pietra dura* inlay, carved marble dado panels on walls, and furnishing fabrics.[1] Even the individuals who passed through these spaces were dressed and accessorized in accordance with the prevailing taste for the flower style. Velvets were prized as furnishing fabrics, used chiefly as hangings, window curtains, and floor-spreads. Lahore and Gujarat are known to have been production centers for velvet since the time of the emperor Akbar (r. 1556–1605),[2] and the material was probably also produced at royal workshops in the capital cities of Delhi and Agra.

This panel has a pattern of alternating rows of seminaturalistic roses and lilies. An additional fragment of the same fabric belongs to the Textile Museum, Washington, D.C.,[3] and a number of variations of this pattern type are also known.[4] Several small surviving

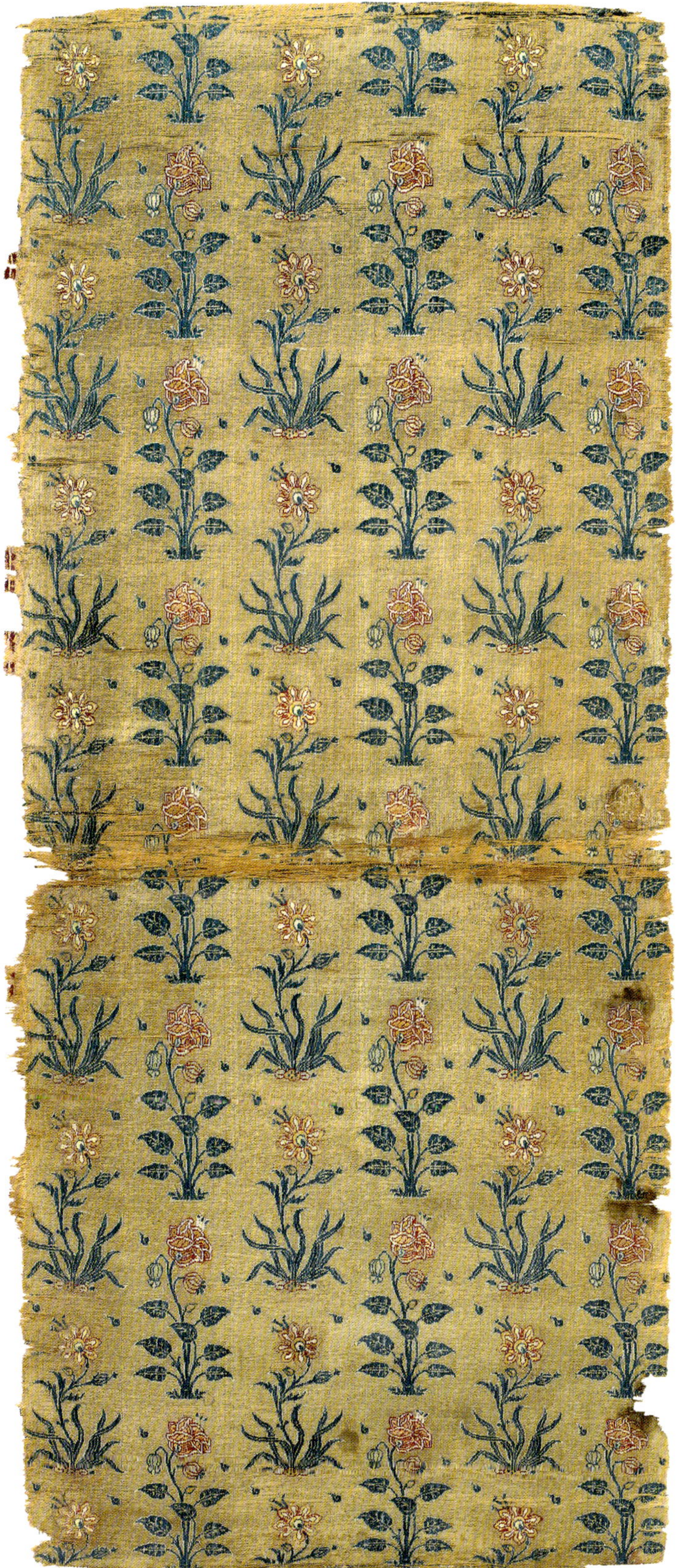

areas of original selvage, showing two red stripes, occur along the left edge. The satin ground in the areas lacking pile—now beige or pale golden yellow, but originally perhaps peach or pink from safflower—contain passes of flat (ungilt) silver strips, now turned black. These were woven with enough space separating them that the ground color would have shown through. The velvet pile has two whites, one bright, the other bluish, which are employed in such a way that subtle diagonal bands slanting down to the right are formed in the pattern. This velvet differs in several respects from Persian examples, even ones with similar patterning (see cat. 175). First, in terms of style and aesthetic, the flowers here do not shift direction from row to row even though the species change; the flowers are therefore inherently more naturalistic, while the pattern is more static. Second, in terms of structure, most noteworthy here is the use of flat metal strips instead of the thin metal sheet wrapped around a silk core found in Persian examples. These strips are passed from edge to edge, running behind the areas of pattern, because Indian weavers found this method more efficient.

The panel is made up of two pieces of velvet that fit together perfectly. By a remarkable stroke of luck, the second piece was donated in 1991 by Alice Heeramaneck, who had no knowledge of the existence of the contiguous piece, purchased from the dealer Joseph Brummer in 1930, which was already in the Metropolitan Museum's collection. DW

1. Two paintings from about 1635 that illustrate the impact of the flower style on Mughal palace interiors may be found in New Delhi and other cities 1997–98, folios 5 and 10.
2. Abu'l Fazl 'Allami 1977, vol. 1, pp. 98–99.
3. No. OC6.150, acquired by museum founder George Hewitt Myers in 1949 from Nasli Heeramaneck.
4. A classic variation is published in Spuhler 1978, pp. 202–3, no. 123. Another important example is the velvet railing hanging in the Chester Beatty Library, Dublin, illustrated in Smart 1986, p. 19, fig. 23. The Chester Beatty velvet bears an inscription indicating that the piece was first inventoried in Amber in February 1648.

Provenance

Acc. no. 30.18: [Brummer Gallery, Inc., New York, until 1930; sold to MMA]

Acc. no. 1991.347.2: The Alice and Nasli Heeramaneck Collection, New York (by 1963–91)

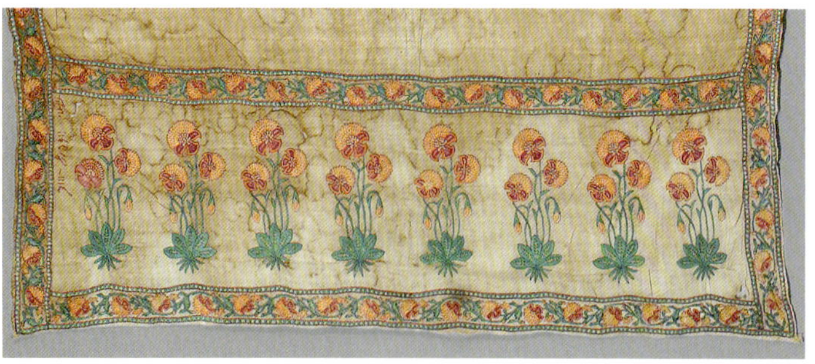

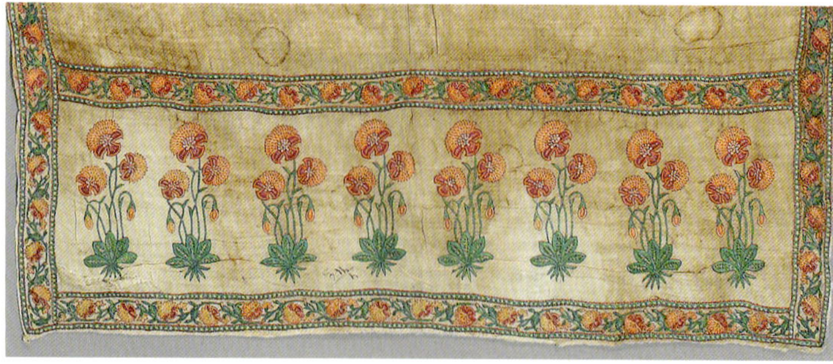

261. Waist Sash (Patka)

India, second half of 17th century
Cotton, silk; plain weave, embroidered
10 ft. 5 in. × 27 in. (317.5 × 68.6 cm)
The Alice and Nasli Heeramaneck Collection, Gift of Alice Heeramaneck, 1983 1983.494.9

The *patka*, an elaborate sash tied around the waist, was a distinctive piece of clothing worn by the Mughal emperors—and by those upon whom the emperors conferred it.[1] The word itself may come from either the Sanskrit *patta*, which means "a bandage, ligature, strip, fillet" of textile, or *pataka*, meaning "girdle, . . . ribbon, piece of cloth."[2] The evolution of the iconography of the *patka*'s decoration reached its zenith after the visit by Emperor Jahangir (r. 1605–27) to Kashmir in 1620. The emperor described this place as the "garden of eternal spring,"[3] and Kashmiri flowers inspired the decorations that became the distinctive element of all artistic Mughal expression, including *patka*,[4] during the reign of his son, Shah Jahan (1627–58).

This sash is representative of the production during Shah Jahan's reign. It is distinctive in its concentration of decoration on the end panels,[5] where a repeated sequence of eight identical poppylike flowers is found. The great naturalistic detail is evident in the thin roots at the bottom of the plant, which fan out below five mint green lanceolate leaves with creamy veining. Five slender intertwining stems rise from the leaves—three opening out into glorious red, pink, and orange corollas, each with a tiny green pistil surrounded by white stamens, and the remaining two bent over with their buds closed. The eight flowers are surrounded by a border with a flowing motif that repeats around the entire outline of the sash. The decoration features the same flowers on a smaller scale, between two narrow bands decorated with small cream-colored beading on a green background and bordered with a red line.[6] This white cotton plain-weave band runs the entire length of the sash. The decoration is embroidered in silk with satin, chain, and stem stitches.

The Mughal *patka* of the Shah Jahani type, with the end panels characteristically decorated with flowering plants on a plain ground, is also found in the Deccan late in the seventeenth century. A number of Deccani paintings of this time from Bijapur and Hyderabad portray figures wearing this type of *patka*.[7] The Mughal style seen here was held in great esteem and strongly influenced the nearby courts, reaching as far as the Rajput courts in Rajasthan and the Punjab Hills. EGM

1. These belts or girdles become in fact something of a marker, as noted in this passage relating to dress from Jahangir's *Tuzuk*: "Having adopted for myself certain special cloths and cloths-stuffs, I gave an order that no one should wear but he on whom I might bestow them" (Jahangir 1909–14, p. 384).
2. Goswamy and Jain 2002, p. 7.
3. Ibid., p. 44.
4. Okada 1995, pp. 5–6.
5. Goswamy and Jain 2002, p. 45.
6. Irwin and Hall 1973a, p. 201, provides a description of silk dyeing in Indian embroidery: "Indigo predominates as the basis for blue, but by double dyeing firstly in indigo and then in one of the many vegetable yellows a glowing dark green is achieved. . . . The range of reds and pink in silk-dyeing derive not from madder, but from *kermes*, a small insect of cochineal type which yields a crimson colorant of soft luminosity."
7. The *patkas* worn by both Muhammad 'Adil Shah and Ikhlas Khan in their double portrait, attributed to the third quarter of the seventeenth century (Los Angeles County Museum of Art), are undoubtedly "northern" (Goswamy and Jain 2002, p. 60, fig. 55). The same *patka* can be seen in portraits from Golconda/Hyderabad (ibid., pp. 62, 65, fig. 56).

PROVENANCE: The Alice and Nasli Heeramaneck Collection, New York (until 1983)

262. Carpet with Pictorial Design

Present-day Pakistan, Lahore, late 16th–early 17th century
Cotton (warp and weft), wool (pile); asymmetrically knotted pile
27 ft. 4 in. × 9 ft. (833.1 × 274.3 cm)
Gift of J. Pierpont Morgan, 1917 17.190.858

Although the advent of carpet weaving in India predates his reign, it was the Mughal emperor Akbar (r. 1556–1605) who established imperial workshops for carpets, as well as a pattern of royal patronage. Carpet workshops were set up first at Fatehpur Sikri, the imperial capital only from 1571 to 1585, then at Lahore and Agra, and then, before 1640, at Kashmir.[1] Not all Indian carpets surviving from these early times necessarily suggest imperial manufacture, so commercial workshops must also have been in full production. Masters and workmen, many undoubtedly Iranian, are known to have come to India to help establish the workshops, and Persian carpets also clearly continued to be imported despite the high quality of local production.[2]

It should not be surprising, then, that this large carpet, representing production dating from late in the reign of Akbar, displays strong Persian influence. The most popular Persian convention was the symmetrical arrangement of scrolling vines with blossoms and leaves, but another approach was the use of pictorial patterns similar to those produced for paintings in royal manuscripts (the two conventions are combined in some examples). The field pattern here combines animals, birds, and vegetation in a pictorial way, that is, they are meant to be seen from one direction and without the matrix of a vine-scroll pattern to connect everything. Pictorial designs can be found in Persian carpets in a few examples of the small "Kashan" rugs and even more in a couple of pieces of the "Sanguszko" group; direct contact of some sort is also implied by the use of certain colors. Counterparts of several animals represented here may be seen in one of the Museum's Persian rugs (cat. 182), notably the leaping ibex, the combat between lion and ibex, and the leaping lion. Flames at the shoulders, indicating supernatural qualities, betray the ultimate Chinese origin of some of these figures, as transmitted to Iran in preceding centuries.

In many respects, however, this carpet is unmistakably Indian. In terms of structure, the cotton warps are eight-ply instead of the four-ply typically found in Persian carpets. As for color, the palette has a brightness, especially in the red, lacking in most Persian pieces, and there is a heavy use of *ton-sur-ton* coloring, juxtaposing similar colors such as red and pink, light and dark blue, and ocher and beige or off-white. The interlocking compartment design of the main border is related to borders found in Persian carpets (see cat. 185), but here it takes a particularly Indian form in its geometricized compartments and the particular silhouette effect of the un-outlined red palmettes and vines set against the white ground. And the palm trees strike an Indian chord. As large as this carpet is, far larger ones are known to have come from Indian looms, including a pair of mid-seventeenth-century audience carpets, each about sixty-three feet long (approximately 19 meters).[3]

Careful observation reveals a feature most unusual in a carpet—the field design consists of a pattern unit of approximately square dimension that is shown four times, each unit reversed in direction. The palm tree marks the top corner of each pattern unit. That the pattern unit at the top of the carpet was unfinished when the border was woven suggests the carpet was woven to a prescribed length. It is important to note that the use of a repeating pattern

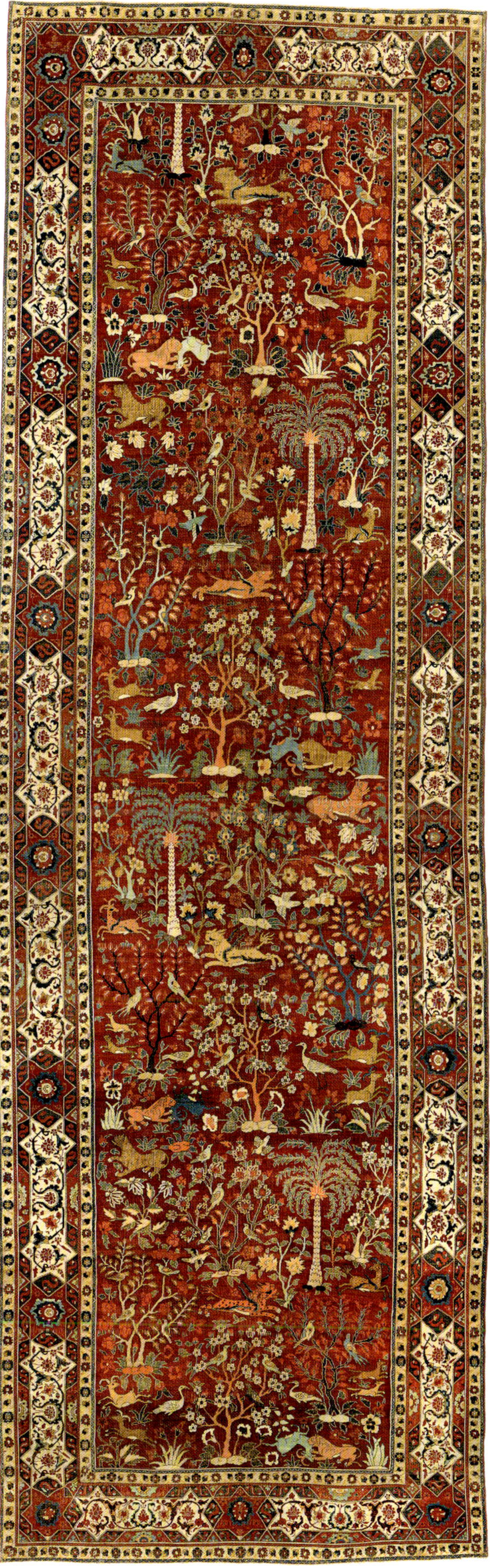

unit is a feature of draw-loom weaving (see cat. 171) because the elaborate preparation of the loom figure harness can be used again and again. But it is of no value as a labor-saving procedure in pile weaving, since all the knots still have to be tied by hand, meaning that the choice of this type of pattern was based on aesthetic preference and not on labor, time, or cost considerations. DW

1. New York 1997–98, pp. 7, 12.
2. Abu'l Fazl 'Allami 1977, vol. 1, p. 57.
3. New York 1997–98, p. 120, fig. 118.

PROVENANCE: Lady Sackville, Knole Park, Kent, England; J. Pierpont Morgan, New York (until 1917)

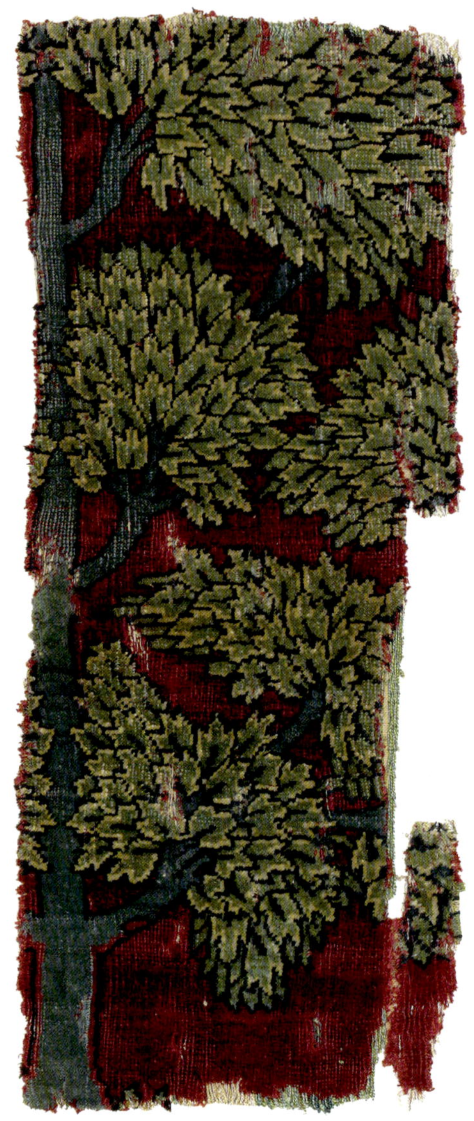

263. *Pashmina Carpet Fragment*

Northern India, first half of 17th century
Silk (warp and weft), *pashmina* wool (pile); asymmetrically knotted pile
13½ × 5¼ in. (34.3 × 13.3 cm)
Rogers Fund, 1908 08.109.20

Pashmina is a type of fine wool made from the undercoat of the Himalayan mountain goat. Exquisite carpets woven of this wool in northern India during the seventeenth century were valued highly not only in India but also in Iran. For instance, two examples dating to this period are preserved in the shrine of Imam Riza in Mashhad.[1] In total, about forty *pashmina* carpets are thought to have survived worldwide, and half of them probably date to the reign of Shah Jahan (1627–58).[2]

This is a fragment of one such luxury carpet. Even in its present form, the delicate, painterly quality of the leaves is apparent. A gradational effect is accomplished by the two tones of blue and green *pashmina* pile set against the finely woven silk ground, which consists of alternating warp bands of white, off-white, green, and blue. The insect-derived vivid red dye used as a background color makes the piece even more attractive.

The fragment once belonged to a famous carpet now in the Frick Collection in New York, and the complete original design of the work has recently been reconstructed. Once extraordinarily large, the carpet had alternating rows of flowering trees and trees in leaf. Surprisingly, in spite of the repetitive design and symmetrical arrangement, the weavers carefully avoided creating identical details.[3] Considering its quality and the luxurious materials used in its production, the carpet is likely to have been made in one of the Mughal royal workshops.

This magnificent carpet was cut up before 1889. Many pieces were then dispersed, and the present fragment was purchased by the Museum in 1908. In 1918 Henry Clay Frick purchased the Frick piece from the dealer Joseph Duveen. Other fragments are in the Victoria and Albert Museum, London; Brooklyn Museum; Museum für Islamische Kunst, Staatliche Museen zu Berlin; and private collections.[4] YK

1. See Gans-Ruedin 1984, pp. 130–33; Cohen and Kajitani 2006, p. 15.
2. New York 1997–98, p. 80.
3. Cohen and Kajitani 2006, pp. 9, 10, 35.
4. Ibid., pp. 9, 11, 15, 19, 26 n. 2.

PROVENANCE: [India, 1880s]; [Dikran G. Kelekian, New York, until 1908; sold to MMA]

264. Carpet with Flower Pattern

India or present-day Pakistan, Kashmir or Lahore, ca. 1650
Cotton (warp and weft); wool (pile); asymmetrically knotted pile
14 ft. 2 in. × 81 3/4 in. (431.8 × 207.6 cm)
Purchase, Florance Waterbury Bequest and Rogers Fund, 1970 1970.321

When the emperor Jahangir (r. 1605–27) made his first spring trip to Kashmir in 1620, he was overwhelmed by the beauty of the flowers coming into bloom. A man with a keen eye and a sensitive soul, Jahangir wanted to record the experience, so he tasked his leading natural-history painter, a gifted artist named Mansur, with painting one hundred flower "portraits."[1] Jahangir's interest in the aesthetics of flowers was perhaps stimulated further by the appearance at court of European herbals; elements of these works, including formal presentations in profile and complementary butterflies and dragonflies, found their way into Indian representations. By about 1630, under Jahangir's son and successor, Shah Jahan (r. 1627–58), the flower style had become the new fashion at the court and appeared in all aspects of the decorative arts—architectural decoration, manuscript binding and illumination, textiles, and objects in various media. The flower style became dominant in carpets a little later, by about 1650. It largely supplanted the Persianate taste for scrolling vines and arabesques, which had previously dominated court circles in India.

This carpet is an excellent example of the type. It has a conventional field pattern consisting of rows of profiled flowers, some identifiable (irises, tulips), others not, but all drawn with a sense of naturalistic individualism and detail. The border is unusual in that it represents a naturalistically drawn and slightly Indianized version of a classic Persian pattern instead of the more expected profiled flowers. Flower carpets with rectangular shapes are outnumbered by arched ones, some of which were made in pairs that may have flanked a raised dais; one circular and one octagonal example are also known. More than fifty examples of such carpets survive.[2] A good number remain in Jaipur and were originally purchased for use in the Amber Fort, ancestral home of the Jaipur rajas, while others have been acquired over the course of the last hundred years by institutions and collectors in the West. Some of the examples now in the West can be traced to Jaipur; this carpet, for example, was observed in Jaipur in 1929, when it still had an inventory label stating that it had been purchased in Lahore in 1656.[3] But it is possible that the royal stores of princely states other than Jaipur also possessed such material. DW

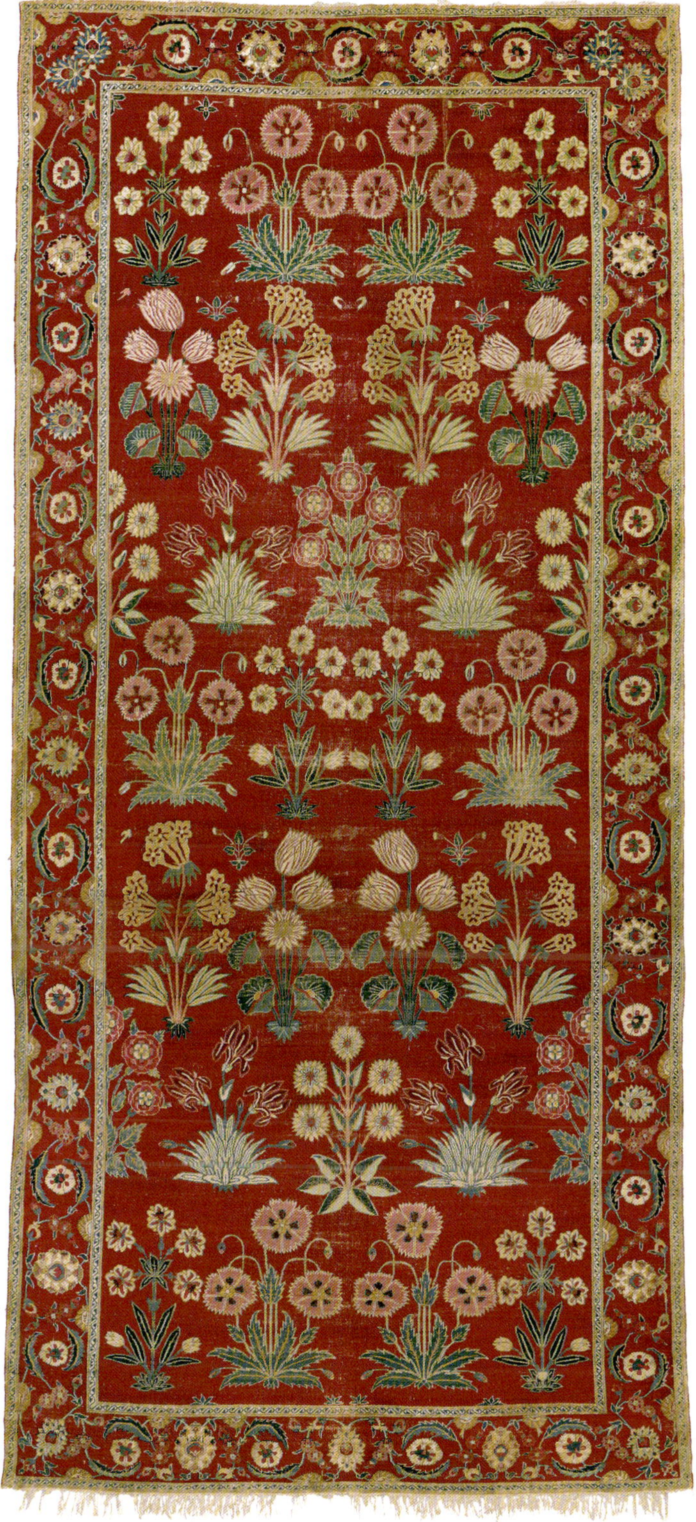

PROVENANCE: Maharaja of Jaipur, India (1656–at least 1929); Hagop Kevorkian, New York (until d. 1962; estate sale, Sotheby's, London, December 11, 1970, lot 8, to MMA)

1. Jahangir 1966, vol. 2, pp. 143–45.
2. New York 1997–98, pp. 86–117, with many illustrations.
3. Ibid., p. 95.

265. *Carpet Fragments with Pattern of Lattice and Blossoms*

India or present-day Pakistan, Kashmir or Lahore, ca. 1650
Silk (warp and weft), *pashmina* wool (pile); asymmetrically knotted pile
12 ft. 11¾ in. × 55¼ in. (395.6 × 140.3 cm)
Bequest of Benjamin Altman, 1913 14.40.723

Among all traditional carpet-weaving societies, northern India during the seventeenth and eighteenth centuries was unique in using the fine underhair of a breed of domesticated goat (*Capra hircus laniger*) over silk as the preferred pile material for the highest grade of carpets.[1] *Pashmina* had a number of advantages over silk as a pile fiber: it was strong, it allowed for an unparalleled fineness of weave, and it absorbed and reflected color at least as well as sheep's wool. The idea for using *pashmina* for carpets, and not only for shawls, seems to have originated in Iran during the second half of the sixteenth century.[2] The earliest surviving Indian example dates from about 1620 to 1625, around the time of Jahangir's initial infatuation with the flowers of Kashmir (see cat. 264). The majority of seventeenth-century examples thus reflect variations of the flower style favored at court after 1630. Late in the century and throughout the next, the fussier *millefleur* style came into fashion, and floral elements became much finer in scale, sometimes clustered in repeating units.[3]

The field pattern of these fragments represents a popular variation of the classic flower style, in which rows of flowers are presented in profile. Here the field is divided into compartments, with a lattice formed by reciprocating serrated vines. Large fantastical blossoms are placed at the points where the vines meet, and smaller blossoms appear in the compartments as part of a secondary vine pattern. The extremely fine weave (just over 1,000 knots per square inch) allows for sublime refinement in drawing and detail. The masterful weavers came to use the pile fiber just as painters use pigments, blending or juxtaposing different colors to create mottled or even shaded effects, as in the leaves of some of the large blossoms or the little hillocks and scudding cloud wisps in the border. Elements in the pattern allow us to estimate the original length at more than twenty-three feet (seven meters), a great size for a carpet of this quality.

Benjamin Altman, the department store magnate who left the Metropolitan Museum his superb collections of old master paintings and Chinese porcelain, should also be remembered for the refinement of his taste in carpets. Not only did he own three of the Museum's small silk "Kashan" rugs (of sixteen known worldwide; see cats. 182 and 183 for two of them), but he collected seven superb examples of Indian *pashmina* carpets, the largest group in any collection.

DW

1. New York 1997–98, pp. 22–23.
2. Ibid., pp. 90–92.
3. Ibid., pp. 119–29.

Provenance: Benjamin Altman, New York (until d. 1913)

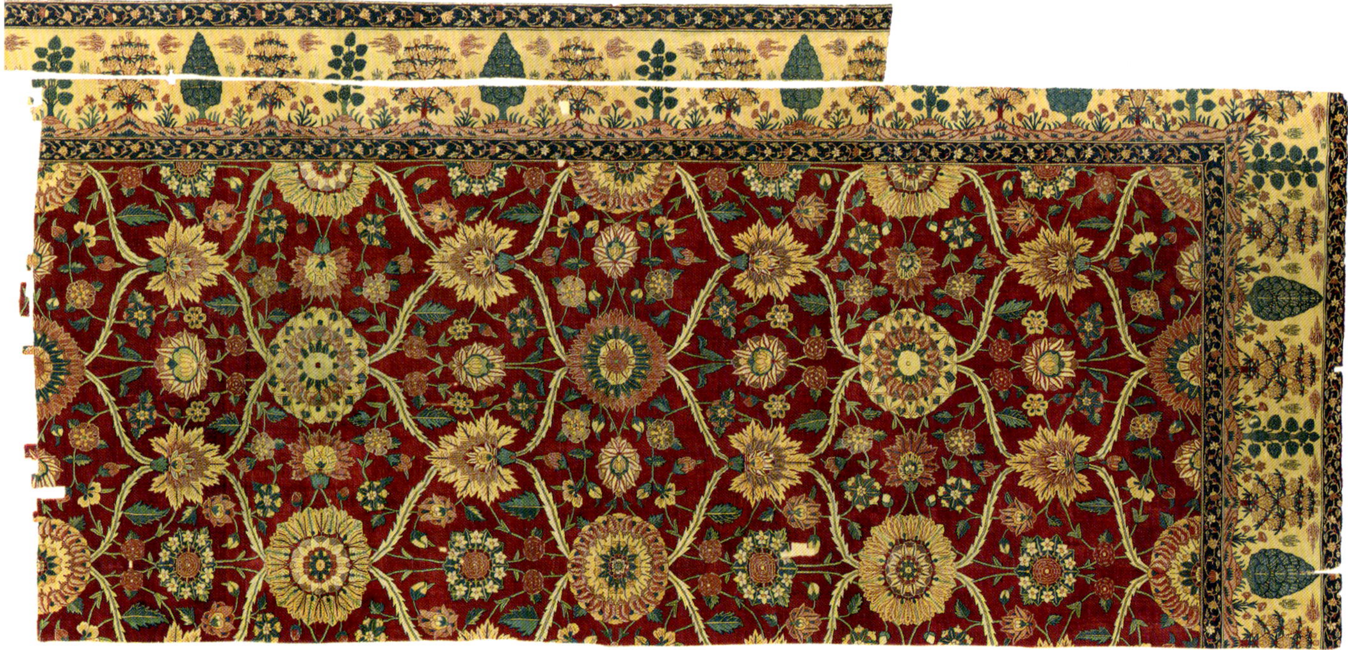

266. Bed Cover or Wall Hanging (Fragment)

India, Gujarat, 17th century
Cotton, silk; plain weave, embroidered, originally quilted
76½ × 45 in. (194.3 × 114.3 cm)
Gift of Victoria and Albert Museum, 1954 54.21

Over the centuries, Gujarat has produced outstanding embroideries both for sale in India and for export. As early as the 1500s, Dutch, English, French, and Portuguese traders brought Indian textiles into the European market, where they continued to be fashionable for the next three centuries.[1] Some of the finest examples of Gujarati embroideries come from the Mochi community; the Cambay area in particular perfected the art of chain-stitch embroidery.[2]

Among the oldest surviving embroidered panels attributed to this seventeenth-century Gujarati production center are those now preserved in the Metropolitan Museum, as well as those in the Victoria and Albert Museum in London.[3] Other panels have been attributed to the same place of production,[4] and one of them bears an inscription in Gujarati on the selvage, further confirming the provenance of the group.[5]

The decorative motifs found on these textiles resulted from a process that began with a request from exporters, who sent prints and drawings from Europe. These artworks were then used by the Indian artists, who sometimes altered the original design to such a degree that the final results were virtually unrecognizable. When the finished pieces were sent back to Europe, customers appreciated them for the exotic allure they had acquired.[6] This is the case with the decorative motifs on the Museum's panel, which feature flowers, birds, cats, and a monkey. These fantastical animals barely resemble their original counterparts. Flowers spread naturalistically across the surface of the textile; the animals, sometimes fanciful and unreal, seem to sit on slender branches.

The silk chain-stitch embroidery—executed in red, pink, yellow, blue, and green silk on a thin white plain-weave quilted cotton background—is of a type produced by the Mochi community. It was done with a special tool (the *ari*), a fine needle hooked at one end that was fitted into a round wooden handle. The *ari* was easy to use, and with it the embroiderer could produce very fine loops to control the progress of the design,[7] thus allowing for a greater degree of detail and refinement. EGM

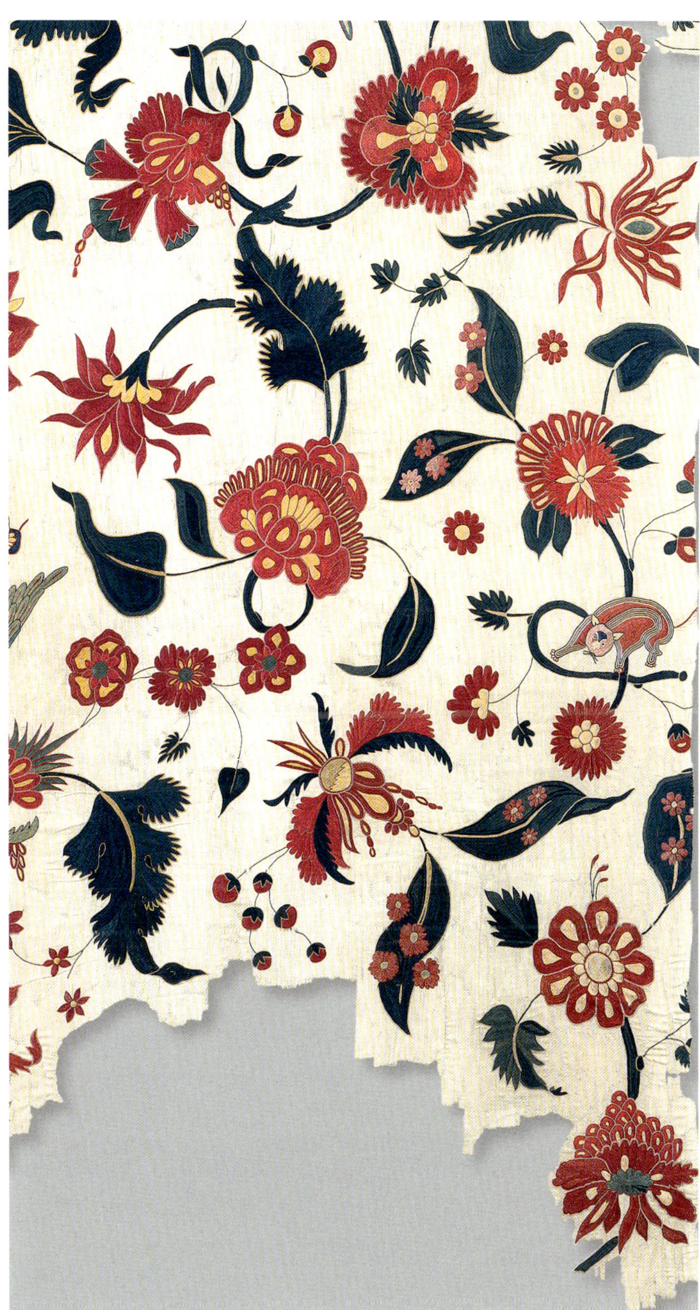

Detail

1. Irwin 1949, p. 51.
2. Crill 1999, p. 8, links Duarte Barbosa's quotation in 1518 regarding the "very beautiful quilts and testers of beds finely worked" with the production of Gujarat chain-stitch embroidery of the Mochi community that was shipped from the port of Cambay.
3. These pieces were part of the Lady Ashburnham Collection in Ashburnham Palace, and at least five of these are mentioned in *The Catalogue of The Important English Furniture etc.* auctioned by Sotheby and Co. on Tuesday, July 7, 1953. It is interesting to note that one of the pieces was purchased by the Museum for the Arts of Decoration of the Cooper Union, as reported in Cooper Union 1954, p. 184.
4. John Irwin (1949, p. 54) has identified other panels that undoubtedly belong to this same place of production.

5. The Gujarati inscription is in seventeenth-century characters, and according to Moti Chandra it reads as follows: "Astar jhahmamak na patar ga.9. Khulat ga. 1 1/4 (The lining of *jhahmām* [?]. Length 9 *gaz*. Breadth 1 1/4 *gaz*)" (from India Office Archives, Court Book IV, 135 [London] as published in Irwin 1949, pp. 55–56 n. 10, pl. 8).
6. The specific request from the European customer who ordered the present piece is referenced in a note attached to the fragment by Sir Leigh Ashton, who in 1954 oversaw its donation to the Metropolitan Museum by the Victoria and Albert Museum, London: "One panel retained by the Victoria and Albert has an inscription in Gujerati: 'which is the first time that anyone has thought that this particular kind of embroidery for the European market was made so far north.' These hangings are completely un-Indian as they never used this kind of thing. They are an example of what English people ordered in the Orient through the East India Company." (Department of Islamic Art curatorial files, gift receipt no. 5947).
7. For an accurate description of the way in which the Mochi community used the *ari* to execute chain stitch, see Irwin and Hall 1973a, pp. 201.

PROVENANCE: Lord Ashburnham, Sussex, England (by descent from late 17th century–1953; sale, Ashburnham Palace, Sussex, through Sotheby's, London, July 7–9, 1953, lot 479; to V&A); Victoria and Albert Museum, London (1953–54; gifted to MMA through Sir Leigh Ashton)

267. Box with Drawer

India, probably Ahmedabad, Gujarat, ca. 1600
Wood (teak); veneered with ebony, inlaid ivory, and lac
3 1/4 × 13 3/8 × 5 3/4 in. (8.3 × 34 × 14.5 cm)
Cynthia Hazen Polsky and Leon B. Polsky Fund, 2000 2000.301

To create the lively decoration on this box, ivory was cut into very thin strips and shaped into tiny flowers and leaves—some stained with color—then inlaid into ebony veneer. The top and sides depict Portuguese hunters riding elephants and horses in a forest setting, and the borders are filled with scrolls, roundels, and stylized bird and animal heads. Such hunting scenes were adapted from Indo-Persian painting to decorate exported furniture, where they depicted European patrons in a princely Indian manner. In this example, the exuberant treatment of foliage, with repeating scrolling vines springing from tree branches and flowers, imbues the decorative scheme with a particular lyricism. The fact that the geometric frieze along the bottom edge is inlaid in lac rather than wood is somewhat unusual and suggests a time of manufacture when craftsmen were shifting from the older technique of lac inlay, for the Ottoman and Persian markets, to hardwood inlay, for the European consumer. During the late sixteenth or early seventeenth century, such inlaid hardwood items were produced for the Portuguese market, possibly in Gujarat and Sind, and exported from Goa and other coastal towns in western India.

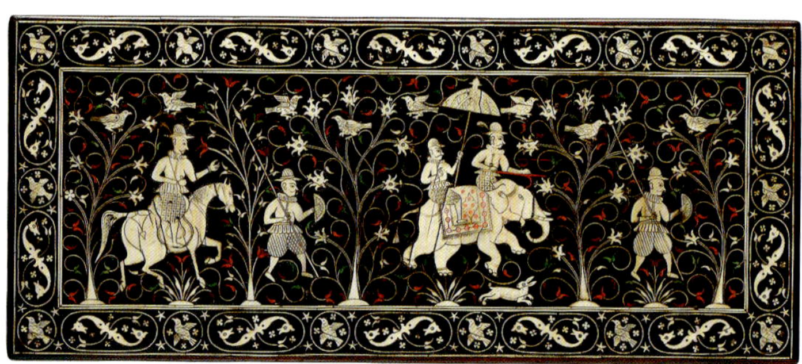

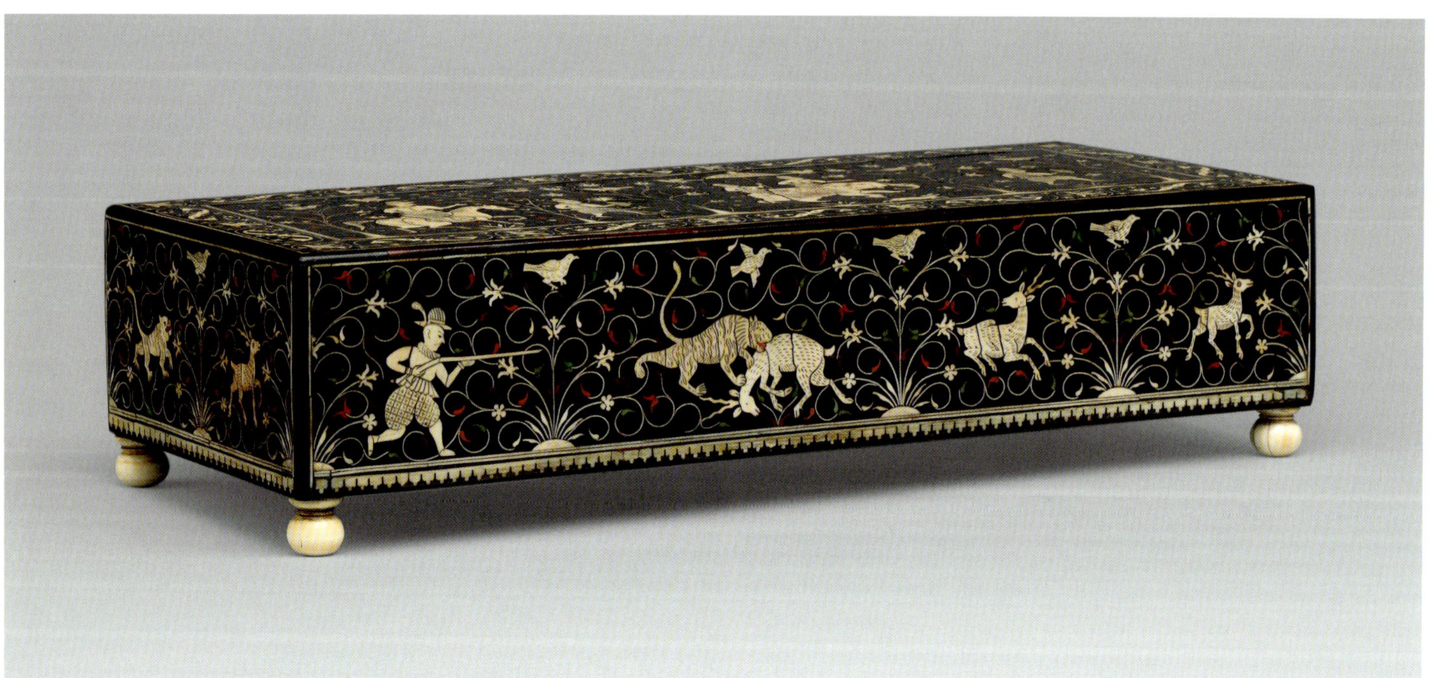

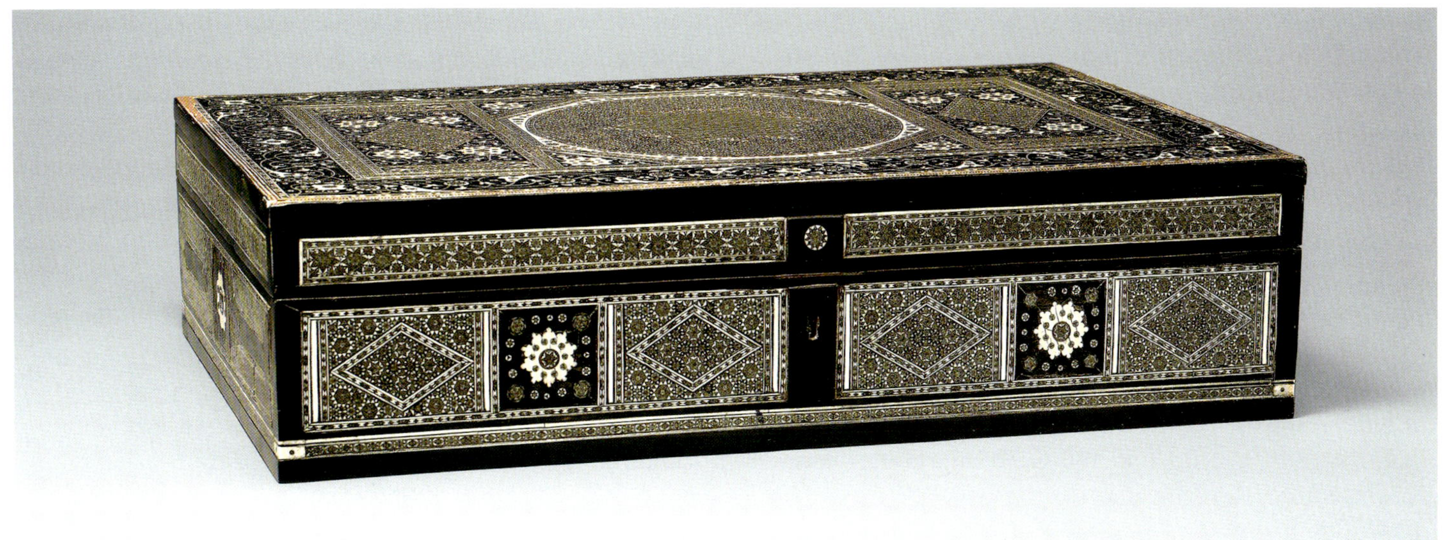

This box can be associated with a group of ivory-inlaid hardwood boxes and furniture that may have been made in the same workshop, the most notable examples of which are a small cabinet in the Cincinnati Museum of Art[1] and another in the Kuwait National Museum, Kuwait City,[2] that bear similar hunting scenes featuring Indian and European figures in a forest. The upper portion of a cabinet in the Museu Nacional de Arte Antiga, Lisbon,[3] exhibits an iconographic program similar to that of the Metropolitan's box, although the Lisbon cabinet's overall iconography is more complex. An altar converted to a tabletop in the Victoria and Albert Museum, London,[4] has almost identical zoomorphic S-shaped motifs in the border pattern. In general, this group of related works reveals consistent decorative principles and details.

The long drawer and relatively simple form of the box are rare, however, and suggest that it may have held writing implements (as an abbreviated form of the larger, more elaborate writing cabinets that are known) or valuable trinkets and personal possessions. Comparable boxes may have been used in the Mughal court as containers for precious objects, but inlaid boxes of this type usually rank among the portable trappings of wealthy European travelers. This particular form of long box with a drawer at one end is found in lac inlaid with mother-of-pearl but not, with the exception of this work, in ivory-inlaid wood.[5] NNH

1. Cincinnati 1985, p. 81, no. 58.
2. Jenkins, ed. 1983, p. 123.
3. Brussels 1991, p. 145.
4. Lisbon 2004, p. 115, no. 84.S; also in Jaffer 2002, pp. 34–35.
5. Digby 1986, p. 221, fig. 12, shows a late sixteenth-century mother-of-pearl box with a scene of very similar composition; London 1982d, p. 162, no. 549.

Provenance: Private collection, Lisbon, Portugal; [Manuel Castilho Antiques, London, until 2000; sold to MMA]

268. Writing Box

India, Gujarat, or Pakistan, Sind, late 16th–early 17th century
Wood; veneered with ebony, inlaid with ivory and bone (partially stained), brass (*sadeli* technique)
5 1/8 × 20 7/8 × 13 1/2 in. (13 × 53 × 34.3 cm)
Purchase, Pat and John Rosenwald Gift, 2004 2004.439

The design on this ebony-veneered box, which is richly inlaid with ivory, bone, and *sadeli* (micromosaic), achieves a pleasing balance between vegetal vine forms in the borders and interspersed floral medallions in the middle ground; its stately geometric patterns include a central star motif, which dominates the main composition. The nature of the decoration, particularly the strong geometric forms, arabesques, and *sadeli* technique, links the box to the larger Islamic world in terms of style and taste, while also exemplifying western India's accomplished tradition of luxury furniture making, which was often oriented, in the late sixteenth century, toward export to Europe or western Asia. Although its

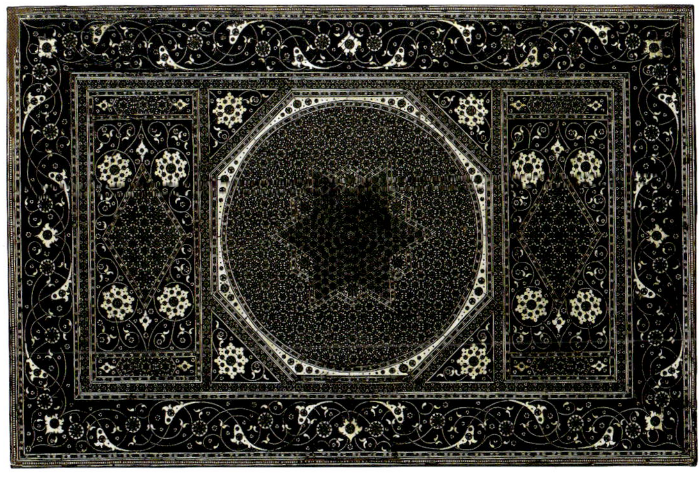

interior is no longer entirely original, the piece is likely to have functioned as a writing box and would presumably have had a number of sections or divisions within to contain various tools and papers.

The *sadeli* technique, which has been in use since antiquity, is particularly associated with the lands of the eastern Mediterranean, from where it spread to Iran and India. The method consists of gluing together geometrically shaped rods or thin strips of diverse materials (such as tin, wood, ivory, horn, and brass), slicing the bundles transversely into thin sheets of repeating patterns, and adhering the sheets to a wooden support. Predating *sadeli* in western India was an earlier method of inlaying mother-of-pearl in wooden objects, which, in the sixteenth century, were destined primarily for the Turkish market.

This box is part of a larger group of related inlaid furniture, some examples of which may have been made in the same workshop. A cabinet on a table stand in the Victoria and Albert Museum, London, regarded as one of the most important works of the type, shows similar radiating-star patterns in *sadeli* on its inner doors and drawers, combined with an elaborate figural and vegetal decorative scheme on its outer surfaces.[1] A cabinet in the Musée des Arts Décoratifs, Paris, contains a similar star pattern in *sadeli* in its inner section.[2] In these examples, however, the medallion-based patterns in *sadeli* are largely restricted to the interiors (probably because of the fragility of the technique), with the outer sections covered instead in figures and flowering plants. Here, in contrast, the medallion style and technique have been elevated to the main surface, and the box thus stands apart from the other pieces in its more archaic and Islamic character. NNH

1. Jaffer 2002, pp. 30–32, no. 8; also, pp. 20–21, no. 4, illustrates a reversible game board with a similar combination of *sadeli* and curving vine forms on the reverse, although, in that case, the areas of *sadeli* are more restrained and less varied.
2. Bordeaux 1998–99, pp. 10–11, 126, no. 83.

Provenance: Private collection, Scotland (by descent from at least 1900–2003); sale, Christie's South Kensington, October 17, 2003, lot 143, to McInerney; [Terence McInerney, New York, 2003–4; sold to MMA]

269. *The House of Bijapur*

Painters: Kamal Muhammad (active 1680s) and Chand Muhammad (active 1680s)
India, Deccan, Bijapur, ca. 1680
Ink, opaque watercolor, gold, and silver on paper
16¼ × 12¾ in. (41.3 × 32.5 cm)
Purchase, Gifts in memory of Richard Ettinghausen; Schimmel Foundation Inc., Ehsan Yarshater, Karekin Beshir Ltd., Margaret Mushekian, Mr. and Mrs. Edward Ablat and Mr. and Mrs. Jerome A. Straka Gifts; The Friends of the Islamic Department Fund; Gifts of Mrs. A. Lincoln Scott and George Blumenthal, Bequests of Florence L. Goldmark, Charles R. Gerth and Millie Bruhl Frederick, and funds from various donors, by exchange; Louis E. and Theresa S. Seley Purchase Fund for Islamic Art and Rogers Fund, 1982 1982.213

Inscribed in Persian in *naskhi* script along upper border:
شاه عباس پادشاه ایران
Shah ʿAbbas King of Iran

Inscribed in Persian in *naskhi* script vertically near left-hand frame:
عمل کمال محمد و چاند محمد
Work of Kamal Muhammad and Chand Muhammad

This image from Bijapur was made for the last of its rulers, Sikandar (r. 1672–86), shown at the far right as a boy, shortly before the fall of the kingdom to Mughal conquerors in 1686. It brings together all nine ʿAdil Shahi sultans in a dynastic assembly that was probably inspired by Mughal paintings illustrating the same idea. The artists, Kamal Muhammad and Chand Muhammad, incorporated the characteristic features of the Bijapur School in this period: great shifts in scale, varying perspectives, and a palette rich in a distinctive pink hue.[1] An "otherworldly" mood (a term often used to characterize Deccani painting) is conveyed by inventive and sometimes illogical juxtapositions, such as the stairs leading up to the carpet with no supporting architectural elements and the soaring mountains of Safavid inspiration in the background. Distant views of water hint at Bijapur's former vastness; at its greatest extent, the kingdom stretched to the Arabian Sea and Goa, a coastal city that was contested several times with the Portuguese over the course of the sixteenth century.

This painting would have the viewer believe that the key of legitimacy, being handed over by Ismaʿil (r. 1501–24), founder of the Safavid dynasty of Iran (here erroneously identified as Shah

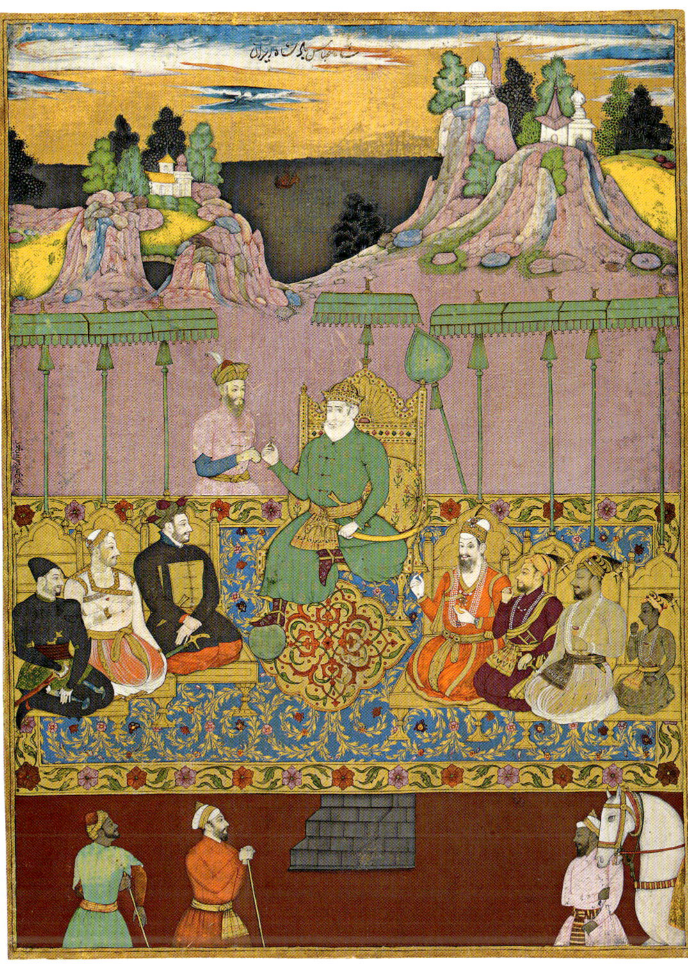

1. The Safavid artist Mu'in Musavvir (active ca. 1638–97) also used this color in his work.
2. New scholarship on Deccani carpets is forthcoming: see Cohen 2011 in the MMA conference volume *Sultans of the South* (Haidar and Sardar, eds. 2011). See also the Ph.D. dissertation by Yumiko Kamada at the Institute of Fine Arts, New York University (Kamada 2011). Thanks to Kurt Behrendt of the Metropolitan Museum's Department of Asian Art for information on the early sculpture of the region.
3. Robbins and McLeod, eds. 2006, p. 34, no. 26; Falk and Archer 1981, no. 404, illustrates a portrait of Ikhlas Khan signed by Chand Muhammad in a similar, though less accomplished, hand. See also, ibid., p. 114, no. 101, illustrating a painting signed by Haidar 'Ali and Muhammad Khan, another example of a collaboration between painters.
4. Later versions include Sotheby's London, *Fine Oriental Manuscripts and Miniatures*, November 21 and 22, 1985, lot 71 (a copy of the MMA painting dated ca. 1750). See also Strzygowski et al. 1933, pp. 42–43, fig. 37 (later, abbreviated version of the MMA painting, now in the Österreichische Nationalbibliothek, Vienna); Duda 1983, p. 266, fol. 20, fig. 458; Taylor 1866 (frontispiece, later version of the MMA painting); Manucci 1906–8, vol. 3, pl. 34.

Provenance: Kevork Essayan, Paris (until d. 1980; estate sale, Nouveau Drouot, Paris, June 24, 1982, lot 67, to John R. Alderman for MMA)

'Abbas in a later inscription), to Yusuf (r. 1489–1510), founder of the Bijapur dynasty, symbolizes the unwavering allegiance of the 'Adil Shahi family to the Shi'i creed. However, Bijapur in its golden period was ruled by Ibrahim II (r. 1579–1626; shown seated third from the right), a self-professed freethinker, whose tolerance of Hinduism and sufism, as well as his formalization of Sunnism as the state religion in 1583, deviated from established tradition.

Certain historicizing details in the composition acknowledge the two-hundred-year span of the family. Two of the early rulers on the left wear hilted daggers—straight split-end western Asian and curving double-leaf South Indian—of an earlier style than the push daggers (*katars*) seen in the belts of the later rulers on the right. Local tastes are seen in the swirling blue carpet and the style of the flat ceremonial umbrellas, which are similar to those found in early Andhra sculpture.[2] Like most painters who were active in the Deccan, Kamal Muhammad and Chand Muhammad remain relatively unknown, with very few attested works, although collaborations such as theirs in the present work are seen elsewhere in Bijapur painting and were standard in Mughal painting.[3] The several later versions of this image that have made their way into notable collections and books illustrate its lasting significance.[4] NNH

270. Buraq: The Celestial Beast

India, Deccan, probably Golconda, ca. 1660–80
Opaque watercolor and gold on paper
8⅝ × 10⅞ in. (21.9 × 27.6 cm)
Purchase, Rogers Fund, Elizabeth S. Ettinghausen Gift, in memory of Richard Ettinghausen and Ehsan Yarshater Gift, 1992 1992.17

The Qur'an contains descriptions of Buraq, the fantastic mount that the Prophet Muhammad rode on his *mi'raj* (night journey) to Paradise. Depicted here without its rider, this hybrid beast has the face of a beautiful woman wearing jewels, the body of a horse with wings, and a knotted tail that terminates in a dragon's head. Buraq's body is inhabited by an assortment of animals, including elephants, lions, fish, and birds. Several lionlike beasts nibble other animals, while the dragon gnaws at Buraq's wings.

The figure is rendered in a subdued palette of beige and green, with gold outlines that show scattered plants in gold against a deep green ground. The combination of a somber palette with the bright natural color in Buraq's face is quite dramatic. The surrounding decorations in gold are related to a late sixteenth-century album border from Golconda;[1] the actual depiction of Buraq is

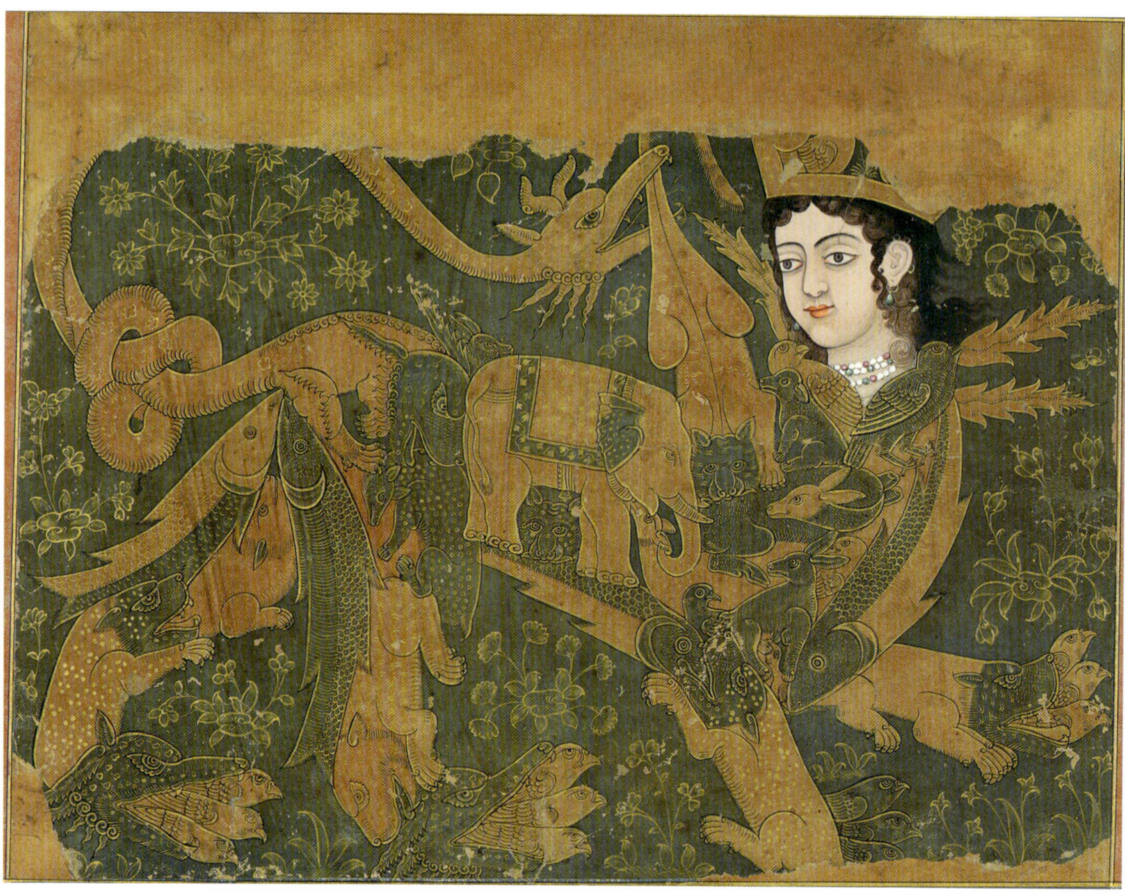

technically and stylistically akin to the painting of a composite horse inhabited by human figures and animals from the early seventeenth century in the Museum für Islamische Kunst, Staatliche Museen zu Berlin, which also displays dark tones similar in feeling to this work.[2] However, in terms of composition, the present painting is closest to a seventeenth-century Mughal composite Buraq with its head turned back (Bodleian Library, Oxford),[3] although the latter, Mughal example differs in treatment and palette from the Museum's.

While composite animals have a long tradition in Iranian and Indian art, and other examples from the Deccan are known, there are few such portrayals of Buraq. Most involve elephants, horses, camels, and lions,[4] depicted with riders. The origins of such images are unknown, although some scholars believe that the concept originated in ancient Central Asia.[5] Several composite paintings of camels and young princes and princesses inhabited by human forms are attributed to sixteenth-century Iran and Central Asia (see cat. 142).[6] In India, there is a long history of similar imagery in Mughal, Deccani, and Hindu traditions. Nevertheless, the composite paintings of Buraq from the Deccan in this distinct style were the ones that served as models for later Indian/Deccan examples.[7]

As scholars have attempted to interpret these images, some have suggested that they reflect the dominion of the heavenly over the natural world and, by implication, the power of a ruler over his land and people.[8] However, these are only hypotheses, and the meaning of these curious paintings remains ambiguous. What is certain is that their playful, enigmatic qualities entertained their patrons and owners in much the same way as they intrigue us today.

ME

1. Zebrowski 1983, pp. 170–72.
2. Ibid., p. 146, pl. 18.
3. MS. Pers. b. 1, f 10r. See Topsfield 2008, pl. 59.
4. There is a composite painting of a lion attributed to the Deccan in the Dorn Album in the National Library of Russia (former Saltykov Shchedrin Library) in St. Petersburg. I would like to thank Navina Haidar for bringing this work to my attention.
5. Del Bontà 1999, p. 70.
6. The composite painting of a princess by Muhammad Shari Musavvir with margins by Muhammad Murad Samarqandi is in the Arthur M. Sackler Gallery, Washington (no. S86.0304), reproduced in Lowry and Nemazee 1988, pl. 67. Its pendant, a composite painting of a seated prince is in the Musée du Louvre, Paris (no. OA 7109). See also cat. 142.
7. Düsseldorf 2003, pp. 153–63.
8. Del Bontà 1999, p. 81.

Provenance: Richard Colley, Marquis of Wellesley (until d. 1842); by descent to his granddaughter-in-law, Mrs. Colley Wellesley (until d. 1941); by descent to the 7th Duke of Wellington (1947–d. 1972); [Terence McInerney, New York, until 1992; sold to MMA]

271. *The Nan va halva (Bread and Sweets) of Muhammad Baha' al-Din al-'Amili*

India, Deccan, Aurangabad, ca. 1690
Ink, opaque watercolor, and gold on paper; leather binding
$9\frac{1}{4} \times 5\frac{1}{2}$ in. (23.5×14 cm)
Purchase, Friends of Islamic Art Gifts, 1999 1999.157

Written by Muhammad Baha' al-Din al-'Amili (1547–1621), also known as Shaikh Baha'i, the text of this manuscript is a *masnavi* poem on the merits of the ascetic life. After serving as the *shaikh al-Islam* of Isfahan, he left the post to travel and write, producing commentaries on the Qur'an, grammar, jurisprudence, and astronomy as well as other subjects.[1] Among the works written during this period was the *Nan va halva* (Bread and Sweets), of which the manuscript here is perhaps the only known illustrated copy. The author's Arabic preface is written in black, with interlinear Persian translations in red, while the poem is given in Persian, in black, with Arabic headings in red. The text is outlined with gold clouds, and several pages have borders with gold lotus flowers in a grid on a silver background. Other borders include fantastical birds and animals in a rocky landscape. Vivid flowering plants flank many of the headings.

The subject of the poem would not seem to lend itself to illustration, but this unknown artist has found humor in the parables sketched by the author. Of his four charming paintings, the first accompanies a chapter on the regrets of a life spent learning things not useful on the day of resurrection. The artist shows a school in which only the sciences are taught, its teachers dozing, meditating, and drinking (opposite page). The second and third paintings illustrate a chapter that relates the story of a recluse who does not receive his accustomed daily bread. When he wanders into town

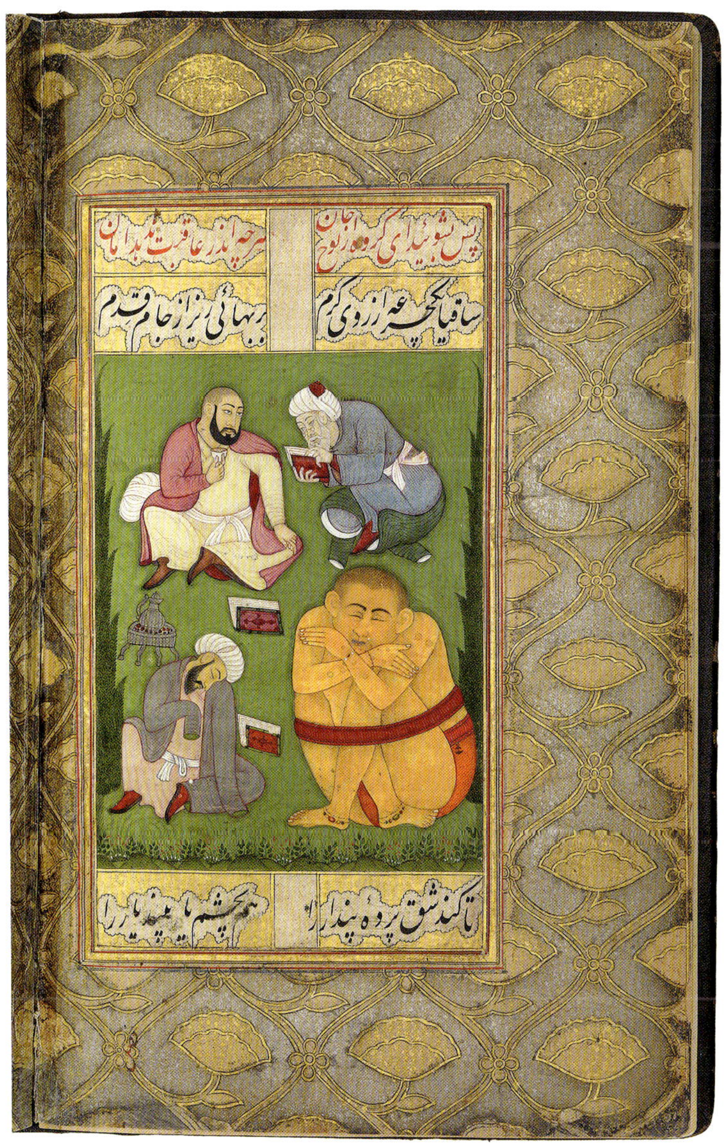

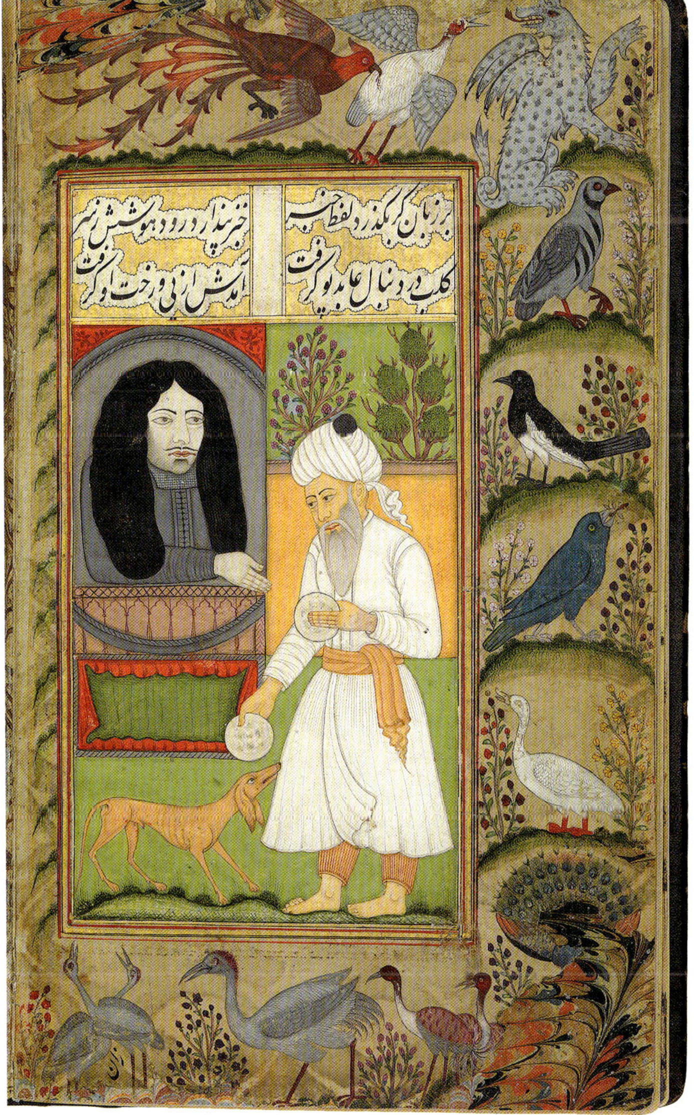

and hungrily accepts bread offered to him by an infidel, a dog scolds him for not having the faith or patience to see whether God would have provided for him. One painting depicts the recluse praying in the wilderness; the second shows the dog chiding him; the infidel in the background is depicted as the English king Charles II (above). In the final painting, the widow Bibi Tamiz sits on a prayer mat with her head turned away, attention diverted. It accompanies a chapter on hypocrisy, for although Bibi Tamiz is ostensibly devout, her real occupation is prostitution.

The manuscript was probably produced in Aurangabad soon after the Mughal conquest of the Deccan, when many northerners had moved into this new province of the empire. While little is known about the court art of this phase, it is assumed that the patronage of many nobles outside the court stimulated a new phase in Deccani art, which began to assimilate elements of Mughal and Rajput painting. MS

1. For Baha' al-Din al-'Amili, see Kohlberg 1989; Stewart 1991, pp. 563–67; Stewart 1996a; Stewart 1996b.

PROVENANCE: [Sam Fogg, London, until 1999; sold to MMA]

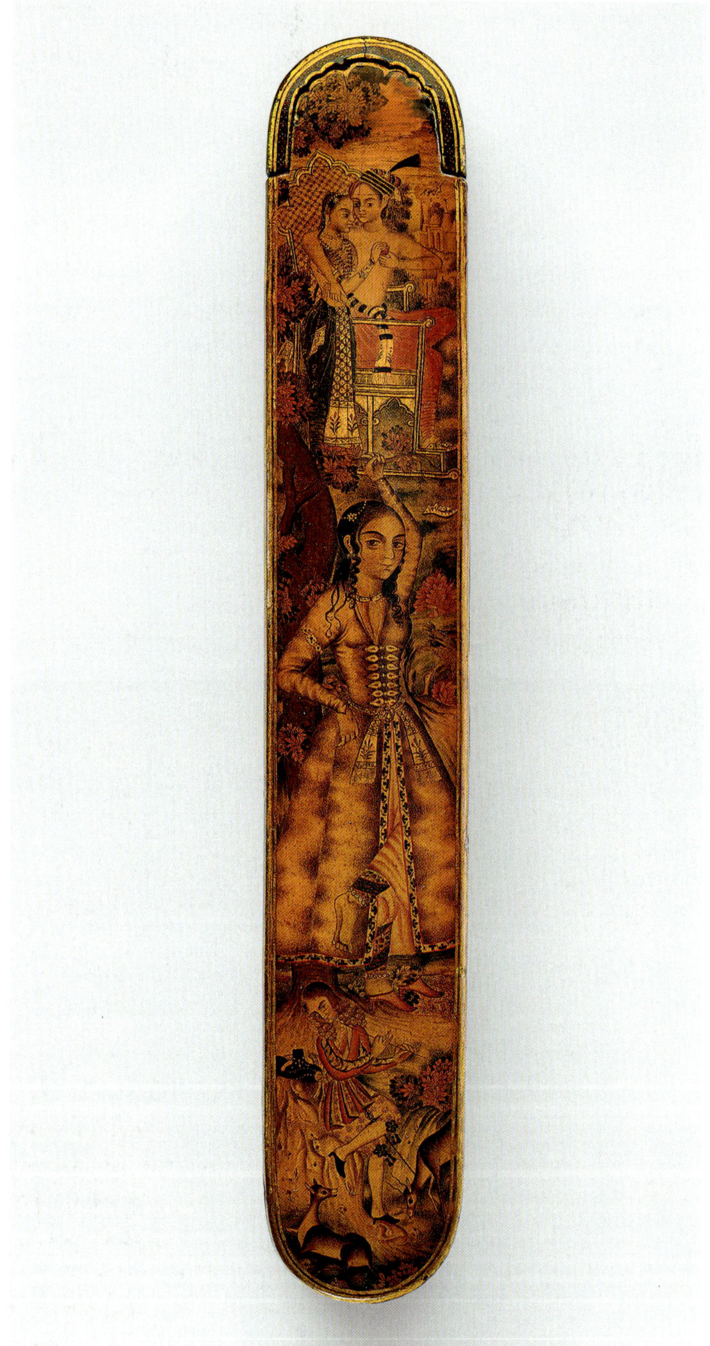

272. Pen Box

Painter: Manohar (active ca. 1582–1624)
India, possibly Deccan or northern India, late 17th–early 18th century
Papier-mâché; painted, gilded, and lacquered
1 1/8 × 9 1/8 × 1 1/2 in. (3 × 23.3 × 3.8 cm)
Cynthia Hazen Polsky and Leon B. Polsky Fund, 2002 2002.416a, b

Inscribed in Persian in *nasta'liq* script in upper right-hand corner of lid:
کمترین منوهر
[Work of] the most humble Manohar

The decoration on this lacquered pen box combines Indian, Persian, and European motifs in a hybrid style first seen in Iran in the late seventeenth century and subsequently in India, particularly in the Deccan. The central image is a young woman in Persian dress holding a branch above her head in the *dohada salabhanjika* (girl who fertilizes a tree) pose, familiar from ancient Indian art. Above her is an amorous couple in Indian dress, the woman standing beside a prince seated on a scalloped-back chair or throne. Below the main figure, a European gallant, perched on a rock, plays his flute as deer graze nearby. The sides of the box are painted with pastoral scenes copied from European masters, including groups of travelers, hunters, a pair of lovers, and views of distant architecture—conventions that were also popular in contemporary Safavid painting. Among the vignettes is one on the lower end of the box that shows two men bearing an oversize bunch of grapes on a pole; this motif was drawn from Nicolas Poussin's allegory of autumn (ca. 1660).[1]

The previously unknown painter of this box, Manohar, is identified by an inscription in Persian near the amorous couple on the lid, at the upper right. He based the individual motifs in the decoration closely on those of a lacquered jewel casket in the Victoria and Albert Museum, London, attributed to the artist Rahim Deccani.[2] The flute-playing figure is also seen in a lightly colored drawing in the Chester Beatty Library, Dublin, that bears an inscription ascribing the work to Rahim Deccani.[3] It is almost certain, therefore, that Manohar had access to the works of Rahim, if not to the painter himself, although the place where those works were produced remains unknown. The *nisba* "Deccani," following Rahim's name, has led scholars to speculate that he must have been active outside the Deccan, although other works of the period attributed to the Deccan indicate that this distinctive style was being practiced there.[4]

Several well-known late-Safavid-period painters introduced both Indian and European motifs and styles into their work, although not necessarily always in combination.[5] These elements were expressed in a tinted drawing technique particularly evident in the works on lacquer of Shaikh 'Abbasi and his sons, 'Ali Naqi and Muhammad Taqi.[6] Contemporary and slightly later painting exhibits a predilection for shaded drawings in a similar style as well as for unusual shifts in scale, as seen in the work of the Persian painter Bahram Sufrakish. Manohar's pen box displays the same exotic combination of motifs along with the shaded-drawing technique. NNH

1. Haidar Haykel 2004, p. 183, fig. 10.
2. Ibid., pp. 179–80, figs. 5, 6, 7.
3. Ibid., p. 181, fig. 8.
4. Jaffer 2002, p. 61, gives an Iranian provenance for the Victoria and Albert Museum's box by Rahim Deccani, suggesting the possibility that he may have been active in Iran.
5. The Safavid painters in question are Shaikh 'Abbasi, 'Ali Naqi, Muhammad Taqi, Bahram Sufrakish, Muhammad Zaman, and 'Ali Quli Jabbadar.
6. Skelton 1985.

PROVENANCE: Private collection, France; Francesca Galloway, London, until 2002; sold to MMA]

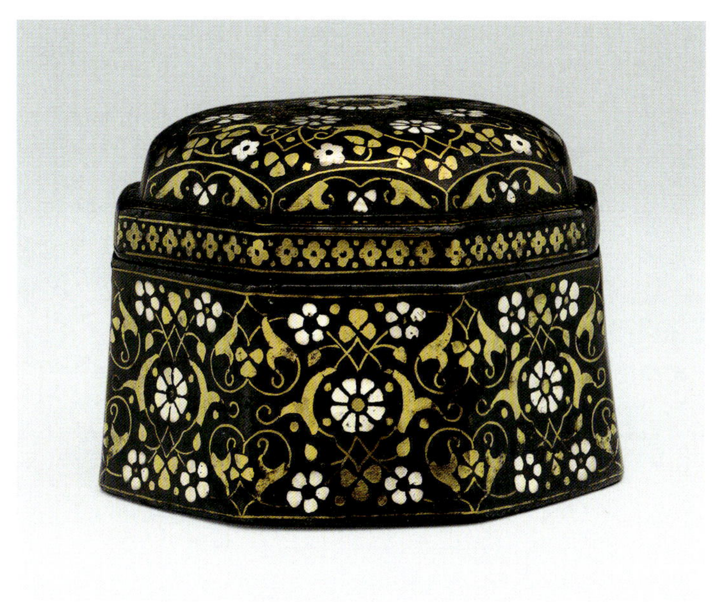

273. Box for Holding Pan

India, Deccan, Bidar, late 16th–early 17th century
Zinc alloy; cast, engraved, inlaid with silver and brass (*bidri* ware)
3⅞ × 5⅜ in. (9.9 × 13.6 cm)
Louis E. and Theresa S. Seley Purchase Fund for Islamic Art and Rogers Fund, 1996 1996.3a, b

Decorated with silver flowers linked to a brass yellow scrolling lattice, this box with sloping sides belongs to a group of Indian octagonal boxes meant to hold *pan*, the *digestif* made of a rolled-up betel leaf filled with lime paste and spices. Since the Museum's box has no interior compartments, it is surmised to have held the completed *pan* rather than the ingredients for making it.[1]

The process for decorating this object, known as *bidri*, is believed to have been invented in the city of Bidar, in the Deccan region of India.[2] In this technique, an object was made from an alloy having zinc and copper as its main components and inlaid with silver and/or brass.[3] A special paste was then applied to the object to render the base material very dark, simultaneously enhancing the contrasting colors of the inlaid metals.

Scholars have long debated how and when this particular technique was developed—a question not to be resolved here—but the decorative forms on this box suggest that it may be one of the oldest surviving examples of *bidri* ware.[4] The sloping walls and low-slung, domed top have been compared to Sultanate and early Bahmani architecture. The scrolling lattice decoration, Persianate in spirit, differs from the friezes of flowering plants on numerous other *bidri* pieces, which are understood as the adoption of the Mughal flower style in the Deccan as a result of mid-seventeenth-century contacts between the two regions.[5] Another early *bidri* object, a footed bowl in the Victoria and Albert Museum, London,[6] is similar in decoration to this box, with flowers on scrolls within cartouches suggested by serrated leaves and bilobed half palmettes. These two examples may predate the earliest dated *bidri* object, a *huqqa* base inlaid with silver and brass now in the Jagdish and Kamla Mittal Museum of Indian Art, Hyderabad, which combines the scrolling floral motif with the tall flowering plants so typical of Mughal portable arts.[7] MS

1. Other octagonal *pan* boxes are illustrated in London 1982d, p. 143, and Zebrowski 1997, pp. 265 and 269.
2. The commonly advanced arguments for this are based on the name of the technique and an eighteenth-century map of Bidar that shows these objects as one of the products of the province (illustrated in London 1982d, p. 49).
3. Susan La Niece and Graham Martin discovered the importance of copper in the alloy for achieving the matte black patina. See La Niece and Martin 1987.

4. This dating was first suggested in Zebrowski 1984, p. 39.
5. See, for example, the *bidri huqqa* base (cat. 274) also discussed and illustrated in this volume.
6. Victoria and Albert Museum, London, no. IS 10-1973, dated to the early seventeenth century, illustrated in Stronge 1985, p. 39.
7. It has an inscription of A.H. 1044/1634 A.D. Published in Zebrowski 1997, p. 232, no. 384.

PROVENANCE: Private collection, England; [John Lawrence Fine Arts Inc., London, until 1996; sold to MMA]

274. *Water Pipe Base*

India, Deccan, Bidar, late 17th century
Zinc alloy; cast, engraved, inlaid with brass (*bidri* ware)
H. 6⅞ in. (17.5 cm); Diam. 6½ in. (16.5 cm)
Louis E. and Theresa S. Seley Purchase Fund for Islamic Art and Rogers Fund, 1984 1984.221

This object is the base of a water pipe, or *huqqa*. Originally, a pipe for inhalation and a long stem supporting a brazier would have been connected to its neck, and the base would have nestled into a ring that kept it steady on the floor. Few if any complete *huqqas* survive from this period, and the bases (a few with matching rings) are what are preserved in museums today; the appearance of the full apparatus can be reconstructed only from paintings. Many of the known *huqqa* bases from the seventeenth and eighteenth centuries were made in the Deccan and decorated with the type of metal inlay known as *bidri*.

With its almost spherical shape, short neck, and everted rim, this object is typical of late-seventeenth-century *bidri huqqa* bases.[1] However, the refined frieze of flowering plants, set against a background lightly sprinkled with blossoms, sets it apart from other, more heavily decorated examples. One might be tempted to see the influence of Mughal aesthetics in the depiction and disposition of elements here. Flowers and plants were the most popular type of decoration for *huqqa* bases, although several examples depicting architectural fantasies and, later in the eighteenth century, Neoclassical motifs are also known. MS

1. See the discussion in Zebrowski 1997, pp. 225–45.

PROVENANCE: [Bashir Muhammad, London, until 1984; sold to MMA]

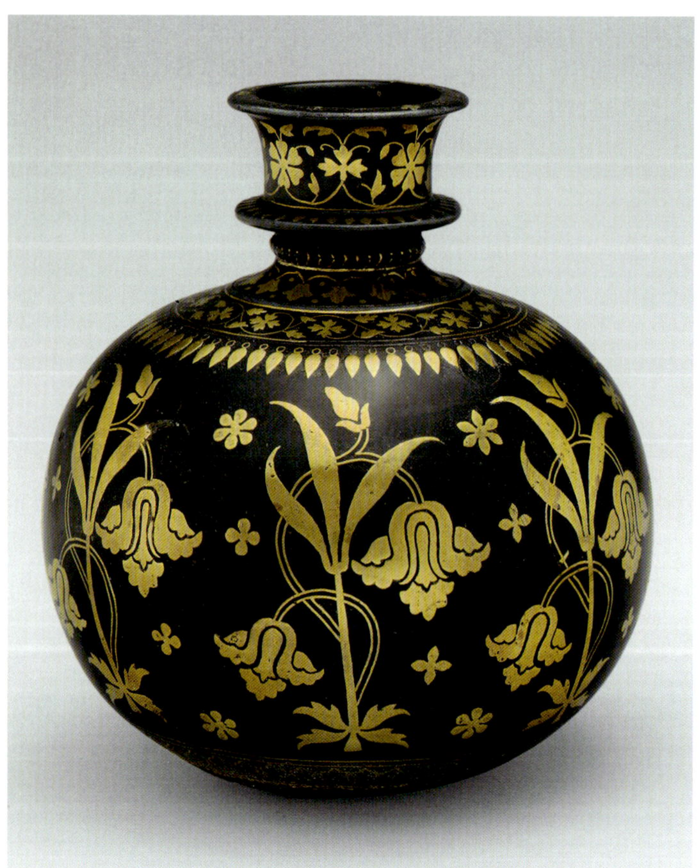

275. *Fountain*

India, Deccan, early 17th century
Brass; cast in sections, joined and engraved
38½ × 36¾ × 26⅝ in. (97.7 × 93.2 × 67.6 cm)
Purchase, Lila Acheson Wallace Gift, 1997 1997.150

An hourglass shape with a rhythmic arrangement of ribs, moldings, and chased designs guides the eye from top to base of this brass fountain in a single fluid motion. The projecting pipe is adorned with the lion mask known as a *kirtimukha* (literally, "face of glory"); this extension would have connected to another pipe that forced water into and through the fountain up to its apex, from which the liquid would have descended. The fountain was formed from seven separately cast parts soldered together in a fashion reminiscent of contemporary cannon construction, and it makes sense that such specialists would have been involved in the casting of such a large and heavy piece.[1]

The decorative motifs of the fountain combine the most distinctive aspects of metalwork from the Deccan, a fusion of strong architectural forms, articulated ribs, and animal motifs—known from numerous ewers and incense burners in the shape of lions, peacocks, geese, or fantastical combinations of the three.

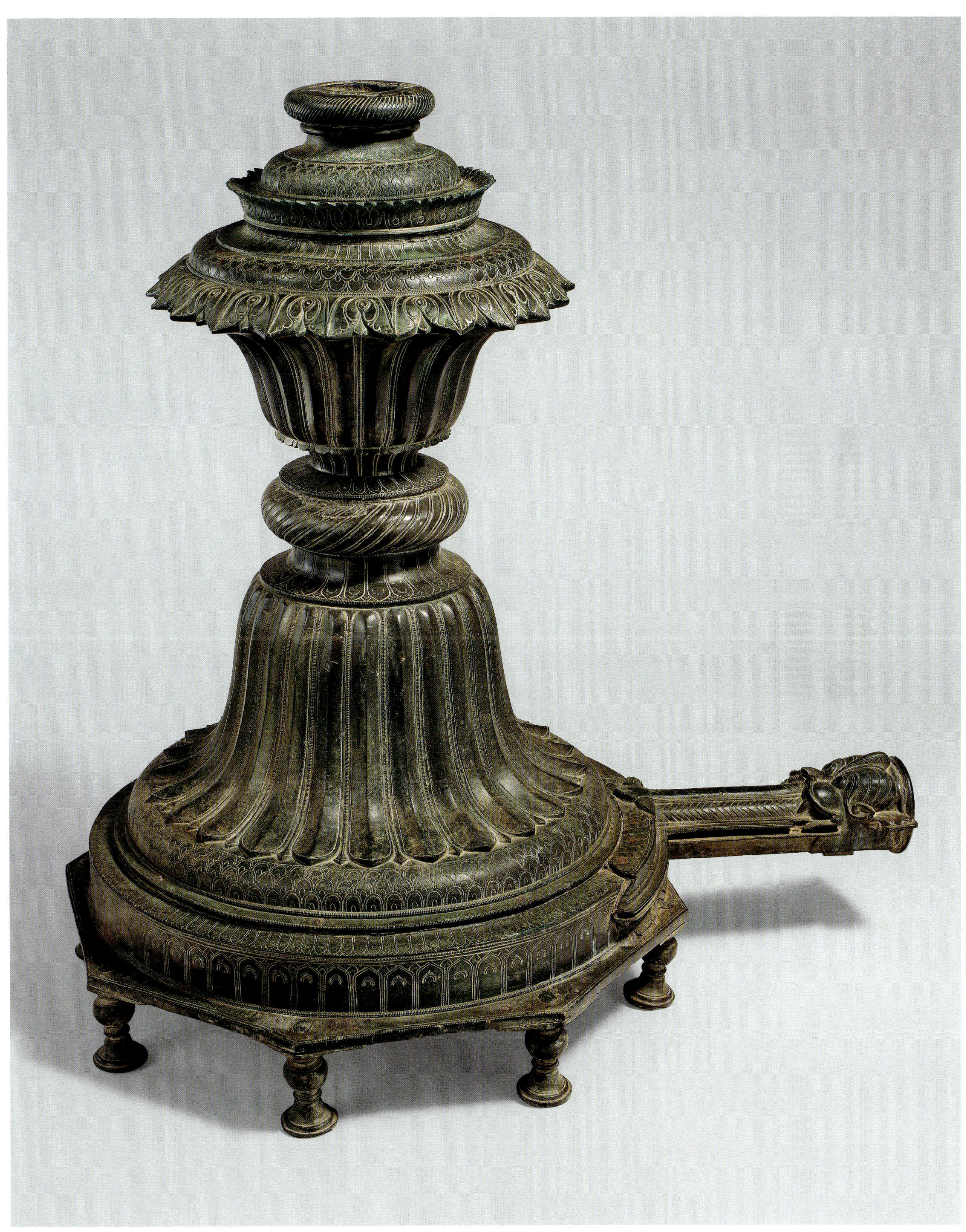

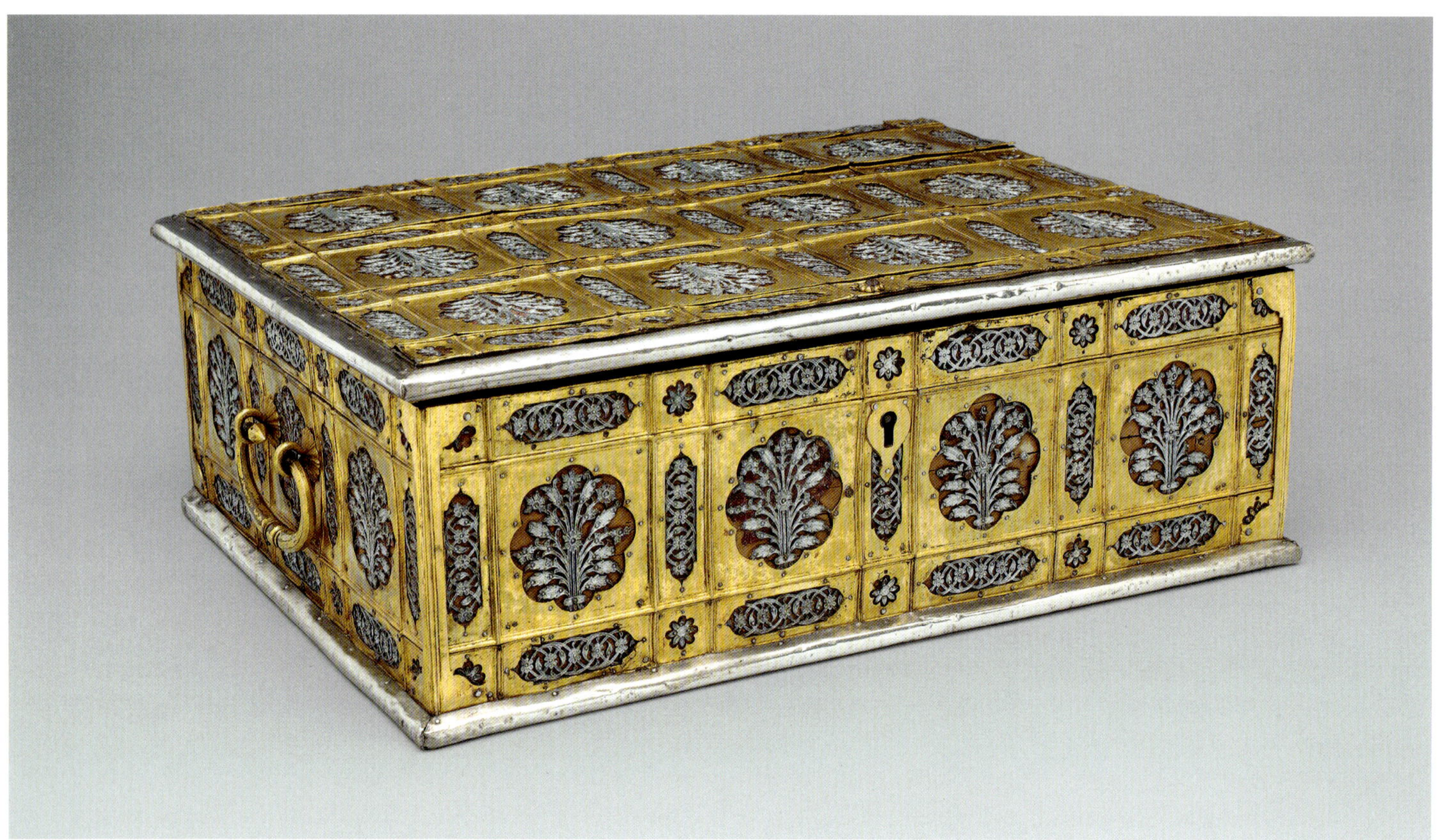

Although no Deccani garden survives in its sixteenth- or seventeenth-century form, study of their physical remains, historical chronicles, and contemporary poetry reveals that they were an important feature of courtly architecture in this region of India.[2] These sources all suggest the importance of water both visually and aurally in the gardens of the period to which this fountain dates, a notion confirmed by studies of the sophisticated water systems that supplied the capitals of Golconda and Bijapur.[3] Two other fountains, both basins, appear to have come from the same garden; they also have petals with chased details, engraved lappets around the base, and a *kirtimukha* spout.[4] Perhaps fountains with different profiles were placed throughout this garden or in a line along a water channel to provide an eye-pleasing arrangement. MS

1. As noted by conservator Richard Stone, see report in curatorial files of the Department of Islamic Art.
2. See, for example, Husain 2000.
3. Among other studies, see Rötzer 2010.
4. One is in the David Collection, Copenhagen, no. 53/1998, published in Folsach 2001, p. 336; the other is in a private collection.

PROVENANCE: Private collection, Europe; [Terence McInerney, New York, until 1997; sold to MMA]

276. Writing Box

India, Mughal or Deccan, possibly Burhanpur, mid-17th century
Wood; overlaid with dyed wool, stamped silver and gilt-copper plaques
5⅜ × 16⅜ × 12⅝ in. (13.6 × 41.5 × 32 cm)
Purchase, Gift of Dr. Mortimer D. Sackler, Theresa Sackler and Family, 1998 1998.434

This portable box with internal compartments and drawers most likely originally held writing implements or other objects for the use of an Indian nobleman, although traces of sandalwood paste within indicate ritual use in a later period. The body of the box was constructed from several pieces of hardwood, probably from the indigenous *shisham* tree, and was outfitted with brass hinges and drawer pulls. In contrast with the unadorned interior, the exterior is sumptuously overlaid with amalgam-gilded copper sheets and ajouré silver plaques stamped with the "lattice-and-flower" pattern that had become popular in the Mughal decorative arts by about 1640. The silver plaques were secured with dome-headed silver nails against a plain-weave woolen backing—now largely lost—that was tinted red with madder lake, a dye derived from plant roots of the Rubiaceae family, which would also have been available in the region.[1]

The technique seen here is familiar from Gujarati wood caskets overlaid with small pieces of mother-of-pearl going back to the

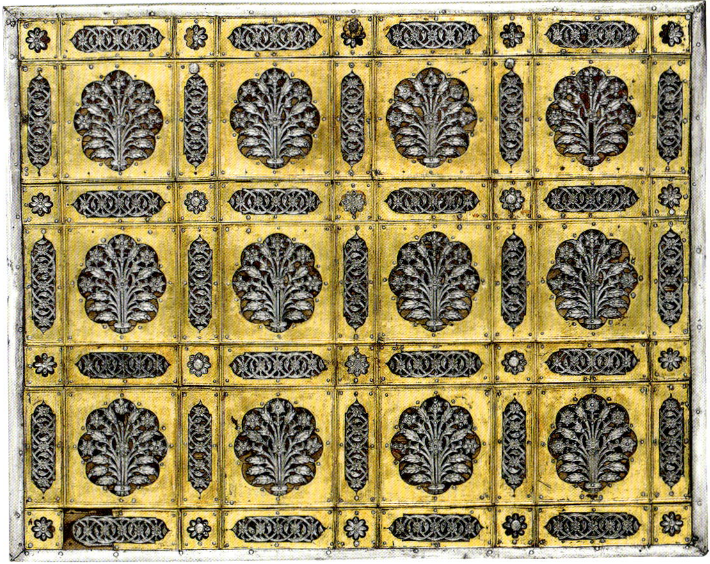

sixteenth century, but such a technique in metalwork is far rarer.[2] It has been noted that a metal overlay tradition existed in sixteenth-century Ottoman Turkey, exemplified by a throne covered with gold sheets held in place by rivets.[3] Such a tradition also existed in Iran, but surviving examples are all later in date, as, for example, a cut-steel plaque of about 1700, backed with a panel of gilt copper.[4] Brass-clad doors embossed with flower-and-star patterns on the Bibi Ka Maqbara of 1661 in Aurangabad, another nearby Mughal center, provide evidence of metal overlay in local Deccani architecture.[5] Taking these points into account, then, the existence of a metal-overlay technique in furniture should not be surprising, even though the proposed box seems to be the sole surviving example.

The decoration and shape of the box have been compared to Indian architectural models, particularly in the integration of surface and form through the grid of strap bands.[6] The flat top and recessed sides recall the profile and elevation of classic Mughal buildings with flat roof, overhanging cornice, raised plinth, and symmetrical columns. While the nature of the decoration is largely Mughal, the taste for opulent gilded objects is associated with southern India. The box has been attributed to Burhanpur in the northern Deccan, an important center for the meeting of Mughal and Deccani traditions, particularly in the production of chintz textiles that share a comparable use of formal repeating flowers contained in lobes or niches. NNH/JFL

1. Lapérouse 2003, pp. 1–3.
2. Folsach 1990, fig. 298, for a Gujarati penbox with comparable technique.
3. Rogers and Köseoğlu 1987, pl. 2. Ottoman Turkey, with its close relations to the Deccan, can be considered a possible source for the technique in India. These are speculations and reflect research by Daniel Walker, who acquired this work for the Museum.
4. Christie's London, April 23, 1996, lot 224.
5. Michell and Zebrowski 1999, p. 134, fig. 99.
6. Loukonine and Ivanov 1996, no. 223, illustrates a Safavid box of comparable shape.

PROVENANCE: Private collection, England; [Terence McInerney, New York, until 1998; sold to MMA]

277. Goa Stone and Container

India, Goa, late 17th century–early 18th century
Container: gold; pierced, repoussé, with cast legs and finials
H. 2⅝ in. (6.7 cm); Diam. 5⅝ in. (14.4 cm)
Goa stone: compound of organic and inorganic materials
Diam. 1⅛ in. (3 cm)
Rogers Fund, 2004 2004.244a–d

An intriguing talismanic object from India's western coast, this Goa stone with opulent gold container is named for the place where such objects are believed to have been manufactured by Jesuits in the late seventeenth century. Like the bezoar stones (natural gallstones of ruminants) of which they are man-made variants, Goa stones were known for their medicinal and protective powers. These treasured objects, encased in elaborate containers made of gold and silver, were often acquired by members of the European nobility; Queen Elizabeth I is said to have worn one as a finger ring. In a letter of 1580, Filippo Sassetti, a Florentine merchant, explained that Goa stones were customarily mounted in gold in order to enhance their powers; thus, there is usually some element of gold or gilding, even in the simplest examples.[1] The stone itself typically consists of a paste of bezoar, clay, silt, crushed shell, amber, musk, resin, narwhal tusk (believed to be unicorn horn), and crushed precious and semiprecious stones, all pressed into a ball and gilded. Scrapings from the ball were ingested as an antidote to poison.

The decorated gold container in this example exhibits an ornate mix of stylistic elements from western Asian, European, and Indian sources. Its globular body is made up of two gold hemispheres, each with an outer layer of pierced, chased, and chiseled foliate openwork. On the base, a scrolling vine arabesque is overlaid by an ogival trellis pattern, the cartouches of which are filled with Indian and Europeanized animals, including mythical beasts such as unicorns and griffins as well as stags, monkeys, gazelles, and foxes. Such elements indicate a diluted Iberian influence, probably due to the Portuguese presence along India's western coast and also are suggestive of European patronage. The tripod

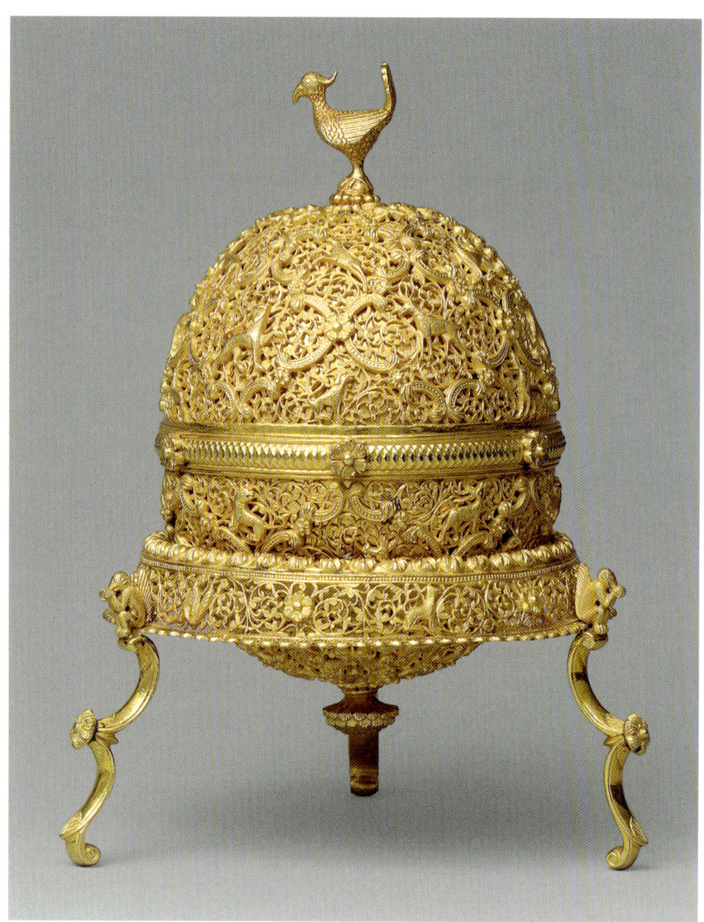

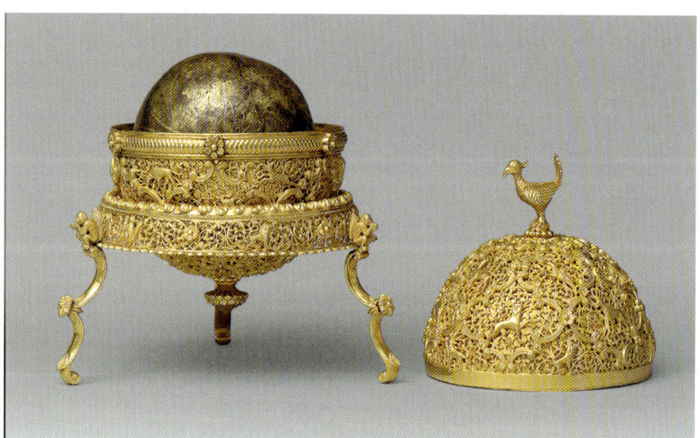

stand can be related to fourteenth-century and earlier southern Indian metalwork models.

Goa stone holders are recorded in European treasuries from about 1750 onward, and one suspension-style holder in gold with floriated openwork scrolls for a bezoar stone has been securely attributed to the last quarter of the sixteenth century.[2] The Gough family with whom the present piece is associated were in western India in the early eighteenth century, and it can therefore be attributed to that period at the latest—though it was more likely made earlier, when there was an active production of such works.[3] The British Museum, London, has three Goa stone holders, including one comparable in shape and decoration to the present piece.[4] Two further examples are in the Henry Wellcome Collection, London, one in silver bearing animal forms and the other executed in gold openwork.[5] There is another smaller silver-gilt example in the Metropolitan Museum.[6] NNH

1. Lisbon and Vienna 2001–2, p. 154.
2. Ibid., p. 151, no. 47, illustrates an example in the Kunsthistorisches Museum, Vienna, made for the Duke of Alba in the last quarter of the sixteenth century; also, p. 154, no. 49, shows an egg-shaped bezoar stone with an inventory record of 1750 from the Schatzkammer, Vienna.
3. Interest in these objects died out over the course of the eighteenth century as, with the rise of more modern medical practices, Goa stones came to be regarded as superstitious objects.
4. Tait, ed. 1984, nos. 407–10.
5. Arnold and Olsen, eds. 2003, nos. SM A 642467, A 642470.
6. The Department of Islamic Art has one other such Goa stone holder (acc. nos. 1980.228.1, .2, .3), but it is far smaller, with a case made mainly of silver. Another example may be seen in a sales catalogue from Bonhams, London, July 25, 2003, lot 60.

PROVENANCE: Gough and Hall families, England, by descent (from early 18th century); Humphrey Farran Hall, England, by descent (until d. 1910); George William Marshall, England (from 1910); sale, Bonhams, London, October 16, 2003, lot 349; [Sam Fogg, London, until 2004; sold to MMA]

278A, B. Two Calligraphic Roundels

A. India, Deccan, probably Hyderabad, late 16th–early 17th century
Sandstone, carved, traces of pigment
Diam. 18 1/2 in. (47 cm)
Edward Pearce Casey Fund, 1985 1985.240.1

Inscription in Arabic in *thuluth* script repeated eight times:
يا عزيز
O Mighty

B. India, Deccan, probably Hyderabad, first half of 17th century
Wood, gesso, painted and metal-leafed with gold and silver
Diam. 19 7/8 in. (50.5 cm)
Purchase, Richard S. Perkins and Alastair B. Martin Gifts and Rogers Fund, 1991 1991.233

Inscription in Arabic in *naskhi* script repeated eight times, of which four appear in mirror image:
يا حي يا قيوم
O, the Ever-Living, the Self-Subsisting

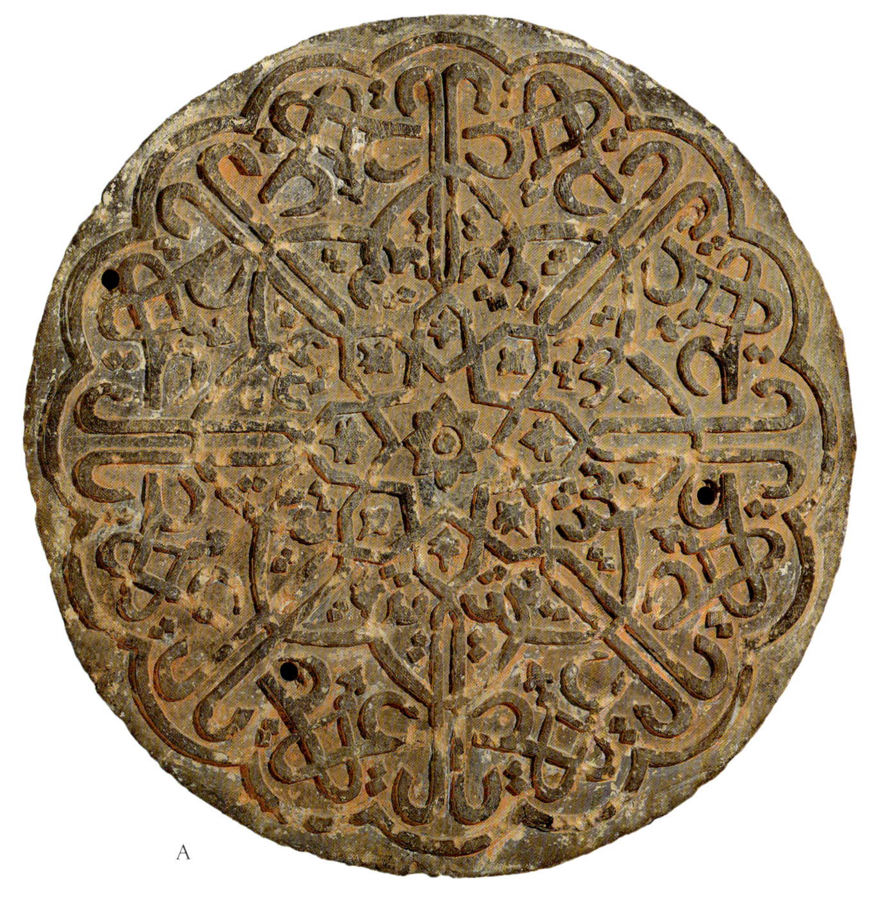

A

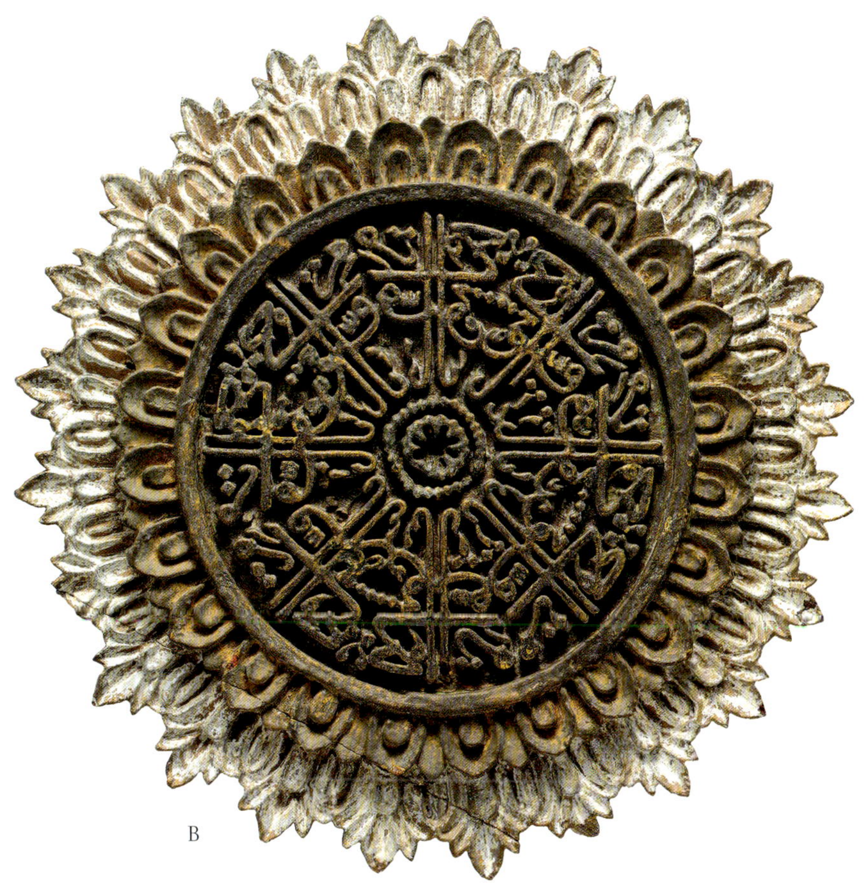

B

Carved sandstone and painted-wood calligraphic roundels like these examples are typically found on the spandrels of the arched portals, niches, and interior walls of sixteenth- and seventeenth-century buildings in the Deccan region of India. The carved inscription in *thuluth* script on cat. 278A repeats "Ya 'Aziz," one of the *asma al-husna* (ninety-nine names of God), eight times in mirror image. The roundel is stylistically related to several carved black basalt examples on the spandrels of the late sixteenth-century Qutb Shahi guesthouse Shaikhpet Sarai (*caravanserai*) in Hyderabad, built under Muhammad Quli Qutb Shah (1580–1611).[1] Similar painted roundels in crimson, brown, and gold outlined in black are also found in the southern hallway of the Bahmanid tomb of Ahmad Shah Wali (r. 1422–36) at Ashtur, near Bidar, which may have served as an earlier source of inspiration for the later examples.[2] The presence of traces of red pigments on the Museum's sandstone example suggests that it was also once painted in a similar palette.

A carved-wood roundel, cat. 278B, from the first half of the seventeenth century contains two of the *asma al-husna*, first written vertically and then in mirror image and repeated eight times around the roundel. The composition springs from two rows of flamelike lappets. Remains of red, blue, yellow, and green paint on this roundel, as well as gold and possibly silver leaf, indicate an originally vibrant palette of decoration, which was likely refinished periodically. While not many wood roundels survive, this one is related to a group of now heavily repainted examples affixed to the upper walls of the Badshahi 'Ashurkhana in Hyderabad (a Shi'i shrine commemorating the martyrdom at Karbala of Husain, the Prophet's grandson, erected in 1593–96 with tiles added in 1611), also built under the patronage of Muhammad Quli Qutb Shah.[3] The building is well known for its large, fine, cut-tile mosaic decoration, particularly the tear-shaped medallions and images of *'alams* (Shi'i processional standards) in a distinct Deccani palette covering its interior walls. In fact, a number of the cut-tile mosaic calligraphic medallions on the two sides of the central niche containing the *'alams* resemble the carved sandstone and basalt roundels discussed here.

Although calligraphic roundels in mirror image are primarily found on architecture, they are also seen in other media, such as metal *'alams*, several of which are preserved in the Badshahi 'Ashurkhana. In a few isolated cases, they appear as illuminations on album pages, as seen in a gold calligraphic roundel in mirror image that is outlined in black and framed by inscriptions containing a hadith of Imam 'Ali in praise of fine penmanship.[4]

Calligraphic roundels are not exclusive to the Deccan or northern India. They are found on the exteriors and interiors of buildings as early as the fourteenth century as far west as Egypt and Turkey[5] and as far east as Iran. However, the compositional characteristics of Deccan examples distinguish them from the others in their persistent use of calligraphy in mirror image (*muthanna*).[6]

Although the origins of this form remain unclear, the type probably entered the Deccan from Iran and Ottoman Turkey in the fifteenth century with the influx into the region of talented Iranian and Ottoman calligraphers, painters, and artisans. The work of these artists was eventually assimilated into the local aesthetic, giving rise to an extended period of creativity and intense artistic exchange that endured into the seventeenth century—as seen in these two Qutb Shahi roundels from Hyderabad. ME

1. I would like to thank Marika Sardar for sharing images of this building with me.
2. See Yazdani 1947. For a detailed discussion of this structure, see Philon 2000.
3. See, for example, Michell, ed. 1986, chapter on Gulbarga, fig. 17, chapter on Bidar, fig. 11, and chapter on Bijapur, fig. 10. I am grateful to my colleague Navina Haidar for sharing the photographs of these buildings, and her expertise, with me.
4. Sotheby's Doha, *Hurouf: The Art of the Word*, December 16, 2010, p. 116, lot 89.
5. Calligraphic roundels and other architectural elements in mirror image are seen as early as 1385 in Artuqid buildings in Mardin, Turkey, and later in Ottoman mosque architecture, such as the Uç Serefeli Mosque (1438–47) in Edirne. For other Ottoman examples, see a carved marble panel from the *qibla* wall of a *sabil*, or fountain, and a woven silk textile panel with niches and suspended mosque lamps in O'Kane, ed. 2006, p. 217, fig. 184, and pp. 212–13.
6. See Yazdani 1947.

Provenance
Cat. 278A: [Vipasha, Ltd., London, until 1985; sold to MMA]
Cat. 278B: [John Lawrence Fine Arts, Inc., London, until 1991; sold to MMA]

279. Hanging

India, Deccan, ca. 1640–50
Cotton; plain weave, mordant-painted and dyed, resist-dyed
8 ft. 4 in. × 78 in. (254 × 198.1 cm)
Gift of Mrs. Albert Blum, 1920 20.79

The impressive figural composition on this hanging, comprising two tiers of large-scale figures posed in an architectural setting with balconies and cupolas containing smaller figures surrounding them, appears to have been painted on the surface of its cotton support, but each element has actually been resist-dyed into the cloth. Reds and purples, for instance, were affixed by first covering those areas with a mordant, or fixative, and then applying a dye over the mordant. Blues were achieved by covering all the

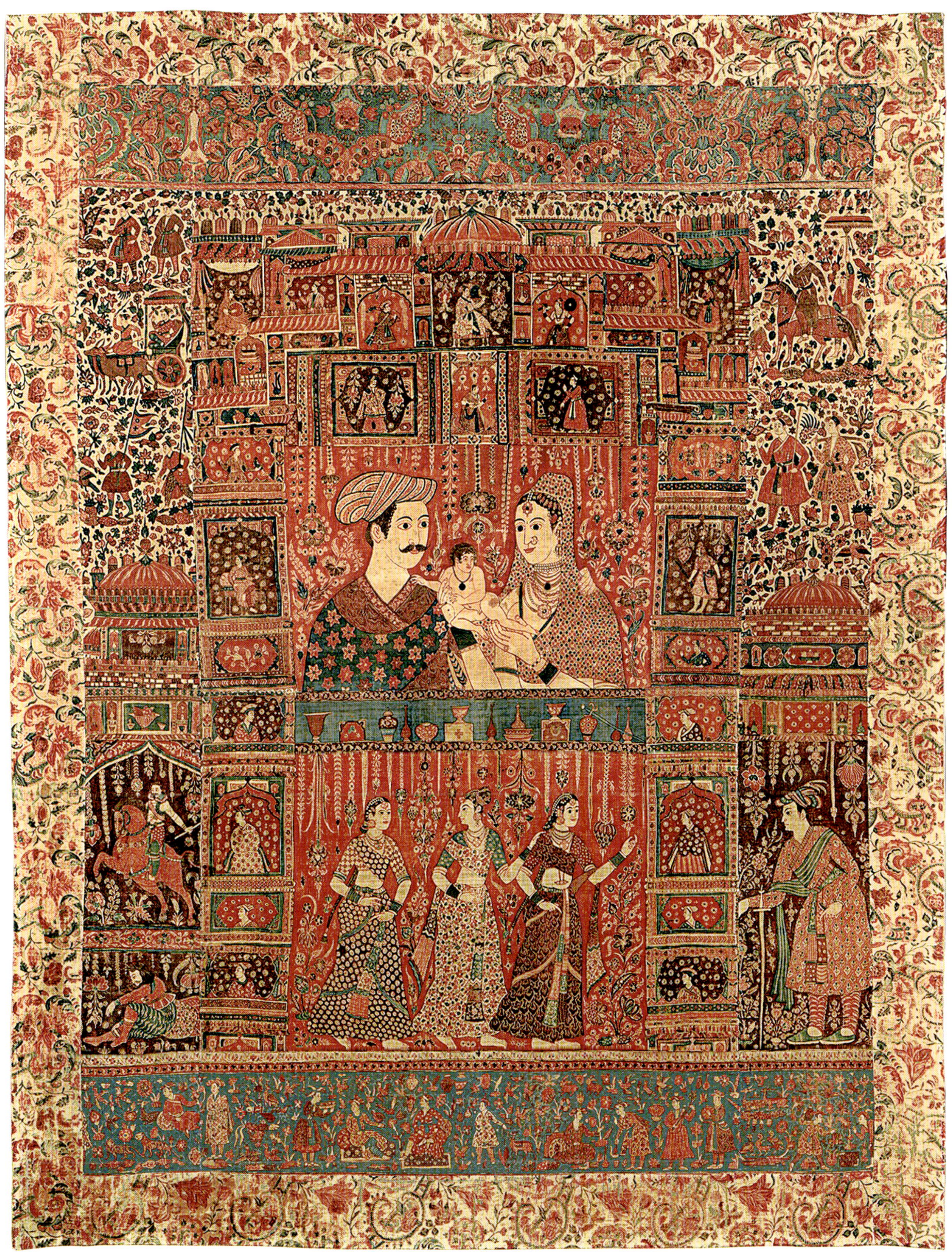

areas not meant to be that color with a coating of wax and then submerging the entire cloth in an indigo bath. Greens were obtained by painting yellow over the blue areas.

Currently, the hanging consists of six separate parts sewn together, with a border made up of seven additional sections from an entirely different piece of fabric. This combination of so many different pieces suggests that the hanging was cut down from a larger work. Indeed, there is a similar piece in the Victoria and Albert Museum, London,[1] that is believed to have once been attached to the Metropolitan Museum's hanging. They were probably joined, along with several other panels, to form a hanging such as one in the Calico Museum of Textiles, Ahmedabad.[2] Displaying a similar arrangement of figures in an architectural framework, it measures, in its current, reduced condition, approximately seven by fourteen feet (213 × 426 cm), which suggests that its original length was at least twenty-eight feet (ca. 853 centimeters).[3]

To understand the composition of this hanging, it helps to look at the local tradition of wall painting, which similarly mixed several subjects in different scales on the same surface.[4] Perhaps this hanging was made to imitate the extensive murals once found in palaces and aristocratic homes in the Deccan. Note, too, that this work prominently features European figures—subject matter that was in vogue during the Mughal period.[5] MS

1. No. 687-1898. See Crill 2008, p. 20.
2. Calico Museum of Textiles, Ahmedabad, no. 403. An appliqué panel in the Victoria and Albert Museum (no. IS.16-1956), with figures very similar to the smaller ones in this hanging, perhaps indicates how other fragments were cut up or otherwise disposed of. See ibid., p. 69.
3. See the discussion in Irwin 1959, pp. 19–27.
4. Nizam al-Din Ahmad 1961, pp. 60–65. This seventeenth-century chronicle describes the walls of the Qutb Shahi royal palaces in Hyderabad as covered with images of the sultan, kings from around the world, and characters from Persian literature.
5. Attesting to the popularity of such images is British Ambassador Sir Thomas Roe's mention that "pictures of the King of England, the Queene, my lady Elizabeth, the Countesse of Sommersett and Salisbury," given to Shah Jahangir by Roe's predecessor, William Edwards, could be found in the *durbar* hall of Mandu, decorated for the celebration of the Persian new year. Quoted in Jaffer et al. 2001, p. 111.

Provenance: Mrs. Albert Blum, New York (until 1920)

280. Tent Panel

India, Deccan, 17th century
Cotton; plain weave, mordant-painted and -dyed, resist-dyed
8 ft. 7 in. × 4 ft. 2 in. (261.6 × 127 cm)
Rogers Fund, 1931 31.82.1

Framed within a cusped arch, a tall plant with purple and red flowers and green leaves, silhouetted against a white background and flanked by smaller plants, forms the central motif of this textile panel. Tiny stylized clouds float above and behind the plant. The size, shape, and design of the panel indicate that it was probably once joined to a series of similar units and used to enclose an outdoor space. The fact that an identical piece is held by the Doris Duke Foundation for Islamic Art, Honolulu,[1] supports this interpretation, as do several contemporary paintings depicting such enclosures, often made of textiles with this exact scheme of ogival frame and flowering plant. These textiles, known as *qanats*, were used in garden spaces within the palace compound and for encampments during journeys. The Mughal chronicle the *A'in-i Akbari* mentions that Emperor Akbar (r. 1556–1605) owned several sets of *qanats* and that they were set up in advance of his arrival at each camping ground.[2]

The production of this textile is attributed to the Deccan region of India, known for the complicated dyeing technique, called *kalamkari*, used to create it. Elements of the drawing and color palette also suggest this place of origin. The panel, however, later found its way to the northern part of the country, as indicated by a seal on the back identical to those on textiles from the treasury of the Kachhwaha rulers at the Amber Palace in Rajasthan.[3] By studying the seals and marks on dozens of textiles, scholars have been able to reconstruct parts of the Kachhwaha collection, which was dispersed around the world in the early twentieth century, and to date many textiles that otherwise lacked a context.[4] This research has brought to light two facts relevant to the Museum's panel: first, that the Kachhwaha treasury contained many dyed textiles from the Deccan, which provide evidence of an Indian market for works otherwise best known in the context of trade with Europe and Iran; and second, that these textiles can be attributed to the seventeenth century or earlier, for that is the date by which they were recorded in the treasury. MS

1. Doris Duke Foundation for Islamic Art, Honolulu, no. DDFIA 83.13.
2. Abu'l Fazl 'Allami 1977, vol. 1, p. 47.
3. The Museum owns three other painted textiles from this collection, all *rumals* decorated with figural scenes (acc. nos. 28.159.1–.3).
4. Smart 1986, and Thompson 1989, pp. 48–51.

Provenance: Kachhwaha Royal Treasury, Amber Palace, Rajasthan, India (in 17th century); [Imre Schwaiger, London, until 1931; sold to MMA]

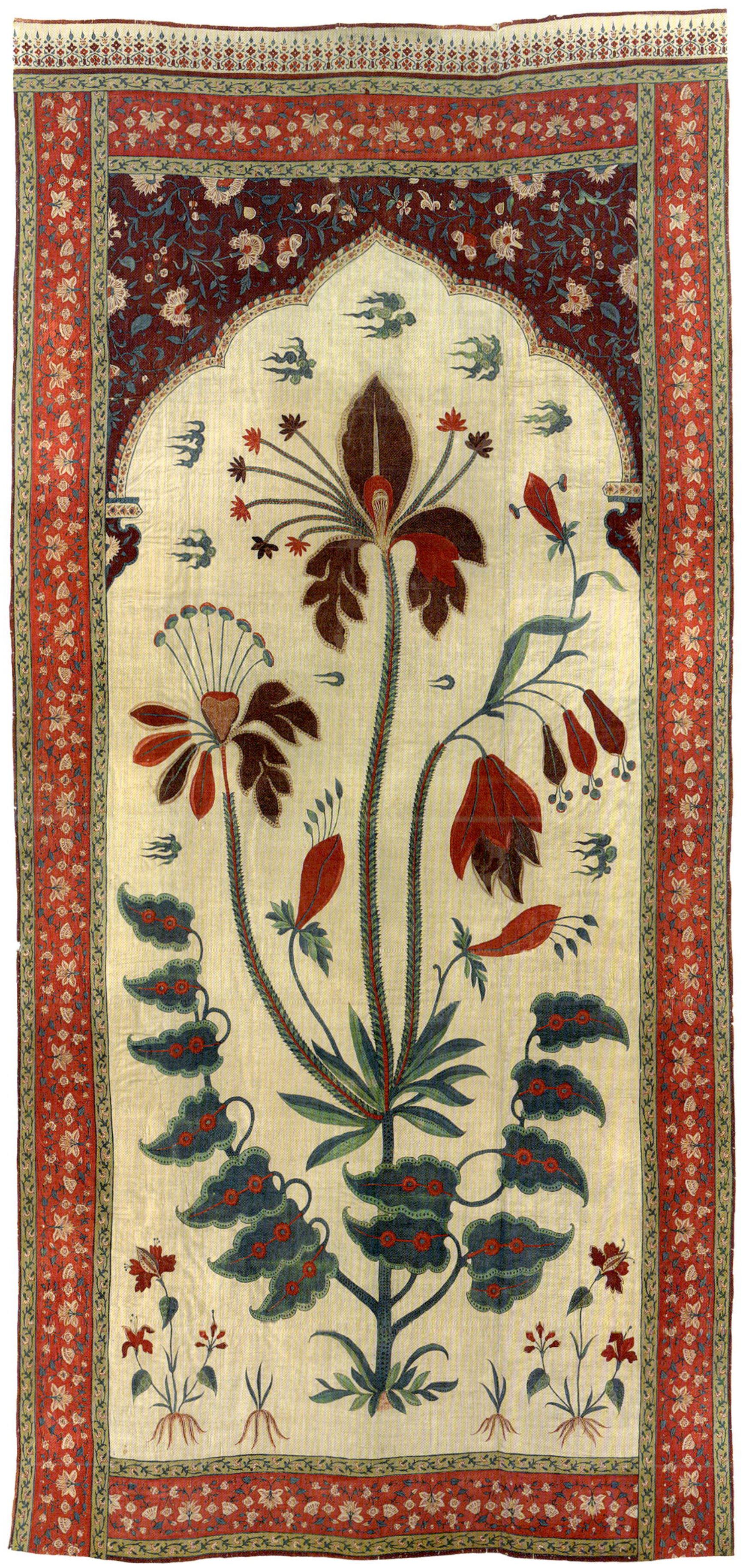

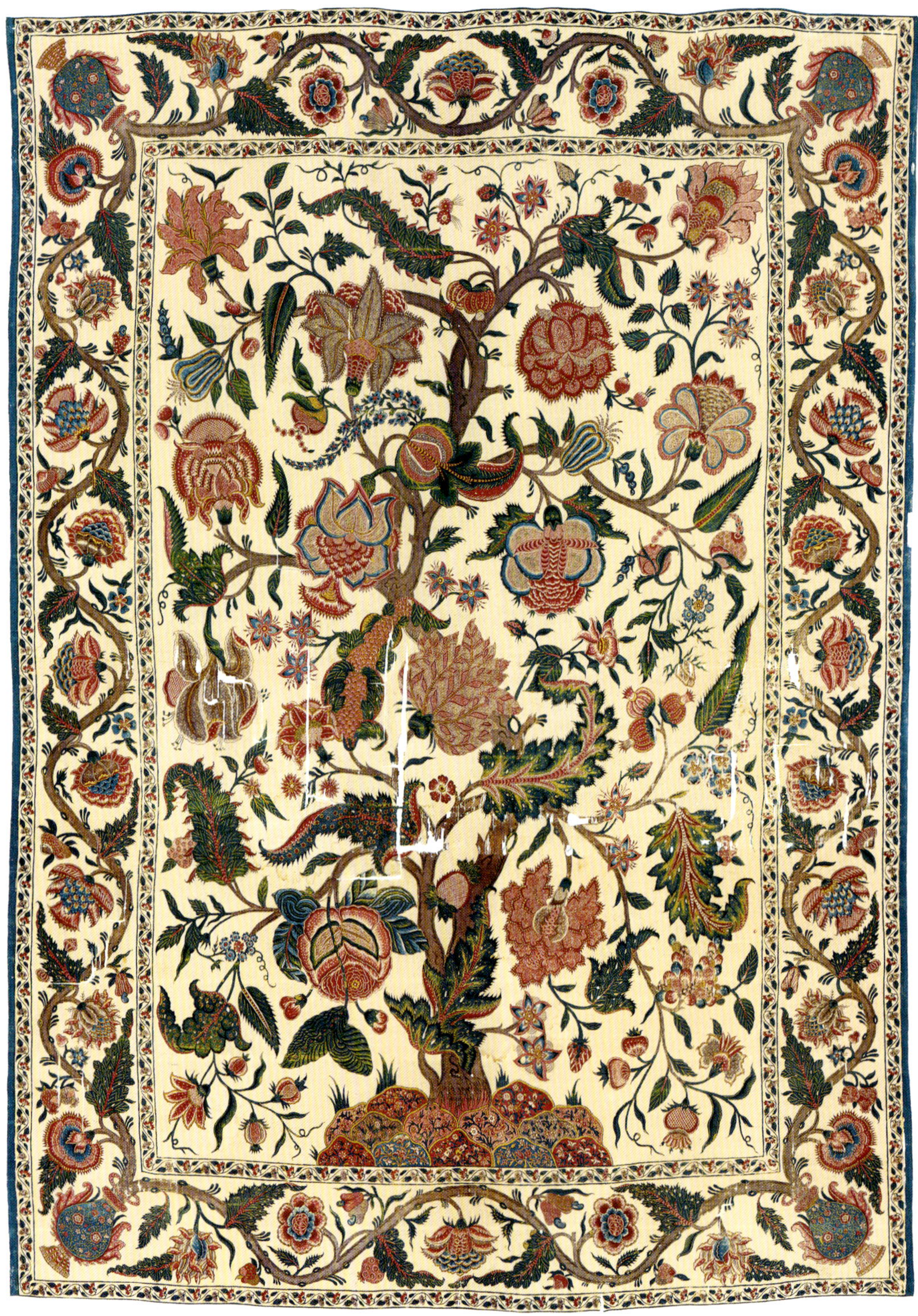

281. Cover (Palampore)

India, Coromandel Coast, 18th century
Cotton; plain weave, mordant-painted and -dyed, resist-dyed
8 ft. 11 in. × 6 ft. 5 in. (271.8 × 195.5 cm)
Purchase, Bequest of George Blumenthal and Gift of Indjoudjian Freres, by exchange, and The Friends of the Islamic Department Fund, 1982 1982.66

At the center of this rectangular panel, a tree growing from a mound is divided into thirteen segments, each framing a flowering plant. Each of the large flowers hanging from the twisting branches of the tree seems to represent a different species. In each corner of the border is a blue vase sprouting two branches that have tendrils, serrated leaves, and pink flowers with blue centers. This type of dyed cotton cloth, known as a *palampore* from the

Hindi term for "bedcover," was produced by the hundreds in the late seventeenth and eighteenth centuries for the European market. Its size and format conformed to tastes and bed sizes in Europe,[1] and the decoration combined patterns from English embroidery, Chinese decorative objects, and Indian textiles, also transformed to suit the intended market.[2] The particularly ripe depiction of the flowers on the Museum's example, the sense of movement in the serrated leaves, and the bold color contrasts throughout are unique attributes and make it an exemplary illustration of the type. MS

1. See the Garrick bed in the Victoria and Albert Museum, London (no. W.70-1916), for instance, for the display of such cloths as they were used in the eighteenth century.
2. The central motif on these *palampores* is often called the "tree of life," but it was first shown by John Irwin and Katharine Brett to be a composite of many sources (Irwin and Brett 1970, pp. 16–21).

PROVENANCE: [Cora Ginsburg, New York, until 1982; sold to MMA]

282. Qur'an Manuscript

India, Kashmir, late 18th–early 19th century
Ink, opaque watercolor, gold on paper; leather binding
6¾ × 4⅝ × 2¼ in. (17.1 × 11.7 × 5.7 cm)
Louis E. and Theresa Seley Purchase Fund for Islamic Art, 2009 2009.294

In the eighteenth century, Kashmir, a predominantly Muslim province in northern India, reemerged as a major art center in the Indian subcontinent after a period of decline. Following the annexation of the province in 1586, talented Kashmiri artists emigrated to the Mughal court; then, in the eighteenth century, the conquest of Kashmir by the Durrani Afghans appears to have spurred a major revival of the arts.[1] Kashmiri artists of this period were actively producing fine Qur'ans, illustrated manuscripts, textiles, and a wide array of decorative objects for a variety of patrons and for the commercial market, including export to other regions of the subcontinent and beyond.[2] Their distinctive style and artistic ingenuity inspired artists elsewhere in the subcontinent and in Iran.

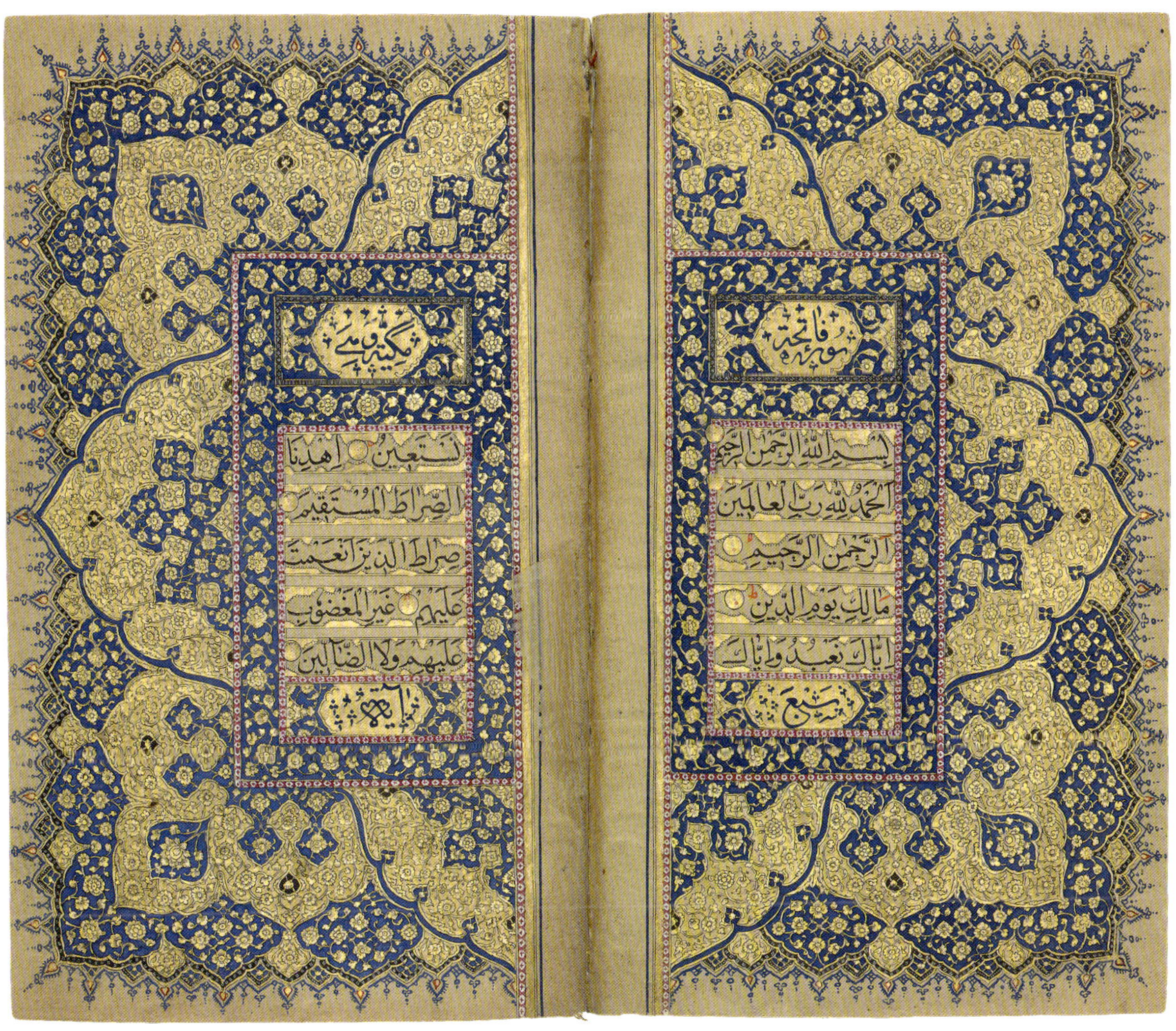

This manuscript is an outstanding example of a Qur'an from Kashmir. Produced in the late eighteenth or early nineteenth century, it has the typical Kashmiri-style gold and blue illumination within a broad frame overlaid by protruding lobed archlike interlacings (the hasp motif) that extend into the margins of the page. The Qur'an has eight lavishly illuminated double pages inserted at the beginning of eight Suras: *al-Fatiha*, *al-Ma'ida*, *Yunus*, *Isra'*, *al-Shu'ara*, *Qaf*, *al-Falaq*, and *al-Nas*. It is written in fine *naskhi* script, which is consistent in quality and evenness throughout the manuscript. The text contains Persian interlinear translations in red *nasta'liq*.

Although Qur'ans in this style were made before the mid-seventeenth century,[3] their production increased significantly in the late eighteenth and early nineteenth centuries. As with other Qur'an manuscripts, these examples are rarely signed, and many (supposedly intended for the local market) are crudely executed. The present work, however, is notable for its fine illumination and outstanding calligraphy. Other fine examples are in the collection of the National Museum, New Delhi, and in the Khalili Collection, London. ME

1. Bayani and Stanley 1999. See also Adamova and Grek 1976.
2. New York and Cincinnati 2007–8.
3. Bayani and Stanley 1999, pp. 230–31.

PROVENANCE: Private collection, England (since 1940s); [Oliver Forge and Brendan Lynch, Ltd., London, until 2009; sold to MMA]

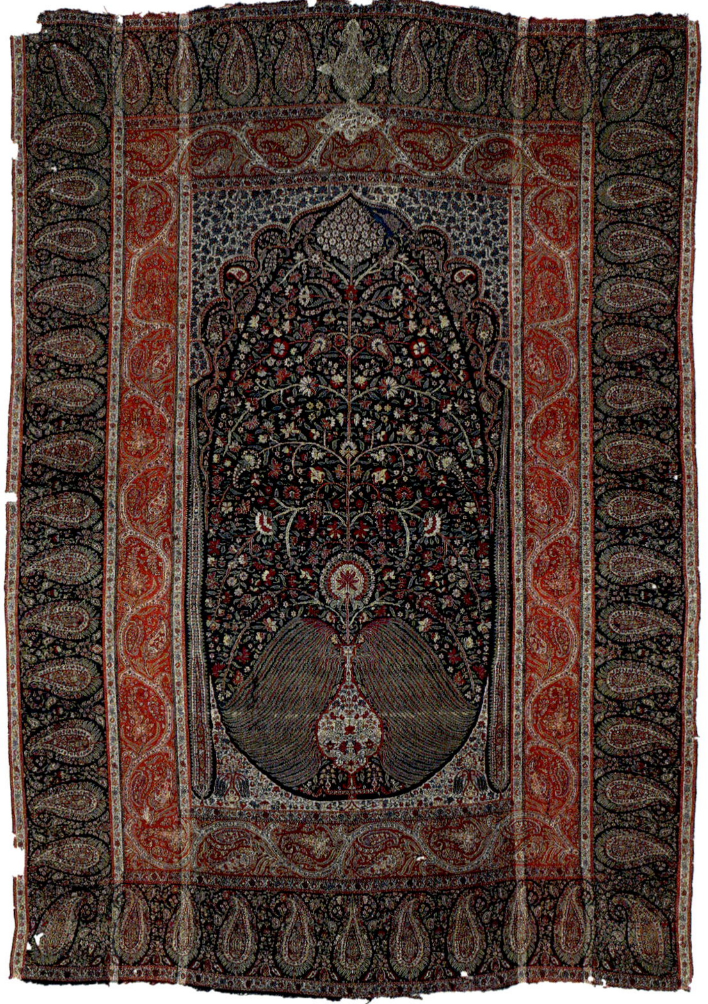

283. Hanging with Design of a Prayer Niche

India, Kashmir, ca. 1820–30
Wool, metal-wrapped thread; double interlocking twill; tapestry weave, embroidered
72 × 51 3/4 in. (182.9 × 131.4 cm)
Museum Accession x.103.4

Inscription in Persian in *nasta'liq* script in cartouche at center of upper frame:

یا حسین
فرمایش نواب اشرف والا
محمد عظیم خان

O Husain, Ordered by the most noble governor, Muhammad 'Azim Khan

At bottom left-hand corner:

برکت یا شاه نجف

Blessing, O King of Najaf[1]

Of the vast and varied textile production of Kashmir, one of the finest, least common types of textile is the hanging with a design of an arch or niche.[2] This example was woven using the typical *kani* shawl technique, which involved three different weaving structures: twill, tapestry, and double-interlocked weft.[3] It belongs to the time known as the Sikh period, when India gained control of Kashmir under Maharaja Ranjit Singh (r. 1801–39).[4] The decorative motifs typical of Kashmir shawls and hangings changed rapidly during this period. The orderly sequence of naturalistic single flowers typical of the Mughal period in Kashmir had previously been replaced during the Afghan occupation by exuberant bouquets that no longer rose from naturalistic roots but rather from a vase placed on a stand. During the Sikh period, the radial shape of the floral composition developed into a teardrop shape with a hooked tip known as the *buta*,[5] which was particularly popular in Iran during the Qajar dynasty.[6]

The *millefleurs* decoration on this *pashmina* hanging immediately brings to mind the shape of a *mihrab* niche, and the hanging may have been placed on a wall to indicate the direction of Mecca. In the central field is a polylobate arch on a plain blue background with a compact, intricate, and colorful pattern: a small stand holds a vase, from which green and red ferns pour in a manner reminiscent of a waterfall. A slender tree of life rises from the mouth of the vase, while a kaleidoscopic effect is created by thin branches covered with a myriad of brightly colored leaves and petals growing out from the central stem. The rectangular field is framed by a sinuous, red vine border that, in turn, is surrounded by a border of large *butas*. By using four bands of white warps instead of blue ones, two at each side, the weaver has produced a ribbon effect that draws attention to the central field.

Directly above the niche, in the outer border, a medallion of loops and arabesques embroidered with loosely twisted *zari*[7] silver thread bears an inscription in white silk with the name of Muhammad ʿAzim Khan, who commissioned the hanging. A second inscription embroidered in white silk chain stitch lies at the lower left-hand corner between the two white bands, proclaiming ʿAli ibn Abi Talib as the king of Najaf. EGM

1. This blessing refers to Imam ʿAli, the first Shiʿa imam, buried in the holy city of Najaf in Iraq.
2. The Metropolitan Museum also owns a rare prayer hanging or mat (acc. no. 17.123.3) that can be attributed to the Afghan period. For other prayer hangings and mats from the Sikh and Afghan periods, see also Ames 1997, pp. 310–12, pls. 179–81; Nemati 2003, pp. 212–15, pls. 45–46; Ames 2007–8, p. 195.
3. Vial 1987, pp. 41–42.
4. Ranjit Singh held sway over Kashmir from 1819 to 1839.
5. Irwin 1973, pp. 11–14. According to Irwin's "Glossary of Terms Used in Kashmir Shawl-Weaving," *buta* is a generic term for the cone and literally means "flower." Ibid., p. 41.
6. Ames 2010, p. 69.
7. The *zari* is a twisted metal (gold or silver) thread wound on silken yarn; Pathak 2003, p. 142.

PROVENANCE: Museum accession; provenance and date of acquisition unknown

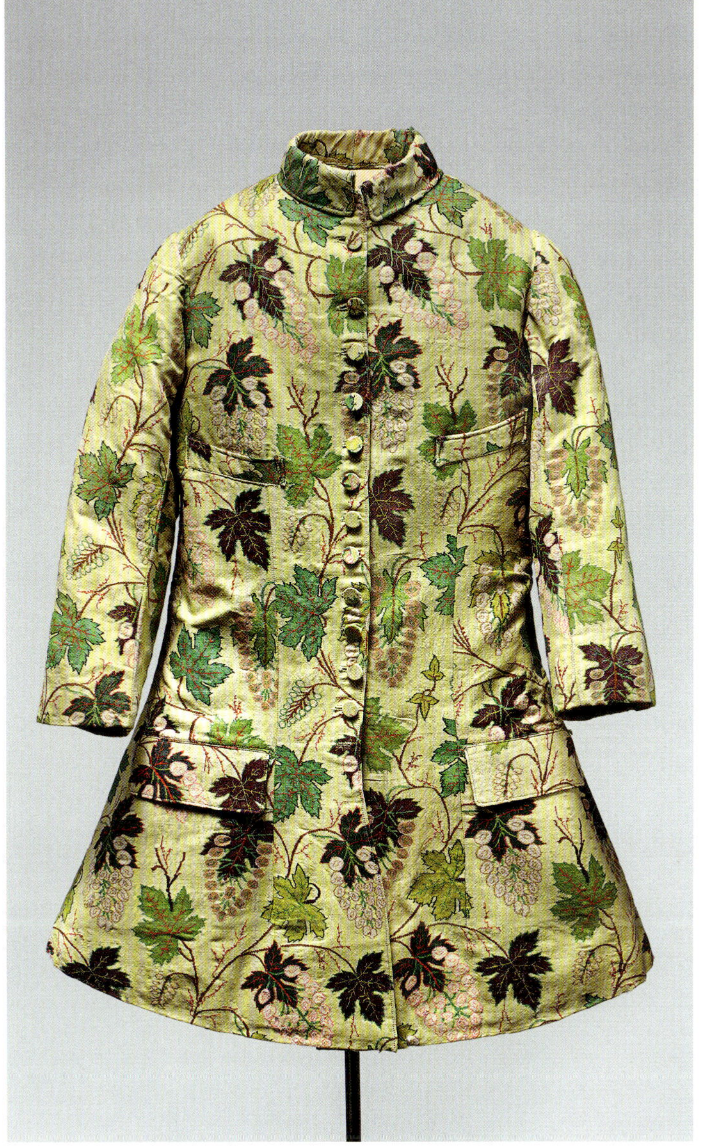

284. Child's Coat

India, Kashmir or Amritsar, late 19th century
Wool; double interlocking twill tapestry weave
28⅝ × 21¼ in. (72.7 × 54.1 cm)
The Alice and Nasli Heeramaneck Collection, Gift of Alice Heeramaneck, 1983 1983.494.10

India has a long and rich history of male costume. Mughal and Deccani illustrated manuscripts and album pages provide examples such as the sleeved coat with flared skirt; later, in the nineteenth century, the assimilation of British clothing styles added fitted jackets and coats to the repertory of Indian costume.[1] Conforming to the Western silhouette, these coats are more tailored than the earlier traditional outer garment for men.[2] This coat, made for a boy, is one such example.

The rows of buttons and buttonholes here represent a marked change in Indian clothing. Additionally, in contrast to the tradition of flat, square sleeves attached to the main body, the sleeves of this coat were attached to round armholes with the aid of a sewing machine—an invention that significantly altered the style of Indian clothes.[3] The Western-looking collar and attached pockets of the coat represent further developments in Indian dress, and the entire garment is carefully lined with fabric made from silk and cotton.

The innovative style and method of the tailoring have been combined with a traditional weaving method. Employing the double interlocking twill tapestry technique, the weaver has filled the light yellow ground with stems bearing European-style vine leaves and grapes. Kashmir was famous for the production of this type of textile. However, during the 1830s, hardships and severe taxation led Kashmiri weavers to leave the country for settlements in the neighboring Punjab Hills.[4] Their emigration might explain why the same type of textile was also made in Amritsar in the Punjab by Kashmiri craftsmen.[5] Men's coats in a similar style with the same kind of fabrics are in the collections of the Museum der Kulturen, Basel, and the Virginia Museum of Fine Arts, Richmond.[6] YK

1. Kumar 1999, p. 201.
2. Ibid.
3. Ibid.
4. Mikosch 1985, p. 8.
5. New York 1985–86, p. 445.
6. Nabholz-Kartaschoff 1986, p. 24; Dye 2001, p. 463, no. 222.

PROVENANCE: The Alice and Nasli Heeramaneck Collection, New York (until 1983)

285. *Fruit Bat*

Painter: Attributed to circle of Bhawani Das
India, Calcutta, ca. 1777–82
Pencil, ink, and opaque watercolor on paper
23½ × 32¾ in. (59.7 × 83.2 cm)
Purchase, Anonymous Gift, Cynthia Hazen Polsky Gift, Virginia G. LeCount Bequest, in memory of The LeCount Family, 2007 Benefit Fund, Louis V. Bell, Harris Brisbane Dick, Fletcher, and Rogers Funds and Joseph Pulitzer Bequest, and Gift of Dr. Mortimer D. Sackler, Theresa Sackler and Family, 2008 2008.312

With its stark composition and subtle coloring, this striking painting transcends its original purpose as a scientific record to become a work of art in its own right. Its subject is the great Indian fruit bat (*Pteropus giganteus*), shown frontally with one wing outstretched and the other folded. The body is depicted in considerable detail, with the fur, claws, veins, and sexual organs articulated in shades of brown and gray. Although the artist is unknown, he is believed to have been among the circle of painters who

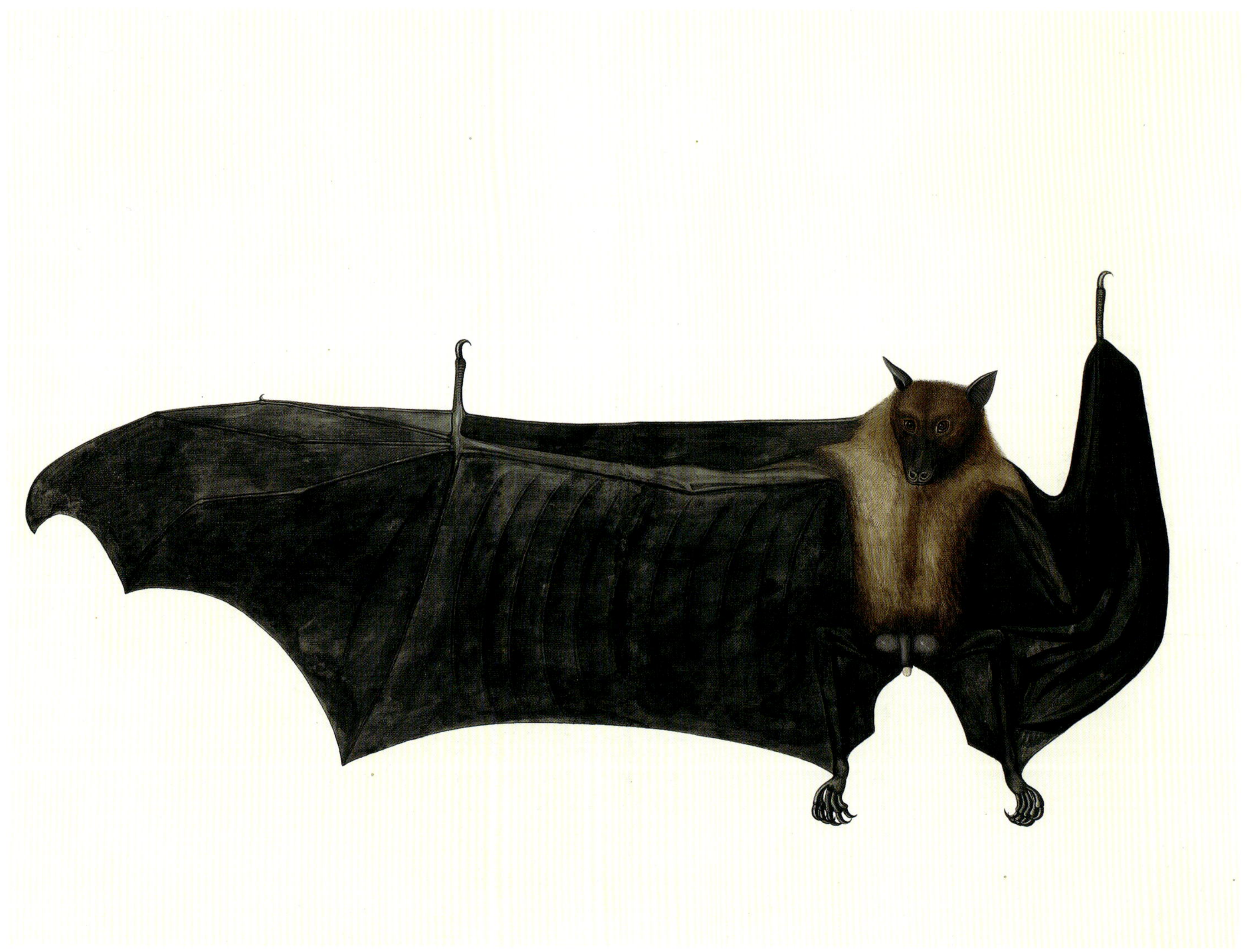

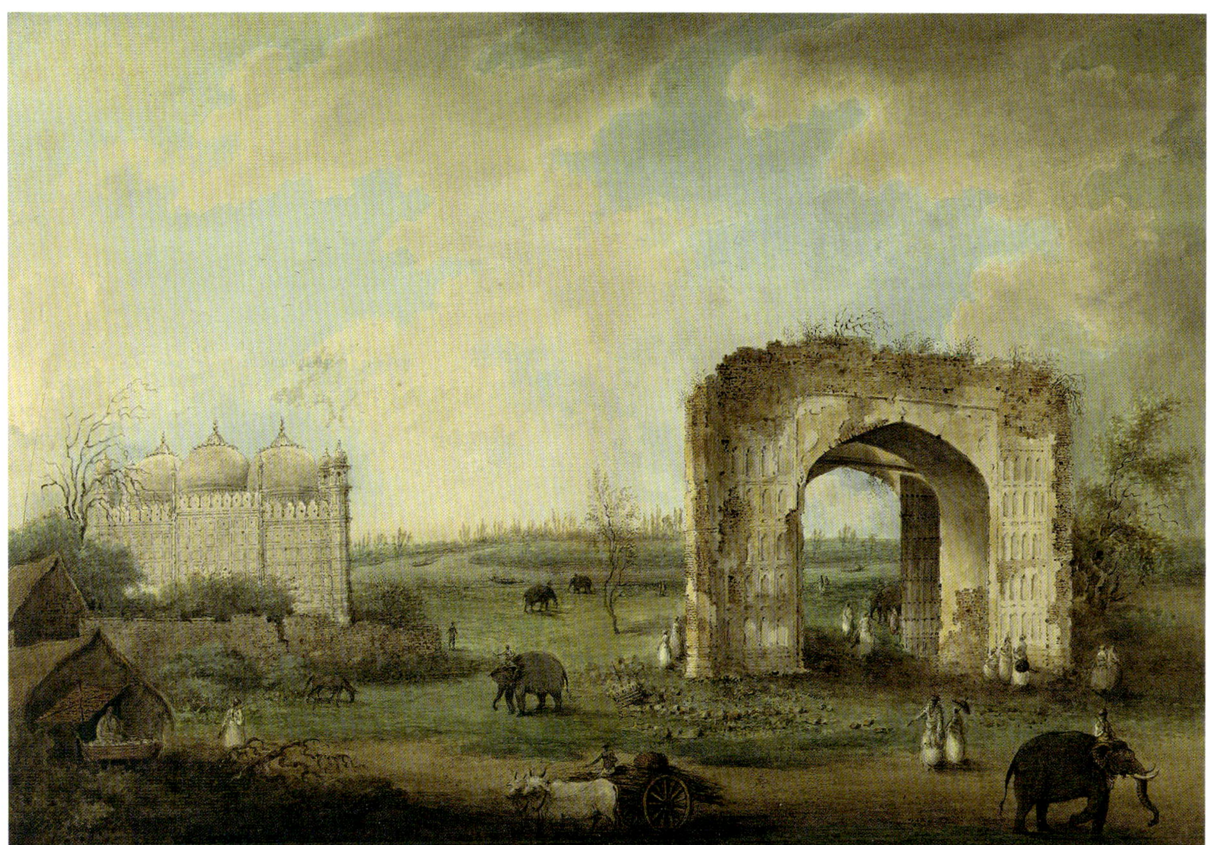

worked for Sir Elijah Impey, chief justice of Bengal from 1774 to 1782, and his wife, Lady Mary. In 1777 the Impeys hired painters to record specimens of flora and fauna that they collected at their Calcutta estate, and, over the next five years 326 paintings of various plants, animals, and birds were made for them.[1] The works tend to show their subjects as fully as possible and with an abundance of detail, against a blank background.

Three of the artists who worked for the Impeys are known: Bhawani Das, Shaikh Zain al-Din, and Ram Das. Their names appear directly on their paintings, alongside the identification of the subject. This painting has not been thus inscribed, but it is closely related to another painting of a bat by Bhawani Das,[2] and it has always been associated with Impey patronage. One can imagine Bhawani Das and the anonymous artist of this painting working side by side, observing the animals, but whereas Bhawani Das's work depicts a tawny-colored female bat centered on the page, with both wings outstretched, his fellow artist has created an asymmetrical composition of an emphatically male bat in shades of gray and black, one wing dramatically unfurled. MS

1. Archer, M. 1992, p. 97. The Impeys' collection was dispersed at an auction in 1810.
2. London 2001a, no. 1; sale, Christie's London, May 22, 2008, lot 7.

PROVENANCE: Niall Hobhouse, London (by 2001–8; cat., 2001, no. 2); Hobhouse sale, Christie's, London, May 22, 2008, lot 8, to MMA

286. *View of a Mosque and Gateway at Motijhil, Bengal*

Painter: Attributed to Sita Ram (active 1814–23)
India, Bengal, ca. 1814–23
Opaque watercolor on paper
13 × 19¼ in. (33 × 48.9 cm)
Cynthia Hazen Polsky and Leon B. Polsky Fund, 2002 2002.461

Recently identified, the subject of this painting is the mosque and gateway of the Sang-i Dalan palace at Motijhil, outside Murshidabad, built in 1743 by Nawazish Muhammad Khan.[1] The artist was probably Sita Ram, an accomplished Bengali painter whose work has been admired since the 1970s, when three albums of his watercolors were sold at auction.[2] It was not until 1995, however, that the patron of the watercolors and the circumstances of their creation were ascertained. Inscriptions in a group of eight albums acquired by the British Library, London, in that year explained that they, along with two albums that had appeared in 1974, had been made for Francis Rawdon (2nd Earl of Moira, later 1st Marquess of Hastings; governor-general of Bengal from 1813 to 1823) on a tour of northern India in 1814 and 1815. In his journal, Hastings had mentioned that, at one point on the tour, "a Bengal draftsman who accompanied us was directed to make a coloured sketch of the scenery,"[3] but the "draftsman" had not previously been identified as Sita Ram, and the "coloured sketch" had not been connected with his magnificent watercolors.[4]

Sita Ram's career can be followed only for the brief but intense span of time when he worked for Hastings, from about 1814 to 1823.[5] During that period, he created the ten albums of the 1814–15 journey and at least two more based on tours in 1817 and 1820–21; contributed to albums of natural history drawings; and made other studies that were later placed in scrapbooks.[6] From this body of work, two facets of Sita Ram's work are apparent. His natural history drawings are characterized by crisp detail, but in his landscapes, he made use of low horizons and warm light and manipulated scale and perspective for greater effect. Like the other works made for Hastings, this painting no doubt captures what the traveling party saw, but it also suffuses both landscape and architecture with a sense of languor, evoking a timeless mood rather than a fleeting moment from a trip. This impression is further emphasized by the artist's decision to depict the Motijhil site from behind, excluding the main palace and emphasizing the state of decay of the remaining buildings. MS

1. This identification was made by J. P. Losty based on a watercolor of an almost identical view in the Album of Bengal Drawings in the possession of the London booksellers Maggs Bros. in 2009. Personal communication to Navina Haidar, February 21, 2010 (curatorial files, Department of Islamic Art). Prior to this identification, Joachim Bautze (in San Francisco and other cities 1998–99, pp. 308–9) and Navina Haidar (in New York 2004–5, p. 218) had suggested that the painting was from a tour of the Gaur district in 1820–21. For Motijhil, see Dani 1961, pp. 276–77.
2. An album of paintings of fruits and plants was sold at Sotheby's London, July 15, 1970. Two albums of views from Murshidabad to Patna and from Sikandra to Agra were sold at Sotheby's London, July 9, 1974.
3. Hastings 1907, p. 133.
4. Losty 1995.
5. Losty has since revised his suggestion (ibid., p. 84 n. 2) that Sita Ram may have worked for Dr. John Fleming before entering Hastings's service; personal communication, September 1, 2010.
6. The albums from Bengal, natural history albums, and scrapbooks were also acquired by the British Library in 1995. See Losty 1995, p. 81. Selected paintings from the 1817 tour were published in Losty 1996.

Provenance: Probably Francis Rawdon, 2nd Earl of Moira, later 1st Marquess of Hastings, governor-general of Bengal (1813–23); private collection, England; Dr. William K. Ehrenfeld, San Francisco (in 1998); [Oliver Forge and Brendan Lynch, Ltd., until 2002; sold to MMA]

287. A Groom Holding Two Carriage Horses

Attributed to Shaikh Muhammad Amir of Karraya (active 1830s–40s)
India, Calcutta, ca. 1845
Opaque watercolor on paper
12 × 20 in. (30.5 × 50.8 cm)
Louis E. and Theresa S. Seley Purchase Fund for Islamic Art and Rogers Fund, 1994 1994.280

This watercolor painting depicts an Indian groom, known as a *syce*, dressed in blue and holding the muzzles of two tall white horses. The trio appears in an almost desolate landscape on the bank of a river; on the opposite bank, a row of low shrubs and bushes is interspersed with small white structures. But these are minute

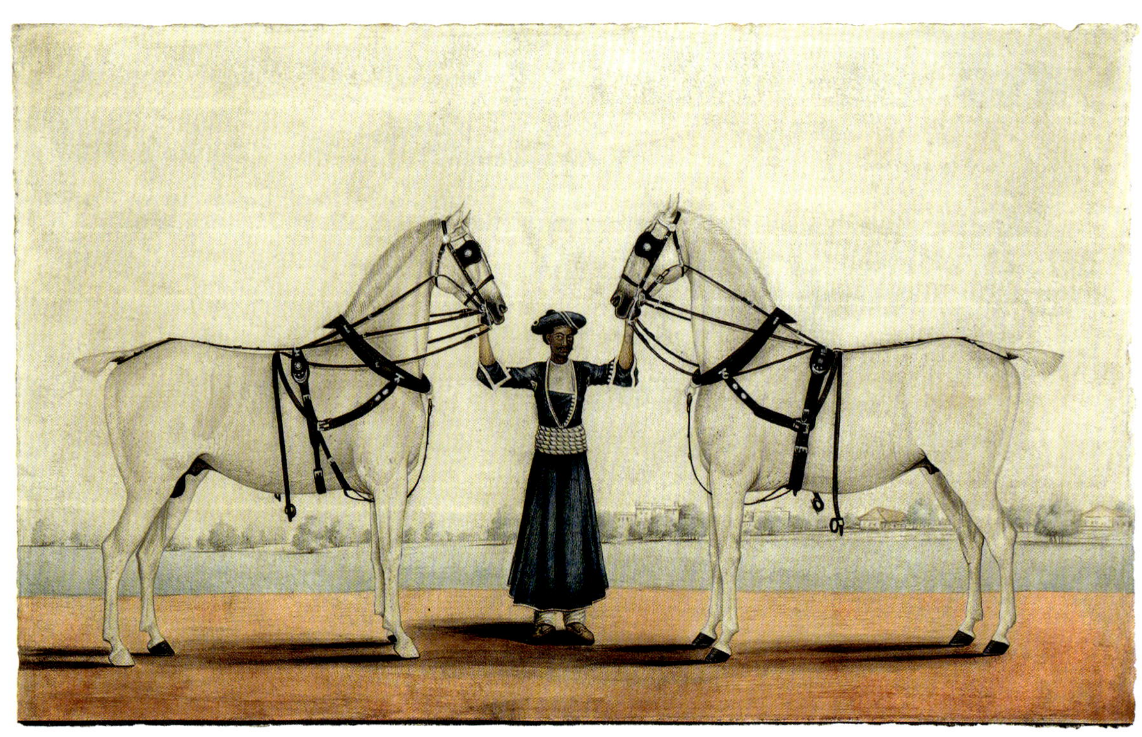

details, and a wide, blank sky constitutes most of the background. The ostensible aim of this painting (a type known from other examples) was to record the property of a British resident in India, but the work seems to have a more particular meaning, in light of the unsettling way in which the groom stares back at us with one eye raised, his two charges blindered.

The painting has been attributed to Shaikh Muhammad Amir of Karraya, one of the three best-known artists working in Calcutta in the nineteenth century, when the city was the capital of the British government and a production center for many works made for British patrons. Whereas the artist Zain al-Din was noted for his plant and animal studies made for Sir Elijah and Lady Mary Impey, and Sita Ram primarily painted landscapes and monuments, Shaikh Muhammad portrayed the members and possessions of British households.

Although this painting does not bear the Persian ascription found on most of Shaikh Muhammad Amir's works, it compares directly with the numerous paintings by this artist that treat the same theme of grooms and horses.[1] He was active in soliciting patrons and created dozens of such works.[2] Finally, the way that the *syce*'s right eye is cocked—a detail found in another painting by the artist of a hookah bearer—ties this work to his oeuvre.[3] MS

1. In the collections of the India Office Library and of the Marquis of Dufferin and Ava (illustrated in New York and other cities 1978–79, pp. 69 and 71); and of Mildred and W. G. Archer (illustrated in Washington, D.C., and other cities 1936, no.79); among others.
2. Pal, ed. 1990, p. 136.
3. Victoria and Albert Museum, London (no. IS 5-1957), illustrated in Archer, M. 1992, p. 103.

PROVENANCE: Robert Edward Master, Esq., England; [Terence McInerney, New York, until 1994; sold to MMA]

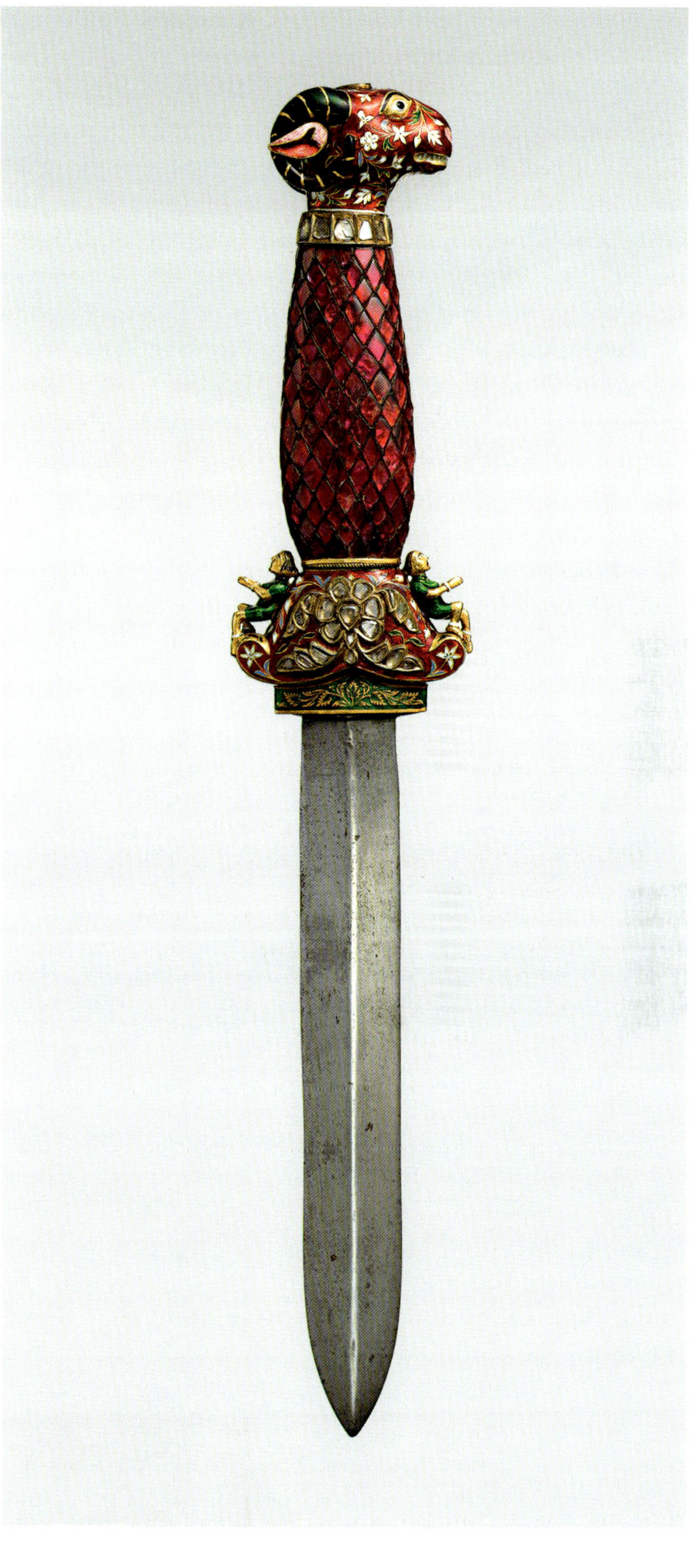

288. Dagger

India, probably Jaipur, 18th–19th century
Hilt: Gold; enameled and set with precious stones; *kundan* technique
Blade: steel
Overall 12¼ × 2¼ in. (31 × 5.7 cm)
Rogers Fund, 1970 1970.180

The sartorial code observed by the nobility of India included highly ornamented daggers that signified the bearer's social standing and prestige.[1] In the mid-seventeenth century, dagger hilts began to be decorated with animal heads, carved from materials such as jade, ivory, and bone, that took on increasingly eccentric and colorful expressions; the trend gained currency throughout northern India during the eighteenth and nineteenth centuries. The hilt of this dagger, which is an example of the latter period, is fashioned in the image of a ram's head.[2] Various techniques have been used in its manufacture. Champlevé enameling and stone-incrustation in the *kundan* technique were employed to decorate the guard and pommel, while the grip is studded with flat-cut stones aligned over red resin to form a lozenge pattern.

The art of enameling became established during the earlier Mughal period, most likely through contact with European traders and jewelers, and it quickly spread over the subcontinent in the following centuries. The enameled floral motifs found on this dagger exhibit a coloring and pattern that closely recall examples attributed to nineteenth-century Jaipur,[3] one of the most reputed centers of enameling. Therefore, the most probable provenance and dating that can be suggested for the hilt are northern India, eighteenth to nineteenth century. The blade, which is made of steel, appears to be a later replacement for the original. An almost identical dagger, certainly coming from the same workshop, was in the collection of James and Marilynn Alsdorf and now belongs to the Art Institute of Chicago.[4] MaB

1. Los Angeles and other cities 1989–91, p. 155.
2. For other examples of ram-headed daggers from the same period, see Pant 1978–83, vol. 2, pls. 97, 117, 174.
3. See Bala Krishnan and Kumar 1999, fig. 159; Antwerp 1997, no. 87.
4. Chicago 1997, no. 331.

Provenance: Peter Marks, New York (until 1970; sold to MMA)

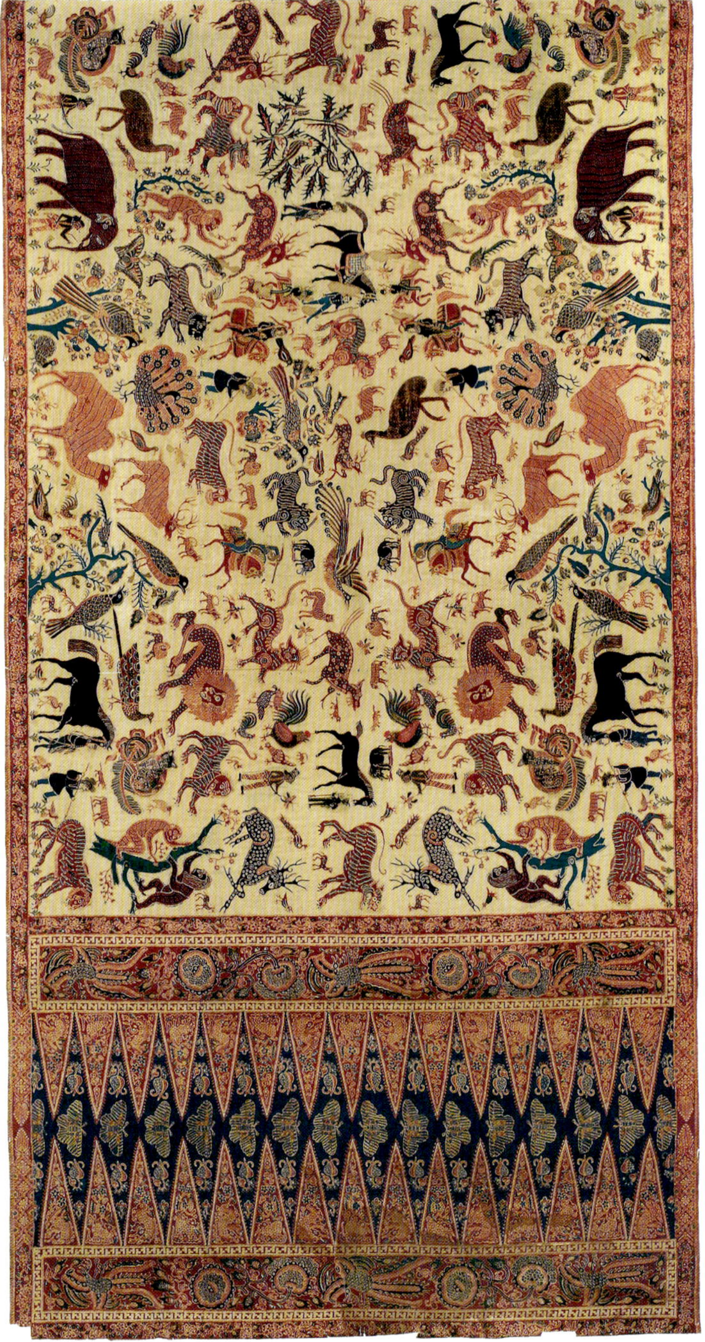

289. *Hip Wrapper (Sarung)*

Indonesia, Java, Pasisir (North Coast) region, mid- to late 19th century
Cotton; plain weave, resist-dyed, painted
44 × 84 in. (111.8 × 213.4 cm)
Purchase, Rogers Fund, 1930 30.88.2

Indonesia, which today has the largest Muslim population of any nation, has long been a crossroads of cultural, religious, and artistic traditions. The center of these interactions is the island of Java, particularly the North Coast region, known as the Pasisir. Over the centuries, Buddhism, Hinduism, and finally Islam have each, in turn, become the dominant faith on the island as waves of Indian, Arab, Persian, Chinese, and, later, European merchants and settlers have visited or made their home on its shores. In the Pasisir, this diversity has resulted in the development of a multiethnic society with arts that reflect a multiplicity of cultural influences.[1]

The diverse cultural influences in Javanese art are evident in the imagery of the distinctive batik textiles made on the island. The term *batik* refers to the technique used to create the images on the cloths, a resist-dyeing process in which the designs are applied to both sides of the cloth in wax, which prevents the absorption of dye. To create the various colors that appear in the final composition, the cloth is then immersed in a succession of dye baths. Between each dye bath, the portions of the designs that are either to receive, or be protected from, each succeeding color are left exposed or protected with wax, as required.[2]

The ends of this work, a hip wrapper, were originally sewn together to form a tubular garment (*sarung*), but the seam was later opened to reveal the complete design. Its imagery and layout indicate a Pasisir origin, and it was probably made in an Indo-European workshop. Operated by women of mixed Javanese and European descent, Indo-European workshops produced batik with imagery

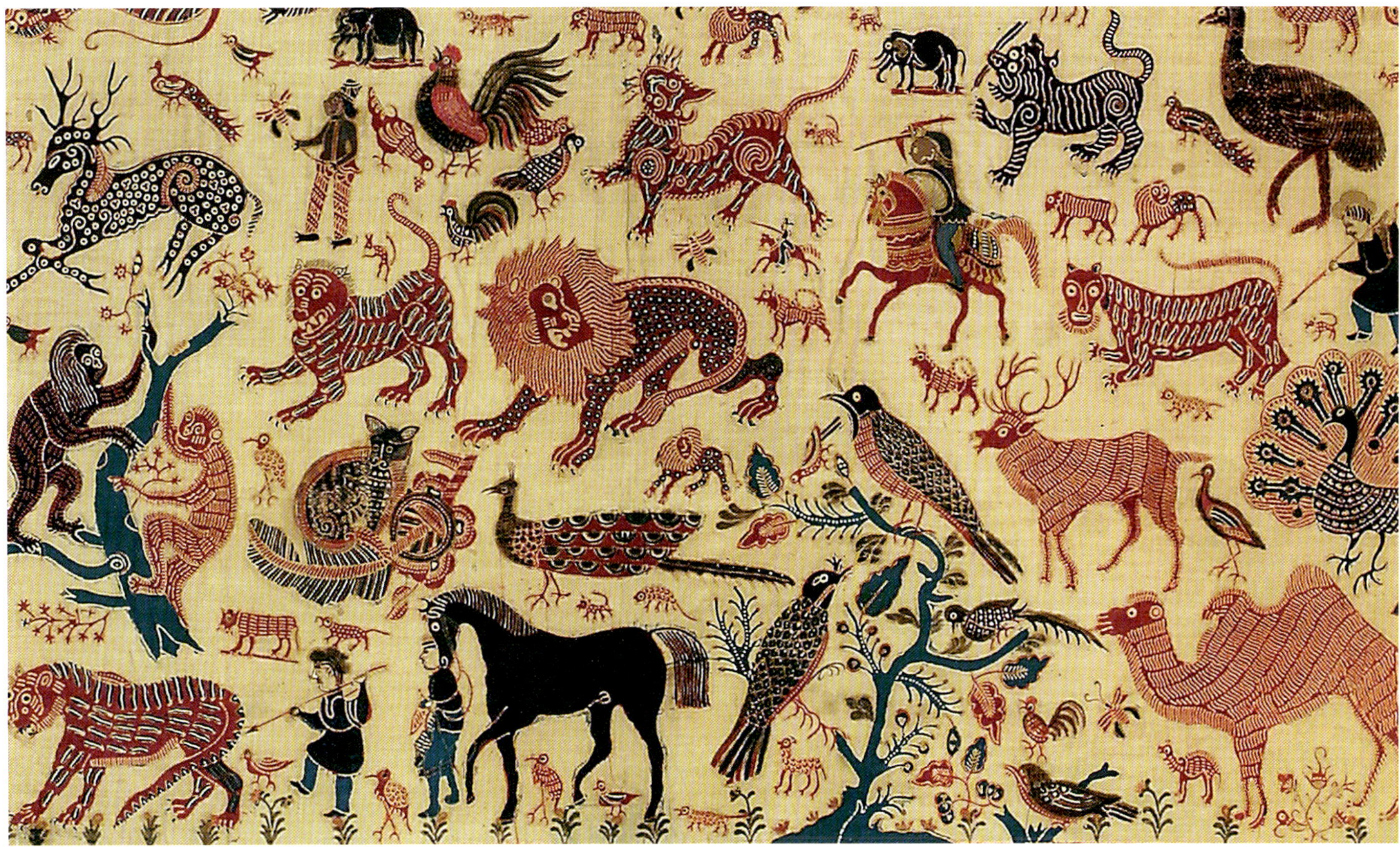

drawn from a variety of sources.[3] The layout and designs on the broad band at the right, called the *kepala* (head) of the cloth, reflect the influence of Indian trade textiles from the Coromandel Coast. Adorning the body (*badan*) of the *sarung* is a fantastic menagerie that includes motifs of Indian and Persian origin such as birds seated in a flowering tree and dancing peacocks, as well as images of felines and leaping deer from Chinese sources. These creatures are accompanied by more naturalistic depictions of two-humped Bactrian camels, lions, tigers, and apes (probably Indonesia's native orangutans). Perhaps the most unusual animal here is the cassowary, a crested ostrichlike bird found only in New Guinea and its adjacent islands and northeastern Australia. The animals are interspersed with images of Europeans riding, leading horses, and hunting with spears; there are also soldiers carrying bayonets and other figures accompanying the elephants. Like Javanese culture itself, this eclectic composition combines a diversity of cultural and artistic influences within an overall Islamic context. EPK

1. For a summary of the complex history of immigration and cultural influences on Java's North Coast, see Carey, P. 1996–97, pp. 21–29.
2. Detailed analysis of the present work by Christine Giuntini, conservator in the Department of the Arts of Africa, Oceania, and the Americas, has revealed that the designs were probably laid out with the aid of pencil guides, drawn on the fabric prior to waxing. The repeated motifs, which are similar but not identical, were likely created with the aid of sketches made on tracing paper that were pinned to the back of the textile, which was then held up to a light source to allow the designs to be copied in wax. The use of this technique in workshops on Java's North Coast is described by Heringa 1996–97a, p. 227. Further details of the designs and some of the smaller motifs were later painted directly onto the surface once dyeing was completed.
3. For discussion of the development, imagery, and production of Indo-European batik and the role of female entrepreneurs, see Legêne and Waaldijk 2001, pp. 43–45; Hout 2001, pp. 143–45; Heringa 1996–97b; and Veldhuisen 1996–97.

Provenance: [Aalderink & Co., Amsterdam, until 1930; sold to A. Vecht for MMA]

GLOSSARY

ʿalam Processional standard used primarily in Iran and India.

aya A verse from the Qur'an.

Buraq Human-headed mount that carried Muhammad on his *miʿraj*, or noctural ascent to the heavens.

caliph Title of the Prophet Muhammad's immediate successors as temporal and spiritual leaders of the Muslim community.

caliphate Office or dominion of a caliph.

çatma Turkish term for cut-and-voided silk velvet; it has a satin-weave ground often embellished with supplementary metal-thread wefts.

chintamani Sanskrit term meaning "auspicious jewel," used to describe an attribute of a bodhisattva and also applied to a motif used in Ottoman art consisting of wavy stripes paired with groups of three or four circular spots.

chuval Knotted-pile storage bag of the Turkmen tribes.

cuerda seca Ceramic decoration technique in which glazes are applied within fields bounded by a wax border to prevent mixing; during firing, the wax carbonizes, leaving discrete zones separated by colored lines.

dervish Individual members of a sufi order, often practicing a type of Islam that stressed spiritual values rather than religious obligations.

div Persian term for a demon usually horned, variously colored, and sometimes furry.

divan Collection of poetry by a single author.

durbar Royal residence, audience hall, or the ceremony held in it.

ebru Marbled paper.

ghazal Short poem with an amorous or erotic theme.

gul-u-bulbul Literally, the rose and the nightingale; used to describe decoration combining birds and flowers that was popular in Iran during the eighteenth to nineteenth century, particularly on lacquerware.

hadith Pronouncement on a religious topic ascribed to the Prophet Muhammad.

hajj Pilgrimage to Mecca.

hatayi Literally, belonging to Hatay or northern China; used in Turkey to describe floral and animal motifs of Chinese origin.

hijra Emigration, specifically that undertaken in 622 by the Prophet Muhammad and his companions from Mecca to Medina; it marks the beginning of an era whose calendar is still in use by the Muslim community.

ikat Both a resist-dyed textile and the technique used to create it; to create a pattern, unwoven warps and/or wefts are bound in specific places to resist dye penetration.

the Jazira Literally, an island; a geographical term applied to the area between the Tigris and Euphrates rivers in present-day Iraq, Syria, and Turkey.

juz' Section comprising one-thirtieth of the Qur'an.

Kaʿba Islam's most sacred building, the cubical structure at the center of the shrine in Mecca used as the focus of prayer.

kalamkari Technique in which cotton cloth is hand-painted to create a pattern.

kani Weaving technique with double interlocking joins that produces a double-sided pattern used particularly to make "Kashmir" or "Kani" shawls.

kashkul Boat-shaped begging bowl of a wandering dervish, used to collect and store alms.

kemha Turkish term for a silk textile woven in lampas with satin-weave ground and twill weave pattern, executed with supplementary wefts of silk and metal thread.

khamsa Five-part narrative poem, especially those written by Nizami Ganjavi and Khusrau Dihlavi.

khilʿa Robe of honor bestowed by a ruler as a special favor or an emblem of office.

lajvardina Modern term, derived from the Persian word for lapis lazuli (*lajvard*), used for glazed ceramics, usually blue, with overglaze decoration in red, white, and gold.

lampas Textile woven in a compound structure, combining two different yet interconnected sets of threads (one for the ground, another for the pattern).

laqab Honorific title.

luster-painting Overglaze technique of ceramic decoration using silver and/or copper oxides that fuse with the glaze during a second firing in a low-oxygen atmosphere to produce a shiny metallic surface.

madrasa A school, especially one offering instruction in Islamic law and theology.

mash'al Columnar lamp stand popular in Iran during the sixteenth to seventeenth century.

mashraba Small drinking vessel, metal or ceramic, with a pot-bellied profile.

masnavi Narrative poem, often of considerable length, composed in rhyming couplets.

mihrab Niche in a mosque's *qibla* wall marking the direction of Mecca and of prayer.

mina'i Modern term, derived from the Persian word for enamel (*mina*), used to describe ceramics with multicolored under- and overglaze-painted decoration.

minbar Raised platform reached by a set of steps, usually situated in a mosque to the right of a *mihrab*; used by speakers to address an assembled group.

mi'raj The Prophet Muhammad's nocturnal ascent to the heavens.

misra' One-half of a poetic couplet.

mulham Fabric combining silk and cotton threads.

muraqqa' Composite book consisting of specimens of calligraphy, paintings, drawings, or designs.

palampore Dyed cotton cloth, from the Hindi word for bedcover.

qibla The direction Muslims face when performing ritual prayers toward the Ka'ba in Mecca.

sadeli Micromosaic technique in which rods of diverse materials are bundled together, sliced transversely, and glued to a wooden support.

safina Small-scale oblong manuscript designed to be held in the hand.

sama' Literally, an audition; a sufi gathering often featuring music and ecstatic dances.

samite Compound-weave textile with both ground and pattern woven entirely in weft-faced complementary twill; can also be enriched with supplementary wefts.

seraser Turkish term for cloth of gold and silver; a silk textile that combines a silk warp with wefts containing both silk and metal-covered threads. (See also *taqueté*.)

shahada Literally, testimony; the Muslim profession of faith: There is no God but Allah and Muhammad is his messenger.

Shahnama Versified history of pre-Islamic Iran composed in the eleventh century by Firdausi.

shamsa Literally, a sun or starburst; form of illumination found in manuscripts as well as in architecture.

simurgh In Persian mythology, a large bird with magical powers believed to nest on Mt. Elburz; sometimes represented in a sinicized form with long colorful feathers.

stonepaste White ceramic body that combines clay, quartz, and ground glass and that approximates the qualities of porcelain.

taqueté Compound-weave textile with both ground and pattern woven entirely in weft-faced complementary plain weave; can also be enriched with supplementary wefts.

tiraz Royal textile workshop or textiles inscribed with royal titles using embroidery, weaving, printing, or painting.

tughra Stylized royal signature containing an Ottoman ruler's name and patronymic along with the phrase "May he reign forever."

yastik Turkish term for a flat bolster pillow, placed against the wall to lean upon.

zilij Architectural tilework used primarily in Morocco; tiles in various shapes are assembled face down and backed with plaster before being affixed to a wall.

BIBLIOGRAPHY

Abdullayev, Fakhretdinova, and Khakimov 1986 Abdullayev, T., D. Fakhretdinova, and A. Khakimov. *Pesn' v metalle: Narodnoe iskusstvo Uzbekistana/A Song in Metal: Folk Art of Uzbekistan*. Tashkent, 1986.

Abu'l Fazl 'Allami 1977 Abu'l Fazl 'Allami. *The A'in-i Akbari by Abu'l Fazl 'Allami*. Translated by H[enry F.] Blochmann and H[enry] S. Jarrett; edited by D[ouglas] C[raven] Phillott. 3rd ed. 3 vols. 1927–49. Calcutta, 1977.

Abu Mansur al-Tha'alibi 1956 Abu Mansur al-Tha'alibi. *Yatimat al-dahr fi mahasin ahl al-'asr*. Edited by Muhammad Muhyi al-Din 'Abd al-Hamid. 2nd ed. 4 vols. in 2. Cairo, 1956.

Acar 1999 Acar, M. Şinası. *Türk hat sanatı (araç, gereç ve formlar)/Turkish Calligraphy (Materials, Tools and Forms)*. Istanbul, 1999.

Ackerman 1938–39a Ackerman, Phyllis. "Standards, Banners and Badges." In Pope, A. U., and Ackerman, eds. 1938–39, vol. 3, pp. 2766–82.

Ackerman 1938–39b Ackerman, Phyllis. "Textiles of the Islamic Periods. A. History." In Pope, A. U., and Ackerman, eds. 1938–39, vol. 5, pp. 1995–2162; vol. 6, pls. 981–1106.

"Acquisitions [MFA]" 1931 "A[c]quisitions, July 3 through September 3, 1931." *Bulletin of the Museum of Fine Arts[, Boston]* 29, no. 175 (October 1931), pp. 94–96.

Adamjee forthcoming Adamjee, Qamar. "The Sultanate Chandayana: An Exemplar of Cultural and Artistic Interaction in Sixteenth Century India." Ph.D. diss., Institute of Fine Arts, New York University, forthcoming.

Adamova 1999 Adamova, Adel T. "Permanent Exhibitions: A Variety of Approaches." *Museum International* (Unesco, Paris) 51, no. 3 (July–September 1999), pp. 4–10.

Adamova 2000 Adamova, Adel T. "On the Attribution of Persian Paintings and Drawings of the Time of Shah 'Abbas I: Seals and Attributory Inscriptions." In *Persian Painting from the Mongols to the Qajars: Studies in Honour of Basil W. Robinson*, edited by Robert Hillenbrand, pp. 17–38. London and New York, 2000.

Adamova and Grek 1976 Adamova, A[del Tigranova], and T[atiana Vladimirovna] Grek. *Miniatiury kashmirskikh rukopiseii/Miniatures from Kashmirian Manuscripts*. Leningrad, 1976.

Adle 1980 Adle, Chahryar. *Écriture de l'union reflets de temps des troubles: Oeuvre picturale (1083–1124/1673–1712) de Haji Mohammad*. Paris, 1980.

Afshar 1969 Afshar, Iraj. *Yadgarha-yi Yazd*. Tehran, 1969.

Afshar 1973 Afshar, Iraj. "Two Twelfth-Century Gravestones of Yazd in Mashad and Washington." *Studia Iranica* 2, no. 2 (1973), pp. 203–11, pls. 41–43.

Afshar 1975 Afshar, Iraj. *Yadgarha-yi Yazd*. Tehran, 1975.

Aga-Oğlu 1935 Aga-Oğlu, Mehmet. *Persian Bookbindings of the Fifteenth Century*. Ann Arbor, 1935.

Aga-Oğlu 1945 Aga-Oğlu, Mehmet. "About a Type of Islamic Incense Burner." *The Art Bulletin* 27, no. 1 (March 1945), pp. 28–45.

Ahmad ibn Mir Munshi 1959 Ahmad ibn Mir Munshi al-Husaini. *Calligraphers and Painters: A Treatise by Qadi Ahmad, Son of Mir-Munshi (circa A.H. 1015/A.D. 1606)*. Translated by V[ladimir] Minorsky. Smithsonian Institution Publication 4339. Freer Gallery of Art Occasional Papers, vol. 3, no. 2. Washington, D.C., 1959.

Akhrarov and Rempel 1971 Akhrarov, I. A., and L. Rempel. *Reznoi shtuk Afrasiaba* (Relief sculpture in Afrasiab). Tashkent, 1971.

Alam and Subrahmanyam 2007 Alam, Muzaffar, and Sanjay Subrahmanyam. *Indo-Persian Travels in the Age of Discoveries, 1400–1800*. Cambridge and New York, 2007.

Ali forthcoming Ali, Daud. *Garden and Landscape Practices in Precolonial India Histories from the Deccan*. London, forthcoming.

Ali-de-Unzaga 2007 Ali-de-Unzaga, Miriam. "Qur'anic Inscriptions on the So-called 'Pennon of Las Navas de Tolosa' and Three Marinid Banners." In *Word of God, Art of Man: The Qur'an and Its Creative Expressions; Selected Proceedings from the International Colloquium, London, 18–21 October 2003*, edited by Fahmida Suleman, pp. 239–70. The Institute of Ismaili Studies, Qur'anic Studies Series, 4. London, 2007.

Allan 1970 Allan, J[ames] W. "Mamluk Sultanic Heraldry and the Numismatic Evidence: A Reinterpretation." *Journal of the Royal Asiatic Society of Great Britain and Ireland*, 1970, no. 2 [*Studies in Honour of Sir Mortimer Wheeler*], pp. 99–112.

Allan 1973 Allan, J[ames] W. "Abu'l-Qasim's Treatise on Ceramics." *Iran* 11 (1973), pp. 111–20.

Allan 1986 Allan, James W. *Metalwork of the Islamic World: The Aron Collection*. London, 1986.

Allan 1991a Allan, James [W]. *Islamic Ceramics*. Ashmolean–Christie's Handbooks. Oxford, 1991.

Allan 1991b Allan, James W. "Metalwork of the Turcoman Dynasties of Eastern Anatolia and Iran." *Iran* 29 (1991), pp. 153–59.

Allan 1995 Allan, J[ames] W. "Silver Door Facings of the Safavid Period." *Iran* 33 (1995), pp. 123–37.

Allan 2003–4 Allan, James W. "Early Safavid Metalwork." In New York and Milan 2003–4, pp. 202–39.

Allan 2004 Allan, James W. *Persian Steel: Masterpieces of Iranian Art*. London, 2004.

Allan and Gilmour 2000 Allan, James [W.], and Brian Gilmour. *Persian Steel: The Tanavoli Collection*. Oxford Studies in Islamic Art, 15. Oxford, 2000.

Allan and Roberts, eds. 1987 Allan, James [W.], and Caroline Roberts, eds. *Syria and Iran: Three Studies in Medieval Ceramics*. Oxford Studies in Islamic Art, 4. Oxford, 1987.

Allan et al. 1979 Allan, James W., et al. *Persian Metal Technology, 700–1300 A.D.* Oxford Oriental Monographs, 2. London, 1979.

Allen 1988 Allen, Terry. *Five Essays on Islamic Art*. [Manchester, Mich.], 1988.

Allgrove McDowell 1989 Allgrove McDowell, Joan. "Textiles." In Ferrier, ed. 1989, pp. 151–70.

Allsen 1997 Allsen, Thomas T. *Commodity and Exchange in the Mongol Empire: A Cultural History of Islamic Textiles*. Cambridge Studies in Islamic Civilization. New York and Cambridge, 1997.

Almagro Gorbea 2007 Almagro Gorbea, Antonio. "Los Palacios de tradición andalusí en la corona de Castilla: Las empresas de Pedro I." In *Simposio Internacional: El legado de al-Andalus; El arte andalusí en los reinos de León y Castilla durante la Edad Media*, edited by Manuel Valdés Fernández, pp. 243–81. Valladolid, 2007.

Alsayyad, Bierman, and Rabbat, eds. 2005 Alsayyad, Nezar, Irene A. Bierman, and Nasser O. Rabbat, eds. *Making Cairo Medieval*. Transnational Perspectives on Space and Place. Lanham, Md., and Oxford, 2005.

Alvi and Rahman 1968 Alvi, M. A., and A. Rahman. *Jahangir: The Naturalist*. The National Institute of Sciences of India Monograph, 3. New Delhi, 1968.

Ames 1997 Ames, Frank. *The Kashmir Shawl and Its Indo-French Influence*. 3rd ed. 1986. Woodbridge, Suffolk, 1997.

Ames 2007–8 Ames, Frank. "Woven Legends: Carpets and Shawls of Kashmir (1585–1870)." In New York and Cincinnati 2007–8, pp. 192–209.

Ames 2010 Ames, Frank. *Woven Masterpieces of Sikh Heritage: The Stylistic Development of the Kashmir Shawl under Maharaja Ranjit Singh (1780–1839)*. Woodbridge, Suffolk, 2010.

Amsterdam 1999–2000 *Earthly Beauty, Heavenly Art: Art of Islam*. Exhibition, De Nieuwe Kerk, Amsterdam. Catalogue by Mikhail B. Piotrovsky, John Vrieze, and others. Amsterdam, 1999.

Amsterdam 2001 *Batik, Drawn in Wax: 200 Years of Batik Art from Indonesia*. Exhibition, Tropenmuseum, Amsterdam. Catalogue by Itie van Hout and others. Amsterdam, 2001.

An 1991 An Jiayao. "Dated Islamic Glass in China." *Bulletin of the Asia Institute*, n.s., 5 (1991), pp. 123–37.

Anderson forthcoming Anderson, Glaire D. "Concubines, Eunuchs and Patronage in Early Islamic Córdoba." In *Reassessing Women's Roles as "Makers" of Medieval Art and Architecture*, edited by Therese Martin. Leiden, forthcoming.

Andrews et al., eds. 1997 Andrews, Walter G., et al., eds. *Ottoman Lyric Poetry: An Anthology*. Austin, 1997.

Anglade 1988 Anglade, Elise. *Catalogue des boiseries de la section islamique, Musée du Louvre*. Paris, 1988.

Angustias Cabrera et al. 2007 Angustias Cabrera, Maria, et al. *7 Paseos por la Alhambra*. Granada, 2007.

Ann Arbor 1967 *Sasanian Silver: Late Antique and Early Mediaeval Arts of Luxury From Iran*. Exhibition, The University of Michigan Museum of Art, Ann Arbor. Catalogue by Oleg Grabar. Ann Arbor, Mich., 1967.

Ann Arbor 1978 *Islamic Art from the University of Michigan Collections*. Exhibition, Kelsey Museum of Archaeology, The University of Michigan, Ann Arbor. Catalogue by Priscilla Parsons Soucek. Ann Arbor, 1978.

al-Ansari 1985 al-Ansari, 'Abd al-Quddus. *Athar al-Madina al-munawwara*. 4th ed. 1935. Medina, 1985.

Antwerp 1997 *Een streling voor het oog: Indische Mogoljuwelen van de 18de en 19de eeuw/Kaleidoscope of Colours: Indian Mughal Jewels from the Eighteenth and Nineteenth Centuries*. Exhibition, Provinciaal Diamantmuseum, Antwerp. Antwerp, 1997.

Arberry 1955 Arberry, Arthur J. *The Koran Interpreted*. New York, 1955.

Arberry 1967 Arberry, Arthur J. *The Koran Illuminated: A Handlist of the Korans in the Chester Beatty Library*. Dublin, 1967.

Arberry et al. 1959–62 Arberry, A[rthur] J., et al. *The Chester Beatty Library: A Catalogue of the Persian Manuscripts and Miniatures*. 3 vols. in 5. Dublin, 1959–62.

Archer, M. 1992 Archer, Mildred. *Company Paintings: Indian Paintings of the British Period*. Victoria and Albert Museum, Indian Art Series. London, 1992.

Archer, W. 1960 Archer, W[illiam] G[eorge]. *Indian Miniatures*. London, 1960.

Arnold and Olsen, eds. 2003 Arnold, Ken, and Danielle Olsen, eds. *Medicine Man: The Forgotten Museum of Henry Wellcome*. London, 2003.

Arslanoglu and Schultz 2009 Arslanoglu, Julie, and Julia Schultz. "Immunology and Art: Using Antibody-based Techniques to Identify Proteins and Gums in Binding Media and Adhesives." *The Metropolitan Museum of Art Bulletin*, n.s., 67, no. 1 [*Scientific Research in The Metropolitan Museum of Art*] (Summer 2009), pp. 40–48.

Aslanapa 1954 Aslanapa, Oktay. "Türkische Miniaturmalerei am Hofe Mehmet des Eroberers in Istanbul." *Ars Orientalis* 1 (1954), pp. 77–82, pls. 1–6.

Atasoy and Raby 1989 Atasoy, Nurhan, and Julian Raby. *Iznik: The Pottery of Ottoman Turkey*. London, 1989.

Atasoy et al. 2001 Atasoy, Nurhan, et al. *Ipek: The Crescent and the Rose; Imperial Ottoman Silks and Velvets*. London, 2001.

Auld 2004 Auld, Sylvia. *Renaissance Venice, Islam and Mahmud the Kurd: A Metalworking Enigma*. London, 2004.

Auld 2009 Auld, Sylvia. "Cross-currents and Coincidences: A Perspective on Ayyubid Metalwork." In *Ayyubid Jerusalem: The Holy City in Context, 1187–1250*, edited by Robert Hillenbrand and Sylvia Auld, pp. 45–71. London, 2009.

Austin 1970 *Treasures of Persian Art after Islam: The Mahboubian Collection*. Exhibition, University Art Museum of The University of Texas at Austin. Catalogue by Mehdi Mahboubian. Austin, 1970.

Ávila 1989 Ávila, Maria Luisa. "Las mujeres 'sabias' en al-Andalus." In *La mujer en al-Andalus*, edited by Maria J. Viguera, pp. 139–84. Madrid and Seville, 1989.

Ávila 2002 Ávila, Maria Luisa. "Women in Andalusi Biographical Sources." In *Writing the Feminine: Women in Arab Sources*, edited by Manuela Marin and Randi Deguilhem, pp. 149–63. The Islamic Mediterranean, 1. London and New York, 2002.

Babaie 2008 Babaie, Sussan. *Isfahan and Its Palaces: Statecraft, Shi'ism and the Architecture of Conviviality in Early Modern Iran*. Edinburgh, 2008.

Bacharach 2010 Bacharach, Jere L. "Signs of Sovereignty: The *Shahada*, Qur'anic Verses, and the Coinage of 'Abd al-Malik." *Muqarnas* 27 (2010), pp. 1–30.

Badr 1993 Badr, 'Abd al-Basit. *Al-Tarikh al-shamil lil-Madina al-munawwara*. 3 vols. Medina, 1993.

Baer 1983 Baer, Eva. *Metalwork in Medieval Islamic Art*. Albany, 1983.

Baer 1989 Baer, Eva. *Ayyubid Metalwork with Christian Images*. Studies and Sources in Islamic Art and Architecture, 4. Leiden, 1989.

Bahari 1996 Bahari, Ebadollah. *Bihzad: Master of Persian Painting*. London and New York, 1996.

Baiqara 1968 Sultan Husain Baiqara. *Divan-i ba-indimam-i risala-yi u*. Edited by Muhammad Ya'qub Vahidi Juzjani. Kabul, 1968.

Baker, C. 2007 Baker, Colin F. *Qur'an Manuscripts: Calligraphy, Illumination, Design*. London, 2007.

Baker, P. 1995 Baker, Patricia L. *Islamic Textiles*. London, 1995.

Bala Krishnan and Kumar 1999 Bala Krishnan, Usha R., and Meera Sushil Kumar. *Dance of the Peacock: Jewellery Traditions of India*. Mumbai, 1999.

Ballard 1916 Ballard, James F. *Illustrated Catalogue and Descriptions of Ghiordes Rugs of the Seventeenth and Eighteenth Centuries from the Collection of James F. Ballard, St. Louis, Mo., U.S.A.* St. Louis, 1916.

Baltimore 2001 *Pearls of the Parrot of India: The Walters Art Museum Khamsa of Amir Khusraw of Delhi*. Exhibition, The Walters Art Museum, Baltimore. Catalogue by John Seyller. *The Journal of the Walters Art Museum*, 58. Baltimore, 2001.

Barbaro and Contarini 1873 Barbaro, Josafa, and Ambrogio Contarini. *Travels to Tana and Persia*. Translated by William Thomas. Works Issued by the Hakluyt Society, 49. London, 1873.

Barcelona 2004 *Mediterraneum: Splendour of the Medieval Mediterranean, Thirteenth–Fifteenth Centuries*. Exhibition, History Museum of Catalunya and Maritime Museum, Barcelona. Catalogue by Joan Alemany, Xavier Barral i Altet, and Joan E. Garcia Biosca. Barcelona, 2004.

Barkan 1972–79 Barkan, Ömer L[ûtfi]. *Süleymaniye Cami ve Imareti Inşaatı (1550–1557)* (The building of the Süleymaniye mosque and its dependencies). Türk Tarih Kurumu yayinlarindan, ser. 6, no. 10. Ankara, 1972–79.

Barrett 1949 Barrett, Douglas [E]. *Islamic Metalwork in the British Museum*. London, 1949.

Bates 1982 Bates, Michael. *Islamic Coins*. A[merican] N[umismatic] S[ociety] Handbook, 2. New York, 1982.

Bates 1986 Bates, Michael. "History, Geography and Numismatics in the First Century of Islamic Coinage." *Revue suisse de numismatique* 65 (1986), pp. 231–62.

Baumeister et al. 2010 Baumeister, Mechthild, et al. "A Splendid Welcome to the 'House of Praises, Glorious Deeds and Magnanimity.'" In *Conservation and the Eastern Mediterranean: Contributions to the 2010 IIC Congress, Istanbul*, pp. 126–33. [London, 2010].

Bayani 1964 Bayani, Mehdi. *Ahval wa athar-i khushnivisan: Nasta'liq nivisan*. Tehran, 1964.

Bayani and Stanley 1999 Bayani, Manijeh, and Tim Stanley. "The 'Kashmiri' Style." In *The Decorated Word: Qur'ans of the Seventeenth to Nineteenth Centuries*, by Manijeh Bayani, Anna Contadini, and Tim Stanley, pp. 228–57. The Nasser D. Khalili Collection of Islamic Art, edited by Julian Raby, vol. 4, pt. 1. London, 1999.

Beach, Fischer, and Goswamy, eds. 2011 Beach, Milo C[leveland], Eberhard Fischer, and B[rijindra] N[ath] Goswamy, eds. *Masters of Indian Painting*. 2 vols. Artibus Asiae Supplementum 48. [Zurich], 2011.

Beg Monshi 1978 Beg Monshi, Iskandar. *History of Shah 'Abbas the Great (Tarik-e 'Alamara-ye 'Abbasi)*. Translated by Roger M. Savory. 2 vols. Persian Heritage Series, 28. Boulder, Colo., 1978.

Behrens-Abouseif 2007 Behrens-Abouseif, Doris. *Cairo of the Mamluks: A History of the Architecture and Its Culture*. London and New York, 2007.

Behrens-Abouseif, ed. 2000 Behrens-Abouseif, Doris, ed. *The Cairo Heritage: Essays in Honor of Laila Ali Ibrahim*. Cairo and New York, 2000.

Ben-Dov 2009 Ben-Dov, Meir. *The Golden Age: Synagogues of Spain in History and Architecture*. Jerusalem, 2009.

Bennett 1987a Bennett, Ian. "Splendours in the City of Silk, Part 3: The Safavid Masterpieces." *Hali*, no. 34 (April–June 1987), pp. 42–50, 103–4.

Bennett 1987b Bennett, Ian. "The Marcy Indjoudjian Cope." *Hali*, no. 35 (July–September 1987), pp. 22–23, 124.

Berchem 1894 Berchem, Max van. *Matériaux pour un corpus inscriptionum Arabicarum*. Part 1, *Égypte*. Vol. 1, *Le Caire*. Mémoires publiés par les membres de la Mission Archéologique Française au Caire, 19; Mémoires publiés par les membres de l'Institut Français d'Archéologie Orientale du Caire, 25, 29, 43–45 (plates), 52. Paris, 1894.

Beresneva 1976 Beresneva, L. *The Decorative and Applied Art of Turkmenia/Dekorativno-prikladnoe iskusstvo Turkmenii*. Leningrad, 1976.

Berlin 1981 *Islamische Kunst: Meisterwerke aus dem Metropolitan Museum of Art, New York/The Arts of Islam: Masterpieces from The Metropolitan Museum of Art New York*. Exhibition, Museum für Islamische Kunst, Berlin. Catalogue by Stuart Cary Welch and others. Berlin, 1981.

Berlin 2007–8 *A Collector's Fortune: Islamic Art from the Collection of Edmund de Unger*. Exhibition, Pergamonmuseum, Berlin. Catalogue by Claus-Peter Haase. Munich, 2007.

Biedrońska-Słota 2010a Biedrońska-Słota, Beata. "Classical Carpets in Poland." *Hali*, no. 163 (Spring 2010), pp. 74–82.

Biedrońska-Słota 2010b Biedrońska-Słota, Beata. "Persian Sashes Preserved in Polish Collections." In Thompson, Shaffer, and Mildh, eds. 2010, pp. 176–85.

Bier and Bencard 1995 Bier, Carol, and Mogens Bencard. *The Persian Velvets at Rosenborg*. Copenhagen, 1995.

Binghamton 1975 *Islam and the Medieval West: A Loan Exhibition at the University Art Gallery, April 6–May 4, 1975*. Catalogue and Papers of the Ninth Annual Conference of the Center for Medieval and Early Renaissance Studies, State University of New York at Binghamton, May 2–4, 1975. Exhibition, University Art Gallery, SUNY, Binghamton. Catalogue by Stanley Ferber and others. Binghamton, 1975.

Binney 1972 Binney, Edwin. "Later Mughal Painting." In *Aspects of Indian Art: Papers Presented in a Symposium at the Los Angeles County Museum of Art, October, 1970*, edited by Pratapaditya Pal, pp. 118–23. Leiden, 1972.

al-Biruni 1936 al-Biruni. *Kitab al-jamahir fi ma'rifat al-jawahir*. Edited by F[ritz] Krenkow. Hyderabad, 1936.

***Bishop Collection* 1909** *The Heber R. Bishop Collection of Jade and other Hard Stones*. The Metropolitan Museum of Art. New York, 1909.

Blair 1984 Blair, Sheila S. "Ilkhanid Architecture and Society: An Analysis of the Endowment Deed of the Rab'-i Rashidi." *Iran* 22 (1984), pp. 67–90.

Blair 1986a Blair, Sheila [S]. "A Medieval Persian Builder." *Journal of the Society of Architectural Historians* 45, no. 4 (December 1986), pp. 389–95.

Blair 1986b Blair, Sheila S. *The Ilkhanid Shrine Complex at Natanz, Iran*. Harvard Middle East Papers, Classical Series, 1. 1980. Cambridge, Mass., 1986.

Blair 1989 Blair, Sheila S. "On the Track of the 'Demotte' Shahnama Manuscript." In *Les manuscrits du Moyen-Orient: Essais de codicologie et de paléographie; Actes du Colloque d'Istanbul (Istanbul, 26–29 mai 1986)*, edited by François Déroche, pp. 125–31. Varia Turcica VIII. Istanbul and Paris, 1989.

Blair 1998 Blair, Sheila S. *Islamic Inscriptions*. Edinburgh, 1998.

Blair 2000 Blair, Sheila S. "Color and Gold: The Decorated Papers Used in Manuscripts in Later Islamic Times." *Muqarnas* 17 (2000), pp. 24–36.

Blair 2002–3 Blair, Sheila [S]. "The Religious Art of the Ilkhanids." In New York and Los Angeles 2002–3, pp. 104–33.

Blair 2004 Blair, Sheila S. "Rewriting the History of the Great Mongol *Shahnama*." In *Shahnama: The Visual Language of the Persian Book of Kings*, edited by Robert Hillenbrand, pp. 35–50. Aldershot, 2004.

Blair 2005 Blair, Sheila S. "Islamic Art as a Source for the Study of Women in Premodern Societies." In *Beyond the Exotic: Women's Histories in Islamic Societies*, edited by Amira el-Azhary Sonbol, pp. 336–46, 448–51. Syracuse, 2005.

Blair 2006 Blair, Sheila S. *Islamic Calligraphy*. Edinburgh, 2006.

Blair 2008 Blair, Sheila S. "A Brief Biography of Abu Zayd." *Muqarnas* 25 [*Frontiers of Islamic Art and Architecture: Essays in Celebration of Oleg Grabar's Eightieth Birthday*, edited by Gülru Necipoğlu and Julia Bailey] (2008), pp. 155–76.

Blair and Bloom 1994 Blair, Sheila S., and Jonathan M. Bloom. *The Art and Architecture of Islam, 1250–1800*. New Haven and London, 1994.

Blair and Bloom 1995 Blair, Sheila [S.], and Jonathan M. Bloom. *The Art and Architecture of Islam, 1250–1800*. Reprint ed. with corrections. 1994. New Haven and London, 1995.

Blair and Bloom 2003 Blair, Sheila S., and Jonathan M. Bloom. "The Mirage of Islamic Art: Reflections on the Study of an Unwieldy Field." *The Art Bulletin* 85, no. 1 (March 2003), pp. 152–84.

Blair and Bloom 2006 Blair, Sheila S., and Jonathan M. Bloom. "Timur's Qur'an: A Reappraisal." In *Sifting Sands, Reading Signs: Studies in Honour of Professor Géza Fehérvári*, edited by Patricia L. Baker and Barbara Brend, pp. 5–13. London, 2006.

Bloom 1989 Bloom, Jonathan M. "The Blue Koran: An Early Fatimid Kufic Manuscript from the Maghrib." In *Les manuscrits du Moyen-Orient: Essais de codicologie et de paléographie; Actes du Colloque d'Istanbul (Istanbul, 26–29 mai 1986)*, edited by François Déroche, pp. 95–99. Varia Turcica VIII. Istanbul and Paris, 1989.

Bloom 2007 Bloom, Jonathan M. *Arts of the City Victorious: Islamic Art and Architecture in Fatimid North Africa and Egypt*. New Haven and London, 2007.

Bloom and Blair 2009 Bloom, Jonathan M., and Sheila S. Blair. "A Global Guide to Islamic Art." *Saudi Aramco World* 60, no. 1 (January–February 2009), pp. 32–43.

Bloom and Blair, eds. 2009 Bloom, Jonathan M., and Sheila S. Blair, eds. *The Grove Encyclopedia of Islamic Art and Architecture*. 3 vols. Oxford and New York, 2009.

Blunt 1948 Blunt, Wilfred. "The Mughal Painters of Natural History." *The Burlington Magazine* 90, no. 539 (February 1948), pp. 48–50.

Bol'shakov 1958–66 Bol'shakov, O. G. "Arabskie nadpisi na polivnoi keramike Srednei Azii." *Epigrafika Vostoka* 12 (1958), pp. 23–38; 15 (1963), pp. 73–87; 16 (1963), pp. 35–55; 17 (1966), pp. 54–62.

Bordeaux 1998–99 *La route des Indes: Les Indes et l'Europe, échanges artistiques et héritage commun, 1650–1850*. Exhibition, Musée des arts décoratifs à Bordeaux; Musée d'Aquitaine de la ville de Bordeaux. Catalogue by Thierry-Nicolas Tchkaloff and others. Paris, 1998.

Borrego Díaz 2005 Borrego Díaz, Pilar. "Análisis técnico del ligamento en los tejidos hispanoárabes." *Bienes culturales*, no. 5 [*Tejidos hispanomusulmanes*] (2005), pp. 75–121.

Boston and Chicago 2006–7 *Cosmophilia: Islamic Art from the David Collection, Copenhagen*. Exhibition, McMullen Museum of Art, Boston College; Alfred and David Smart Museum of Art, University of Chicago. Catalogue by Sheila S. Blair, Jonathan M. Bloom, and others. Chestnut Hill, Mass., 2006.

Bosworth 1996 Bosworth, Clifford Edmund. *The New Islamic Dynasties: A Chronological and Genealogical Manual*. Enl. and updated ed. 1967. Edinburgh, 1996.

Bowersock 2006 Bowersock, G[len] W. *Mosaics as History: The Near East from Late Antiquity to Islam*. Revealing Antiquity, 16. Cambridge, Mass., and London, 2006.

Bowersock 2007 Bowersock, G[len] W. "Hellenism and Islam." In *Late Antique and Medieval Art of the Mediterranean World*, edited by Eva R. Hoffman, pp. 85–96. Malden, Mass., and Oxford, 2007.

Brac de la Perrière 2008 Brac de la Perrière, Éloise. *L'art du livre dans l'Inde des sultanats*. Paris, 2008.

Bradford and London 1988–89 *A Golden Treasury: Jewellery from the Indian Subcontinent*. Exhibition, Cartwright Hall, Bradford Art Galleries and Museums, Bradford; Zamana Gallery, London. Catalogue by Susan Stronge, Nima Smith, and J. C. Harle. New York, 1988.

Breck 1920 B[reck], J[oseph]. "The William Milne Grinnell Bequest." *The Metropolitan Museum of Art Bulletin* 15, no. 12, pt. 1 (December 1920), pp. 273–75.

Breck 1932 Breck, Joseph. "The Department of Near Eastern Art." *The Metropolitan Museum of Art Bulletin* 27, no. 1 (January 1932), pp. 18–19.

Brend 1986 Brend, Barbara. "The British Library's *Shahnama* of 1438 as a Sultanate Manuscript." In *Facets of Indian Art: A Symposium Held at the Victoria and Albert Museum on 26, 27, 28 April and 1 May 1982*, edited by Robert Skelton et al., pp. 87–93. London, 1986.

Brend 1988–89 Brend, Barbara. "Akbar's *Khamsah* of Amir Khusrau Dihlavi: A Reconstruction of the Cycle of Illustration." *Artibus Asiae* 49, no. 3–4 (1988–89), pp. 281–315.

Brend 1991 Brend, Barbara. *Islamic Art*. Cambridge, Mass., 1991.

Brend 2002 Brend, Barbara. *Perspectives on Persian Painting: Illustrations to Amir Khusrau's Khamsah*. New York, 2002.

Brend 2004 Brend, Barbara. "On the Borders: A Possible Source for Naturalistic Floral Decoration at the Mughal Court." In *Arts of Mughal India: Studies in Honour of Robert Skelton*, edited by Rosemary Crill, Susan Stronge, and Andrew Topsfield, pp. 138–40. London and Ahmedabad, 2004.

Bretanitskii and Veimarn 1976 Bretanitskii, L[eonid] S[emenovich], and B[oris] V[ladimirovich] Veimarn. *Iskusstvo Azerbaidzhana, IV–XVIII vekov*. Ocherki istorii i teorii izobrazitel'nykh iskusstv. Moscow, 1976.

Brooklyn 1987 *The Collector's Eye: The Ernest Erickson Collections at The Brooklyn Museum*. Exhibition, The Brooklyn Museum. Catalogue by Linda S. Ferber and others. Brooklyn, 1987.

Brooklyn 1998–99 *Royal Persian Paintings: The Qajar Epoch, 1785–1925*. Exhibition, The Brooklyn Museum of Art. Catalogue by Layla S. Diba, Maryam Ekhtiar, and others. Brooklyn, 1998.

Brown 1989 Brown, Peter. *The World of Late Antiquity, AD 150–750*. Rev. ed. 1971. New York, 1989.

Brussels 1991 *Via Orientalis*. Exhibition, Galerie de la CGER, Brussels. Catalogue by Ezio Bassani and others. Brussels, 1991.

Buffalo 1926 *Catalog of Oriental Rugs in the Collection of James F. Ballard*. Exhibition, Buffalo Fine Arts Academy, Albright Art Gallery. Buffalo, 1926.

Bulliet 1976 Bulliet, Richard W. "Medieval Nishapur: A Topographic and Demographic Reconstruction." *Studia Iranica* 5, no. 1 (1976), pp. 67–89, pls. 1–2.

Burckhardt 1976 Burckhardt, Titus. "Introduction to Islamic Art." In London 1976c, pp. 31–38.

Burgoyne 1987 Burgoyne, Michael Hamilton. *Mamluk Jerusalem: An Architectural Study*. London, 1987.

Busbecq 1927 Busbecq, Ogier Ghiselin de. *The Turkish Letters of Ogier Ghiselin de Busbecq, Imperial Ambassador to Constantinople, 1554–1562*. Translated by Edward Seymour Forster. Oxford, 1927.

Bush 2006 Bush, Olga. "'When My Beholder Ponders': Poetic Epigraphy in the Alhambra." *Artibus Asiae* 66, no. 2 [*Pearls from Water, Rubies from Stone: Studies in Islamic Art in Honor of Priscilla Soucek, Part 1*, edited by Linda Komaroff and Jaclynne J. Kerner] (2006), pp. 55–67.

Bush 2009 Bush, Olga. "The Writing on the Wall: Reading the Decoration of the Alhambra." *Muqarnas* 26 (2009), pp. 119–47.

Bussagli and Chiappori 1991 Bussagli, Mario, and Maria Grazia Chiappori. *Arte del vetro*. Rome, 1991.

Çağman 1981 Çağman, Filiz. "On the Contents of the Four Istanbul Albums H. 2152, 2153, 2154, 2160." *Islamic Art* 1 (1981), pp. 31–36, figs. 1–490 passim.

Çağman and Tanındı 1979 Çağman, Filiz, and Zeren Tanındı. *Topkapı Sarayı Müzesi İslâm Minyatürleri*. Tercüman sanat ve kültür yayınları, 1. Istanbul, 1979.

Çağman, Tanındı, and Rogers 1986 Çağman, Filiz, and Zeren Tanındı. *The Topkapı Saray Museum: The Albums and Illustrated Manuscripts*. Translated and expanded by J. M[ichael] Rogers. 1979. Boston, 1986.

Cairo 1931 *L'exposition persane de 1931*. Exhibition, Musée arabe du Caire. Catalogue by Gaston Wiet. Cairo, 1933.

Cambridge, Mass., and New York 1973–74 *Shah 'Abbas and the Arts of Isfahan*. Exhibition, Asia House Gallery, New York; Fogg Art Museum, Harvard University, Cambridge, Mass. Catalogue by Anthony Welch. New York, 1973.

Cammann 1972 Cammann, Schuyler V. R. "Symbolic Meanings in Oriental Rug Patterns." *Textile Museum Journal* 3, no. 3 (December 1972), pp. 5–54.

Canby 1993 Canby, Sheila R. *Persian Painting*. New York, 1993.

Canby 1996a Canby, Sheila [R]. "Farangi Saz: The Impact of Europe on Safavid Painting." In *Silk and Stone: The Art of Asia*, pp. 46–59. The Third Hali Annual. London, 1996.

Canby 1996b Canby, Sheila R. *The Rebellious Reformer: The Drawings and Paintings of Riza-yi 'Abbasi of Isfahan*. London, 1996.

Canby 1999a Canby, Sheila [R]. "The Curator's Dilemma: Dispelling the Mystery of Exotic Collections." *Museum International* (Unesco, Paris) 51, no. 3 (July–September 1999), pp. 11–15.

Canby 1999b Canby, Sheila R. *The Golden Age of Persian Art, 1501–1722*. London, 1999.

Canby 2000 Canby, Sheila [R]. "Islamic Archaeology: By Accident or Design?" In *Discovering Islamic Art: Scholars, Collectors and Collections, 1850–1950*, edited by Stephen Vernoit, pp. 128–37. London, 2000.

Canby 2007 Canby, Sheila R. "Royal Gifts to Safavid Shrines." In *Muraqqa'e Sharqi: Studies in Honor of Peter Chelkowski*, edited by Soussie Rastegar and Anna Vanzan, pp. 57–68, 220–29. Dogana and Serravalle, Republic of San Marino, 2007.

Canby 2010 Canby, Sheila R. "An Illustrated *Shahnameh* of 1650: Isfahan in the Service of Yazd." *The Journal of the David Collection* 3 (2010), pp. 54–113.

Canby, ed. 1990a *Marg* 41, no. 3 [*Painters of Persia and Their Art*, edited by Sheila R. Canby] ([1990]).

Canby, ed. 1990b Canby, Sheila R., ed. *Persian Masters: Five Centuries of Painting*. Bombay, 1990.

Canepa 2009 Canepa, Matthew P. *The Two Eyes of the Earth: Art and Ritual of Kingship between Rome and Sasanian Iran*. The Transformation of the Classical Heritage, 45. 2004. Berkeley and Los Angeles, 2009.

Carboni 1987 Carboni, Stefano. "Two Fragments of a Jalayirid Astrological Treatise in the Keir Collection and in the Oriental Institute in Sarajevo." *Islamic Art* 2 (1987), pp. 149–86, pl. 9.

Carboni 1994 Carboni, Stefano. "The Illustrations in the *Mu'nis al-ahrar*." In New York 1994, pp. 8–47.

Carboni 1999 Carboni, Stefano. "Glass Production in the Fatimid Lands and Beyond." In *L'Égypte fatimide, son art et son histoire: Actes du colloque organizé à Paris les 28, 29 et 30 mai 1998*, edited by Marianne Barrucand, pp. 169–77, pls. 7–8. Paris, 1999.

Carboni 2000 Carboni, Stefano. "Panel of Four Calligraphic Tiles." *The Metropolitan Museum of Art Bulletin*, n.s., 58, no. 2 (Fall 2000), p. 16.

Carboni 2001 Carboni, Stefano. *Glass from Islamic Lands*. The al-Sabah Collection, Kuwait National Museum. New York, 2001.

Carboni 2002–3 Carboni, Stefano. "Synthesis: Continuity and Innovation in Ilkhanid Art." In New York and Los Angeles 2002–3, pp. 196–225.

Carboni 2004 Carboni, Stefano. "Fifteenth-Century Enameled and Gilded Glass Made for the Mamluks: The End of an Era, the Beginning of a New One." *Orient: Reports of the Society for Near Eastern Studies in Japan* 39 (2004), pp. 69–78.

Carboni, Walker, and Moore 1998 Carboni, Stefano, Daniel Walker, and J. Kenneth Moore. "Recent Acquisitions: A Selection, 1997–1998; Islam." *The Metropolitan Museum of Art Bulletin*, n.s., 56, no. 2 (Fall 1998), pp. 11–13.

Carboni, Walker, and Swietochowski 1999 Carboni, Stefano, Daniel Walker, and Marie Lukens Sw[ie]tochowski. "Recent Acquisitions: A Selection, 1998–1999; Islam." *The Metropolitan Museum of Art Bulletin*, n.s., 57, no. 2 (Fall 1999), pp. 10–13.

Carey, M. 2001 Carey, Moya. "Painting the Stars in a Century of Change: A Thirteenth-Century Copy of al-Sufi's Treatise on the Fixed Stars (British Library, Or. 5323)." Ph.D. diss., School of Oriental and African Studies, University of London, 2001.

Carey, P. 1996–97 Carey, Peter. "The World of the Pasisir." In Los Angeles 1996–97, pp. 20–29.

Carswell 1972a Carswell, John. *Kütahya Tiles and Pottery from the Armenian Cathedral of St. James, Jerusalem*. 2 vols. Oxford, 1972.

Carswell 1972b Carswell, John. "Six Tiles." In Ettinghausen, ed. 1972, pp. 99–123.

Carswell 1998 Carswell, John. *Iznik Pottery*. London, 1998.

Casal 1978 Casal, Geneviève. "Description des peintures de la grande salle d'audience du château du sud à Lashkari Bazar (automne 1949)." In *Lashkari Bazar: Une résidence royale ghaznévide et ghoride*, vol. 1A, *L'architecture*, edited by Daniel Schlumberger, pp. 101–8; pls. 13–15, 121–24. Mémoires de la Délégation Archéologique Française en Afghanistan. Paris, 1978.

Cassavoy 2004 Cassavoy, Kenneth. "The Gaming Pieces." In *Serçe Limani: An Eleventh-Century Shipwreck*, vol. 1, *The Ship and Its Anchorage, Crew, and Passengers*, by George F. Bass et al., pp. 328–43. College Station, Tex., 2004.

Castéra 1999 Castéra, Jean-Marc. *Arabesques: Decorative Art in Morocco*. Courbevoie, 1999.

Chamberlain 1994 Chamberlain, Michael. *Knowledge and Social Practice in Medieval Damascus, 1190–1350*. Cambridge Studies in Islamic Civilization. Cambridge and New York, 1994.

Chandra, M. 1949 Chandra, Moti. *The Technique of Mughal Painting*. Lucknow, 1949.

Chandra, P. 1957–59 Chandra, Pramod. "A Series of Ramayana Paintings of the Popular Mughal School." *Prince of Wales Museum Bulletin*, no. 6 (1957–59), pp. 64–70, figs. 18–27.

Chandra, P. 1960 Chandra, Pramod. "Ustad Salivahana and the Development of Popular Mughal Art." *Lalit Kala*, no. 8 (October 1960), pp. 25–46, pls. 5–18.

Charleston 1974 Charleston, R. "Glass in Persia in the Safavid Period and Later." *Art and Archeology Research Papers* 5 (June 1974), pp. 12–27.

Chelkowski and Soucek 1975 Chelkowski, Peter J., and Priscilla P. Soucek. *Mirror of the Invisible World: Tales from the Khamseh of Nizami*. New York, 1975.

Chicago 1922–23 *Descriptive Catalogue of an Exhibition of Oriental Rugs from the Collection of James Franklin Ballard, Exhibited in Gallery Fifty and on the Main Staircase from November 28, 1922 to February 1923*. Exhibition, The Art Institute of Chicago. Chicago, 1922.

Chicago 1997 *A Collecting Odyssey: Indian, Himalayan, and Southeast Asian Art from the James and Marilynn Alsdorf Collection*. Exhibition, The Art Institute of Chicago. Catalogue by Pratapaditya Pal, with Stephen Little. Chicago, 1997.

Chicago 2007 *Perpetual Glory: Medieval Islamic Ceramics from the Harvey B. Plotnick Collection*. Exhibition, The Art Institute of

Chicago. Catalogue by Oya Pancaroğlu with Manijeh Bayani. Chicago, 2007.

Cilento and Vanoli 2007 Cilento, Adele, and Alessandro Vanoli. *Arabs and Normans in Sicily and the South of Italy*. New York, 2007.

Cincinnati 1985 *Pride of the Princes: Indian Art of the Mughal Era in the Cincinnati Art Museum*. Exhibition, Cincinnati Art Museum. Catalogue by Ellen S. Smart, Daniel S. Walker and others. Cincinnati, 1985.

Cleveland and New York 1997–98 *When Silk was Gold: Central Asian and Chinese Textiles*. Exhibition, Cleveland Museum of Art; The Metropolitan Museum of Art, New York. Catalogue by James C. Y. Watt, Anne E. Wardwell, and Morris Rossabi. New York, 1997.

Codrington 1904 Codrington, O[liver]. *A Manual of Musalman Numismatics*. Asiatic Society Monographs, 7. London, 1904.

Cohen 1995 Cohen, Steven. "A Group of Early Silks: A Tree Motif." In *The Woven Silks of India*, edited by J. Dhamija, pp. 17–36. Bombay, 1995.

Cohen 2001 Cohen, Steven. "Safavid and Mughal Carpets in the Gulbenkian Museum, Lisbon." *Hali*, no. 114 (January–February 2001), pp. 75–88, 99.

Cohen 2011 Cohen, Steven. "Deccani Carpets: Creating a Corpus." In Haidar and Sardar, eds. 2011, pp. 112–31.

Cohen and Kajitani 2006 Cohen, Steven, and Nobuko Kajitani. *Gardens of Eternal Spring: Two Newly Conserved Seventeenth-Century Mughal Carpets in the Frick Collection*. New York, 2006.

Combe 1939 Combe, Étienne. "Natte de Tibériade au Musée Benaki à Athènes." In *Mélanges Syriens offerts à Monsieur René Dussaud*, vol. 2, pp. 841–44. 2 vols. Bibliothèque archéologique et historique, 30. Paris, 1939.

Contadini 1995 Contadini, Anna. "Islamic Ivory Chess Pieces, Draughtsmen and Dice." In *Islamic Art in the Ashmolean Museum, Part 1*, edited by James [W.] Allen, pp. 111–54. Oxford Studies in Islamic At, 10. Oxford, 1995.

Contadini 1998 Contadini, Anna. *Fatimid Art at the Victoria and Albert Museum*. London, 1998.

Coomaraswamy 1929 Coomaraswamy, Ananda K. *Les miniatures orientales de la collection Goloubew au Museum of Fine Arts de Boston*. Ars Asiatica, 13. Paris and Brussels, 1929.

Cooper Union 1954 "Recent Additions to the Museum Collections." *Chronicle of the Museum for the Arts of Decoration of the Cooper Union* 2, no. 6 (June 1954), pp. 180–93.

Copenhagen 1993 *Woven Treasures: Textiles from the World of Islam*. Exhibition, The David Collection, Copenhagen. Catalogue by Kjeld von Folsach and Anne-Marie Keblow Bersted. Copenhagen, 1993.

Copenhagen 1996 *Sultan, Shah, and Great Mughal: The History and Culture of the Islamic World*. Exhibition, National Museum, Copenhagen. Catalogue by Kjeld von Folsach, Torben Lundbaek, Peder Mortensen, and others. Copenhagen, 1996.

Corning, London, and Cologne 1987 *Glass of the Caesars*. Exhibition, The Corning Museum of Glass; British Museum, London; Römisch-Germanisches Museum, Cologne. Catalogue by Donald B. Harden and others. Milan, 1987.

Corning, New York, and Athens 2001–2 *Glass of the Sultans*. Exhibition, The Corning Museum of Glass; The Metropolitan Museum of Art, New York; The Benaki Museum, Athens. Catalogue by Stefano Carboni, David Whitehouse, and others. New York, 2001.

Cornu et al. 1992 Cornu, Georgette, et al. *Tissus Islamiques de la collection Pfister*. Vatican City, 1992.

Cortese and Calderini 2006 Cortese, Delia, and Simonetta Calderini. *Women and the Fatimids in the World of Islam*. Edinburgh, 2006.

Crane 1940 Crane, Mary E. "Notes: A Fourteenth-Century Mihrab from Isfahan." *Ars Islamica* 7, pt. 1 (1940), pp. 96–100.

Cressier 1995 Cressier, Patrice. "Los capiteles del Salón Rico: Un aspecto del discurso arquitectónico califal." In *Madinat al-Zahra: El Salón de 'Abd al-Rahman III*, edited by Antonio Vallejo Triano, pp. 83–106. Cordoba, 1995.

Creswell 1959 Creswell, K[eppel] A[rchibald] C[ameron]. *The Muslim Architecture of Egypt*. Vol. 2. Oxford, 1959.

Crill 1999 Crill, Rosemary. *Indian Embroidery*. Victorian and Albert Museum. London, 1999.

Crill 2008 Crill, Rosemary. *Chintz: Indian Textiles for the West*. Victorian and Albert Museum. London, 2008.

Crill and Stanley 2006 Crill, Rosemary, and Tim Stanley. *The Making of the Jameel Gallery of Islamic Art at the Victoria and Albert Museum*. London, 2006.

Crowe 1996 Crowe, Yolande. "The Chiselled Surface: Chinese Lacquer and Islamic Design." In *Silk and Stone: The Art of Asia*, pp. 60–69, 189. The Third Hali Annual. London, 1996.

Crowe 2002 Crowe, Yolande. *Persia and China: Safavid Blue and White Ceramics in the Victoria and Albert Museum, 1501–1738*. [Geneva], 2002.

Cutler 1994 Cutler, Anthony. *The Hand of the Master: Craftsmanship, Ivory, and Society in Byzantium (Ninth–Eleventh Centuries)*. Princeton, N.J., 1994.

Cutler 2001 Cutler, Anthony. "Gifts and Gift Exchange as Aspects of the Byzantine, Arab, and Related Economies." *Dumbarton Oaks Papers* 55 (2001), pp. 247–78.

Cutler 2009 Cutler, Anthony. *Image Making in Byzantium, Sasanian Persia and the Early Muslim World: Images and Cultures*. Variorum Collected Studies. Farnham, Surrey, 2009.

Daggett 1910 Daggett, William G. *A History of the Class of Eighty, Yale College, 1876–1910*. [New Haven], 1910.

Daiber and Becker, eds. 2004 Daiber, Verena, and Andrea Becker, eds. *Raqqa III: Baudenkmäler und Paläste I*. Deutsches Archäologisches Institut. Mainz am Rhein, 2004.

Daneshvari 1981 Daneshvari, Abbas. "Symbolism of the Rabbit in the Manuscript of Warqa wa Gulshah." In *Essays in Islamic Art and Architecture in Honor of Katharina Otto-Dorn*, edited by Abbas Daneshvari, pp. 21–28, figs. 1–10. Malibu, 1981.

Dani 1961 Dani, Ahmad Hasan. *Muslim Architecture in Bengal*. Asiatic Society of Pakistan Publications, 7. Dacca, 1961.

Danishpazhuh 1988 Danishpazhuh, M.-T. "Bayaz." In *Encyclopaedia Iranica, Online Edition*, December 15, 1988, available at http://www.iranicaonline.org/articles/bayaz.

Das 1998 Das, Asok Kumar. "Farrukh Beg: Studies of Adorable Youths and Venerable Saints." In Das, ed. 1998a, pp. 20–35, and/or Das, ed. 1998b, pp. 96–111.

Das 1999 Das, Asok Kumar. "The Elephant in Mughal Painting." In *Flora and Fauna in Mughal Art*, edited by Som Prakash Verma, pp. 36–54. Mumbai, 1999.

Das, ed. 1998a *Marg* 49, no. 4 [(Mughal Masters issue), edited by Asok Kumar Das] (June 1998).

Das, ed. 1998b Das, Asok Kumar, ed. *Mughal Masters: Further Studies*. Mumbai, 1998.

Daskalakis-Mathews 1997 Daskalakis-Mathews, Annie-Christine. "A Room of 'Splendor and Generosity' from Ottoman Damascus." *Metropolitan Museum Journal* 32 (1997), pp. 111–39.

Daskalakis-Mathews 2004 Daskalakis-[Mathews], Annie-Christine. "Damascus Eighteenth- and Nineteenth-Century Houses in the *Ablaq-'Ajami* Style of Decoration: Local and International Significance." Ph.D. diss., Institute of Fine Arts, New York University, 2004.

Daskalakis-Mathews 2006 Daskalakis-Mathews, Annie-Christine. "Mamluk Elements in the Damascene Decorative System of the Eighteenth and Nineteenth Centuries." *Artibus Asiae* 66, no. 2 [*Pearls from Water, Rubies from Stone: Studies in Islamic Art in Honor of Priscilla Soucek, Part 1*, edited by Linda Komaroff and Jaclynne J. Kerner] (2006), pp. 69–96.

Da'vadar Qummi 1986 Da'vadar Qummi, Rukn al-Din. *Divan-i Rukn al-Din Da'vadar Qummi*. Edited by 'Ali Muhaddith. Tehran, 1986.

Davidovich 1960 Davidovich, E. A. "Dva Samarkandskikh kuvshina s datoi i imenem mastera i nadpisi." *Kratkie soobshcheniya i dokladakh i polevykh issledovaniyakh Instituta Istorii Material'noi Kultury* 80 (1960), pp. 109–13.

Day 1950 Day, Florence E. "Silks of the Near East." *The Metropolitan Museum of Art Bulletin*, n.s., 9, no. 4 (December 1950), pp. 108–17.

Day 1952 Day, Florence E. "The Tiraz Silk of Marwan." In *Archaeologica Orientalia in Memoriam Ernst Herzfeld*, edited by George C[arpenter] Miles, pp. 39–61, pl. 6. Locust Valley, N.Y., 1952.

Degeorge and Porter 2002 Degeorge, Gérard, and Yves Porter. *The Art of the Islamic Tile*. 2001. Paris, 2002.

DeJong 1992 DeJong, Frederick, "Pictorial Art of the Bektashi Order." In *The Dervish Lodge: Architecture, Art, and Sufism in Ottoman Turkey*, edited by Raymon Lifchez, pp. 228–41. Berkeley, 1992.

Del Bontà 1999 Del Bontà, Robert J. "Reinventing Nature: Mughal Composite Animal Painting." In *Flora and Fauna in Mughal Art*, edited by Som Prakash Verma, pp. 69–82. Mumbai, 1999.

Denamur 2003 Denamur, Isabelle. *Moroccan Textile Embroidery*. Paris, 2003.

Denamur 2010 Denamur, Isabelle. "A Stitch in Good Time." *Hali*, no. 164 (Summer 2010), pp. 57–59.

Denny 1972 Denny, Walter B. "Ottoman Turkish Textiles." *Textile Museum Journal* 3, no. 3 (December 1972), pp. 55–66.

Denny 1974a Denny, Walter B. "A Group of Silk Islamic Banners." *Textile Museum Journal* 4, no. 1 (December 1974), pp. 67–81.

Denny 1974b Denny, Walter B. "Blue-and-White Islamic Pottery on Chinese Themes." *Boston Museum Bulletin* 72, no. 368 (1974), pp. 76–99.

Denny 1977 Denny, Walter B. *The Ceramics of the Mosque of Rüstem Pasha and the Environment of Change*. [Garland] Outstanding Dissertations in the Fine Arts. 1970. New York and London, 1977.

Denny 1983 Denny, Walter B. "Dating Ottoman Turkish Works in the Saz Style." *Muqarnas* 1 (1983), pp. 103–21.

Denny 1996 Denny, Walter B. "Mirror. IV. Islamic Lands." In *The Dictionary of Art*, edited by Jane [S.] Turner, vol. 21, pp. 717–18. 34 vols. London and New York, 1996.

Denny 1998 Denny, Walter [B]. *Gardens of Paradise: Sixteenth Century Turkish Ceramic Tile Decoration*. [Istanbul], 1998.

Denny 2004 Denny, Walter B. *Iznik: The Artistry of Ottoman Ceramics*. London and New York, 2004.

Denny 2006–7 Denny, Walter B. "Oriental Carpets and Textiles in Venice." In *Venice and the Islamic World, 828–1797*, pp. 174–91. Exhibition, Institut du Monde Arabe, Paris; The Metropolitan Museum of Art, New York. Catalogue by Stefano Carboni and others. New York, 2007.

Déroche 1988–89 Déroche, François. "Les origines de la calligraphie islamique." In Geneva and other cities 1988–89, pp. 21–29.

Déroche 1992 Déroche, François. *The Abbasid Tradition: Qur'ans of the Eighth to the Tenth Centuries A.D.* The Nasser D. Khalili Collection of Islamic Art, edited by Julian Raby, vol. 1. London, 1992.

Déroche 1999 Déroche, François. "Notes sur les fragments coraniques anciens de Katta Langar (Ouzbékistan)." *Cahiers d'Asie Centrale* 7 (1999), pp. 65–73, pl. 7. http://www.asiecentrale.revues.org/index557.html.

Déroche 2004a Déroche, François. "Colonnes, vases et rinceaux sur quelques enluminures d'époque omeyyade." *Comptes-rendus des séances de l'Académie des Inscriptions et Belles-Lettres* 148, no. 1 (2004), pp. 227–64. http://www.persee.fr/web/revues/home/prescript/article/crai_0065-0536_2004_num_148_1_22702.

Déroche 2004b Déroche, François. *Le livre manuscrit arabe: Préludes à une histoire*. Conférences Léopold Delisle, Bibliothèque nationale de France [November 2001]. Paris, 2004.

Déroche and Gladiss 1999 Déroche, François, and Almut von Gladiss. *Der Prachtkoran im Museum für Islamische Kunst: Buchkunst zur Ehre Allahs*. Veröffentlichungen des Museums für Islamische Kunst, 3. Berlin, 1999.

DeShazo and Bates 1974 DeShazo, A. S., and Michael Bates. "The Umayyad Governors of al-'Iraq and the Changing Annulet Patterns on Their Dirhams." *Numismatic Chronicle*, ser. 7, 14 (August 1974), pp. 110–18, pl. 11.

Dhaky 1965 Dhaky, Madhusudan A. *The Vyala Figures on the Mediaeval Temples of India*. Indian Civilization Series, 2. Varanasi, 1965.

Diba 1983 Diba, Layla Soudavar. "Glass and Glassmaking in the Eastern Islamic Lands: Seventeenth to Nineteenth Century." *Journal of Glass Studies* 25 (1983), pp. 187–93.

Diba 1989 Diba, Layla S[oudavar]. "Persian Painting in the Eighteenth Century: Tradition and Transmission." *Muqarnas* 6 (1989), pp. 147–60.

Diba 1994 Diba, Layla S[oudavar]. "Lacquerwork of Safavid Persia and Its Relationship to Persian Painting." Ph.D. diss., [Institute of Fine Arts], New York University, 1994.

Diba et al. 2011 Diba, Layla S[oudavar], et al. *Turkmen Jewelry: Silver Ornaments from the Marshall and Marilyn R. Wolf Collection.* New York, 2011.

Dickinson 1949 Dickinson, Eric. "'The Way of Pleasure': The Kishangarh Paintings." *Marg* 3, no. 4 (1949), pp. 29–35.

Dickinson and Khandalavala 1959 Dickinson, Eric, and Karl Khandalavala. *Kishangarh Painting.* Lalit Kala Series of Indian art, 4. [New Delhi], 1959.

Dickson and Welch 1981 Dickson, Martin Bernard, and Stuart Cary Welch. *The Houghton Shahnameh.* 2 vols. Cambridge, Mass., 1981.

Digby 1973 Digby, Simon. "The Fate of Daniyal, Prince of Bengal, in the Light of an Unpublished Inscription." *Bulletin of the School of Oriental and African Studies, University of London* 36, no. 3 (1973), pp. 588–602.

Digby 1986 Digby, Simon."The Mother-of-Pearl Overlaid Furniture of Gujarat: The Holdings of the Victoria and Albert Museum." In *Facets of Indian Art: A Symposium Held at the Victoria and Albert Museum on 26, 27, 28 April and 1 May 1982*, edited by Robert Skelton et al., pp. 213–22. London, 1986.

Dimand 1924 Dimand, M[aurice S]. *Die Ornamentik der ägyptischen Wollwirkereien: Stilprobleme der spätantiken und koptischen Kunst.* Leipzig, 1924.

Dimand 1926 Dimand, M[aurice] S. "Near Eastern Metalwork." *The Metropolitan Museum of Art Bulletin* 21, no. 8 (August 1926), pp. 193–99.

Dimand 1927 Dimand, M[aurice] S. "Persian Velvets of the Sixteenth Century." *The Metropolitan Museum of Art Bulletin* 22, no. 4 (April 1927), pp. 108–11.

Dimand 1930 Dimand, M[aurice] S. *A Handbook of Mohammedan Decorative Arts.* The Metropolitan Museum of Art. New York, 1930.

Dimand 1932a Dimand, M[aurice] S. "Arabic Woodcarvings of the Ninth Century." *The Metropolitan Museum of Art Bulletin* 27, no. 5 (May 1932), pp. 135–37.

Dimand 1932b Dimand, M[aurice] S. "A Recent Gift of Egypto-Arabic Textiles." *The Metropolitan Museum of Art Bulletin* 27, no. 4 (April 1932), pp. 92–96.

Dimand 1933a D[imand], M[aurice] S. "A Gift of Early Egypto-Arabic Textiles." *The Metropolitan Museum of Art Bulletin* 28, no. 6 (June 1933), p. 112.

Dimand 1933b Dimand, M[aurice] S. "Eighth-Century Arabic Woodcarvings." *The Metropolitan Museum of Art Bulletin* 28, no. 8 (August 1933), pp. 134–35.

Dimand 1936 Dimand, M[aurice] S. "Three Syrian Capitals of the Eighth Century." *The Metropolitan Museum of Art Bulletin* 31, no. 8 (August 1936), pp. 153, 155–57.

Dimand 1937 Dimand, Maurice S. "Studies in Islamic Ornament: I. Some Aspects of Omaiyad and Early 'Abbasid Ornament." *Ars Islamica* 4 (1937), pp. 293–337.

Dimand 1940a Dimand, M[aurice] S. "Notes; A Persian Garden Carpet in the Jaipur Museum." *Ars Islamica* 7, pt. 1 (1940), pp. 93–96.

Dimand 1940b Dimand, M[aurice] S. "Two Iranian Silk Textiles." *The Metropolitan Museum of Art Bulletin* 35, no. 7 (July 1940), pp. 142–44.

Dimand 1944a Dimand, M[aurice] S. *A Handbook of Muhammadan Art.* 2nd ed. 1930. New York, 1944.

Dimand 1944b Dimand, M[aurice] S. "An Enameled-Glass Bottle of the Mamluk Period." *The Metropolitan Museum of Art Bulletin*, n.s., 3, no. 3 (November 1944), pp. 73–77.

Dimand 1952 Dimand, Maurice S. "A Saljuk Incense Burner." *The Metropolitan Museum of Art Bulletin*, n.s., 10, no. 5 (January 1952), pp. 150–53.

Dimand 1955 Dimand, Maurice S. "Rugs in the Altman Collection." *The Metropolitan Museum of Art Bulletin*, n.s., 13, no. 5 (January 1955), pp. 177–80.

Dimand 1957 Dimand, Maurice S. "The Horace Havemeyer Bequest of Islamic Art." *The Metropolitan Museum of Art Bulletin* 15, no. 9 (May 1957), pp. 208–12.

Dimand 1971 Dimand, Maurice S. "Persian Hunting Carpets of the Sixteenth Century." *Boston Museum Bulletin* 69, no. 355–56 [Persian Carpet Symposium] (1971), pp. 15–20, 46–53.

Dimand and Mailey 1973 Dimand, M[aurice] S., and Jean Mailey. *Oriental Rugs in The Metropolitan Museum of Art.* New York, 1973.

Dodd 1972 Dodd, Erica Cruikshank. "On a Bronze Rabbit from Fatimid Egypt." *Kunst des Orients* 8, nos. 1–2 (1972), pp. 60–76.

Dodds 1990 Dodds, Jerrilynn D. *Architecture and Ideology in Early Medieval Spain.* University Park, Pa., 1990.

Dodds 1992 Dodds, Jerrilynn D. "The Great Mosque of Córdoba." In Granada and New York 1992, pp. 10–25.

Dodds, Menocal, and Krasner Balbale 2008 Dodds, Jerrilynn D., María Rosa Menocal, and Abigail Krasner Balbale. *The Arts of Intimacy: Christians, Jews, and Muslims in the Making of Castilian Culture.* New Haven and London, 2008.

Doha 2004 *Silk, Thirteenth to Eighteenth Centuries: Treasures from the Museum of Islamic Art, Qatar.* Exhibition, Sheraton Doha Hotel, Doha, Qatar. Catalogue by Jon Thompson. Doha, 2004.

Duda 1971 Duda, Dorothea. *Innenarchitektur syrischer Stadthäuser des 16. bis 18. Jahrhunderts: Die Sammlung Henri Pharaon in Beirut.* Beiruter Texte und Studien, 12. Beirut, 1971.

Duda 1983 Duda, Dorothea. *Islamische Handschriften.* Vol. 1. *Persische Handschriften.* Veröffentlichungen der Kommission für Schrift- und Buchwesen des Mittelalters. Ser. 1, Die Illuminierten Handschriften und Inkunabeln der Österreichischen National-bibliothek, 4. Vienna, 1983.

Düsseldorf 2003 *Das endlose Rätsel: Dali und die Magier der Mehrdeutigkeit.* Exhibition, Museum Kunst Palast, Düsseldorf. Catalogue by Jean-Hubert Martin, Stephan Andreae, and Uta Husmeier. Düsseldorf, 2003.

Dye 2001 Dye, Joseph M., III. *The Arts of India: Virginia Museum of Fine Arts.* Richmond, 2001.

Eaton 2005 Eaton, Richard M. *A Social History of the Deccan, 1300–1761: Eight Indian Lives.* The New Cambridge History of India, 1, 8. Cambridge and New York, 2005.

Edinburgh 1977 *Imperial Images in Persian Painting.* Exhibition, Scottish Arts Council Gallery, Edinburgh. Catalogue by Robert Hillenbrand and others. Edinburgh, 1977.

***EI2* 1960–2009** *The Encyclopaedia of Islam.* New ed. 11 vols.; supplements 1–6; index. 1913–36. Leiden, London, and Boston, 1960–2009.

Ekhtiar 2006 Ekhtiar, Maryam. "Innovation and Revivalism in Later Persian Calligraphy: The Visal Family of Shiraz." In *Islamic Art in the Nineteenth Century: Tradition, Innovation and Eclecticism*, edited by Doris Behrens-Abouseif and Stephen Vernoit, pp. 257–79. Islamic History and Civilization, Studies and Texts, 60. Leiden and Boston, 2006.

Ellis, C. 1965 Ellis, Charles Grant. "Some Compartment Designs for Carpets, and Herat." *Textile Museum Journal* 1, no. 4 (December 1965), pp. 42–56.

Ellis, C. 1972 Ellis, Charles Grant. "The Portuguese Carpets of Gujarat." In Ettinghausen, ed. 1972, pp. 267–89.

Ellis, C. 1982 Ellis, Charles Grant. "Garden Carpets and Their Relation to Safavid Gardens." *Hali* 5, no. 1 [no. 17] (1982), pp. 10–17.

Ellis, M., and Wearden 2001 Ellis, Marianne, and Jennifer Wearden. *Ottoman Embroidery.* London, 2001.

***Encyclopaedia Iranica* 1985–** Yarshater, Ehsan, ed. *Encyclopaedia Iranica.* London, Costa Mesa, Calif., and New York, 1985– ; and/or *Encyclopaedia Iranica, Online Edition*, n.d., available at http://www.iranica.com.

Erdmann 1970 Erdmann, Kurt. *Seven Hundred Years of Oriental Carpets.* 1966. Berkeley and Los Angeles, 1970.

Erdmann 1976 Erdmann, Kurt. *Oriental Carpets: An Account of Their History.* 1960. Fishguard, Wales, 1976.

Erdmann, with Grabar and Hahnloser 1971 Erdmann, Kurt, with André Grabar and Hans R. Hahnloser. "Opere islamiche." In *Il tesoro di San Marco*, vol. 2, *Il tesoro e il museo*, edited by H. R. Hahnloser, pp. 103–8. Florence, 1971.

Errera 1927 Errera, Isabelle. *Catalogue d'étoffes anciennes et modernes.* 3rd ed. Musées Royaux d'Art et d'Histoire, 3. Brussels, 1927.

Ettinghausen 1936 Ettinghausen, Richard. "Evidence for the Identification of Kashan Pottery." *Ars Islamica* 3, pt. 1 (1936), pp. 44–75.

Ettinghausen 1938–39 Ettinghausen, Richard. "Dated Faience." In Pope, A. U., and Ackerman, eds. 1938–39, vol. 2, pp. 1667–96; vol. 5, pt. 1, pls. 734–35, 738.

Ettinghausen 1952 Ettinghausen, Richard. "The 'Beveled Style' in the Post-Samarra Period." In *Archaeologica Orientalia in Memoriam Ernst Hertzfeld*, edited by George C[arpenter] Miles, pp. 72–83, pls. 9–16. Locust Valley, N.Y., 1952.

Ettinghausen 1954 Ettinghausen, Richard. "Some Paintings in Four Istanbul Albums." *Ars Orientalis* 1 (1954), pp. 91–103, pls. 24–26.

Ettinghausen 1955 Ettinghausen, Richard. "An Illuminated Manuscript of Hafiz-i Abru in Istanbul, Part 1." *Kunst des Orients* 2 (1955), pp. 30–44.

Ettinghausen 1959 Ettinghausen, Richard. "New Light on Early Animal Carpets." In *Aus der Welt der islamischen Kunst: Festschrift für Ernst Kühnel zum 75. Geburtstag am 26.10.1957*, edited by Richard Ettinghausen, pp. 93–116. Berlin, 1959.

Ettinghausen 1970a Ettinghausen, Richard. "Islamic Carpets: The Joseph V. McMullan Collection." *The Metropolitan Museum of Art Bulletin*, n.s., 28, no. 10 (June 1970), pp. [400–433].

Ettinghausen 1970b Ettinghausen, Richard. "The Flowering of Seljuq Art." *Metropolitan Museum Journal* 3 (1970), pp. 113–31.

Ettinghausen 1971 Ettinghausen, Richard. "The Boston Hunting Carpet in Historical Perspective." *Boston Museum Bulletin* 69, no. 355–56 [Persian Carpet Symposium] (1971), pp. 35–41, 54–81.

Ettinghausen 1979 Ettinghausen, Richard. "The Taming of the Horror Vacui in Islamic Art." *Proceedings of the American Philosophical Society* 123, no. 1 (February 20, 1979), pp. 15–28.

Ettinghausen 1984 Ettinghausen, Richard. "Decorative Arts and Painting: Their Character and Scope [1974]." In *Islamic Art and Archaeology: Collected Papers*, edited by Myriam Rosen-Ayalon, pp. 22–48. Berlin, 1984.

Ettinghausen and Grabar 1987 Ettinghausen, Richard, and Oleg Grabar. *The Art and Architecture of Islam, 650–1250.* The Pelican History of Art. Harmondsworth, Middlesex, 1987.

Ettinghausen and Yarshater, eds. 1979 Ettinghausen, Richard, and Ehsan Yarshater, eds. *Highlights of Persian Art.* Boulder, Colo., 1979.

Ettinghausen, ed. 1972 Ettinghausen, Richard, ed. *Islamic Art in The Metropolitan Museum of Art.* New York, 1972.

Ettinghausen et al. 1975a Ettinghausen, Richard, et al. "Islamic Art." *The Metropolitan Museum of Art Bulletin*, n.s., 33, no. 1 (Spring 1975), pp. 2–53.

Ettinghausen et al. 1975b Ettinghausen, Richard, et al. *Notes on Islamic Art in Its Historical Setting.* The Metropolitan Museum of Art. New York, 1975.

Ettinghausen, Grabar, and Jenkins-Madina 2001 Ettinghausen, Richard, Oleg Grabar, and Marilyn Jenkins-Madina. *Islamic Art and Architecture, 650–1250.* 2nd ed. Pelican History of Art. 1987. New Haven and London, 2001.

Falk and Archer 1981 Falk, Toby, and Mildred Archer. *Indian Miniatures in the India Office Library.* London, 1981.

Farhad 1990 Farhad, Massumeh. "The Art of Mu'in Musavvir: A Mirror of His Times." In Canby, ed. 1990b, pp. 113–28.

Farhad 2004 Farhad, Massumeh. "Military Slaves in the Provinces: Collecting and Shaping the Arts." In *Slaves of the Shah: New Elites of Safavid Iran*, by Sussan Babaie et al. London, 2004.

Fehérvári 1972 Fehérvári, Géza. "Tombstone or Mihrab? A Speculation." In Ettinghausen, ed. 1972, pp. 241–54.

Fehérvári 1976 Fehérvári, Géza. *Islamic Metalwork of the Eighth to the Fifteenth Century in the Keir Collection.* London, 1976.

Fehérvári 2000 Fehérvári, Géza. *Ceramics of the Islamic World in the Tareq Rajab Museum.* London and New York, 2000.

Feliciano 2005 Feliciano, María Judith. "Muslim Shrouds for Christian Kings?: A Reassessment of Andalusi Textiles in Thirteenth-Century Castilian Life and Ritual." In Robinson, C., and Rouhi, eds. 2005, pp. 101–31.

Feliciano, Rouhi, and Robinson, eds. 2006 *Medieval Encounters* 12, no. 3 [*Interrogating Iberian Frontiers*, (edited by Maria Judith Feliciano, Leyla Rouhi, and Cynthia Robinson)] (2006).

Fendall 2003 Fendall, Ramsey. *Islamic Calligraphy*. London, 2003.

Feng 2004–5 Feng Zhao. "The Evolution of Textiles Along the Silk Road." In *China: Dawn of a Golden Age, 200–750 A.D.*, pp. 66–77. Exhibition, The Metropolitan Museum of Art, New York. Catalogue by James C. Y. Watt and others. New York, 2004.

Ferdowsi 1997 Ferdowsi, Abu'l-Qasem. *The Shahnameh (The Book of Kings)*. Vol. 5. Edited by Djalal Khaleghi-Motlagh. Bibliotheca Persica. Costa Mesa, Calif., and New York, 1997.

Ferdowsi 2006 Ferdowsi, Abolqasem. "The Discovery of Fire and the Establishment of the Feast of Sadeh." In *Shanameh: The Persian Book of Kings*, pp. 3–4. Translated by Dick Davis. New York, 2006.

Fernández González 2007 Fernández González, Etelvina. "Que los reyes vestiessen paños de seda, con oro, e con piedras preciosas." In *Simposio Internacional: El legado de al-Andalus; El arte andalusí en los reinos de León y Castilla durante la Edad Media*, edited by Manuel Valdés Fernández, pp. 365–408. Valladolid, 2007.

Fernández-Puertas 1973 Fernández-Puertas, Antonio. "Un paño decorativo de la Torre de las Damas." *Cuadernos de La Alhambra* 9 (1973), pp. 37–52.

Fernández-Puertas 1997 Fernández-Puertas, Antonio. *The Alhambra*. Vol. 1. London, 1997.

Ferrier, ed. 1989 Ferrier, R[onald] W., ed. *The Arts of Persia*. New Haven, 1989.

Fierro 2004 Fierro, Maribel. "Madinat al-Zahra, el paraíso y los Fatimíes." *Al-Qantara* 25, no. 2 (2004), pp. 299–327.

Fino 2010 Fino, Elizabeth V. "Ctesiphon." In *Discovering the Art of the Ancient Near East: Archaeological Excavations Supported by The Metropolitan Museum of Art, 1931–2010*, edited by Yelena Rakic, pp. 12–15. New York, 2010.

Fletcher 1968 Fletcher, Joseph F. "China and Central Asia, 1368–1884." In *The Chinese World Order: Traditional China's Foreign Relations*, edited by John King Fairbank, pp. 206–24, 345–68. Harvard East Asian Series, 32. Cambridge, Mass., 1968.

Flood 2001 Flood, Finbarr Barry. *The Great Mosque of Damascus: Studies on the Makings of an Umayyad Visual Culture*. Islamic History and Civilization, Studies and Texts, 33. Leiden, 2001.

Flood 2009 Flood, Finbarr B[arry]. *Objects of Translation: Material Culture and Medieval "Hindu-Muslim" Encounter*. Princeton, N.J., 2009.

Floor 1999 Floor, Willem M. *The Persian Textile Industry in Historical Perspective, 1500–1925*. Moyen Orient et Océan Indien, XVIe–XIXe s., 11. Paris, 1999.

Flury 1925 Flury, S[amuel]. "Le décor épigraphique des monuments de Ghazna." *Syria* 6, no. 1 (1925), pp. 61–90.

Folsach 1990 Folsach, Kjeld von. *Islamic Art: The David Collection*. Copenhagen, 1990.

Folsach 1993 Folsach, Kjeld von. "Dating and Localizing Islamic Textiles: Some Methods and Problems." In Copenhagen 1993, pp. 26–64.

Folsach 2001 Folsach, Kjeld von. *Art from the World of Islam in the David Collection*. Rev. and enl. ed. 1990. Copenhagen, 2001.

Folsach 2006–7 Folsach, Kjeld von. "The David Collection: The Museum's History, Character, and Various Reflections on the Reinstallation of the Islamic Collection." In Boston and Chicago 2006–7, pp. 31–38.

Folsach 2011 Folsach, Kjeld von. *Art from the World of Islam in the David Collection*. Copenhagen, 2011.

Folsach and Meyer, eds. 2005 *Journal of the David Collection* 2, pts. 1–2 [*The Ivories of Muslim Spain: Papers from a Symposium held in Copenhagen from the 18th to the 20th of November 2003*, edited by Kjeld von Folsach and Joachim Meyer] (2005).

Fowden 1993 Fowden, Garth. *Empire to Commonwealth: Consequences of Monotheism in Late Antiquity*. Princeton, N.J., 1993.

Fowden 2004 Fowden, Garth. *Qusayr 'Amra: Art and the Umayyad Elite in Late Antique Syria*. The Transformation of the Classical Heritage, 36. Berkeley and Los Angeles, 2004.

Fraad and Ettinghausen 1971 Fraad, Irma L., and Richard Ettinghausen. "Sultanate Painting in Persian Style, Primarily from the First Half of the Fifteenth Century: A Preliminary Study." In *Chhavi, Golden Jubilee Volume*, edited by Anand Krishna, pp. 48–66, figs. 133–67. Banaras, 1971.

Franses 1993a Franses, Michael. "The Caucasus or North-East Persia: A Question of Attribution." In Hamburg and Stuttgart 1993, pp. 94–102.

Franses 1993b Franses, Michael. "The 'Historical' Carpets from Anatolia." In Hamburg and Stuttgart 1993, pp. 266–69, 373.

Frelinghuysen 1993 Frelinghuysen, Alice Cooney. "The Forgotten Legacy: The Havemeyers' Collection of Decorative Arts." In *Splendid Legacy: The Havemeyer Collection*, pp. 98–113. Exhibition, The Metropolitan Museum of Art, New York. Catalogue by Alice Cooney Frelinghuysen, Gary Tinterow, and others. New York, 1993.

Frembgen 2010–11 Frembgen, Jürgen Wasim. "Harmony of Line, Islamic Calligraphy from Ottoman Dervish Lodges." In Munich 2010–11, pp. 79–89.

Froom 2008 Froom, Aimée. *Persian Ceramics from the Collections of the Asian Art Museum*. San Francisco, 2008.

Frothingham 1951 Frothingham, Alice Wilson. *Lustreware of Spain*. Hispanic Notes and Monographs. New York, 1951.

Frye, ed. 1973 Frye, Richard N., ed. *Sasanian Remains from Qasr-i Abu Nasr: Seals, Sealings, and Coins*. Harvard Iranian Series, 1. Cambridge, Mass., 1973.

Fukai and Horiuchi 1984 Fukai, Shinji, and Kiyoharu Horiuchi. *Taq-i Busutan/Taq-i-bustan*. Vol. 4. Report, Tokyo University Iraq-Iran Archaeological Expedition, 20. Tokyo, 1984.

Gadon 1986 Gadon, Elinor W. "Dara Shikuh's Mystical Vision of Hindu–Muslim Synthesis." In *Facets of Indian Art: A Symposium Held at the Victoria and Albert Museum on 26, 27, 28 April and 1 May 1982*, edited by Robert Skelton et al., pp. 153–57. London, 1986.

Gairola 1970 Gairola, C. Krishna. "Paintings from India, Nepal and Tibet." *Arts in Virginia* 2, no. 1 (Fall 1970), pp. 4–23.

Galán y Galindo 2005 Galán y Galindo, Ángel. *Marfiles medievales del Islam*. 2 vols. Cordoba, 2005.

Galloway 2009 Galloway, Francesca. *Global India: Court, Trade and Influence, 1300–1900*. Dealer catalogue. London, 2009.

Galloway 2011 Galloway, Francesca. *Islamic Courtly Textiles and Trade Goods, Fourteenth–Nineteenth Century*. Dealer catalogue. London, 2011.

Gans-Ruedin 1978 Gans-Ruedin, E[rwin]. *The Splendor of Persian Carpets*. New York, 1978.

Gans-Ruedin 1984 Gans-Ruedin, E[rwin]. *Indian Carpets*. New York, 1984.

García Gómez 1996 García Gómez, Emilio. *Poemas árabes en los muros y fuentes de la Alhambra*. Publicaciones del Instituto Egipcio de Estudios Islámicos. 2nd ed. 1985. Madrid, 1996.

Gaube 1994 Gaube, Heinz. "Das Mausoleum des Yusuf Gardizi in Multan." *Oriens* 34 (1994), pp. 330–47.

de Gayangos 1840–43 de Gayangos, Pascual. *The History of the Muhammedan Dynasties in Spain*. 2 vols. London, 1840–43.

Gayraud 1995 Gayraud, Roland-Pierre. "Istabl 'Antar (Fostat) 1994: Rapport de fouilles." *Annales Islamologiques* 29 (1995), pp. 1–24.

Genequand 2008 Genequand, Denis. "An Early Islamic Mosque in Palmyra." *Levant* 40, no. 1 (April 2008), pp. 3–15.

Geneva 1985 *Treasures of Islam*. Exhibition, Musée Rath, Geneva. Catalogue by Toby Falk and others. London, 1985.

Geneva 1995 *Empire of the Sultans: Ottoman Art from the Collection of Nasser D. Khalili*. Exhibition, Musée Rath, Geneva. Catalogue by J. M[ichael] Rogers. Geneva, 1995.

Geneva and other cities 1988–89 *Calligraphie islamique: Textes sacrés et profanes/Islamic Calligraphy: Sacred and Secular Writings*. Exhibition, Musée d'Art et d'Histoire, Geneva, and other venues. Catalogue by David [Lewis] James and others. Geneva, 1988.

Geneva and Paris 1993–94 *Tissus d'Égypte: Témoins du monde arabe VIIIe–XVe siècles: Collection Bouvier*. Exhibition, Musée d'Art et d'Histoire, Geneva; Institut du Monde Arabe, Paris. Geneva and Paris, 1993.

George 2010 George, Alain. *The Rise of Islamic Calligraphy*. London, 2010.

Gerspach 1885 Gerspach, É[douard]. *L'art de la verrerie*. Bibliothèque de l'enseignement des beaux-arts. Paris, [1885].

al-Ghazali 1989 al-Ghazali. *The Remembrance of Death and the Afterlife/Kitab dhikr al-mawt wa-ma ba'dahu*. Translated by T. J. Winter. Cambridge, 1989.

Ghouchani 1986 Ghouchani, A[bdullah]. *Katibaha-yi sufal-i Nishabur/Inscriptions on Nishabur Pottery*. Tehran, 1986.

Ghouchani 2004 Ghouchani, Abdullah. *Research on Inscriptions of Architectural Structures of Yazd/Barrasi-i katibaha-yi binaha-yi Yazd*. Tehran, 2004.

Gibb 1901 Gibb, E[lias] J[ohn] W[ilkinson]. *Ottoman Literature: The Poets and Poetry of Turkey*. New York and London, 1901.

Gibson forthcoming Gibson, Melanie. "A Symbolic *Khassakiyah*: Representations of the Palace Guard in Murals, Stucco, and Ceramic Sculpture." In *Art, Architecture and Material Culture, New Perspectives: Proceedings from a Workshop held at the Centre for the Advanced Study of the Arab World*, edited by Margaret S. Graves. British Archaeological Reports. Oxford, forthcoming.

Gildemeister 1885 Gildemeister, J[ohann]. *Idrisi's Palaestina und Syrien im arabischen Text*. Beilage zu der *Zeitschrift des Deutschen Palaestina-Vereins* 8. Bonn, 1885.

Gillow 2010 Gillow, John. *Textiles of the Islamic World*. New York, 2010.

Gilmartin and Lawrence, eds. 2000 Gilmartin, David, and Bruce B. Lawrence, eds. *Beyond Turk and Hindu: Rethinking Religious Identities in Islamicate South Asia*. Gainesville, Fla., 2000.

Glidden and Thompson 1989 Glidden, Harold W., and Deborah Thompson. "Tiraz in the Byzantine Collection, Dumbarton Oaks. Parts Two and Three: Tiraz from the Yemen, Iraq, Iran, and an Unknown Place." *Bulletin of the Asia Institute*, n.s., 3 (1989), pp. 89–105.

Goitein 1967–93 Goitein, S[olomon] D. *A Mediterranean Society: The Jewish Communities of the Arab World as Portrayed in the Documents of the Cairo Geniza*. 6 vols. Berkeley and Los Angeles, 1967–93.

Goitein 1983a Goitein, S[olomon] D. *A Mediterranean Society: The Jewish Communities of the Arab World as Portrayed in the Documents of the Cairo Geniza*. Vol. 4, *Daily Life*. Berkeley and Los Angeles, 1983.

Goitein 1983b Goitein, S[olomon] D. "Clothing and Jewelry." In Goitein 1983a, pp. 150–226.

Goldin 1976 Goldin, Amy. "Islamic Art: The Met's Generous Embrace." *Artforum* 14, no. 7 (March 1976), pp. 44–51.

Golombek 1991 Golombek, Lisa. "Golden Garlands of the Timurid Epoch." In *Jewellery and Goldsmithing in the Islamic World: International Symposium, The Israel Museum, Jerusalem 1987*, edited by Na'ama Brosh, pp. 63–71. [Jerusalem], 1991.

Golombek 2003 Golombek, Lisa. "The Safavid Ceramic Industry at Kirman." *Iran* 41 (2003), pp. 253–70.

Golombek et al. 1988 Golombek, Lisa, et al. *The Timurid Architecture of Iran and Turan*. 2 vols. Princeton Monographs in Art and Archaeology, 46. Princeton, N.J., 1988.

Golombek, Mason, and Proctor 2001 Golombek, Lisa, Robert B. Mason, and Patty Proctor. "Safavid Potters' Marks and the Question of Provenance." *Iran* 39 (2001), pp. 207–36.

Gonosovà 1989 Gonosovà, Anna. "Textiles." In *Beyond the Pharaohs: Egypt and the Copts in the Second to the Seventh Centuries A.D.*, pp. 65–72. Exhibition, Museum of Art, Rhode Island School of Design, Providence, R.I. Catalogue by Florence D. Friedman and others. Providence, R.I., 1989.

Gonzalez 1999 Gonzalez, Valérie. "Pratique d'une technique d'art Byzantine chez les Fatimides: L'émaillerie sur métal." In *L'Égypte fatimide, son art et son histoire: Actes du colloque organizé à Paris les 28, 29 et 30 mai 1998*, edited by Marianne Barrucand, pp. 197–217, pl. 10. Paris, 1999.

Goodwin 1977 Goodwin, Godfrey. "The Reuse of Marble in the Eastern Mediterranean in Medieval Times." *Journal of the Royal Asiatic Society of Great Britain and Ireland,* 1977, no. 1, pp. 17–30.

Goswamy and Bhatia 1999 Goswamy, B[rijindra] N[ath], with Usha Bhatia. *Painted Visions: The Goenka Collection of Indian Paintings.* New Delhi, 1999.

Goswamy and Jain 2002 Goswamy, B[rijindra] N[ath], and Rahul Jain. *Patkas: A Costume Accessory in the Collection of the Calico Museum of Textiles.* Indian Costumes, 2. Ahmedabad, 2002.

Grabar 1975 Grabar, Oleg. "The Visual Arts. I. Architecture and Its Decoration." In *The Cambridge History of Iran,* vol. 4, *The Period from the Arab Invasion to the Saljuqs,* edited by R. N. Frye, pp. 331–51, figs. 1–13. Cambridge, 1975.

Grabar 1976 Grabar, Oleg. "An Art of the Object." *Artforum* 14, no. 7 (March 1976), pp. 36–44.

Grabar 1978 Grabar, Oleg. *The Alhambra.* Cambridge, Mass., 1978.

Grabar 1987a Grabar, Oleg. *The Formation of Islamic Art.* Rev. ed. 1973. New Haven and London, 1987.

Grabar 1987b Grabar, Oleg. "The Symbolic Appropriation of the Land." In Grabar 1987a, pp. 41–73.

Grabar 1998 Grabar, Oleg. "The Shared Culture of Objects." In *Byzantine Court Culture, 829 to 1204,* edited by Henry Maguire, pp. 115–29. Cambridge, Mass., 1998.

Grabar and Blair 1980 Grabar, Oleg, and Sheila [S.] Blair. *Epic Images and Contemporary History: The Illustrations of the Great Mongol Shahnama.* Chicago, 1980.

Granada and New York 1992 *Al-Andalus: The Art of Islamic Spain.* Exhibition, Alhambra, Granada; The Metropolitan Museum of Art, New York. Catalogue by Jerrilynn D. Dodds and others. New York, 1992.

Gray 1977 Gray, Basil. *Persian Painting.* New York, 1977.

Grube 1963a Grube, Ernst J. "Four Pages from a Turkish Sixteenth-Century Shahnama in the Collection of the Metropolitan Museum of Art in New York." In *Beiträge zur Kunstgeschichte Asiens: In Memoriam Ernst Diez,* edited by Oktay Aslanapa, pp. 237–55. Istanbul, 1963.

Grube 1963b Grube, Ernst J. "The Miniatures of Shiraz." *The Metropolitan Museum of Art Bulletin,* n.s., 21, no. 9 (May 1963), pp. 285–95.

Grube 1963c Grube, Ernst J. "Three Miniatures from Fustat in the Metropolitan Museum of Art in New York." *Ars Orientalis* 5 (1963), pp. 89–95, pls. 1–6.

Grube 1978 Grube, Ernst J. *Persian Painting in the Fourteenth Century: A Research Report.* Istituto Universitario Orientale, Supplemento, no. 17, agli Annali, 38 (1978), no. 4. Naples, 1978.

Grube 1981 Grube, Ernst J. "The Problem of the Istanbul Album Pantings." *Islamic Art* 1 (1981), pp. 1–30, addenda [n.p.], figs. 1–490 passim.

Grube and Tonghini 1988–89 Grube, Ernst J., and Cristina Tonghini. "Towards a History of Syrian Islamic Pottery before 1500." *Islamic Art* 3 (1988–89), pp. 59–93, pls. 10–12.

Grube et al. 1968 Grube, Ernst J., et al. "The Ottoman Empire." *The Metropolitan Museum of Art Bulletin,* n.s., 26, no. 5 (January 1968), pp. 204–24.

Grube et al. 1994 Grube, Ernst J., et al. *Cobalt and Lustre: The First Centuries of Islamic Pottery.* The Nasser D. Khalili Collection of Islamic Art, edited by Julian Raby, vol. 9. Oxford and New York, 1994.

Guérard 1974 Guérard, Martha. "Contribution à l'étude de l'art de la broderie au Maroc: Les Broderies de Chéchaouen." *Hespéris Tamuda* 15 (1974), pp. 225–50, pls. 68–91.

Guest and Kendrick 1932 Guest, Rhuvon, and A[lbert] F[rank] Kendrick. "The Earliest Dated Islamic Textiles." *The Burlington Magazine for Connoisseurs* 60, no. 349 (April 1932), pp. 185–87, 191.

Guha-Thakurta 2004 Guha-Thakurta, Tapati. *Monuments, Objects, Histories: Institutions of Art in Colonial and Postcolonial India.* Calcutta, 2004.

Guidetti 2010 Guidetti, Mattia. "Churches and Mosques in the Cities of Bilad al-Sham: Coexistence and Transformation of the Urban Fabric." In *Islamic Cities in the Classical Age,* edited by Nasser Rabbat. Boston, 2010.

Gunter 2004–5 Gunter, Ann C. "Chess and Its Visual Culture in West, South, and Southeast Asia." In *Asian Games: The Art of Contest,* pp. 136–67. Exhibition, Asia Society Museum, New York; Arthur M. Sackler Gallery, Smithsonian Institution, Washington, D.C. Catalogue by Colin Mackenzie, Irving Finkel, and others. New York, 2004.

Gunter and Hauser, eds. 2004 Gunter, Ann C., and Stefan R. Hauser, eds. *Ernst Herzfeld and the Development of Near Eastern Studies, 1900–1950* [Papers originally delivered at the symposium . . . held from 3–5 May 2001 at the Freer Gallery of Art and Arthur M. Sackler Gallery, Smithsonian Institution, Washington, D.C.]. Leiden, 2004.

Gutas 1998 Gutas, Dimitri. *Greek Thought, Arabic Culture: The Graeco-Arabic Translation Movement in Baghdad and Early 'Abbasid Society (Second–Fourth/Eighth–Tenth Centuries).* London and New York, 1998.

Guy 1998 Guy, John. *Woven Cargoes: Indian Textiles in the East.* New York, 1998.

Haase 2007 Haase, Claus-Peter. "The Development of Stucco Decoration in Northern Syria of the Eighth and Ninth Centuries and the Bevelled Style of Samarra." In *Facts and Artefacts, Art in the Islamic World: Festschrift for Jens Kröger on His 65th Birthday,* edited by Annette Hagedorn and Avinoam Shalem, pp. 439–60. Leiden and Boston, 2007.

Haidar 1995 Haidar, Navina [Najat]. "The Kishangarh School of Painting, c. 1680–1850." Ph.D. diss., University of Oxford, 1995.

Haidar and Sardar, eds. 2011 Haidar, Navina Najat, and Marika Sardar, eds. *Sultans of the South: The Arts of India's Deccan Courts, 1323–1687.* The Metropolitan Museum of Art Symposia. New York, 2011.

Haidar Haykel 2004 Haidar Haykel, Navina N[ajat]. "A Lacquer Pen-box by Manohar: An Example of Late Safavid-style Painting in India." In *Arts of Mughal India: Studies in Honour of Robert Skelton,* edited by Rosemary Crill, Susan Stronge, and Andrew Topsfield, pp. 176–89. London and Ahmedabad, 2004.

***Hali* 1990** "An Early Animal Rug at The Metropolitan Museum." *Hali,* no. 53 (October 1990), pp. 154–55.

Hallett 2010 Hallett, Jessica. "From the Looms of Yazd and Isfahan: Persian Carpets and Textiles in Portugal." In Thompson, Shaffer, and Mildh, eds. 2010, pp. 90–123.

Hamburg and Stuttgart 1993 *Orient Stars, A Carpet Collection.* Exhibition, Deichtorhallen, Hamburg; Linden-Museum, Stuttgart. Catalogue by Heinrich Kirchheim and others. London and Stuttgart, 1993.

Hamm and other cities 1996–98 *Ägypten, Schätze aus dem Wüstensand: Kunst und Kulture der Christen am Nil.* Exhibition, Gustav-Lübcke-Museum der Stadt Hamm and other venues. Catalogue by Arne Effenberger and others. Wiesbaden, 1996.

Hanover and other cities 1991–92 *Images of Paradise in Islamic Art.* Exhibition, Hood Museum of Art, Dartmouth College, Hanover, N.H., and other venues. Catalogue by Sheila S. Blair, Jonathan M. Bloom, and others. Hanover, N.H., 1991.

Hansford 1950 Hansford, S. Howard. *Chinese Jade Carving.* London, 1950.

Hansford 1968 Hansford, S. Howard. *Chinese Carved Jades.* Greenwich, Conn., 1968.

Harari 1938–39 Harari, Ralph. "Metalwork after the Early Islamic Period." In Pope, A. U., and Ackerman, eds. 1938–39, vol. 3, pp. 2466–529; vol. 6, pt. 2, pls. 1276–404.

Hardie 1998 Hardie, Peter. "Mamluk Glass from China?" In Ward, ed. 1998, pp. 85–90, 193–96, pl. G.

Harper 1972 Harper, Prudence Oliver. "An Eighth Century Silver Plate from Iran with a Mythological Scene." In Ettinghausen, ed. 1972, pp. 153–68.

Harris 2005 Harris, Julie A. "Good Jews, Bad Jews, and No Jews at All: Ritual Imagery and Social Standards in the Catalan Haggadot." In *Church, State, Vellum, and Stone: Essays on Medieval Spain in Honor of John Williams,* edited by Therese Martin and Julie A. Harris, pp. 275–96. The Medieval and Early Modern Iberian World, 26. Leiden, 2005.

Hasan 2007 Hasan, Perween. *Sultans and Mosques: The Early Muslim Architecture of Bangladesh.* London and New York, 2007.

Hasson 1998 Hasson, Rachel. "An Enamelled Glass Bowl with 'Solomon's Seal': The Meaning of a Pattern." In Ward, ed. 1998, pp. 41–44, 174–75, pl. F.

Hastings 1907 Hastings, Francis Rawdon-Hastings, Marquess of. *The Private Journal of the Marquess of Hastings, edited by His Daughter the Marchioness of Bute.* Reprint of 2nd ed. 1858. Allahabad, 1907.

Hauser and Wilkinson 1942 Hauser, Walter, and Charles K. Wilkinson. "The Museum's Excavations at Nishapur." *The Metropolitan Museum of Art Bulletin* 37, no. 4 (April 1942), pp. 83–119.

Havemeyer 1993 Havemeyer, Louisine W. *Sixteen to Sixty: Memoirs of a Collector.* Introduction by Gary Tinterow. Annotated by Susan Alyson Stein. 1961. New York, 1993.

Hawley 1979 Hawley, John Stratton. "Krishna's Cosmic Victories." *Journal of the American Academy of Religion* 47, no. 2 (June 1979), pp. 201–21.

Heckscher 1995 Heckscher, Morrison H. "The Metropolitan Museum of Art, An Architectural History." *The Metropolitan Museum of Art Bulletin,* n.s., 53, no. 1 (Summer 1995), pp. 1, 4–80.

Heidemann 1998 Heidemann, Stefan. "The Merger of Two Currency Zones in Early Islam: The Byzantine and Sasanian Impact of the Circulation in Former Byzantine Syria and Northern Mesopotamia." *Iran* 36 (1998), pp. 95–112.

Heidemann 2003 Heidemann, Stefan. "Die Geschichte von ar-Raqqa/ar-Rafiqa—ein Überblick." In Heidemann and Becker, eds. 2003, pp. 9–56, 259–76.

Heidemann 2010 Heidemann, Stefan. "The Evolving Representation of the Early Islamic Empire and Its Religion on Coin Imagery." In *The Qur'an in Context: Historical and Literary Investigations into the Qur'anic Milieu,* edited by Angelika Neuwirth, Nicolai Sinai, and Michael Marx, pp. 149–95. Leiden and Boston, 2010.

Heidemann and Becker, eds. 2003 Heidemann, Stefan, and Andrea Becker, eds. *Raqqa II: Die Islamische Stadt.* Deutsches Archäologisches Institut. Mainz am Rhein, 2003.

d'Hennezel 1930 d'Hennezel, Henri. *Decorations and Designs of Silken Masterpieces Ancient and Modern: Original Specimens in Colours Belonging to the Textile Historical Museum of Lyon.* Musée Historique des Tissus de Lyon. New York, 1930.

Herbert 1928 Herbert, Thomas. *Travels in Persia, 1627–1629.* London, [1928].

Heringa 1996–97a Heringa, Rens. "Appendix 3: Materials and Techniques." In Los Angeles 1996–97, pp. 224–30.

Heringa 1996–97b Heringa, Rens. "Batik Pasisir as Mestizo Costume." In Los Angeles 1996–97, pp. 46–69.

Herrmann 1987 Herrmann, Eberhart. "A Great Discovery." *Hali,* no. 36 (October–December 1987), pp. 48–51, 105–6.

Herzfeld 1923 Herzfeld, Ernst. *Der Wandschmuk der Bauten von Samarra und seine Ornamentik.* Forschungen zur islamischen Kunst, 2. Ausgrabungen von Samarra, 1. Berlin, 1923.

Herzig 1992 Herzig, Edmund M. "The Volume of Iranian Raw Silk Exports in the Safavid Period." *Iranian Studies* 25, nos. 1–2 [*The Carpets and Textiles of Iran: New Perspectives in Research*] (1992), pp. 61–79.

Hewitt 1907 H[ewitt], C[onrad]. "The Edward C. Moore Collection." *The Metropolitan Museum of Art Bulletin* 2, no. 6 (June 1907), pp. 105–6.

Hillenbrand, C. 2000 Hillenbrand, Carole. *The Crusades, Islamic Perspectives.* 1999. New York, 2000.

Hillenbrand, R. 1992 Hillenbrand, Robert. "'The Ornament of the World': Medieval Córdoba as a Cultural Centre." In *The Legacy of Muslim Spain,* edited by Salma Khadra Jayyusi, pp. 113–35. Handbuch der Orientalistik/Handbook of Oriental Studies, 12. Leiden, 1992.

Hillenbrand, R. 1996 Hillenbrand, Robert. "The Iconography of the Shah-nama-yi Shahi." In *Safavid Persia: The History and Politics of an Islamic Society,* edited by Charles Melville. London, 1996.

Hillenbrand, R. 1998 Hillenbrand, Robert. "The Sarcophagus of Shah Isma'il at Ardabil." In *Society and Culture in the Early Modern Middle East: Studies on Iran in the Safavid Period,* edited by Andrew J. Newman, pp. 165–90. Edinburgh, 1998.

Hillenbrand, R. 1999 Hillenbrand, Robert. *Islamic Art and Architecture*. London, 1999.

Hoffman 1999 Hoffman, Eva R. "A Fatimid Book Cover: Framing and Re-framing Cultural Identity in the Medieval Mediterranean World." In *L'Égypte fatimide, son art et son histoire: Actes du colloque organizé à Paris les 28, 29 et 30 mai 1998*, edited by Marianne Barrucand, pp. 403–19, pls. 29–31. Paris, 1999.

Hoffman 2000 Hoffman, Eva R. "The Beginnings of the Illustrated Arabic Book: An Intersection between Art and Scholarship." *Muqarnas* 17 (2000), pp. 37–52.

Hoffman 2001 Hoffman, Eva R. "Pathways of Portability: Islamic and Christian Interchange from the Tenth to the Twelfth Century." *Art History* 24, no. 1 (February 2001), pp. 17–50.

Hoffman 2004 Hoffman, Eva R. "Christian-Islamic Encounters on Thirteenth-Century Ayyubid Metalwork: Local Culture, Authenticity, and Memory." *Gesta* 43, no. 2 (2004), pp. 129–42.

Hoffman 2007 Hoffman, Eva R. "Introduction: Remapping the Art of the Mediterranean." In *Late Antique and Medieval Art of the Mediterranean World*, edited by Eva R. Hoffman, pp. 1–8. Malden, Mass., and Oxford, 2007.

Hoffman 2008 Hoffman, Eva R. "Between East and West: The Wall Paintings of Samarra and the Construction of Abbasid Princely Culture." *Muqarnas* 25 [*Frontiers of Islamic Art and Architecture: Essays in Celebration of Oleg Grabar's Eightieth Birthday*, edited by Gülru Necipoğlu and Julia Bailey] (2008), pp. 107–32.

Holod 1992 Holod, Renata. "Luxury Arts of the Caliphal Period." In Granada and New York 1992, pp. 40–47.

Hoskins 2004 Hoskins, Nancy Arthur. *The Coptic Tapestry Albums and the Archaeologist of Antinoé, Albert Gayet*. Seattle, 2004.

Housego 1989 Housego, J. "Carpets." In Ferrier, ed. 1989, pp. 118–49.

Houston 2010 *Light of the Sufis: The Mystical Arts of Islam*. Exhibition, Museum of Fine Arts, Houston. Catalogue by Ladan Akbarnia with Francesca Leoni. Houston, 2010.

Hout 2001 Hout, Itie van. "Batik on Batik: A Wayang Story as a Record of Batik Design." In Amsterdam 2001, pp. 143–45.

Howe 1913 Howe, Winifred E. *A History of the Metropolitan Museum of Art, with a Chapter on the Early Institutions of Art in New York*. Vol. 1. New York, 1913.

Humlebaek 2007–8 *For the Privileged Few: Islamic Miniature Painting from the David Collection*. Exhibition, Louisiana Museum of Modern Art, Humlebaek. Catalogue by Kjeld von Folsach. Copenhagen, 2007.

Humphreys 1977 Humphreys, R. Stephen. *From Saladin to the Mongols: The Ayyubids of Damascus, 1193–1260*. Albany, N.Y., 1977.

Hunarfar 1971 Hunarfar, Lutfullah. *Ganjina-yi asar-i tarikhi-yi Isfahan*. Isfahan, 1971.

Husain 2000 Husain, Ali Akbar. *Scent in the Islamic Garden: A Study of Deccani Urdu Literary Sources*. Oxford, 2000.

Ibn Silm 1993 Ibn Silm, Ahmad Sa'id. *Al-Madina al-munawwara fi al-qarn al-rabi' 'ashar al-hijri*. Heliopolis, 1993.

Indictor, Koestler, Blair, and Wardwell 1988 Indictor, Norman, R. J. Koestler, C. Blair, and Anne Wardwell. "The Evaluation of Metal Wrappings from Medieval Textiles Using Scanning Electron Microscopy–Energy Dispersive X-Ray Spectrometry." *Textile History* 19, no. 1 (1988), pp. 3–22.

Inner Mongolia Institute 1993 Nei Menggu zizhiqu wen wu kao gu yan jiusuo (Inner Mongolia Institute of Cultural Relics and Archaeology), and Zhelimu meng bo wuguan (Zhelimu League Museum). *Liao Chen guo gong zhu mu* (Tomb of the Princess of the Chen State). Beijing, 1993.

Irvine 1903 Irvine, William. *The Army of the Indian Moghuls, Its Organization and Administration*. London, 1903.

Irwin 1949 Irwin, John. "The Commercial Embroidery of Gujarat in the Seventeenth Century." *Journal of the Indian Society of Oriental Art* 17 (1949), pp. 51–56, pls. 7–10.

Irwin 1959 Irwin, John. "Golconda Cotton Paintings of the Early Seventeenth Century." *Lalit Kala*, no. 5 (April 1959), pp. 11–48, pls. 1–20.

Irwin 1973 Irwin, John. *The Kashmir Shawl*. [Victoria and Albert] Museum Monograph, no. 29. London, 1973.

Irwin and Brett 1970 Irwin, John, and Katharine B. Brett. *Origins of Chintz, with a Catalogue of Indo-European Cotton-Paintings in the Victoria and Albert Museum, London, and the Royal Ontario Museum, Toronto*. London, 1970.

Irwin and Hall 1973a Irwin, John, and Margaret Hall. "Glossary of Embroidery Stitches." In Irwin and Hall 1973b, pp. 201–15.

Irwin and Hall 1973b Irwin, John, and Margaret Hall. *Indian Embroideries*. Historic Textiles of India at the Calico Museum, Ahmedabad, vol. 2. Ahmedabad, 1973.

***Islamic Art* 1981** "Concordance of Figures and Folio Numbers in the Istanbul Albums." *Islamic Art* 1 (1981), pp. 164–65, figs. 1–490 passim.

Issa 1994 Issa, Ahmad Mohammed. *Islamic Art Terms (Lexicon Explained and Illustrated)*. Research Centre for Islamic History, Art and Culture, Islamic Arts and Crafts Series, 8. Istanbul, 1994.

Istanbul 1998a *Osmanli sanatinda hat*. Exhibition, Topkapı Palace Museum, Istanbul. Catalogue by Filiz Çağman and and Sule Aksoy. Istanbul, 1998.

Istanbul 1998b *Sultanlarin Aynaları/The Sultans' Mirrors*. Exhibition, Topkapı Palace Museum, Istanbul. Catalogue by Filiz Çağman and others. Istanbul, 1998.

Istanbul 2008 *Three Capitals of Islamic Art, Istanbul, Isfahan, Delhi: Masterpieces from the Louvre Collection*. Exhibition, Sabancı University, Sakıp Sabancı Museum, Istanbul. Istanbul, 2008.

Ivanov 1979 Ivanov, A. A. "The Life of Muhammad Zaman: A Reconsideration." *Iran* 17 (1979), pp. 65–70.

Jaffer 2002 Jaffer, Amin. *Luxury Goods from India: The Art of the Indian Cabinet Maker*. London, 2002.

Jaffer et al. 2001 Jaffer, Amin, et al. *Furniture from British India and Ceylon: A Catalogue of the Collections in the Victoria and Albert Museum and the Peabody Essex Museum*. London, 2001.

Jahangir 1909–14 Jahangir. *The Tuzuk-i Jahangiri*. Translated by Alexander Rogers and edited by Henry Beveridge. 2 vols. London, 1909–14.

Jahangir 1968 Jahangir. *The Tuzuk-i Jahangiri or Memoirs of Jahangir*. Translated by Alexander Rogers and edited by Henry Beveridge. Reprint ed. 2 vols. 1909–14. Delhi, 1968.

Jahangir 1999 Jahangir. *The Jahangirnama: Memoirs of Jahangir, Emperor of India*. Translated, edited, and annotated by Wheeler M. Thackston. Washington, D.C., New York, and Oxford, 1999.

James 1988 James, David Lewis. *Manuscripts of the Holy Qur'an from the Mamluk Era*. King Faisal Centre for Research and Islamic Studies. London, 1988.

James 1992a James, David [Lewis]. *After Timur: Qur'ans of the Fifteenth and Sixteenth Centuries*. The Nasser D. Khalili Collection of Islamic Art, edited by Julian Raby, vol. 3. London, 1992.

James 1992b James, David [Lewis]. *The Master Scribes: Qur'ans of the Tenth to Fourteenth Centuries, A.D.* The Nasser D. Khalili Collection of Islamic Art, edited by Julian Raby, vol. 2. London, 1992.

James 1999 James, David [Lewis]. *Manuscripts of the Holy Qur'an from the Mamluk Era*. King Faisal Centre for Research and Islamic Studies. 1988. Riyadh, 1999.

James 2009 James, David [Lewis]. "Qur'ans and Calligraphers of the Ayyubids and Zangids." In *Ayyubid Jerusalem: The Holy City in Context, 1187–1250*, edited by Robert Hillenbrand and Sylvia Auld, pp. 348–59. London, 2009.

James and Ettinghausen 1977 James, David Lewis, and Richard Ettinghausen. *Arab Painting*. New York, 1977.

al-Janabi 1983 al-Janabi, Tariq. "Islamic Archaeology in Iraq: Recent Excavations at Samarra." *World Archaeology* 14, no. 3 [*Islamic Archaeology*] (February 1983), pp. 305–27.

Jarrar 1999 Jarrar, Salah. *Diwan al-hamra': al-ash'ar al-'arabiyya al-manqutha fi mabani Qasr al-Hamra' wa-Jannat al-'Arif bi-Gharnata*. Beirut, 1999.

Jaubert, ed. 1936–40 Jaubert, P. Amédée, trans. and ed. *Géographie d'Édrisi traduite de l'arabe en français d'après deux manuscrits de la Bibliothèque du roi et accompagnée de notes*. 2 vols. in 4. Paris, 1936–40.

al-Jawhari 1954 Mansur al-Katib al-'Azizi al-Jawhari. *Sirat al-ustadh Jawhar wa-bihi tawqi 'at al-a'immat al-fatimiyyin*. Edited by Muhammad Kamil Husayn and Muhammad 'Abd al-Hadi Shu'aira. Cairo, 1954.

al-Jawhari 1958 Mansur al-Katib al-'Azizi al-Jawhari. *Vie de l'Ustadh Jaudhar (contenant sermons, lettres et rescrits des premiers califes fâtimides) écrite par Mansûr le secrétaire à l'époque du calife al-'Azîz billâh (365–386/975–996)*. Translated by Marius Canard. Publications de l'Institut d'Études Orientales de la Faculté des Lettres d'Alger, ser. 2, vol. 20. Algiers, 1958.

al-Jazari 1974 al-Jazari, Isma'il ibn al-Razzaz. *The Book of Knowledge of Ingenious Mechanical Devices*. Translated and annotated by Donald R. Hill. Dordrecht and Boston, 1974.

Jenkins 1968a Jenkins, Marilyn. "Muslim: An Early Fatimid Ceramist." *The Metropolitan Museum of Art Bulletin*, n.s., 26, no. 9 (May 1968), pp. 359–69.

Jenkins 1968b Jenkins, Marilyn. "The Palmette Tree: A Study of the Iconography of Egyptian Lustre Painted Pottery." *Journal of the American Research Center in Egypt* 7 (1968), pp. 119–26, pls. 1–9.

Jenkins 1972 Jenkins, Marilyn. "An Eleventh-Century Woodcarving from a Cairo Nunnery." In Ettinghausen, ed. 1972, pp. 227–40.

Jenkins 1984 Jenkins, Marilyn. "Mamluk Underglaze-Painted Pottery: Foundations for Future Study." *Muqarnas* 2 [*The Art of the Mamluks*] (1984), pp. 95–114.

Jenkins 1986 Jenkins, Marilyn. "Islamic Glass: A Brief History." *The Metropolitan Museum of Art Bulletin*, n.s., 44, no. 2 (Fall 1986), pp. 1–56.

Jenkins 1988 Jenkins, Marilyn. "Mamluk Jewelry: Influences and Echoes." *Muqarnas* 5 (1988), pp. 29–42.

Jenkins 1992 Jenkins, Marilyn. "Early Medieval Islamic Pottery: The Eleventh Century Reconsidered." *Muqarnas* 9 (1992), pp. 56–66.

Jenkins, ed. 1983 Jenkins, Marilyn, ed. *Islamic Art in the Kuwait National Museum: The al-Sabah Collection*. London, 1983.

Jenkins-Madina 2000 Jenkins-Madina, Marilyn. "Collecting the 'Orient' at the Met: Early Tastemakers in America." *Ars Orientalis* 30 [*Exhibiting the Middle East: Collections and Perceptions of Islamic Art*] (2000), pp. 69–89.

Jenkins-Madina 2006 Jenkins-Madina, Marilyn. *Raqqa Revisited: Ceramics of Ayyubid Syria*. New York, 2006.

Jenyns 1988 Jenyns, Soame. *Ming Pottery and Porcelain*. The Faber Monographs on Pottery and Porcelain. 2nd ed. 1953. London, 1988.

Jerusalem 1987 *Early Islamic Jewellery*. Exhibition, L.A. Mayer Memorial Institute for Islamic Art, Jerusalem. Catalogue by Rachel Hasson. Jerusalem, 1987.

Jesús Fuente 2009 Jesús Fuente, Maria. "Christian, Muslim and Jewish Women in Late Medieval Iberia." *Medieval Encounters* 15 (2009), pp. 319–33.

Kahl 2008 Kahil, Abdallah. *The Sultan Hasan Complex in Cairo, 1357–1364: A Case Study in the Formation of Mamluk Style*. Beiruter Texte und Studien, 98. Würzburg and Beirut, 2008.

Kalter and Pavaloi 1987 Kalter, Johannes, and Margareta Pavaloi. *Linden-Museum Stuttgart, Abteilungsführer Islamischer Orient*. Stuttgart, 1987.

Kamada 2010 Kamada, Yumiko. "A Taste for Intricacy: An Illustrated Manuscript of *Mantiq al-Tayr* in the Metropolitan Museum of Art." *Orient: Reports of the Society for Near Eastern Studies in Japan* 45 (2010), pp. 129–75.

Kamada 2011 Kamada, Yumiko. "Flowers on Floats: The Production, Circulation, and Reception of Early Modern Indian Carpets." Ph.D. diss., Institute of Fine Arts, New York University, 2011.

Karev 2005 Karev, Yuri. "Qarakhanid Wall Paintings in the Citadel of Samarqand: First Report and Preliminary Observations." *Muqarnas* 22 (2005), pp. 45–84.

Karim 2002 Karim, Chahinda. "The Mosque of Amir Qawsun in Cairo (730/1330)." In *Historians in Cairo: Essays in Honor of George Scanlon*, pp. 29–48. Cairo and New York, 2002.

Karimzada Tabrizi 1990 Karimzada Tabrizi, Muhammad Ali. *Ahval va Asar-i Naqqashan-i Qadim-i Iran*. Vol. 2. London, 1990.

Karnouk 1981 Karnouk, Gloria S. "Form and Ornament of the Cairene Bahri Minbar." *Annales islamologiques* 17 (1981), pp. 113–39, pls. 1–6.

al-Kashani 1966 Abu 'l-Qasim 'Abdallah al-Kashani. *'Arayis al-jawahir wa nafayis al-atayib*. Edited by Iraj Afshar. Tehran, 1966.

Katzenstein and Lowry 1983 Katzenstein, Ranee A., and Glenn D. Lowry. "Christian Themes in Thirteenth-Century Islamic Metalwork." *Muqarnas* 1 (1983), pp. 53–68.

Kayaoğlu 2000 Kayaoğlu, I. Gundag. "Divitler." In *M. Uğur Derman Festschrift: Papers Presented on the Occasion of His Sixty-fifth Birthday*, edited by Irvin Cemil Schick, pp. 354–68. Istanbul, 2000.

Keene 2004 Keene, Manuel. "The *Kundan* Technique: The Indian Jeweller's Unique Artistic Treasure." In *Arts of Mughal India: Studies in Honour of Robert Skelton*, edited by Rosemary Crill, Susan Stronge, and Andrew Topsfield, pp. 190–202. London and Ahmedabad, 2004.

Keene 2008 Keene, Manuel. "Jade. iii. Jade Carving, Fourth Century B.C.E. to Fifteenth Century C.E." In *Encyclopaedia Iranica* 1985– , vol. 14 (2008), pp. 326–39; or in *Encyclopaedia Iranica, Online Edition*, n.d., available at http://www.iranica.com/articles/jade-iii.

Kendrick 1924 Kendrick, A[lbert] F[rank]. *Catalogue of Muhammadan Textiles of the Medieval Period*. Victoria and Albert Museum, Department of Textiles. London, 1924.

Kennedy 1993 Kennedy, H[ugh]. "Al-Mu'tamid 'ala 'llah." In *EI2* 1960–2009, vol. 7 (1993), pp. 765–66.

Kennedy, ed. 2001 Kennedy, Hugh, ed. *The Historiography of Islamic Egypt (c. 950–1800)*. The Medieval Mediterranean, 31. Leiden, 2001.

Kenney 2004 Kenney, Ellen [V]. "Power and Patronage in Mamluk Syria: The Architecture and Urban Works of Tankiz al-Nasiri, 1312–1340." Ph.D. diss., Institute of Fine Arts, New York University, 2004.

Kenney 2009 Kenney, Ellen V. *Power and Patronage in Medieval Syria: The Architecture and Urban Works of Tankiz al-Nasiri*. Chicago Studies on the Middle East. Chicago, 2009.

Keyvani 1982 Keyvani, Mehdi. *Artisans and Guild Life in the Later Safavid Period: Contributions to the Socio-Economic History of Persia*. Islamkundliche Untersuchungen, 65. Berlin, 1982.

Khalili, Robinson, and Stanley 1996–97 Khalili, Nasser D., B[asil] W. Robinson, and Tim Stanley with Manijeh Bayani. *Lacquer of the Islamic Lands*. 2 parts. The Nasser D. Khalili Collection of Islamic Art, edited by Julian Raby, vol. 22. London, 1996–97.

Khan 1983 Khan, Ahmad Nabi. *Multan, History and Architecture*. Islamabad, 1983.

Khoury 1992 Khoury, Nuha N. N. "The Mihrab Image: Commemorative Themes in Medieval Islamic Architecture." *Muqarnas* 9 (1992), pp. 11–28.

Khoury 1998 Khoury, Nuha N. N. "The Mihrab: From Text to Form." *International Journal of Middle East Studies* 30, no. 1 (February 1998), pp. 1–27.

Khusifi Birjandi 2002 Khusifi Birjandi, Ibn Hisham. *Khavaran nama: Nigara-ha, va tadhhib-ha-yi Farhad-i Naqqash-i sada-yi nuhum-i hijri*. Tehran, 2002.

Kia 2006 Kia, Chad. "Is the Bearded Man Drowning?: Picturing the Figurative in a Late-Fifteenth-Century Painting from Herat." *Muqarnas* 23 (2006), pp. 85–105.

King 1983 King, David A. *Mathematical Astronomy in Medieval Yemen: A Biobibliographical Survey*. Catalogs (American Research Center in Egypt), 4. Malibu, 1983.

King 1985 King, David A. "The Medieval Yemeni Astrolabe in the Metropolitan Museum of Art in New York City." *Zeitschrift für Geschichte der arabisch-islamischen Wissenschaften* 2 (1985), pp. 99–122; 4 (1987–88), pp. 268–69 [errata].

King 2005 King, David A. *In Synchrony with the Heavens: Studies in Astronomical Timekeeping and Instrumentation in Medieval Islamic Civilization*. Vol. 2, *Instruments of Mass Calculation: Studies X–XVIII*. Islamic Philosophy, Theology, and Science, 55. Leiden, 2005.

Klose 1978 Klose, Christine. "Betrachtungen zu nordwestpersischen Gartenteppichen des 18. Jahrhunderts." *Hali* 1, no. 2 [no. 2] (Summer 1978), pp. 112–21.

Klose 2010 Klose, Christine. "Traces of Timurid Carpets in Contemporary and Later Carpets from the Near East." In Thompson, Shaffer, and Mildh, eds. 2010, pp. 72–89.

Koch 2006 Koch, Ebba. *The Complete Taj Mahal and the Riverfront Gardens of Agra*. London, 2006.

Kogman-Appel 2004 Kogman-Appel, Katrin. *Jewish Book Art between Islam and Christianity: The Decoration of Hebrew Bibles in Medieval Spain*. The Medieval and Early Modern World, 19. Leiden, 2004.

Kohlberg 1989 Kohlberg, Etan. "Baha'-al-Din 'Ameli, Shaikh Mohammad." In *Encyclopaedia Iranica* 1985– , vol. 3 (1989), pp. 429–30.

Komaroff 1979–80 Komaroff, Linda. "Timurid to Safavid Iran: Continuity and Change." *Marsyas* 20 (1979–80), pp. 11–16, pls. 9–12.

Komaroff 1992a Komaroff, Linda. *Islamic Art in The Metropolitan Museum of Art: The Historical Context*. New York, 1992.

Komaroff 1992b Komaroff, Linda. *The Golden Disk of Heaven: Metalwork of Timurid Iran*. Costa Mesa, Calif., 1992.

Komaroff 2000 Komaroff, Linda. "Exhibiting the Middle East: Collections and Perceptions of Islamic Art." *Ars Orientalis* 30 [*Exhibiting the Middle East: Collections and Perceptions of Islamic Art*, edited by Linda Komaroff] (2000), pp. 1–8.

Komaroff 2002–3 Komaroff, Linda. "The Transmission and Dissemination of a New Visual Language." In New York and Los Angeles 2002–3, pp. 168–95.

Krachovskaya 1949 Krachovskaya, V. A. "Evolyutsiya kuficheskogo pis'ma v Srednei Azii." *Epigrafika Vostoka* 3 (1949), pp. 3–27.

Krachovskaya 1955 Krachovskaya, V. A. "Arabskoe pis'mo na pamyatnikakh Srednei Azii i Zakavkaz'ya IX–XI VV." *Epigrafika Vostoka* 10 (1955), pp. 38–60.

Kröger 1993 Kröger, Jens. "Crystal, Rock. ii. In the Islamic Period." In *Encyclopaedia Iranica* 1985– , vol. 6 (1993), pp. 440–41; or in *Encyclopaedia Iranica, Online Edition*, December 15, 1993, available at http://www.iranica.com/articles/crystal-rock-bolur-bolur-e-kuhi.

Kröger 1995 Kröger, Jens. *Nishapur: Glass of the Early Islamic Period*. New York, 1995.

Kröger 2005 Kröger, Jens. "Scratched Glass." In *Glass: From Sasanian Antecedents to European Imitations*, edited by Sidney M. Goldstein, pp. 140–47. The Nasser D. Khalili Collection of Islamic Art, edited by Julian Raby, vol. 15. London, 2005.

Kronk 1998 Kronk, Gary W. *Comets: A Descriptive Catalogue*. 1984. Hillside, N.J., 1998.

Kühnel 1934 Kühnel, Ernst. "Die 'abbasidischen Lüsterfayencen." *Ars Islamica* 1, pt. 2 (1934), pp. 148–59.

Kühnel 1938 Kühnel, Ernst. *Die Sammlung türkischer und islamischer Kunst im Tschinili Köschk*. Meisterwerke der archäologischen Museen in Istanbul, vol. 3. Berlin and Leipzig, 1938.

Kühnel 1952 Kühnel, Ernst. "Neue Beiträge zur Tiraz-Epigraphik." In *Documenta Islamica Inedita*. pp. 163–71, figs. 1–9. Berlin, 1952.

Kühnel 1971 Kühnel, Ernst. *Die islamischen Elfenbeinskulpturen, VIII.–XIII. Jahrhundert*. Berlin, 1971.

Kühnel and Bellinger 1952 Kühnel, Ernst, and Louisa Bellinger. *The Textile Museum Catalogue of Dated Tiraz Fabrics: Umayyad, Abbasid, Fatimid*. Washington, D.C., 1952.

Kühnel and Bellinger 1953 Kühnel, Ernst, and Louisa Bellinger. *Catalogue of Spanish Rugs: Twelfth Century to Nineteenth Century*. The Textile Museum, Catalogue raisonné. Washington D.C., 1953.

Kulkarni 2004 Kulkarni, Prashant P. "Die Linkage of the Zodiacal Mohurs of Jahangir." *The Journal of the Numismatic Society of India* 66 (2004), pp. 68–84.

Kumar 1999 Kumar, Ritu. *Costumes and Textiles of Royal India*. London, 1999.

Kunz 1903 Kunz, George Frederick. "Heber Reginald Bishop and His Jade Collection." *American Anthropologist*, n.s., 5, no. 1 (January–March 1903), pp. 111–17.

Kuwait 1990 *Bada'i' al-fann al-islami fi Mathaf al-Hirmitaj bil-Ittihad al-Sufyiti / Shedevry islamskogo iskusstva v Ermitazha SSSR* (Masterpieces of islamic art in the Hermitage Museum). Exhibition, Dar al-Athar al-Islamiyya, Kuwait. Kuwait, 1990.

Labarta and Barceló 1987 Labarta, Ana, and Carmen Barceló. "Las fuentes árabes sobre al-Zahra: Estado de la cuestión." *Cuadernos de Madinat al-Zahra* 1 (1987), pp. 93–106.

Labatt and Appleyard 2004 Labatt, Annie, and Charlotte Appleyard. "Byzantine Art under Islam." In *Heilbrunn Timeline of Art History*. The Metropolitan Museum of Art. New York, 2000– . http://www.metmuseum.org/toah/hd/bzis/hd_bzis.htm (October 2004).

Lace 2006 Lace, William W. *The Unholy Crusade: The Ransacking of Medieval Constantinople*. San Diego, 2006.

Lafontaine-Dosogne 1981 Lafontaine-Dosogne, Jacqueline. *Textiles islamiques*. Vol. 1, *Iran et Asie Centrale*. Brussels, 1981.

Lamm 1928 Lamm, Carl Johan. *Das Glas von Samarra*. Forschungen zur islamischen Kunst, 2; Die Ausgrabungen von Samarra, 4. Berlin, 1928.

Lamm 1936 Lamm, Carl Johan. "Fatimid Woodwork, Its Style and Chronology." *Bulletin de l'Institute d'Égypte* 18 (1936), pp. 59–91.

Lamm 1937 Lamm, Carl Johan. *Cotton in Mediaeval Textiles of the Near East*. Paris, 1937.

Lamm 1985 Lamm, Carl Johan. *Carpet Fragments: The Marby Rug and some Fragments of Carpets Found in Egypt*. Stockholm: Nationalmuseum, 1985.

Landau 2006 Landau, Amy S. "Farangi-Sazi at Isfahan: The Court Painter Muhammad Zaman, the Armenians of New Julfa and Shah Sulayman (1666–1694)." Ph.D. diss., University of Oxford, 2006.

Landau 2011 Landau, Amy S. "From Poet to Painter: Allegory and Metaphor in a Seventeenth Century Painting by Muhammad Zaman, Master of *Farangi-sazi*." *Muqarnas* 28 (2011), forthcoming.

Lane 1946 Lane, Arthur. "Early Hispano-Moresque Pottery: A Reconsideration." *The Burlington Magazine for Connoisseurs* 88, no. 523 (October 1946), pp. 246, 248–53.

Lane 1957 Lane, Arthur. "The Ottoman Pottery of Isnik." *Ars Orientalis* 2 (1957), pp. 247–81, pls. 1–14.

Lane 1971 Lane, Arthur. *Later Islamic Pottery: Persia, Syria, Egypt, Turkey*. Revised by Ralph Pinder-Wilson. 2nd ed. 1957. London, 1971.

La Niece and Martin 1987 La Niece, Susan, and Graham Martin. "The Technical Examination of Bidri Ware." *Studies in Conservation* 32, no. 3 (August 1987), pp. 97–101.

Lapérouse 2003 Lapérouse, Jean-François de. "Mixed Media: An Islamic Writing Cabinet." *Met Objectives: The Sherman Fairchild Center for Objects Conservation, Treatment and Research Notes* 4, no. 2 (2003), pp. 1–3.

Lassikova 2010 Lassikova, Galina. "Hushang the Dragon-Slayer: Fire and Firearms in Safavid Art and Diplomacy." *Iranian Studies* 43, no. 1 (February 2010), pp. 37–40.

Lawrence, Kans., and San Francisco 1994 *Latter Days of the Law: Images of Chinese Buddhism, 850–1850*. Exhibition, Spencer Museum of Art, University of Kansas, Lawrence; Asian Art Museum of San Francisco. Catalogue by Marsha Weidner and others. Lawrence, Kans., 1994.

Leach 1995 Leach, Linda York. *Mughal and Other Indian Paintings from the Chester Beatty Library*. Vol. 1. London, 1995.

Leach 1998 Leach, Linda York. "Mir Kalan Khan and Provincial Mughal Painting of the Later Eighteenth Century." In *Paintings from India*, by Linda York Leach, pp. 166–87. The Nasser D. Khalili Collection of Islamic Art, edited by Julian Raby, vol. 8. London, 1998.

Leatham 2000 Leatham, Victoria. *Burghley: The Life of a Great House*. 1992. London, 2000.

Lefevre and Thompson 1977 Lefevre, Jean, and Jon Thompson. *The Persian Carpet*. London, 1977.

Legêne and Waaldijk 2001 Legêne, Susan, and Berteke Waaldijk. "Reverse Images—Patterns of Absence: Batik and the Representation of Colonialism in the Netherlands." In Amsterdam 2001, pp. 43–45.

Leisten 2003 Leisten, Thomas. *Excavation of Samarra*. Vol. 1, *Architecture: Final Report of the First Campaign, 1910–1912*. Mainz am Rhein, 2003.

Leithe-Jasper and Distelberger 1998 Leithe-Jasper, Manfred, and Rudolf Distelberger. *The Kunsthistorisches Museum,*

Vienna: The Imperial and Ecclesiastical Treasury. London, 1998.

Lentz 1990 Lentz, Thomas W. "Changing Worlds: Bihzad and the New Painting." In Canby, ed. 1990a and/or Canby, ed. 1990b, pp. 39–54.

Lev 1999 Lev, Yaacov. *Saladin in Egypt*. Medieval Mediterranean, 21. Leiden, 1999.

Levanoni 1995 Levanoni, Amalia. *A Turning Point in Mamluk History: The Third Reign of al-Nasir Muhammad ibn Qalawun, 1310–1341*. Leiden, 1995.

Lings 2005 Lings, Martin. *Splendours of Qur'an Calligraphy and Illumination*. 2004. Vaduz, Liechtenstein, 2005.

Lisbon 2004 *Goa and the Great Mughal*. Exhibition, Museu Calouste Gulbenkian, Lisbon. Catalogue by Nuno Vassallo e Silva and Jorges Flores. London, 2004.

Lisbon and Vienna 2001–2 *Exotica: The Portuguese Discoveries and the Renaissance Kunstkammer*. Exhibition, Museu Calouste Gulbenkian, Lisbon; Kunsthistorisches Museum, Vienna. Catalogue by Nuno Vassallo e Silva, Helmut Trnek, and others. Lisbon, 2001.

Llewellyn-Jones, ed. 2003 Llewellyn-Jones, Rosie, ed. *Lucknow, Then and Now*. Mumbai, 2003.

Loehr 1954 Loehr, Max. "The Chinese Elements in the Istanbul Miniatures." *Ars Orientalis* 1 (1954), pp. 85–89, pls. 20–23.

London 1967 *Persian Miniature Painting from Collections in the British Isles*. Exhibition, Victoria and Albert Museum, London. Catalogue by B[asil] W[illiam] Robinson. London, 1967.

London 1976a *Islamic Metalwork from Iranian Lands (Eighth–Eighteenth Centuries)*. Exhibition, Victoria and Albert Museum, London. Catalogue by A[ssadullah] S[ouren] Melikian-Chirvani. London, 1976.

London 1976b *Persian and Mughal Art*. Exhibition, P. and D. Colnaghi, London. Catalogue by B[asil] W[illiam] Robinson. London, 1976.

London 1976c *The Arts of Islam*. Exhibition, Hayward Gallery, London. London, 1976.

London 1980 *Qur'ans and Bindings from the Chester Beatty Library: A Facsimile Exhibition*. Exhibition, Leighton House Gallery, London. Catalogue by David [Lewis] James. London, 1980.

London 1982a *Indian Painting, 1525–1825*. Exhibition, David Carritt Limited, London. Catalogue by Terence McInerney. London, 1982.

London 1982b *In the Image of Man: The Indian Perception of the Universe through 2000 Years of Painting and Sculpture*. Exhibition, Hayward Gallery, London. Catalogue by George Michell, Catherine Lampert, and Tristram Holland. London, 1982.

London 1982c *The Art of the Book in India*. Exhibition, British Library, Reference Division, London. Catalogue by Jeremiah P. Losty. London, 1982.

London 1982d *The Indian Heritage: Court Life and Arts under Mughal Rule*. Exhibition, Victoria and Albert Museum, London. [Catalogue by Robert Skelton.] London, 1982.

London 1983 *The Eastern Carpet in the Western World from the Fifteenth to the Seventeenth Century*. Exhibition, Hayward Gallery, London. Catalogue by Donald King and David Sylvester. London, 1983.

London 1990–91 *The Raj, India and the British, 1600–1947*. Exhibition, National Portrait Gallery, London. Catalogue by C[ristopher] A[lan] Bayly. London, 1990.

London 2001a *Indian Painting for the British, 1780–1889*. Exhibition Walpole Gallery, London. Catalogue by Niall Hobhouse. London, 2001.

London 2001b *The Lucknow Menagerie: Natural History Drawings from the Collection of Claude Martin (1735–1800)*. Exhibition, Walpole Gallery, London. Catalogue by William Chubb. London, 2001.

London 2004 *Encounters: The Meeting of Asia and Europe, 1500–1800*. Exhibition, Victoria and Albert Museum, London. Catalogue by Anna Jackson, Amin Jaffer, and others. London, 2004.

London 2005 *Turks: A Journey of a Thousand Years, 600–1600*. Exhibition, Royal Academy of Arts, London. Catalogue by David J. Roxburgh and others. London, 2005.

London 2009 *Shah 'Abbas: The Remaking of Iran*. Exhibition, The British Museum, London. Catalogue by Sheila R. Canby and others. London, 2009.

London 2009–10 *Maharaja: The Splendour of India's Royal Courts*. Exhibition, Victoria and Albert Museum, London. Catalogue by Amin Jaffer, Anna Jackson, and others. London, 2009.

London and Lisbon 2008 *Kraak Porcelain: The Rise of Global Trade in the Late Sixteenth Century and Early Seventeenth Centuries*. Exhibition, Jorge Welsh, London; Jorge Welsh, Lisbon. Catalogue by Luisa Vinhais and Jorge Welsh. London, 2008.

London and other cities 1983 *Indian Drawing*. Exhibition, Hayward Gallery, London, and other English venues. Catalogue by Howard Hodgkin and Terence McInerney. London, 1983.

London and other cities 2001 *Treasury of the World: Jewelled Arts of India in the Age of the Mughals*. Exhibition, British Museum, London, and other cities. Catalogue by Manuel Keene with Salam Kaoukji. London, 2001.

London, Cambridge, Mass., and Zurich 1998–99 *Princes, Poets and Paladins: Islamic and Indian Paintings from the Collection of Prince and Princess Sadruddin Aga Khan*. Exhibition, The British Museum, London; Arthur M. Sackler Museum, Harvard University Art Museums, Cambridge; Museum Rietberg Zürich. Catalogue by Sheila R. Canby. London, 1998.

London, Washington, D.C., and Cambridge, Mass. 1979–80 *Wonders of the Age: Masterpieces of Early Safavid Painting, 1501–1576*. Exhibition, British Library, London; National Gallery of Art, Washington, D.C.; Fogg Art Museum, Cambridge, Mass. Catalogue by Stuart Cary Welch and others. Cambridge, Mass., 1979.

London, Washington, D.C., Zurich, and Oxford 1991–93 *Indian Paintings and Drawings from the Collection of Howard Hodgkin*. Exhibition, British Museum, London; Arthur M. Sackler Gallery, Smithsonian Institution, Washington, D.C.; Museum Rietberg Zürich; Ashmolean Museum, Oxford. Catalogue by Andrew Topsfield and Milo Cleveland Beach. New York and London, 1991.

Loring 2001 Loring, John. *Magnificent Tiffany Silver*. New York, 2001.

Los Angeles 1996–97 *Fabric of Enchantment: Batik from the North Coast of Java from the Inger McCabe Elliot Collection at the Los Angeles County Museum of Art*. Exhibition, Los Angeles County Museum of Art. Catalogue by Rens Heringa and others. Los Angeles and New York, 1996.

Los Angeles and other cities 1989–91 *Romance of the Taj Mahal*. Exhibition, Los Angeles County Museum of Art and other venues. Catalogue by Pratapaditya Pal and others. Los Angeles and London, 1989.

Losty 1995 Losty, J[eremiah] P. "The Governor-General's Draughtsman: Sita Ram and the Marquess of Hastings' Albums." *Marg* 47, no. 2 (1995), pp. 80–84.

Losty 1996 Losty, J[eremiah] P. "Early Views of Gaur and Pandua by the Indian Artist Sita Ram." *Journal of Bengal Art* 1 (1996), pp. 189–203.

Losty 2002 Losty, J[eremiah] P. "Towards a New Naturalism: Portraiture in Murshidabad and Avadh, 1750–80." In *After the Great Mughals: Painting in Delhi and the Regional Courts in the Eighteenth and Nineteenth Centuries*, edited by Barbara Schmitz, and/or Marg 53, no. 4 (June 2002), pp. 34–55. Mumbai, 2002.

Loukonine and Ivanov 1996 Loukonine, Vladimir, and Anatoli Ivanov. *Lost Treasures of Persia: Persian Art in the Hermitage Museum*. Washington, D.C., 1996.

Lowry and Nemazee 1988 Lowry, Glenn D., with Susan Nemazee. *A Jeweler's Eye: Islamic Arts of the Book from the Vever Collection*. Washington D.C., 1988.

Lowry et al. 1988 Lowry, Glenn D., et al. *An Annotated and Illustrated Checklist of the Vever Collection*. Washington, D.C., 1988.

Lugano 1994 *The St. Petersburg Muraqqa' Album of Indian and Persian Miniatures of the Sixteenth–Eighteenth Centuries and Specimens of Persian Calligraphy of 'Imad al-Hasani*. Exhibition, ARCH Foundation, Villa Favorita, Lugano. Catalogue by Oleg F. Akimushkin. Lugano, 1994.

Luschey-Schmeisser 1978 Luschey-Schmeisser, Ingeborg. *The Pictorial Tile Cycle of Hast Behest in Isfahan and Its Iconographic Tradition*. Centro studi e scavi archeologici in Asia: Reports and Memoirs, 14. Rome, 1978.

MacKenzie 1992 MacKenzie, Neil D. *Ayyubid Cairo: A Topographical Study*. Cairo, 1992.

Mackie 1984 Mackie, Louise W. "Toward an Understanding of Mamluk Silks: National and International Considerations." *Muqarnas* 2 [*The Art of the Mamluks*] (1984), pp. 127–46.

MacWilliam 2006 MacWilliam, Ian. "Tashkent's Hidden Islamic Relic." BBC News, London, January 5, 2006. http://www.news.bbc.co.uk/2/hi/asia-pacific/4581684.stm.

Maddison and Savage-Smith 1997 Maddison, Francis, and Emilie Savage-Smith. *Science, Tools and Magic*. Pt. 1, *Body and Spirit, Mapping the Universe*. The Nasser D. Khalili Collection of Islamic Art, edited by Julian Raby, vol. 12. [London], 1997.

Madinat al-Zahra' 2001 *El esplendor de los Omeyas cordobeses: La civilización musulmana de Europa Occidental; Catálogo de piezas*. Exhibition, Madinat al-Zahra' and Cordoba. Catalogue by María Jesús Viguera Molins and Concepción Castillo. 2 vols. Granada, 2001.

Madrid 2005 *Vestiduras ricas: El Monasterio de las Huelgas y su época, 1170–1340*. Exhibition, Palacio Real de Madrid. Catalogue by Rafael López Guzmán, Antonio Vallejo Triano, and others. Madrid, 2005.

Maguire 1990 Maguire, Henry. "Garments Pleasing to God: The Significance of Domestic Textile Designs in the Early Byzantine Period." *Dumbarton Oaks Papers* 44 (1990), pp. 215–24, figs. 1–36.

Makariou, ed. 2002 Makariou, Sophie, ed. *Nouvelles acquisitions, arts de l'Islam, 1988–2001*. Musée du Louvre, Département des Antiquités Orientales; Catalogue. Paris, 2002.

***Mamluk Studies Review* 1997–** *Mamluk Studies Review/Majallat al-dirasat al-Mamlukiyya*. Middle East Documentation Center, University of Chicago, 1997– .

Manucci 1906–8 Manucci, Niccolao. *Storia do Mogor*. Translated and annotated by William Irvine. 4 vols. London, 1906–8.

al-Maqrizi 1853–54 Taqi al-Din Ahmad al-Maqrizi. *Al-Mawa'iz wal-i'tibar bi-dhikr al-khitat wal-athar* (Exhortations and instructions on the districts and antiquities). 2 vols. Cairo, 1853–54.

al-Maqrizi 1967–73 Taqi al-Din Ahmad al-Maqrizi. *Itti'az al-hunafa' bi-akhbar al-a'imma al-fatimiyyin al-khulafa'* (Admonitions of the orthodox on the most important information about the Fatimid caliphate). Cairo, 1967–73.

al-Maqrizi 2003–4 Taqi al-Din Ahmad al-Maqrizi. *Al-Mawa'iz wal-i'tibar bi-dhikr al-khitat wal-athar* (Exhortations and instructions on the districts and antiquities). Edited by Ayman Fu'ad Sayyid. 1853. London, 2003–4.

Marçais and Poinssot 1948–52 Marçais, Georges, and Louis Poinssot. *Objets kairouanais, IXe au XIIIe siècle*. 2 vols. Tunis, 1948–52.

Marefat 1991 Marefat, Roya. "Beyond the Architecture of Death: The Shrine of the Shah-i Zinda in Samarqand." Ph.D. diss., Harvard University, Cambridge, Mass., 1991.

Marek and Knízková 1963 Marek, J[iri], and H[ana] Knízková. *The Jenghiz Khan Miniatures from the Court of Akbar the Great*. London, 1963.

***Marg* 1965** "II. Historical Carpets. 3. Important Carpets in U.S.S.R." *Marg* 18, no. 4 [*Carpets of India*] (September 1965), p. 20.

Marín 2000 Marín, Manuel[a]. *Mujeres en Al-Ándalus*. Estudios onomástico-biográficos de Al-Andalus, 11. Madrid, 2000.

Markel 1991 Markel, Stephen. "Indian and 'Indianate' Glass Vessels in the Los Angeles County Museum of Art." *Journal of Glass Studies* 33 (1991), pp. 82–92.

Marshak 1971 Marshak, Boris I. *Sogdiiskoe serebro: Ocherki po vostochnoi torevtike*. Moscow, 1971.

Marshak 1986 Marshak, Boris I. *Silberschätze des Orients: Metallkunst des 3.–13. Jahrhundert und ihre Kontinuität*. Leipzig, 1986.

Martin 1908 Martin, Fredrik R. *A History of Oriental Carpets before 1800*. Vienna, 1908.

Martin 1912 Martin, F[redrik] R. *The Miniature Painting and Painters of Persia, India and Turkey, from the Eighth to the Eighteenth Century*. 2 vols. London, 1912.

Martínez Núñez 1995 Martinez Núñez, Ma[ria] Antonia. "La epigrafia del Salón de 'Abd al-Rahman III." In *Madinat al-Zahra: El Salón de 'Abd al-Rahman III*, editied by Antonio Vallejo Triano, pp. 107–52. Cordoba, 1995.

Martinovich 1925 Martinovich, Nicholas N. "The Life of Mohammad Paolo Zaman, the Persian Painter of the Seventeenth Century." *Journal of the American Oriental Society* 45 (1925), pp. 106–9.

Mason 2003 Mason, Robert B. "Petrography of Pottery from Kirman." *Iran* 41 (2003), pp. 271–78.

Mason 2004 Mason, Robert B. J. *Shine Like the Sun: Lustre-Painted and Associated Pottery from the Medieval Middle East*. Bibliotheca Iranica: Islamic Art and Architecture Series, 12. Costa Mesa, 2004.

Masuya 1997 Masuya, Tomoko. "The Ilkhanid Phase of Takht-i Sulaiman." Ph.D. diss., Institute of Fine Arts, New York University, 1997.

Masuya 2000 Masuya, Tomoko. "Persian Tiles on European Walls: Collecting Ilkhanid Tiles in Nineteenth-Century Europe." *Ars Orientalis* 30 [*Exhibiting the Middle East: Collections and Perceptions of Islamic Art*, edited by Linda Komaroff] (2000), pp. 39–54.

Masuya 2002–3 Masuya, Tomoko. "Ilkhanid Courtly Life." In New York and Los Angeles 2002–3, pp. 74–103.

Matthee 1994 Matthee, Rudi. "Coffee in Safavid Iran: Commerce and Consumption." *Journal of the Economic and Social History of the Orient* 37, no. 1 (1994), pp. 1–32.

May 1957 May, Florence Lewis. *Silk Textiles of Spain, Eighth to Fifteenth Century*. Hispanic Notes and Monographs. New York, 1957.

Mayer, C. 1969 Mayer, Christa Charlotte. *Masterpieces of Western Textiles from the Art Institute of Chicago*. Chicago, 1969.

Mayer, L. 1933 Mayer, L[eo] A[ry]. *Saracenic Heraldry: A Survey*. Oxford, 1933.

Mayer, L. 1952 Mayer, L[eo] A[ry]. *Mamluk Costume: A Survey*. Geneva, 1952.

Mayer, L. 1956 Mayer, L[eo] A[ry]. *Islamic Astrolabists and Their Works*. Geneva, 1956.

McAllister 1939 McAllister, Hannah E. "Tughras of Sulaiman the Magnificent." *The Metropolitan Museum of Art Bulletin* 34, no. 11 (November 1939), pp. 247–48.

McChesney 1988 McChesney, R. D. "Four Sources on Shah 'Abbas's Building of Isfahan." *Muqarnas* 5 (1988), pp. 103–34.

McMullan 1965 McMullan, Joseph V. *Islamic Carpets*. New York, 1965.

McWilliams 1987 McWilliams, Mary Anderson. "Prisoner Imagery in Safavid Textiles." *Textile Museum Journal* 26 (1987), pp. 4–23.

Meinecke 1972 Meinecke, Michael. "Zur mamlukischen Heraldik." *Mitteilungen des Deutschen Archäologischen Instituts: Abteilung Kairo* 28 (1972), pp. 213–87, pls. 52–67.

Meinecke 1988 Meinecke, Michael. "Syrian Blue-and-White Tiles of the Ninth/Fifteenth Century." *Damaszener Mitteilungen* 3 (1988), pp. 203–14, pls. 37–44.

Meinecke 1991 Meinecke, Michael. "Materialien zu fatimidischen Holzdekorationen in Kairo II: Die Holzpaneele der Moschee des Ahmad Bay Kuhya." *Mitteilungen des Deutschen Archäologischen Instituts: Abteilung Kairo* 47 (1991), pp. 235–42, pls. 25–26.

Meinecke 1992 Meinecke, Michael. *Die mamlukische Architektur in Ägypten und Syrien (648/1250 bis 923/1517)*. 2 vols. Abhandlungen des Deutschen Archäologischen Instituts Kairo. Islamische Reihe, 5. Glückstadt, 1992.

Meinecke 1998 Meinecke, Michael. "'From Mschatta to Samarra': The Architecture of ar-Raqqa and Its Decoration." In *Colloque international d'archéologie islamique, IFAO, Le Caire, 3–7 février 1993*, edited by Roland-Pierre Gayraud, pp. 141–48. Cairo, 1998.

Meinecke 1999 Meinecke, Michael. "'Abbasidische Stuckdekorationen aus ar-Raqqa." In *Rezeption in der islamischen Kunst: Bamberger Symposium vom 26.6–28.6.1992*, edited by Barbara Finster, Greta Fragner, and Herta Hafenrichter, pp. 247–67, pls. 32–34. Beiruter Texte und Studien, 61. Stuttgart, 1999.

Meinecke and Schmidt-Colinet 1993 Meinecke, Michael, and Andreas Schmidt-Colinet. "Palmyra und die frühislamische Architekturdekoration von Raqqa." In *Syrien von den Aposteln zu den Kalifen*, edited by Erwin M. Ruprechtsberger, pp. 352–59. Linz, 1993.

Meinecke-Berg 1980 Meinecke-Berg, Viktoria. "Die Vervendung von Spolien in der mamlukischen Architektur von Kairo." In *XX. Deutscher Orientalistentag vom 3. bis 8. Oktober 1977 in Erlangen: Vorträge*, edited by Wolfgang Voigt, pp. 530–32. Zeitschrift der Deutschen Morgenländischen Gesellschaft, Supplement 4. Wiesbaden, 1980.

Meinecke-Berg 1991 Meinecke-Berg, Viktoria. "Materialien zu fatimidischen Holzdekorationen in Kairo I: Holzdecken aus dem fatimidischen Westpalast in Kairo." *Mitteilungen des Deutschen Archäologischen Instituts: Abteilung Kairo* 47 (1991), pp. 227–33, pls. 23–24.

Melikian 2001 Melikian, Souren. "Illusion and Delusion." *Art and Auction* 23, no. 3 (March 2001), pp. 94–101.

Melikian-Chirvani 1969 Melikian-Chirvani, A[ssadullah] S[ouren]. "L'école de Shiraz et les origins de la miniature Moghole." In *Paintings from Islamic Lands*, pp. 124–41. Oxford, 1969.

Melikian-Chirvani 1973 Melikian-Chirvani, A[ssadullah] S[ouren]. *Le bronze iranien*. Musée des arts décoratifs. Paris, 1973.

Melikian-Chirvani 1974 Melikian-[C]hirvani, A[ssadullah] S[ouren]. "Safavid Metalwork: A Study in Continuity." *Iranian Studies* 7, nos. 3–4 [*Studies on Isfahan: Proceedings of The Isfahan Colloquium, Part 2*] (Summer–Autumn 1974), pp. 543–95.

Melikian-Chirvani 1982a Melikian-Chirvani, A[ssadullah] S[ouren]. "Essais sur la sociologie de l'art islamique—L'argenterie et la féodalité dans l'Iran médiéval." In *Art et société dans le monde iranien*, edited by Chahryar Adle, pp. 143–76. Paris, 1982.

Melikian-Chirvani 1982b Melikian-Chirvani, A[ssadullah] S[ouren]. *Islamic Metalwork from the Iranian World, Eighth–Eighteenth Centuries*. London, 1982.

Melikian-Chirvani 1984 Melikian-Chirvani, A[ssadullah] S[ouren]. "Le Shah-name: La Gnose soufie et le Pouvoir mongol." *Journal asiatique* 277, no. 3–4 (1984), pp. 249–337.

Melikian-Chirvani 1987a Melikian-Chirvani, A[ssadullah] S[ouren]. "The Lights of Sufi Shrines." *Islamic Art* 2 (1987), pp. 117–47, pls. 6–8.

Melikian-Chirvani 1987b Melikian-Chirvani, A[ssadullah] S[ouren]. "The Transition to the Safavid Period: The Evidence of Metalwork and Its Epigraphy." In *Transition Periods in Iranian History: Actes du Symposium de Fribourg-en-Brisgau (22–24 Mai 1985) Studia Iranica. Cahier 5*, 1987, pp. 181–203. Paris, 1987.

Melikian-Chirvani 1988 Melikian-Chirvani, A[ssadullah] S[ouren]. "Banners." In *Encyclopaedia Iranica, Online Edition*, December 15, 1988, available at http://www.iranicaonline.org/articles/banners-alam-derafs.

Melikian-Chirvani 1990–91 Melikian-Chirvani, A[ssadullah] S[ouren]. "From the Royal Boat to the Beggar's Bowl." *Islamic Art* 4 (1990–91), pp. 3–111, pl. 1.

Melikian-Chirvani 1991 Melikian-Chirvani, A[ssadullah] S[ouren]. "Le livre des rois, miroir du destin." *Studia Iranica* 20, no. 1 (1991), pp. 33–148, pls. 1–16.

Melikian-Chirvani 2002 Melikian-Chirvani, Assadullah Souren. "Of Prayers and Poems on Safavid Bronzes." In *Safavid Art and Architecture*, edited by Sheila R. Canby, pp. 86–94, figs. 16.1–16.8. London, 2002.

Menocal 2002 Menocal, Maria Rosa. *The Ornament of the World: How Muslims, Jews, and Christians Created a Culture of Tolerance in Medieval Spain*. Boston, 2002.

Menshikova 2006 Menshikova, Maria L. "Chinese Textiles for Islamic Countries." In *Beyond the Palace Walls: Islamic Art from the State Hermitage Museum*, pp. 94–97. Exhibition, National Museums of Scotland, Edinburgh. Catalogue by Mikhail B. Piotrovsky, Anton D. Pritula, and others. St. Petersburg, 2006.

Mexico City 1994–95 *Arte islámico del Museo Metropolitano de Arte de Nueva York*. Exhibition, Colegio de San Ildefonso, Mexico City. Catalogue by Daniel Walker, Arturo Ponce Guadián, and others. Mexico City, 1994.

Michell 2011 Michell, George. "Indic Themes in the Design and Decoration of the Ibrahim Rauza in Bijapur." In Haidar and Sardar, eds. 2011, pp. 236–51.

Michell and Zebrowski 1999 Michell, George, and Mark Zebrowski. *The Architecture and Art of the Deccan Sultanates*. The New Cambridge History of India, 1, no. 7. Cambridge and New York, 1999.

Michell, ed. 1986 Michell, George, ed. *Islamic Heritage of the Deccan*. Bombay, 1986.

Mikosch 1985 Mikosch, Elisabeth. "The Scent of Flowers: Kashmir Shawls in the Collection of The Textile Museum." *Textile Museum Journal* 24 (1985), pp. 6–22.

Milan 1982 *Il tappeto orientale dal XV al XVIII secolo*. Exhibition, Eskenazi, Milan. Milan, 1982.

Milan 2006 *Milestones in the History of Carpets*. Exhibition, Gallery Moshe Tabibnia, Milan. Catalogue by Jon Thompson. Milan, 2006.

Miles 1974 Miles, George C. "The Inscriptions of the Masjid-i Jami' at Ashtarjan." *Iran* 12 (1974), pp. 89–98.

Mills 1978 Mills, John. "Early Animal Carpets in Western Paintings: A Review." *Hali* 1, no. 3 [no. 3] (Autumn 1978), pp. 234–43.

Milwright 2001 Milwright, Marcus. "Fixtures and Fittings: The Role of Decoration in Abbasid Palace Design." In *A Medieval Islamic City Reconsidered: An Interdisciplinary Approach to Samarra*, edited by Chase F. Robinson, pp. 79–109. Oxford Studies in Islamic Art, 14. Oxford, 2001.

Minneapolis 1922 *Loan Exhibition of Oriental Rugs from the Collection of James F. Ballard*. Exhibition. Minneapolis, 1922.

Minorsky 1958 Minorsky, Vladimir. *The Chester Beatty Library: A Catalogue of the Turkish Manuscripts and Miniatures*. Dublin, 1958.

Mirtaheri 2005 Mirtaheri, Fatemeh. "La cérémonie du henné en Iran central: Le chant des femmes." *Cahiers de musiques traditionnelles* 18 [*Entre femmes*] (2005), pp. 67–78.

Mittal 1963 Mittal, Jagdish. "Paintings of the Hyderabad School." *Marg* 16, no. 2 (March 1963), pp. 43–56.

***MMA Annual Report* 1871–** *Annual Report of the Trustees of The Metropolitan Museum of Art* 1– (1871–). [The annual report ran within the MMA *Bulletin* series from the 77th report, for 1946, to the 100th, for 1969–70, first in the no. 1 (Summer) issue and then, beginning in 1956, in the no. 2 (October) issue. Separate publication resumed with the 101st report for 1970–71.]

***MMA Bulletin* 1905–** *The Metropolitan Museum of Art Bulletin* 1– (1905–).

***MMA Bulletin* 1930** "The Bequest of Theodore M. Davis." *The Metropolitan Museum of Art Bulletin* 25, no. 11 (November 1930), pp. 230–31.

Moraitou 2001 Moraitou, Mina. "Umayyad Ornament on Early Islamic Woodwork: A Pair of Doors in the Benaki Museum." *Mouseio Benake* 1 (2001), pp. 159–71.

Morris 1914 M[orris], F[rances]. "An Early Seventeenth-Century Cope." *The Metropolitan Museum of Art Bulletin* 9, no. 6 (June 1914), pp. 147–48.

Mortel 1998 Mortel, Richard T. "Ribats in Mecca during the Medieval Period: A Descriptive Study Based on Literary Sources." *Bulletin of the School of Oriental and African Studies, University of London* 61, no. 1 (1998), pp. 29–50.

Mouawad and Carswell 2004 Mouawad, Robert, and John Carswell. *The Future of the Past: The Robert Mouawad Private Museum*. Beirut, 2004.

Munich 1910–12 *Die Ausstellung von Meisterwerken muhammedanischer Kunst in München*, 1910. Exhibition, Munich. Catalogue by Friedrich Sarre and F[redrik] R. Martin. 3 vols. Munich, 1912.

Munich 1987–88 *Yemen: 3000 Years of Art and Civilization in Arabia Felix*. Exhibition, Staatliches Museum für Völkerkunde München. Catalogue by Werner Daum. Innsbruck and Frankfurt/Main, [1987].

Munich 2010–11 *The Aura of Alif: The Art of Writing in Islam*. Exhibition, Staatliches Museum für Völkerkunde München. Catalogue by Jürgen Wasim Frembgen and others. Munich and London, 2010.

al-Muqaddasi 1906 al-Muqaddasi. *Ahsan at-taqasim fi ma'rifat al-aqalim/Descriptio imperii Moslemici*. Edited by M[ichael] J[an] de Goeje. Bibliotheca geographorum Arabicorum, 3. Leiden, 1906.

Murphy 1987 Murphy, Veronica. *Vastra, the Fabric of Indian Art: Origins of the Mughal Flowering Plant Motif*. London, 1987.

Nabholz-Kartaschoff 1986 Nabholz-Kartaschoff, Marie-Louise. *Golden Sprays and Scarlet Flowers: Traditional Indian Textiles from The Museum of Ethnography, Basel, Switzerland/Indo no dentō senshoku: Suisu/Bāzeru Minzokugaku Hakubutsukan zō*. Museum für Völkerkunde und Schweizerisches Museum für Volkskunde, Basel. Kyoto, 1986.

Nasir al-Din Khusrau 1881 Nasir al-Din Khusrau. *Sefer Nameh/Relation du Voyage de Nassiri Khosrau en Syrie, en Palestine, en Égypte, en Arabie et en Perse, pendant les années de l'hégire 437–444* (1035–1042). Edited and translated by Charles Henri Auguste Schefer. 2 vols. Publications de l'École des Langues Orientales Vivantes, ser. 2, vol. 1. Paris, 1881.

Nasir al-Din Tusi 1969 Nasir al-Din Tusi. *Tansukhnama-yi Ilkhani*. Tehran, 1969.

Necipoğlu 1990 Necipoğlu, Gülru. "From International Timurid to Ottoman: A Change of Taste in Sixteenth-Century Ceramic Tiles." *Muqarnas* 7 (1990), pp. 136–70.

Nemati 2003 Nemati, Parviz. *Shawls of the East from Kerman to Kashmir*. New York, 2003.

Neumann and Murza 1988 Neumann, Reingard, and Gerhard Murza. *Persische Seiden: Die Gewebekunst der Safawiden und ihrer Nachfolger*. Leipzig, 1988.

Neumeier 2006 Neumeier, Emily. "Early Koranic Manuscripts: The Blue Koran Debate." *Elements: Boston College Undergraduate Research Journal* 2, no. 1 (Spring 2006), pp. 10–19.

New Delhi and other cities 1997–98 *King of the World: The Padshahnama, an Imperial Mughal Manuscript from the Royal Library, Windsor Castle*. Exhibition, National Museum of India, New Delhi, and other venues. Catalogue by Milo Cleveland Beach and Ebba Koch with Wheeler [M.] Thackston. London and Washington, D.C., 1997.

New Haven 1981 *A Sense of Pattern: Textile Masterworks from the Yale University Art Gallery*. Exhibition, Yale University Art Gallery, New Haven. Catalogue by Loretta N. Staples. New Haven, 1981.

New York 1921 *Loan Exhibition of Oriental Rugs from the Collection of James F. Ballard, Saint Louis, Mo*. Exhibition, The Metropolitan Museum of Art, New York. Catalogue by Joseph Breck. New York, 1921.

New York 1930 *Loan Exhibition of Persian Rugs of the So-called Polish Type*. Exhibition, The Metropolitan Museum of Art, New York. Catalogue by Maurice S. Dimand. New York, 1930.

New York 1935 *A Guide to an Exhibition of Oriental Rugs and Textiles*. Exhibition, The Metropolitan Museum of Art, New York. Catalogue by M[aurice] S. Dimand. New York, 1935.

New York 1961 *Peasant and Nomad Rugs of Asia: Catalogued with an Introductory Text*. Exhibition, The Metropolitan Museum of Art, New York. Catalogue by Maurice S. Dimand. New York, 1961.

New York 1963–64 *The Art of Mughal India: Paintings and Precious Objects*. Exhibition, The Asia House Gallery, New York. Catalogue by Stuart C[ary] Welch. New York, 1963.

New York 1966 *The Kevorkian Foundation Collection of Rare and Magnificent Oriental Carpets: Special Loan Exhibition, a Guide and Catalog*. Exhibition, The Metropolitan Museum of Art, New York. Catalogue by Maurice S. Dimand. New York, 1966.

New York 1972 *A King's Book of Kings: The Shah-nameh of Shah Tahmasp*. Exhibition, The Metropolitan Museum of Art, New York. Catalogue by Stuart Cary Welch. New York, 1972.

New York 1978 *The Royal Hunter: Art of the Sasanian Empire*. Exhibition, Asia House Gallery, New York. Catalogue by Prudence Oliver Harper and others. New York, 1978.

New York 1979 *Calligraphy in the Arts of the Muslim World*. Exhibition, Asia House Gallery, New York. Catalogue by Anthony Welch. Austin, 1979.

New York 1983 *Islamic Jewelry in the Metropolitan Museum of Art*. Exhibition, The Metropolitan Museum of Art, New York. Catalogue by Marilyn Jenkins and Manuel Keene. New York, [1983].

New York 1985–86 *India: Art and Culture, 1300–1900*. Exhibition, The Metropolitan Museum of Art, New York. Catalogue by Stuart Cary Welch. New York, 1985.

New York 1987–88 *The Emperors' Album: Images of Mughal India*. Exhibition, The Metropolitan Museum of Art, New York. Catalogue by Stuart Cary Welch, Annemarie Schimmel, Marie L[ukens] Swietochowski, and Wheeler M. Thackston. New York, 1987.

New York 1989 *Persian Drawings in The Metropolitan Museum of Art*. Exhibition, The Metropolitan Museum of Art, New York. Catalogue by Marie Lukens Swietochowski and Sussan Babaie. New York, 1989.

New York 1992–93 *Tiraz: Inscribed Textiles from Islamic Workshops*. Exhibition, The Metropolitan Museum of Art, New York. Exhibition pamphlet by Daniel Walker and Aimée Froom. New York, 1992.

New York 1993 *Persian Tiles*. Exhibition, The Metropolitan Museum of Art, New York. Catalogue by Stefano Carboni and Tomoko Masuya. New York, 1993.

New York 1994 *Illustrated Poetry and Epic Images: Persian Painting of the 1330s and 1340s*. Exhibition, The Metropolitan Museum of Art, New York. Catalogue by Marie Lukens Swietochowski, Stefano Carboni, and others. New York, 1994.

New York 1995–96 *Textiles of Late Antiquity*. Exhibition, The Metropolitan Museum of Art, New York. Catalogue by Annemarie Stauffer, Marsha Hill, Helen C. Evans, and Daniel Walker. New York, 1995.

New York 1997a *Following the Stars: Images of the Zodiac in Islamic Art*. Exhibition, The Metropolitan Museum of Art, New York. Catalogue by Stefano Carboni. New York, 1997.

New York 1997b *Indian Court Painting: Sixteenth–Nineteenth Century*. Exhibition, The Metropolitan Museum of Art, New York. Catalogue by Steven [M.] Kossak. New York, 1997.

New York 1997c *The Glory of Byzantium: Art and Culture of the Middle Byzantine Era, A.D. 843–1261*. Exhibition, The Metropolitan Museum of Art, New York. Catalogue by Helen C. Evans, William D. Wixom, and others. New York, 1997.

New York 1997–98 *Flowers Underfoot: Indian Carpets of the Mughal Era*. Exhibition, The Metropolitan Museum of Art, New York. Catalogue by Daniel Walker. New York, 1997.

New York 2004–5 *In the Realm of Gods and Kings: Arts of India*. Exhibition, The Metropolitan Museum of Art, New York; Asia Society Museum, New York. Catalogue by Andrew Topsfield and others. London, 2004.

New York and Cincinnati 2007–8 *The Arts of Kashmir*. Exhibition, Asia Society and Museum, New York; Cincinnati Art Museum. Catalogue by Pratapaditya Pal and others. New York and Milan, 2008.

New York and Los Angeles 1998–99 *Letters in Gold: Ottoman Calligraphy from the Sakıp Sabancı Collection, Istanbul*. Exhibition, The Metropolitan Museum of Art, New York; Los Angeles County Museum of Art. Catalogue by M. Uğur Derman and others. New York, 1998.

New York and Los Angeles 2002–3 *The Legacy of Genghis Khan: Courtly Art and Culture in Western Asia, 1256–1353*. Exhibition, The Metropolitan Museum of Art, New York; Los Angeles County Museum of Art. Catalogue by Linda Komaroff, Stefano Carboni, and others. New York, 2002.

New York and Milan 2003–4 *Hunt for Paradise: Court Arts of Safavid Iran, 1501–1576*. Exhibition, Asia Society Museum, New York; Museo Poldi Pezzoli and Palazzo Reale, Milan. Catalogue by Jon Thompson, Sheila R. Canby, and others. New York, 2003.

New York and other cities 1978–79 *Room for Wonder: Indian Painting During the British Period, 1760–1880*. Exhibition, The American Federation of Arts, New York, and other venues. Catalogue by Stuart Cary Welch. New York, 1978.

New York and other cities 1984–87 *Indian Miniatures: The Ehrenfeld Collection*. Exhibition, American Federation of Arts, New York, and other venues. Catalogue by Daniel J. Ehnbom, with Robert Skelton and Pramod Chandra. New York, 1985.

New York and Venice 1962 *Muslim Miniature Paintings from the XIII to XIX Century from Collections in the United States and Canada*. Exhibition, The Asia Society, New York; Giorgio Cini, Venice. Catalogue by Ernst J. Grube. Venice, 1962.

New York and Washington, D.C. 2004–5 *Asian Games: The Art of Contest*. Exhibition, Asia Society Museum, New York; Arthur M. Sackler Gallery, Smithsonian Institution, Washington, D.C. Catalogue by Colin Mackenzie, Irving Finkel, and others. New York, 2004.

New York and Washington, D.C. 2008–9 *Timbuktu to Tibet: Exotic Rugs and Textiles from New York Collectors*. Exhibition, New-York Historical Society; The Textile Museum, Washington, D.C. Catalogue by Jon Thompson. New York, 2008.

***New York Times* 1901** "Mrs. Osgood Field Dead: Husband's Bric-a-Brac Collection Now Goes to the Metropolitan Museum of Art." *The New York Times*, August 19, 1901, p. 7.

***New York Times* 1902a** "Death of Heber R. Bishop: He Was Interested in Management of Many Important Corporations." *The New York Times*, December 11, 1902, p. 9.

***New York Times* 1902b** "Will of Heber R. Bishop: Provision for Preservation of Famous Jade Collection; Now in Metropolitan Museum—Estate of $3,500,000 Goes to Family of Testator." *The New York Times*, December 18, 1902, p. 9.

***New York Times* 1921** "Rare Oriental Rugs Loaned to Museum: Sixty-nine From James F. Ballard's Noted Collection; Early Spanish Weaves . . . Among Features." *The New York Times*, October 7, 1921, p. 17.

de la Nézière 1921 de la Nézière, J[oseph]. *Les monuments mauresque du Maroc*. Paris, [1921].

de la Nézière 1924 de la Nézière, J[oseph]. *La décoration marocaine*. Paris, [1924].

Nizam al-Din Ahmad 1961 Nizam al-Din Ahmad, Mirza. *Hadiqat al-Salatin Qutbshahi*. Hyderabad, 1961.

Nizam al-Mulk 1891–97 Nizam al-Mulk. *Siasset namèh, traité de gouvernement*. Edited and translated by Charles Scheffer. 3 vols. Paris, 1891–97.

Nora 1989 Nora, Pierre. "Between Memory and History: *Les lieux de mémoire*." Translated by Marc Roudebush. *Representations*, no. 26 [*Memory and Counter-Memory*] (Spring 1989), pp. 7–24.

Norman 1982 Norman, A. V. B. "Some Princely Arms from India and Persia in the Wallace Collection." In *Islamiske våben i dansk privateje/Islamic Arms and Armour from Private Danish Collections*. Exhibition, Davids Samling, Copenhagen. Copenhagen, 1982.

Northedge 2005 Northedge, Alastair. *The Historical Topography of Samarra*. Samarra Studies, 1. London, 2005.

Okada 1995 Okada, Amina. "À propos du motif floral dans l'art moghol." In *Le motif floral dans les tissus moghols: Inde XVIIe et XVIIIe siècles*, by Krishna Riboud, Amina Okada, and Marie-Hélène Guelton, pp. 5–6. Paris, 1995.

O'Kane 1987 O'Kane, Bernard. *Timurid Architecture in Khurasan*. Costa Mesa, Calif., 1987.

O'Kane, ed. 2006 O'Kane, Bernard, ed. *The Treasures of Islamic Art in the Museums of Cairo*. Cairo and New York, 2006.

Olagnier Bey 1961 Olagnier Bey, Riottot. "Influence turque dans la broderie de Tétouan au Maroc." *First International Congress of Turkish Art: Communications Presented to the Congress . . . (Nineteenth–24th October, 1959)*, pp. 291–96. Institute of History of Turkish and Islamic Arts, Publication No. 6. Ankara, 1961.

Ölçer and Denny 1999 Ölçer, Nazan, and Walter [B.] Denny. *Anatolian Carpets: Masterpieces from the Museum of Turkish and Islamic Arts, Istanbul*. 2 vols. Bern, 1999.

Orbeli 1938–39 Orbeli, Josef. "Sassanian and Early Islamic Metalwork." In Pope, A. U., and Ackerman, eds. 1938–39, vol. 1, pp. 716–70, vol. 4, pt. 1, pls. 204–46.

Orihuela Uzal 1995 Orihuela Uzal, Antonio. *Casas y palacios nazaríes, siglos XIII–XV*. Barcelona, 1995.

Otto-Dorn 1941 Otto-Dorn, Katharina. *Das islamische Iznik*. Archäologisches Institut des Deutschen Reiches, Istanbuler Forschungen 13. Berlin, 1941.

Owen 2002 Owen, Antoinette. "Technical Aspects of the *Hamzanama* Manuscript." In Washington, D.C. 2002, pp. 280–84.

Pal 1993 Pal, Pratapaditya. *Indian Painting*. Vol. 1, 1000–1700. A Catalogue of the Los Angeles County Museum of Art Collection. Los Angeles, 1993.

Pal 1997 Pal, Pratapaditya. *Divine Images, Human Visions: The Max Tanenbaum Collection of South Asian and Himalayan Art in the National Gallery of Canada*. Ottowa, 1997.

Pal, ed. 1990 Pal, Pratapaditya, ed. *Changing Visions, Lasting Images: Calcutta Through 300 Years*. Bombay, 1990.

Pal, ed. 1991a *Marg* 42, no. 4 [*New Studies in Mughal Painting*, edited by Pratapaditya Pal] (June 1991).

Pal, ed. 1991b Pal, Pratapaditya, ed. *Master Artists of the Imperial Mughal Court*. Bombay, 1991.

Pancaroğlu 2002 Pancaroğlu, Oya. "Serving Wisdom: The Contents of Samanid Epigraphic Pottery." In *Studies in Islamic and Later Indian Art from the Arthur M. Sackler Museum, Harvard University Art Museums*, pp. 58–75. Cambridge, Mass., 2002.

Pant 1978–83 Pant, G[ayatri] N[ath]. *Indian Arms and Armour*. 3 vols. New Delhi, 1978–83.

Paquin 1992 Paquin, Gerard. "Çintamani." *Hali*, no. 64 (August 1992), pp. 104–19, 143–44.

Paret 1960 Paret, R. "Ashab al-Kahf." In *EI2* 1960–2009, vol. 1 (1960), p. 691.

Paris 1878 *Livret-guide du visiteur à l'exposition historique du Trocadéro*, 1878. Exhibition, Salle Polonaise, Palais de Trocadéro, Exposition Universelle de 1878, Paris. Catalogue by Philibert Breban. Paris, 1878.

Paris 1982–83 *De Carthage à Kairouan: 2000 ans d'art et d'histoire en Tunisie*. Exhibition, Musée du Petit Palais de la Ville de Paris. Catalogue by Adeline C. Bissy, Judith Petit, and others. Paris, 1982.

Paris 2000 *Les Andalousies de Damas à Cordue*. Exhibition, Institut du Monde Arabe, Paris. Catalogue by Marthe Bernus-Taylor and others. Paris, 2000.

Paris 2001a *L'étrange et le merveilleux en terres d'Islam*. Exhibition, Musée du Louvre, Paris. Catalogue by Marthe Bernus-Taylor and others. Paris, 2001.

Paris 2001b *L'orient de Saladin: L'art des Ayyoubides*. Exhibition, Institut du Monde Arabe, Paris. Paris, 2001.

Paris 2001–2 *L'art du livre arabe: Du manuscrit au livre d'artiste*. Bibliothèque nationale de France, Paris. Catalogue by Marie-Geneviève Guesdon, Annie Vernay-Nouri, and others. Paris, 2001.

Paris 2002–3 *Chevaux et cavaliers arabes dans les arts d'Orient et d'Occident*. Exhibition, Institut du Monde Arabe, Paris. [Paris], 2002.

Paris 2007 *Chefs-d'oeuvre islamiques de l'Aga Khan Museum*. Exhibition, Musée du Louvre, Paris. Catalogue by Sophie Makariou and others. Paris and Milan, 2007.

Paris 2007–8 *Le chant du monde: L'art de l'Iran safavide*, 1501–1736. Exhibition, Musée du Louvre, Paris. Catalogue by Assadullah Souren Melikian-Chirvani. Paris, 2007.

Paris, Caen, and Toulouse 1992–93 *Terres secrètes de Samarcande: Céramiques du VIIIe au XIIIe siècle*. Exhibition, Institut du Monde Arabe, Paris; Musée de Normandie, Caen; Musée des Augustins, Toulouse. Paris, 1992.

Parodi, ed. forthcoming Parodi, Laura E., ed. *Art Patronage and Society in the Muslim Deccan from the Fourteenth Century to the Present Day* [Proceedings of a symposium, Oxford, July 4–6, 2008]. Oxford, forthcoming.

Partearroyo Lacaba 1992 Partearroyo [Lacaba], Cristina. "Almoravid and Almohad Textiles." In Granada and New York 1992, pp. 104–13.

Partearroyo Lacaba 1995 Partearroyo Lacaba, Cristina. "Los tejidos nazaríes." In *Arte islámico en Granada: Propuesta para un Museo de la Alhambra*, pp. 116–31. Exhibition, Museo de La Alhambra, Granada. Catalogue by Jesús Bermúdez López and others. Granada, 1995.

Partearroyo Lacaba 2005 Partearroyo Lacaba, Cristina. "Estudio histórico-artístico de los tejidos de al-Andalus y afines." *Bienes culturales*, no. 5 [*Tejidos hispanomusulmanes*] (2005), pp. 37–74.

Pathak 2003 Pathak, Anamika. *Pashmina*. New Delhi, 2003.

Pauty 1931a Pauty, Edmond. *Les bois sculptés jusque'à l'époque ayyoubide*. Catalogue général du Musée Arabe du Caire; Musée National de l'Art Arabe. Cairo, 1931.

Pauty 1931b Pauty, Edmond. "Sur une porte en bois sculpté provenant de Bagdad [*sic*]." *BIFAO: Bulletin de l'Institut français d'archéologie orientale* 30 (1931), pp. 77–81, pls. 1–6.

Peck et al. 1996 Peck, Amelia, et al. *Period Rooms in The Metropolitan Museum of Art*. New York, 1996.

Petersen 1954 Petersen, Theodore C. "Early Islamic Bookbindings and Their Coptic Relations." *Ars Orientalis* 1 (1954), pp. 41–64 and errata.

Petry 2001 Petry, Carl F. "Robing Ceremonials in Late Mamluk Egypt: Hallowed Traditions, Shifting Protocols." In *Robes and Honor: The Medieval World of Investiture*, edited by Stewart Gordon, pp. 353–77. New York, 2001.

Philadelphia 2001 *Intimate Worlds: Indian Paintings from the Alvin O. Bellak Collection*. Exhibition, Philadelphia Museum of Art. Catalogue by Darielle Mason and others. Philadelphia, 2001.

Phillips 2004 Phillips, Jonathan. *The Fourth Crusade and the Sack of Constantinople*. New York, 2004.

Philon 1980 Philon, Helen. *Early Islamic Ceramics: Ninth to Late Twelfth Centuries*. Mouseio Benake Catalogue of Islamic Art, vol. 1. London, 1980.

Philon 2000 Philon, Helen. "The Murals in the Tomb of Ahmad Shah near Bidar." *Apollo* 152, no. 465 (2000), pp. 3–10.

Philon, ed. 2010 Philon, Helen, ed. *Silent Splendour: Palaces of the Deccan, Fourteenth–Nineteenth Centuries*. Mumbai, 2010.

Phipps 2010 Phipps, Elena. "Cochineal Red: The Art History of a Color." *The Metropolitan Museum of Art Bulletin*, n.s., 67, no. 3 (Winter 2010), pp. 1–48.

Pickett 1984 Pickett, Douglas. "Inscriptions by Muhammad Rida al-Imami." *Iran* 22 (1984), pp. 91–102.

Pinder-Wilson 1959 Pinder-Wilson, Ralph. "An Early Fatimid Bowl Decorated in Lustre." In *Aus der Welt der islamischen Kunst: Festschrift für Ernst Kühnel zum 75. Geburtstag am 26.10.1957*, edited by Richard Ettinghausen, pp. 139–43. Berlin, 1959.

Pires 1944 Pires, Tomé. *The Suma Oriental of Tomé Pires, an Account of the East, from the Red Sea to Japan, Written in Malacca and India in 1512–1515, and the Book of Francisco Rodrigues, Rutter of a Voyage in the Red Sea, Nautical Rules, Almanack and Maps: Written and Drawn in the East Before 1515, Transl. from the Portuguese Ms in the Bibliothèque de la Chambre des Députés, Paris*. Edited by Armando Cortesão. Hakluyt Society, Works Ser. 2, 89–90. London, 1944.

Pisarev 1905 Pisarev, S[tepan] I[vanovic]. *Samarkandskii kuficheskii Koran, po predaniiu pisannyi sobstvennoruchno tret'im khalifom Osmanom (644–656)/Coran coufique de Samarcand, écrit d'après la tradition de la propre main du troisième calife Osman (644–656) qui se trouve dans la Bibliothèque Impériale Publique de St. Petersbourg*. St. Petersburg, 1905.

Pittsburgh 1923 *An Exhibition of Oriental Rugs Lent by James Franklin Ballard*. Exhibition. Pittsburgh, 1923.

Polo 1875 Polo, Marco. *The Book of Ser Marco Polo, the Venetian, Concerning the Kingdom and Marvels of the East*. Translated by Henry Yule. 2nd ed. 2 vols. 1871. London, 1875.

Pope, A. U., and Ackerman, eds. 1938–39 Pope, Arthur Upham, and Phyllis Ackerman, eds. *A Survey of Persian Art from Prehistoric Times to the Present*. 6 vols. in 9. London and New York, 1938–39.

Pope, J. A. 1956 Pope, John Alexander. *Chinese Porcelains from the Ardebil Shrine*. Smithsonian Institution Publication 4231. Washington, D.C., 1956.

Pope, J. A. 1972 Pope, John A[lexander]. "Chinese Influences on Iznik Pottery: A Re-Examination of an Old Problem." In Ettinghausen, ed. 1972, pp. 124–39.

Porter, V. 1981 Porter, Venetia. *Medieval Syrian Pottery (Raqqa Ware)*. Oxford, 1981.

Porter, V. 1987–88 Porter, Venetia. "The Art of the Rasulids." In Munich 1987–88, pp. 232–53.

Porter, V. 1995 Porter, Venetia. *Islamic Tiles*. New York, 1995.

Porter, V. 1998 Porter, Venetia. "Enamelled Glass Made for the Rasulid Sultans of the Yemen." In Ward, ed. 1998, pp. 91–95, 197–99.

Porter, V. 2007 Porter, Venetia. "Amulets Inscribed with the Names of the 'Seven Sleepers' of Ephesus in the British Museum." In *Word of God, Art of Man: The Qur'an and Its Creative Expressions; Selected Proceedings from the International Colloquium, London, 18–21 October 2003*, edited by Fahmida Suleman, pp. 123–34. The Institute of Ismaili Studies, Qur'anic Studies Series, 4. Oxford, 2007.

Porter, V., and Watson 1987 Porter, Venetia, and Oliver Watson. "'Tell Minis' Wares." In *Syria and Iran: Three Studies in Medieval Ceramics*, edited by James [W.] Allan and Caroline Roberts, pp. 175–248. Oxford Studies in Islamic Art, 4, pt. 2. Oxford, 1987.

Porter, Y. 1994 Porter, Yves. *Painters, Paintings and Books: An Essay on Indo-Persian Technical Literature, Twelfth–Nineteenth Centuries*. New Delhi, 1994.

Portland and other cities 1973–74 *Indian Miniature Painting from the Collection of Edwin Binney, 3rd*. Vol. 1, *The Mughal and Deccani Schools with Some Related Sultanate Material*. Exhibition, Portland Art Museum and other venues. Catalogue by Edwin Binney, 3rd. Portland, Ore., 1973.

Portland and other cities 1979 *Turkish Treasures from the Collection of Edwin Binney, 3rd*. Exhibition, Portland Art Museum and other venues. Catalogue by Edwin Binney, 3rd, and Walter [B.] Denny. Portland, 1979.

Poullada 2006 Poullada, S. Peter. "Kizil Ayak and Ali Eli Chuvals: Turkmen Weavings of the Middle Amu Darya." *Hali*, no. 148 (September–October 2006), pp. 66–73.

Prado-Vilar 1997 Prado-Vilar, Francisco. "Circular Visions of Fertility and Punishment: Caliphal Ivory Caskets from al-Andalus." *Muqarnas* 14 (1997), pp. 19–41.

Prado-Vilar 2005 Prado-Vilar, Francisco. "Enclosed in Ivory: The Miseducation of al-Mughira." In Folsach and Meyer, eds. 2005, pt. 1, pp. 138–63.

Prisse d'Avennes 1877 Prisse d'Avennes, [Achille-Constant-Théodore-Émile]. *L'art arabe d'après les monuments du Kaire depuis le VIIe siècle jusqu'a la fin du XVIIIe*. Paris, 1877.

Pruitt 1998 Pruitt, Bettye Hobbs. *Timken: From Missouri to Mars—A Century of Leadership in Manufacturing*. Boston, 1998.

Puerta Vílchez 1990 Puerta Vilchez, José Miguel. *Los códigos de utopía de la Alhambra de Granada*. Biblioteca de ensayo, 20. Granada, 1990.

Puerta Vílchez 2007 Puerta Vilchez, José Miguel. "La Alhambra de Granada o la caligrafía elevada al rango de arquitectura." In Angustias Cabrera et al. 2007, pp. 301–86.

al-Qaddumi 1990 [al-]Qaddumi, Ghada al-Hijjawi. "A Medieval Islamic Book of Gifts and Treasures: Translation, Annotation, and Commentary on the 'Kitab al-Hadaya wa al-Tuhaf.'" Ph.D. diss., Harvard University, 1990.

al-Qaddumi, ed. 1996 al-Qaddumi, Ghada al-Hijjawi, ed. and trans. *Book of Gifts and Rarities (Kitab al-Hadaya wa al-Tuhaf): Selections Compiled in the Fifteenth Century from an Eleventh-Century Manuscript on Gifts and Treasures*. Cambridge, Mass., 1996.

Qaisar 1996 Qaisar, Ahsan Jan. "Muhammad Zaman: A Seventeenth Century Controversial Artist." In *Art and Culture: Endeavours in Interpretation*, edited by Ahsan Jan Qaisar and Som Prakash Verma, pp. 79–92. New Delhi, 1996.

Rabbat 1993 Rabbat, Nasser [O]. "The Dome of the Rock Revisited: Some Remarks on al-Wasiti's Accounts." *Muqarnas* 10 [*Essays in Honor of Oleg Grabar, Contributed by His Students*] (1993), pp. 66–75.

Rabbat 1995 Rabbat, Nasser O. *The Citadel of Cairo: A New Interpretation of Royal Mamluk Architecture*. Islamic History and Civilization, Studies and Texts, 14. Leiden and New York, 1995.

Raby 1977–78 Raby, Julian. "Diyarbekir: A Rival to Iznik." *Istanbuler Mitteilungen* 27–28 (1977–78), pp. 429–59.

Raby 1986 Raby, Julian. "Looking for Silver in Clay: A New Perspective on Samanid Ceramics." In *Pots and Pans: A Colloquium on Precious Metals in the Muslim, Chinese and Greco-Roman Worlds, Oxford, 1985*, edited by Michael Vickers, pp. 179–204. Oxford, 1986.

Raby and Johns, eds. 1992 Raby, Julian, and Jeremy Johns, eds. *Bayt-al-Maqdis: 'Abd-al-Malik's Jerusalem*. Part 1. Oxford Studies in Islamic Art, 9. Oxford, 1992.

Raby and Tanındı 1993 Raby, Julian, and Zeren Tanındı. *Turkish Bookbinding in the Fifteenth Century: The Foundation of an Ottoman Court Style*. London, 1993.

Raemdonck 2006 Raemdonck, Mieke van. "Isabella Errera and the Brussels Royal Museum." *Hali*, no. 148 (September–October 2006), pp. 74–79.

Rageth 2004 Rageth, Jürg. "Dating the Dragon and Phoenix Fragments: A Newcomer Unmasked and a Genuine New Discovery." *Hali*, no. 134 (May–June 2004), pp. 106–9.

Rawson 1984 Rawson, Jessica. *Chinese Ornament: The Lotus and the Dragon*. London, 1984.

Reath and Sachs 1937 Reath, Nancy Andrews, and Eleanor B. Sachs. *Persian Textiles and Their Technique from the Sixth to the Eighteenth Centuries Including a System for General Textile Classification*. Florence House Memorial Collection. New Haven and London, 1937.

Renda 2008 Renda, Günsel. "The Decorative Program of the Ottoman House and Reflections of the Provinces: The Aleppo Room." In *Angels, Peonies, and Fabulous Creatures: The Aleppo Room in Berlin*, edited by Julia Gonella and Jens Kröger, pp. 119–26. Berlin, 2008.

***Repèrtoire chronologique d'épigraphie arabe* 1932** Institut français d'archéologie orientale du Caire. *Repèrtoire chronologique d'épigraphie arabe* 2 (1932).

Ribeiro 2009 Ribeiro, Maria Queiroz. *Iznik Pottery and Tiles in the Calouste Gulbenkian Collection*. Lisbon, 2009.

Riboud et al. 1998 Riboud, Krishna, et al. *Samit et lampas: Motifs indiens/Indian Motifs*. Association pour l'étude et la documentation des textiles d'Asie. Calico Museum of Textiles. Paris and Ahmedabad, 1998.

Rice, D. S. 1949 Rice, D. S. "The Oldest Dated 'Mosul' Candlestick, A.D. 1225." *The Burlington Magazine* 91, no. 561 (December 1949), pp. 334, 336–41.

Rice, D. S. 1957 Rice, D. S. "Inlaid Brasses from the Workshop of Ahmad al-Dhaki al-Mawsili." *Ars Orientalis* 2 (1957), pp. 283–326, pls. 1–16.

Rice, D. T. 1934 Rice, D[avid] Talbot. "The Oxford Excavations at Hira." *Ars Islamica* 1, pt. 1 (1934), pp. 51–73, figs. 1–24.

Rich 1987 Rich, Vivian A. "Mughal Floral Painting and Its European Sources." *Oriental Art*, n.s., 33, no. 2 (Summer 1987), pp. 183–89.

Riefstahl 1916 Riefstahl, R[udolf] Meyer. "Oriental Carpets in American Collections: Part One, Three Silk Rugs in the Altman Collection." *Art in America* 4 (1916), pp. 147–61.

Riefstahl 1931 Riefstahl, Rudolf Meyer. "Persian Islamic Stucco Sculptures." *The Art Bulletin* 13, no. 4 (December 1931), pp. 438–63.

Riefstahl 1937 Riefstahl, Rudolf Meyer. "Early Turkish Tile Revetments in Edirne." *Ars Islamica* 4 (1937), pp. 249–81.

Rieu 1966 Rieu, Charles. *Catalogue of the Persian Manuscripts in the British Museum*. Reprint ed. 3 vols. 1879. London, 1966.

Riis and Pousen 1957 Riis, P. J., and Vagn Pousen. *Les verreries et poteries médiévales*. Hama: Fouilles et recherches de la Fondation Carlsberg 1931–38, vol. 4, pt. 2. Copenhagen, 1957.

Riyadh 1985 *The Unity of Islamic Art: An Exhibition to Inaugurate the Islamic Art Gallery of the King Faisal Center for Research and Islamic Studies, Riyadh, Saudi Arabia, 1405AH/1985AD*. Exhibition, Islamic Art Gallery, Riyadh. Catalogue by Oliver Hoare and Esin Atil. Riyadh, 1985.

Rizzo et al. 2011 Rizzo, Adriana, et al. "A Multi-Analytical Approach for the Identification of Aloe as a Colorant in Oil-Resin Varnishes." *Analytical and Bioanalytical Chemistry* 399 (March 2011), pp. 3093–107.

Rizzo et al. forthcoming Rizzo, Adriana, et al. "A Rediscovered Opulence: The Surface Decoration of an Early Eighteenth Century Damascene Reception Room at The Metropolitan Museum of Art." In *Post Prints of the 4th International Architectural Paint Research Conference, Sharing Information, Sharing Decisions [August 3–6, 2010]*, forthcoming.

Robbins and McLeod, eds. 2006 Robbins, Kenneth X., and John McLeod, eds. *African Elites in India: Habshi Amarat*. Ahmedabad, 2006.

Robinson, B. 1957 Robinson, B[asil] W[illiam]. "Prince Baysonghor's Nizami: A Speculation." *Ars Orientalis* 2 (1957), pp. 383–91, pls. 1–7.

Robinson, B. 1958 Robinson, B[asil] W[illiam]. *A Descriptive Catalogue of the Persian Paintings in the Bodleian Library*. Oxford, 1958.

Robinson, B. 1976 Robinson, B[asil] W[illiam]. "Isma'il II's Copy of the Shahnama." *Iran* 14 (1976), pp. 1–8.

Robinson, B. 1991 Robinson, B[asil] W[illiam]. *Fifteenth Century Persian Painting: Problems and Issues*. Hagop Kevorkian Series on Near Eastern Art and Civilization. New York, 1991.

Robinson, B. 1992 Robinson, B[asil] W[illiam]. "Muhammadi and the Khurasan Style." *Iran* 30 (1992), pp. 17–29.

Robinson, B. 1993 Robinson, B[asil] W[illiam]. "The Dunimarle Shahnama: A Timurid Manuscript from Mazandaran." In *Studies in Persian Art*, by B[asil] W[illiam] Robinson, vol. 2, pp. 193–204. 2 vols. London, 1993.

Robinson, B. 2005 Robinson, B[asil] W[illiam]. "Shah Isma'il II's Copy of the Shah-Nama: Additional Material." *Iran* 43 (2005), pp. 291–99.

Robinson, B., and Sims 2007 Robinson, B[asil] W[illiam], and Eleanor Sims. *The Windsor Shahnama of 1648*. London, 2007.

Robinson, B., ed. 1988 Robinson, B[asil] W[illiam], ed. *Islamic Art in the Keir Collection*. Keir Collection, vol. 5. London, 1988.

Robinson, C. 2003 Robinson, Cynthia. "Mudéjar Revisited: A Prolegoména to the Reconstruction of Perception, Devotion, and Experience at the Mudéjar Convent of Clarisas, Tordesillas, Spain (Fourteenth Century A.D.)." *RES: Anthropology and Aesthetics*, no. 43 [*Islamic Arts*] (Spring 2003), pp. 51–77.

Robinson, C. 2008 Robinson, Cynthia. "Marginal Ornament: Poetics, Mimesis, and Devotion in the Palace of the Lions." *Muqarnas* 25 [*Frontiers of Islamic Art and Architecture: Essays in Celebration of Oleg Grabar's Eightieth Birthday*, edited by Gülru Necipoğlu and Julia Bailey] (2008), pp. 185–214.

Robinson, C., and Pinet, eds. 2008 Robinson, Cynthia, and Simone Pinet, eds. *Courting the Alhambra: Cross-Disciplinary Approaches to the Hall of Justice Ceilings*. Special offprint of *Medieval Encounters* 14, nos. 2–3 (2008). Leiden, 2008.

Robinson, C., and Rouhi, eds. 2005 Robinson, Cynthia, and Leyla Rouhi, eds. *Under the Influence: Questioning the Comparative in Medieval Castile*. The Medieval and Early Modern Iberian World, 22. Leiden, 2005.

de Roddaz 1882 de Roddaz, Camille. *L'art ancien à l'exposition nationale belge*. Brussels, 1882.

Rogers 1989 Rogers, J. M[ichael]. "Exhibition Reviews; Washington and Los Angeles, Timurid Art." *The Burlington Magazine* 131, no. 1036 (July 1989), pp. 509–10.

Rogers 1992 Rogers, J. Michael. "Chinese-Iranian Relations. iv. The Safavid Period, 907–1145/1501–1732." In *Encyclopaedia Iranica* 1985– , vol. 5 (1992), pp. 436–38.

Rogers and Köseoğlu 1987 Rogers, J. M[ichael], and Cengiz Köseoğlu. *The Topkapi Saray Museum, The Treasury*. Boston, 1987.

Rome 1956 *Mostra d'arte iranica: Catalogo/Exhibition of Iranian Art: Catalogue*. Exhibition, Palazzo Brancaccio, Rome. Catalogue by Mario Bussagli and others. Milan, 1956.

Rosen-Ayalon 1991 Rosen-Ayalon, Myriam. "The Islamic Jewellery from Ashkelon." In *Jewellery and Goldsmithing in the Islamic World: International Symposium, The Israel Museum, Jerusalem 1987*, edited by Na'ama Brosh, pp. 9–19. [Jerusalem], 1991.

Rosenthal 1975 Rosenthal, Franz. *Gambling in Islam*. Leiden, 1975.

Rosenthal 1997 Rosenthal, F[ranz]. "Shatrandj." In *EI2* 1960–2009, vol. 9 (1997), pp. 366–68.

Rosser-Owen 2010 Rosser-Owen, Mariam. *Islamic Arts from Spain*. London, 2010.

Rötzer 2010 Rötzer, Klaus. "Hydraulic Works and Gardens." In Philon, ed. 2010, pp. 106–13.

Roxburgh 1998 Roxburgh, David J. "Disorderly Conduct?: F. R. Martin and the Bahram Mirza Album." *Muqarnas* 15 (1998), pp. 32–57.

Roxburgh 2000 Roxburgh, David J. "Kamal al-Din Bihzad and Authorship in Persianate Painting." *Muqarnas* 17 (2000), pp. 119–46.

Roxburgh 2005a Roxburgh, David. "Reinventions of the Book." In Roxburgh 2005b, pp. 148–79, 339–42.

Roxburgh 2005b Roxburgh, David J. *The Persian Album, 1400–1600: From Dispersal to Collection*. New Haven and London, 2005.

Roxburgh 2005c Roxburgh, David J. "The Timurids and Turkmen." In London 2005, pp. 190–259.

Roxburgh 2007 Roxburgh, David J. *Writing the Word of God: Calligraphy and the Qur'an*. Houston, 2007.

Rubiera Mata 1970 Rubiera Mata, María Jesús. "Los poemas epigráficas de Ibn al-Yayyab en la Alhambra." *Al-Andalus* 35 (1970), pp. 453–73.

Rubiera Mata 1981 Rubiera [Mata], María Jesús. "Poesía epigráfica en la Alhambra y Generalife." *Poesía*, no. 12 (Fall 1981), pp. 17–76.

Rubiera Mata 1994 Rubiera Mata, María Jesús. *Ibn al-Yayyab: El otro poeta de la Alhambra*. Publicaciones del Patronato de la Alhambra, 4. 1982. Granada, 1994.

Ruggles 1997 Ruggles, D. Fairchild. "The Eye of Sovereignty: Poetry and Vision in the Alhambra's Lindaraja Mirador." *Gesta* 36, no. 2 (1997), pp. 180–89.

Ruggles 2000 Ruggles, D. Fairchild. *Gardens, Landscape, and Vision in the Palaces of Islamic Spain*. University Park, Pa., 2000.

Ruggles 2004a Ruggles, D. Fairchild. "Mothers of a Hybrid Dynasty: Race, Genealogy, and Acculturation in al-Andalus." *The Journal of Medieval and Early Modern Studies* 34, no.1 (Winter 2004), pp. 65–94.

Ruggles 2004b Ruggles, D. Fairchild. "The Alcazar of Seville and Mudejar Architecture." *Gesta* 43, no. 2 (2004), pp. 87–98.

Rührdanz 1995 Rührdanz, Karin. "Zur Ikonographie der Wandmalereien in Tepe Madraseh (Nishapur)." In *Proceedings of the Second European Conference of Iranian Studies held in Bamberg, 30th September to 4th October 1991, by the Societas Iranologica Europaea*, edited by Bert G. Fragner, pp. 589–95. Serie orientale Roma, 73. Rome, 1995.

Ruiz Souza 1998 Ruiz Souza, Juan Carlos. "El Patio del Vergel del real monasterio de Santa Clara de Tordecillas y la Alhambra de Granada: Reflexiones para su estudio." *al-Qantara* 19, no. 2 (1998), pp. 315–37.

Ruiz Souza 2004 Ruiz Souza, Juan Carlos. "Castilla y Al-Andalus: Arquitecturas aljamiadas y otros grados de asimilación." *Anuario del Departamento de Historia y Teoría del Arte* [U.A.M.] 16 (2004), pp. 17–43.

Rumi 1984 Rumi, Jalal al-Din. *Kulliyat-i shams-i tabrizi ya divan-i kabir*. Edited and annotated by Badi' al-Zaman Furuzanfar. 8th ed. Tehran, 1984.

Sa'di 1974 Muslih al-Din Sa'di. *Morals Pointed and Tales Adorned: The Bustan of Sa'di*. Translated by G. M. Wickens. Toronto, 1974.

Sa'di 1989 Muslih al-Din Sa'di. *Bustan*. Edited by Ghulam Husayn Yusufi. Tehran, 1989.

Safadi 1981 Salah al-Din Khalil ibn Aybak al-Safadi. *Kitab al-wafi bil-wafayat/Das biographische Lexikon des Salahaddin Halil Ibn Aibak as-Safadi*. Edited by Shukir Faysal. Tamir bis al-Hasan, 11. Wiesbaden, 1981.

Safwat and Zakariya 1996 Safwat, Nabil F., and Mohamed Zakariya. *The Art of the Pen: Calligraphy of the Fourteenth to Twentieth Centuries*. The Nasser D. Khalili Collection of Islamic Art, edited by Julian Raby, vol. 5. London, 1996.

Şahin 2009 Şahin, Seracettin. *The Museum of Turkish and Islamic Arts: Thirteen Centuries of Glory from the Umayyads to the Ottomans*. New York, 2009.

Saint Laurent 1989 Saint Laurent, Beatrice. "The Identification of a Magnificent Koran Manuscript." In *Les manuscrits du Moyen-Orient: Essais de codicologie et de paléographie; Actes du Colloque d'Istanbul (Istanbul, 26–29 mai 1986)*, edited by François Déroche, pp. 115–24. Varia Turcica VIII. Istanbul and Paris, 1989.

Sakisian 1929 Sakisian, Arménag Bey. *La miniature persane du XIIe au XVIIe siècle*. Paris and Brussels, 1929.

Saliba 2002 Saliba, George. "Greek Astronomy and the Medieval Arab Tradition." *American Scientist* 90, no. 4 (July–August 2002), pp. 360–67.

Saliba 2004 Saliba, George. "The World of Islam and Renaissance Science and Technology." In *The Arts of Fire: Islamic Influence on Glass and Ceramic of the Italian Renaissance*, edited by Catherine Hess, pp. 55–73. Los Angeles, 2004.

Saliba 2007 Saliba, George. *Islamic Science and the Making of the European Renaissance*. Transformations. Cambridge, Mass., 2007.

Salmon 1971 Salmon, Larry. "Appendix: Description of the Boston Carpet." *Boston Museum Bulletin* 69, no. 355–56 [Persian Carpet Symposium] (1971), pp. 35–41, 82–87.

Samadi 1950 Samadi, H. *Museum of Meshed*. [Tehran, 1950].

Sana'i 1983–84 Abu l-Majd Majdud ibn Adam Sana'i. *Divan-i hakimi Abu l-Majd Majdud ibn Adam Sana'i Ghaznavi*. Edited by Muhammad Taqi Mudarris Razavi. N.p., 1983–84.

Sanders 1994 Sanders, Paula. *Ritual, Politics, and the City in Fatimid Cairo*. SUNY Series in Medieval Middle East History. Albany, N.Y., 1994.

San Francisco and Cambridge, Mass. 2004–5 *From Mind, Heart, and Hand: Persian, Turkish, and Indian Drawings from the Stuart Cary Welch Collection*. Exhibition, Asian Art Museum of San Francisco—Chong-Moon Lee Center for Asian Art and Culture; Arthur M. Sackler Museum, Harvard University Art Museums, Cambridge, Mass. Catalogue by Stuart Cary Welch and others. New Haven and London, 2004.

San Francisco and other cities 1998–99 *Interaction of Cultures: Indian and Western Painting 1780–1910, the Ehrenfeld Collection*. Exhibition, M. H. de Young Memorial Museum, San Francisco, and other venues. Catalogue by Joachim K. Bautze. Alexandria, Va., 1998.

Sarre 1934 Sarre, Friedrich. "Die Bronzekanne des Kalifen Marwan II im arabischen Museum in Kairo." *Ars Islamica* 1, pt. 1 (1934), pp. [6], 10–15.

Sarre and Herzfeld 1911–20 Sarre, Friedrich, and Ernst Herzfeld. *Archäologische Reise im Euphrat- und Tigris-Gebiet*. 4 vols. Forschungen zur islamischen Kunst, 1. Berlin, 1911–20.

Sarre and Trenkwald 1926–29 Sarre, Friedrich, and Hermann Trenkwald. *Old Oriental Carpets*. 2 vols. 1892; 1908. Vienna and Leipzig, 1926–29.

Sarre et al. 1925 Sarre, Friedrich, et al. *Die Keramik von Samarra*. Forschungen zur islamischen Kunst, 2. Die Ausgrabungen von Samarra, 2. Berlin, 1925.

Sarre, Schulz, and Krecker 1901–10 Sarre, Friedrich, Bruno Schulz, and Georg Krecker. *Denkmäler persischer Baukunst: Geschichtliche Untersuchung und Aufnahme muhammedanischer Backsteinbauten in Vorderasien und Persien*. 2 vols. Berlin, 1901–10.

Savory 1998 Savory, Roger. "Ebn Bazzaz, Darvis Tawakkoli." In *Encyclopaedia Iranica* 1985– , vol. 8 (1998), p. 8.

Scanlon and Pinder-Wilson 2001 Scanlon, George T., and Ralph Pinder-Wilson. *Fustat Glass of the Early Islamic Period: Finds Excavated by The American Research Center in Egypt, 1964–1980*. London, 2001.

Scarce 1996 Scarce, Jennifer [M]. *Domestic Culture in the Middle East: An Exploration of the Household Interior*. Edinburgh, 1996.

Scharrahs 2008 Scharrahs, Anke. "Ajami Rooms—Polychrome Wooden Interior Decorations from Syria of the Seventeenth to the Nineteenth Centuries: A View into Art Technology and Conservation Problems." *ICOM Committee for Conservation* 2 (2008), pp. 918–23.

Scharrahs 2011 Scharrahs, Anke. *Ajami Interiors: Forgotten Jewels of Interior Design*. London, 2011.

Schimmel 1992 Schimmel, Annemarie. "Calligraphy and Sufism in Ottoman Turkey." In *The Dervish Lodge: Architecture, Art, and Sufism in Ottoman Turkey*, edited by Raymon Lifchez, pp. 242–52. Berkeley, 1992.

Schimmel and Rivolta 1992 Schimmel, Annemarie, and Barbara Rivolta. "Islamic Calligraphy." *The Metropolitan Museum of Art Bulletin*, n.s., 50, no. 1 (Summer 1992), pp. 1, 3–56.

Schlumberger 1952 Schlumberger, Daniel. "Le palais ghaznévide de Lashkari Bazar." *Syria* 29, no. 3–4 (1952), pp. 251–70.

Schmitz et al. 1992 Schmitz, Barbara, et al. *Islamic Manuscripts in The New York Public Library*. New York and Oxford, 1992.

Schmoranz 1898 Schmoranz, Gustav. *Altorientalische Glas-Gefässe*. Ministerium für Cultus und Unterricht. K.K. Österreichisches Handelsmuseum. Vienna, 1898.

Schneider 1973 Schneider, Laura T. "The Freer Canteen." *Ars Orientalis* 9 [*Freer Gallery of Art Fiftieth Anniversary Volume*] (1973), pp. 137–56, pls. 1–13.

Serjeant 1972 Serjeant, R[orbert] B[ertram]. *Islamic Textiles: Materials for a History up to the Mongol Conquest*. 1942–51. Beirut, 1972.

Setton et al. 1985 Setton, Kenneth M., et al. *A History of the Crusades*. Vol. 5, *The Impact of the Crusades on the Near East*. Edited by Norman P. Zacour and Harry W. Hazard. Madison, Wisc., 1985.

Seyller 1985 Seyller, John. "Model and Copy: The Illustration of Three *Razmnama* Manuscripts." *Archives of Asian Art* 38 (1985), pp. 37–66.

Seyller 1990 Seyller, John. "Codicological Aspects of the Victoria and Albert Museum *Akbarnama* and Their Historical Implications." *Art Journal* 49, no. 4 (Winter 1990), pp. 379–87.

Seyller 1997 Seyller, John. "The Inspection and Valuation of Manuscripts in the Imperial Mughal Library." *Artibus Asiae* 57, no. 3–4 (1997), pp. 243–349.

Seyller 1999 Seyller, John. *Workshop and Patron in Mughal India: The Freer Ramayana and Other Illustrated Manuscripts of 'Abd al-Rahim*. Artibus Asiae Supplementum, 42. Zurich, 1999.

Shahbazi 1999 Shahbazi, A. Shapur. "Flags. i. Of Persia." In *Encyclopaedia Iranica, Online Edition*, December 15, 1999, available at http://www.iranicaonline.org/articles/flags-i.

Shalem 1996 Shalem, Avinoam. *Islam Christianized: Islamic Portable Objects in the Medieval Church Treasuries of the Latin West*. Ars faciendi: Beiträge und Studien zur Kunstgeschichte, 7. Frankfurt am Main, 1996.

Shalem 1997 Shalem, Avinoam. "Jewels and Journeys: The Case of the Medieval Gemstone Called al-Yatima." *Muqarnas* 14 (1997), pp. 42–56.

Shalem 1998 Shalem, Avinoam. *Islam Christianized: Islamic Portable Objects in the Medieval Church Treasuries of the Latin West*. 2nd ed. Ars faciendi, 7. 1996. Frankfurt am Main and New York, 1998.

Shalem 2004a Shalem, Avinoam. "Objects as Carriers of Real or Contrived Memories in a Cross-Cultural Context: The Case of Medieval Diplomatic Presents." In *Migrating Images: Producing . . . Reading . . . Transporting . . . Translating*, edited by Petra Stegmann and Peter C. Seel, pp. 36–52. Berlin, 2004.

Shalem 2004b Shalem, Avinoam. *The Oliphant: Islamic Objects in Historical Context*. Islamic History and Civilization, Studies and Texts, 54. Leiden, 2004.

Shani 2006 Shani, Raya Y. "Illustrations of the Parable of the Ship of Faith in Firdausi's Prologue to the *Shahnama*." In *Shahnama Studies I*, edited by Charles Melville. Cambridge, 2006.

Sharaf al-din 'Ali Yazdi 1957 Sharaf al-din 'Ali Yazdi. *Zafarnamah: Tarikh-i 'umumi-yi mufassal-i Iran dar dawra-yi*. 2 vols. Tehran, 1957.

Sheffield and Birmingham 1976 *Carpets of Central Persia, with Special Reference to Rugs of Kirman*. Exhibition, Mappin Art Gallery, Sheffield; City Museum and Art Gallery, Birmingham. Catalogue by May H. Beattie. [London], 1976.

Shepherd 1943 Shepherd, Dorothy G. "The Hispano-Islamic Textiles in the Cooper Union Collection." *Chronicle of the Museum for the Arts of Decoration of the Cooper Union* 1, no. 10 (December 1943), pp. 356–401.

Shepherd 1957 Shepherd, Dorothy G. "A Dated Hispano-Islamic Silk." *Ars Orientalis* 2 (1957), pp. 373–82, pls. 1–10.

Sherrill 1996 Sherrill, Sarah B. *Carpets and Rugs of Europe and America*. New York, 1996.

Shillington, ed. 2005 Shillington, Kevin, ed. *Encyclopedia of African History*. 3 vols. New York, 2005.

Shirvani 1987 Shirvani, Jamal Khalil. *Nuz'hat al-majalis*. Edited by Muhammad Amin Riyahi. Tehran, 1987.

Shokoohy 2003 Shokoohy, Mehrdad. *Muslim Architecture of South India: The Sultanate of Ma'bar and the Traditions of the Maritime Settlers on the Malabar and Coromandal Coasts*. New York, 2003.

Shorter 1957 Shorter, Alfred H. *Paper Mills and Paper Makers in England, 1495–1800*. Monumenta chartae papyraceae historiam illustrantia, 6. Hilversum, 1957.

Shovelton 2009 Shovelton, Emily Phillida. "Sultanate Painting from the North Indian Subcontinent: Three Fifteenth-Century Persian Illustrated Manuscripts." Ph.D. diss., School of Oriental and African Studies, University of London, 2009.

Shtrum et al. 2010 Shtrum, Batyah et al. "The Metropolitan Museum of Art's 'Spanish Ceiling' Project: Interpretation and Conservation." *Journal of Architectural Conservation* 16, no. 3 (November 2010), pp. 29–50.

Siddiq 2009 Siddiq, Mohammad Yusuf. *Historical and Cultural Aspects of the Islamic Inscriptions of Bengal: A Reflective Study of Some New Epigraphic Discoveries*. Studies of Bengal Art, 10. Dhaka, 2009.

Simon-Cahn 1993 Simon-Cahn, Annabelle. "The Fermo Chasuble of St. Thomas Becket and Hispano-Mauresque Cosmological Silks: Some Speculations on the Adaptive Reuse of Textiles." *Muqarnas* 10 [*Essays in Honor of Oleg Grabar, Contributed by His Students*] (1993), pp. 1–5.

Simpson 1979 Simpson, Marianna Shreve. *The Illustration of the an Epic: The Earliest Shahnama Manuscripts*. [Garland] Outstanding Dissertations in the Fine Arts. 1978. New York, 1979.

Simpson 1980 Simpson, Marianna Shreve. *Arab and Persian Painting in the Fogg Art Museum*. Fogg Art Museum Handbooks, 2. Cambridge, Mass., 1980.

Simpson 1981 Simpson, Marianna Shreve. "The Narrative Structure of a Medieval Iranian Beaker." *Ars Orientalis* 12 (1981), pp. 15–24, pls. 1–7.

Sims 1990–91 Sims, Eleanor. "Ibrahim-Sultan's Illustrated *Zafar-nameh* of 839/1436." *Islamic Art* 4 (1990–91), pp. 175–217, pls. 8–13.

Sims 2001 Sims, Eleanor. "Toward a Monograph on the Seventeenth-Century Iranian Painter Muhammad Zaman ibn Haji Yusuf." *Islamic Art* (2001), pp. 183–99.

Sims 2002 Sims, Eleanor. "A Dispersed Late-Safavid Copy of the *Tarikh-i Jahangusha-yi Khaqan Sahibqiran*." In *Safavid Art and Architecture*, edited by Sheila R. Canby, pp. 54–57. London, 2002.

Sims, Marshak, and Grube 2002 Sims, Eleanor, Boris I. Marshak, and Ernst J. Grube. *Peerless Images: Persian Painting and Its Sources*. New Haven and London, 2002.

Skelton 1970 Skelton, Robert. "Mughal Painting from Harivamṣa Manuscript." *Victoria and Albert Museum Yearbook* 2 (1970), pp. 41–54.

Skelton 1972a Skelton, Robert. "A Decorative Motif in Mughal Art." In *Aspects of Indian Art: Papers Presented in a Symposium at the Los Angeles County Museum of Art, October 1970*, edited by Pratapaditya Pal, pp. 147–52. Leiden, 1972.

Skelton 1972b Skelton, Robert. "Migrations of Miniature Painters Between Iran and India During the Sixteenth and Seventeenth Centuries." Unpublished lecture, VIth International Congress of Iranian Art and Archaeology, Oxford, 1972.

Skelton 1985 Skelton, Robert. "'Abbasi, Sayk." In *Encyclopaedia Iranica* 1985– , vol. 1 (1985), pp. 86–88.

Skelton 1988 Skelton, Robert. "Imperial Symbolism in Mughal Painting." In *Content and Context of Visual Arts in the Islamic World: Papers from A Colloquium in Memory of Richard Ettinghausen, Institute of Fine Arts, New York University, 2–4 April 1980*, edited by Priscilla P. Soucek, pp. 177–91. University Park, Pa., and London, 1988.

Skelton 2000 Skelton, Robert. "Ghiyath al-Din 'Ali-yi Naqshband and an Episode in the Life of Sadiqi Beg." In *Persian Painting from the Mongols to the Qajars: Studies in Honour of Basil W. Robinson*, edited by Robert Hillenbrand, pp. 249–63. London and New York, 2000.

Smart 1986 Smart, Ellen S. "A Preliminary Report on a Group of Important Mughal Textiles." *Textile Museum Journal* 25 (1986), pp. 5–23.

Smith 1987–88 Smith, G. Rex. "The Political History of the Islamic Yemen Down to the First Turkish Invasion (1–945/622–1538)." In Munich 1987–88, pp. 129–39.

Snelders 2010 Snelders, Bas. *Identity and Christian-Muslim Interaction: Medieval Art of the Syrian Orthodox from the Mosul Area*. Leiden, 2010.

Sokoly 2002 Sokoly, Jochen A. "Tiraz Textiles from Egypt: Production, Administration and Uses of Tiraz Textiles from Egypt under the Umayyad, 'Abbasid and Fatimid Dynasties." Ph.D. diss., University of Oxford, 2002.

Sonday 1987–88 Sonday, Milton. "Pattern and Weaves: Safavid Lampas and Velvet." In Washington, D.C. 1987–88, pp. 57–84.

Soucek 1990 Soucek, Priscilla [P]. "Sultan Muhammad Tabrizi: Painter at the Safavid Court." In Canby, ed. 1990a and/or Canby, ed. 1990b, pp. 55–70.

Soucek 1997 Soucek, Priscilla [P]. "Byzantium and the Islamic East." In New York 1997b, pp. 402–11, 517.

Soucek 1999 Soucek, Priscilla [P]. "Ceramic Production as Exemplar of Yuan-Ilkhanid

Relations." *RES: Anthropology and Aesthetics*, no. 35 [*Intercultural China*] (Spring 1999), pp. 125–41.

Soucek 2003–4 Soucek, Priscilla [P]. "Calligraphy in the Safavid Period, 1501–76." In New York and Milan 2003–4, pp. 48–71.

Soudavar 1996 Soudavar, Abolala. "The Saga of Abu Sa'id Bahador Khan: The Abu-Sa'idname." In *The Court of the Il-khans, 1290–1340*, edited by Julian Raby and Teresa Fitzherbert, pp. 95–218. Oxford Studies in Islamic Art, 12. Oxford, 1996.

Soudavar 2000 Soudavar, Abolala. "The Age of Muhammadi." *Muqarnas* 17 (2000), pp. 53–72.

Soudavar and Beach 1992 Soudavar, Abolala, with Milo Cleveland Beach. *Art of the Persian Courts: Selections from the Art and History Trust Collection*. New York, 1992.

Sourdel-Thomine 1978 Sourdel-Thomine, Janine. *Le décor non figuratif et les inscriptions*. Lashkari Bazar, une résidence royale ghaznévide et ghoride, 1B. Paris, 1978.

Sourdel-Thomine et al. 1973 Sourdel-Thomine, Janine, et al. *Die Kunst des Islam*. Propyläen-Kunstgeschichte, 4. Berlin, 1973.

Souto 2007 Souto, Juan A. "La Mezquita Aljama de Córdoba." *Artigrama*, no. 22 (2007), pp. 37–72.

Spallanzani 2009 Spallanzani, Marco. "Carpets at the Medici Court in the Second Half of the Sixteenth Century." *Oriental Art* 6 (2009), pp. 206–9.

Spuhler 1978 Spuhler, Friedrich. *Islamic Carpets and Textiles in the Keir Collection*. Translated by George and Cornelia Wingfield Digby. London, 1978.

Spuhler 1979 Spuhler, Friedrich. "Das Teppich-Museum in Tehran: Ein vorläufiger Bericht über seine Bestände an klassischen Orientteppichen." *Hali* 2, no. 2 [no. 5] (Summer 1979), pp. 97–100.

Spuhler 1987 Spuhler, Friedrich. *Oriental Carpets in the Museum of Islamic Art, Berlin*. Translated by Robert Pinner. Washington, D.C., 1987.

Spuhler, Mellbye-Hansen, and Thorvildsen 1987 Spuhler, Friedrich, Preben Mellbye-Hansen, and Majken Thorvildsen. *Denmark's Coronation Carpets*. The Royal Collections, Rosenborg Palace. Copenhagen, 1987.

Stanley 1999 Stanley, Tim. "North Africa: The Maintenance of a Tradition." In *The Decorated Word: Qur'ans of the Seventeenth to Nineteenth Centuries*, by Manijeh Bayani, Anna Contadini, and Tim Stanley, pp. 42–45. The Nasser D. Khalili Collection of Islamic Art, edited by Julian Raby, vol. 4, pt. 1. London, 1999.

Stchoukine 1954 Stchoukine, Ivan. *Les peintures des manuscrits timurides*. Institut Français d'Archéologie de Beyrouth, Bibliothèque archéologique et historique, 60. Paris, 1954.

Stchoukine 1964 Stchoukine, Ivan. *Les peintures des manuscrits de Shah 'Abbas Ier à la fin des Safavis*. Bibliothèque archéologique et historique, 76. Paris, 1964.

Stein 1986–87 Stein, Roger B. "Artifact as Ideology: The Aesthetic Movement in Its American Cultural Context." In *In Pursuit of Beauty: Americans and the Aesthetic Movement*, pp. 23–51. Exhibition, The Metropolitan Museum of Art, New York. Catalogue by Alice Cooney Frelinghuysen and others. New York, 1987.

Stevens 1974 Stevens, Roger. "European Visitors to the Safavid Court." *Iranian Studies* 7, no. 3–4 [*Studies on Isfahan: Proceedings of The Isfahan Colloquium, Part 2*] (Summer–Autumn 1974), pp. 421–57.

Stewart 1991 Stewart, Devin J. "A Biographical Notice on Baha' al-Din al-'Amili (d. 1030/1621)." *Journal of the American Oriental Society* 111, no. 3 (July–September 1991), pp. 563–71.

Stewart 1996a Stewart, Devin J. "Taqiyyah as Performance: The Travels of Baha' al-Din al-'Amili in the Ottoman Empire, 991–93/1583–85." *Princeton Papers in Near Eastern Studies* 4 (1996), pp. 1–70.

Stewart 1996b Stewart, Devin J. "The First *Shaykh al-Islam* of the Safavid Capital Qazvin." *Journal of the American Oriental Society* 116, no. 3 (July–September 1996), pp. 387–405.

Stone 1985 Stone, Caroline. *The Embroideries of North Africa*. Burnt Mill, Harlow, Essex, 1985.

St. Petersburg 1996 *Persidskaia zhivopis' i risunok XV–XIX vekov v sobranii Ėrmitazha: Katalog vystavki/Persian Painting and Drawing of the Fifteenth–Nineteenth Centuries from the Hermitage Museum*. Exhibition, Hermitage Museum, Saint Petersburg. Catalogue by Adel T. Adamova. Saint Petersburg, 1996.

Stronge 1985 Stronge, Susan. *Bidri Ware: Inlaid Metalwork from India*. Victoria and Albert Museum. London, 1985.

Strzygowski et al. 1933 Strzygowski, Josef, et al. *Asiatische Miniaturenmalerei im Anschluss an Wesen und Werden der Mogulmalerei*. Arbeiten des I. Kunsthistorischen Institutes der Universität Wien (Lehrkanzel Strzygowski), 50. Klagenfurt, 1933.

Sumahendra 1995 Sumahendra [M. K. Sharma]. *Splendid Style of Kishangarh Painting*. Jaipur, 1995.

Sumi 2004 Sumi, Akiko Motoyoshi. *Description in Classical Arabic Poetry: Wasf, Ekphrasis, and Interarts Theory*. Brill Studies in Middle Eastern Literatures, 25. Leiden and Boston, 2004.

Sun 2010–11 Sun, Zhixin Jason. "Dadu: Great Capital of the Yuan Dynasty." In *The World of Khubilai Khan: Chinese Art in the Yuan Dynasty*, pp. 40–63. Exhibition, The Metropolitan Museum of Art, New York. Catalogue by James C. Y. Watt and others. New York, 2010.

Swietochowski 1978 Swietochowski, Marie Lukens. "Persian Painting." *The Metropolitan Museum of Art Bulletin*, n.s., 36, no. 2 (Autumn 1978), pp. 3, 6–33, frontispiece, cover ill.

Swietochowski 1994 Swietochowski, Marie Lukens. "The Metropolitan Museum of Art's Small *Shahnama*." In New York 1994, pp. 67–127.

Sychova 1981 Sychova, Natalya. *The Museum of Oriental Art, Moscow*. Leningrad, 1981.

Tabbaa 1997 Tabbaa, Yasser. *Constructions of Power and Piety in Medieval Aleppo*. University Park, Pa., 1997.

Taipei 1990 *Luohan hua/Bian ji zhe Guo li gu gong bo wu yuan bian ji wei yuan hui*. [On cover:] *Catalogue for Exhibition on Paintings of Lohans*. [Table of contents and introduction in English.] Exhibition, The Palace Museum, Taipei. Catalogue by Li Yumin and others. Taipei, 1990.

Tait, ed. 1984 Tait, Hugh, ed. *The Art of the Jeweller: A Catalogue of the Hull Grundy Gift to the British Museum: Jewelry, Engraved Gems and Goldsmiths' Work*. London, 1984.

Tanındı 1984 Tanındı, Zeren. *Siyer-i Nebi*. [Istanbul], 1984.

Tashköprüzade 1985 Ahmad Tashköprüzade. *Al-Shaqa'iq al-Nu'maniyya fi ulama' al-daula al-'uthmaniyya*. Edited by Ahmet Subhi Furat. Istanbul, 1985.

Tavernier 1889 Tavernier, Jean Baptiste. *Travels in India*. Translated by V[alentine] Ball. 2 vols. London and New York, 1889.

Taylor 1866 Taylor, Meadows. *Architecture at Beejapore*. London, 1866.

Teece 2006 [Teece, Denise-Marie.] "Storage Bag (Chuval) [Turkoman/Arabatchi, Central Asia] (22.100.40.a)." In *Heilbrunn Timeline of Art History*. The Metropolitan Museum of Art. New York, 2000– . http://www.metmuseum.org/toah/ho/10/nc/ho_22.100.40.a.htm (October 2006).

Teng 2004 Teng Shu-p'ing. "On the Eastern Transmission of Islamic-style Jades during the Ch'ien-lung and Chia-ch'ing Reigns." *National Palace Museum Bulletin* 37, no. 2 (September 2004), pp. 25–138.

Thackston 1989 Thackston, W[heeler] M. *A Century of Princes: Sources on Timurid History and Art*. Cambridge, Mass., 1989.

Thackston 2001 Thackston, W[heeler] M. *Album Prefaces and Other Documents on the History of Calligraphers and Painters*. Studies and Sources in Islamic Art and Architecture, 10. Leiden and Boston, 2001.

Thomas 2007 Thomas, Thelma K. "Coptic and Byzantine Textiles Found in Egypt: Corpora, Collections, and Scholarly Perspectives." In *Egypt in the Byzantine World, 300–700*, edited by Roger S. Bagnall, pp. 137–62. New York and London, 2007.

Thompson 1977 Thompson, Jon. "The Anatomy of a Carpet–3." In Lefevre and Thompson 1977, pp. 65–77.

Thompson 1989 Thompson, Jon. "Shaped Carpets Found in the Jaipur Treasury." In *In Quest of Themes and Skills: Asian Textiles*, edited by Krishna Riboud, pp. 48–51. Bombay, 1989.

Thompson 2003–4 Thompson, Jon. "Early Safavid Carpets and Textiles." In New York and Milan 2003–4, pp. 270–317.

Thompson 2010 Thompson, Jon. "Carpets in the Fifteenth Century." In Thompson, Shaffer, and Mildh, eds. 2010, pp. 30–57.

Thompson, Shaffer, and Mildh, eds. 2010 Thompson, Jon, Daniel Shaffer, and Pirjetta Mildh, eds. *Carpets and Textiles in the Iranian World 1400–1700: Proceedings of the Conference held at the Ashmolean Museum on 30–31 August 2003*. Oxford and Genoa, 2010.

Titley 1983 Titley, Norah M. *Persian Miniature Painting and Its Influence on the Art of Turkey and India: The British Library Collections*. London, 1983.

Tokatlian 2007 Tokatlian, Armen. *Falnamah: Livre royal des sorts*. Montreuil, 2007.

Tonghini 1994 Tonghini, Cristina. "The Fine Wares of Ayyubid Syria." In *Cobalt and Lustre: The First Centuries of Islamic Pottery*, edited by Ernst J. Grube, pp. 248–93. The Nasser D. Khalili Collection of Islamic Art, edited by Julian Raby, vol. 9. Oxford and New York, 1994.

Topsfield 2008 Topsfield, Andrew. *Paintings from Mughal India*. Bodleian Library, University of Oxford. Oxford, 2008.

Treadwell 2009 Treadwell, Luke. "'Abd al-Malik's Coinage Reforms: The Role of the Damascus Mint." *Revue numismatique* 165 (2009), pp. 357–81.

Turin 2010 *L'India dei Rajput: Miniature dalla Collezione Ducrot*. Exhibition, Museo d'Arte Orientale, Turin. Catalogue by Claudia Ramasso and others. Milan, 2010.

Uluç 1994 Ulu[ç], Lâle. "A Persian Epic, Perhaps for the Ottoman Sultan." *Metropolitan Museum Journal* 29 (1994), pp. 57–69.

Uluç 2006 Uluç, Lâle. *Turkman Governors, Shiraz Artisans, Ottoman Collectors: Sixteenth Century Shiraz Manuscripts*. Istanbul, 2006.

Uzunçarşılı 1984 Uzunçarşılı, I. Hakkı. *Anadolu Baylikieri ve Akkoyunlu, Karakoyunlu Devetleri*. 2nd ed. 1969. Ankara, 1984.

Valdés Fernández, ed. 2007 Valdés Fernández, Manuel, ed. *Simposio Internacional: El legado de al-Andalus; El arte andalusí en los reinos de León y Castilla durante la Edad Media*. Valladolid, 2007.

Valentiner 1913 V[alentiner], W[illiam] R. "The Cochran Collection of Persian Manuscripts." *The Metropolitan Museum of Art Bulletin* 8, no. 4 (April 1913), pp. 80–86.

Veldhuisen 1996–97 Veldhuisen, Harmen C. "The Role of Entrepreneurs in the Stylistic Development of *Batik Pasisir*." In Los Angeles 1996–97, pp. 70–81.

Venice 1993–94 *Eredità dell'Islam/Mirat al-Islam: Arte islamica in Italia*. Exhibition, Palazzo Ducale, Venice. Catalogue by Bianca Maria Alfieri, Giovanni Curatola, and others. Milan, 1993.

Ventrone 1974 Ventrone, G. "Iscrizioni inedite su ceramica samanide in collezioni italiane." In *Gururajamanjarika: Studi in onore do Giuseppe Tucci*, pp. 221–32. Instituto Universitario Orientale. Naples, 1974.

Verma 1994 Verma, Som Prakash. *Mughal Painters and Their Work: A Biographical Survey and Comprehensive Catalogue*. Delhi, 1994.

Vernoit 1998 Vernoit, Stephen [J]. "Islamic Gilded and Enamelled Glass in Nineteenth-Century Collections." In Ward, ed. 1998, pp. 110–15, 206–10, pl. E.

Vernoit, ed. 2000 Vernoit, Stephen, ed. *Discovering Islamic Art: Scholars, Collectors and Collections, 1850–1950*. London and New York, 2000.

Vial 1987 Vial, Gabriel. "La technique du châle indien." In *Quelques aspects du châle cachemire*, pp. 38–50, figs. 1–22. A.E.D.T.A. Paris, 1987.

Vivier 2002–3 Vivier, Marie-France. "Urban Textiles: Embroideries." In *The Fabric of Moroccan Life*, pp. 41–97. Exhibition, Indianapolis Museum of Art; National Museum of African Art, Smithsonian Institution, Washington, D.C. Catalogue by Niloo Imami Paydar, Ivo Grammet, and others. Indianapolis, 2002.

Völker 2001 Völker, Angela. *Die orientalischen Knüpfteppiche im MAK*. Österreichisches Museum für Angewandte Kunst. Vienna, Cologne, and Weimar, 2001.

Volov 1966 Volov, Lisa. "Plaited Kufic on Samanid Epigraphic Pottery." *Ars Orientalis* 6 (1966), pp. 107–33, pls. 1–6.

Wace 1935 Wace, A. J. B. *Mediterranean and Near Eastern Embroideries from the Collection of Mrs. F. H. Cook*. 2 vols. London, 1935.

Walker, D. 1990 Walker, Daniel. "Carpets. ix. Safavid Period." In *Encyclopaedia Iranica* 1985– , vol. 4 (1990), pp. 866–75.

Walker, D. 1993 Walker, Daniel. "Recent Acquisitions: A Selection, 1992–1993; Islam; Flask in the Shape of a Mango." *The Metropolitan Museum of Art Bulletin*, n.s., 51, no. 2 (Fall 1993), p. 23.

Walker, D. 1994 Walker, Daniel. "Metropolitan Quartet." *Hali*, no. 76 (August–September 1994), pp. 104–7, 120.

Walker, D. 1995–96 Walker, Daniel. "Textiles in The Metropolitan Museum of Art; Islamic." *The Metropolitan Museum of Art Bulletin*, n.s., 53, no. 3 (Winter 1995–96), pp. 28–34, ills. pp. 14–17.

Walker, D. 2006 Walker, Daniel. "Carpets of Khorasan." *Hali*, no. 149 (November–December 2006), pp. 72–77.

Walker, J. 1941 Walker, John. *A Catalogue of the Muhammadan Coins in the British Museum*. Vol. 1, *A Catalogue of the Arab-Sassanian Coins: Umaiyad Governors in the East, Arab-Ephthalites, 'Abbasid Governors in Tabaristan and Bukhara*. London, 1941.

Walker, J. 1956 Walker, John. *A Catalogue of the Muhammadan Coins in the British Museum*. Vol. 2, *A Catalogue of the Arab-Byzantine and Post-Reform Umaiyad Coins*. London, 1956.

Walker, P. 2002 Walker, Paul E. *Exploring an Islamic Empire: Fatimid History and Its Sources*. London, 2002.

Wallis 1904 Wallis, Henry. *Italian Ceramic Art: The Albarello; A Study in Early Renaissance Maiolica*. London, 1904.

Wannell 2011 Wannell, Bruce. "The Epigraphic Program of the Ibrahim Rauza in Bijapur." In Haidar and Sardar, eds. 2011, pp. 252–67.

Ward 1990–91 Ward, Rachel [M]. "Incense and Incense Burners in Mamluk Egypt and Syria." *Transactions of the Oriental Ceramic Society* 55 (1990–91), pp. 67–82.

Ward 1993 Ward, Rachel [M]. *Islamic Metalwork*. London, 1993.

Ward 2004 Ward, Rachel M. "Brass, Gold and Silver from Mamluk Egypt: Metal Vessels Made for Sultan Al-Nasir Muhammad: A Memorial Lecture for Mark Zebrowski, Given at the Royal Asiatic Society on 9 May 2002." *Journal of the Royal Asiatic Society* 14, no. 1 (April 2004), pp. 59–73.

Ward 2005 Ward, Rachel M. "Style versus Substance : The Christian Iconography on Two Vessels Made for the Ayyabid Sultan al-Sahik Ayyub." In *The Iconography of Islamic Art: Studies in Honour of Robert Hillenbrand*, edited by Bernard O'Kane, pp. 309–24. Edinburgh, 2005.

Ward, ed. 1998 Ward, Rachel [M]., ed. *Gilded and Enamelled Glass from the Middle East*. London, 1998.

Wardwell 1983 Wardwell, Anne E. "A Fifteenth-Century Silk Curtain from Muslim Spain." *The Bulletin of the Cleveland Museum of Art* 70, no. 2 (February 1983), pp. 58–72, and cover ill.

Wardwell 1987 Wardwell, Anne E. "Flight of the Phoenix: Crosscurrents in Late Thirteenth- to Fourteenth-Century Silk Patterns and Motifs." *The Bulletin of the Cleveland Museum of Art* 74, no. 1 (January 1987), pp. 2–35, cover ill.

Wardwell 1988–89 Wardwell, Anne E. "*Panni Tartarici*: Eastern Islamic Silks Woven with Gold and Silver (Thirteenth and Fourteenth Centuries)." *Islamic Art* 3 (1988–89), pp. 95–173, pls. 8–9.

Wardwell 1992 Wardwell, Anne E. "Two Silk and Gold Textiles of the Early Mongol Period." *The Bulletin of the Cleveland Museum of Art* 79, no. 10 (December 1992), pp. 354–78.

Warner 2005 Warner, Nicholas. *The Monuments of Historic Cairo: A Map and Descriptive Catalogue*. American Research Center in Egypt Conservation, 1. Cairo and New York, 2005.

Washington, D.C. 1973 *The Splendor of Turkish Weaving: An Exhibition of Silks and Carpets of the Thirteenth–Eighteenth Centuries*. Exhibition, The Textile Museum, Washington, D.C. Catalogue by Louise W. Mackie. Washington, D.C., 1973.

Washington, D.C. 1975 *Art of the Arab World*. Exhibition, Freer Gallery of Art, Smithsonian Institution, Washington, D.C. Catalogue by Esin Atil. Washington, D.C., 1975.

Washington, D.C. 1980 *Turkmen: Tribal Carpets and Traditions*. Exhibition, The Textile Museum, Washington, D.C. Catalogue by Louise W. Mackie and Jon Thompson. Washington, D.C., 1980.

Washington, D.C. 1981–82 *The Imperial Image: Paintings for the Mughal Court*. Exhibition, Freer Gallery of Art, Smithsonian Institution, Washington, D.C. Catalogue by Milo Cleveland Beach. Washington, D.C., 1981.

Washington, D.C. 1985–86 *Islamic Metalwork in the Freer Gallery of Art*. Exhibition, Freer Gallery of Art, Smithsonian Institution, Washington, D.C. Catalogue by Esin Atil and others. Washington, D.C., 1985.

Washington, D.C. 1987–88 *Woven from the Soul, Spun from the Heart: Textile Arts of Safavid and Qajar Iran Sixteenth–Nineteenth Centuries*. Exhibition, The Textile Museum, Washington, D.C. Catalogue by Carol Bier and others. Washington, D.C., 1987.

Washington, D.C. 2000 *Flowers of Silk and Gold: Four Centuries of Ottoman Embroidery*. Exhibition, The Textile Museum, Washington, D.C. Catalogue by Sumru Belger Krody. London and Washington, D.C., 2000.

Washington, D.C. 2002 *The Adventures of Hamza: Painting and Storytelling in Mughal India*. Exhibition, Arthur M. Sackler Gallery of Art, Smithsonian Institution, Washington, D.C. Catalogue by John Seyller, with Wheeler M. Thackston, Ebba Koch, Antoinette Owen, and Rainald Franz. Washington, D.C., and London, 2002.

Washington, D.C. 2002–3 *The Classical Tradition in Anatolian Carpets*. Exhibition, The Textile Museum, Washington, D.C. Catalogue by Walter B. Denny and Sumru Belger Krody. Washington, D.C., 2002.

Washington, D.C. 2004 *Caliphs and Kings: The Art and Influence of Islamic Spain; Selections from the Hispanic Society of America, New York*. Exhibition, Arthur M. Sackler Gallery, Smithsonian Institution, Washington, D.C. Catalogue by Heather Ecker. New York, 2004.

Washington, D.C. 2009–10 *Falnama: The Book of Omens*. Exhibition, Arthur M. Sackler Gallery, Smithsonian Institution, Washington, D.C. Catalogue by Massumeh Farhad, Serpil Bağci, and others. Washington, D. C., 2009.

Washington, D.C., and Los Angeles 1989 *Timur and the Princely Vision: Persian Art and Culture in the Fifteenth Century*. Exhibition, Arthur M. Sackler Gallery, Smithsonian Institution, Washington, D.C.; Los Angeles County Museum of Art. Catalogue by Thomas W. Lentz and Glenn D. Lowry. Los Angeles, 1989.

Washington, D.C., and other cities 1936 *Indian Miniatures from the Collection of Mildred and W. G. Archer, London*. Exhibition, Smithsonian Institution, Washington, D.C. Catalogue by Mildred and W. G. Archer. Washington, D.C., 1936.

Washington, D.C., and other cities 1981–82 *Renaissance of Islam: Art of the Mamluks*. Exhibition, National Museum of Natural History, Washington, D.C., and other venues. Catalogue by Esin Atil. Washington, D.C., 1981.

Washington, D.C., and other cities 2004–6 *Palace and Mosque: Islamic Art from the Victoria and Albert Museum*. Exhibition, National Gallery of Art, Washington, D.C.; Kimbell Art Museum, Fort Worth; Setagaya Art Museum, Tokyo; Millennium Galleries, Sheffield. Catalogue by Tim Stanley, Mariam Rosser-Owen, and Stephen Vernoit. London, 2004.

Washington, D.C., and other cities 2008–9 *Muraqqa': Imperial Mughal Albums from the Chester Beatty Library, Dublin*. Exhibition, Arthur M. Sackler Gallery, Smithsonian Institution, Washington, D.C.; Detroit Institute of Arts; Honolulu Academy of Arts; Nelson-Atkins Museum of Art, Kansas City, Mo.; Denver Art Museum, 2008–9. Catalogue by Elaine Wright, Susan Stronge, and Wheeler [M.] Thackston. Alexandria, Va., 2008.

Washington, D.C., Chicago, and New York 1987–88 *The Age of Sultan Süleyman the Magnificent*. Exhibition, National Gallery of Art, Washington, D.C.; The Art Institute of Chicago; The Metropolitan Museum of Art, New York. Catalogue by Esin Atil. Washington, D.C., 1987.

Watson 1983 Watson, O[liver]. "Abu Taher." In *Encyclopaedia Iranica, Online Edition*, December 15, 1983, available at http://www.iranica.com/articles/abu-taher-family-of-leading-potters-from-kasan-known-through-four-generations-602-734-1205-1333.

Watson 1985 Watson, Oliver. *Persian Lustre Ware*. The Faber Monographs on Pottery and Porcelain. London and Boston, 1985.

Watson 2004 Watson, Oliver. *Ceramics from Islamic Lands*. Kuwait National Museum, the al-Sabah Collection. New York, 2004.

Watson 2006 Watson, Oliver. "Pottery under the Mongols." In *Beyond the Legacy of Genghis Khan*, edited by Linda Komaroff, pp. 325–45, 527, 600–611. Islamic History and Civilization, Studies and Texts, 64. Leiden and Boston, 2006.

Watt and Wardwell 1997–98 Watt, James C. Y., and Anne E. Wardwell. "Luxury-Silk Weaving under the Mongols." In Cleveland and New York 1997–98, pp. 126–63.

Weber 2002 Weber, Stefan. "Images of Imagined Worlds: Self-Image and Worldview in Late Ottoman Wall Painting." In *The Empire in the City: Arab Provincial Capitals in the Late Ottoman Empire*, edited by J. Hanssen, T. Philipp, and S. Weber, pp. 145–71. Beirut, 2002.

Weber 2009 Weber, Stefan. *Damascus: Ottoman Modernity and Urban Transformation, 1801–1918*. Proceedings of the Danish Institute in Damascus, 5. [Aarhus and Copenhagen, 2009].

Weibel 1952 Weibel, Adèle Coulin. *Two Thousand Years of Textiles: The Figured Textiles of Europe and the Near East*. Detroit Institute of Arts. New York, 1952.

Weill 1931–36 Weill, Jean David. *Les bois à épigraphes*. 2 vols. Catalogue général du Musée Arabe du Caire; Musée National de l'Art Arabe. Cairo, 1931–36.

Welch, A. 1974 Welch, Anthony. "Painting and Patronage under Shah 'Abbas I." *Iranian Studies* 7, nos. 3–4 [*Studies on Isfahan: Proceedings of The Isfahan Colloquium, Part 2*] (Summer–Autumn 1974), pp. 458–507.

Welch, A. 1976 Welch, Anthony. *Artists for the Shah: Late Sixteenth-Century Painting at the Imperial Court of Iran*. New Haven and London, 1976.

Welch, A. 1996 Welch, Anthony. "A Medieval Center of Learning in India: The Hauz Khas Madrasa in Delhi." *Muqarnas* 13 (1996), pp. 165–90.

Welch, S. C. 1963 Welch, Stuart C[ary]. "Mughal and Deccani Miniature Paintings from a Private Collection." *Ars Orientalis* 5 (1963), pp. 221–33, pls. 1–15.

Welch, S. C. 1971 Welch, Stuart C[ary]. "Two Shahs, Some Miniatures, and the Boston Carpet." *Boston Museum Bulletin* 69, no. 355–56 [Persian Carpet Symposium] (1971), pp. 6–14, 35–45.

Welch, S. C. 1987 Welch, Stuart Cary. "Islamic Art; A Safavid Pierced-Steel Plaque." In *Recent Acquisitions: A Selection, 1986–1987; The Metropolitan Museum of Art*, p. 11. New York, [1987].

Welch, S. C. 1995 Welch, Stuart Cary. "The Two Worlds of Payag—Further Evidence on a Mughal Artist." In *Indian Art and Connoisseurship: Essays in Honour of Douglas Barrett*, edited by John Guy, pp. 320–41. New Delhi, 1995.

Welch, S. C., et al. 1987 Welch, Stuart Cary, et al. *The Islamic World*. The Metropolitan Museum of Art Series, 11. New York, 1987.

Welch, S. C., Jenkins, and Kane 1983–84 Welch, Stuart Cary, Marilyn Jenkins, and Carolyn Kane. "Islamic Art." In *Notable Acquisitions [The Metropolitan Museum of Art]*, 1983–1984, pp. 4–8. New York, 1984.

Wellesz 1959 Wellesz, Emmy. "An Early al-Sufi Manuscript in the Bodleian Library in Oxford: A Study in Islamic Constellation Images." *Ars Orientalis* 3 (1959), pp. 1–26, pls. 1–27.

Wenzel 1993 Wenzel, Marian. *Ornament and Amulet: Rings of the Islamic Lands*. The Nasser D. Khalili Collection of Islamic Art, edited by Julian Raby, vol. 16. London, 1993.

Weyl et al. 1995 Weyl, Martin, et al. *The Israel Museum, Jerusalem*. London, 1995.

Whelan 1986 Whelan, Estelle. "The Origins of the *Mihrab Mujawwaf*: A Reinterpretation." *International Journal of Middle East Studies* 18, no. 2 (May 1986), pp. 205–23.

Whelan 1990a Whelan, Estelle. "Early Islam: Emerging Patterns (622–1050)." In *Islamic Art and Patronage: Treasures from Kuwait* [The al-Sabah Collection], pp. 40–93. Exhibition, The State Hermitage Museum, St. Petersburg, and other venues. Catalogue edited by Esin Atil. New York, 1990.

Whelan 1990b Whelan, Estelle. "Writing the Word of God: Some Early Qur'an Manuscripts and Their Milieux, Part I." *Ars Orientalis* 20 (1990), pp. 113–47.

Whelan 1998 Whelan, Estelle. "Forgotten Witness: Evidence for the Early Codification of the Qur'an." *Journal of the American Oriental Society* 118, no. 1 (January–March 1998), pp. 1–14.

Whitcomb 1985 Whitcomb, Donald S. *Before the Roses and Nightingales: Excavations at Qasr-i Abu Nasr, Old Shiraz*. New York, 1985.

Whitehouse 2001–2 Whitehouse, David. "Imitations of Islamic Glass." In Corning, New York, and Athens 2001–2, pp. 297–311.

Wiet 1929 Wiet, Gaston. *Lampes et bouteilles en verre emaillé*. Catalogue général du Musée Arabe du Caire; Musée National de l'Art Arabe. Cairo, 1929.

Wilber 1939 Wilber, Donald N. "The Development of Mosaic Faïence in Islamic Architecture in Iran." *Ars Islamica* 6, pt. 1 (1939), pp. 16–47.

Wilber 1955 Wilber, Donald [N]. *The Architecture of Islamic Iran: The Il Khanid Period*. Princeton Monographs in Art and Archaeology, 29. Princeton, N.J., 1955.

Wilckens 1992 Wilckens, Leonie von. *Mittelalterliche Seidenstoffe: Seidenstoffe des 5.–14. Jahrhunderts im Berliner Kunstgewerbemuseum*. Bestandskatalog des Kunstgewerbemuseum, 18. Berlin, 1992.

Wilkinson 1943 Wilkinson, Charles K. "A Thirteenth-Century Morality." *The Metropolitan Museum of Art Bulletin*, n.s., 2, no. 1 (Summer 1943), pp. 47–55.

Wilkinson 1973 Wilkinson, Charles K. *Nishapur: Pottery of the Early Islamic Period*. New York, [1973].

Wilkinson 1986 Wilkinson, Charles K. *Nishapur: Some Early Islamic Buildings and Their Decoration*. New York, 1986.

Williams Jackson and Yohannan 1914 Williams Jackson, A[braham] V[alentine], and Abraham Yohannan. *A Catalogue of the Collection of Persian Manuscripts, Including Also Some Turkish and Arabic, Presented to the Metropolitan Museum of Art, New York, by Alexander Smith Cochran*. Columbia University Indo Iranian Series, 1. New York, 1914.

Williamstown, Mass., Baltimore, Boston, and New York 1978–79 *The Grand Mogul: Imperial Painting in India, 1600–1660*. Exhibition, Sterling and Francine Clark Art Institute, Williamstown, Mass.; Walters Art Gallery, Baltimore; Museum of Fine Arts, Boston; Asia House Gallery, New York. Catalogue by Milo Cleveland Beach, with Stuart Cary Welch and Glenn D. Lowry. Williamstown, Mass., 1978.

Wilson 2005 Wilson, Verity. *Chinese Textiles*. London, 2005.

Winter 1986 Winter, H. J. J. "Persian Science in Safavid Times" In *The Cambridge History of Iran*, vol. 6, *The Timurid and Safavid Periods*, edited by Peter Jackson and Laurence Lockhart, pp. 581–609. London and New York, 1986.

Wolfe 1990 Wolfe, Richard J. *Marbled Paper: Its History, Techniques, and Patterns with Special Reference to the Relationship of Marbling to Bookbinding in Europe and the Western World*. A Publication of the A. S. W. Rosenbach Fellowship in Bibliography. Philadelphia, 1990.

Yazdani 1947 Yazdani, G[hulam]. *Bidar: Its History and Monuments*. London, 1947.

Yoltar-Yildirim 2005 Yoltar-Yildirim, Ayşin. "A 1498–99 *Khusraw va Shirin*: Turning the Pages of an Ottoman Illustrated Manuscript." *Muqarnas* 22 (2005), pp. 95–109.

Zebrowski 1983 Zebrowski, Mark. *Deccani Painting*. London and Berkeley and Los Angeles, 1983.

Zebrowski 1984 Zebrowski, Mark. "Ornamental Pandans of the Mughal Age." In *Symbols and Manifestations of Indian Art*, edited by Saryu Doshi, pp. 32–40. Bombay, 1984.

Zebrowski 1997 Zebrowski, Mark. *Gold, Silver and Bronze from Mughal India*. London, 1997.

Zuka 1962 Zuka, Yahya. "Muhammad Zaman: Avvalin naqqashi-i Irani ki ba-urupa raft'." *Sukhan* 12, no. 9–10 (1962), n.p.

Zuka 1963 Zuka, Yahya. "Khawaran Nama." *Hunar va Mardum*, no. 20 (1963), pp. 17–29.

Zurich and New York 2011–12 *Wonder of the Age: Master Painters of India, 1100–1900*. Exhibition, Museum Rietberg Zürich; The Metropolitan Museum of Art, New York. Catalogue by John Guy and Jorrit Britschgi. New York, 2011.

INDEX

Page numbers in **bold** refer to main catalogue entries. Page numbers in *italics* refer to figures.

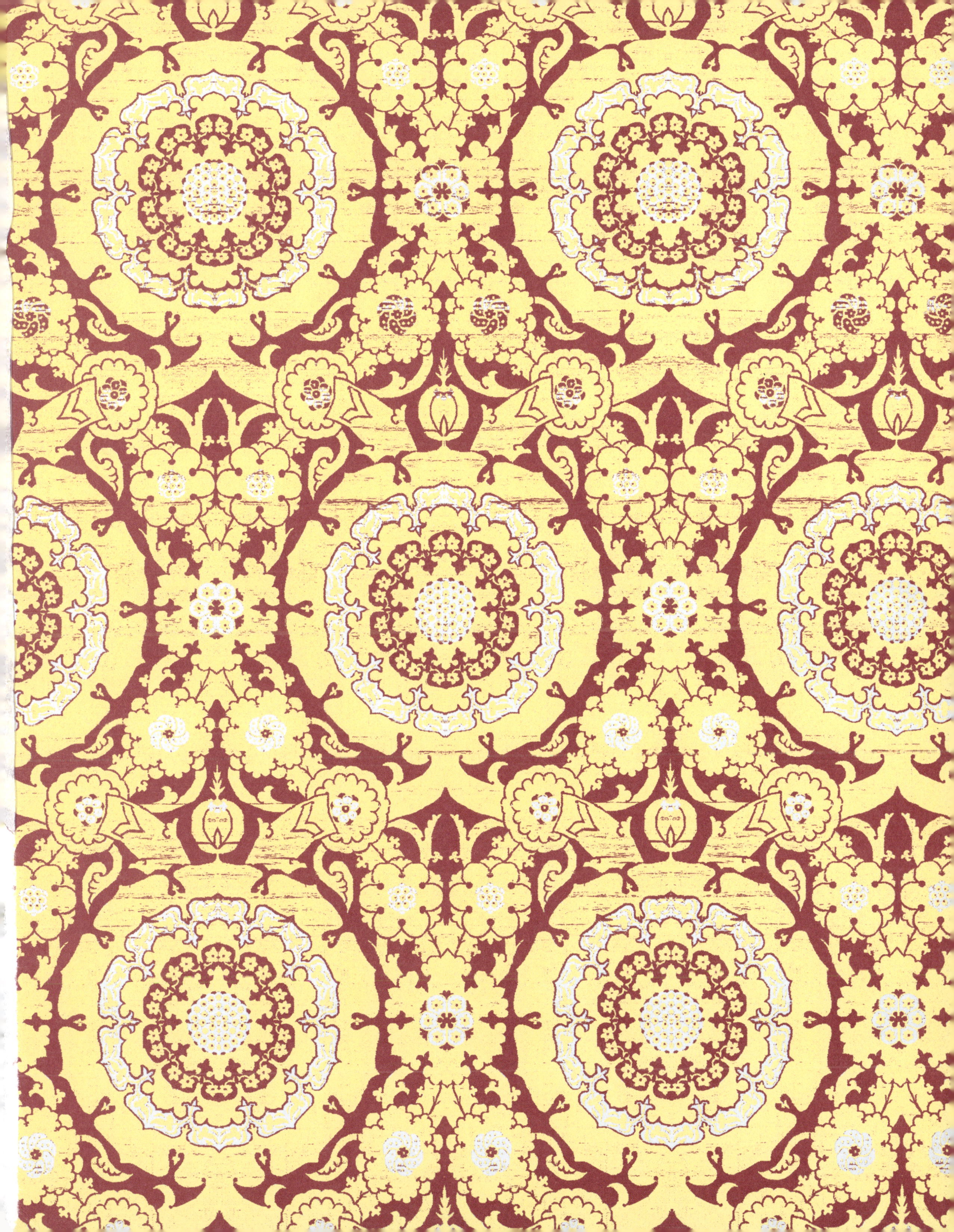

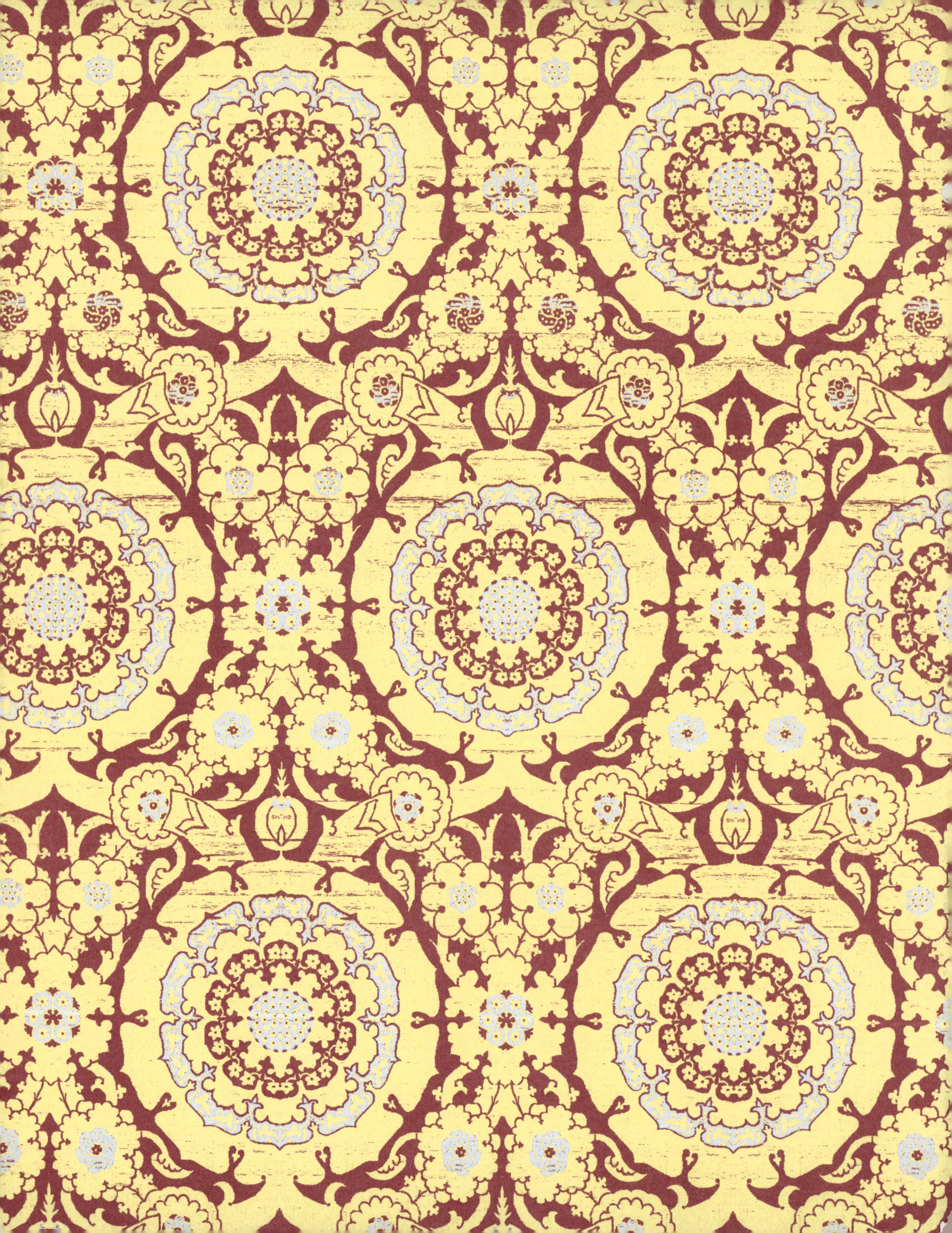